THREE CENTURIES OF HARPSICHORD MAKING

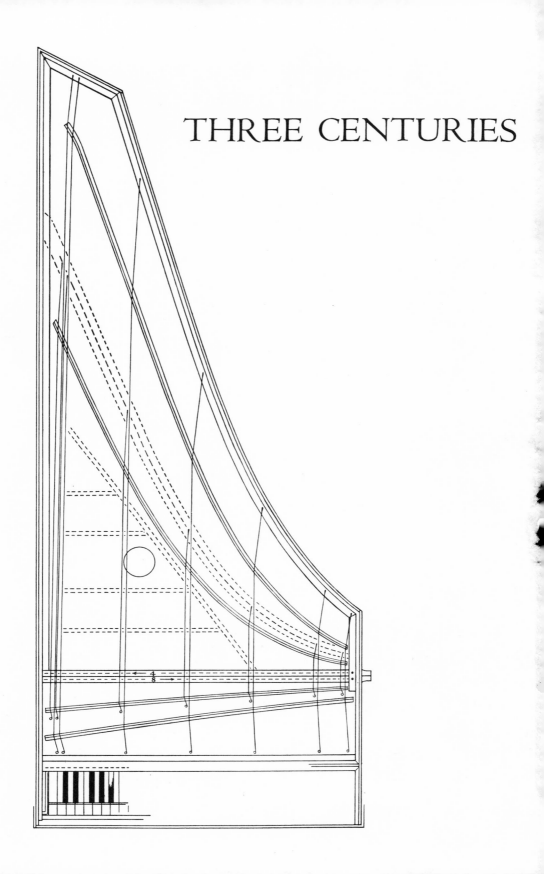

THREE CENTURIES

OF HARPSICHORD MAKING

BY FRANK HUBBARD

HARVARD UNIVERSITY PRESS

CAMBRIDGE, MASSACHUSETTS

Distributed in Great Britain by Oxford University Press, London

Publication of this book has been aided by a grant from the Ford Foundation

Library of Congress Catalog Card Number 65–12784

SBN 674–88845–6

The two lines of T. S. Eliot used as an epigraph are from "The Love Song of J. Alfred Prufrock," which is included in *Collected Poems 1909–1962*, published by Harcourt, Brace and World and by Faber and Faber. The lines are quoted by permission of the publishers.

Printed in the United States of America

Original plates by Frank L. Hubbard

Book Design by David Ford

FOREWORD

At some time in the late 1940's, on the occasion of a concert in Cambridge, I was told of two graduate students in English at Harvard who had built what I believe was a clavichord. Such reports usually arrive with an invitation to inspect a cherished and totally unplayable instrument. Having contrived politely to dodge the invitation, I never found out what the qualities of this instrument might have been. But not long afterwards it became perfectly clear to me that Frank Hubbard and William Dowd did not in any way embody the enthusiastic ineptitude that so frequently is to be encountered among those persons infatuated with old instruments. At about the same time it must have become clear to these two young men that there was a mission to perform, that a career in harpsichord building was at the outset more challenging and in the end perhaps more productive than one in university teaching. The pursuit of the Ph.D. was dropped, and the two separated for a period of apprenticeship.

Dowd went to Detroit for a year to work in the shop of John Challis, whose work from the thirties onward, together with that of his teacher and predecessor of a quarter-century earlier, Arnold Dolmetsch, laid the foundations of twentieth century harpsichord building in the United States. Frank Hubbard, on his side, departed for England to gather what he could of the Dolmetsch tradition and to make a study of ancient keyboard instruments in public and private collections in England and on the Continent.

At the end of their period of apprenticeship, Hubbard and Dowd returned to Boston to collaborate in a partnership that lasted until 1958. From this they both emerged as consummate craftsmen, second to none in skill, intelligence, and experience, having accomplished the major revolution of this century in harpsichord building. This revolution was simply a return to seventeenth and eighteenth century traditions and principles of construction that had hitherto been practiced only in isolated instances. Without Frank Hubbard's historical studies this would not have been possible. These studies he pursued at intervals throughout his collaboration with Dowd and subsequently, to such an extent that he unquestionably knows more about the history and construction of harpsichords than anyone alive today. The bulk of this knowledge, guided by the disciplines of the scholar and illuminated by the insights and experience of the craftsman, is set forth in this book.

Despite the proliferation of harpsichord builders since the beginning of this century, there has been regrettably little connection between most modern harpsichords and their supposed prototypes of the seventeenth and eighteenth centuries. Modern harpsichord building, since its inception by Pleyel and Erard at the end of the last century, has been largely in the hands of piano makers dominated by nineteenth century notions of technological progress. It has seldom occurred to any of them to question the assumed superiority of modern methods over the experience accumulated by the great harpsichord makers of an earlier day. (I long ago observed an inveterate temptation to reinvent the piano.) The traditions of an earlier day, however, were not easy to come by. Either they were buried in books and documents, hence inaccessible to the non-scholarly builder, or they were embodied in old instruments that for the most part had fallen into such neglect or that had been so badly restored that they exhibited few qualities that seemed worthy of admiration and emulation. Indeed, the condition of most old instruments would reinforce any piano builder's belief in progress.

If builders were not always equipped to address themselves to the lessons of the past, scholars and musicians were not always equipped to guide them. Uncritical acceptance of historic instruments, without rigorous examination of their history of decay and restoration, has brought about some unfortunate "copies" and "authentic models." Moreover, sufficient insight into the manner of playing has often not been available either to scholars or musicians. There were of course remarkable and fortunate exceptions to these tendencies, most notably set forth in the early work of Arnold Dolmetsch and in the work of some more recent instrument makers. But the time has long been ripe for a more adequate fusion of the scholar's knowledge, the musician's insight, and the builder's craftsmanship. To such a fusion, as represented by the constant interchange and cross-fertilization among American harpsichord builders, young and serious harpsichord players, and inquiring and knowledgeable scholars, Frank Hubbard has made an incalculable contribution.

It is a matter of lasting regret that my friend Raymond Russell, whose *The Harpsichord and Clavichord* preceded this book, and who so generously shared his material with Frank Hubbard, should not have lived to see its influence and that of the instruments of his collection brought to such a flowering, one that by no means has ceased to unfold.

The effect of this book for one reader, to speak for myself, has been to clear away many of the preconceptions and erroneous notions with which the aesthetic of the modern harpsichord has been burdened. It immensely clarifies the performer's ideas of the manner in which harpsichord composers used the instruments available to them, and it makes possible for the harpsichord builder a total and in many cases highly desirable re-examination of his craft. It is unlikely that a book will soon again appear that will have such a far-reaching influence in the harpsichord world.

Ralph Kirkpatrick

PREFACE

In this book my purpose has been to record the traditions of harpsichord making as they might have been transmitted to young apprentices in any one of the several countries in which the craft flourished. I have intended to give enough information to make it possible for builders of harpsichords to base their work on certain knowledge of the designs and methods of earlier makers; to guide players of the harpsichord in their search for appropriate instruments, dispositions, and registrations in re-creating the music of the past; and to serve as a useful body of information for historians and editors of early keyboard music. I do not pretend to have dealt with the purely musical side of the subject. The reader will find few discussions of the literature, employment, or styles of performance appropriate to the harpsichord.

A chapter each is devoted to the five most important schools of harpsichord making. A series of plates illustrates the most typical harpsichords of each country. Ordinarily each group of plates includes a plan and elevation drawn to scale, a drawing in perspective of the interior of the instrument, and miscellaneous details of action and construction. These plates are supplemented by many reproductions of illustrations taken from early sources.

Before modern times there were no books on harpsichord making, and the literature of the subject was scattered in relatively short chapters and chance remarks occurring in works covering an enormous range of subject matter. The usual bibliographical sailing directions which modern scholars have come to expect from their predecessors had not been compiled when I undertook this project. My necessarily desultory search for material has unearthed significant passages in encyclopedias, musical, commercial, and philological dictionaries, treatises on musical theory and history, travelers' tales, notarial records, public archives, newspapers, musical periodicals, almanacs, reminiscences, diaries, manuals on subjects from forestry and mining to piano tuning and gilding, the advertising puffs of inventors, technical publications of scientific academies, and commonplace books. These sources are so diverse and difficult of access that I have felt it worthwhile to attempt to reprint in translation most of those of note which have not already been made available by Raymond Russell in *The Harpsichord and Clavichord, An Introductory Study* (London: Faber and Faber, 1959) or other accessible modern editions. It may seem that this policy has resulted in a somewhat cumbrous apparatus and overmeticulous documentation. However it must be remembered that this book is intended as much as an anthology of early sources as it is a treatise on the history of harpsichord making. Unless otherwise noted all translations are my own.

Once found, these documents are often difficult of interpretation. Harpsichord makers as a whole were neither inclined nor able to write accurately of their trade and those who did attempt to deal with it were chiefly amateurs, cranks, or dilettantes. To bolster this somewhat feeble documentation I have turned to the instruments which chance, curiosity, or avarice have preserved. I have disassembled and measured some hundreds of harpsichords, and the experience of ten years making my own instruments and restoring antiques has been of considerable assistance in assessing what I have seen. But even here I have been able to hold only a cloudy glass up to nature, for the typical harpsichord one finds in a museum is an agglomeration of accretions, *ravalements*, and redecorations. Fakers have been active without cessation from at least the beginning of the seventeenth century. Even more misleading is the tendency of harpsichords to have been preserved because they were atypical. Thus the statistician finds himself listing and computing the vagaries of freaks which were originally prized as curiosities. Then the catastrophes of war have not destroyed instruments impartially. The turmoil of the seventeenth century in Germany may have wiped out the early examples of the harpsichord maker's art in that country almost completely. They certainly do not exist now; one can only guess whether they ever did. On the other hand the tranquil course of the eighteenth century in England left a great many fine harpsichords as part of its monument and one is tempted to grant them more than their due importance on the basis of their number. Again, the intense preoccupation of the French upper classes with the ephemera of fashion caused the destruction of many more harpsichords as they became obsolete than seems to have been the case among France's more conservative neighbors.

For the purposes of this book I have arbitrarily decided to consider only the period from about 1500 to 1800. It must be admitted that the least assiduous niggler could find ample evidence of the existence of harpsichord making on either side of these limiting dates. However, very little concrete can be known of the exact nature of the harpsichord before 1500, and after 1800 its nature is no longer of any musicological significance.

This study is designed to continue and amplify the recent books of Raymond Russell and of Donald Boalch (*Makers of the Harpsichord and Clavichord, 1440 to 1840*, London: George Ronald, 1956). Mr. Russell's lucid discussion of the elements of the subject has made repetition of that material unnecessary here and has permitted a more technical and detailed history of the instrument than might otherwise have been comprehensible. Mr. Boalch's biographical dictionary of the makers has served as an indispensable source and has freed me from the necessity of rehearsing biographical detail except in the rare cases where I have been able to provide new information or where the identification of makers has been pertinent to my argument.

The unstinting assistance of Mr. Russell and Mr. Boalch in my project immeasurably improved the resulting book and added not a little to my pleasure in writing it. Pierre J. Hardouin generously made available the results of his researches at the Archives Nationales. John Rackliffe, Gustav Leonhardt, and Ralph Kirkpatrick read the manuscript and made extremely useful suggestions. Mr. Kirkpatrick has contributed a foreword which must greatly enhance the value of the work for those who know him as a musician and a scholar. It is to Mr. Leonhardt that I owe my acquaintance with the *Verhandeling over de Muziek*. Charles P. Fisher was of the greatest assistance in the basic planning of the form of the book and several of the plates were originally designed by him. The final execution of the plates I owe to my father, Frank L. Hubbard, who has devoted many hours of work and many miles of travel to the project.

I must express gratitude to the following persons who have been of great help in the collecting of material: Sidney Beck, Alfred Berner, Mme. de Chambure, the late Erwin Bodky, Thurston Dart, William R. Dowd, Friedrich Ernst, Mrs. Elisabeth van Asbeck Feldbrugge, Mrs. Anne Gombosi, Hugh Gough, Eric Herz, Robert Johnson, R. Kenneth Lee, Victor Luithlen, Miss Sibyl Marcuse, J. H. van der Meer, Fritz Neumeyer, George Pahud, J. Ricart Matas, Edwin Ripin, William Post Ross, the late Ulrich Rück, H. C. August Wenzinger, and Miss Narcissa Williamson. Mrs. Betsy G. Moyer edited and typed the manuscript with unusual care. Miss Diane Goetz, Mrs. Elizabeth Griffin,

Mark William Kramer, and Mrs. Ingeborg von Huene aided in the final preparation of the manuscript.

The staffs of the following institutions have generously assisted me beyond the call of their duty: Belle Skinner Collection (now part of the Yale collection of musical instruments); Benton Fletcher Collection, London; Boston Public Library; Carl Claudius Collection, Copenhagen; Conservatoire National de Musique, Paris; Conservatoire Royal de Musique, Brussels; Donaldson Collection, London; Musikinstrumenten-Museum der Karl-Marx-Universität, Leipzig; Kunsthistorisches Museum, Vienna; Metropolitan Museum of Art, New York; Musikhistorisk Museum, Copenhagen; Museum of Art, Rhode Island School of Design, Providence; Rushworth and Dreaper Collection, Liverpool; Smithsonian Institution, Washington, D.C.; Victoria and Albert Museum, London; The Vleeschhuis, Antwerp; and Württembergisches Landesgewerbemuseum, Stuttgart.

This project was made possible by a grant from the American Philosophical Society, a Fulbright Fellowship for research, and a C.R.B. Fellowship from the Belgian-American Educational Foundation.

It should be noted that throughout the book proper names are spelled as they appear on the instrument or in the document under consideration. In many cases this policy has produced apparent inconsistencies in spelling.

In this second printing a few corrections have been made and Appendix I has been added.

F. H.

CONTENTS

TABLES

PLATES

THREE CENTURIES OF
HARPSICHORD MAKING

. . . 'I am Lazarus, come from the dead,
Come back to tell you all, I shall tell you all' —

T. S. Eliot

CHAPTER ONE · ITALY

"But, to say the truth," wrote Charles Burney in 1771,[1] "I have neither met with a *great* player on the harpsichord, nor an original composer for it throughout Italy. There is no accounting for this but by the little use which is made of that instrument there, except to accompany the voice. It is at present so much neglected both by the maker and player, that it is difficult to say whether the instruments *themselves*, or their performers are worst." In the greater leisure of his footnotes Burney was able to expand this somewhat complacent observation:

To persons accustomed to English harpsichords, all the keyed instruments on the continent appear to great disadvantage. Throughout Italy they have generally little octave spinets to accompany singing, in private houses, sometimes in a triangular form, but more frequently in the shape of our old virginals; of which the keys are so noisy, and the tone so feeble, that more wood is heard than wire. The best Italian harpsichord I met with for touch, was that of Signor Grimani at Venice; and for tone, that of Monsignor Reggio at Rome; but I found three English harpsichords in the three principal cities of Italy, which are regarded by the Italians as so many phenomena. One was made by Shudi, and is in the possession of the Hon. Mrs. Hamilton at Naples. The other two, which are of Kirkman's make, belong to Mrs. Richie at Venice, and to the Hon. Mrs. Earl, who resided at Rome when I was there.

Another observer, Nicolas Hullmandel, a brilliant harpsichordist who had studied with C. P. E. Bach and who was well known in both Paris and London, agreed with Burney that the Italians were not particularly interested in the harpsichord. "The Italians did not profit by the new progress of the harpsichord and continued to make theirs with two unisons and one keyboard. Since these instruments were almost entirely destined for composers and were used especially to accompany the voice, a sweet sound was all that was sought." [2]

The attitude which Burney and Hullmandel noted in Italy during

[1] Charles Burney, *The Present State of Music in France and Italy* (London, 1771), p. 288.
[2] "Musique," *Encyclopédie méthodique* (Paris, 1791), I, 286b.

the eighteenth century seems to have been characteristic of Italian musicians and instrument makers in much earlier times and is probably responsible for the scarcity of written descriptions of the harpsichord in Italian. Theorists of the Renaissance and Baroque frequently discussed various elaborations of the standard keyboard which were intended to eliminate the necessity for temperament in the tuning of harpsichords, but they seldom seem to have regarded any other aspect of the instrument worthy of comment. This tendency of the Italian theorists seems to have wearied Burney, and it must be admitted that anyone writing on early Italian instruments feels a certain sympathy for his frustration.

During the sixteenth century, and a great part of the next, many of the most eminent musical theorists of Italy employed their time in subtle divisions of the scale, and visionary pursuits after the ancient Greek genera; nor was this a rage wholly confined to theorists, but extended itself to practical musicians, ambitious of astonishing the world by their deep science and superior penetration, though they might have employed their time more profitably to themselves, and the art they professed, in exploring the latent resources of harmonic combinations and effects in composition, or in refining the tone, heightening the expression, and extending the powers of execution, upon some particular instrument. These vain enquiries certainly impeded the progress of modern Music; for hardly a single tract or treatise was presented to the public, that was not crowded with circles, segments of circles, diagrams, divisions, subdivisions, commas, modes, genera, species, and technical terms drawn from Greek writers, and the now unintelligible and useless jargon of Boethius.[3]

The efforts of Donald Boalch [4] have recalled to our attention the names of several fifteenth century Italian makers who were active as early as 1419, but even his industry has been powerless to provide any sort of description of their product or to ascertain whether Italians were primarily responsible for its invention. It is curious that while nearly all of the earliest extant harpsichords are Italian the first written descriptions of the instrument were made mostly north of the Alps. Fourteenth century sources in England, France, Spain, and in the realm of the Dukes of Burgundy mention a so-called *eschequier* (the word is cognate to "checker," probably in reference to the black and white pattern of the keyboard) which was described in a letter of John I of Aragon to Philip the Bold of Burgundy in 1387 as "an instrument like an organ which sounds by means of strings." [5]

[3] Charles Burney, *A General History of Music* (London, 1776–1788), III, 161.
[4] Donald Boalch, *Makers of the Harpsichord and Clavichord* (London, 1955).
[5] Edmond van der Straeten, *La Musique aux Pays-Bas* (Brussels, 1885), VII, 40. The spelling is *exaquir*.

If the identity of the *eschequier* is dubious, an unequivocal drawing of the harpsichord and several suggested mechanisms for jacks with a discussion of their operation is contained in the mid-fifteenth century manuscript of Arnault de Zwolle,[6] a member of the retinue of the Duke of Burgundy. Other early representations are French, German, and English in origin.[7] The first years of the fifteenth century saw the spread of this device into Italy, and no less than fourteen makers can be named to demonstrate the bare fact that the Italians were practicing the art of harpsichord making at an early date.

Deprived of the written documents which might have illuminated our history, we are forced to turn to the extant instruments as the only materials for study, and it is fortunate that so many have survived. Italian harpsichords are found with dates from 1521,[8] and those originating in the sixteenth century are fairly common considering their extreme age. The degree of standardization which is evidenced by the early sixteenth century Italian harpsichords supports the feeble written evidence we have of an older Italian tradition in the craft. The very earliest Flemish instruments, on the other hand, were not standardized, and there seems to have been a period of development and experimentation in Flanders which is recorded to some extent in the surviving examples. Since these first Flemish efforts (the oldest is dated 1548) are very like contemporary Italian instruments, it is obvious that there was a connection between the two schools. Whether it was a question of direct Flemish imitation of Italian practice or of a heritage common to both is difficult to determine. One would naturally assume that Flanders was part of the Burgundian ambience, but if this is true it is curious that the makers of the older Burgundian-Flemish tradition would appear to be fumbling their way through a phase of experimental evolution while the ostensibly younger Italian school was already firm in the possession of a settled practice.

In any case there is no doubt that northern Italy was the world center of harpsichord making during the sixteenth century and that instru-

[6] Edited from MS fonds Latin 7295, Bibliothèque Nationale, Paris, by G. le Cerf and E. R. Labande, *Instruments de musique du XVᵉ siècle* (Paris, 1932).

[7] For a more extended discussion of the earliest traces of the harpsichord see Curt Sachs, *The History of Musical Instruments* (New York, 1940), pp. 334–339.

[8] In Sienna there is a harpsichord inscribed and dated 1516 by a certain "Vicentius." According to Hugh Gough, who has examined it, the nameboard does not appear to belong to this instrument, although it is undoubtedly a genuine part of another harpsichord. There is a spinet by Alessandro Pasi, dated 1493, in the museum at Perugia. I have not examined it, but those who have doubt its genuineness. See Raymond Russell, *The Harpsichord and Clavichord* (London, 1959), p. 27.

ments were sent from there to all parts of Europe. The extreme rarity of non-Italian harpsichords until the rise of the Ruckers family in Antwerp toward the end of the century is ample demonstration of this fact. Furthermore, various small signs indicate that the Italian tradition was known and accepted as normal throughout Europe. For example, in Germany Praetorius shows an obviously Italian harpsichord, spinet, clavicytherium, and clavichord to illustrate those instruments in the *Syntagma musicum*;[9] the French spinets of the sixteenth century reveal what is either an Italian or a Burgundian influence in the provision of an outer case completely independent of the spinet itself; and in England Elizabeth's own "virginal," preserved in the Victoria and Albert Museum, is an Italian pentagonal spinet. Even more significant of English familiarity with Italian instruments is a remark made in 1588 by Thomas Hariot in the course of his narrative of Raleigh's fourth voyage to America.[10] Hariot was giving a list of "marchantable commodities" found in those foreign climes. Under "cedar" we read: "A very sweet wood & fine timber; whereof if nests of chests be there made, or timber thereof fitted for sweet & fine bedsteads, tables, deskes, lutes, virginalles & many things else." No school of instrument makers except the Italians ever used cedar or a cedarlike wood for harpsichords or spinets. It seems very likely that Hariot was thinking of Italian keyboard instruments.

Italian harpsichord production was not concentrated in one city as it was in Flanders, France, and England. However, there was never much activity in the south, and Venice seems to have been the most important center of the trade during the sixteenth century. About half of the extant Italian harpsichords are unsigned and undated, and many of the signed ones give no indication of the place of origin. Thus even the loosest generalization about the organization of harpsichord making based on this evidence is shaky. A random sampling of sixty-one fifteenth and sixteenth century makers whose dates and locales are known can be broken down in the following proportions: fifteen were found in Venice, eight in Modena, six in Ferrara, three each in Florence, Milan, Mantua,

---

[9] Praetorius' plates VI, XIV, and XV are reproduced here as Plates XXIV, XXV, and XXVI.

[10] Thomas Hariot, *A Briefe and True Report of the New Found Land of Virginia* (London, 1588), p. B2 (verso). On p. D3 Hariot wrote, "Some of our company which haue wandered in some places where I haue not been haue made certain affirmation of *cyprus* which for such & other excellent vses, is also a wood of price and no small estimation." Here Hariot was in error. The European cypress (*Cupressus sempervirens*) is a light brown, aromatic wood, indigenous to the shores of the Mediterranean, and not to be confused with the American cypress. Hariot's confusion, however, emphasizes the association of cedar with cypress in his mind.

Padua, Rome, and Verona, and the remaining fourteen were scattered over twelve cities, chiefly in the north.[11]

The oldest harpsichord to have survived is included in the collection of the Victoria and Albert Museum in London. It is inscribed "Hieronymus Bononiensis Faciebat Romae MDXXI." Nothing further is known of the "Gerolamo of Bologna" who made it. The extraordinary fact about this 1521 harpsichord is that it can scarcely be distinguished from Italian harpsichords made one hundred and fifty years later. It very strongly resembles, for instance, the harpsichord made in 1677 which is the most important source for Plates I–III. As much variation as is seen here could easily be found between two harpsichords made in the same year by different makers.

Like almost all Italian harpsichords, the Hieronymus Bononiensis instrument is composed of two major parts: a light and exceedingly graceful instrument made of cypress, and an outer case with hinged lid containing the harpsichord. In this example the outer case is covered with tooled leather of much later date. The stand is missing. The apparent range of the single keyboard is E–d''' (47 keys),[12] but the actual range was C–d'''[13] for, like the organs of the time, the bass octave of harpsichords in the sixteenth and seventeenth centuries was almost always "short."[14] The apparent low E was tuned to C, and D and E were provided respectively by the apparent F♯ and G♯. Thus the lowest octave of the keyboard sounded only one chromatic, B♭. Plate IV, figure 7, will make this arrangement clear. We symbolize the bottom note of this harpsichord thus: C/E.

There are two choirs of strings, tuned in unison at eight-foot pitch (termed a 2x8′ disposition), and plucked by two registers of quilled jacks. No provision of any kind is made for changing stops while playing. The registers are movable, but one must push the jack rail aside in order to reach them. It seems that they were made movable only to assist in tuning, when it would be essential to be able to sound one choir at a time. The existence of certain Italian virginals and harpsichords

[11] Based on information in Boalch, *Makers of the Harpsichord.*

[12] In this system for symbolizing the notes on the keyboard the bottom note of a five-octave keyboard (two and one-half octaves below middle C) would be shown as FF. Eight-foot C (on the second line below the bass clef) would be C, and the successive C's in ascending order would be c, c′ (middle C), c″, and c‴. The top note of most five-octave keyboards would be shown as f‴.

[13] The range of keyboards such as this one with a short octave to C will be symbolized C/E–d‴.

[14] See Georg Kinsky, "Kurze Oktaven auf besaiteten Tasteninstrumenten: Ein Beitrag zur Geschichte des Klaviers," *Zeitschrift für Musikwissenschaft,* 2 (1920): 65.

with a 2x8′ disposition which cannot be varied at all leads one to suspect that Italian musicians considered the eight-foot unison tone basic and that they felt no need to produce other effects. Four-foot stops exist on Italian harpsichords, but they are excessively rare. Italian harpsichords with four-foot were usually disposed 1x8′, 1x4′. It is interesting to note that not much more effort was made to provide stop mechanisms for harpsichords with four-foot than for those with eight-foot unisons. A fine claviorganum by Alexander Bortolotti, 1585, now in the Conservatoire Royal de Musique, Brussels, provides three draw stops for the organ division, but the harpsichord has none, even though it is disposed 1x8′, 1x4′. Another harpsichord disposed 1x8′, 1x4′, inscribed "Francisci Patari Ni Dicti, Ongaro 1561," in the Deutsches Museum, Munich, has registers provided with metallic extensions protruding through the right side of the case. It is difficult to determine whether this arrangement is original. The present metal knobs are modern, but they may be replacements of original ones in wood, metal, or ivory. Any stop-changing mechanism was unusual in Italian harpsichords until toward the end of the seventeenth century.

Buff stops were exceedingly rare on Italian harpsichords, possibly because the short strings do not sustain long enough to sound well while being damped by a buff pad. A harpsichord signed by Faby Bononiensis in 1677, now in the Conservatoire National de Musique, Paris, has two narrow battens standing on the edge in the gap behind the registers. Each is armed with small vertical iron pins, one for each string. These battens are controlled by two hand stops which cause them to advance until the iron pins touch the strings, producing a jarring sound. This device is quite like that described by Praetorius[15] under the term *Arpichordum*. Certain Flemish virginals were equipped with a similar stop.

Outline, scaling, stringing, case construction, and soundboard details are the most important factors in tone production. These elements combine to produce a timbre which can be manipulated and varied by the substitution of plectra of nonstandard materials or by moving the plucking point, but a fundamentally bad sound cannot be made good by changing plectra or plucking points, nor, within reasonable limits, can a good sound be made really bad by a poor choice of plectra or plucking points. I propose to discuss each of these points with an eye to the Hieronymus Bononiensis harpsichord, and it is suggested that the reader refer frequently to Plates I, II, and III, both to render the technical jargon a little more comprehensible and to convince himself of the re-

[15] *Syntagma musicum*, p. 67.

markable similarity existing between these two harpsichords so remote
from each other in time. Unfortunately for our purpose, even four hundred dry winters have not opened large enough cracks in the bottom or
the soundboard of the Hieronymus Bononiensis harpsichord to permit
us to see into the interior, and we are forced to base our discussion of
the frame and underside of the soundboard on other and later Italian
harpsichords. Since the Bononiensis conforms to the Italian tradition in
every observable characteristic, I feel reasonably secure in predicting that
a restorer of the future will find an interior structure very like that
shown in Plate II.

The outline of a harpsichord is determined by the sounding length
of the strings and their lateral spacing. It is common knowledge that the
string length theoretically doubles for each octave descended; this is
termed a "just" scale. In practice this scheme is seldom followed rigor-
ously because it would produce an extremely elongated instrument. Normally the strings are "foreshortened" in the bass and are made of thicker
wire in order to compensate. It should be noted that no old harpsichords
ever used the overspun strings so frequently found in modern instruments, except occasionally for the bass of the sixteen-foot. (See page 265.)
Most Italian harpsichords have just scales from the top to c, below which
the string lengths are arbitrarily reduced. Thus, if we are given the
string length of any of the higher pitched c's, we can easily calculate the
length of any of the others above middle c. The convention I have followed in this book is to specify the length of c'' (one octave above middle
c), and, in the case of instruments with unison choirs, to measure the
shorter string. I find that by comparison with the northern European
traditions of harpsichord making, the Italians generally used a very short
scale.

The octave span of the keyboard determines the lateral spacing of the
strings since the key levers of harpsichords are nearly always straight.
Italian makers ordinarily used a larger octave span than is found in the
north, and their strings, therefore, were somewhat more widely spaced.
These two elements, the short scale and the wide octave span, tended
to produce an instrument with a very deeply incurved bentside. Since
the Italians carried the just proportion of their scale to c (and even to C
in rare cases) — a full octave lower than the practice of the north European makers — the Italian harpsichords, proportionately, have longer and
more slender tails. This characteristic difference of form can easily be
seen by comparing Plate I, figure 1, which represents a typical Italian
harpsichord, with Plate VI, figure 1, which shows a Flemish harpsi-

chord of nearly the same range. Table 1 compares the Bononiensis string lengths and plucking points to those of the eight-foot choirs of a typical Flemish harpsichord. The Flemish harpsichord has much longer strings in the treble but its more severe foreshortening produces a bass string of almost exactly the same length as the Italian.

Table 1. Comparison of Italian and Flemish harpsichord scales

| | Italian (Bononiensis) | | Flemish (Andreas Ruckers, 1648) | |
	String length	Distance to plucking point	String length	Distance to plucking point [a]
d'''	4¹⁄₁₆ inches	1¼ inches	––	––
c'''	4¾	1⅜	7 inches	2⅝ inches
c''	10⅛	2⅝	13½	3¼
c'	18¾	3⅝	25½	4
c	40⅝	4⅞	40½	5
C/E	58	5⅛	––	––
C	––	––	54½	6

[a] By convention we give the plucking point of the front jack. The plucking point is defined as the distance from the end of the string nearest the player to the point where it is plucked by the jack. Add ¾ inch to the plucking point given to obtain that of the second jack.

The translation of this concept of scale and outline into terms of wood and wire was remarkably consistent throughout the history of the Italian harpsichord. Italian harpsichords were usually formed of very thin (³⁄₁₆ inch) sides of cypress nailed and glued around the edge of a full-length deal bottom (½ inch). These sides were reinforced on the inside by deal knees (⅝ inch) of triangular form standing vertically along the edges of the bottom, and by small sloping struts between the knees which extended from a point just under the soundboard downward to the center of the bottom. Two heavy blocks were glued to the sides and to the bottom behind the nameboard, and the wrest plank was posed on these. Parallel to the rear edge of the wrest plank and removed from it by the space required for the registers (about 1½ inches) was a member called the belly rail. This consisted of a plank of deal (6⅝ inches x ¾ inch) standing on edge and glued to the bottom and to the wrest plank blocks. The front edge of the soundboard rested on the upper edge of the belly rail to which it was glued. Battens (1¼ inches x ½ inch), called liners, were glued all the way around the inner edge of the case at the height of the top of the belly rail to serve as supports for the remaining three edges of the soundboard.

The interior construction of Italian harpsichords gives the impression of quick but competent work. Most of the parts which were fastened to the bottom were nailed and glued, the nails probably serving as clamps until the glue had set. One has the impression that an Italian harpsichord maker could make a case in three or four days.

With extremely thin sides of cypress and a well-planned frame, the Italian makers were able to make a harpsichord weighing little more than a modern bass viol, yet which was capable of withstanding the stresses imposed by the strings. This very lightness of construction reduced the stress the instruments were required to bear as the following will make apparent.

If one tunes a harpsichord string down in pitch, listening carefully to the timbre as the pitch falls, a point will be reached where the tone becomes false and weak. Careful listening will identify the sensory cause of this effect. With the ictus at the pluck the pitch is high, and as the string sounds with attenuating volume the pitch falls slightly. This phenomenon is usually accompanied by beats so that the total effect of the tone is of a lack of homogeneity and force. In tuning the string down one has really been shortening its scale. One can compensate to some extent for this shortening of scale by using a heavier string, but a short thick string does not produce quite the same timbre as a long thin one. The sound of the thick string is likely to be less thin and bright, more of a "plunk" than a "plink." [16]

If the same experiment is attempted with an Italian harpsichord of light construction, one will soon find that a short scale sounds better than it would on a heavier instrument. Furthermore, given an identical scale, the light harpsichord will demand a thinner string than the heavier harpsichord. This effect produces the seeming paradox that the Italian harpsichords with their short scales actually require thinner strings than their longer scaled and heavier northern European counterparts. Old stringing lists consistently take this phenomenon into account. Smaller and shorter scaled instruments were assigned thinner strings by Flemish and Dutch experts of the seventeenth and eighteenth centuries (see Douwes' stringing list, Appendix A).

Since the treble strings of an Italian harpsichord are both shorter and thinner, and the Italian bass strings, although of similar length, are thinner than those of a northern European harpsichord, the total tension imposed upon the Italian harpsichord is considerably less than that borne by a northern instrument of the same range and disposition. Thus,

[16] It is this effect which is the chief cause of the tonal weakness of many modern

Italian harpsichords, despite the extreme lightness of their construction, are more often found undistorted by the long continued tension of their strings than the instruments of any other nation.

Table 2 compares the stringing list of a 1694 Italian harpsichord on which the strings appear to be pre-nineteenth century to that used by me in the restoration of a harpsichord by Franciscus Marchionus, Rome, 1666. The 1666 harpsichord is similar to the Bononiensis. The second list was arrived at by experiment. Data on the string sizes actually used in old Italian harpsichords are so scarce that we cannot afford to discard the stringing list in Table 2 that is derived by the measurement of old strings. However, the real date of those strings is dubious enough. The evidence of my ears argues so strongly against them and so much in favor of the empirical stringing list that I have little hesitation in stating that the original stringing of most Italian harpsichords must have resembled the empirical stringing list more closely than the stringing found on the 1694 harpsichord.

During the sixteenth century Italian harpsichord soundboards were almost always made of the same cypress as the case. In the best examples this was quartersawed in order to reduce the shrinking and swelling as much as possible. In the seventeenth century one finds both cypress and the spruce or fir (see page 202), which all other schools of harpsichord makers favored. Although the cypress soundboards were sometimes sawed on the slab, the spruce soundboards never were. Cypress is not as stiff by weight as spruce. It seems that Italian makers attempted to compensate by planing spruce soundboards somewhat thinner than cypress soundboards. A typical cypress soundboard (1677)[17] which I examined, was thick under the bridge and tapered rather sharply to all the edges. Under the bridge the thickness ranged from ¹⁰⁄₆₄ inch to ¹³⁄₆₄ inch and around the edges from ⁵⁄₆₄ inch to ⁶⁄₆₄ inch. Spruce soundboards averaged about ⅛ inch. Whether this marked taper was deliberate or not cannot be determined. If the maker had no caliper, he would estimate the thickness of the soundboard by its appearance at the edges, and he would be likely to leave the center thick. However, the taper at the

harpsichords. In an endeavor to make them strong their makers increase the size and number of frame parts. They soon discover that in order to make such heavy instruments sound at all well the strings must be heavier and longer than the norm for old instruments, but such a scale and stringing greatly increase the total tension. The next step is to install even more weighty members to hold the instruments together. Ironically, the revivalists of the harpsichord find themselves involved in the spiral which produced the modern piano in the first place.

[17] The harpsichord is unsigned except for the inscription "F. A. 1677" on two key levers.

Table 2. Italian harpsichord string diameters (in inches)[a]

	Measurement of old strings	Empirical stringing list		Measurement of old strings	Empirical stringing list
c‴	.010 Steel	.008 Steel	c#′	.012 Steel	.010 Steel
b″			c′	.012 Steel	.010 Steel
a#″			b	.016 Steel	.011 Steel
a″			a#		.011 Steel
g#″			a		.012 Steel
g″			g#		[.012 Steel / .013 Steel][b]
f#″					
f″			g		
e″			f#		.013 Steel
d#″		[.008 Steel / .009 Steel][b]	f		.014 Steel
d″			e		
c#″			d#		
c″			d		
b′			c#		
a#′			c	.016 Steel	
a′	.010 Steel		B	.018 Steel	
g#′	.012 Steel		A#	.018 Steel	
g′			A	————	
f#′		.009 Steel	G	————	
f′		.010 Steel	F	————	[.014 Steel / .016 Steel][b]
e′			E/G#	————	.016 Brass
d#′			D/F#	.020 Steel	.022 Brass
d′	.012 Steel	.010 Steel	C/E	.020 Steel	.022 Brass

[a] See text for instruments compared.
[b] This harpsichord has a variable intonation keyboard with many split sharps and extra courses of strings. The crossover points from one string size to the next often fall on these doubled notes. See below, page 35, for a discussion of this type of keyboard. See also Table 18 for a seventeenth century Italian stringing list.

narrow part of the tail seems extreme enough to have been deliberate. It has been my experience, moreover, that soundboards which are thick under the bridge and thinner along the edges produce a better tone.

As important in the production of tone as the material and thickness of the soundboard are the structures which are glued to it. In the Italian instruments these structures consisted of an eight-foot bridge, some sort of ribbing on the underside, and often a rose. The rose does not seem to have a great influence on tone. Many fine Italian harpsichords have no rose, and no particular pains seem to have been taken by their makers to make another opening somewhere in the case to compensate. The characteristic Italian rose was a complex confection in the Gothic style of parchment and thin veneer, sometimes projected into the third dimension by a cylindrical extension into the cavity of the harpsichord. Curiously enough, the most elaborate roses are usually found in spinets, not harpsichords, and this observation can be extended to the generalization that the most ornate of the Italian instruments were spinets.

Italian harpsichord bridges were smaller in section than those of the north, and they frequently had none of the bass-to-treble taper which was characteristic of the northern harpsichord. The section of the Italian bridge was almost invariably similar to that illustrated in Plate II, figure 5, and it was frequently executed in walnut instead of the harder beech commonly used in the north. Most northern harpsichord eight-foot bridges end in a sawed bend, more or less abrupt in curvature, but Italian makers usually mitered a short piece to the main part of the bridge in the extreme bass (Plate II, figure 5). Occasionally Italian bridges have no hook or miter of any kind at the end but terminate in a straight sweep like northern four-foot bridges. Still another variation was to arrange one or several short pieces nearly parallel to the main bridge in the bass and disconnected from it, each of which carried a few courses of strings. The advantage of this system was to leave the soundboard more flexible in the narrow part of the tail and thus resonant to a lower frequency. Among the charming details of Italian instruments were the small carved scrolls with which the bridge and nut were frequently terminated. The relatively light bridge is probably an important element in the complex which combines to produce the tone peculiar to Italian harpsichords.

Italian makers seem to have used two systems of ribbing on the underside of the soundboard. The more common type is illustrated in Plate II, figure 4, in which four or five ribs, which are invariably of spruce even when the soundboard is of cypress, are glued diagonally across the soundboard. This arrangement has the disadvantage that ribs cross the bridge at several points. The strings near the intersection of bridge and rib tend to have a thin, tight sound, lacking in fundamental. The harpsichord maker William Dowd reports that an Italian harpsichord dated 1693 (in the Smithsonian Institution, Washington, D.C.) but unsigned is ribbed diagonally, but that the maker has cut out the ribs for about 1½ inches where they pass under the bridge. The tone is said to be good. However, ordinarily harpsichords ribbed in this manner produce a harder and less resonant tone than that of instruments ribbed in the second fashion (Plate II, figure 3). Here one large rib, the cutoff bar, is glued tangent to the bridge but distant from it about two inches at the nearest point. That section of the soundboard beyond the cutoff bar is then stiffened by one or more smaller ribs. This method of ribbing is much more like that employed in northern Europe and produces a tone of greater depth and resonance. It has the disadvantage that the soundboard is not held as flat by the ribs as in the transverse system.

Despite the strictures of Burney and Hullmandel and the disinclination of Italian writers to stir in the defense of their national type of harpsichord, it must not be assumed that Italian harpsichords were contemptible. The strong sense of form and organization which has always been characteristic of Italian art produced a consistent design which is inferior to no other in terms of either appearance or sound. More elaborate and powerful harpsichords were developed outside of Italy, and music was composed for them which exceeded the possibilities of range and registration inherent in the Italian instruments. But no harpsichords ever excelled the Italian in their dry sparkle or in the flexibility of phrasing made available to the player by the clarity and precision of their speech. The northern instruments overwhelm the senses in the rushing, reedy brilliance of treble and drumlike boom of bass. The evener and more meticulous articulation of the Italian harpsichords is less likely to tire and confuse the listener.

Italian harpsichord tone begins with a sharp pop and decays very rapidly. Damping is quick so that the instrument distinguishes sharply between legato and staccato phrasing. Strangely enough it is not difficult to provide the illusion of a cantabile connection between notes even though, in cold fact, one string has often ceased to sound before the next begins. The tone is fairly loud and the timbre is rather plain, being marked by less of a specific vowel color than that found in the north. The bass is hard and clean and balances well against the treble.

As Burney and Hullmandel remarked, Italian harpsichords were chiefly used for accompaniment and it is precisely in this employment that they are most successful. The marked attack and brittle timbre permit them to be heard among an ensemble of other instruments. Still it must not be thought that any harpsichord ever dominated an orchestra as a piano is able to do (it is this notion which produces so much dissatisfaction with the continuo harpsichord in orchestra performances), but the Italian harpsichord strikes the best balance between blending with other instruments and making its own voice heard.

A close examination of the typical action of Italian harpsichords, though perhaps tedious, is essential to an understanding of the means through which the peculiar musical effect of Italian instruments was produced. The action of any harpsichord is made up of three constituents: the keyboard with its key bed, the registers and stop mechanism, and the jacks. The Bononiensis harpsichord is typical of later Italian practice in all of these details.

The keyboard is mounted on a three-rail key bed similar to that illustrated in Plate III, figure 1. The keys are maintained in position by a balance pin passing through a mortise and by a wooden slip glued into the rear end of the key lever. This "rack pin" slides in a groove sawed into a block which is mounted on the back rail of the key bed, just behind the key levers (Plate III, figures 1 and 4). This structure, known as the rack or diapason, is typical of nearly all single manual harpsichord keyboards and the lower manuals of double harpsichords. In England during the eighteenth century the rack was replaced by the modern system wherein a second pin is driven into the front rail and works in a mortise cut into the bottom of the key lever (Plate XXII, figures 1 and 2). In the Italian rack the slips fixed to the keys are made of wood; in the Flemish, French and German rack they consist of iron or brass pins. The northern racks sometimes had a padded rail mounted above, which limited the key dip (Plate XVIII, figure 3), but the Italian makers padded the front rail, which served to stop the keys.

Italian key levers were generally balanced well forward of the center and thus return to the position of rest without extra weighting. Since the thin strings of Italian instruments do not require a strong pluck, a rather short stroke at the jack is sufficient, and the key dip is usually shallow. The forward balance point, with its adverse mechanical advantage, gives the player a vivid sensation of the action of plucking the string and produces a crisp and rapid action. The natural key levers of the Bononiensis are 14⅛ long and were originally balanced 5⅛ inches from the front. (The balance points were later moved back ⅞ inch to permit the installation of pull-down pedals.) The key levers are made of poplar, but beech is more often found in Italian harpsichords. The use of hardwood for key levers seems to have been characteristically Italian. Pine or lime was generally employed by makers in other countries.

The most common type of register found in Italian harpsichords is that known as a box slide (Plate III, figure 4, and Plate I, figure 2). That of the Bononiensis is a typical example. In the northern harpsichord making shops each rank of jacks worked in mortises cut into two battens about the size of a narrow yardstick (Plate XXII, figure 10). One of these, the lower guide, was immovably fixed inside the case of the harpsichord just above the rear of the key levers. The other, the register, was placed flush with the surface of the soundboard in the gap and was movable from side to side for a distance of about ⅛ inch to permit the jacks to be brought in and out of play. The Italian makers incorporated these two pierced battens into one structure about two inches thick which was movable. Since the box slide (or register) was so thick, no second bearing was required for the jacks. The problem of cutting accurate mortises through so thick a member was sometimes met by building the register up of shaped blocks, glued together, but other examples appear to have been cut out of a single piece of wood. The most common material seems to have been beech.

The Italian box slide is certainly sturdier than the north European registers, but it entails certain disadvantages. With so much wood in contact with the jack the mortises must be given more clearance than the thin northern registers require. Hence the Italian instruments are more likely to produce the rattling noises Burney so resented. Repairs which require the removal of the registers are also more difficult to perform on an Italian harpsichord. Since the cross-sectional area of the northern registers was small, their makers were able to cut a small hole in the spine through which the registers could be withdrawn. However, the Italian box slides are so large that the thin Italian harpsichords would have been seriously weakened by such holes. The only method of removing an Italian box slide is by first unstringing the harpsichord and then lifting the box slide out vertically.

Italian harpsichord makers bordered the soundboard and wrest plank with charming and light moldings no more than 3/16 inch thick (Plate II, figures 7 and 10). In order to make the box slides look well from above, their upper surfaces were almost flush with the top of these moldings and hence were higher than the soundboard. The raised register in conjunction with the low Italian bridge means that the working part of the jack must descend into the mortise when the key is at rest. In order to give clearance to the tongue and its spring, many Italian box slides were cut out in a form similar to that of the English spinet register (Plate XXIII, figure 4). Often this cutout was made both before and behind the jack so that one cannot tell from the form of the box slide which direction the jack originally faced.

Another type of register is occasionally found which seems to derive its decorative features from the box slide but which is similar in principle to the registers found in the north (Plate III, figure 3). Thin mortised battens are placed over the gap, overlapping the wrest plank and soundboard to either side. Slots are cut in the extreme edges of these battens through which fixed screws or pins pass into the soundboard (over the belly rail) and wrest plank to maintain the battens in place. The edges of these battens are molded to imitate the effect of the box slides between their moldings. A lower guide is affixed as I have described above.

The regulation of the motion of the registers is an exceedingly important part of the harpsichord action, and on the precision and stability of its management depend the reliability and evenness of touch. No maker before modern times devoted enough effort to this mechanism, and nearly all old harpsichords are less stable than they might have been. Almost any effective system of the regulation of movements of very small magnitude must depend ultimately on a screw, but we are probably safe in assuming that the cost and relative difficulty of obtaining or making suitable screws was enough to dissuade the average harpsichord maker from their use. There are no screws of any kind to be found in Italian harpsichords, and they were rare in any harpsichord until toward the end of the eighteenth century. The Italian makers were content to glue a small chamfered block to the upper surface of the box slide at each end, overhanging slightly, which provided a stop to the motion by coming into contact with the case. These blocks were very easy to install in the first instance since the maker had only to put the register into the correct position and glue on the block, making sure that it touched the case. Then, moving the box slide to the opposite extreme of its given motion, he could apply the second block to the other end. The disadvantage of this system is the inconvenience of the inevitable subsequent adjustment.

The jacks rest upon the rear of the key levers with their plectra facing either to the right or to the left. In an instrument with two eight-foot strings for each key, one string will be supported above and parallel to the right edge of the key lever, and the other will be over the left edge. The observer who views the string band from above will notice that the strings are gathered into pairs and will be tempted to reason from his experience with pianos that the strings of each pair are tuned in unison. A little reflection, however, will demonstrate to him that the jacks are *between* the unisons, and that the strings, then, which are closest to each other are actually tuned a semitone apart. The wide pairs are at unison. If the harpsichord has a four-foot choir, these strings are at a lower level and each is almost under one of the eight-foot strings, generally the one to the left. The four-foot string is slightly offset from the eight-foot string toward the jacks on that key so that the four-foot plectrum and damper will not touch the eight-foot string above when the key is fully depressed. If there is a sixteen-foot choir, it is placed at a level above the eight-foot strings, and each string is displaced slightly away from the jacks in order to keep it away from the eight-foot plectra.

I have adopted the following convention to express a given harpsichord disposition. An arrow symbolizes a jack and gives the direction in which it faces. Thus $\rightarrow 8'$ indicates a jack that is plucking an eight-foot string to the right. A simple 2x8′ single-manual harpsichord might be diagramed thus:

$$\rightarrow 8'$$
$$\leftarrow 8'.$$

Now we are told that the front eight-foot jack (which plucks closest to the end of the string) is sounding the string on the right, and the back jack, the left string. A three register double might appear thus:

$$\rightarrow 8'$$
$$- - - - - -$$
$$\leftarrow 4'$$
$$\leftarrow 8'.$$

The front jack, plucking to the right, is an eight-foot, the second jack, plucking to the left, is a four-foot, and the rear jack, plucking to the left, is another eight-foot. The broken line symbolizes the division between the manuals. Thus, the front eight is on the upper manual and the back eight and the four are on the lower manual. The bracket indicates the existence of a manual coupler. Thus all three stops can be controlled from the lower manual through the coupler.

A typical Italian jack is illustrated in Plate III, figure 3. It is difficult to specify any peculiarly Italian characteristic which is invariably present, but it is quite possible to distinguish certain features which often appear and mark a jack with certainty as Italian. The usual Italian jack was rather thicker than those of other areas (between ⅛ inch and ³⁄₁₆ inch) and normally had two dampers and a tongue of the simple section illustrated. They were seldom made of pear, favored by all other harpsichord makers, but are found in a variety of woods including beech, yew, and walnut. The spring behind the tongue was most commonly of bristle, but sometimes a leaf-spring of thin brass or quill was substituted.

Since documents contemporary to the age of harpsichord building almost always mention quill as the only possible plectrum, and never included sole leather in the number of exotic substitutes which were tried from time to time in the effort to find a more durable material, it is with exceeding diffidence that I suggest that the Italian makers occasionally used leather plectra. Yet a significant number of Italian harpsichords and spinets with apparently old jacks are fitted with leather plectra giving every appearance of age. I have never seen a non-Italian harpsichord with leather plectra [18] in which it was not perfectly obvious that the jacks had been replaced or reworked. Admittedly, the only alteration required is the enlargement of the mortise in the tongue, and the skeptic might argue that this change has been made to all Italian instruments presently fitted with leather plectra. But then the skeptic must explain why the restorers uniformly have been so clever in hiding the traces of their work on Italian harpsichords and so gauche when they work on others. It seems simpler to me to admit the existence of leather plectra in Italian harpsichords.

Italian harpsichords, as we have seen, consisted of an instrument inserted into a box. The decorations applied to the box and to the instrument must be considered independently, since they frequently date from different epochs and involve unrelated techniques. Harpsichord owners apparently had their instruments redecorated regularly to keep them abreast of current styles. Most of the outer boxes which survive reflect the rococo taste of the eighteenth century even when the instrument they contain is much earlier. It seems likely that harpsichord makers did not make the boxes at all but left them to other hands.

There is some evidence that at one time Italian harpsichords were withdrawn from their cases and placed on a table in order to be played. The care devoted to the adornment of the exterior of the harpsichord itself, particularly noticeable in the earlier examples, would lead one to suspect this, for these details are hidden when the instrument is in a box. The suspicion becomes a certainty in view of the numerous con-

---

[18] A clear distinction must be made between the plectra of hard cowhide with which we are dealing and the soft *peau de buffle*, buffalo hide, of the French eighteenth century makers. The two have nothing in common but a remote zoological affinity.

The *Encyclopédie méthodique*, "Arts et métiers méchaniques" (Paris, 1785), IV, 11, contains an article by an unknown V.A.L. which had been printed in earlier editions of the *Encyclopédie*. In outlining the history of the spinet, the author makes the following reference to leather plectra: "The mechanism of the keys was almost like that of today except that in place of quill the jack was provided with a piece of leather almost in the same manner as that practiced today by M. de Laine, teacher of the hurdy-gurdy, and M. Paschal [Pascal Taskin], harpsichord maker, both living in Paris." De Laine, so far as we can tell, and Pascal Taskin, most certainly, did not use hard leather plectra. Theirs were the soft *peau de buffle* which were sometimes used to provide a pianissimo and a stop somewhat sensitive to force of touch. It may be that V.A.L. was confused, since he had never seen leather plectra other than *peau de buffle*.

temporary representations of Italian instruments, uncased, being played upon tables. In this connection it is interesting to note the fine clavi-organum by Alexander Bortolotti, 1585,[19] in the collection of the Conservatoire Royal in Brussels. This instrument consists of an uncased Italian-style harpsichord mounted upon a largish box which contains the organ wind chest and pipes. It is unquestionably in its original form, and if it had been usual for Italian harpsichords to be encased at the period, Bortolotti presumably could have made some sort of covering for the harpsichord.

A storage box generally must have been provided for the harpsichord, and this box may gradually have evolved a hinged lid and legs in order to save players the trouble of clearing a table and dragging the instrument out each time it was to be used. The period at which the storage box became a true outer case is difficult to specify. Just as the human figure was frequently depicted undraped, the greater grace of unboxed harpsichords might have tempted artists to continue to portray them in that state even after it had become usual to play them in their boxes. The best guess I am able to make is that the change was taking place during the seventeenth century. Many of the ornate outer cases do preserve seventeenth century decoration, and the harpsichords begin to show tell-tale signs of their incarceration. For example, an instrument which bears the legend "F. A. 1677" is lacking all the moldings which would be hidden by a box, although those are present which would show even when the instrument was boxed. The moldings along the bottom edge of the harpsichord begin bravely and disappear behind the sides of the box, where they soon come to an illogical and ignominious termination. On the other hand, paintings from the same period show unboxed harpsichords in use. In the Prado there is a canvas by Castiglione,[20] which was painted about 1670, showing an uncased Italian harpsichord which is resting on a table and is being played by a standing performer. (Traces of the high legs of tables, preserved in the tall stands commonly found under Italian harpsichords, testify that it could not have been usual to sit in the position assumed by modern players until late in the eighteenth century.) But the title page of the *Frottole intabulate da sonare organi*, published at Rome in 1517,[21] contains a vignette showing an Italian single-manual harpsichord being played upon a table. The instrument is in a lidded box; the large section of the lid is closed, but the break

[19] Illustrated in Russell, *The Harpsichord and Clavichord*, plate 8.

[20] No. 652, entitled (by the museum) "Concierto."

[21] Reproduced as frontispiece to Claudio Sartori, *Bibliografia della musica strumentale Italiana* (Florence, 1952).

over the keyboard has been folded back. It appears that the instrument has been drawn slightly forward out of the box in order to be played, for the keyboard with its molded brackets protrudes slightly.

One of the clues we have to the date of the shift from the uncased to the cased instrument is found in the occasional appearance of a type of case I have designated as the "false inner-outer." This curious hybrid is a sort of *trompe l'oeil* which pretends to be a normal Italian instrument inside its box. However, the construction is actually similar to the northern harpsichords where the box *is* the harpsichord. In this sort of construction a radical departure has been made from the usual Italian practice. The case is now about ½ inch thick instead of ³⁄₁₆ inch and is made of a softer deal rather than cypress. The inner edge above the soundboard has been adorned by a molding which masquerades as the upper edge of an inner instrument. Cypress veneer, applied to the inside of the case above the soundboard and around the keyboard well, completes the illusion. It is certain that this sort of case could not have been conceived before the public had become accustomed to the appearance of an instrument in its box. The earliest example of which I am aware is a virginal inscribed "Johannes Batt. Boni da Cortona fecit anno 1617," now in the collection of the School of Music at Yale University. Another harpsichord of this type turns up in 1670 by "Joannes Tollenari Fianmengo Nell'Aquila," (Württembergisches Landesgewerbemuseum, Stuttgart), and other examples were made from time to time until well into the eighteenth century. (See Plate IV which illustrates an early seventeenth century virginal of this type. Figure 3 shows how the illusion is produced.) The sound of instruments made in this style is frequently not very good for the scale is too short for the heavy case.

To return to the description of the more usual type of Italian harpsichord with independent outer case, the form of the oiled or unfinished cypress case of the inner instrument was emphasized by continuous moldings at top and bottom. The commonest form of lower molding is shown in Plate II, figure 12. The complex of moldings at the upper edge generally consisted of a small cyma glued to the side of the case to act as console for the superimposed projecting cap (Plate II, figure 8). Occasionally, as in the illustrated example, the cyma was replaced by a reduced version of the lower edge molding. A second cyma was sometimes applied to the inner edge of the case. The cap molding and its consoles were carried right across the top of the nameboard, dividing the keyboard well from the body of the instrument. Forward of the nameboard, the spine and cheekpiece encompassed the keyboard and were usually given the form in profile of elaborate brackets (Plate II, figure 9). Sometimes, however, a more austere style was adopted in which a flat end block met the vertical block retaining the nameboard with no elaboration other than the smallest ovolo molding framing the upper surfaces of both blocks (Plate I, figure 2). It will be seen that the Flemish makers continued the molding formed in the inner edge of the case to the squared front of the harpsichord, including the keyboard well in the instrument (Plate VII, figure 1). The isolated keyboard of the Italian harpsichord is undoubtedly related in concept to the protruding keyboard of the Italian spinet, just as the integrated keyboard of the Flemish harpsichord is analogous to the recessed keyboard of the Flemish virginals.

Many of the earlier harpsichords are lacking the cap molding entirely, whereupon the console is generally thicker and more elaborate. A line of contrasting color may be inlaid into the upper edge of the case to conceal the joint between the side of the case and the console molding and to accent the pleasing outline of the instrument.

The soundboard and wrest plank were nearly always bordered by a very small molding (most often an ovolo), sometimes of a contrasting color. This molding was generally so narrow that the hitchpins did not pass through it.

Many Italian harpsichords were much more richly ornamented than the common instrument I have been describing. Understandably enough the most elaborate ornamentation was not often lavished on the exterior of the instrument where it would be hidden by the outer case. The most beautifully decorated and the best executed of the Italian harpsichords seem to date from the sixteenth century. In these the inner edge of the case above the soundboard and the nameboard were often adorned by a combination of veneer, inlay, and painting which produced a diapered or floral design. The upper surface of the cap molding and the keyboard brackets was sometimes accented by turned ivory studs inserted every few inches. The scrolled keyboard brackets might be replaced by a pair of carved figures. Frequently the soundboard roses were extremely elaborate, and the blocks supporting the ends of the jack rail often assumed complex forms, of which a partially unrolled scroll was the most usual (Plate II, figure 1). The jack rail itself, normally a simple bar with molded edges (Plate II, figure 11), could be divided by small moldings in frame and panel style. Sixteenth century Italian harpsichords exist which were veneered inside and out with ebony, against which inlaid lines of ivory stand out boldly.

The best Italian makers were wise enough to contrive that their ornament emphasize the elegant and logical form which was derived directly
from acoustical necessity. Possibly it is this unity of form and function
which enables a good Italian harpsichord to withstand as severe and
loving an examination as a violin. The Ruckers harpsichords are charming, but their naïve crudity is to the sophisticated Italian harpsichord
as a cuckoo clock to Brunelleschi's Duomo.

Great numbers of spinets and virginals were produced by the Italian
makers throughout the period of their activity. The construction of these
is analogous to that of the harpsichords. The remarks I have made on
materials, outer boxes, and moldings may be applied equally well to
the smaller instruments. We find again the extremely light cypress instrument, protected by its painted deal box; and although a greater number of spinets than harpsichords are highly ornamented, the type of
ornamentation is quite similar.

The smaller instruments at eight-foot pitch fall into two groups, both
with the usual range of C/E–f'''. The virginal is shown in plan in
Plate IV. It will be seen that its form is that of a rectangle with protruding keyboard, the rear right-hand corner beveled off. A closer examination would show the hitchpin rail, roughly parallel to the line of
jacks, sloping across the instrument from the spine at the right to a
point near the middle of the left end. The string band, then, is bounded
by the wrest plank at the right (note that the wrest plank turns abruptly
after abutting the right end for a short distance), the spine and hitchpin
rail behind, the left end, and the front. If one were to draw a line around
these limits of the string band, then make the two front corners more
acute in order to improve the appearance of the instrument, the form
of the second type of eight-foot instrument would be produced. This
type of spinet, generally called pentagonal, is far more common than the
virginal, but is inferior in tone. It appears in several minor variants.
Sometimes the right end is composed of two pieces meeting at a very
obtuse angle. Rarely the keyboard is partially recessed, and even more
rarely, completely recessed. The proportions and overall dimensions
were subject to a good deal of individual manipulation (see Plate XXV,
figure 2).

The frame of these spinets and virginals is so simple as to be almost
nonexistent. Like the harpsichords, the smaller instruments are built
on a full bottom, and the soundboard is supported by a liner (1¼ inches
x ⅝ inch) glued to the inside of the case. At the right end the liner is
wider, although no deeper, and is made of a hard wood to serve as the
wrest plank. There is no special reinforcement of any kind, the sole sup-

port being provided by the glue joint to the end of the case. In the pentagonal spinets the hitchpin rail is identical with the liner, but the virginals have an extra piece (1¼ inches deep x ¾ inch wide) glued to the underside of the soundboard where it receives the hitchpins. The only frame members are two planks which run from front to rear of the case at either end of the keyboard. These are cut down as shown in Plate IV, figure 1, so that the enclosed volume of the box is not divided. The register is similar to the box slide of the harpsichords, but it is glued to the underside of the soundboard, which is mortised to clear the jacks (Plate IV, figures 2 and 7). Where the register intersects the two frame members it is usually glued. Thus the soundboard is divided diagonally by the rigid register which is securely anchored to the frame.

Soundboard ribbing is equally simple (Plate IV, figure 2) and generally consists of from two to four ribs, more or less perpendicular to the register, running from that member to the front of the instrument. When there are two ribs, they are usually placed to either side of the rose, which in an instrument of C/E to f‴ compass is most frequently centered on the line of g″, midway from the front of the case to the register. Thus the practice of the spinet makers seems to corroborate my dictum that bridges are to be placed between two rigid members. The nut (the rearmost bridge) lies between the hitchpin rail (or liner in the case of the pentagonal spinets) and the register, and the bridge is bounded by the wrest plank and the rib to the right of the rose.

The scales of the spinets and virginals are consistently longer than those of the harpsichords, so much so in fact, that the spinet scales are more like those of the Flemish than the Italian harpsichords. For example, c″ averages between twelve and fourteen inches in length whereas the Italian harpsichord c″ seldom exceeds twelve inches, and more often is between ten and eleven inches. Spinet makers were able to burden their slight instruments with these long scales only because there were half as many strings in the 1x8′ spinets as in the 2x8′ harpsichords. The scale and plucking points on an Italian virginal inscribed "Ioannes Antonius Baffo Venetus F MDLXXXI" (now in the collection of Rushworth and Dreaper, Ltd., Liverpool) are typical.

String	String length	Distance to plucking point
f‴	4½ inches	2⅛ inches
c‴	6½	3
c″	13	4
c′	26	6½
c	45¾	10¾
C	57½	10¾

If this scaling is compared to that of the Bononiensis harpsichord, given in Table 1, it will be seen that the tenor of the virginal, as well as the treble, is longer and that the harpsichord equals the virginal in string length only in the extreme bass.

The plucking points of Italian virginals were much closer to the center of the strings than those of the harpsichords. Table 3 compares the percentage of the string length represented by the distance to the plucking point in the Bononiensis harpsichord and the virginal specified above.

Table 3. Percentage of string length represented by distance to plucking point, Italian harpsichord and virginal [a]

	Harpsichord	Virginal
f'''	----	47.2%
d'''	30.6%	----
c'''	28.9	46.2
c''	25.9	30.8
c'	19.3	25.0
c	12.0	23.5
C/E	8.8	----
C	----	18.2

[a] See text for instruments compared.

Italian virginals have a remarkably good tone, which is quite different from that of the harpsichords. The timbre is rounder, revealing a stronger box resonance; the bass is less hard, more "tubby," and the treble is purer, although less brilliant. This characteristic tone is the result of the combination of the plan and the enclosed volume of the instrument, of the scale and plucking point, and of the placement of the nut as well as the bridge on the soundboard. Much has been made of the last as the basis of an immutable distinction between the harpsichord and the virginal, but it is quite possible to find harpsichords in which the nut as well as the bridge is mounted on free soundboard.[22] Nevertheless it cannot be denied that the placement of the nut on the soundboard influences the tone significantly, reinforcing the fundamental at the expense of the partials. If the ability of the nut of a virginal to transmit vibrations to the soundboard is inhibited by resting a heavy mass on it, the tone becomes noticeably thinner and more wiry. The precise role played by each factor

[22] An undated Italian harpsichord owned in 1958 by Raymond Russell of London has the top surface of the wrest plank hollowed away under the nut which then rests on a sort of deck the thickness of the soundboard. A claviorganum made in London by the Fleming, Lodowicus Theewes, in 1579, now in the Victoria and Albert Museum, is constructed in a similar manner.

I have specified is impossible to determine unless by arduous and dubious experimentation. The rounder quality of tone is doubtless due in part to the plucking point, which, farther from the end of the string than that of the harpsichord, would produce a weaker series of partials.

Italian pentagonal spinets are not nearly so good as the virginals. Since they are identical with the virginals in all respects but outline, it seems fair to put the difference down to that factor. Their tone is weaker, less "tubby," more hard and unresonant. The pentagonal cases do enclose less volume, but I suspect that the more generous margin of soundboard around the bridge and nut of the virginals (even when isolated by the hitchpin rail) is of greater significance than the reduced volume.

I shall not pause long over the four-foot ottavini, common as they were, because they are nearly devoid of interest for modern musicians. Suffice to say that the most common outline was roughly rectangular and the usual keyboard ranges were from C/E to c′′′ and from GG/BB to c′′′ (sounding an octave higher). They were generally of heavier construction than the larger instruments, often exhibiting false inner-outer cases.

Of much more interest are the bentside spinets, similar in form to the common English late seventeenth and eighteenth century instruments (see Plate XXIII). In outline these are not unlike a very small harpsichord except that the spine is set at an angle of about thirty degrees to the keyboard instead of being perpendicular. The earliest spinet of this shape known to me was made by Hieronymus de Zentis in 1631.[23] It is quite possible that Zentis was the inventor of the type so widely copied in other countries. It is interesting to note that the French referred to the bentside spinet as the *épinette à l'italienne* as early as 1682.[24] Zentis' spinet shows all the typical features of the Italian style and is protected by an outer box. Although the instrument is at eight-foot pitch with a range of C/E to c′′′, the straight side is only four feet long and the scale is 11⅛ inches with a C/E of forty-three inches. Some later examples are larger and built more heavily in integral cases.[25]

Although the near absence of progressive development in Italian harpsichords is the despair of the historian, there was a great deal of

[23] Not 1637, as several writers have stated. The instrument is now in the Conservatoire Royal de Musique, Brussels.

[24] The bare term appears in an inventory of that year (Archives Nationales, Minutier Central CXXI, 135, Pierre Baillon). It is explained in the *Encyclopédie méthodique,* "Arts et métiers mécaniques," IV, 11a. The wide dissemination of the *épinette à l'italienne* may have been the result of Zentis' travels, for he is known to have worked both in England and France. See H. C. de Lafontaine, *The King's Musick* (London, 1909), p. 465, *s.v.* Andrea Testa.

[25] A particularly good example of the type was restored by Edwin Ripin of Forest Hills, New York, and is owned by Mrs. Thomas Furness of Middleburg, Va.

almost random variation which duty forces him to chronicle and, wherever possible, to document with less mutable references than the instruments chance has preserved. I have described the most typical instruments of the Italian production in what I fear has proved to be painful
detail. We should now turn to the variants of those types. Since this subject will immediately plunge us into a wave of niggling details which
are not easily restrained in the mold of English syntax, I shall employ
a harsher method and freeze them into the form of tables and lists.

The group of instruments upon which this documentation is based

Table 4. Sample ranges of Italian instruments

Eight-foot spinets and virginals		
Date	Type	Range
1523	Pentagonal	C/E–f'''
1537	"	C/E–f'''
1540	"	C/E–f'''
1548	"	GG/BB–c'''
1555	"	C/E–f'''
1556	"	C/E–f'''
1561	"	C/E–c'''
1564	"	C/E–e'''
1568	"	C/E–f'''
1570	"	C/E–f'''
1571	"	C–f'''
1572	"	C/E–f'''
1573	"	C/E–f'''
1581	Virginal	C–f'''
1586	Pentagonal	C/E–f'''
1601	Virginal	C/E–f'''
1608	"	C/E–f'''
1610	"	C/E–f'''
1610	Pentagonal	C/E–f'''
1617	Virginal	C/E–f'''
1618	Pentagonal	C/E–c'''
1620	Virginal	C/E–f'''
1631	Bentside	C/E–c'''
1684	"	C/E–c'''
1693	Special [a]	C–c'''
1694	Pentagonal	C/E–c'''
1705	Bentside	C–c'''
1711	Virginal	C/E–f'''
1726	Virginal [b]	C/E–c'''
1734	Bentside	GG/BB–c'''

Table 4 (cont'd)

Harpsichords			
Date	Range	Date	Range
1521	C/E–d'''	1666	AA–f'''
1533	C/E–f'''	1666	C/E–c'''
1538	D–e''' ᶜ	1670	C–c'''
1546	C/E–c'''	1672	C/E–f'''
1554	C/E–c'''	1676	AA–d'''
1559	C/E–c'''	1677	C/E–d'''
1560	C/E–f'''	1677	C/E–c'''
1561	GG/BB–c'''	1682	C/E–c'''
1574	C–f'''	1683	D–c'''
1579	AA–f'''	1684	C–c'''
1580	C–f'''	1689	C/E–c'''
1581	GG–c'''	1690	C/E–c'''
1581	GG–f'''	1691	GG/BB–c'''
1585	GG/BB–c'''	1693	GG–c''' ᵃ
1592	C/E–c'''	1695	GG–f'''
1602	C/E–f'''	1696	FF–c'''
1605	GG–f'''	1697	GG–c'''
1612	C/E–c'''	1701	C–c'''
1613	C/E–f'''	1702	C–c'''
1614	C/E–c'''	1702	C–f'''
1615	C/E–c'''	1722	C/E–c'''
1619	C/E–c'''	1757	C–g'''
1631	C–f'''	1759	D–c'''
1643	C/E–c'''	1761	C/E–f'''
1646	GG–f'''	1762	FF–e'''
1656	C/E–c'''	1779	FF–f'''
1658	C/E–c'''	1780	FF–f'''
1665	C/E–c'''	1792	FF–f'''

ᵃ A spinet of peculiar shape by Cristofori, Heyer Collection.
ᵇ Recessed keyboard. All corners are beveled off. Claudius Collection.
ᶜ Possibly extended in 1669.
ᵈ No GG♯.

is by no means exhaustive, but it probably represents a fair cross section of Italian harpsichords and spinets. I have examined every instrument that chance or industry has put within my reach, and I have extracted the descriptions of others from the pages of catalogues. It is to be hoped that the vicissitudes of four hundred years have produced a truly random sample. Some of my lists may appear unduly short, but it must be remembered that only half of the existing Italian instruments are dated (and for most of our purposes an instrument of unknown date is useless), that the remnant must be culled of obvious frauds, that full information for a variety of reasons is not available on others, and that frequently only one specific type is relevant, a limitation which imposes a further division on my waning statistical sample.

I shall treat these variants under two headings: first, purely musical characteristics such as the range, disposition, and special keyboards planned for variable intonation; second, the various details which affect tone, such as the soundboard material, scale, plectrum material, and case construction.

Table 4 lists sample ranges of various sorts of Italian instruments. It will be seen that C/E–f′′′ was almost standard for the spinets and virginals although C/E–c′′′ was not uncommon. Strangely enough, the shorter ranges are more frequently found in the later spinets than in those dating from the sixteenth century, a possible indication that spinets were no longer taken seriously as musical instruments in the later period. Range seems to have varied more in the harpsichords than in the spinets, but it shows little more tendency toward a continuous trend. It is significant that all the harpsichords dated after 1762 have the full five-octave range, but this was more than half a century after that range had been introduced elsewhere.

In my opinion no extant Italian harpsichord with more than one manual is genuine. The few which I have not been able to examine are considered dubious by their owners. Except for the instruments fitted with elaborate arrangements of keys devised to provide for nonenharmonic tuning it has been assumed that all Italian harpsichords originally had one manual only. The great majority were disposed 2x8′, but four-foot stops appear irregularly. Rather than construct a long and monotonous list nearly all disposed 2x8′, I itemize in Table 5 only the instruments which depart from that norm.

Table 5. Selected Italian harpsichords with unusual dispositions

Date	Disposition	Remarks	Identification
1533	1x8′	[a]	Dominicus Pisavrensis, Heyer Collection, Leipzig [b]
1538	1x8′, 1x4′		Alexandri Trasontini, Brussels Conservatory
1543	2x4′	Only 45⅛ inches in length	Dominicus Pisaurensis, Paris Conservatory
1554	2x8′	One register a "lute" very close to the nut	Padre Stoppacio (?), Vassar College
1561	1x8′, 1x4′		Francisci Patari, Deutsches Museum, Munich

Table 5 (*cont'd*)

Date	Disposition	Remarks	Identification
1579	1x8', 1x4'	Now 2x8' but the soundboard shows traces of an earlier 4' bridge and a line of 4' hitch-pin holes. There is no 4' hitchpin rail under the sound-board, but it appears that each hitchpin was anchored by a drop of glue	Antonius Baffo, Paris Conservatory
1585	1x8', 1x4'	Claviorganum. The 4' is old, but the 8' bridge has two pins for each note as if the instrument had 2x8' at one time	Alexander Bortolotti, Brussels Conservatory
1590	2x8', 1x4'	Kinsky[c] doubts authenticity but apparently only because the disposition is unusual	Two signatures: Francesco da Brescia, Dominicus Pisauren-sis, Dublin Museum
1600	2x8', 1x4' (?)	1938 Sotheby's sale catalogue shows "three stops"	Dominicus Pisaurensis (Boalch no. 11)
1619	1x8'	[a]	Gio. Battista Boni, Brussels Conservatory
1676	2x8', 1x4'		Ioannes Baptista Giusti, Heyer Collection, Leipzig
1683	(?x?), 1x4'	Now two manuals, 1x16', 1x8', 1x4'. Originally one manual. The 16' is a mod-ern addition. The 4' is origi-nal	Ionnes De Perticis, Heyer Collection, Leipzig[b]
1690	1x8'	[a]	Giovanni Andrea Menegoni, Smithsonian Institution, Wash-ington, D.C.
1694	2x8', 1x4'	No 4' hitchpin rail. The con-struction is similar to that of the 1579 Baffo except that a small block is glued to the soundboard where each four-foot hitchpin is driven	Nicolavs DeQvoco, Smithso-nian Institution, Washington, D.C.
1696	3x8'		Antonius de Migliais, Schloss Charlottenburg, Berlin
1726	1x8', 1x4', 1x2'	Kinsky gives the disposition: 1x16', 1x8', 1x4'. I follow Paul Rubardt of the museum staff	Bartholomaeus de Christo-phoris, Heyer Collection, Leipzig
1757	3x8'		Gio. Francesco Franco, Heyer Collection, Leipzig

[a] It seems likely that these 1x8' Italian harpsichords were intended to be strung in gut.

[b] Based on information kindly provided by Paul Rubardt of the Musikinstrumenten-Museum der Karl-Marx-Universität, Leipzig.

[c] Georg Kinsky, *Musikhistorisches Museum von Wilhelm Heyer in Cöln, Katalog* (Cologne, 1910), I, 224.

In reopening the question of keyboards devised to provide a diversity of intonations by dividing the octave into many parts, the historian finds himself skirting the boggy ground which engulfed so many of the Italian theorists of the sixteenth and seventeenth centuries. The stale disputes between the proponents of the "ancient" theories of harmony and the "modern" are inextricably intertwined with the problems of temperament, and these in turn involve keyboards and harpsichords. Unfortunately very little solid information on instruments is to be found. Several writers discuss certain harpsichords with multiple division keyboards, but nothing beyond the configuration of those keyboards is dealt with.

Possibly the central figure in the controversies that produced the multiple division keyboards of the sixteenth and seventeenth centuries was the choirmaster of the d'Este family, a certain Dom Nicola Vicentino. Vicentino had been a student of the famous Flemish musician Adrian Willaert, but he had become obsessed by an interest in what he considered to be ancient music and was dominated by the misguided hope of reviving the chromatic and enharmonic genera of the Greeks. He published a volume of madrigals (1546) which pretended to exemplify his system, but it provoked little notice. In order to make possible the performance of his music on keyboard instruments he invented a harpsichord which he called the "arcicembalo," equipped with a special keyboard containing enough keys in each octave to produce the various intonations required by each of the genera. According to Bottrigari[26] this instrument was first invented in 1555. Since Vicentino's book on theory was published in 1555, it seems likely that Bottrigari assigned that date without further thought. The instrument was probably made a few years earlier. It had "six rows of keys, comprehending in their division the three harmonic genera." Meanwhile Vicentino had started a singing school which undertook to provide vocalists with the technique required by his system, but he declined to reveal the details of his theory to the world until he had been sufficiently recognized. This prudent decision had to be cast aside when a private discussion with the Portuguese musician Vicente Lusitano broadened into a formal and public disputation. The point at issue was the theoretical analysis of a particular piece of music, Vicentino holding that modern music was formed of a mélange of the three genera, Lusitano that it could be analyzed in terms of the diatonic. Judges were appointed, stakes posted, and the contest took place. Vicentino was adjudged to have lost. Chagrined by his defeat,

[26] Alemanno Benelli (pseudonym for Ercole Bottrigari), *Il Desiderio ovvero de'concerti di varii stromenti musicali* (Bologna, 1590).

he devoted himself to the production of a book which should vindicate his position. In 1555 *L'Antica musica ridotta alla moderna pratica* was published in Rome, and in Book V one can read the description of his instrument. Three plates at the end of the volume further clarify the details of Vicentino's division of the octave. In 1561 a further description of the harpsichord appeared,[27] and it was stated that Vincenzo Colombo had actually built the instrument to Vicentino's specifications.

Vicentino was not to find much support, for he was soon attacked bitterly by Artusi, Zarlino, and Doni.[28] However, his party could not have suffered complete annihilation; as late as 1606 a harpsichord was built to his prescription by Vito de Trasuntinis. This instrument is preserved in the Museo Civico at Bologna and has a compass of four octaves, each octave having thirty-one keys.[29]

Although Zarlino disposed of Vicentino's theory, he was not to be so fortunate with the sad arithmetic of sound. The crux of the problem of temperament lies in the fact that a circle of perfect fifths will not produce perfect octaves. If one begins with c, ascends to g, to d′, to a′, to e″, and so forth, producing a perfect fifth each time, one would sound the following notes successively: c, g, d^1, a^1, e^2, b^2, $f\#^3$, $c\#^4$, $g\#^4$, $d\#^5$, $a\#^5$, $e\#^6$, $b\#^6$. Descending from the stratosphere of $b\#^6$ by perfect octaves, one would soon discover that the b♯ one had produced was not identical with the c with which one had commenced. It would be sharp by a small interval known as the "comma of Pythagoras." A little knowledge of arithmetic might enable one to predict this issue. The ratio of vibrations from the lower note of a perfect fifth to the upper note is 2:3. The ratio of vibrations of an octave is 1:2. A series of ratios of 2:3 simply will not combine to form the ratio 1:2. Thus we are faced with the fact that each fifth is too large and that a perfect fifth cannot be admitted into a musical scale in which the octaves are to be perfect. Similar reasoning will show that perfect fourths are too small to produce perfect octaves.

It has only been admitted in relatively modern times that the obvious solution is to divide the comma of Pythagoras evenly throughout each

[27] Nicola Vicentino, *Descrizione dell' arciorgano* (Venice, 1561).

[28] Giovanni Maria Artusi, *L'Artusi, ovvero delle imperfezzioni della moderna musica* (Venice, 1600), p. 28. Gioseffo Zarlino, *Instituzioni harmoniche* (Venice, 1558). Giovanni Battista Doni, *Commentarii de Lyra Barberina* (Florence, 1763; written ca. 1635); and *Compendio del trattatto dei generi e modi della musica* (Rome, 1635).

[29] It is inscribed: "Solus/ Camillus Gonzaga Novellariae comes// Clavemusicum omnitonum/ Modulis diatonicis, chromaticis et enharmonicis// A docto manu tactum/ Insigne/ Vito de Trasuntinis veneto auctore/ MDCVI." See Russell, *The Harpsichord and Clavichord*, plates 13A and 13B for photographs of this instrument. Russell errs in stating that there are 32 keys per octave; there are 31, or a total of 125 for the keyboard.

octave (equal temperament) by narrowing each fifth very slightly and widening each fourth.[30] The ancients failed to arrive at this solution, not because they were stupid but because their ears had not been dulled as ours have been. Up to the sixteenth century the musical culture had been predominantly vocal, and temperament is not necessary in vocal music. When a choir produces the perfect fifth a♯–e♯, they need not replace the e♯ with an f as the pianist must do. Their ears automatically direct them to sing the pitch[31] which bears the relationship to the a♯ of 3:2 and they sound a beatless interval. I have used the example of a fifth for reasons of simplicity and brevity. In point of fact, the difference between a tempered fifth and a perfect fifth is so slight that it is almost impossible to determine which a choir sings. It is in the thirds and sixths that the great difference between true and tempered intonation is found. The miserable thirds produced by the system of equal temperament seemed intolerable in early times, and many solutions were devised to avoid them. Broadly speaking, these solutions can be divided into two groups. In the first system extra keys were provided to sound the required notes. For example, to avoid the difficulty noted above, the b♯ which is not identical with c, a special key would have been added to sound b♯. The second system juggled the tuning of the twelve semitones which make up an octave in various ways in order to minimize the difficulty. Certain remote keys were jettisoned altogether so that it would be possible to tune the others to a closer approximation of just intonation. In other words, instead of dividing the comma of Pythagoras evenly throughout the octave, they threw all the error onto a few rarely used intervals and improved the most common keys significantly. (It is quite likely that the real variation in intonation between various keys which once existed is at the root of the dogma still held by musicians that each key has its characteristic color.)

Zarlino was to provide several solutions of his own to the problem, although none was quite as elaborate as that of Vicentino. Plate V, which is reproduced from the *Instituzioni harmoniche*,[32] shows a typical Italian

---

[30] Without the use of logarithms it is very difficult to calculate the frequency ratios of a scale of twelve equal semitones, but they are not difficult to arrive at in practice by listening to beats. Many theoreticians prior to Napier gave practical rules for equal temperament.

[31] J. Murray Barbour would object to this statement, arguing that the technique of most singers is not accurate enough to permit them to vary the pitch of notes according to their context. Although I am inclined to concur with Dr. Barbour's gloomy view, I have arrived at the opposite conclusion. It seems to me that it would be much more difficult to intone the wolfs inherent in meantone or Pythagorean tuning than to mitigate their harshness by small changes in pitch. See J. Murray Barbour, *Tuning and Temperament* (East Lansing, Mich., 1953).

[32] I, 164.

harpsichord in which all the sharps are split and extra keys are provided between E and F, and B and C, giving nineteen divisions to the octave, which as Barbour points out would be most suitable for Zarlino's temperament.[33] Zarlino remarks that this instrument was made for him by "Maestro Dominico Pesarese raro & eccellente fabricattore di simili instrumente." ("Master Dominico Pesarese, rare and excellent maker of such instruments.") [34]

Burney saw this instrument in 1770, when he wrote:

At Florence, I found the harpsichord of Zarlino, which is mentioned in the second part of his Harmonical Institutions, p. 140 [incorrect citation]. This instrument was invented by Zarlino, in order to give the temperament and modulation of the three *genera*, the diatonic, chromatic, and enharmonic; and was constructed, under his direction, in the year 1548, by Dominico Pesarese: it is now in the possession of Signora Moncini, widow of the late composer Piscetti. I copied Zarlino's instructions for tuning it, from his own handwriting, on the back of the foreboard; but I shall reserve them, and the particular description of this curious instrument, for the History of Music, to which they more properly belong.[35]

Unfortunately, Burney does not give this information in his history or even refer to Zarlino's invention. Apparently his slender patience with Italian theoreticians had been exhausted by the time he had reached the appropriate part of his great work (III, 161), for there we find the diatribe on the Italian preoccupation with intonation I have quoted above.

According to Sir John Hawkins,[36] Zarlino's harpsichord produced more of a *succès d'estime* than anything else, for the multitude of "chords" in this astonishing instrument rendered it difficult to tune and more so to play. The most skillful players were seldom bold enough to meddle with it, although the Duke of Ferrara's organist, Luzzasco, was able to play on it well. And well he might, for Fétis has this to say of Luzzasco Luzzaschi: "The abbé Requeno cites Luzzasco Luzzaschi among the musicians of the sixteenth century who attempted to resuscitate the enharmonic genus of the Greeks and assures us that he had made a harpsichord in which the keyboard was so arranged as to make possible the performance of music in three genera, diatonic, chromatic, and enharmonic." [37] Further investigation in the same work reveals the

[33] *Tuning and Temperament*, p. 33.
[34] Dominicus Pisaurensis seems to have been a very well-known instrument maker in Venice. Fourteen instruments ranging in date from 1533 to 1600 have survived. If all of these are genuine, there may have been two makers of the same name.
[35] *The Present State of Music in France and Italy*, p. 253.
[36] *A General History of Music*, p. 446 in the Novello edition of 1875.
[37] *Biographie universelle* (Brussels, 1835), VI, 215a.

Abbé Requeno to have been a crank who held that the Greeks practiced equal temperament and that Pythagoras and Ptolemy were the destruction of Greek music by the *invention* of their intervals (VII, 406).

Having directed his attack against the already vanquished and long dead Vicentino, Doni provided his versions of harpsichords with variable intonation. One type had three manuals (or rows of keys; it is likely that there were not really three manuals but that one keyboard had keys arranged with their tops at three levels in place of the two found normally) transposed in various ways like the Flemish transposing doubles.[38] This instrument was called the "pentarmonico." Doni's friend Pietro Valle had another type built under the master's direction which was known as the "triarmonico."[39] This one also had three manuals. To round the series out we find two double manual harpsichords, the "tetrarmonico" and the "diarmonico."[40]

Fétis (s.v. Doni) mentions having found the description in an unpublished manuscript by Doni of a "clavecin transpositeur" built by a certain "Jacques Ramarin." He gives the pertinent passage in French translation as follows: "Enfin la diversité des tons d'aujourd'hui n'est autre que celle qu'on entend au clavecin fabriqué par Jacques Ramarin, Floréntin; auquel, par le changement des ressorts, le même clavier sert à divers ton differens par dégrés semitoniques." ("Finally the variety of today's pitches is the same as may be heard on a harpsichord made by Jacques Ramarin, a Florentine, in which by moving a mechanism [spring] the one keyboard serves for different pitches by steps of a semitone.") Athanasius Kircher reports that *Nicolaus* Ramarinus invented a keyboard in 1640, simple in its division, but changeable by means of registers.[41] On the basis of Fétis' quotation and Kircher's description it seems that this instrument did not transpose in the sense of changing a C to C♯ but by varying certain intervals slightly in order to provide various scales in nearly perfect intonation. This would be quite possible if one had an instrument with several choirs of strings, each of which was given a different temperament. By changing registers one would "transpose": that is, provide the correct intonations for the new key.

Robert Smith [42] describes such a mechanism with exceedingly clever details. He does not provide complete alternate choirs but many extra

---

[38] "Trattando secundo sopra gl'instrumenti di tasti," *Lyra Barberina*, I, 328.
[39] *Ibid.*, I, 330. See Barbour, *Tuning and Temperament*, p. 111, for a discussion.
[40] *Lyra Barberina*, I, 332.
[41] *Musurgia universalis* (Rome, 1650), I, 461. Walther and Adlung also mention him without adding anything new.
[42] *Harmonics or the Philosophy of Musical Sounds* (London, 1759), p. 168.

strings. His registers are of thin metal, superimposed, six deep. Each jack fits one of the six superimposed registers tightly while the other five have large enough mortises to clear the jack. Thus the stops advance certain groups of jacks selectively, and if the strings are tuned appropriately, his harpsichord could play in several keys with perfect intonation.

Kircher devoted the most elaborate discussion of any contemporary writer to the subject of multiple division keyboards.[43] Although German by birth, Kircher spent the greater part of his life in Rome and was more Italian than German in his approach to musical problems. He seems to have been attracted by the one problem in our field that ever appeared worthy of discussion to the Italian authors of theoretical treatises. Kircher provides us with a recapitulation of the achievements of Vicentino and Doni, and discusses a keyboard by the mid-seventeenth century theoretician Galeazzi Sabbatini of thirty-eight keys to the octave. Six keyboards with from twelve to thirty-one keys per octave are illustrated.[44] Some of these are of uncertain value since the cut was poorly proofread; and, by what may have been an engraver's error, several of the vibration numbers are reversed in order, creating some doubt as to the range of the keyboard segments Kircher was attempting to illustrate.

All of this is pretty dry fare and will hardly stimulate the desire for emulation in modern makers. As Hullmandel put it, "An attempt has been made to eliminate this failure to give the difference between the sharps and flats by adding keys. This kind of improvement will be difficult to introduce because of the problems which it presents to players and to tuners." It is to be doubted whether many performers ever learned to manage any of these mechanical marvels with any degree of facility.

A much more laudable innovation was that type of keyboard which, attempting less, achieved more. Generally speaking, the meantone system of tuning produced six practicable major scales (C, G, D, A, F, and Bb), and three minor scales (A, D, and G). The farther one modulated from C, the less satisfactory the intonation became. In order to improve the most remote of the practicable keys and to add certain others to those which could be employed, makers sometimes divided some of the sharps into two halves in order to permit alternative tunings for each. The sharps

---

[43] *Musurgia universalis.* Volume I, book VI, is of the most interest to us since it contains Kircher's description of the instruments of music. Unfortunately he says little that cannot be better learned elsewhere, and his plates bear a suspicious resemblance to those of Mersenne. It is worth adding here that Kircher's illustration of a harpsichord (plate IV, facing p. 454) shows an instrument disposed 1x8', 1x4', and a single manual with the range C to c'''. Nothing about the construction seems to have been uniquely Italian.

[44] Plate VI, facing p. 456.

most often "split" were G♯, A♯, and D♯. In this way one could provide a better B♭ major and make E♭ major possible, as well as improve A major and add E major to the list of keys.

According to De la Borde, "Ce sont les clavecins que les Italiens appelent brisés (Spezzati), & il parait qu'on en faisait beaucoup plus d'usage en Italie, lorsque les principes de la Musique y étaient en vigueur, & que l'ignorance, soit des chanteurs, soit des autres practiciens, quant à l'intonation n'y avait pas pris le dessus." ("These are the harpsichords that the Italians call broken, and it appears that they were used more in Italy when the principles of music were still vigorous there and ignorance either of singers or of other performers as to intonation had not taken over.") [45]

A reasonable number of Italian instruments with split sharps have survived; it is worthwhile to itemize some of these.

Date	Maker	Type	Range	Sharps split
1601	Viti de Trasvntini	Virginal	C/E–f'''	F♯, G♯ (short octave), d♯, g♯, d♯', g♯', d♯'', g♯''
1617	Joannes Batt. Boni [46]	Harpsichord	C/E–f'''	F♯, G♯ (short octave), d♯, g♯, d♯', g♯'
1619	Gio. Battista Boni	Harpsichord	C/E–c'''	F♯, G♯ (short octave), d♯, g♯, d♯', d♯''
1666	Franciscus Marchionus	Harpsichord	C/E–c'''	F♯, G♯ (short octave), d♯, g♯, a♯, d♯', g♯', a♯'
1670	Joannes Tollenari	Harpsichord	C–c'''	C♯, D♯, c♯, d♯
1683	Girolamo Zenti	Harpsichord	D–c'''	F♯, G♯, d♯, g♯, d♯', g♯'
1711	Petrus Centamin	Virginal	C/E–f'''	F♯, G♯ (short octave), d♯, g♯, d♯', g♯'

A clear distinction should be made between sharps split to obtain an alternate intonation and those split to fill out the short octave. Frequently an instrument descending to C/E will be equipped with split sharps for the apparent low F♯ and G♯. The extra keys thus obtained are used to provide a real F♯ and G♯, since those notes are lacking in the ordinary short-octave arrangement. Similar split sharps were sometimes used to fill the GG short octaves which appear to begin with BB. In the short-octave examples here one half of the F♯ key would sound D and the other half would sound F♯. One half of the G♯ key would sound E; the other half, G♯. I am unable to explain why sharps in the top octave

[45] Jean Benjamin de la Borde, *Essai sur la musique ancienne et moderne* (Paris, 1780), I, 344.

[46] Mersenne (*Harmonie universelle*, Paris, 1636, p. 215) remarks that Boni made good harpsichords with split keys that one could tune perfectly, following the mathematical proportions of the intervals.

were never split. Poor intervals sound worse in the treble than in the bass.

No harpsichord with an original pedal board has survived, but a few instruments from almost every country where harpsichords were made show traces of "pull-downs."[47] Apparently a pedal board was placed under the harpsichord and connected to the keys of the manual by cords or trackers. Thus it would be possible to practice some organ music on the harpsichord, although notes would be missing if the pedal part ever coincided with that of the left hand. The range of these pull-down pedal boards must always have been small, because the greater octave span of the pedals would require a roller board if many pedal keys were to be provided. The traces of pull-downs which one finds in harpsichords generally consist of holes in the bottom of the instrument, under the keys, and some sort of device applied to the key levers to permit the attachment of the cords. Often this was no more than a vertical hole through the key (behind the nameboard) through which a knotted cord might pass. Other instruments show iron staples or other hardware. Since the addition of pull-downs to a harpsichord was so simple and required so little alteration, it is impossible to specify which harpsichords possessed original pedal boards and to which instruments the traces of pedal boards were later accretions. The improvised character of much of the work connected with pull-downs makes me suspect that they were not often original. The following Italian instruments were equipped with pull-downs at one time. (The two undated instruments are probably seventeenth century.)

Date	Maker	Type	Range	Range of pedal board	
1521	Hieronymus Bononiensis	Harpsichord	C/E–d'''	C/E–f♯	(15 keys)
1625	Valerius Peres	Harpsichord	C/E–c'''	C/E–c	(9 keys)
1694(?)	Unsigned	Pentagonal spinet	C/E–c'''	C/E–c	(9 keys)
1694	Nicolavs Deqvoco	Harpsichord	C–c'''	C–B	(11 keys)[48]
1697	Elpedius Gregori	Harpsichord	C/E–d'''	C/E–B	(8 keys)
Undated	Unsigned	Pentagonal spinet	C/E–f'''	C/E–B	(8 keys)
Undated	Unsigned	Quadrangular spinet	C/E–c'''	C/E–c	(9 keys)

[47] See below, p. 112 for a description of a French harpsichord with a pedal board which is probably at least partly original. R. K. Lee has informed me that the Valdrighi collection at Modena contains a somewhat dubious pedal board intended to be placed beneath a harpsichord to which it was connected by pull-down cords. There are eight pedal keys, C/E to B.

[48] This harpsichord lacks C♯. It is quite common for Italian instruments which do not have a bass short octave to lack certain chromatics. If the range descends below C it becomes almost the rule.

Certain elements of the physical design of Italian harpsichords were experimented with in a casual way by their makers. These changes would not be worthy of record if they were really as petty as they seem, but several of the features which were subject to frequent change are closely connected with tone quality. Table 6 collects the information on soundboard material, scale, plectrum material, case construction, and angle

Table 6. Variations in Italian harpsichords which affect tone

Date	Maker	Soundboard material	Scale (inches)	Plectrum material	Case type [a]	Tail angle
1521	Bononiensis	Cypress	10⅛	Quill	Inner-outer	Medium
1531	Trasuntini	Cypress	9⅞	Quill	Inner-outer	Pointed
1533	Pisavrensis	Cypress	11¾	Leather	No outer	Medium
1538	Trasontini	Cypress	10¾	Quill	Inner-outer	Medium
1543	Pisaurensis [b]	Cypress	5⅝	Leather	No outer	Medium
1546	Pesaurensis	Cypress	10	————	Inner-outer	Square
1554	Stoppacio [c]	Spruce	7	Leather	Inner-outer	Pointed
1554	Pisauri	Cypress	9½	————	Inner-outer	Medium
1559	Salodiensis	Cypress	10¾	————	Inner-outer	Pointed
1560	Transvntinis [d]	Cypress	————	Quill	No outer	Medium
1561	Patari	Cypress	12¾	Quill	No outer	Medium
1574	Baffo	Cypress	12¾	Leather	Inner-outer	Square
1579	Baffo	Cypress	11	Leather	No outer	Medium
1580	Baffo (?)	Cypress	12³⁄₁₆	Quill	Inner-outer	Square
1581	Bortolotti [e]	Cypress	9¾	Quill	No outer	Square
1592	Donatus	Spruce	10⅞	Quill	Inner-outer	Medium
1605	Celestini	Spruce	11³⁄₁₆	Leather	Inner-outer	Pointed
1612	Pratensis	Cypress	9⅛	Leather	Inner-outer	Pointed
1612	Dequoco	Spruce	10½	Leather	Inner-outer	Square
1613	Querci	Cypress	11½	Quill	Inner-outer	Square
1614	Quercius	Cypress	————	————	Inner-outer	————
1615	Dequoco [f]	Cypress	9½	————	Inner-outer	Pointed
1619	Boni	Cypress	10¼	Quill	Inner-outer	Pointed
1625	Peres	Cypress	10⅝	Quill	Inner-outer	Pointed
1631	Bolcionus	Cypress	9¾	————	Inner-outer	Square
1643	Albana	Cypress	11⅜	Quill	Inner-outer	Medium
1646	Mondini	Cypress	11⁵⁄₁₆	————	Inner-outer	Medium
1654	————	Cypress	10¼	————	Inner-outer	Pointed
1656	Zentis	Spruce	10¾	Quill	Inner-outer	Medium
1658	Zentis	Spruce	11¼	Quill	Non-inner-outer	Medium
1665	Rodolphus	Cypress	10	Leather	Inner-outer	Medium
1666	Marchionus	Cypress	10⅝	Quill	Inner-outer	Medium
1666	Zenti [g]	Cypress	10¾	Leather	Inner-outer	Square
1670	Tollenari	Cypress	12⅛	————	False inner-outer	Square
1672	Perticis	Cypress	10⁹⁄₁₆	Leather	False inner-outer	Pointed
1676	Givsti [h]	Cypress	9⅞	Quill	Inner-outer	Square
1677	Faby	Cypress	10⅛	Quill	Inner-outer	Medium
1677	————	Cypress	10³⁄₁₆	Quill	Inner-outer	Square
1682	Ridolfi	Spruce	11	————	Inner-outer	Medium
1683	Zenti	Cypress	10⅛	————	Inner-outer	Pointed
1689	Magniai	Cypress	————	————	Inner-outer	Pointed
1689	Cargnonvs	Cypress	9	Quill	Inner-outer	————
1690	Menegoni	Spruce	10¹³⁄₁₆	————	Inner-outer	Square

Table 6 (cont'd)

Date	Maker	Soundboard material	Scale (inches)	Plectrum material	Case type [a]	Tail angle
1691	Faby	Cypress	10⅜	Quill	Inner-outer	Medium
1693	————	Spruce	10½	Quill	Inner-outer	Medium
1694	Deqvoco	Spruce	10	Leather	Inner-outer	Medium
1695	Nobili	Spruce	9⅜	————	Non-inner-outer	Square
1696	Menegoni	Cypress	9⅞	Quill (?)	Inner-outer	————
1697	Grimaldi	Spruce	10¾	Quill	Inner-outer	Square
1697	Gregori	Cypress	9¼	Leather	False inner-outer	Medium
1699	Ferrini	Cypress	9⅞	————	Inner-outer	Pointed
1702	Migliais	Cypress	10¼	————	Inner-outer	Medium
1722	G. S.[i]	Spruce	10½	————	False inner-outer	Square
1726	Christophoris	Cypress	10⁹⁄₁₆	————	False inner-outer	Square
1729	G. S.	Cypress	10⁷⁄₁₆	————	Inner-outer	Square
1757	Franco	Cypress	————	Quill	Inner-outer	Medium
1759	Rossi	Cypress	10⁵⁄₁₆	————	Inner-outer	Pointed
1761	Berera	Cypress	12½	Quill	Inner-outer	Pointed
1762	————[j]	Spruce	————	————	Non-inner-outer	Medium
1773	Leoni	Cypress	9¹⁄₁₆	Quill	Inner-outer	Medium
1780	Sodi [k]	————	————	————	Non-inner-outer	Medium
1783	————[l]	Spruce	12	————	Inner-outer	Medium

[a] The terms specifying case type are defined thus:
Inner-outer: An inner instrument in an outer case. The normal Italian construction.
No inner-outer: No outer case and no trace of one ever having been present.
Non-inner-outer: The case and the instrument are one and the same. No camouflage is applied to make it appear to be an inner-outer instrument.
False inner-outer: An instrument with the appearance of an inner-outer but which in fact has no separate outer case.
[b] At 4' pitch.
[c] High pitch (?).
[d] Originally 1x8', 1x4'.
[e] Claviorganum 1x8', 1x4'.
[f] Nut mounted on free soundboard.
[g] Four separate bridges in bass.
[h] 2x8', 1x4'.
[i] Soundboard is not sawed on the quarter.
[j] Grain of soundboard is perpendicular to the bentside.
[k] Has double-tongued jacks.
[l] 2x8', 1x4'.

of the tail for as many dated and genuine Italian harpsichords as I have been able to marshal. It will be noted that there are many blanks in the entries. For the most part these represent information that can never be provided since the work of earlier restorers has so altered the instruments that their original form in these respects cannot be known. In some few cases the omissions indicate instruments which are in collections not now accessible but of which I have been informed by catalogues which do not provide sufficient data.

It remains to assess the effect of each of the elements compared in

Table 6. In the absence of controlled experiments the opinion of the most experienced maker must be mere prejudice, though acquired with more than ordinary effort. Every maker has certainly found that nominally identical harpsichords can sound quite different. How then to judge the exact role played by each part of several unlike harpsichords?

In general, harpsichords with cypress soundboards sound less well than those with spruce soundboards. If there is a difference not due to other concurrent factors, those instruments with cypress soundboards have less volume of sound, quicker attenuation, and a higher percentage of false or "wolf" notes.

The effect of scale on tone quality, as we have explained, is dependent on the weight of construction and the diameter of the strings. If the weight of the instrument and the thickness of the strings remain constant as the scale is progressively elongated, the tone will become louder and plainer, losing the silvery "fuzz" of rich harmonic development until, finally, it is dull and coarse. If the scale is shortened, the tone becomes weaker and more and more complex until it is so ridden with overtones and beats that the ear rejects it as false. Given the average construction of an Italian harpsichord with outer case, the ideal length of c″, judged by modern ears, lies between ten and eleven inches. The best Italian harpsichord known to me has a ten-inch c″, a spruce soundboard, a medium-angle tail, and leather plectra. (It is undated and for that reason omitted from Table 6.)

However, there seems to be more to the question of Italian scales than the simple preference of each maker for a particular tone quality. John D. Shortridge [49] has called attention to an interesting correlation between the ranges and scales of Italian sixteenth and seventeenth century instruments. He argues that those instruments with ranges which ascend to f‴ tend to have longer scales (12.78 inches is the average) than the instruments with keyboards ending on c‴ (10.45 inches average). From this observation Shortridge deduces that the longer-range instruments were tuned a fourth lower than standard pitch (their f‴ would then sound c″) and that they thus represent a parallel development to the transposing double harpsichords made in Flanders at the same period.

In assembling his data Shortridge has considered spinets, virginals, and harpsichords in one group. The neatness of his conclusion and the ingenuity of his argument can be somewhat damaged if we distinguish

[49] "Italian Harpsichord Building in the 16th and 17th Centuries," U. S. National Museum Bulletin (Washington, D.C.), no. 225 (1960), p. 95.

between the various instrumental types. The theory seems to fit the facts best in the case of polygonal spinets. Here there is a clear correlation between scale and range. However, since nearly all Italian rectangular virginals have the extended range and long scales, no comparisons or deductions can be made within this second group. In the case of the harpsichords there is some correlation between scale and range, but not nearly so much as Shortridge's overall figures would indicate. Table 7

Table 7. Scale and range in selected Italian harpsichords

Date	Scale (inches)	Range	Disposition	Maker	Location
1560	10⁹⁄₁₆	C/E–f'''	2x8'	Trasuntinus	Schloss Charlottenburg, Berlin
1574	12¾	C–f'''	2x8'	Baffo	Victoria and Albert Museum, London
1579	11	AA–f'''	2x8'	Baffo	Conservatoire National de Musique, Paris
1602	13	C/E–f'''	2x8', 1x4'	Remoti	Landesgewerbmuseum, Stuttgart
1605	11³⁄₁₆	GG–f'''	2x8'	Celestini	Gemeente-Museum, The Hague
1613	11½	C/E–f'''	2x8'	Querci	Smithsonian Institution, Washington, D.C.
1631	9¾	C–f'''	2x8'	Bolcionius	Museum, Rhode Island School of Design, Providence, R.I.
1646	11⁵⁄₁₆	GG–f'''	2x8'	Mondini	Information from Howard Graves
1689	9	C/E–f'''	2x8'	Cargnonus	Alain Vian, Paris (1957)

shows the scale and range of eight harpsichords with extended ranges which Shortridge does not take into account and which are added to his single example. We find that of a total of nine harpsichords three have standard Italian scales (under 11 inches), four have medium long scales (between 11 inches and 12 inches), and only two have long scales (over 12 inches). Whereas Shortridge finds the average scale of all instrumental types with an extended range to be 12.78 inches, the average scale of these nine harpsichords with extended range is only 11.08 inches. This is to be compared to 10.45 inches which is Shortridge's average for short-range instruments. Shortridge was forced to gloss over the fact that his ratios of long to short scales were not large enough to account for a transposition of a fourth. These new ratios are obviously much too close to support any such transposition.

Of the other factors listed in Table 6, the effect of the plectrum material is very subtle and depends a good deal on the instrument. If the harpsichord as an "amplifier" is capable of reproducing an extended series of partials one can easily distinguish between leather and quill. A tone plucked by quill begins with a click and is cleaner and brighter than that produced by leather. With many harpsichords this effect is not noticeable at any distance from the keyboard. Since Italian harpsichord tone begins with a pop and is quite sharp in any case, it is possible that leather might be considered preferable to quill for them. This is not true of the northern instruments.

As for tail angle, Italian harpsichords are found with three sorts. Some are almost square, others long and pointed. The majority fall between the two extremes. The tail angle affects the amount of soundboard around the bass end of the bridge. Generally speaking, a bridge well away from the sides and end of the case produces a more sonorous tone. A square tail tends to provide more space for the bridge than a pointed one. Roughly, the square tails approach a 90° angle, the medium are about 60°, and the pointed may be as acute as 45°.

These fragile and slender harpsichords which we have examined in such pitiless detail may have been scorned by Burney and Hullmandel and largely neglected by modern makers who have generally sought a model for their products among the north European styles, yet it must be remembered that the ubiquitous Italian instruments were probably the commonest of all harpsichords. Every Renaissance or Baroque composer must have been familiar with their possibilities and limitations. The chief obstacle in the way of their resurrection is the unresolved problem of the pitch appropriate to the scale. Once a viable solution has been found it is likely that the more purist among players will quickly discover that a great deal of keyboard music will seem more interesting in the dry and transparent voice of the Italian harpsichord than when intoned by the more sonorous but less lucid north European instruments.

CHAPTER TWO · FLANDERS

More scholarly effort has been devoted to the study of the group of harpsichord makers which gathered in Antwerp during the sixteenth century than to any other branch of the craft. In view of the immense influence of the Flemish style which was exerted in every part of Europe except Italy until harpsichords ceased to be made, this study has not been misplaced. Unfortunately the early students and editors of the primary documents were not always accurate, nor were they well enough informed to put the Flemish school into its proper historical perspective. That a great deal of confusion exists in the standard accounts is due partly to their errors and partly to the inherent difficulty of the subject.[1]

To judge by the dominance of Italian harpsichords among extant instruments dated before 1590, one would think that the Italian makers had enjoyed an almost complete monopoly of their trade during the sixteenth century. Yet, as we have seen, many of the earliest documents referring to plucked keyboard instruments are French or Burgundian in origin, and there is evidence of such instruments having been made in Tournai as early as 1385. The rolls of the Guild of St. Luke, in Antwerp, to which all harpsichord makers of that city eventually belonged, reveal a flourishing group of harpsichord makers established there almost as

---

[1] Modern writers on the history of the harpsichord in Flanders have generally relied on three sources: the guild rolls as published by Ph. Rombouts and Th. Van Lerius (*Les Liggeren et autres archives historiques de la gilde anversoise de Saint Luc*, vol. I, Antwerp, 1872; vol. II, The Hague, n. d.); the historical studies of the Chevalier Léon de Burbure, which took into account not only the guild rolls but also many supporting documents from the archives of the guild and of several local parishes (*Recherches sur les facteurs de clavecins et les luthiers d'Anvers*, Brussels, 1863); and the even more broadly based studies of E. van der Straeten (*La Musique aux Pays-Bas*). Rombouts added punctuation to the guild rolls at the peril of sense. Van der Straeten had very little specialized knowledge of the harpsichord, and while dissipating his energy in a fruitless attack on Fétis, presented inaccurate material which is disorganized to an almost incredible degree. De Burbure is by all odds the worst of the three. To the self-defeating activity of translating all proper names into French (which failing he shares even with many modern scholars who write in that language) he turns one of those minds which seems perpetually incapable of getting anything straight.

early as the date of the oldest surviving Italian instruments. An apprentice clavichord maker, Goosent Kareest, is listed in 1519, and when he was admitted to the guild as master in 1529, he was only following the example of a relative, Joos Kerrest, who had been admitted in 1523. Nineteen more harpsichord makers were received into the guild before 1579, the year of the admission of Hans Ruckers. It is tempting to assume that these twenty-one constituted the entire community of their craft prior to Ruckers, but it is quite possible that there were others whose names have been lost, for it is not until 1557 that we have any assurance that all of the harpsichord makers in Antwerp were members of the guild.

In that year ten makers applied for guild regulation of harpsichord making.[2] Apparently most of the group of applicants had been carrying on their trade without benefit of guild sanction up to that point, and it was to obtain that form of legal regulation and protection against competition that application was made to the authorities requesting admission without presentation of the traditional masterwork. A favorable reply was made to the first overture, a meeting was held, and agreement was reached on the basic rules under which the harpsichord making craft would thenceforth operate. This tentative arrangement was submitted to the chiefs of the commune, and on March 28, 1558, the formal statute was received from the royal representative in Antwerp, Jan Van Immerseele.[3] The only stipulation of special note is the last, which called for maker's marks to be affixed to all harpsichords made in Antwerp. The initialed rose of gilded pipe metal which was invariably set in the soundboards of Flemish harpsichords was the result.

The ramifications of the tradition represented by this group of makers are difficult to trace. Somewhat surprisingly in view of all the documentary evidence of active and productive makers in Flanders, there are almost no extant Flemish instruments made before the rise of the Ruck-

---

[2] Those listed were Joos Carest, Marten Blommesteyn, Jacop Theeuwes, Aelbrecht Van Neeren, Hans d'orgelmakere, Christoffel Blommesteyn, Ghoosen Carest, Jacop Aelbrechts, Marten Van der Biest, and Lodewyck Theeuwes. In 1557 Ghoosen Carest, Joos Carest, Marten Blommesteyn, and Christoffel "Blomsteen" were already masters, but there were several other makers admitted between 1523 and 1557 whose names do not appear on the application. Perhaps they were no longer living. The rolls for 1557 show three of the applicants admitted: Marten Van der Biest, Hans Bos (d'orgelmakere), and Jacop Aelbrechts. For some reason, Jacop Theeuwes, Aelbrecht Van Neeren, and Lodewyck Theeuwes are not so shown. On the other hand, four non-applicants were admitted in 1557. In 1561 a Lodewyk Teeus appears in a list of sons of masters who are being admitted. This entry must refer to Lodewyk Teeus (II), the son of Lodewyk (I).

[3] A translation of this document may be found in app. 4 of Russell, *The Harpsichord and Clavichord.*

ers family. Yet there still exist a great many harpsichords and spinets made in Italy during the sixteenth century. It seems most likely that accidents of violence and changing taste have destroyed the Flemish product while that of Italy has been preserved. Since the Italian harpsichord, as compared to the Flemish, changed very little throughout its history, it can be assumed that there was less likelihood of an old harpsichord in Italy being discarded as outmoded.

One instrument, a spinet by Ioes Karest in 1548,[4] seems to represent an intermediate between the Flemish and Italian styles. In the absence of other examples demonstrating a gradual evolution of style it is risky to assume that the Flemish instruments are ultimately derived from the Italian. Indeed it seems to me as likely that both the Flemish and the Italian instruments owe something to an earlier type which is now represented mainly by the "exaquir" references and Arnault de Zwolle's manuscript. For lack of a better term and more exact information this tradition might be called "Burgundian." But before we can trace the transition of the Flemish instruments from their early style to their final form, we must examine the instruments as they eventually emerged.

The obvious fact about the Flemish harpsichords, as compared to the Italian, is their greater weight of structure and more bulky outline. In place of the extremely thin cypress case, ribbed by the cap moldings like a Gothic vault, we find half-inch softwood covered by paint or paper. This outline and structure is the result of a longer scale and greater tension. The string c″ in Flemish harpsichords is usually about fourteen inches long, three or four inches longer than the Italian norm. When this scale is laid out on a string band, the resulting curve of the bridge is much less extreme than that produced by a ten-inch scale. As we have seen, the Italian makers tended to double the length of their strings for each octave of descent until far into the bass, and sometimes for the entire range of the instrument. The Flemish makers were much less rigorous in their bass scaling, and we find their instruments shorter than theory might demand from about c′ to the bottom. As a practical matter their bass strings are of the same order of length as those of all but the longest Italian harpsichords, but their longer c″ theoretically implies a much longer bass. An examination of Plate VI, which shows a Flemish harpsichord in plan, will demonstrate the form of bentside produced by this new approach to scaling. The steepest part of the curve

---

[4] "Ioes Karest de Colonia 1548." The maker is almost certainly that Joos Karest who was admitted to the Antwerp guild in 1523 as clavichord maker. Apparently originally from Cologne, we know that he was still living in 1557 when his name headed the group petition for admission.

is very mild compared to the Italian form, and the sweep is carried smoothly to the end of the bentside. The more gradually increasing length of the bass strings produces a broader tail. The increased tension above c′ is met by case scantlings about three times as heavy as the Italian practice and by a new type of frame (see Plate VII, figure 1).

Examination of Plates VI and VII, which show a typical Flemish harpsichord of the seventeenth century, will clarify some of the details of its decor. The chief features to be noted are the square profile in front, the gilded ogee molding running around the inner edge of the case, the absence of molding around the base of the exterior of the case, and the elimination of the Italian style outer case and of the Italian carved details. Flemish keyboards were almost invariably made with naturals of bone and sharps of hardwood, stained black. Four lines were scored in the key tops, the rearmost line flush with the front of the sharp. Ordinarily a round notch was filed between the two innermost lines, a vestigial survival of the very early organ key detail.[5]

Originally the interior of the case and lid of the Flemish harpsichords or virginals was covered with block printed paper in one of several standard patterns.[6] This paper was often further adorned on the inside of the lid by Latin mottoes, painted in large black roman letters. The soundboard was always painted in tempera, the naïve designs including flowers, prawns, birds, and insects, bordered rather elaborately by arabesques executed in black, dark green, or blue. A gilded metal rose carrying the maker's initials was a prominent feature of the soundboard decoration. The inscription was usually painted on a brown batten over the keys in black roman letters which extended the full width of the keyboard, but the date often appears on the soundboard as well. The inscription was usually placed on the jack rail of virginals.

Sometimes the exterior of the harpsichord was also covered with a printed paper. Several small harpsichords have survived with this decoration. Another common method of adornment was to paint the exterior in imitation of marble. Still other instruments appear to have been painted a flat color, most often dark green.

It is interesting to note in this regard that the Guild of St. Luke contained painters, carvers, sculptors, framers, panel makers, and a variety

[5] See Praetorius, *Theatrum instrumentorum*, plates XXIV, XXVII, XXVIII, XXXV.

[6] See E. Closson, "L'Ornementation en papier imprimé des clavecins anversois," *Revue belge d'archéologie et d'histoire de l'art*, 2 (1932): 105–112, and D. F. Lunsingh Scheurleer, "Over het Ornament en de Authenticiteit van bedrukte Papierstrooken in twee Clavierinstrumenten," *Medelingen van de Dienst voor Kunsten en Wetenschappen* (Gemeente Museum, The Hague), 6 (1939): 45–49.

of craftsmen connected with the production of books, such as binders, printers, and dealers. The harpsichord makers, who were a very minor part of this assemblage, made use of the techniques of both the painters and of the printers in the decoration of their instruments. It is difficult to say whether the Flemish harpsichords were decorated with block printed papers and painting because their makers were members of the guild and thus authorized to practice those crafts, or that the Flemish harpsichord makers joined the Guild of St. Luke because they were already block printers and painters. If any Flemish instruments were known which were made prior to the legal regulation of harpsichord making and by nonmembers of the guild, this question might be answered. The earliest, a spinet by Ioes Karest dated 1548, was made by one of those who had joined the Guild independently before the adoption of the statute of 1558, and it is neither painted nor decorated with block printed paper.

Original Flemish stands are rare, but they appear to have had heavy melon-turned or baluster legs, and the stretchers were placed near the floor level. Sometimes the stretcher ran lengthwise under the center line of the instrument and carried several finials or balusters. Many contemporary depictions of harpsichords show stands in which the front legs are flush with the keyboard corners of the instrument. These stands were quite high, and the harpsichords were often played from a standing position or from high stools like those now used by double bass players.[7]

Along with this broader and heavier harpsichord the Flemish introduced a new type of oblong virginal using the long scale and heavy construction. In the place of the protruding keyboards of the Italian virginals and spinets we find a keyboard recessed into the front of the instrument. The Italian box slide, glued to the underside of the soundboard, has been replaced by a two-part structure. A strip of leather is glued to the upper surface of the soundboard, and the mortises for the jacks are cut or punched out of the leather. No partitions exist between the mortises of adjacent jacks. Thus two jacks work in each mortise. The soundboard itself is mortised with sufficient clearance so that only the leather touches the jack. Under the soundboard and just above the key levers there is a light batten which is mortised for the jacks and acts as a lower bearing. Sometimes this lower guide is supported by light sides glued to the underside of the soundboard so that the structure

[7] A. M. Pols, *De Ruckers en de Klavierbouw in Vlaanderen* (Antwerp, 1942), has a chapter on the iconography of Flemish seventeenth century instruments.

superficially resembles an Italian box slide. But the essential distinction is almost always present: the Flemish jack is guided by an upper and lower bearing, and the Italian jack by one thick bearing. On the whole, the Flemish did not make the Italian pentagonal spinet and the bentside spinet.

The 1548 spinet by Ioes Karest suggests the path taken by the Flemish makers in the development of their characteristic virginal from the earlier pentagonal spinet. This instrument is very satisfying to the instincts of the orderly historian since it shares Italian (Burgundian?) and Flemish characteristics most accommodatingly. In outline [8] it is quite similar to those Italian pentagonal spinets which have two-piece right ends. The range is C/E to c''' (four octaves) and there is one choir of eight-foot strings which were plucked by quill. The recessed keyboard which we find on this instrument is only rarely seen on Italian spinets and is quite the rule with Flemish virginals. The sides of the case are as thin as the Italian norm and are stiffened at the upper edge in the Italian manner with a cap molding. They are not made of cypress, but of a sort of softwood which is difficult to identify but which may be lime, a wood used by later Flemish makers. The bridge is not Italian in section, nor Flemish, but shares elements of both. The naturals are covered with a hard brown wood similar to the Italian boxwood, but the key levers use metal pins to engage the rack at the rear instead of the usual Italian wooden pins. This is a familiar feature in Ruckers keyboards.

There is a sort of counter-soundboard 2⅝ inches below the usual soundboard to which it is not connected in any way. The jacks pass through mortises cut into this second soundboard which thus forms the lower guide. This device is so cumbersome and unlike anything which had gone before that it might be dismissed as a freak except that we find it again in another instrument in the same collection — an undated virginal signed "Iohannes Gravwels." (Grauwels was admitted to the guild in 1579.) One finds the double soundboard occasionally in English virginals of the seventeenth century; for example, one by Adam Leversidge, 1666, now at Yale. And there are reminiscences of it in English seventeenth and early eighteenth century harpsichords; for example, a harpsichord by Johannes Haward, 1622, at Knole Park, Sevenoaks, Kent, and one by Thomas Hitchcock, undated, circa 1700, Victoria and Albert Museum.

---

[8] Illustrated in Franz Josef Hirt, *Meisterwerke des Klavierbaus* (Olten, Switz., 1955), p. 171.

It is reasonable to assume that the Flemish makers prior to Hans Ruckers made harpsichords as well as spinets. We have seen in the case of Karest that Italian influence was strong in Antwerp, and so we might expect the members of the Guild of St. Luke to make some adaptation of the Italian harpsichord to their new tradition. The earliest extant harpsichord made by a Fleming is a combination harpsichord-organ now in London at the Victoria and Albert Museum.[9] Unfortunately, it is not early enough to throw real light on the nature of the transitional stages in the development of the Flemish harpsichord. The inscription reads, "Lodowicvs Theewes Me Fesit 1579." Two harpsichord makers of this name were members of the guild in Antwerp. The first, Lodewyck Theeuwes (I), was one of the 1557 applicants. The second, Lodewyck "Teeus" (II), was admitted in 1561, the son of a master. The present instrument seems to have been made by the latter, who was probably a nephew of Lodewyck I. The instrument was probably constructed in London rather than Antwerp, for its maker's name appears as a resident on the parish records of St. Martin's le Grand.[10]

This claviorganum[11] consists of a single-manual harpsichord resting on a large oblong organ case which seems to have originally contained five stops. The harpsichord has a range of four octaves, C to c′′′, and three choirs of strings, two at eight-foot pitch and one at four-foot. The plectra are of quill. It is the earliest three-choired instrument known to me, and this disposition is unquestionably original. There is no connection between the harpsichord and the organ except that a space for stickers has been left beneath the harpsichord keyboard. Stop levers are provided for both organ and harpsichord so that either division could be played independently or pipe and string could be heard in any combination. This, incidentally, is the oldest example of stop levers to have come to my attention. They are moved in and out rather than from side to side.

[9] There is a single-manual harpsichord with a Hans Ruckers rose, dated 1573, in the Deutsches Museum, Munich. I am unable to accept the date. This is six years before Rucker's admission to the guild. The instrument has been extensively restored.

[10] The *Publications of the Huguenot Society*, vol. X, pt. 3, p. 435, shows the following entry in a list of aliens (1568): "A denizen. Lodewyke Tyves, virginall maker, a Ducheman, and denizen, with his wyffe, Pavyll Fandevell his seruant, and Jacob Albright, who do lie in his howse; thy go to the Duche churche." Again in 1583 (vol. X, pt. 2, p. 348): "Lodwicke Thewes, musycion, borne under the Dominion of the King of Spaine, was made denizent the XXIIIth day of Januarye, anno nono predicte Regine, paeth tribute to no Company, and is of the Dutche churche." Thus Theewes had been naturalized in 1567. His name appears once more in 1585.

[11] See Appendix H for a general account of the claviorganum. For a close description of this instrument see Frank Hubbard, "Two Early English Harpsichords," *The Galpin Society Journal*, 3 (1950): 12.

The general outline of the case is clearly Flemish, closely resembling the instruments of the Ruckers family in the bentside form and the angle of the tail, although the case is somewhat narrower toward the small end. However, it is not typical of Flemish instruments in being constructed of oak. The scaling is based upon a fourteen-inch pitch c″, and descends to a sixty-six-inch bass C. This string length was to become quite standard for the harpsichords of the Ruckers family.

The decoration is not entirely typical of the Flemish tradition, even though many of the usual elements are present. The exterior of the case is covered with tooled leather, an adornment sometimes found on the outer cases of Italian harpsichords. The usual ogee molding is cut into the top inner edge of the case, and the soundboard shows traces of floral paintings in the Flemish manner. The bridge and nut sections are not Flemish, but are closer to the Italian. It is interesting to note that both this instrument and the Karest spinet show bridge sections which vary from the later Flemish practice (though the two bridges are not alike).

The registers of this harpsichord are most interesting in that they seem to indicate that Theewes had not yet established his harpsichord building methods but was reasoning still from knowledge of the virginal. It appears to have been a characteristic of the Flemings to refuse to follow the lead of the Italians in register making. As we have seen, the Flemish virginals substituted an upper and a lower bearing for the one-piece Italian register. Theewes used the same type of upper register as Karest, gluing leather to the soundboard and piercing that for the upper bearing. Since this instrument had three stops and thus required movable registers for tuning purposes (if not for registration), Theewes was forced to make his bottom guides movable. This is the only case I have seen in which the lower guide moves rather than the register. It is possible that Theewes was led into this peculiar design not by the example of the structure of the Flemish virginal register and guide, but by a more fundamental consideration: virginal makers, of course, mounted both nut and bridge on a true soundboard, whereas harpsichord makers glued the nut to the solid wrest plank. (See Plate XVIII, figures 1 and 5, which show an English virginal, a type which is quite similar to the Flemish virginal.) Both ends of a virginal string pass over structures designed to transmit vibrations into the air, but usually only one end of a harpsichord string is so placed. We find that this clavi-organum resembles a virginal in this respect. The soundboard is continuous from the tail to the nameboard and is glued to the upper surface of an extremely narrow wrest plank at the keyboard end. There is no gap for the registers in the usual sense since the soundboard spans the point where the gap would normally be found. Thus the nut as well as the bridge rests on open soundboard and performs an important acoustical function. Given this soundboard construction, Theewes had no alternative but to make his lower guide movable.

Few other Flemish instruments of any kind made by the predecessors of Ruckers exist, and none that throw any light on the evolution of his design. Hans Ruckers' career as an independent maker seems to have commenced in 1579,[12] for in that year the guild admitted a "Hans Ruyckers, claversinbalmakeere."[13] Our specific knowledge of the Ruckers family is quite meager, dependent as it is on nine entries on the guild rolls and a scattering of parish accounts. The dynasty seems to have been founded by a Frans Ruckers, possibly a harpsichord maker himself, in Malines, where his son Hans was born about 1555. By 1575 Hans Ruckers was living in Antwerp where he was married, according to its register, in Onze Lieve Vrouwekerk on June 25 of that year. The earliest Hans Ruckers instrument[14] known to me is a fine double virginal made in 1581 which was found in Peru where it apparently was taken in the sixteenth century. Ruckers seems to have practiced the trade of organ tuner and repairman in addition to that of harpsichord maker, for the accounts of Onze Lieve Vrouwekerk show him receiving payment for this service in 1598 and 1599. There are other organ tuning accounts at the St. Jacobskerk for a Hans Ruckers in 1617, and he appears to have maintained the organ there until 1623. Although his death duties were paid in 1598, Hans Ruckers seems to have lived until sometime after 1623. His last surviving instrument was made in 1620.

Two of Ruckers' sons followed him in his chosen trade — Hans (II), baptized in 1578, and Andreas (I), baptized in 1579. In 1611 "Hans Rukers sone claversigmaker" appeared in a list of sons of the masters admitted to the guild. Considerable controversy exists over the identity of this maker. Some authorities have held that the entry refers to Hans II, the son of a harpsichord maker; others that the son of Hans Ruckers the harpsichord maker is intended, and that the person in question could be either Hans II or Andreas I. In any case, the earliest instrument to carry the "AR" rose (Andreas) is dated 1608. The earliest Hans II

[12] Not 1575, the date given in *Grove's Dictionary of Music and Musicians*.
[13] All references to guild admissions are taken from Rombouts and Van Lerius, *Les Liggeren*.
[14] See above, note 9.

instrument is a harpsichord dated 1612, now at the Conservatoire in Paris. Between 1631 and 1634 a Hans Ruckers, now certainly Hans II, tuned the organ at the St. Jacobskerk, and in 1643 the arrears in his organ tuning accounts were paid to his heirs. According to the accounts of Onze Lieve Vrouwekerk, Hans II was buried in 1642.

In 1637 we find a "Rickart, Claversingelmaker, Wynmeester" admitted to the guild. This may refer to Andreas II, who was born in 1607, the son of Andreas I. Two undated virginals also exist by a mysterious Christophel Ruckers whose connection with the rest of the family is unknown.

The successor to the Ruckers reputation and business seems to have been a nephew of Hans II named Joannes, or Jan, Couchet. He was received into the guild in 1642/3 and repaired the organ of Onze Lieve Vrouwekerk several times. He was buried in 1655. His son, Jan Couchet (Joannes II), was admitted into the guild in 1655/6. Two more members of the family, Joseph (probably the son of Joannes I) and Abraham, were admitted in 1666/7. A harpsichord exists which is signed by a Petrus Ioannes Couchet,[15] whose relationship to the other members of the family is unknown. In 1693/4 there is an entry in the guild accounts for the widow of Jan Couchet, so that it is certain that Joannes II was dead before that date. After 1693 there is no further mention of any member of the Ruckers family in the guild records.

About one hundred thirty-five harpsichords and virginals made by the Ruckers family still exist, spanning a period of almost exactly one hundred years, from 1581 to 1680.[16] This relatively large number of surviving instruments is surprising in view of the fact that there now exist few Flemish instruments made by contemporaries of the Ruckers family. It is true that Ruckers harpsichords were always highly prized, particularly in France, where they almost stifled the native product, and that they were rebuilt over and over, continuing in use until the end of the eighteenth century. This sort of care and esteem would, of course, improve their chances of survival, but hardly enough to account for the overwhelming predominance we have noticed. Other harpsichord makers continued to be admitted to the guild in Antwerp at about the same rate after Hans Ruckers' admission as before, so that it cannot be argued

[15] Boalch, *Makers of the Harpsichord and Clavichord*, identifies Petrus Ioannes with Joannes II.

[16] For a list of surviving Ruckers instruments, see the article "Ruckers" in *Grove's Dictionary of Music and Musicians* (5th ed., London, 1954), or Boalch, *Makers of the Harpsichord and Clavichord*. To these lists I am able to add only one instrument, a single-manual harpsichord by Andreas II, dated 1646, formerly the property of Alphonse van Neste of Brussels, and now owned by William Post Ross of Berea, Ky.

that the Ruckers firm eliminated their competition at the outset. One is forced to the disquieting conclusion that some of the instruments now accepted as Ruckers did not begin their existence as such. The high prices that Ruckers harpsichords fetched in Paris in the eighteenth century would certainly have provided strong motivation to unscrupulous makers to attempt to pass other old Flemish harpsichords, and possibly even new instruments, as original Ruckers.

No direct evidence can be adduced to prove this assertion, but one can find considerable material which tends to strengthen the suspicion. The most elaborate alterations were being made to Ruckers harpsichords by the French harpsichord makers between 1675 and 1790. Most of the extant Ruckers passed through these Paris workshops, some of them more than once. This means that the French makers had an exhaustive knowledge of the most minute details of the Ruckers style and were in a position to copy it. Their customers were accustomed to seeing Ruckers instruments that had been more or less worked over and were not likely to suspect the genuineness of an instrument because of evidence of alteration. Furthermore, we know that parts of Ruckers harpsichords and virginals were being used in the construction of new instruments. Hullmandel wrote in 1791,[17] "Il ne reste plus de virginales; les épinettes disparoissent, on les démolit pour employer leurs vieilles tables à la construction d'instrumens plus modernes." ("There are no more virginals remaining; spinets are disappearing, they are being demolished so that their old soundboards can be used in the construction of more modern instruments.") And van Blankenburg describes in some detail the rebuilding of Ruckers harpsichords (see Appendix A).

The researches of Pierre Hardouin in the Archives Nationales at Paris have produced a considerable number of inventories of the contents of the workshops of Parisian harpsichord makers taken during the seventeenth and eighteenth centuries (for excerpts from these see Appendix C). Many of the entries in these documents show that old Ruckers instruments were being broken up for their materials. With this sort of activity being pursued on a large scale it is certain that many makers yielded to the temptation to ascribe an instrument to Ruckers when only a part of it was by that maker. It seems quite likely that Ruckers harpsichords in bad condition were being disassembled not only for their useful old materials but to be reassembled with the liberal addition of new parts into hybrid instruments which could be passed

[17] "Clavecin," *Musique*, I, p. 286, which is part of the *Encyclopédie méthodique*, Paris, from 1785.

off as genuine Ruckers. Apparently, even virginal soundboards were sometimes rebuilt into soundboards for harpsichords which were then ascribed to Ruckers. For example, we find the following in François Etienne Blanchet's workshop in 1726: "Dix espinettes de flandre toutes Riguerses." ("Ten Flemish virginals all Ruckers.")[18] At that date there was certainly no demand for virginals per se for they were completely outmoded. Yet in 1737 we find that Blanchet still maintained a stock of Flemish virginal soundboards: "Trois autres clavecins de Jean Ruckers & quatre tables d'epinette de Flandres." ("Three other harpsichords of Hans Rucker and four Flemish virginal soundboards.")[19]

An extant Hans Ruckers harpsichord[20] has a soundboard which was clearly made at least in part from an old virginal soundboard, for one of the planks from which it is formed shows a row of plugged mortises of a size and arrangement that indicate that they were the mortises originally cut into a virginal soundboard to serve as register for the jacks. We know that this instrument passed through the workshop of Blanchet's successor, Pascal Taskin, for it was inscribed by that maker in 1774. So far the historian would have a fairly strong case for ascribing this instrument to Taskin and assuming that Taskin used one of the virginal soundboards with a Ruckers rose which might still have been knocking about the workshop. And Taskin did have a stock of old Ruckers instruments which he cannibalized.[21] A typical complication, however, is introduced by the paintings on the case which were ascribed in the eighteenth century to Van der Meulen (1634–1690),[22] a judgment which has been upheld by modern authority. Thus a harpsichord which seems at first sight to have been an obvious confection of unrelated parts

[18] Archives Nationales, Minutier Central, CXV, 445, Jan. 15, 1726.

[19] Ibid., IX, 646, May 9, 1737.

[20] Boalch no. 17.

[21] An inventory of his shop prepared in 1777 contains the following item: "Deux petits clavecins Ruckers pour prendre la table." ("Two small Ruckers harpsichords for taking the soundboards.") Archives Nationales, Minutier Central, CI, 621, April 24, 1777.

[22] This instrument can be identified in an advertisement inserted in Les Affiches: "Clavecin à grand rav. fait en 1612 par Rukers superieurement peint par Van der Meulen, orné de bronzes. Il a été mis en état par le sieur Pascal Taskin, artiste celebre. Il contient 4 registres, dont six mouvements que l'on change avec le genou sans retirer les mains de dessus le clavier; ce qui donne le piano, le forte et le crescendo de la manière la plus nette et la plus sensible. Pris: 260 louis comptant, chez le sieur de la Chevardiere, maître de musique, rue de Roule, 23 janv. 1777." ("Harpsichord with full range made in 1612 by Ruckers, superbly painted by Van der Meulen, adorned with bronzes. It has been put in condition by Mr. Pascal Taskin, the well-known artist. It has 4 registers with six mechanisms which one changes with the knee without withdrawing one's hands from the keyboard; these give the piano, the forte, and the crescendo in the clearest and most sensitive manner. Price: 260 louis cash, at the house of Mr. Chevardiere, music master, Roule Street, January 23, 1777.")

turns out to be much older than the period in which the faking would have been done and must be accepted as genuine. Even Ruckers, then, was using parts taken from older instruments.

The Blanchet shop was not the only establishment producing fake Ruckers and bringing genuine ones into doubt. An inventory of Jacques Goerman's possessions, made in 1789, specifies the ultimate fate of many old Flemish instruments: "Trois clavecins vieux pour mettre en pièce." ("Three old harpsichords to be taken to pieces.")[23] The new instruments produced by the French makers out of these old bits and pieces are sometimes frankly described as such in the inventories: "Un clavecin fait par Goujon et qui a pour titre Hans Ruckers" ("A harpsichord made by Goujon and which has for inscription Hans Ruckers");[24] or, "Un clavesin contrefait de Ruquestre a petit ravalement" ("A harpsichord falsely ascribed to Ruckers with the narrow range").[25] The inevitable confusion produced by this mélange of old and new is revealed in the following: "Un clavecin a ravalement Flamand par Belot sur son pied doré" ("A full range Flemish harpsichord by Belot on its gilded stand").[26] Louis Bellot was a French eighteenth century maker.

It is through this environment of doubt and alteration that the historian must pick his uncertain way as he attempts to deduce the nature of the various models of harpsichords originally produced by the Ruckers family. Not only is it doubtful whether any given instrument is genuinely by Ruckers, but also one has to contend with the extensive alterations and enlargements applied from time to time to nearly all Ruckers harpsichords in order to keep them abreast of changing times. In the case of virginals this *ravalement* usually did not change the basic outside dimensions of the case, but the *ravalement* of harpsichords was a more elaborate undertaking, and many Ruckers harpsichord cases are now far from their original dimensions. By assembling long lists of harpsichord dimensions and specifications, culling them of obvious frauds, and arranging them in the order of increasing range, I have found that certain combinations of range and dimensions appear repeatedly enough to reveal the successive steps of *ravalement*. After weighting these data with information acquired from contemporary documents, it is possible to identify several standard models. The Ruckers "catalogue" thus acquired has a fair degree of internal consistency, and as new instruments come to light they can generally be identified as one or another of the

[23] Archives Nationales, Minutier Central, XLVI, 538, May 6, 1789.
[24] *Ibid.*, CIX, 728, Sept. 28, 1769 (Jean Henry Hemsch).
[25] *Ibid.*, LXXXIII, 461, May 14, 1759 (Jean Marie Galland).
[26] *Ibid.*, XCI, 758, March 2, 1737 (Jacques Bourdet).

known types. It must not be imagined, however, that the instruments made in the Ruckers workshops were completely standardized. The methods of design and marking-out were loose enough to permit a good deal of variation.

The Ruckers seem to have built three sizes of single-manual harpsichord, one double harpsichord, two types of eight-foot virginals, several kinds of raised-pitch virginals, two four-foot virginals, and a double virginal (that is, two instruments in one box). In addition, there were various experimental instruments which never were made in any number. Among these were a spinet[27] of similar form to the Karest already described and several oblong harpsichords[28] which had a C/E–c''' four-foot virginal built into that side which would normally be curved. Tables 8 and 9 give the salient characteristics of the standard Ruckers instruments.

The cases of all the Ruckers instruments ordinarily were made of lime or linden, a soft and close-textured wood, rather light in weight and quite stable in dimension. Bottoms and frame members were usually of pine or lime of lower quality than the sides of the case. The wrest planks were of oak veneered on its upper surface to resemble the soundboard. Quartered spruce, probably *Picea excelsa,* was used for the soundboard and its ribs. In the eighteenth century French sources refer to this wood as "sapin de Hollande,"[29] but it is not likely that even in the seventeenth century the large, clear planks necessary for soundboards originated in that country. It is more probable that it was sawed into thin planks in Holland,[30] which was famous for that trade, but that the timber itself came from southern Germany and Switzerland. An eighteenth century Dutch work[31] gives the country of origin as Switzerland. Under the soundboard, the four-foot hitchpin rail was of lime. For both nuts and bridges the Ruckers used beech, probably because beech is quite easy to bend after soaking or steaming. The bridges were reinforced from the underside of the soundboard by iron nails.

[27] Illustrated in Boalch, *Makers of the Harpsichord and Clavichord,* Plate VIII (Hans the Elder no. 5).

[28] In the Plantin-Moretus museum in Antwerp there is a similar harpsichord by Iohannes Iosephus Coenen, dated 1735.

[29] *Encyclopédie* (Paris, 1751–1778), "Clavecin."

[30] J. Savary des Bruslons, *Dictionnaire universel de commerce* (1759–1766; 1st ed., 1741), "Bois." "Il se fait à Amsterdam un très grand commerce de toutes sortes de Bois, mais particuliérement de ce qui sont propres à la teinture, à la marqueterie & à la tabletterie." ("At Amsterdam there is carried on a very large business in all kinds of wood but particularly in that suitable for dyeing, marquetry, and inlay work.")

[31] Anonymous, *Verhandeling over de Muziek* (The Hague, 1772), p. 200, "vuuren-hout, dat uit Zwitzerland koomt."

Table 8. Catalogue of Ruckers harpsichords

Model number	Number of manuals	Range	Average dimensions (inches)	Pitch and number of choirs	Number of registers	Scale (length of c" string in inches)	Remarks and optional features
I	one	C/E–c''' (45 keys)	48 long 27 wide	1x8', 1x4' →8' ←4'	2	9⅜	2x8' in the place of 1x8', 1x4'. Possibly tuned a fifth high.
II	one	C/E–c''' (45 keys)	72 long 28 wide	1x8', 1x4' →8' ←4'	2	13½	2x8' in the place of 1x8', 1x4'. Third slide available later (ca. 1648) giving 2x8', 1x4'
III	one	Variable, but extended below C. May have been as large as GG/BB-f'''	86½ long 34⅞ wide	1x8', 1x4' →8' ←4'	2	13⅝	This is the enlarged version of model II mentioned in the Huyghens-Duarte correspondence. Later a third slide was available (ca. 1648) giving 2x8', 1x4'
IV	two (transposing)	C/E–c''', upper; C/E–f''' (50 keys), lower; (c''' of upper manual directly over f''' of lower)	88 long 31 wide	1x8', 1x4' →8' ←4' - - - →8' ←4'	4	14 (upper manual)	See text for explanation. Since c''' is over f''' each manual has its own scale. Ruckers evidently considered the upper to be basic since he gave it his usual scale

Table 9. Catalogue of Ruckers virginals

Model number	Single or double	Range	Dimensions (inches)	Pitch actually sounded by C key	Scale (length of c″ string in inches)	Position of keyboard
V	Single	C/E–c‴ (45 keys)	66–68 long 18½–19½ wide	C (8 foot)	13–14	Recessed, right or left
VI [a]	Single	C/E–c‴ (45 keys)	44–56 long	D♯ (raised 3 semitones) [b] F (raised fourth) G (raised fifth)	11¾ (D♯) 10¾ (F) 9½ (G)	Recessed, right or left
VII	Single	C/E–c‴ (45 keys)	31½ long 12½ wide	C (4 foot)	6¼–7¼	Protruding, center
VIII [c]	Single	C/E–c‴ (45 keys)	32¼ long 15⅝ wide	C (4 foot)	7¼	Recessed, center
IX [d]	Double	C/E–c‴ (45 keys)	67–69 long 17½–19½ wide	C (8 foot)	14	Recessed, right (ottavino to left) [e]

[a] Raised pitch. I have grouped together three types of these virginals.
[b] This type may actually have sounded at eight-foot pitch with a somewhat short scale.
[c] Ottavino in double virginals.
[d] Eight-foot virginal with model VIII inserted into recess in case.
[e] Two double virginals by Grovvelus (n. d.) and Van der Biest (1580) have the keyboard of the eight-foot virginal to the left and the ottavino to the right.

Among the action parts, Ruckers harpsichord registers were cut out of beech, and the lower guides of lime, covered on the upper surface with leather, and underneath with cloth or parchment. The jacks were of pear with holly tongues and quill plectra. Key levers were made of lime and the natural key heads were covered with bone or ivory. The sharp key tops were usually of pear stained black, but occasionally one finds ebony. The key beds were made of any softwood that Ruckers found handy but most often of pine or lime.

Among the distinctive features of the Ruckers harpsichords which should be noted in Plates VI and VII are the layout and the framing. The layout is largely the logical development of the scaling and the octave span of the keyboard. However, the placement of the bridge on the soundboard and the exact form of the bentside should be examined. The arrangement of ribs under the soundboard and the dimensions of those ribs is traditionally the central mystery of the harpsichord builder. It will be noticed that each of the bridges lies between structures on the underside of the soundboard which tend to form nodal points. The eight-foot bridge is placed between the bentside and the four-foot hitch-pin rail, and the four-foot bridge is between the four-foot hitchpin rail and the cut-off bar. The precise placement of these elements is important and it is illustrated in Plate VI, figure 1, and in Plate VII, figure 2, which is based on a Ruckers soundboard that has never been altered. Many Ruckers instruments now have a variety of ribs which pass under the bridges, but after careful examination of many examples, I am convinced that Ruckers never glued any ribs under the bridges. Those instruments which now show them were rebuilt long after Ruckers' time, and the restorers were probably attempting to level the old soundboards which had warped.

The thickness of the soundboard of course is also an important element in tone production. Ruckers soundboards are not very consistent in the minor details of taper, and it is probable that their makers were not attempting to produce any very subtle gradation of thickness. As I conjectured in the case of the Italian soundboards, it is most likely that Ruckers planed by eye and did not use a caliper to ensure a perfectly even thickness throughout. In general, the Ruckers soundboards are the thinnest we will find in any reputable instruments. They average about 3/32 inch but sometimes have areas as thin as 1/16 inch along the belly rail. A double harpsichord may have a soundboard as much as 1/8 inch thick near the rose, but the bulk of its soundboard is likely to measure 3/32 inch. There seems to have been a sensible tendency to make the smaller soundboards somewhat thinner than the large ones. It must be remembered that Ruckers soundboards are three hundred years old and that repeated repairs as well as possible rejointing of harpsichords with *ravalement* has worn their substance away. Eighteenth century harpsichords of the various schools derived from the Flemish usually possess soundboards of about ⅛ inch in thickness, and it is possible that the Ruckers soundboards were once nearly that thick. The anonymous author of the *Verhandeling over de Muziek* [32] instructs the harpsichord maker to plane the soundboard until it is a little less than ¼ *duim* in thickness (almost exactly ¼ inch), thinner in the treble and between the bridge and the bentside. To prevent sagging he suggests that it be left thicker around the rose. I have found that it is wise to plane soundboards considerably thinner than ¼ inch and would suggest ⁵⁄₃₂ inch as the absolute maximum.

The basic concept of the Ruckers framing seems to have been similar to that of the Italian makers, but the method of attaining the desired result is entirely different. Both Flemings and Italians seem to have grasped the fact that for a harpsichord case to be rigid it is only necessary to maintain an unchanged outline in plan at the top and at the bottom of the case. A harpsichord fails structurally when the cheekpiece cocks upward so that the front is high and the bentside cheekpiece corner is low. For this situation to arise the bentside must curve inward more sharply at the top than at the bottom. It is the role of the frame to prevent the bentside from sagging inward. At its lower edge the bentside is extremely rigid since the bottom supports it at every point. The lower-level frames are planned to prevent the bottom from bowing up or down. So long as it is flat and uncracked, its outline must remain unchanged. The upper-level frames carry the thrust of the bentside across the instrument to the spine which is maintained in a vertical position by its own stiffness and by the deep lower braces. It is possible that this concentration of stress on the upper part of the spine is not as effective as the Italian design which carries the thrust of the bentside to the bottom by means of sloping braces, for despite the heavier construction used by the Ruckers, their instruments are more prone to distortion than those of the Italians. However, it must be remembered that the Ruckers are under considerably greater tension, not only because of their longer scale, but because of heavier stringing.

Model I (see Table 8) in the Ruckers "catalogue" was a very small

---

[32] Page 200, paragraph 85.

single-manual harpsichord, a very good example of which is to be found in the collection of the Gemeente Museum at The Hague. In 1648 Gaspard Duarte wrote to the famous Constantijn Huyghens describing the contemporary output of the Ruckers workshop: [33] "About the little harpsichords with unisons or a four-foot—a matter of taste—they are usually a tone higher and are my invention of a few years ago, serving in small rooms for the performance of courants, allemandes, and sarabandes." [34] It is interesting that one could have the instrument with a disposition of 2x8' or 1x8', 1x4'. To judge from surviving examples there were no stop levers with which to move the slides. By an elongation these passed through the cheekpiece and could be reached by the player with a long reach and supple joints. It is not known whether a buff stop was provided on this instrument. However, since most Ruckers harpsichords had buff stops, there is no reason to expect that it would not be available on this one. In its usual form the Ruckers buff stop was divided at about the middle of the range so that either treble or bass could be buffed independently. The treble half of the buff batten extended through the cheekpiece, and the bass half was moved by means of a block glued to the batten at the bass end inside the harpsichord.

The question of pitch in this model is more complicated. A glance at Table 8 will show that the apparent compass was C/E to c'''.[35] At present a string of 13⅜ inches is sounded by the b' key and the keyboard range is A to f'''. This scale, short by Ruckers standards, might imply a pitch raised one tone as Duarte mentions. However, traces of the original arrangement of the wrestpins show that the original range was C/E to c''' and the scale 9⅜ inches. This is clearly too short to be that of a unison instrument but would work well enough for an instrument tuned a fifth sharp.

The instrument which Huyghens was most interested in and which he had asked his friend Duarte to look into for him was model III, the large single. In the early days of the firm the single-manual harpsichords

[33] W. J. A. Jonckbloet and J. P. N. Land, eds., *Musique et musiciens au XVII*° *siècle, correspondence et oeuvre musicales de Constantin Huygens* (Leyden, 1882), p. cxci.

[34] Many of the amateurs who enter the workshops of harpsichord makers in modern times torment themselves and the proprietors of the establishment by attempting to extemporize improvements to the current product. It is amusing to note that seventeenth century visitors had the same habits. It seems doubtful that this particular type of harpsichord was the invention of Duarte, a prosperous diamond dealer. Furthermore an example in the Gemeente Museum is dated 1627, twenty-one years before Duarte wrote to Huyghens, a period of time which seems to exceed "a few years."

[35] My information on this instrument was kindly supplied by Dr. J. H. van der Meer. See his article in *The Galpin Society Journal*, no. 18 (1965).

usually had had a range of four octaves from C with short-octave bass, and as late as 1644 we find Andreas Ruckers making a single-manual harpsichord (model II) with that range. (This harpsichord, which is in the Vleeshuis Museum, Antwerp, now has a range of four octaves chromatic from C, but four notes have been added in the bass, and the original range must have extended only to E, implying a short octave, C/E.) However, Duarte reports that in 1648 Couchet had already made four instruments with an extended range, chromatic from GG. Although he does not mention the top note, it was probably c'''.[36]

An even more important innovation was the addition of a third register and choir at eight-foot pitch giving the disposition 2x8', 1x4'. Duarte wrote, "The extreme length of the large harpsichords is around eight feet; at choir pitch with three registers, there are three different strings, that is to say, two strings at unison and one at the octave; all three can be played together or each string alone." Not all of the large singles (model III) had three registers, however. An example in the Vleeshuis in Antwerp has two registers, 1x8', 1x4'.

Fifty years later Klaas Douwes was to write, "But I should say further that such harpsichords [clavicimbel] as are called six-foot harpsichords are not fully six feet in length but about one-third of a foot shorter. Likewise, those of five, four, and three feet too have not quite the full length but are usually somewhat shorter." [37] The foot at Antwerp in this period contained only eleven divisions and was just over eleven modern inches in length.[38] Eight feet in Antwerp would have contained 90.3 inches. If we subtract the four-inch allowance that Douwes permits us, we find that Duarte's eight-foot harpsichord may actually have been about 86 inches in length. This corresponds perfectly with the length (86½ inches) of a Hans II single-manual harpsichord (model III) which was made in 1629. I have examined this harpsichord with the greatest care, and I am convinced that the case has not been enlarged although a few extra strings have been crowded in. Therefore, it seems that Hans II was making the model III long before Couchet, despite Duarte's implication that the type was first made by Couchet. It is possible that Couchet introduced the third slide.

In the end Huyghens ordered the extended single (model III) but

[36] Klaas Douwes, *Grondig Ondersoek van de Toonen der Musijk* (Amsterdam, 1699), p. 107: "But some large harpsichords [*steertstuks*] go down further to 'G' or 'F' like some large organs, and include four octaves and a fifth." A harpsichord by Hans Moermans in 1584 possesses the original range GG/BB to f''', single manual, 1x8', 1x4'. It is 83⅛ inches in length, 33⅜ inches in width.

[37] *Ibid.*, p. 107.

[38] Horace Doursther, *Dictionnaire universel des poids et mesures anciens et modernes* (Brussels, 1840).

without the four-foot, preferring the somewhat less common 2x8′ disposition. He settled on one with unusual range FF to d‴, "at unison in the normal choir pitch, the lowest which was made, with a full keyboard in the bass to the octave ef fa ut and in the treble to the cadence of la sol re." Later he seems to have purchased a Couchet double. The extended single would certainly have its slides and the treble half of the buff stop batten protruding through the cheekpiece to the right to permit manipulating of the registers. As Duarte said, the tone was at choir pitch. Praetorius defines choir pitch as one tone lower than chamber pitch, and Mendel [39] has found that Praetorius' chamber pitch stood a minor third higher, more or less, than our modern pitch. Thus, Praetorius' choir pitch would be one semitone higher than modern pitch. However, Praetorius remarks that, "In England formerly, and in the Netherlands still today, most of the wind instruments are tuned a minor third lower than our present chamber pitch, so that their 'F' is, in our chamber pitch, 'D,' and their 'G' our 'E.' And the excellent instrument maker at Antwerp, Johannes Bossus,[40] made most of his harpsichords and spinets, as well as pipe-works built there, tuned to this same low pitch." [41] A minor third lower than Praetorius' chamber pitch would be more or less our modern pitch, and this seems to have been the pitch of Huyghens' harpsichord.

Models II and III, when equipped with three choirs of strings, provided more possibilities for varied registration than any other Ruckers harpsichord. They represent a considerable advance on the Italian singles by virtue of their four-foot choir and the buff stop, both of which were extremely rare in Italy. Furthermore, the simple expedient of prolonging the registers to the outside of the instrument, where the player could reach them, immensely increased the flexibility of the harpsichord. The divided buff stop permitted the player to produce two tone colors at once and to provide muted accompaniments to cantabile lines. It suffered from the limitation of all such devices, that one crossed the division point at one's peril. Later owners of Ruckers instruments frequently bound the divided battens together.

Discussion of model IV, the transposing double, requires that we plunge even more deeply into the complicated problem of pitch. It is possible that early Italian harpsichords were tuned to a higher pitch than the Flemish and that this is the explanation of the longer Flemish

[39] Arthur Mendel, "Pitch in the 16th and Early 17th Centuries," *Musical Quarterly,* Jan., 1948.

[40] As we have seen, Hans Bos was admitted to the guild in 1557 as organ maker.

[41] Michael Praetorius, *Syntagma musicum,* pt. II, *De Organographia,* p. 14, quoted and translated by Mendel, "Pitch in the 16th and Early 17th Centuries."

scale.[42] Schlick [43] points out that the lowest tone on the pedal of an organ (the pipe length being fixed) can be called either F (FF) or C. Thus two standards of pitch are set up a fifth apart; the C pitch being the *lower* one, as Mendel specifies,[44] since the C in question is above the F (FF) in question. Thus a harpsichord tuned to the pitch of an organ with a C pipe eight feet in length would sound a fifth lower than a harpsichord tuned to an organ with an eight-foot FF pipe.

Flemish harpsichord scales were more standard than those of the Italians. As we have seen the Italian c″ string varied in length from about 9¼ inches to over 12 inches. If we assume that the shortest Italian scales were actually tuned to the F pitch and calculate the theoretical length of a string at the same tension sounding the C pitch, we arrive almost exactly at the Flemish scale. This pretty arithmetic ignores the longer Italian scales which are much too long to have sounded a fifth sharp. In any case, any sort of reasoning which attempts to deduce the pitch of harpsichords from string length rests on very shaky foundations since it is possible for a string of a given length to vary about a fifth in pitch and still sound fairly well.

The two possible pitches, C and F, play a more obvious and forthright role in the Ruckers two-manual harpsichords.[45] Here we find one instrument which is able to be played at both pitches by the simple expedient of providing both a C keyboard and an F keyboard for one string band. It is as if Schlick's dilemma of what to call the eight-foot organ pipe had been solved by calling it both C and F. These transposing harpsichords, as they are usually called, had a range of C/E to c‴ (45 notes) on the upper manual, and C/E to f‴ (50 notes) on the lower manual. Both manuals sounded the identical strings: one eight-foot choir and one four-foot choir. From the designer's point of view the upper manual is the basic one, for c″ corresponds to the 14-inch string. The harpsichord is disposed:

$$\rightarrow 8'$$
$$\leftarrow 4'$$
- - - - -
$$\rightarrow 8'$$
$$\leftarrow 4'.$$

---

[42] Praetorius (*ibid.*, chap. II) to the contrary: "The Italians believe, and not without reason, that singing in the high register is very unpleasant and without charm, and that it causes the text to be obscured, sounding like the shrill bawling of a harvester maid."

[43] Arnolt Schlick, *Spiegel der Orgelmacher und Organisten* (Mainz, 1511).

[44] In "Pitch in the 16th and Early 17th Centuries."

[45] For an excellent article on the subject of transposing harpsichords see Sibyl Marcuse, "Transposing Keyboards on Extant Flemish Harpsichords," *The Musical Quarterly* 38.3 (July 1952): 414.

The keys were arranged so that the topmost note of the upper manual (c‴) was directly over the topmost note of the lower manual (f‴). Thus a performer playing on the lower manual would hear the piece a fourth lower (or a fifth higher) than if he played on the upper manual.

Since the upper manual had only 45 notes to the lower manual's 50, the upper manual did not activate the lowest string of the harpsichord but ended five notes short of the lower keyboard (over the lower manual A). This confusing arrangement is made more complicated by the short-octave basses of both keyboards. As we have seen in dealing with the Italian harpsichords, most seventeenth century instruments lacked the chromatics in the lowest octave. A keyboard apparently ending on E actually descended to C. (See Plate IV, figure 7.) This was ordinarily managed easily enough by tuning the lowest string down to C, the apparent F♯ down to D, and the apparent G♯ down to E. No extra mechanism was needed, and in the case of organs, four large and expensive pipes were saved in each rank. It was not so easy in the case of the transposing harpsichords. Since the upper manual short-octave strings were required by the lower manual, tuned to their correct diatonic sequence, they could not be tuned to fit the requirements of the upper manual. Instead, Ruckers had to contrive a rather elaborate device in which the keys of the upper manual which require an altered pitch were splayed downward to reach the string sounding the appropriate note.[46] The upper manual apparent E key, which is intended to sound C and which is over A, must reach down so that its jack can pluck the same string as the lower manual F key, its equivalent in pitch. The F♯ must reach down to G, and the G♯ to A. Thus each of these three upper-manual keys must be cranked downward to the fourth key lever below. In the case of the F♯ and G♯ this means that they must cross over the straight F and G levers.

A minor riddle which further confounds the problem of Ruckers transposing harpsichords is the apparent existence in former times of an extra string, both 8′ and 4′, for every D♯ throughout the range.[47] The double harpsichord now preserved in the Vleeshuis at Antwerp has an extra wrest pin, bridge pin, and hitchpin for each D♯, and the nut has a little metal plate inlaid at each point where the D♯ strings were pinned. These plates could only have served to raise the extra strings above the general level of their choirs at the nuts. This device could be set aside as a freakish aberration except that a subsequent examination of several

---

[46] Such a keyboard is illustrated in Russell, *The Harpsichord and Clavichord*, plate 35.

[47] I am indebted to Raymond Russell for calling my attention to this feature of the Ruckers harpsichords.

Ruckers doubles has shown little blocks let into the nuts at the D♯ strings, obviously to fill in the gaps left after the removal of the metal plates. Traces of the extra wrest pins and bridge pins can also frequently be found. I was at a loss to explain the purpose of this peculiar arrangement until Gustav Leonhardt made a suggestion so ingenious in its simplicity that it seems almost certainly correct. The meantone system of temperament which was in use at the time of the Ruckers' activity did not attempt to provide an equally feasible intonation in all keys. The notes which were usually made available were as follows: c, c♯, d, e♭, e, f, f♯, g, g♯, a, b♭, and b. The arrangement of the keyboards in the Ruckers transposing harpsichords raised the pitch of the lower manual a fifth to place its f in unison with the upper manual c. If we arrange the notes provided by the meantone tuning in the orientation of the transposing keyboards we find that each pair represents an acceptable fifth except one: g♯–e♭. Here one requires a d♯ in the place of the e♭ of the upper manual, hence the alternate string for each upper manual e♭. The following schematic diagram may make the problem Ruckers faced more easily understood:

Upper manual: c, c♯, d, e♭, e, f, f♯, g, g♯, a, b♭, b, c, c♯, d, e♭, e, f
Lower manual: g, g♯, a, b♭, b, c, c♯, d, e♭, e, f, f♯, g, g♯, a, b♭.

It seems most likely that the lower manual g♯ jacks were of such a length that their plectra would not slip beneath the lower level string, and the upper manual e♭ jacks were short enough (and the key dip was limited enough) so that they could sound only the lower string. Thus, the upper string would be tuned to g♯ and the lower string to e♭; the lower level string would be sounded from the upper manual (which usually produces a shorter stroke at the jack) and the upper string from the lower manual.

Praetorius[48] describes a somewhat similar device contrived to extricate the meantone tuner from certain difficulties produced by transposition. He would provide extra keys as well as extra strings: "The harpsichord, symphony and the like, otherwise called *Instruments* (though incorrectly, as mentioned before) are rather incomplete and imperfect in that they do not afford chromatic tones such as can be produced on lutes and viols da gamba. On this account various harpsichords, in accordance with the specifications of good organists, have been provided with two different keys for the D♯, such that in the aeolian mode transposed a fourth lower, the third falling between the B [B♭] and F♯ may be had

[48] *Syntagma musicum*, pt. II, chap. XL.

in a pure and correct form." F#–Bb is not a third, but if the Bb is replaced by an A#, that interval is obtained in "a pure and correct form." Thus, Praetorius would have an alternate Bb–A# intonation, but since he is discussing a situation in which the pitch has been transposed down a fourth, the actual key he would split is the D#–Eb.

The musical employment of the Ruckers transposing harpsichords seems to have presented a problem to their foreign contemporaries as well as to modern musicologists. There has been preserved a most illuminating correspondence which passed between the painter Balthazar Gerbier in Brussels and Sir Francis Windebank in London during the year 1638.[49] Sir Francis, like Huyghens after him, was interested in purchasing a harpsichord from the famous Ruckers establishment, and he made use of a correspondent on the spot to inform him as to the details. Gerbier wrote: "The Virginall I do pitch upon is an excellent piece, made by Johanees Rickarts att Antwerp. Its a dobbel staert stick [steertstuk, a bentside harpsichord] as called, hath foure registers, the place to play on att the inde." In other words, it was a standard Ruckers transposing double. After several letters (reproduced in full in Appendix A) the harpsichord was purchased and sent to London. There Sir Francis was appalled by the transposing keyboards and wrote: "The Virginal wch you sent me, is com safe, and I wish it were as useful as I know you intended it. But the workman, that made it, was much mistaken in it, and it wants 6 or 7 keyes [referring to the unequal range of upper and lower manuals] so that it is utterly unserviceable. If either he could alter it, or wolde change it for another that may have more keyes, it were well; but as it is, our musick is marr'd." This request was transmitted by Gerbier to Ruckers, "who saith this Virginall cannot be altered, and none elce made here on saille." (Certainly it would not have been difficult for Ruckers to have rebuilt this instrument into a normal double if the concept of such an instrument had been familiar to him.)

In 1739 the Dutch organist Quirinus van Blankenburg was almost as shocked at the idea of the Ruckers transposing harpsichords.[50] He wrote:

At that time (the beginning of the seventeenth century) they were so inexperienced in transposing that in order to transpose a piece a fourth lower, they made expressly a special second keyboard in the harpsichord. This seems

[49] W. Noël Sainsbury, ed., *Original Unpublished Papers Illustrative of the Life of Sir Peter Paul Rubens* (London, 1859), p. 208. See Appendix A.
[50] Quirinus van Blankenburg, *Elementa musica* (The Hague, 1739), p. 142.

incredible, but the proof (which is very remarkable) will confirm this [statement]: namely, that the famous Ruckers, from the beginning of the previous [seventeenth] century until more than thirty years later only made instruments in which, first, there were for the two keyboards only two [sets of] strings, but nevertheless, four registers (for there is no indication even then of a unison), so that one keyboard had to be silent when the other was sounding; secondly, the lower keyboard stood a fourth lower than organ pitch, and had at the top five keys too many so that the upper keyboard could have had the same overflow in the bass, but instead of making the beautiful bass of the lower keyboard sound to this end, they not only left it without keys but they made in their place a wooden block, and next to it a short octave — and this with great difficulty, because the keys, on account of the recently mentioned rearranged notes had to reach over each other. This proves how little importance was attached at that time to the filling in of notes in the bass.

It should be mentioned that van Blankenburg was wrong in saying that there were no unisons; unisons were not used on transposing doubles, to be sure, but they appeared on singles.

Actually, van Blankenburg had not been careful enough in thinking through the problem of the short octave in transposing harpsichords. As he pointed out, the lower keyboard had to extend to f''' in the treble in order to permit the upper to reach c'''. Even using the short octave in the bass of the lower to provide a C required fifty keys, rather a large number for that period. It is not a matter of surprise that Ruckers did not add four more to provide a chromatic bass on the lower manual. Once he had retuned the lower manual F♯ and G♯ strings to D and E respectively, he had made it impossible to have a chromatic bass on the upper manual, for these strings would be required in their normal chromatic sequence for the upper manual C♯ and D♯.

The transposing doubles limited the player to a much narrower range of registrations than the large single. The lower manual appeared to provide a higher compass in the treble, but the music of the time did not demand these notes, and they could not have been much used. Once the player had decided the *tessitura* in which he desired to play, he had available, really, only a single manual with 1x8', 1x4', and buff stop, as in the early forms of the single-manual harpsichords. It was more difficult for him to change registration during a piece since the longer cheekpiece and wider keyboard of the double forced him to stretch further to reach the protruding slides.

The question whether the Ruckers family ever produced a double harpsichord in which the second manual was used for expressive purposes rather than for transposition is extremely important and even more difficult to answer. The question can be attacked from two sides.

First: Since transposing instruments were conceived as two equal harpsichords at different pitches, there must always have been an even number of registers, and for practical reasons this number is limited to four. A three-register double harpsichord, on the other hand, could not have been so divided and must have been originally conceived as an expressive instrument, unless one insists that it transposed with a single eight at one pitch and an eight and four at the other. This seems unlikely since there is no evidence to support that possibility. If, then, we could produce an original three-register Ruckers two-manual harpsichord, we should have answered our question in the affirmative.

Second: If one could find documentary evidence which described a Ruckers expressive double, one could be moderately satisfied that the family had built such instruments. In this case, one could accept the theory that some of their four-register instruments were not originally equipped with transposing keyboards but employed the four registers to pluck three choirs in the disposition frequently found in eighteenth century Flemish and French harpsichords.[51]

There are many three-register doubles existing at present which carry the Ruckers inscription. However, none of these can be demonstrated to have been originally so disposed. All of them have been rebuilt extensively and their original disposition is uncertain. In the normal course of *ravalement* of a Ruckers harpsichord, the original wrest plank was usually replaced with a longer one to suit the wider harpsichord made necessary by the extended range. The new wrest plank could easily be made slightly wider, the extra width filling in the front of the gap and thus concealing the fact that the gap had once been wide enough to contain four registers. This operation would change the plucking points slightly, but by making each of the three new registers somewhat wider than the old ones, it would not be necessary to narrow the gap by the width of one full register. The nut could be advanced toward the gap, thus reducing the plucking distances to something like their original magnitudes at the expense of the scale. By skillful juggling, each of the three variables — gap width, plucking point, and scale — could be brought within the fairly flexible range of standard Ruckers variation, and a spurious three-register double would then exist which

---

[51] A harpsichord signed by Joannes Couchet in the Metropolitan Museum of Art, New York, may turn out to fit this prediction. I have not been able to examine it with sufficient care to draw any conclusions.

would be very difficult to distinguish from an original one. I have made a careful analysis of the dimensions of many such harpsichords, and I have not been able to find enough consistency to imply the existence of a standard three-register double. In fact, they all seem to be either rebuilds of the four-register type or enlargements of three-register singles.[52]

The documentary evidence at present available seems to deny the existence of a Ruckers expressive double. In the passage quoted above van Blankenburg states that all Ruckers double harpsichords were transposing instruments until after 1630. Writing in Holland in 1699, Klaas Douwes[53] does not mention double harpsichords. It is likely that he knew them chiefly as outmoded transposing devices and was not clearly aware of the expressive role which could be given to the second manual, although it must be confessed that 1699 seems a little late for such ignorance.

Our best clue comes from a letter written by De la Barre, *organiste du Roi*, to Huyghens on October 15, 1648. Apparently Huyghens had written to him to ask about the possibilities of buying a harpsichord for himself in Paris. It is likely that Huyghens only bought his Couchet because of De le Barre's delay in answering. In any case, De la Barre wrote: "As far as the price of harpsichords in Paris is concerned about which you wrote me, I thought I had sent you the facts but possibly, despite myself, I have expressed myself badly. Because the truth is that this master, who is still young, originally discovered the invention of making harpsichords with two manuals, not in the style of Flanders which play only the same strings, but different in that these make different strings sound from each keyboard; and to speak correctly, they are two harpsichords joined together, and as a result, the work is double."[54]

In 1648, then, "the style of Flanders," in so far as two-manual harpsichords are concerned, refers only to transposing instruments. It is possible that the Couchets began to produce expressive doubles toward the end of their careers. Van Blankenburg states that transposing instruments began to be altered about 1675,[55] but his claim to have discovered as late as 1708 an expressive use for the fourth register certainly implies that

---

[52] Van Blankenburg (*Elementa musica*, p. 144) alludes to the latter practice and warns prospective purchasers against it.

[53] *Grondig Ondersoek.*

[54] Jonckbloet and Land, eds., *Musique et musiciens*, p. cxlix.

[55] On page 142 van Blankenburg wrote that transposing doubles were made from the beginning of the seventeenth century until more than thirty years later. In the next page we learn that the rebuilding of these instruments began about fifty years afterward, probably about 1675–1690.

instruments in which that register was so used were not being produced commercially. Although much of the evidence which has been adduced is negative, I am inclined to believe that the Ruckers family never made expressive two-manual harpsichords.

In the most general way the concepts of harpsichord timbre must be divided into a North European and a South European school. In our consideration of the Italian harpsichords I have tried to describe the loud but rather plain quality of the Southern instruments with their hard basses and brittle trebles. I have called attention to the short sustaining power and the attendant clarity of articulation of Italian harpsichords. The heavier construction and longer scales of the Ruckers harpsichords produce a tone in which the initial energy imparted to the string by the pluck is not drained off quite so quickly. The sound begins with less ictus and attenuates more slowly. The general effect is of greater smoothness but of somewhat less definition. The basses, although still clear, are not as hard as the Italian and have more of what we call "boom," that is, a drumlike resonance which produces an effect of great nobility and power. In most examples the treble tends to be slightly weak in comparison to the bass which must, therefore, be quilled with great care. The best Ruckers tone has enough individuality to be interesting, but does not impose its characteristic upon the performer. Very few modern harpsichords approach the Ruckers in freedom of sound production and interest of harmonic development. In comparison to a Ruckers, modern harpsichords are likely to have a weak, wiry sound much like that produced by a Ruckers when a heavy mass such as a hammer or flatiron is permitted to rest on the bridge near the string being sounded.

Just as harpsichord makers never use mutation stops because the partials in question are already strongly present in the tone produced by vibrating strings, the Italian makers never found the four-foot very successful. Their instrument seems to have produced a rather powerful second partial, and to reinforce this by the addition of a second string provided the unpleasant effect of parallel octaves. The Ruckers harpsichords with their smoother eight-foot tone give the impression of having either an evener or a weaker series of partials, and are able to make use of the four-foot choir. When a properly voiced four-foot is employed the tone becomes more brilliant, but one is not disturbed by the effect of parallels. There is no doubt that the sound becomes less smooth. Possibly this is the effect of parallel octaves barely heard.

The various virginals made by the Ruckers family do not require as full a treatment as the harpsichords. Their chief importance lies in the ubiquitous role they played as instruments for house music and for the music lessons of young ladies. There can be no doubt that nearly every prosperous bourgeois household in the Low Countries possessed a virginal. Their frequent appearance in contemporary Netherlands and Flemish painting bears witness to that. It also seems plain that the mid-seventeenth century English virginal owes a large debt to the Flemish design. But a lengthy discussion would be comparable to extensive efforts of some future historian to describe the twentieth century upright piano. Alec Hodsdon and Cecil Clutton [56] have argued that the virginal was an instrument distinct from the harpsichord and possessing its own literature. This seems to me to be pushing a good thing too far, particularly in the case of the Flemish virginals, which simply are not as good as the harpsichords. If one must be an enthusiast of the virginal, let it be for the Italian virginals, which had a much better sound. The English and Flemish virginals were unresonant, thin, and sour.

As Table 9 makes clear, all of the standard models of Ruckers virginals had a range of four octaves, C/E to c''', and, of course, only one choir of strings. The main features of their construction have already been described. Although Plate XVIII illustrates an English virginal, it can be illuminating in the present context since English and Flemish virginals were quite similar in many details of design. It should be noted that the keyboards of models V and VI are found either to the right or left of center. This variation is important because the position of the keyboard in a virginal determines the plucking point. Those virginals with the keyboard to the right are plucked nearer to the center of the string than those with the keyboard to the left.

The center plucking type is much more frequently encountered than that with the keyboard to the left. This is curious when considered in the light of the critical opinion of van Blankenburg,[57] who may be taken as a good judge of instruments. Although removed by one hundred years from the milieu in which the Ruckers instruments were produced, he might still be expected to have many of the same criteria: "Of the virginals [vierkante] we will say in passing that those whose keyboard stands toward the left are even [regelmatig] and playable—these are called spinets [spinetten]; but those which have the keyboard on the

[56] Alec Hodsdon and Cecil Clutton, "Defining the Virginal," *The Musical Times*, May 1947.
[57] Page 142.

right-hand side are good in the right hand, but grunt in the bass like young pigs. It is impossible to prevent this, because the jack in falling divides the string into two parts, which are of such a length that they can sound against each other." (Van Blankenburg is referring to the difficulty of damping a string when the damper falls in the center of the string. Instead of ceasing to sound, the tone leaps upward an octave and continues to reverberate.) Douwes [58] is more explicit about the terminology of the two types: "There are various kinds. In some the jacks stand about half way between the bridges, and these are the most common; they are called '*muselars.*' In some the jacks stand close to the bridge, on the left hand; and these are called spinets [*spinetten*]. The small ones are called '*scherpen*' because they are high and sharp in sound."

Model VI covers a group of virginals which vary from the standard eight-foot virginals only in their smaller size and shorter scales. It is a reasonable guess that the scales imply a pitch or pitches higher than normal, a suspicion which is borne out by the variable standard of pitch revealed in the Duarte-Huyghens correspondence [59] and by a remark of Praetorius: "The spinet (Italian, *spinetto*) is a small quadrangular instrument which is tuned an octave or a fifth higher than normal pitch. It is generally placed on top of larger keyboard instruments." [60] However, since even these smaller Flemish virginals range from forty-four to fifty-six inches in length, they seem a bit large to be placed in this manner. Furthermore, a passage in van Blankenburg leads one to suspect that they might have sounded the pitch of the larger instruments, scale notwithstanding. Van Blankenburg is discussing the method of stringing harpsichords and the material of which the strings are made: "but since they [copper strings] do not sound as clear as iron ones in the treble, harpsichords are seldom made in this way. There is a difference in the string lengths: a top c of iron is seven inches long, but of copper five and one half; an octave lower down the measurement of the iron string is fourteen inches, of the copper one eleven . . . The little oblong virginals, which are called 'five-footers,' are suited to copper stringing." [61] Van Blankenburg's physics demand a constant pitch, since a copper—or as we would say, brass—string of eleven inches can barely sound pitch c'' without breaking, and cannot sound a higher pitch. On

[58] *Grondig Ondersoek*, p. 104.
[59] See Russell, *The Harpsichord and Clavichord*, p. 150.
[60] *Syntagma musicum*, chap. XXXVIII.
[61] *Elementa musica*, p. 175.

the other hand, van Blankenburg wrote one hundred years after Ruckers built virginals, and it is likely that the necessities which had forced Ruckers to make instruments in a variety of pitches had ceased to exist.

The scales of the shorter virginals include c″ at 9½ inches, 10¾ inches, and 11¾ inches. It is simple to calculate that these scales imply a departure from the normal tone sounded by the fourteen-inch c″ of three semitones, a fourth, and a fifth. However, it is possible to tune harpsichord strings of a fixed length over so large a range that it is a most dubious proceeding to base on the scale a theory of the pitch sounded by any instrument.

Douwes[62] gives tables of the string lengths of harpsichords (klavecimbels) six, five, four, and three feet in length. These scales are respectively fourteen, thirteen, ten, and seven inches. The first three could conceivably sound normal eight-foot pitch, but the last could not and certainly is the scale of an instrument at four-foot pitch. The ten-inch scale, although quite normal for an Italian harpsichord, is so short that here it probably represents some sort of raised pitch. Unfortunately, Douwes does not say anything about the pitches sounded by these instruments. He is not thinking of brass scales, however, because later[63] he gives the wire diameters and materials for these scales, and the trebles of even the shortest are in steel.

Praetorius describes a device which is occasionally found on Ruckers virginals of model VI: "The *Arpichordum* is a *Symphony* or *Virginall* on which a harplike sound is produced by means of a special stop which governs brass hooks under the strings."[64] Such a device takes the form of brass or iron pins, bent like staples into a U shape, which are driven into a batten working under the strings and attached to the bridge like a buff stop batten. When this batten is moved to bring the staples into contact with the strings, a jarring sound is produced. Since a virginal bridge has a sharp bend at about a′, the stop operates only from the bass to that point. A somewhat similar stop is to be found on the Theewes claviorganum.[65]

Model VII is a perfectly straightforward ottavino at four-foot pitch, which varies from the other Ruckers virginals in having a protruding rather than a recessed keyboard. This was obviously a space-saving device, for a virginal only 12½ inches wide does not have room for en-

[62] *Grondig Ondersoek,* p. 106.
[63] Pages 120–122.
[64] *Syntagma musicum,* chap. XLIII.
[65] See Hubbard, "Two Early English Harpsichords." See also below, page 270, Adlung's remarks on this stop.

closed key levers of sufficient length, particularly in the bass. By permitting the keyboard to protrude Ruckers could make the body of the instrument narrower than would otherwise be possible.

Model VIII appears only as the octave instrument inserted into the body of the double virginals, model IX. Like the virginals of models V and VI, the keyboard is recessed, but it resembles the other ottavino (model VII) in the placement of that keyboard in a centered position. The scales and dimensions of models VII and VIII are similar except that the recessed keyboard of model VIII required that Ruckers make the case nearly three inches wider in order to obtain a reasonable key lever length.

Model IX is the famous double virginal. An ottavino of model VIII is inserted into the case of the virginal like a drawer slipping into a bureau. When it was desired to use the ottavino, it could be drawn forward, either remaining partly in the eight-foot case or being removed completely and placed on top of the eight-foot virginal, thus forming a second keyboard at four-foot pitch. The surviving examples of Ruckers double virginals show the ottavino to the left, and hence the keyboard of the eight-foot virginal to the right (*muselar*), but a double virginal by Grovvelus and another by Van der Biest reverse this arrangement by placing the ottavino to the right and the keyboard of the eight-foot instrument to the left. It seems likely that Ruckers also made this model since all of his other virginals appear with the keyboard in either position. At least one Flemish ottavino (Hans Ruckers, 1610) has been coupled to the manual of its companion eight-foot virginal. The eight-foot virginal jack rail is removed and the ottavino set in its place. The eight-foot jacks rise through mortises cut in the bottom of the ottavino and push the ottavino key levers upward. This instrument has been so much altered that it is difficult to guarantee that this arrangement was original. Reynvaan described the double virginal thus: "There are also even virginals which have two keyboards; but the second keyboard is really a separate small harpsichord or little spinet which is placed on the rectangular harpsichord, being built for this purpose. This kind is called the Mother with the Child." [66]

This catalogue of instruments, with the possible addition of an expressive double by the Couchets, seems to have satisfied the clients of the Ruckers family until the workshop was finally closed. The last entries of harpsichord makers in the guild rolls are those for Abraham and Joseph

[66] Joos Verschuere Reynvaan, *Muzykaal Kunst-Woordenboek* (Amsterdam, 1795), p. 115.

Couchet, who were admitted in 1666. The international reputation of the Flemish school seems to have declined very rapidly after this date, and the traditions of the Ruckers were inherited by the French, who apparently altered their own native product in the last decade of the century to imitate the Flemish instruments. It is not difficult to assign reasons for the decay of the community of harpsichord makers in Antwerp; indeed one is surprised that any industry of that moribund city ever gained such pre-eminence. Assisted in its rise to the commercial leadership of Europe by the inundations of Zeeland at the beginning of the fifteenth century, which had enlarged the western Scheldt and afforded a direct route to the sea, and by a liberal municipal organization, Antwerp had seized the initiative from Bruges and had assumed all the financial and commercial functions of that center. But the wars and sieges associated with the revolt of the Low Countries against their Spanish and Austrian masters at the end of the sixteenth century left Antwerp prostrate. Fifty percent of the population of the surrounding provinces was gone and the Dutch were blocking the Scheldt, as they were destined to do until the end of the eighteenth century. The effect of these events is vividly reported in a letter written by Sir Dudley Carleton to John Chamberlaine in 1616:

Hagh, Sept 5/15, 1616

untill we came to *Antwerp*, wch I must confesse exceedes any I ever saw any where else, for the bewtie and the uniformity of buildings, heith and largeness of streetes, and strength and fairness of the rampars . . . But I must tell you of the state of this towne in a word, so as you take it literally, *magna civitas magna solitudo*, for in ye whole time we spent there I could never sett my eyes in the whole length of a streete uppon 40 persons at once: I never mett coach nor saw man on horseback: none of owr companie (though both were workie dayes) saw one pennie worth of ware ether in shops or in streetes bought or solde. Two walking pedlers and one ballad-seller will carrie as much on theyr backs at once as was in that royall exchange ether above or below. The English house is filled wth schooleboyes under the Jesuits discipline, and the Esterlings stands emptie. In many places grasse growes in the streetes, yet (that wch is rare in such solitariness) the buildings are all kept in perfect reparation. Theyr condition is much worse (wch may seem strange) since the truce than it was before; and the whole country of Brabant was suitable to this towne; *splendida paupertas*, faire and miserable.[67]

This dreary desolation was not to be filled until long after the last harpsichord was made in Antwerp. Off on his musical journey to Germany, Burney passed through Antwerp more than one hundred fifty

[67] Sainsbury, ed., *Original Unpublished Papers*, p. 11.

years later and found it an excellent occasion to compose an elegant *memento mori*:

I arrived here Friday evening, July 17th: it is a city that fills the mind with more melancholy reflections concerning the vicissitudes of human affairs, and the transient state of worldly glory, than any other in modern times: the exchange which served as a model to Sir Th. Gresham, when he built that of London, and which, though still intire, is as useless to the inhabitants, as the *coloseo* at Rome: the Town-house, constructed as a tribunal, for the magistrates, at the head of two hundred thousand inhabitants, which are now reduced to less than twenty thousand: the churches, the palaces, the squares, and whole streets, which, not two hundred years ago, were scarce sufficient to contain the people for whom they were designed, and which are now almost abandoned: the spacious and commodious quays, the numerous canals, out with such labour and expence, the noble river Schelde, wider than the Thames at Chelsea-reach, which used to be covered with ships from all quarters of the world, and on which now, scarce a fishing boat can be discovered: all contribute to point out the instability of fortune, and to remind us that, what Babylon, Carthage, Athens, and Palmyra now are, the most flourishing cities of the present period, must in the course of time, inevitably become.[68]

Although the guild rolls are silent on the course of harpsichord making in Antwerp after the admission of the last two Couchets, there is considerable evidence to be found of the harpsichord making which continued in Flanders but now probably only to meet local requirements. The corpus of extant instruments pertinent to this part of our investigation is not large, and only about twenty are known to me. These include a 1710 Jacobus van den Elsche double harpsichord; an "H.V.L." double of 1702; several Ioannes Daniel Dulcken instruments, dated between 1745 and 1769; three Albertus Delin harpsichords, including two clavicytheria from the middle of the century; and, finally, four Joannes Bull harpsichords built between 1776 and 1789. Burney gives us a glimpse of the state of affairs at the time of his visit in 1772:

The harpsichord maker of the greatest eminence, after them, [the Ruckers] was J. Dan. Dulcken;[69] he was a Hessian. At present there is a good workman at Antwerp, of the name of Bull, who was Dulcken's apprentice, and who sells his double harpsichords for a hundred ducats each, with only plain painted cases, and without swell or pedals; the work, too, of Vanden

[68] Charles Burney, *The Present State of Music in Germany, the Netherlands, and United Provinces* (London, 1773), p. 28.

[69] Dulcken died in 1763, but the business was carried on by his widow and his son. Apparently conditions were more favorable in Brussels, for in 1763 she requested the rights of *bourgeoise* in Brussels. Although she met with a refusal, she established her business there and seems to have done rather poorly, for she soon received a remission of taxes. (Van der Straeten, *La Musique aux Pays-Bas.*)

Elsche, a Flamand, has a considerable share of merit; but, in general, the present harpsichords, made here after the Rucker model, are thin, feeble in tone, and much inferior to those of our best makers in England.[70]

We cannot rely very heavily on Burney's estimate of these harpsichords because at every step he has demonstrated himself to have been a poor judge of musical traditions alien to his own. In Germany, for example, when confronted with the superb organs of the school of Schnitger, so remarkable for their ensemble tone, he judged them almost entirely as a collection of solo stops, thus revealing his ignorance of the concept held by their makers. To begin with, it is an oversimplification to describe the instruments of van den Elsche, Bull, and Dulcken as of the Ruckers model. They owe a great deal to Ruckers, as do all harpsichords made outside of Italy, but they are hardly closer to Ruckers than are the Kirckmans and Shudis of England. Burney's remark that Bull sold double harpsichords without swell or pedals for one hundred ducats may have been true, but the implication that Bull and his school made no pedals is a distortion of fact. In place of pedals, knee levers may be employed to change stops. The only surviving van den Elsche known to me had two knee levers; of seven Dulckens, two have knee levers; and two out of the four existing Bulls each have a knee lever.

A list of late Flemish harpsichords showing their tonal specifications poses fundamental problems in the history of disposition. It has seemed convenient to assume that all of the instruments of the Ruckers school conformed to a rigid norm and that variants were the result of later tinkering. This thesis is quite defensible so long as one confines oneself to instruments made before about 1645. However, the late Ruckers and Couchet harpsichords are not easy to reconcile in some details with the standard accounts. Van Blankenburg, viewing the development of the Flemish harpsichord from the vantage point of the year 1739, has written a most lucid account of the revision of the Ruckers transposing keyboards [71] and the addition of the second eight-foot choir. His first assumption was that once the transposing keyboards had been reconciled, one had use for only three registers of jacks, one for each choir; and he devoted considerable ingenuity to finding a use for the fourth register.

Just as we have been unable to assign a precise date to the first expressive double harpsichord, we are unable to define the period of the

---

[70] *Ibid.*, p. 47.

[71] For an analysis of the transformations undergone by a 1620 Andreas Ruckers transposing harpsichord, see Alfred Berner, "Zum Klavierbau im 17 und 18 Jahrhunderts," in (Kongress-Bericht) *Gesellschaft für Musikforschung* (Lüneburg, Germ., 1950).

last transposing harpsichord. If van Blankenburg's attitude was generally held by harpsichord makers we could be confident in our assumption that any four-register instrument up to the date of his discovery of a use for the fourth register (1708) must have been designed as a transposing instrument, yet van Blankenburg himself gives 1650 as the approximate date of the last of the transposing harpsichords, and it does not seem likely that it was much later. Most of the surviving Flemish instruments of the second half of the seventeenth century are indeed four-jackers, and the type continues into the eighteenth century without the hiatus one might expect between the demise of the transposing harpsichord and the general acceptance of van Blankenburg's device. It is easy to discount van Blankenburg's natural enthusiasm for his invention but not his unawareness of any prior expressive use for a fourth register. Whether the late seventeenth century harpsichords were transposing instruments or expressive instruments is not possible to discover. Unfortunately, all the specimens known to me have been rebuilt extensively and offer no clue to the enigma of their original nature.

Van Blankenburg's employment of the fourth register, whether original or not, is highly significant in the development of some of the characteristic eighteenth century dispositions in Flanders, Germany, and especially England. He removed the front eight-foot slide from its position beside the other slides and placed it in a special gap cut through the wrest plank nearly parallel to the eight-foot nut. The very close plucking point provided by these jacks produced an extremely nasal tone. In England, where this stop was most used, it was known as the "lute stop," and thus we shall refer to it here. Van Blankenburg's second move was to add a projection (dogleg) to the rear of the second jack (8'), now the foremost rank in the main gap, so that the front edge of the jack rested on the rear of the upper-manual key lever and the long dogleg reached downward to rest upon the lower-manual key lever. Thus the jack was moved by either the upper- or the lower-manual key. His harpsichord would now be disposed 2x8' on the upper manual (lute and dogleg 8'), and 2x8', 1x4' on the lower manual (one of the eight-foot jacks being, of course, the dogleg). (Plate XX, which shows the plan and elevation of a typical English double harpsichord, will clarify the details of van Blankenburg's invention.) Later Flemish makers arranged the two upper manual jacks to face in opposite directions so that a true unison was available on that keyboard. The lute and the back eight-foot jack plucked the same choir and the player had to be careful to cancel one when he wished to play the other.

Whatever the role we assign to van Blankenburg in the development of the typical disposition of the eighteenth century Flemish harpsichord and however we dispose of the seventeenth century instruments, which in their present form at least seem to antedate his innovations, there can be no doubt that the instrument he described became one of the commonest types constructed in Antwerp. Dulcken, particularly, seems to have provided his double harpsichords with the lute stop and the dogleg eight. In some cases he has made this disposition somewhat more flexible by mounting the upper manual key bed on supports which permit it to slide in and out a short distance, thus engaging and disengaging the upper manual key lever from the dogleg jack.

The following is the most typical Dulcken disposition:

$$\leftarrow \text{Lute (8')}$$
$$\rightarrow \text{8' (Dogleg)}$$
- - - - - - - - - -
$$\leftarrow \text{4'}$$
$$\leftarrow \text{8'.}$$

It will be understood, of course, that the dogleg jack works from both manuals. At first glance this disposition, which is controlled by hand stops, seems to be extremely flexible. There are three eight-foot tones, ranging from the nasal lute through the bright dogleg to the dark back eight. One has available two distinct eight-foot unisons: on the upper manual there is the bright lute and dogleg combination which sounds almost as if the four-foot were included in the ensemble, or, on the lower manual, the darker and more used back eight and dogleg unison. Similarly, there are two eight and four combinations provided: dogleg and four, and back eight and four. In addition to all of these there is the full harpsichord registration: dogleg, back eight, and four from the lower manual.

The vital limitation of Dulcken's disposition operates when one attempts to divide voices between manuals, employing different tone colors simultaneously. Since the lute jack and the back eight-foot jack are plucking the same string, it follows that they are also damping the same string. Thus, if the lute is left "on" with its dampers resting on the strings the back eight will not sound because the strings it is plucking are damped. In the same way the lute will not sound unless the back eight-foot slide is first moved to the right. Thus it is impossible to produce a dialogue between the lute and any of the lower keyboard combinations which employ the back eight-foot. A further limitation is produced by the dogleg jack. Since it is always moved by a lower-manual key, it follows that if one attempts to use it from the upper manual in dialogue with lower manual registrations and the parts cross, one will find notes on the upper manual missing because they have already been sounded from the lower manual. Even more annoying is the discovery that one cannot use the dogleg in dialogue with the back eight. If the dogleg stop is drawn, that stop will sound from the lower manual and with the back eight will produce an eight-foot unison. In the case of the instruments in which Dulcken fitted a sliding upper manual, it is possible to dialogue the lute against the dogleg by disengaging the dogleg from the upper manual and playing it from the lower manual, but this is a rather glittering combination for continual use. One is forced to the conclusion that Dulcken did not think in terms of true two-manual performance in which the various stops are used more or less consistently to give a distinct personality to each voice. At most, his second manual is an aid to sudden contrasts of tone and timbre.[72]

There is a two-manual Bull harpsichord, dated 1789 (now in the Conservatoire Royal de Musique, Brussels), disposed:

$$\rightarrow 8'$$
$$- - - - -$$
$$\rightarrow 8'$$
$$\leftarrow 8'$$
$$\leftarrow 4'.$$

It is surprising that this instrument has no coupler. Without it the registration is even worse than Dulcken's, for one cannot even contrast the quiet upper manual against the forte lower since there is damper interference between the upper eight and the front eight of the lower manual. This instrument has a buff stop which operates on both eight-foot strings simultaneously at the touch of a knee lever. The registers are operated by hand stops.

Another and rather clever disposition used by Bull in 1778 is the following:

$$\leftarrow 8' \text{ (Lute)}$$
$$\leftarrow \!\!\rightarrow 8' \text{ (Dogleg)}$$
$$- - - - - - - - - -$$
$$\leftarrow 8' \text{ (Peau de buffle)}$$
$$\leftarrow 4'.$$

[72] The Flemish dogleg, so inferior to the disposition with manual coupler used in France, may have been adopted in the interests of a light action, which was regarded as a desirable attribute.

The dogleg jack is extra wide and contains two tongues facing in opposite directions permitting the jack to pluck either eight-foot choir. Thus a 2x8′ unison is available on either manual. If the lower-manual unison is to be used, the lute must be "off" to avoid damper interference. Then the available registrations would be:

Upper: 1x8′ (Dogleg)
Lower: 2x8′ (Dogleg and back eight)
or
2x8′, 1x4′.

If the brighter upper-manual unison were to be employed the registrations would be:

Upper: 2x8′ (Dogleg and lute)
Lower: 1x8′ (Dogleg)
or
1x8′ (Dogleg), 1x4′.

Even with Bull's best disposition one does not have two completely independent eight-foot stops to dialogue.

The late Flemish makers seem to have made single harpsichords as well as the doubles we have been describing. These are normally found with three choirs, 2x8′, 1x4′, disposed:

$\rightarrow 8′$
$\leftarrow 8′$
$\leftarrow 4′$.

The registers were moved by hand stops, often of the push-pull variety. Frequently they were provided with a buff stop consisting of a bar of metal, covered with action cloth, which was mounted over the eight-foot nut so that it could be lowered into contact with the strings at the touch of a knee lever.

Delin, particularly, seems to have concentrated on upright harpsichords (clavicytheria). In principal, these are only 2x8′ single harpsichords standing vertically. The keyboard, of course, remained horizontal, and a special action had to be devised to transmit the motion of the keys to the jacks. Aside from their orientation, Delin's instruments vary in no important detail from earlier Flemish singles. He even retained the primitive projecting slides in the place of hand stops. The tone of Delin's clavicytheria is particularly good.

Apart from disposition the chief distinctions between the eighteenth century Flemish practice and that of the seventeenth century lay in the choice of materials and in the dimensions and form of the cases. Scales remained about the same. Most of the late instruments were originally built with a compass of five full octaves (FF to f''') and are much wider than the four-octave Ruckers. This produced more of a hook to the bentside in the treble and less curve as the bentside approached the joint with the tail. Dulcken's double harpsichords average fourteen inches longer than a Ruckers transposing harpsichord.

Bull experimented more boldly with his case outline and produced harpsichords in which the tail is curved and made of a piece with the bentside. This form of case appeared intermittently in various countries. It was to be found in the seventeenth century in both France and England, became completely standard among the Hamburg makers of the eighteenth century, and crops up occasionally in late Italian harpsichords with integral outer cases. It is slightly more difficult to make than the usual type since it requires a more elaborate mold.

We find the last Flemish harpsichord makers abandoning soft wood as the only possible material for cases and sometimes turning to hardwoods such as oak, walnut, and even maple. These harpsichords are likely to show the natural surface of the wood and often reveal dovetails at the corners. The old Ruckers style moldings which ran around the inside edge of the case at the top are sometimes omitted. Despite these changes in decor, the Flemish makers seem to have remained generally faithful to their bone or ivory natural key tops to the very end.

Although the Flemish makers continued to be active for more than one hundred years after the last Ruckers instruments were built they no longer stood in the main stream. The great Flemish contribution to the history of the instrument was the tonal concept created by Hans Ruckers. The methods which produced that sound had long since been taken up by others who refined the disposition and extended the range but never abandoned the central facts of his design.

CHAPTER THREE · FRANCE

In Italy our studies have been aided by the existence of a great many old harpsichords and hampered by the lack of descriptive texts. French source materials, on the other hand, consist almost entirely of documents; the instruments themselves are exceedingly rare. In France, for both the seventeenth and eighteenth centuries, we are fortunate in possessing general compendia which contain more specific information than that found in any other language, with the possible exception of German. The *Harmonie universelle*[1] of Mersenne and the various articles contained in the *Encyclopédie*[2] provide for their respective periods a framework of solid information around which one can arrange the details derived from slightly less substantial sources. The French genius for red tape has provided archives of unequaled richness which have been hardly touched by scholars in this field and which undoubtedly still contain a great deal of undiscovered information.

Toward the middle of the eighteenth century the liberal movement of opposition to the obfuscation and technical conservatism of the guilds was sufficiently powerful to bring about the production of many volumes on the techniques of contemporary arts and trades. Those published by the Académie Royale des Sciences are particularly noteworthy. In addition to such formal treatises on particular trades as the volumes of Dom Bedos and Roubo,[3] the Académie published shorter papers on a tremendous variety of subjects, many of which are pertinent to our investigations.

The bulk of the records of the Guild of Master Makers of Musical Instruments of the City and Suburbs of Paris (*La Communauté des maîtres*

---

[1] F. Marin Mersenne, *Harmonie universelle, contenant la théorie et la pratique de la musique* (Paris, 1636).

[2] Denis Diderot and Jean le Rond d'Alembert, eds., *Encyclopédie ou Dictionnaire raisonné des sciences, des arts, et des métiers* (Paris, 1751–1778). For a discussion of this source see Frank Hubbard, "The *Encyclopédie* and the French Harpsichord," *The Galpin Society Journal*, 9 (1956): 37.

[3] Dom François Bedos de Celles, *L'Art du facteur d'orgues* (Paris, 1766–1778); André Jacob Roubo, *L'Art du menuisier* (Paris, 1769–1774).

faiseurs d'instruments de musique de la ville et faubourgs de Paris) have been lost, and with them we lost the possibility of clear knowledge of the names and numbers of harpsichord makers working in Paris on any given date. But the documents preserved in the Minutier Central of the Archives Nationales have more than made up that deficiency by providing us with very detailed information about a few specific makers.

It does not appear that harpsichord making was carried on as early in Paris as in Italy or Antwerp. No instruments have survived which were made before the middle of the seventeenth century, although we have traces of several makers who were working one hundred years earlier. One can view the French trade as divided into two distinct schools. The earlier was a group of seventeenth century makers, working in an indigenous tradition and providing innovations of an extremely original nature. Toward the end of the century this group was superseded by those who devoted themselves to the rebuilding of Ruckers harpsichords to suit the taste of changing times and to the making of new instruments in imitation of the Ruckers. This tremendous and somewhat unhealthy enthusiasm for Ruckers harpsichords ended by almost destroying the local product, although, as we have seen, that product went underground and many so-called Ruckers instruments were undoubtedly French in origin.

The majority of the harpsichord makers were regulated by the statute of 1599, issued by Henry IV and confirmed by Louis XIV in 1679,[4] which established a separate guild for instrument makers.[5] There were, however, certain categories of workers who enjoyed traditional immunities. Members of the royal family could issue letters of mastery and frequently did so to imported artisans of various sorts. Furthermore, masters and workers attached to the court were protected as were the residents of a few specified localities.

We like to think of the guilds as organizations of ruggedly independent bourgeois, jealous of their privileges and immunities, the cradle of freedom and the school of the arts; but a glance at the guild statute of 1599 will reveal in pitiless detail the basis of economic monopoly and technical restraint on which those organizations rested. To the nepotism

---

[4] Reproduced in Constant Pierre, *Les Facteurs d'instruments de musique, les luthiers et la facture instrumentale, précis historique* (Paris, 1893), p. 10.

[5] Before this time instrument makers apparently joined that guild whose members were authorized to employ the material of which their particular instruments were made. Constant Pierre (*Les Facteurs d'instruments de musique*) has demonstrated, for example, that trumpet makers at the end of the thirteenth century were members of the guild of iron and copper pot makers.

implicit in the prohibition of the trade to all who were not members of the guild and the easing of membership qualifications for the sons of masters must be added the methodical elimination of true competition between the masters, and the protection of the incompetent makers at the expense of the talented. Article 10 provided that any material bought outside of the country must be offered to all the masters of the guild impartially so that no maker, even through his own enterprise, could have the advantage of superior materials. Each master was limited to one apprentice at a time, and this regulation tended to prevent the art from developing as it must if apprentices were able to seek out the best masters with whom to study. The limitation of each master to one shop tended to prevent the most talented makers from exploiting their superiority and to reduce all firms to one level. Savary des Bruslons wrote:

> Everywhere abuses are introduced. In effect these guilds have special rules almost all of which are opposed to the general welfare and to the purpose of the legislator. The first and most dangerous is that which erects barriers to industry in multiplying the expense and formalities of admission. In some guilds where the number of members is limited and in those where the possibility of joining is restricted to the sons of masters, one can see only a monopoly contrary to the laws of reason and of the state and almost failing in those of conscience and religion . . .
>
> "The certain profit of the artisans and merchants renders them indolent and lazy while they exclude the clever men to whom necessity would provide industry." [6]

The exceedingly slow development until 1775 of all technology including harpsichord making is certainly due in part to the leaden hand of the guilds on the individual artisan. Decades produced only slight improvements, and most makers undoubtedly ended their lives making instruments identical to those which they had studied as apprentices.

The only evidences we have of harpsichord making in Paris during the sixteenth century are the names of a few makers attached to the court. Jean Potin, "faiseur d'épinettes du roy" ("harpsichord maker to the king"),[7] is mentioned in 1561, and he was succeeded in his office by Merry Lorillart, Antoine Potin and Pierre Lorillart. The families of Potin, Lorillart, and Dugué seem to have produced several makers each. The Denis and Jacquet dynasties which were founded in this century continued into the next. Mersenne mentions "Antoine Potin, & Emery

---

[6] *Dictionnaire universel de commerce*, II, 130. The second paragraph was quoted by Savary from the *Mémoires* of Jean de Wit, chap. X, pt. 1.

[7] François Lesure, "La Facture instrumentale à Paris au seizième siècle," *The Galpin Society Journal*, 7 (1954): 11.

ou Mederic [possibly Merry Lorillart], que l'on recognoist auoir esté les meilleurs Facteurs de France" ("Antoine Potin and Emery or Mederic who are recognized as having been the best makers in France").[8]

Something can be learned about these makers from inventories of their shops. For example, an inventory of the shop of Yves Mesnager in 1556, included:

Item   an old spinet [espinette] four and one-half feet long closing with a key . . .
Item   another spinet three feet long or thereabouts . . .
Item   a double clavichord [manicordion] three and one-half feet long or thereabouts . . .
Item   the wood of an unfinished clavichord . . .[9]

Mesnager, then, possessed two small spinets (one of them certainly at four-foot pitch) and a clavichord with two choirs of strings. The fourth item is the most significant: if Mesnager had the wood for an unfinished clavichord in his shop, he must have been a maker. We will see that the clavichord turns up fairly frequently in French documents during the sixteenth and the first half of the seventeenth century. For example, the apprenticeship papers of Antoine Gourdin, March 15, 1557,[10] bind Guillaume Raguenet, organist, to teach young Gourdin "à jouer du manicordion et de l'espinette" ("to play the clavichord and the spinet"). And Nicolas Robillard, "joueur d'instruments" ("player of instruments"), who died in 1557, possessed "ung manycordion" (a clavichord) but no espinette. I am not aware of any extant French clavichords.

The inventory of the effects of Claude Denis, "facteur d'instruments" ("maker of instruments"), dead in 1587, includes several spinets:

Item   1 old spinet so so . . .
Item   1 spinet five feet long . . .
Item   1 spinet of "bure" [?], covered with red leather . . .
Item   1 clavichord . . .
Item   1 old spinet three feet long . . .[11]

When Robert Denis the Younger died in 1589, besides a tremendous collection of instruments which show him to have been a dealer on a large scale, he possessed:

Item   nine spinets covered as well as not covered and of several sizes . . .

[8] Mersenne, Harmonie universelle, book 3, p. 159.
[9] Lesure, "La Facture instrumentale," p. 24.
[10] Ibid.
[11] Ibid.

Item   three spinet locks and two for lute [cases] furnished with their keys and "danyes" [?] . . .

Item   two dozen spinet tuning hammers . . .[12]

The French had a tendency to use the word "épinette" in a general way, as the English employed "virginal." Even in the eighteenth century one finds the phrase "épinette ordinaire" used to mean harpsichord.[13] The small size of most of the instruments cited above makes it obvious that the word refers to spinets and not to harpsichords. This conclusion is reinforced by Mersenne's remark, "Il semble que ceux de l'autre siecle n'ont point eu de Clavecins, ny d'Epinettes à deux ou plusieurs ieux" ("It seems that those of the other century had no harpsichords at all nor spinets of two or several stops").[14]

It will be noted that the cases of many of these spinets were covered with leather or cloth. This is a feature often found on Italian instruments with independent outer cases, but it is exceedingly rare on integral instruments. The seventeenth century French spinets which still survive seem to display certain details which might refer back to a period of separate inner and outer cases. It is by no means impossible that the instruments cited above were constructed in that manner.

When the organist of Notre Dame de Paris, Pierre Chabanceau (De la Barre), died in 1600, he left behind rather a large collection of keyboard instruments, including the first *clavecin* we meet: [15]

Item   a harpsichord [*clavesin*] covered with red *bazanne* [a thin sheepskin still used by bookbinders] without iron work or other furnishings . . .

Item   a little clavichord of white wood . . .

Item   a spinet covered with red *bazanne* with a lock that doesn't close furnished with two trestles . . .

Item   another little spinet of black leather lined with green Burgos satin with a closing lock furnished with its trestles of oak wood . . .

The last item offers a clue to the nature of the leather covered instruments which seem to have been so common. It is just possible that a spinet with integral outer case could be covered with leather — after all, the claviorganum by Theewes (1579) was so adorned — but surely no one would line a spinet case with green satin unless the case were in the nature of an outer box enclosing the instrument itself.

Mersenne, writing in the middle of the seventeenth century, consid-

[12] *Ibid.*

[13] *Encyclopédie*, "Epinette" (appeared originally in the Geneva edition of 1777).

[14] Mersenne, *Harmonie universelle*, book 3, p. 160.

[15] Lesure, "La Facture instrumentale," p. 45.

ered "the best makers at present" to be "Iean Iacquet, le Breton, & Iean Denys."[16] In 1603 we find Jacques Le Breton being bound apprentice to "Mederic Lorillart,"[17] and the career begun thus auspiciously was to be embellished by the titles of "maitre joueur d'espinette du roi" ("master spinet player to the King") in 1624, "maitre faiseur d'espinettes du roi" ("master maker of spinets to the King") in 1627, and "maitre faiseur d'instruments ordinaire du roy" ("master maker of instruments in ordinary to the King") in 1656.

Jean Jacquet died in 1632 and the inventory of his goods has fortunately survived. We find "in the shop being beside the said kitchen":

Item three harpsichords [*clavessins*] of which one barred [*barré*; Mersenne uses the word to refer to both the frame members and the soundboard ribs] . . .

Item two spinets three feet in length or thereabouts . . .

Item three other little spinets of which two of two and one-half feet and one of two feet . . .

Item a clavichord . . .

Item two spinet cases [*bastimes*] of three and one-half feet and one of two feet . . .

Item three bad benches, three jointing planes, two large and one small, a plane, six saws, large and small, three rules, twelve bad bit braces, three bar clamps, and four holdfasts, all of them in iron, a knife, three small hammers and other similar tools.[18]

It seems that Jacquet was devoting most of his efforts to spinet making, although the more expensive harpsichord was beginning to overtake its rival. Against the three harpsichords in his workshop we can place five completed spinets and two under construction. A matter of interest is the extremely small size of nearly all the spinets described up to this point. The ottavino now seems to be more of a plaything than a musical instrument, and yet a great many of them seem to have been made and placed in the possession of musicians.

Benches and jointing planes traditionally belonged to the class of tools called *d'affutage*[19] which were provided by masters to their workmen. Since Jean Jacquet owned three benches and three jointing planes it is likely that the total staff of his workshop consisted of three men. One of these could legally have been an apprentice, and the other a journeyman. Perhaps one was Claude Jacquet, of whom we have an inventory in 1661.

[16] *Harmonie universelle*, book 3, p. 159.
[17] Lesure, "La Facture instrumentale," p. 46.
[18] Archives Nationales, Minutier Central, VII, 21, April 2, 1632.
[19] See below, Chap. 6, and Roubo, *L'Art du menuisier*, pt. I, chap. 5.

In the course of a discussion of string sizes Michel Corrette gives us a list of seventeenth century makers: "Quand l'ut d'en haut A n'a que 5 pouces il faut monter le clavecin en cordes jaunes tels sont ceux de Geronimo, de la Couture, Roze. Pour les jacquet, Denis, Barbier, Dufour, Dumont, Richard, Rigault, Dastenet, Verjure, Rastoin suivent a peu de chose près les mêmes proportions que ceux des habiles Facteurs de ce Siècle. La même chose pour les Epinettes du ton." ("When the C of upper A [c′′′] is only five inches long, it is necessary to string the harpsichord with yellow strings [brass] such as on those of Geronimo, De la Couture, Roze. However, the Jacquets, Denis, Barbier, Dufour, Dumont, Richard, Rigault, Dastenet, Verjure, and Rastoin followed nearly the same measurements as those of the clever makers of this [the eighteenth] century. The same is true of eight-foot spinets.") [20]

It is interesting to attempt to identify the makers Corrette cites. Particularly since he used a short scale, Geronimo sounds like Hieronymus de Zentis of Rome, possibly the best Italian maker of his time. He seems to have worked in both London and Paris. In 1668 there was a petition by a certain Andrea Testa to Charles II of England for a pension "as formerly granted to Gerolamo Zenti, harpsicall maker, whose place he supplies, being sent over by Zenti, who went to Paris, and died in the French King's service." [21] The name Jerosme occurs sometimes in eighteenth century advertisements and may refer to Zentis. A harpsichord thus inscribed was in the possession of the maker Joseph Treyer, "dit l'Empereur," in 1779. Several harpsichords and spinets by Zentis have survived, but all of those inscribed with a place name are dated from Rome. Kinsky [22] reports one, dated 1683, which implies either another maker of the same name, a false inscription, or a typographical error. Bontempi credits Zentis with the invention of a harpsichord in the form of a triangle with unequal sides. [23] The two keyboards and three registers were placed on the shortest side of the triangle. This instrument is supposed to have produced as much sound as the largest harpsichord.

Pierre de la Couture was received into the guild on October 24, 1678. I have found no record of Roze except that the name occurs in an inventory of 1769. [24] "Les Jacquet" must include Jean, already mentioned;

---

[20] *Le Maître de clavecin*, chap. XXI, p. 82.

[21] Lafontaine, *The King's Musick*, p. 465.

[22] Georg Kinsky, *Musikhistorisches Museum von Wilhelm Heyer in Cöln, Katalog* (Cologne, 1910), p. 94.

[23] Giovanni Andrea Bontempi, *Historia musica* (Perugia, 1695), p. 47.

[24] Archives Nationales, Minutier Central, CIX, 728, Sept. 28, 1769, effects of Henry Hemsch include "Un clavecin de Roze."

Nicolas, who was apprenticed to Robert Despont; and Claude, who died in 1661, and with whom I shall deal at length below. The harpsichord makers of the Denis family during the seventeenth century included Jehan; Jean (II), his eldest son, of whom we have an inventory in 1686;[25] and Philippe, Jehan's second son, dead in 1705, of whom a spinet, dated 1672, is to be found at the Conservatoire in Paris. In 1905 a harpsichord by Philippe Denis of the year 1691 was said to be in existence, but all trace of it has since been lost. M. and A. Saloman of Paris once owned another Philippe Denis harpsichord, dated 1674. The library of the Musée des Arts Decoratifs in Paris has a photo of this instrument.[26] We have a short inventory of Philippe's possessions made after his death.[27] Several advertisements for instruments by Louis Denis, the third brother, were printed during the eighteenth century in Les Affiches, annonces, et avis divers, including one for a harpsichord which had been made in the year 1702. The cursory inventory which made part of the scellé (a preliminary inventory made at the time of death) of Jean Ferchur (1729)[28] included "[Un] autre clavessin ledit doré dedans et dessus fait par Pierre Denis." ("Another harpsichord the said gilded inside and out, made by Pierre Denis.") Pierre, the son of Philippe, is thus the sixth member of this family known to us. Ferchur, incidentally, is probably the "Verjure" mentioned by Corrette.

Antoine Barbier was called in as consulting expert in 1686 when the inventory of the workshop of Jean Denis (II) was in preparation. An instrument by Dufour was advertised for sale in 1753 in the pages of Les Affiches. Nicolas Dumont, who was received into the guild July 20, 1675, has left a harpsichord, dated 1697, which is to be found at the Conservatoire in Paris. There are numerous other references to his instruments in inventories and advertisements.

Michel Richard left two spinets (1672 and 1693) and signed the underside of the soundboard of a Hans Ruckers (I) harpsichord[29] in 1688: "Faict par Michel Richard a Parice Rue du Paon 1688." Apparently he was responsible only for the ravalement, although the wording of his inscription is a little ambiguous. Hullmandel[30] remembered him in 1791 as a good seventeenth century maker. Besides fairly frequent

---

[25] Ibid., LXIV, 206, Jan. 4, 1686. He is probably the author of the Traité de l'accord de l'espinette (Paris, 1650).

[26] No. 322–17, page 39.

[27] Archives Nationales, Minutier Central, LXXII, 178, July 21, 1705. It lists two benches, a few tools, and one unfinished harpsichord.

[28] Ibid., Y 15323, Jan. 30, 1729.

[29] Boalch, Makers of the Harpsichord and Clavichord, no. 18.

[30] "Musique," Encyclopédie méthodique, I, 286b.

references in *Les Affiches* we have several documents[31] referring to Richard, including the apprenticeship papers of a certain Gilbert des Ruisseaux, dated January 20, 1670.[32] Des Ruisseaux will concern us further, since he is the maker of one of the very few seventeenth century French harpsichords still in existence. There is a harpsichord now to be found in the Conservatoire des Arts et Métiers in Paris which has been ascribed to Richard. The rose carries the initials "MR," but this is hardly enough on which to base an ascription. The harpsichord has been very thoroughly rebuilt, perhaps in 1792 by Joachim Swann in Paris,[33] and the original workmanship has been quite thoroughly effaced.

Jean Baptiste Rigault is represented by two notices in *Les Affiches*. A will exists for his widow which contains nothing of interest for us. Dastenet is unknown to me. Honoré Rastoin is otherwise known only by one advertisement in *Les Affiches*. We do know, however, that Rastoin's son, Louis Jacques, was admitted to the guild on March 27, 1747.

The group represented by the nineteen makers cited above can be enlarged somewhat. Documents in the Minutier Central preserve traces of members of the Despont family who were following the trade well back in the sixteenth century. During the first half of the seventeenth century we find three brothers, Antoine, Luc, and Robert; the sons of Antoine: Antoine (II), Jean, Philippe, and Robert; two sons of Luc: Louis and Philippe (II); and Pierre Despont. Henry Dulong is termed "facteur d'epinettes" in 1645. Michel Douvé, "aussy m̄r a la dit voccation" ("also master of the said vocation"), was called in as expert for the preparation of the Claude Jacquet inventory of 1661. Jacques Bourdet was received into the guild October 24, 1678, and became *juré* in 1689. We have an inventory prepared after his death in 1737.[34] We must also admit a provincial maker, Vincent Tibaut of Toulouse, for in 1679 he made a harpsichord which is still preserved in the Conservatoire Royal at Brussels.

Since we do not have examples available of the work of all the seventeenth century makers we have been enumerating, it is not possible to determine completely which among them belonged to that tradition which we have designated native, and which to the Franco-Flemish

[31] Archives Nationales, Minutier Central, XII, Sept. 12, 1659, agreement to teach Elie Jame to play the violin; XLIII, 169, June 11, 1679, apprenticeship articles of André Guignard.

[32] *Ibid.*, XLIII, 134, Jan. 20, 1670.

[33] This guess is based upon the fact that one of the jacks is dated and that the external veneer (obviously from the eighteenth century) and the stand are almost identical with those of an instrument by Swann in the same collection.

[34] Archives Nationales, Minutier Central, XCI, 758, March 2, 1737.

school which eventually was to triumph. We know that Dumont certainly belonged to the latter, for we have an instrument to prove it, and we can assume that the very early seventeenth century makers such as Jean Jacquet belonged to the first tradition. The Des Ruisseaux harpsichord is a primary document in defining the native French tradition; we can assume that its maker's master, Richard, also worked in that style, an assumption borne out by Richard's spinets. The Philippe Denis spinet[35] like Vincent Tibaut's harpsichord is in the native French style.

Corrette divided the group of makers he cited into two sections apparently on the basis of scale. The c''' of five *pouces* which he specified implies a scale just over ten inches. Geronimo, De la Couture, and Roze seem to have worked to that measure. Corrette considered the remaining makers in his list to have followed proportions identical to those of the eighteenth century in scaling. The scanty information I have been able to assemble on late seventeenth century French harpsichords shows that indeed they did have scales longer than ten inches, although not so long as those by Blanchet and Taskin. It is not likely that Des Ruisseaux used a shorter scale than that of his master, Richard, who was included in the longer-scaled group by Corrette. Des Ruisseaux's harpsichord was designed to a scale of 12⅛ inches. His design certainly looks backward toward the earlier seventeenth century rather than forward to the more massive concept of the Franco-Flemish school. Thus, we cannot take Corrette's division as a reliable appraisal of the two tendencies.

Nor can we rely on the descriptions we have of the seventeenth century instruments. Mersenne devoted twenty-five folio pages[36] of slippery ambiguities to his discussion of the spinet and the harpsichord — a tremendous supply of material for a field with such meager resources as ours. It must, however, be assessed with exceeding caution. For example, two pages are adorned with tables purporting to specify the appropriate wire sizes for each string of a harpsichord. The calculations have been carried out with the utmost rigor to the third decimal place. Although this stern matter, cast in its forbidding format, has exacted faint praise from generations of browbeaten commentators, it is a compound of absurdities based on a false assumption. Mersenne started with the mistaken premise that a string sounding great C must have sixteen times the circumference of a string sounding c''', four octaves above,[37] for-

---

[35] Conservatoire National, Paris. Others mentioned are privately owned in Paris.

[36] See *Harmonie universelle*, pp. 155f.

[37] The ratio of vibrations of C to c''' is 1 to 16, but assuming equal length and equal tension, it is the cross-sectional area which varies in that ratio and not the circumference.

getting completely that harpsichord designers provide for the various pitches by halving the length of the strings for each octave ascended.

If one were to be guided by theory alone, all the strings in a harpsichord would be of one circumference. In practice, they are not of equal circumference but become larger in the bass, although in nothing like the ratio of sixteen to one. His oversight is more difficult to understand since he has provided the lengths of each string in a harpsichord as one of the elements of his table. The recommended string sizes are ridiculous, not only as the result of this fundamental error but also because they attenuate to such small diameters in the treble (.001 inch) that the wire could not have been drawn at all. From all Mersenne's effort we glean only one dubious fact about string sizes: "la plus grosse chorde a ⅕ de ligne, & 5. pieds de longueur, comme a pour l'ordinaire la plus grosse chorde des Epinettes & des Clauecins" ("the thickest string is ⅕ of a line and five feet long as is ordinarily the thickest string of spinets and harpsichords").[38] Elsewhere Mersenne has mentioned both G and C as the lowest note of the keyboard. Thus, that string, whichever it was, had a diameter of .0178 inches. (The *pied du Roi*, which contained 144 *lignes*, equaled 12.789 modern inches.[39])

"But because the strings are sometimes larger than ⅗ of a line," Mersenne wrote at the foot of his first page of tables, "as is the case with large harpsichords of 12, 15, or of 20 feet, I place a table here." [40] Even with the assumption that Mersenne is dealing with pitches rather than dimensions, it is not easy to reconcile this passage with the instruments of his time which show no trace of sixteen-foot pitch. An open organ pipe twelve feet long sounds FF (the lowest eight-foot note of the modern harpsichord), one of fifteen feet sounds CC♯, and of twenty feet, GGG♯. The lowest sixteen-foot tone of a harpsichord with keyboard descending to FF is FFF. It is possible that Mersenne had various large instruments in mind, not at standard pitch, which had one choir tuned an octave below the "unison" pitch. The lower choir might then sound at fifteen- or twenty-foot pitch. This conjecture is weakened, however, by the description Mersenne provided a little later of the largest harpsichord he knew: "Il semble que ceux de l'autre siecle n'ont point eu de Clauecins, ny d'Epinettes à deux ou plusieurs ieux, comme nous en auons maintenant, qui ont quatre ieux, & quatre rangs de chordes, & que l'on nomme *Eudisharmoste*, dont le plus grand respond au 12

---

[38] *Harmonie universelle*, book 3, p. 120.
[39] See Doursther, *Dictionnaire universel*.
[40] *Harmonie universelle*, book 3, p. 121.

pieds de l'Orgue, le second est à l'Octaue, le 3 à la Douziesme, & le 4
à la Quinziesme en haut, soit qu'ils n'ayent qu'vn clauier, ou qu'ils en
ayent doux ou trois." ("It seems that those of the other [sixteenth] century had no harpsichords at all, nor spinets with two or several stops like
those we have now which are called *Eudisharmostes* and which have
four stops and four choirs of strings. The deepest corresponds to the
twelve-foot of the organ, the second is the octave, the third to the twelfth,
and the fourth to the fifteenth above whether they have only one keyboard or two or three.") [41]

It will be seen immediately that this instrument does not correspond
with the type he first referred to. There is no stop deeper than eight-foot,
but the keyboard descended to FF (12 foot), quite a possible range, as
we have seen in Flanders. The first key sounded strings tuned to FF,
F, c, and f, and the harpsichord thus contained the following stops:
eight-foot, four-foot, quint, and two-foot.

Those attempting to demonstrate the existence of sixteen-foot harpsichords in the seventeenth century often adduce the following passage
from Chapter XXXIX of Praetorius' *De Organographia* (1619). "The
Clavicymbalum or *Gravecymbalum* is a longish *Instrument* which to
some is a wing because it is almost in that shape: by others (but badly)
it would be called a pig's head because it ends in a point like the head
of a wild boar; and it has a strong, bright, rather lovely tone and resonance, more than the others, because of the doubled, tripled, even
quadrupled strings; just as one I saw which had two eight-foot unisons,
a quint, and a little octave of strings; and quite sweetly and splendidly
they rang amongst one another."

Both Mersenne and Praetorius, then, when they specifically describe
a four-choired harpsichord, give eight-foot as the lowest stop. Praetorius'
harpsichord seems to have been disposed 2x8', 1x4', and quint. Thus
Mersenne's twenty-foot harpsichord is deprived of its external documentary support and Mersenne, himself, seems to have abandoned the
idea when he specifically described a large harpsichord.

According to Mersenne, the eudisharmoste could have as many as
three keyboards. Most multimanual harpsichords do not bear close examination. If they are described in documentary sources, it generally
turns out that the writer had in mind some more or less elaborate division of the octave into many tones in order to avoid enharmonic tuning.
Thus, in effect these instruments had only one manual. A few three-
manual harpsichords still exist, but with two exceptions these have

[41] *Ibid.,* p. 160.

proved fraudulent, the work of nineteenth and twentieth century dealers. Although it must be admitted that there is too much evidence of its
occasional construction for it to be entirely ignored, the three-manual
harpsichord certainly never represented a norm nor played a significant
role in either the history of music or of the harpsichord.[42] The *Diction-
aire des arts, et des sciences*[43] contains the following reference: "Il y a
des clavessins à un seul clavier. D'autres en ont deux, & quelquefois
jusqu'a trois." ("There are harpsichords with one keyboard. Others have
two and sometimes up to three.") The compiler may have been following Mersenne. There are certain slight similarities in phrase which support this suspicion. However, Adlung[44] certainly stood on his own feet,
and he had this to say: "Man kann aber die Clavicymbel auch so machen,
dass 2 oder 3 Claviere übereinander stehen" ("However, one can make
a harpsichord in such a way that two or three keyboards are placed one
above the other"). But it must be remembered that Adlung was writing
nearly one hundred fifty years after Mersenne, and also that there is
sound evidence of three-manual harpsichord building in Hamburg
during the eighteenth century.[45]

The quint, which the large harpsichords known to both Praetorius
and Mersenne seem to have contained, was one of the mutation stops
characteristic of the organ. Another mutation in common use was the
tierce, and Mersenne suggests adding it to the ensemble of the eudisharmoste.[46] "L'on peut encore y adiouster vn nouueau ieu à la Tierce
maieure, ou plustost à la Dixiesme ou Dixseptiesme maieure, qui sont les
repliques de ladite Tierce: ce qui pourroit seruir à la speculation de
la nature, en considerant pourquoy deux chordes qui sont à la Quinte
n'azardent, & quel effet ont celles qui font la Tierce soit maieure ou
mineure, &c." ("Again one can tune another stop to the major third,
or rather to the major tenth or seventeenth which are the replicas of the
said third: which can be useful in speculations on nature in considering
why two strings which are at the quint [a twelfth apart] sound nasal

[42] The library of the Musée des Arts Décoratifs in Paris contains a tremendous collection of scrapbooks made up of pictures of every conceivable object clipped from various
unnamed sources. Vol. 322–17, p. 31, contains two identical prints, one labeled "d'après
une estampe de Bonnart" and the other "d'après la gravure d'Arnault," the second
dated 1688; both show a lady playing a three-manual harpsichord which looks Franco-
Flemish. See also the 1702 inventory of instruments belonging to Claude Jacquet,
Appendix C and the ms. of Trichet in Appendix I.

[43] "M.D.C." [Thomas Corneille], *Dictionnaire des arts, et des sciences* (Paris, 1694),
I, 222.

[44] Jakob Adlung, *Musica mechanica organoedi* (Berlin, 1768), II, 110.

[45] See below, Chap. 5.

[46] *Harmonie universelle*, book 3, p. 160.

and what the effect is of those at the tierce [a tenth apart] either major or minor, etc.") Racketts, shawms, and krummhorns are sufficient evidence of the baroque taste for shrill and brilliant sounds. Apparently even that wide tolerance was exceeded by the cacophony which mutations must have produced on harpsichords, for we hear no more of them after this period. The organ builder who employs mutation stops is merely replacing natural constituents which happen to be weak or lacking in the tone produced by his pipe. A vibrating string, on the other hand, already possesses a very complete series of partials, and the ear finds the artificial reinforcement of any of them other than the second partial (octave) too much of a good thing.

Whether Mersenne was indulging his penchant for theoretical speculation or soberly describing an instrument he had seen, the most important aspect of the passages we have quoted is the unvoiced assumption that the possibility of producing a great variety of tone colors is to be sought. This turn of ear has always been characteristic of French musicians and was to transform the beautiful but rigid Flemish harpsichord into the supple and colorful instrument of Rameau and Couperin. "Or encore qu'il n'y ayt que quatre ieux dans l'Eudisarmoste, neantmoins on les varie en plusieurs manieres suiuant le nombre des combinations, conternations & conquaternations qui se peuuent faire de quatre choses differentes, dont i'ay parlé fort amplement dans le liure des Airs & des Chants." ("But even though there are only four stops in the eudisharmoste yet one varies them in several ways according to the numbers of combinations, 'conternations' and 'conquaternations' [permutations ?] which can be made of the four different things I have spoken of very fully in the book of Airs and Chants.") [47]

Elsewhere Mersenne amplified this theme:

Or il n'est pas necessaire de remarquer que l'on fait maintenant des Claue-cins, qui ont sept ou huict sortes de ieux, & deux ou trois clauiers, & que ces ieux se varient, & se tirent, se ioigent, meslent ensemble comme ceux de l'Orgue, par le moyen de plusieurs petits registres, cheuilles & ressorts, qui font que les sautereaux ne touchent qu'vn seul rang de chordes, ou qu'ils en touchent deux, ou plusieurs, par ce que la veüe & l'experience en fera plus comprendre que le discours: c'est pourquoy ie viens à l'explication d'vne autre sorte d'Epinette, dont on n'vse pas en France, & qui est en vsage dans l'Italie, apres auoir remarqué que plusieurs ayment mieux se seruir du seul Clauier qui se pousse, & se tire pour changer les ieux, que des susdits ressorts, qui ne sont pas ordinairement si iustes; que d'autres vsent de 2. ou 3. clauiers pour varier les ieux, & qu'il y a encore plusieurs inuentions qui se peuuent

⁴⁷ Ibid., p. 160.

adiouster à cet instrument, dans lequel on a remarqué plus de quinze cens pieces toutes differentes.

(But it is not necessary to note that now harpsichords are made with seven or eight kinds of stops and two or three keyboards, and that these stops may be changed and drawn and joined, mixing together like those of the organ by means of several little registers, pins and springs which cause the jacks to touch only a single choir of strings, or two, or several — but seeing and trying will make this more comprehensible than a discussion. That is why I turn to the explanation of another type of spinet which is not in use in France and which is used in Italy, after having remarked that several have done better by using a single keyboard which can be pushed and pulled to change the stops than [by using] the said springs which are not usually so accurate; as others use two or three keyboards to vary the stops and that there are several more inventions that can be fitted to this instrument in which someone has noted more than fifteen hundred different parts.)[48]

(The spinet in use in Italy turns out to be a clavicytherium, and the device for changing stops by pushing or pulling the keyboard is described more fully by Adlung.)[49]

Mersenne's ottavino, which seems quite similar to those small spinets we have found in the inventories of the sixteenth and seventeenth centuries, is illustrated in isometric projection and a rather crude plan view (see Plates VIII and IX). The range is somewhat uncertain. Mersenne states that there are thirty-one keys from "C sol," and that the first sharp is split into two notes. The artist has drawn a keyboard of this range, but the keys are mislabeled to show a range of "G" to "C," two octaves and a fourth. If we assume that the description and drawing are correct and ignore the names of the keys, we find an apparent range of c to f″, at four-foot pitch.[50] "Mais ces feintes seruent pour descendre à la Tierce, & à la Quarte de la premiere marche, ou du C sol, afin d'arriuer à la 3. octaue, car les 18. marches principales font seulement la Dix-huictiesme, c'est à dire la Quarte sur deux octaues" ("but these sharps serve to descend to the third and fourth from the first key, or from C sol, in order to reach the third octave, because the eighteen principal keys only make an eighteenth, that is to say, two octaves and a fourth").[51] A fourth below c is G, which is not "the octave" as specified

[48] *Ibid.,* p. 112.

[49] *Musica mechanica organoedi,* II, 108.

[50] "Or cette Epinette de deux pieds & demy est à l'Octaue du ton de Chapelle: & celle que l'on faict de 3 pieds & ½ de long, de 17 poulces de large, & de 5 poulces de haut en oeuure, est à la Quarte dudit ton de Chappelle, auquel descend celle de cinq pieds de long." ("But this two and one-half foot spinet is an octave above the chapel tone: and the one which is made three and one-half feet long, seventeen inches wide, and five inches high is a fourth above the said chapel tone to which the one which is five feet long descends.") *Harmonie universelle,* book 3, p. 158.

[51] *Ibid.,* p. 107.

by Mersenne. We should have to descend a fifth to F to meet that stipulation. However, the short octaves that Mersenne is thinking about are easy to reconstruct. In the first, the two halves of "c♯" produced G and A, and "d♯" provided B. There could have been no chromatics in the lowest octave. If the range reached only to A, we should require the two halves of "c♯" for A and B, but we should have d♯ available as a normal chromatic.

The ottavino was about two and one-half feet long, sixteen inches wide, and four and one-half inches deep. The keyboard was recessed and placed in the center and the key fronts were carved into a sort of double arcade which seems to have been characteristic of early French work. There was a separate register and lower guide just as there was on the Flemish virginals. A piece of leather was glued to the upper surface of the soundboard to act as the register. Two quilled jacks worked in each mortise, but a piece of wire placed across the mortise prevented them from touching one another. The frame and ribbing of the soundboard were similar to that found on extant instruments. (Mersenne's diagram of the ribbing is one of the very few realistic ones to be found in old sources. See Plate IX.) The materials were those used in Flemish and French construction (lime and pine), although Mersenne does mention the possibility of cypress for the soundboard. The layout of the string band, in which both bridge and nut were composed of straight lines, seems to have been a characteristic of French ottavini of this type. The strings of the lowest octave were of brass, in three gauges beginning with "number three." The remainder of the strings were of steel, of which there were also three sizes. The recommended wire size for c, two feet six inches long, in Mersenne's table is .009 inches (too light), but we are already too far from his point of departure (C) for this to have much meaning. The table does not show gauge numbers.

Mersenne's harpsichord is shown only in a perspective drawing which reveals a four-octave single-manual instrument with two choirs of strings, 1x8', 1x4' (Plate X). The range is C–c''' chromatic and no devices are provided to change the stops. Because the drawing is rather crude, very little can be ascertained of the decor or basic outline. However, the general impression produced is of Flemish rather than Italian influence. The jacks are described in considerable detail and appear to have been perfectly standard examples of the northern European type, with two dampers, quill plectra, and bristle spring, in distinction to the Italian jacks which often had brass leaf springs and sometimes leather plectra. The basic dimensions of the harpsichord were 67⅛ inches long by 28¾ inches wide by 7½ inches deep. The wrest plank seems to have been

Table 10. Specifications of four French seventeenth century harpsichords

	Jacquet (1652)	Des Ruisseaux (after 1670)	Vincent Tibaut (1679)	Unsigned instrument
Disposition	2x8′, 1x4′, two manuals. (No jacks or keys)	2x8′, 1x4′, two manuals. (Modern jacks and slides, manual coupler probably modern)	2x8′, 1x4′, two manuals. Once had buff stop. (Modern jacks, manual coupler probably modern)	2x8′, 1x4′, two manuals. ← 4′ dogleg - - - - - - - → 8′ ← 8′
Range	GG/BB–c‴	GG/BB–c‴	GG/BB–c‴	GG–c‴
Means of expression	Two handstops on name-board with levers under veneer of wrest plank	Two handstops on name-board with levers on upper surface of wrest plank	Two handstops on name-board with levers on under surface of wrest plank	Four handstops on name-board (two operate the back 8′)
Dimensions (inches)				
length	87	84	81¾	98½
width	30⅝	30¼	30½	32 13/16
depth of case	9½	9 5/16	9	10¼
length of cheekpiece	25⅜	27 13/16	————	28¾
Tail angle	about 60°	round tail	about 60°	about 45°
Scale (inches)	c‴ – 6¼ c″ – 11 15/16 c′ – 23⅛ c – 42¾ C – 63¼	c‴ – 6 7/16 c″ – 12⅛ c′ – 24⅜ c – 47⅝ C – 61⅝	c‴ – 6¼ c″ – 12 5/16 c′ – 22⅛ c – 36⅞ C – 60⅜	c‴ – 7 c″ – 13¼ c′ – 24⅞ c – 44 C – 68½

tapered about two inches in width, the bass end being wider. We have seen this as a persistent feature of Italian harpsichords, but it is not as commonly found in the north. The effect is to provide a more distant plucking point in the bass. In sum, this harpsichord resembled the Ruckers single-manual harpsichord, model II, except that it was about five inches shorter, two inches shallower, and did not use the short octave in the bass. The scales which Mersenne gives are not possible if one assumes his table to begin with C. In that case c″ would be seventeen inches long. On the other hand, if he took G as the bass note, as it was on his ottavino, one arrives at a c″ of twelve inches, which corresponds fairly well to that of the extant French seventeenth century instruments.

Very few harpsichords have survived which were made in France during the seventeenth century. Details of the four most representative specimens of the native school that I have been able to examine are included in Table 10. Unfortunately, none of these dates from the early years of the century. The earliest is marked "Iacquet Fecit 1652." Another is inscribed "Fait par moy Vincent Tibaut a Tolose 1679." The third carries a mark made by a metal die in the wrest plank: "DESRUISSEAVX"; I assume that the maker is that Gilbert des Ruisseaux who was apprenticed to Michel Richard in 1670. At that time Des Ruisseaux was eighteen years of age and was bound to Richard for only two years. He must, therefore, have commenced his apprenticeship under another master. In any case, it is not likely that this harpsichord could date much earlier than 1675, since enough time must have passed for Des Ruisseaux to have been admitted to the guild and to have established his own workshop. The last instrument (formerly in the collection of De Bricqueville) is neither signed nor dated, but it is a fine specimen and has so many features in common with the first two that I have not hesitated to ascribe it to the same period and school.

All four of these harpsichords are two-manual instruments with three choirs, 2x8′, 1x4′, and three registers. Three of them, the Jacquet, the Des Ruisseaux, and the Tibaut, have a range of GG/BB–c‴, and the two lowest sharps of the Tibaut are split. The keyboard of the unsigned instrument has the range GG–c‴, chromatic. In view of their period it is not surprising that these instruments show a larger compass than that mentioned by Mersenne, but it is interesting that the extremes of the compass are those of Mersenne's spinet with one more octave added to the bass. The details of Mersenne's short octave have been refined to permit more chromatics in the lowest octave by the addition of the apparent BB.

It is very difficult to determine the original disposition of all four of these early French harpsichords since each lacks essential bits of evidence. The key levers and jacks of the Jacquet are missing, the Tibaut has modern jacks, and the Des Ruisseaux has both modern registers and modern jacks. The obvious rebuilding of the actions of the Tibaut and Des Ruisseaux harpsichords makes it impossible to know whether their present couplers, are original, but the fact that the unsigned harpsichord has no coupler may imply that they are not. The key beds of the Jacquet indicate that the upper manual of that instrument could never have slid in and out, but it is just possible that the lower manual did. However, a sliding lower manual is atypical of later French work, and it seems more likely that Jacquet's instrument had no coupler.

The unsigned harpsichord has what appear to be old jacks and may still possess its original disposition:

$$\leftarrow 4' \ \text{dogleg}$$
$$\text{-- -- -- -- --}$$
$$\rightarrow 8'$$
$$\leftarrow 8'.$$

This arrangement, with the four-foot dogleg on the upper manual, is not quite so bizarre as it seems at first glance. We have already quoted a remark of Praetorius to the effect that small four-foot virginals were frequently placed on top of larger eight-foot instruments to provide a second manual at four-foot pitch. Furthermore, we have some evidence that Richard may have disposed his instruments thus. I have restored, with William Dowd, a Ruckers harpsichord which Michel Richard rebuilt in 1688 and which was found with the four-foot on the upper manual. It was disposed:

$$\leftarrow 4'$$
$$\text{-- -- -- --}$$
$$\leftarrow 8'$$
$$\rightarrow 8'.$$

Admittedly, this harpsichord had been restored subsequent to Richard's work, but it is likely that the later restorer copied the original disposition; for otherwise he would probably have put an eight-foot on the upper manual in accordance with the more usual practice.[52]

[52] An ambiguous entry in an inventory of the workshop of Jean Denis in 1672 seems to describe a harpsichord in which one manual sounds an octave higher than the other. "Une epinette en forme de clavecin a deux demi claviers l'un comme l'autre jouant a l'octave l'un de l'autre." ("A spinet in the form of a harpsichord with two half keyboards one like the other and playing at the octave, one of the other.") See Appendix C.

The dogleg in place of the coupler finds support, if not precedent, in the dispositions of the eighteenth century Flemish makers, who, it will be remembered, never employed a coupler, but retained the dogleg to the end. One can hazard the guess that their disposition represents the persistence of a tradition which had been formed in the seventeenth century, and that all of the early expressive two-manual harpsichords were provided with a dogleg jack. Another straw in the uncertain wind which tempts one to accept the upper-manual dogleg four-foot disposition as fundamental to this school is the passage from Mersenne quoted above which describes the ensemble use of several stops at one time. Mersenne does not mention a manual coupler, yet he is clearly thinking of two- and three-manual harpsichords. The only possible alternative to a coupler to provide a *plein jeu*, a full harpsichord, on such instruments is the dogleg.

If we are correct in our suspicion that

$$\leftarrow 4' \text{ dogleg}$$
$$\text{- - - - - - - -}$$
$$\rightarrow 8'$$
$$\leftarrow 8'$$

was the typical disposition of French seventeenth century double harpsichords, it is obvious that contemporary players were not particularly subtle in their registration. A duet of upper and lower manual would be difficult to manage since any registration on the lower manual would automatically have the four-foot of the upper manual added to it, and there could be no question of equal balance of dynamics. The usual employment of the upper manual must have been to provide echo responses, in a very different timbre and register, to statements made by the lower manual. Some pieces of a light character could have been performed entirely on the upper manual. Hand stops were provided to make changes of registration possible at certain moments during the performance of a piece.

The constructional design of this native French school of the seventeenth century gave a lighter and more transient quality of tone than that of the Ruckers instruments. The most important factor leading to this result was the shortened scale, which varied between 11^{15}⁄₁₆ inches and 13¼ inches and was thus about 1½ inches shorter on the average than the Ruckers scale. The effect of this scale was enhanced by the light construction. We find case scantlings between ⁹⁄₃₂ inch and ⅜ inch in place of the ½ inch normally employed by the Ruckers, although Jacquet's scantlings were ½ inch. Bridge sections and dimensions frequently showed an Italian influence, and the bridges were always lighter than those of the Flemish tradition. In general, one can say that these harpsichords stood midway between the Italian instruments and the Flemish, and their tone reflects this fact. Percussive and thin with very little sustaining power or majesty of effect, they seem to combine the worst qualities of both schools, lacking the brittle excitement of the Italian harpsichords and the darker brilliance of the Flemish.

Two interesting details of construction which we shall refer to again in discussing English seventeenth century harpsichords were the employment of solid walnut for the sides of the case and, in one example, the round tail. The decor shows a mixture of influences ranging from Italian harpsichords to French furniture fifty years earlier. Scrolled end blocks were sometimes glued to the inside surfaces of the cheekpiece and spine at the keyboard well, perhaps in a reminiscence of the appearance of an Italian harpsichord with scrolled cheeks inside its outer case. A further reminder of that construction is the nameboard, which is not flush with the top edge of the case as the Ruckers always left it, but is lowered a short distance. Sometimes it is cut down in the middle to the level of the wrest plank and rises at either end in a series of simple coves and fillets executed with a fret saw. Like the Italian nameboards, these are removable. The inner edges of the cases, above the soundboards, were often ornamented with block-printed papers. The Tibaut harpsichord is beautifully adorned with inlay work and marquetry and the Des Ruisseaux is covered on the exterior with painted flowers. The most common sort of stand was a twist-turned trestle with a straight stretcher running close to the floor clear around the harpsichord. Keyboards were black with bone topped sharps, and the peculiar type of double arcade, carved directly into the ends of the key levers, which was illustrated by Mersenne is frequently found.

We shall not pause long over the ottavini made by members of this school. The most notable are those by Richard, dated 1672 and 1693, and one by Philippe Denis, 1672.[53] All three have a range of GG/BB–c′′′ at four-foot pitch. They average about three feet long with a variety of case outlines in which all sides are straight. They tend to show the vestigial Italian features we found in the nameboards and applied scrollwork of the harpsichords. They demonstrate the same resolute northern

[53] The first was formerly in the Sammlung alter Musikinstrumente, Staatlichen Hochschule für Musik, Berlin. See the catalogue by Curt Sachs (Berlin, 1922). The other Richard and the Denis are in the collection of the Conservatoire National, Paris.

insistence on separate registers, and lower guides that the Flemish makers manifested and also have the piece of wash leather glued to the sound-board through which the jacks pass.

Although the native school of French seventeenth century makers does not seem to have made particularly good harpsichords, their development of the expressive two-manual instrument represents one of the most significant advances in the entire history of the harpsichord. It seems likely that the possibilities provided by harpsichords such as we have been describing were grasped by the later French school of Ruckers imitators, and the same principles of disposition were applied to the much more successful Ruckers design. Except for occasional monsters of the eudisharmoste sort it seems likely that the usual French expressive double of the seventeenth century had three registers. It was only later when the restorers and makers had inherited the four registers of the Ruckers transposing harpsichords that they began to apply their expressive principles to that format, and very often they suppressed the fourth register in returning to three.

In his letter of October 15, 1648, to Constantijn Huyghens, De la Barre makes a clear distinction between the Flemish tradition of transposing doubles and the new French expressive doubles: "Because the truth is that this master who is still young invented harpsichords with two manuals in the first place, not in the manner of Flanders where they only play the same strings, but different in that they sound different strings on each keyboard; and to speak properly, there are two harpsichords combined into one, and consequently the work is double." [54] The distinction De la Barre makes between the Flemish tradition of transposing doubles and the new, French, expressive double gives us one of the few precise points of departure our subject affords. A few years later the existence of the French expressive double is confirmed in an inventory of the effects of the maker Claude Jacquet (1661): "Premierement deux clavecins dont l'un desquels faict et parfait, à trois cordes et deux claviers" ("First two harpsichords of which one is made and complete with three strings and two keyboards").[55] A three-choir instrument could not have been a transposing harpsichord since those always require an even number of registers and choirs. It can be assumed that Jacquet's harpsichords were similar to those under discussion.

This inventory of the contents of Claude Jacquet's workshop is worth

[54] De la Barre to Constantin Huyghens, Oct. 15, 1648. See Jonckbloet and Land, eds., *Musique et musiciens*, p. cxlix. See Appendix A.
[55] Archives Nationales, Minutier Central, LXVIII, 155, Jan. 27, 1661.

examining at length, for it gives a very good idea of the scale and nature of the business carried on by Jacquet and his contemporaries.

First	two harpsichords of which one is made and complete with three strings and two keyboards	200 l[ivres]
	and the other unfinished	100 l.
Item	another harpsichord which is not finished	30 l.
Item	another harpsichord with two manuals of which the soundboard is glued	75 l.
Item	another harpsichord with two manuals of which the keyboards are made	40 l.
Item	a three and one-half foot spinet and another little one and a case [outer case ?] both half made	25 l.
Item	six dozen and five pieces of pine [sappin] to make spinet soundboards	10 l.
Item	fifty-five planks of pine wood five and six feet in length, twenty-six of pine wood from five to eight feet in length	8 l.
Item	six other planks of beech wood eight feet long	48 s[ols]
Item	fifteen other planks of white wood [deal] six feet long	4 l. 10 s.
Item	six other planks of Flemish wood [bois de flandre] [56] six feet long	3 l.
Item	three spinet assemblies and a clavichord assembly	4 l. 10 s.
Item	a spinet all finished and a case	24 l.
Item	three benches of beech wood	5 l. 10 s.
Item	five holdfasts, a little vise and two hatchets	40 s.
Item	a ripsaw and eleven other small saws, five triangles and two bitbraces	3 l.
Item	nineteen items such as jointing planes, planes and such like	3 l.
Item	several small measuring tools serving the said trade and vocation of said deceased	30 s.
Item	three small harpsichord locks two hooks and other small objects	25 s.
Item	three small packets of spinet strings both brass and steel	20 s.

At the time of Jacquet's death his shop contained one completed two-manual harpsichord, four unfinished harpsichords of which at least two were doubles, one finished and five unfinished spinets, and an unfinished clavichord. Thus, he appears to have had ten instruments under construction, a sizable project. We find the same number of benches as the establishment had possessed thirty years before in the time of Jean Jacquet. One wonders if they were the identical "trois mechants establis" ("three bad benches"). The staff, in any case, does not seem to have been enlarged under Claude Jacquet beyond the three workers we found in 1632.

[56] Probably refers to soundboard wood. This was often called sapin de Hollande.

Two of the spinets are listed with *coffrets* as if they had distinct outer cases. One must admit the possibility that these *coffrets* represent spinets at a very early stage of construction when they were composed only of sides attached to the bottom. This theory is weakened by the use of *assemblage*, apparently to describe an instrument in an early stage.

An inventory of the workshop of Jean Denis (II), 1686, contains an entry which strengthens my theory that the smallest variety of French spinets sometimes had a separate outer case in the Italian manner: "quatre corps d'Epinettes l'un a l'Italienne et les trois autres quarré dont deux a deux coffrets et l'un qui n'a que le clavier, les petites sont garnys de leurs tables, et celle à l'Italienne aussy" ("four spinet cases one in the Italian style and the three others square of which two have two cases and one has only the keyboard, the small ones are provided with their soundboards, and the one in the Italian style also").[57] Two of the three square spinets, or virginals as we should call them, had two cases or boxes and, therefore, must have been made in what we think of as the Italian manner. What, then, did the expert drawing up the inventory mean by "à l'Italienne?" He implies that the square instruments were smaller than the one "à l'Italienne," and that somehow the distinction also lay in the fact that the latter was not square. The article "Epinette" printed in the Livorno edition of the *Encyclopédie* states that spinets "à l'Italienne ont à-peu-près la figure du clavecin" ("in the Italian style have almost the shape of the harpsichord"). Hieronymus de Zentis had been working in Paris some years before the date of this Denis inventory, and a bentside spinet of his make, dated 1631, is still to be found in the collection of the Brussels Conservatory. It is quite possible that Zentis was the inventor of this form of instrument and that the French called them *à l'Italienne* after him. (See Plate XXIII for an illustration of an English bentside spinet which has roughly the shape of a Zentis *épinette à l'Italienne.*)

Item   a harpsichord with two manuals made by the said deceased [Jean Denis] painted in the Chinese style equipped with its stand in the same style[58]   150 l.

Item   another harpsichord also with two keyboards made by the said deceased Sieur Denis, which is in white wood, the soundboard painted in miniature, found in the said attic shop   132 l.

Item   in the same [place] . . . found one triangular harpsichord

[57] Archives Nationales, Minutier Central, LXIV, 206, Jan. 4, 1686.
[58] *Chinoiserie* seems to have been quite popular. Several instruments have survived which are thus adorned.

	case barred with frame wood [that is, with liners and frame members]	8 l.
Item	two spinets with painted soundboards which are not finished	44 l.
Item	four spinet cases one *à l'Italienne* and the three others square of which two have two outer cases [*coffrets*] and one has only the keyboard, the small ones are provided with their soundboards, and the one in the Italian style also	12 l.
Item	four benches of which three in the said shop and one other in the small room	12 l.
Item	fourteen saws both large and small of which two are ripsaws	7 l.
Item	three jointing planes, six smooth planes, two rabbet planes, two fillister planes, two bitbraces, three marking gauges, two triangles and other small tools	4 l.
Item	five bar clamps for gluing and jointing and a bitbrace	20.1
Item	iron holdfasts and a lead glue pot	3 l.
Item	forty tools good and bad	25 l.
Item	twenty-one clamps good and bad	3 l.
Item	in the said small room are found two keyboards ready to receive the ebony and also several pieces of lime wood for making keyboards, forty pieces of white wood and several short pieces of wood of different kinds	6 l.
Item	seventy-five pieces of pine soundboard wood	18 l.
Item	three planks of walnut, nineteen planks of pine and a plank of beech and some pieces of wood of different kinds	6 l.
Item	a *disposition* to make a harpsichord case with two wrest planks [59]	20 s.
Item	two trestles, eight small bar clamps and three spinet stands	3 l.
Item	a harpsichord with one keyboard which transposes one tone, with a pedal board harpsichord	120 l.
Item	a small spinet two feet in length, the soundboard painted	15 l.
Item	three spinet cases of which one is without soundboard and the two others with their soundboards	4 l.
Item	a spinet four and one-half feet long, the soundboard painted	3 l.
Item	a spinet *à l'Italienne* all finished the soundboard painted	15 l.
Item	a little bag in which there are iron wrest pins for harpsichords and spinets	[no value given]
Item	a packet of brass strings for spinets of several weights and colors weighing 10 pounds	4 l.
Item	a packet of silver strings for spinets	12 l. 13 s.

[59] The *disposition* is possibly a drawing. The value seems too low for this item to represent either dimensioned wood for a harpsichord or a fixture of some sort. The dubious punctuation of the *notaire* makes it difficult to guess whether this item refers to a vis-à-vis harpsichord or to a harpsichord and two wrest planks. The *Mercure de France*, April 1712, mentions a "clavessin tres-particulier et tres-beau — A quatre Claviers sçavoir deux à chaque bout, il est utile pour ceux qui font des concerts & pour ceux qui veulent entendre jouer des pieces de clavessin à un bout & les accompagner de l'autre; le nom de l'autheur Phillippe Devis [sic]" ("Very special and very beautiful harpsichord — with four keyboards, viz. two at each end, it is useful for those who play ensemble music and for those who wish to hear harpsichord pieces played at one end and to accompany them at the other; the name of the maker Phillippe [Denis]").

Denis seems to have worked on much the same scale as Jacquet. Although his shop contained more finished instruments than that of Jacquet, the unfinished batch of eight instruments — two harpsichords and six spinets — is comparable. His staff, too, seems to have been about equal to Jacquet's. We find four benches instead of three, but one of these was tucked away in a small room and may not have represented another workman. Roubo describes a small enclosure, equipped with fireplace, called a *sorbonne* or *étuve*, which usually made part of the establishment of a *menuisier*. The *sorbonne* was used as a hot room for gluing and frequently contained a bench. The *bouge*, a small room, may have served that function in Denis' workshop.

The most interesting of the instruments in Denis' possession were the harpsichord with one keyboard which transposes one tone and the pedal-board harpsichord ("clavecin à un clavier qui se transpose d'un ton, avec un clavecin de pedalle"). The transposition was undoubtedly carried out by shifting the keyboard sideways to bring each key lever under the adjacent jack. Apparently the total possible displacement of this keyboard was about one inch, which would provide a transposition of two key levers, or one tone. Descriptions of such transposing keyboards are not uncommon. However, a trap is baited for the unwary in the many accounts of nonenharmonic keyboards, and a clear distinction must be made. The nonenharmonic keyboard was provided with extra notes in each octave to make it possible to play with just intonation in all keys. The harpsichord Praetorius called the *Clavicymbalium Universale* had a keyboard of this type. Praetorius stated that it could be raised seven times in pitch, but he did not mean that the transpositions were carried out mechanically. Schlick describes a true transposing keyboard of the type mentioned in this inventory, but in his example it was applied to the organ.[60] During the eighteenth century the Germans seem to have taken up the idea again. Johann Wilhelm Völcker, organist at Arnstadt, is said to have "invented" such an instrument in 1758 which could transpose four semitones up or down.[61] Adlung[62] provided another description in 1768 of a harpsichord which transposed from a semitone above choir pitch to chamber pitch, three semitones below choir pitch. In 1771 Burney found the German form of the device imported into Italy:

He [Count Taxis] is possessed of a very curious keyed instrument which was made at Berlin, under the direction of his Prussian majesty: it is in

[60] Schlick, *Spiegel der Orgelmacher und Organisten*, p. 19. See also the discussion of Nicolas Ramarinus' keyboard above, Chap. 1.

[61] Fétis, *Biographie universelle*, "Voelcker."

[62] *Musica mechanica organoedi*, II, 107. Also *Anleitung zu der musikalischen Gelahrtheit* (Erfurt, 1758), p. 553.

shape, like a large clavichord, has several changes of stops, and is occasionally a harp, a harpsichord, a lute, or piano forte; but the most curious property
of this instrument is, that by drawing out the keys the hammers are trans-
ferred to different strings, by which means a composition may be transposed
half a note, a whole note, or a flat third lower at pleasure, without the em-
barrassment of different notes or clefs, read or imaginary.[63]

The *"clavecin de pedalle,"* or pedal-board harpsichord, is as elusive as
the shy unicorn and possessed of the same menacing charm. Some of its
power to bewitch rests in the ambiguity of the name; one is never quite
sure whether one is dealing with a harpsichord with stops changed by
pedals or with a true pedal board. No pedal-board harpsichords have survived. Those that have been cited are not original.[64] However, there do
exist a fair number of harpsichords which show traces of the previous
attachment of pull-downs on the underside of the keys. These instruments were provided at some time with a pedal board which was connected by cords or trackers to the bottom few keys of the lower manual.
The only seventeenth century instruments with traces of pull-downs
which are known to me are Italian. Their pedal boards (all missing)
ranged from eight to fifteen keys (C/E–B, C–f).[65] Pedal-board clavichords seem to have been more common than pedal-board harpsichords.
Such a clavichord made by Johann David Gerstenberg in 1760 is preserved in the Heyer collection at Leipzig. It is probable that most pedal-
board clavichords were intended as practice instruments for organists.

[63] Burney, *The Present State of Music in France and Italy*, p. 181. Count Taxis'
instrument was a square piano with the strings running transversely. Hence the transposing keyboard would move in and out rather than from side to side as it must in a
transposing harpsichord.

[64] The illustration in Athanasius Kircher, *Phonurgia nova* (Kempten, Germ., 1673),
p. 167, and *Neue Hall- und Thon-Kunst* (Nordlingen, Germ., 1684), p. 120, cited by
Susi Jeans ("The Pedal Clavichord and Other Practice Instruments of Organists,"
Proceedings of the Royal Musical Association, 77 [1950–1951]:1) as the depiction of
a clavicytherium with pedal board, cannot be admitted. The instrument Kircher was
describing was an elaborate concoction produced after eighteen years of unremitting
effort by an ex-musette player called Michele Todini; it was essentially a collection of
four harpsichords, one of which was upright, two *geigenwerken*, and an organ, all played
from a one-manual console with pedal board. There is no indication that the pedal
board activated any of the harpsichord stops, and even if it did, any conclusions based
on such a contraption must be irrelevant to normal practice.
  See Todini's own account of his creation: *Dichiaratione della galleria armonica
eretta in Roma da Michele Todini, Piemontese di Saluzzo nella sua habitatione posta
all'arco della Ciambella* (Rome, 1676). See also Filippo Bonanni, *Gabinetto armonico*
(Rome, 1722), plate XXXIII; Joseph Jérôme de la Lande, *Voyage d'un français en
Italie* (Paris, 1769; 2nd ed., 1786), IV, 499; Burney, *The Present State of Music in
France and Italy*, p. 392; Jean Benjamin de la Borde, *Essai sur la musique* (Paris 1780),
III, 538. Fétis has given a full account: *Biographie universelle*, "Todini."

[65] See page 37 for a list of these Italian harpsichords and page 272 for Adlung's comments on this arrangement.

The true pedal-board harpsichord was a separate instrument placed on the floor beneath a conventional harpsichord. We have almost no idea of the range, the number of choirs, or the means for varying registration. There are no pertinent instruments and only feeble descriptions. One can merely assume that the range and philosophy of disposition were related to those of contemporary organs. What little light is ours to throw on the shadowy role played by the pedal-board harpsichord in the history of music is best reserved for the chapter on the development of harpsichord making in Germany; but I fear that even in that limited ambience I shall not be able to satisfy the eager curiosity of a certain section of my public. A hopelessly ambiguous remark in a document concerning the distribution of Bach's estate and a cryptic indication on the holograph of the Trio Sonatas have been set up as holy writ by the organ world, and such airy vessels of musicological speculation have been launched that the cursory descriptions of Adlung, Halle, Mattheson, and Türk, which constitute the only available factual ballast, must seem quite inadequate.

That Denis' pedal-board harpsichord was not an isolated phenomenon is demonstrated by two other items found in the Archives Nationales. In 1684 Jean LeBègue possessed a "clavecin de pedalle — (le clavecin à deux claviers qui allait avec est deja vendu)" ("pedal harpsichord — the harpsichord with two keyboards that went with it is already sold").[66] We cannot tell if the single-manual harpsichord which was listed with the pedal instrument in the Denis inventory belonged to that pedal board or not. In the case of LeBègue's harpsichord one can be sure that the total instrument consisted of two manuals and pedal. This information is amplified by the description of an instrument in the possession of the organist Nicolas Gigault in 1701: "Un clavecin à double claviers a l'unison . . . un clavecin de pedalles a l'octave le tout au ton de chambre" ("A harpsichord with two keyboards at unison [eight-foot] pitch . . . a pedal harpsichord at four-foot pitch, both at chamber pitch").[67] It is difficult to believe that a two-manual harpsichord could have had only two eight-foot stops. The expert drawing up the inventory probably meant to say that the fundamental pitch of the harpsichord was at eight-foot and the pedal at four-foot. The harpsichord was almost certainly three-choired, as all the French doubles of this period seem to have had 2x8', 1x4', and the pedal might have had only a single four-foot choir.

Apparently the pedal-board harpsichord dropped out of use with the decline of the native French tradition of harpsichord making. We hear

[66] See Appendix C.
[67] See Appendix C.

little more about it[68] until the very end of the eighteenth century when certain makers began to attach pianoforte pedal boards to their harpsichords: "One must not omit the invention of a double bottom by means of which one applies to the underside of the harpsichord, or piano, strings which are struck by hammers which are activated by pedals similar to those of the organ. Silbermann at Strassburg and Peronard[69] at Paris have carried this idea out very well; originally it was due to Schobert, the celebrated harpsichordist. It enriches the harpsichord with two octaves of bass notes and an infinity of harmonic resources."[70] A harpsichord by Joachim Swann or Swanen, 1786, Paris, now in the Conservatoire des Arts et Métiers, fits this description perfectly. Heavy strings are stretched underneath the bottom. The pedal board operates heavy hammers which sound the strings. Surprisingly, the mechanism is patently modern. It may be that the string band was originally arranged in this way and that the pedal board, which had been lost, was supplied later.

After the Revolution, when Antonio Bartholomeo Bruni, violinist at the Comédie Italienne and one of the delegates to the Convention, drew up an inventory of musical instruments seized on the premises of *émigrés* who had fled, he listed one pair of instruments which may be pertinent to our purpose: "Un clavecin en acajou, superbe, bande et pieds dorés et sculptés, sans nom d'auteur et sans pupitre . . . Un petit clavecin pour mettre dessous" ("A harpsichord in mahogany, superb, banded, stand gilded and carved, without maker's name and without music desk . . . A small harpsichord to put underneath").[71] This is the last twinkle of the unicorn's horn.

The history of the harpsichord in France during the eighteenth century is primarily the story of the *ravalement* and redisposition of the Ruckers instruments inherited from the previous age, and the construction of new instruments in their image. In 1771 Bemetzrieder[72] gave a thumbnail sketch of the gradual increase of range imposed on the Ruckers instruments. He pointed out that at one time harpsichords had had a compass of four octaves from C and that seven keys were added succes-

[68] There is a mention in the inventory of the effects of Pierre de Machy (Archives Nationales, Minutier Central, LXII, 340, April 26, 1726): "un pied de pedal dont le corpse est de bois de sapin" ("a pedal stand the body of which is of pine").

[69] Contemporary references exist to harpsichords by this maker dated 1760 and 1777.

[70] *Encyclopédie méthodique*, "Musique," I, 287a.

[71] J. Gallay, ed., *Un Inventaire sous la Terreur, état des instruments de musique relevé chez les émigrés et condamnés* (Paris, 1890).

[72] Anton Bemetzrieder, *Leçons de clavecin, et principes d'harmonie* (Paris, 1771), p. 13. This work was "edited" by Diderot, who polished Bemetzrieder's Germanic French.

sively in the bass: BB, BBb, AA, AAb, GG, GGb, and FF; and five keys in the treble: c#''', d''', d#''', e''', and f'''. The most extended harpsichords of Bemetzrieder's day had a compass of five octaves from FF and were called *clavecins à grand ravalement*. Those instruments which had more than four octaves from C and less than five octaves from FF were termed *à ravalement*. Although there was a tendency to extend the bass before the treble, a confusion of ranges existed throughout the period, and it is impossible to establish a series of definite steps by which the range was extended from the C/E–c''' of Ruckers to the FF–f''' of Bemetzrieder. We have seen that Mersenne knew the range C–c''' chromatic, and that the Ruckers had occasionally extended the compass of their instruments in the bass. It seems likely that the most frequent first step was to fill out the bass short octave. From that point, the rebuilders seem to have treated each instrument as an individual problem and fitted as many additional keys as the space and available money made possible.

The earliest documented *ravalement* which has come to my attention was that performed in 1688 by Michel Richard, to which I have already referred. Richard seems to have transformed a Flemish single[73] into a three-register double, GG/BB–c''' with the disposition 2x8', 1x4', the four-foot on the upper manual, with manual coupler and two hand stops, one for the back eight-foot and the other for the buff stop. It is probable that the *chinoiserie* which adorns the case of this harpsichord dates from Richard's restoration, for we have seen that Denis owned a harpsichord "peint en manier de le chine" ("painted in Chinese style") in 1686.

The inventory[74] of the workshop of Nicolas Blanchet (1722), the founder of the firm which was later the most renowned for reconstructions of Ruckers harpsichords, shows "un petit clavesin trois Epinettes et un autre petit clavesin demembré le tout de flandres" and "un vieux clavesin flandres" ("a little harpsichord, three spinets, and another little dismantled harpsichord, all Flemish" and "an old Flemish harpsichord"). It seems, however, that most French harpsichord makers did not imme-

---

[73] Since Ruckers doubles were about 88 inches long by 31 inches wide and this harpsichord is 76½ inches long by 32½ inches wide, it seems that it could not have been a double to begin with. It is almost exactly the length of a Ruckers single (72 inches) plus the extra length required for the second manual (4¼ inches). The problem of the width is not quite so easy to resolve. Ruckers singles (C/E–c''') averaged about 28 inches wide. The five extra naturals required to provide the compass mentioned by Duarte as the largest made by the Ruckers family would increase the width to 32⅝ inches, almost exactly right. The weakness in this conjecture is that it seems unlikely that Richard would have rebuilt a single with the range GG–c''' into a double of GG/BB–c'''. Furthermore, there is no evidence that Ruckers built harpsichords with deepened basses as early as 1613.

[74] Archives Nationales, Minutier Central, CXV, 403, July 17, 1772. See Appendix C.

diately desert their own tradition to devote their energies to the restoration of Ruckers harpsichords, for we have inventories of the workshops
of Pierre de Machy in 1726[75] and Jean Ferchur in 1729[76] which do not
contain any instruments recognisable as Flemish. But it is clear that
about the turn of the century the French makers began to be strongly influenced by the Antwerp school. In the Musée Instrumental du Conservatoire National de Musique in Paris one can see a two-manual harpsichord by Nicolas Dumont (1697) which is very similar in design to a
Ruckers double. The instrument is inscribed "Nicolas Dumont à Paris
1697," and on the wrest plank, "Refait par Pascal Taskin à Paris, 1789."
The length (89 inches) and scale (14 inches) are patently Flemish in
inspiration, and the instrument has four registers like the transposing
doubles. (It is unlikely that Taskin added the fourth register to an original three.) The original range of this instrument has been permanently
obscured by the restoration made nearly one hundred years later by Pascal Taskin, the successor to the Blanchet family concern. It must have
been considerably less than the present five octaves, FF–f''', since the
interior of the case shows quite clearly that Taskin was forced to increase
the width of the instrument in order to accommodate his new keyboards.

Dumont's harpsichord is thoroughly Flemish in material, decor, and
most of the details of design, but it shows one characteristically French
feature which we are to find in all of the Franco-Flemish harpsichords.
Ruckers invariably carried the sweep of the bentside to the tail in one
smooth curve. In contrast, the bentsides of French harpsichords, including this Dumont, approached straightness for about one half of their
length. The same observation can be applied with somewhat less assurance to the eight-foot bridges of harpsichords of the two schools. The
resulting difference in dimensions is quite small, but the visual effect is
marked. (Compare Plate XI, figure 1, with Plate VI, figure 1.)[77]

[75] *Ibid.*, LXII, 340, April 26, 1726. See Appendix C.
[76] *Ibid.*, *scellé*, Jan. 30, 1729, Y 15323. See Appendix C.
[77] The bentsides of English harpsichords also have a straight section, but their
characteristic outline is distinguished from the French in that the straight section is
longer. All of the curve in an English bentside is concentrated in an abrupt hook near
the joint between the cheekpiece and bentside. It is not so easy to generalize about
German bentsides which vary more than the French and English partly as a result of
the national partiality to the S-curved bentside and the sixteen-foot, either of which
obscures any consistent curve the makers might have tended to follow. However, it is
relatively safe to say that the German makers favored a bend which was more abrupt
than the French but less so than the English. If one were to arrange the national styles
of bentside in order from the smoothest curve with the least change from end to end to
that which varies most from perfectly straight at the tail-bentside corner to a curve of
short radius at the cheekpiece corner, the list would be: Flemish, French, German,
English. The short scales of the Italian harpsichords produced quite a different curve

So far as one can judge, harpsichord making was carried on during the first quarter of the eighteenth century in individual shops of much the same sort as those of the seventeenth century. De Machy had two benches, Ferchur had only one, and Nicolas Blanchet in 1722 had three. Pierre de Machy seems to have operated chiefly as a dealer, for we find in his possession thirteen harpsichords, ten spinets, *un pied de pedal* (a pedal stand), and a theorbo, but no sign of instruments under construction or stocks of wood and other materials. The stock of harpsichords owned by De Machy seems to have included several of seventeenth century French origin, for we find four harpsichords with the walnut cases which were typical of that tradition, and four painted black, which could pertain to either school of French construction. Five harpsichords were made of pine and perhaps represent newer instruments in the imitation Flemish style. Of the spinets, six out of ten had walnut cases, two were painted, and two are unspecified. Possibly this can be taken as an indication that the spinet was becoming somewhat outmoded and that a rather large percentage of the extant spinets at that time were old.

Unfortunately we have only the preliminary inventory routinely executed as part of the *scellé* for Jean Ferchur. The records of the notary who prepared a more elaborate inventory are missing for 1729. Since Ferchur had a bench, tools, and wood, as well as two harpsichord cases not yet supplied with strings and keyboards, there can be no doubt that he was actively engaged in the construction of harpsichords. Instruments found in his workshop underline the fact that this was the moment of transition from the indigenous to the imported tradition. One was made by a representative of the local school, Pierre Denis, and the other by "Belot pere" (Louis Bellot),[78] an ardent disciple of the Flemish.

Well over sixty harpsichord makers are known to have worked in Paris during the eighteenth century, and it seems remarkable that there are no extant instruments by the great majority of these. Probably some were dealers and made no instruments, others made harpsichords we now know as Ruckers, and almost the total output of the remainder has been destroyed. There can be no doubt that the violence of the Revolution, particularly since it came at the moment of transition to the piano, was

---

than any of these. Like the Flemish it was usually continuous but much more deeply incurved.

[78] A two-manual harpsichord, undated, signed Louis Bellot, is to be found in the Crosby Brown Collection of the Metropolitan Museum of Art in New York. A single with the soundboard inscribed "Le Pere Bellot," and dated 1729, is to be found in the Archiepiscopal palace at Chartres. It may be that Louis is not "Bellot le pere," but the "Belot le jeune" referred to in *Les Affiches*, Sept. 4, 1752.

responsible for the destruction of a large number of harpsichords. There seems to have been extant until recently a manuscript [79] list of instruments, the former property of *émigrés*, that had been assigned to the newly founded Conservatoire in Paris in 1794. Sixty-one harpsichords and seven spinets were among more than three hundred fifty musical instruments of all kinds. In 1890 Jean Baptiste Weckerlin, librarian of the Conservatoire, gave the following account of their fate. (It should be noted that the exceptions he speaks of are not included in the totals I have given above.)

Even if all these instruments (excepting those for which specific directions were given) were intended for the Conservatoire, I do not know if they all arrived there. I recall very well that some old employees of that establishment told me in 1844 that these harpsichords served to heat the classrooms, a purpose for which some were taken from time to time from the garret: the fact is that the Conservatoire does not possess a single instrument which made a part of that donation of the government, enumerated below, and forty years ago when I was a student, there remained only some huge packing cases twelve or fifteen feet long which I saw taken out into the courtyard; it was said that these instruments served for the celebrations of the First Empire: they were burned. [80]

Destruction on such a grand scale goes far toward explaining the present scarcity of French harpsichords.

The most eminent of the creators of these vanished masterpieces were the members of the Blanchet [81] family, who maintained their supremacy in the field from the last years of the seventeenth century until the end of the eighteenth. Five makers made up the dynasty, beginning with Nicolas Blanchet, who established his workshop in the Rue St. Germain l'Auxerrois a little before 1686, and ending with Pascal Joseph Taskin (II), who outlived the era of the harpsichord. Nicolas Blanchet is the first maker who seems to have devoted himself extensively to the restoration of Ruckers instruments, for not only do we find several Flemish harpsichords in his possession in 1722 but he appears to have sold a re-

---

[79] It is ironic that the manuscript on which Weckerlin based his account of the vandalism of previous administrations should be missing in its turn from the library of the Conservatoire. I was able to find no trace of it. This is not Bruni's list, but many of the instruments are the same.

[80] J. B. Weckerlin, *Nouveau musiciana* (Paris, 1890), p. 143. For other details of this affair see Constant Pierre, ed., *Le Conservatoire national de musique et de déclamation, documents* (Paris, 1900), p. 94.

[81] See Pierre J. Hardouin, "Harpsichord Making in Paris, Part I, Eighteenth Century," translated with a technical introduction and explanatory footnotes by Frank Hubbard, *The Galpin Society Journal*, vol. 10 (1957).

built Hans Ruckers harpsichord for the immense sum of three thousand livres to Garnier, *organiste du Roi*, in 1721.[82] From 1722 until Nicolas' death in 1731 the business was conducted as a formal partnership between Nicolas and his second son, François Etienne (I) (ca. 1695–1761). An undated Nicolas Blanchet harpsichord sold by Sotheby and Company on June 29, 1956, seems typical of the productions of the firm: two manuals, three registers, FF–f''', 2x8', 1x4', with eight-foot and four-foot on the lower manual and one eight-foot on the upper manual, sliding upper manual coupler, buff stop on the lower manual eight-foot, and hand stops. The form and construction of the case is nearly identical to Ruckers' except that the painted decorations are in the style of Louis XV. Another instrument, almost identical, dated 1730 and signed "N. et François Blanchet," is owned by Charles P. Fisher of Framingham, Massachusetts.

François Etienne I was followed in turn by his son, François Etienne (II) (1729–1766). Seven months after the premature death of François Etienne II his widow married a Belgian who had been assisting her in the business, Pascal Joseph Taskin (I).[83] Taskin combined an inventive mind with a firm competence in his craft. He raised the French harpsichord to its highest level, and, indeed, his harpsichords are among the best ever made in any country. I have chosen a Taskin I double harpsichord, made in 1769, as the model for Plate XII. Taskin probably died in 1793, when he was succeeded by his nephew, Pascal Joseph Taskin II, who, confusingly, married a daughter of François Etienne II by his second wife — who was later the wife of Pascal Joseph Taskin I.

We are fortunately able to provide inventories at several points in the history of the Blanchet firm (see Appendix C). The earliest[84] specifies the contents of Nicolas Blanchet's shop in 1722. The second (1726)[85] covers the period of the joint proprietorship of Nicolas and François Etienne I. The third (1737)[86] derives from the time of François Etienne I while his son, François Etienne II, was still a child. The fourth (1761)[87] was prepared on the occasion of the death of François Etienne

---

[82] Archives Nationales, Minutier Central, CXVII, 322. "Inventaire après le décès de G. Garnier."

[83] See Ernest Closson, "Pascal Taskin," *Sammelbände des Internationalen Musikgesellschaft*, 1910–1911, p. 234.

[84] Archives Nationales, Minutier Central, CXV, 403, July 17, 1722, Nicolas Blanchet.

[85] *Ibid.*, CXV, 445, Jan. 15, 1726, François Estienne Blanchet.

[86] *Ibid.*, IX, 646, May 9, 1737, François Estienne Blanchet.

[87] *Ibid.*, CI, 511, Dec. 18, 1761, François Etienne Blanchet.

I and represents the state of affairs at the moment when François Etienne II was taking over. The fifth (1766) [88] marks the death of François Etienne II and substantially defines the business that Taskin I was soon to take charge of. The sixth inventory (1777) [89] provides a glimpse into the shop after several years of Taskin's direction, and the last document (1783) [90] shows a prosperous enterprise increasingly concerned with the piano.

A succession of favorable marriages, plus the increasing reputation of the Blanchet instruments and restorations, brought about a steady improvement in the family fortune. Sometime in the stewardship of François Etienne I there seems to have been an increase of staff from the three we found in Nicolas' time. The inventory of 1761 seems exceedingly sparse, but in reality it marks a very prosperous point in the affairs of the firm. During the final illness of François Etienne I, his son took the work in hand from the workshop in the Rue de la Verrerie to his own home, in Rue St. Bon, and only the establishment in the Rue de la Verrerie was inventoried. An unknown number of benches and workers were employed in the Rue St. Bon, and all the instruments of value were there. In 1766 we find six benches in all, a doubling of the staff of Nicolas' time.

An interesting item in the inventory of 1726 gives us an insight into the number of new harpsichords built at one time. We find seven spines, seven bentsides, and wood roughed out for fourteen key beds, all listed in one group; it seems obvious that François Etienne I and Nicolas were beginning a batch of seven two-manual harpsichords. With the six-man staff of 1766 it is probable that even larger projects were undertaken.

The fine four-register Ruckers rebuilds that one associates with the names of Blanchet and Taskin distract one from the realization that there is no evidence whatsoever that the instruments constructed by French eighteenth century makers ever had more than three registers. The few instruments that survive all have three registers. It might be objected that the Nicolas Dumont harpsichord which we have already described has four registers and that it surely could not have been an isolated phenomenon. On the other hand, it must be remembered that Taskin rebuilt that instrument as late as 1789 and that he was forced to take it all to pieces in order to widen the case. It would have been a very easy matter to add a fourth register in the course of such an extensive project. A passage

[88] *Ibid.*, CI, 545, June 18, 1766, François Etienne Blanchet.
[89] *Ibid.*, CI, 621, April 24, 1777, Pascal Joseph Taskin.
[90] *Ibid.*, XIV, Feb. 22, 1793, Pascal Taskin.

from the *Encyclopédie méthodique*[91] gives us an idea of the complete-
ness with which the Ruckers harpsichords were rebuilt in the Blanchet
shop:

It is in the art of enlarging the Flemish harpsichords of the Ruckers and
of Couchet that Blanchet, a French maker, has perfectly succeeded. Yet he
has been surpassed by M. Paschal Taskin, his pupil. Anyway, here is the
procedure for enlarging harpsichords: To accomplish this it is necessary to
cut them in treble and bass, then to widen and even elongate the whole case
of the harpsichord, and finally to add old resonant pine, the most even-
grained one can find, to the soundboard to give it its new width and length.
The wrest plank is replaced in this sort of harpsichord which, all considered,
keeps of its original state only the soundboard and around two and one-half
feet of the old right side. The accessory parts, such as keyboards, jacks, and
registers, are made now with much more accuracy than the Flemish masters
made them in the last century. A harpsichord of the Ruckers or of Couchet,
artistically cut and enlarged with jacks, registers and keyboards by a clever
modern maker such as Blanchet or Paschal has become an infinitely precious
instrument.

If the Dumont had the same treatment, and there is no reason why it
should not have had, the addition of a fourth register would have been an
insignificant detail.

The 1769 Taskin illustrated in Plate XII and the Hemsch in Plate XI
are fine examples of their type and should be studied carefully by those
interested in assimilating the central mysteries of the craft. With two
manuals FF–f''', 2x8', 1x4', three registers disposed

$$\left\{ \begin{array}{l} \leftarrow 8' \\ \text{- - - - - - - -} \\ \leftarrow 4' \\ \rightarrow 8', \end{array} \right.$$

the Taskin is quite similar to the two Blanchets already mentioned, although slightly superior to them in workmanship. A comparison of the
structural details and design to those of a Ruckers transposing harpsichord
is instructive. The string band and plan is built upon a scale very slightly
shorter than the most common Ruckers measurement, 13⅜ inches in the
place of an average very close to 14 inches for Ruckers, and the plucking
points of the front jacks are very similar. In comparing the dimensions of
the two harpsichords we must consider the Ruckers as BB–c''', not the
C/E–c''' that the musician would find. Ruckers scaling is designed to fit

[91] "Arts et métiers," Paris, 1785, IV, 8. The same article may be found in the quarto
editions of the *Encyclopédie*.

the upper manual, not the lower. The upper manual ends on an apparent E, but there are five more keys in the lower manual which would carry the range to BB if tuned diatonically.

Table 11 compares the string lengths (shorter eight-foot) and plucking point of the front eight-foot jack of the 1769 Taskin and of a 1615 transposing Ruckers now exhibited in the Vleeshius at Antwerp. The most significant difference is to be observed in the extreme treble and this

Table 11. French and Flemish eight-foot scales [a]

| | Ruckers | | | | Taskin | | |
| | | Distance to plucking point | | | | Distance to plucking point | |
String	Length (inches)	Inches	Percent [b]	String	Length (inches)	Inches	Percent [b]
c'''	6⅞	2⅛	31	c'''	7	2	29
c''	13¹³⁄₁₆	2¹¹⁄₁₆	19	c''	13⅜	2¾	21
c'	27¼	3⁷⁄₁₆	13	c'	26¾	3⅝	14
c	47⁹⁄₁₆	4⅜	9	c	45	4⅝	10
C	65¼	5½	9	C	64	5⅝	9

[a] Measurements are of a 1615 Ruckers and a 1769 Taskin (see text).
[b] That is, the percent of the total string length represented by the distance to the plucking point.

is the result of the more extended range of the Taskin. Since the f''' string must span the gap and the space occupied by the four-foot nut, bridge, and wrest pins, Taskin has had to elongate his treble scale slightly, and we observe the traces of this alteration at c'''. At c Taskin is considerably shorter than Ruckers. Two factors produce this result. One is the straight section in the bridge and bentside of French harpsichords mentioned above. Ruckers pulled his bridge back a bit more in the tenor in continuing the sweep of its curve, and this produced a longer c. The other factor is again the increased range. Taskin is crowding more strings into a case only three inches longer than the Ruckers. His string sounding c is farther from the spine than that of Ruckers, farther up along the curve of the bridge, and thus is shorter. The fact to be remembered, however, is not the difference between the two instruments but their resemblance in scale, which is about as close as that existing between two Ruckers.

Table 12 compares the string lengths and plucking points of the four-foot string band of the same two instruments. The four-foot jack is the second from the front in both cases. It will be noticed that the Ruckers has the longer scale throughout and the Taskin the more distant plucking point. In other words, the four-foot nut of the Taskin is farther from the gap, and the four-foot bridge is closer to the gap than in Ruckers' design. If we consider the four-foot string band as superimposed on the eight-foot string band, its whole orientation has been moved slightly forward toward the keyboard, thus giving the eight-foot bridge more unobstructed space on the soundboard.

Table 12. French and Flemish four-foot scales [a]

	Ruckers				Taskin		
		Distance to plucking point				Distance to plucking point	
String	Length (inches)	Inches	Percent [b]	String	Length (inches)	Inches	Percent [b]
c'''	3⁷⁄₁₆	1	29	c'''	3¼	1⁵⁄₁₆	40
c''	6⅞	1½	22	c''	6	1⁹⁄₁₆	26
c'	13¾	1¹¹⁄₁₆	12	c'	13¼	2	15
c	24⅜	2	8	c	24	2⅞	12
C	36¾	2¼	6	C	35	3⅜	10

[a] Measurements are of a 1615 Ruckers and a 1769 Taskin (see text).
[b] That is, the percent of the total string length represented by the distance to the plucking point.

Although the Ruckers and the Taskin have frames which are similar in conception, the Taskin is better worked out in detail. Where the Ruckers had three upper-level braces, Taskin employed four, and by fixing them almost perpendicular to the bentside he increased their effectiveness. Another improvement was the placing of the first two braces in a position to conduct the load on the bentside to the belly rail and to the junction of belly rail and spine respectively. It will also be noted that Taskin affixed a member to the rear of the upper section of his belly rail, thus giving that piece a T-section, and greatly increasing its stiffness. The rounded section of Taskin's frames seems characteristic of his work.

The materials employed by Taskin and Ruckers are identical, but Taskin tended to increase the thickness of each part slightly. Table 13 compares the outside dimensions and the scantlings of some of the major constituents of the two instruments.

This bog of tabular detail has been introduced not to demonstrate the slight deviation the French introduced into the Flemish tradition but to make apparent the remarkable similarity of instruments separated by one hundred and fifty years, the products of dissimilar national cultures.

Table 13. French and Flemish case and scantling dimensions (inches) [a]

	Ruckers	Taskin
	Case dimensions	
Total length	88	91¼
Total width	31⅟16 (50 keys)	36¹¹⁄16 (61 keys)
Total depth	10½	11
Length of cheekpiece	26	27⅜
Length from front to nameboard	9½	9½
Length of tail [b]	11⅝	10¼
	Scantling dimensions	
Cheekpiece	9⁄16	¾
Bentside	½	13⁄16
Tail	⅝	13⁄16
Spine	9⁄16	⅞
Wrest plank		
rear	1 15⁄16	2½
front	2⅛	
Bottom	½	½
Soundboard		
at belly rail	3⁄32	
at rose	⅛	7⁄64

[a] Measurements are of a 1615 Ruckers and a 1769 Taskin (see text).
[b] This measurement is the width of the tailpiece itself. The Ruckers tail angle is slightly more acute than the Taskin.

The really important French innovations were musical and not structural.

We have already seen how the French seventeenth century makers turned the two-manual format to expressive ends by giving each manual its particular choir or choirs of strings. At first the *plein jeu* seems to have been produced by means of the dogleg, but sometime toward the end of the seventeenth century the manual coupler was introduced. Mersenne does not mention it, and I have not been able to find a direct reference to its invention. Jean Denis (1650)[92] makes one exceedingly obscure remark which may imply the existence of a manual coupler: "Voila tout ce qui se peut dire de l'accord du plus bel Instrument du monde, & le plus parfaict; veu qu'il ne se peut faire de Musique qu'il n'exprime & n'execute tout seul, ayant des clavecins à deux claviers, pour passer tous les Vnissons; ce que le Luth ne sçauroit faire: & les Orgues en ont quatre

[92] Jean Denis, *Traité de l'accord de l'espinette* (Paris, 1650), p. 13.

pour jouër toute sorte de Musique." ("Here is all that can be said of the tuning of the most beautiful instrument in the world, and the most perfect; even if one wished it so music cannot be written which it [the harpsichord] cannot express and execute by itself, there being harpsichords with two keyboards for passing all the unisons; a thing the lute cannot do: and organs have four of them for playing all kinds of music.")

Denis contrasts the ability of the harpsichord with two keyboards to "passer tous les Vnissons" ("pass all the unisons") with the inability of the lute to do the same thing. He seems to be referring to the crossing of voices, which a harpsichord with two independent manuals can manage very well, but which is awkward on the lute. A harpsichord with a dog-leg jack does not have two independent manuals since the upper is always coupled, in effect, to the lower. Thus Denis may be referring to a double equipped with coupler. Organ couplers were in existence long before this period, but it is impossible to guess exactly how long the inherent conservatism of harpsichord makers prevented them from applying the manual coupler to their own instruments.

The coupler, as it finally appeared on French and German harpsichords, was a simple and effective device. Plate XV, taken from the *Encyclopédie*, will provide illustration of its construction. See also Plate XIII, figures 1 and 2. The "dogs" are the wooden uprights firmly attached to the upper surface of the lower manual key levers. The upper manual is able to slide in and out a short distance on the supports provided by the sides of the lower-manual key bed. When the upper manual is drawn forward, the dogs rise behind the rear of its key levers, and the manuals are independent. If the upper manual is pushed to the rear, the dogs, in rising, carry the upper manual levers with them, and the upper is coupled to the lower. Obviously, lower-manual jacks cannot be operated from the upper manual, even when the coupler is engaged. Thus, the upper-manual disposition is still available for sudden pianos in contrast to the forte of the lower.

The upper-manual key bed is moved by grasping the end blocks at bass and treble and pushing or pulling. Usually there is too much friction to permit the coupler to be operated from one end alone. Moreover, if an attempt is made to engage the coupler while a lower-manual key is depressed, the dog will be broken off. Therefore, the coupler could have been engaged or disengaged only at pauses in the music. None of the modern types of manual coupler which can be engaged or disengaged while holding lower manual keys down were known in the eighteenth century.

It is as action makers that the French harpsichord makers were most famous, and in this company the Blanchet family was pre-eminent. Hullmandel, himself a virtuoso and former student of C. P. E. Bach, praised them thus: "One hundred years later Blanchet surpassed them [Richard and his contemporaries] in the agreeable tone of his harpsichords, and principally in the extreme lightness of his keyboards, which contributed a great deal to the progress of the instrument in France. Blanchet remade the keyboards of a great number of Ruckers harpsichords, to which he added four bass notes and as many in the treble." [93] Burney also mentions the light touch characteristic of these instruments:

After church M. Balbastre invited me to his house, to see a fine Rucker harpsichord which he has had painted inside and out with as much delicacy as the finest coach or even snuff-box I ever saw at Paris. On the outside is the birth of Venus; and on the inside of the cover the story of Rameau's most famous opera, Castor and Pollux; earth, hell, and elysium are there represented: in elysium, sitting on a bank, with a lyre in his hand, is that celebrated composer himself; the portrait is very like, for I saw Rameau in 1764. The tone of this instrument is more delicate than powerful; one of the unisons is of buff, but very sweet and agreeable; the touch is very light, owing to the quilling, which in France is always weak.[94]

The *peau de buffle* unison which Burney mentions makes it very likely that Taskin had performed the *ravalement*.

Taskin and Blanchet produced their light actions not by any remarkable tricks but by clean and accurate workmanship and meticulous quilling. Plate XIII, figures 2 and 6, will make clear the details of Taskin's key beds and key levers. He had inherited the metal pin rack of the Flemings and, while improving the execution, retained the principle. For his upper manual he refined the Ruckers system by cutting mortises through the rear of the key levers for the rear guide pins instead of placing the guide pins between the keys (figure 7). The key levers are balanced just in front of the midpoint ($9\frac{3}{16}$ for a $20\frac{3}{16}$ lever), where Ruckers balanced them considerably more forward ($7\frac{3}{4}$ for a $20\frac{3}{4}$ lever). This balance point reduces the mechanical disadvantage inherent in the Ruckers design and produces a lighter action. At the same time it increases the required key dip, at least theoretically, but Taskin minimized this effect by cutting his jacks to exactly the right length and eliminating as much lost motion as possible. Taskin key levers are not usually weighted, but they are cut away under the key heads to reduce the weight

[93] *Encyclopédie méthodique*, "Musique" (1791), I, 286b.
[94] *The Present State of Music in France and Italy*, p. 38. Burney's host is Claude Balbastre (1729–1799), organist at Notre Dame and a pupil of Rameau.

forward of the balance rail (figure 10). Thus the key loading consists essentially of the weight of the jacks (without leads), and the resistance of the string and quill at the moment of plucking constitutes a considerable proportion of the total effort required of the player. A crisp, positive touch is the result, and the player has the sensation of absolute control.

Taskin, in common with all the French makers, deviated from the Ruckers type of registers. The Ruckers had always employed a simple wooden batten appropriately mortised for the jacks. The French covered a softwood batten with thin leather and punched the mortises with great accuracy through the leather. The batten was mortised much oversize so that the jacks bore only on the leather. The lower guide is similar in principle except that the leather was applied to the lower side instead of the upper.

Taskin's jacks are tapered so that they fit tightly in the slides only when the jack is in its lowest position. This characteristic was probably adopted for ease in fitting rather than for any peculiar effect. Like his keyboards, Taskin's jacks are remarkable for the finish and accuracy of their workmanship, but they do not vary in design from those of his contemporaries. Plate XIII, figure 9, shows a typical French jack. Characteristic features are the simple section of the tongue, the single damper, and the bristle spring. The jacks are of pear wood with holly tongues. Taskin normally dated the first jack of each register.

From 1770 the portents of the ultimate destruction of the art of the harpsichord maker by that of the piano maker become more and more ominous. The piano, of course, had been in existence since before 1711, when Maffei [95] first saw four pianofortes of Cristofori's construction in Florence. Scattered inventors and builders had either taken up the idea or developed it independently during the eighteenth century, but the piano did not represent a serious threat to the ascendancy of the harpsichord until the philosophy of musicians began to change. So long as there was no general demand for the nuance of dynamic offered by the piano mechanism, there was no reason for musicians to wish to exchange the brilliant and clean tone of the harpsichord for the false and dull sound of the earliest pianos. Before 1750 one can easily find printed praise of the harpsichord in the most unreserved terms. Jean Denis, for example, called it the most beautiful instrument in the world, and the most perfect. Couperin *le Grand* said in 1725 that "le clavecin a dans son espéce un brillant et une netteté qu'on ne trouve guères dans les autres instruments"

[95] See "Nueva invenzione d'un gravecembalo etc.," *Giornale de letterati d'Italia* (Venice), V (1711).

("The harpsichord has in its way a brilliance and a crispness that one hardly finds in other instruments").[96] The fact that the inflexible dynamic level of the harpsichord was not regarded as a flaw in earlier times is clearly demonstrated by the neglect and eventual abandonment of Haward's seventeenth century invention of pedals to change the stops. The limitation began to appear crippling in the last half of the eighteenth century, and criticism of the instrument was general, sometimes explicit, and often implied in the ingenious efforts which were devoted to the attempt to provide the instrument with the capacity for nuance. The following passage is typical of the attacks made on the harpsichord during the eighteenth century.

Le prix éxhorbitant que coûte un bon clavessin, la difficulté de son transport, la place qu'il occupe, la dépense de son entretien, le mistère de son accord ou partition, dont le tempérament arbitraire n'est fondé que sur une longue expérience. Cet accord, si sujet au changement des tems, que l'on ne peut pas s'assurer d'en joüer, si l'on n'a pas un Facteur auprès de soi pour l'accorder à chaque Concert, & pour réparer les accidens fréquens du clavier, froid en hyver, & l'impossibilité d'enfler & de diminuer les sons, rebutent aujourd'huy les Dames de bon goût qui préférent la Vielle dans laquelle elles ne trouvent aucun de ces défauts.

(The exorbitant price of a good harpsichord, the difficulty of moving it, the space that it occupies, the expense of its upkeep, the mystery of its tuning, of which the arbitrary temperament is founded only on long experience. That tuning so subject to the change of weather that one cannot assure oneself of playing if one does not have a maker near enough to tune for each performance and to repair the frequent accidents to the keyboard, cold in winter, and the impossibility of increasing and diminishing the sound today repel women of good taste who prefer the hurdy-gurdy in which they find none of these failings.) [97]

One must distinguish between two fundamental sorts of expression. The first is the ability to express the vertical structure of a movement of music by the exposition of its various sections in different timbres or at several dynamic levels. Corollary to this is the underlining of the horizontal elements by clothing each voice in a specific color. The baroque organ and the double harpsichord with hand stops are superbly fitted to perform these functions. The second sort of expression is that which attempts to expound the internal structure of a musical phrase by the manipulation of dynamic and timbre. The harpsichord is not suited to

[96] François Couperin, *Apothéose, composé à la memoire immortelle de l'incomparable M. de Lully* (Paris, 1725), "Avis."
[97] From *Lettre de M. l'Abbé Carbasus à M. de—— sur la mode des instrumens de musique* (Paris, 1739), p. 20. Variously ascribed to the Abbé Goujet and François Campion, and addressed to Voltaire.

this purpose, and it is the violation of this limitation which vitiates the performances of many modern players.

All art gains force and intensity by the compression of its matter by its means, the reduction of nature to order. It is precisely the statement of a sinuous and elusive musical line in the geometric terms of the harpsichord which provides the keyboard works of the baroque with their tension. More than any other style the baroque depends on the conflict of substance and medium. Carved into the rigid stones of its architecture we find the flowing lines of natural forms, on the static panels of its painting we feel the exuberance of motion, and upon hearing its music we sense the endless tension between the implied nuance of the line and the meticulous but rigid statement. To express every implication is to deflate the music utterly.

Yet this is exactly what the French set out to do. The history of the harpsichord in France through the last half of the eighteenth century is a series of attempts to free the instrument from the inherent limitation of its design. The details of these inventions become more and more academic as the death dates of Bach, Handel, Scarlatti, and Couperin recede into the past, and in the end the story belongs to the historian of the burgeoning era of the piano (see the list of inventions in Appendix D).

The most significant of these attempts was that of Taskin. Essentially he was coping with the problem that had occupied van Blankenburg at the beginning of the century: to find an employment for the fourth register of a Ruckers double. If one simply quilled it as an extra eight-foot stop on the lower manual, it was not of much practical value. It could not offer a great deal of color contrast since its jacks necessarily must be adjacent to one of the other eight-foot registers. If its jacks were faced to pluck the same string as the other lower-manual eight-foot, the two could not produce a true unison ensemble, and were only of use for the slight variation of 1x8′ tone quality they offered. If the third eight-foot jack plucked the choir of the upper manual, one was involved in the more serious difficulty of damper interference, since the dampers pertaining to one manual were resting quietly on the strings which one was attempting to pluck from the other. The dampers had to be cut very short in order that the cloth would not be in contact with the strings when the jacks were in the off position. This did not work at all well. When the register was moved toward the string, sixty-one dampers were buckled between the jacks and the strings and tended to push the register off again. Furthermore, one had to be careful to take off the upper-manual register (thus muting one manual) when using the extra eight-foot on the lower.

Taskin's solution was to consider the fourth register as a solo eight-foot stop of peculiar characteristics. It was arranged so that it plucked the choir of the lower-manual eight-foot jacks (thus eliminating damper interference) and was provided with plectra of *peau de buffle*. (See Plate XXIX, figures 8 and 9, for an illustration of a *peau de buffle* plectrum.) By the use of this substance Taskin hoped to achieve the dynamic sensitivity to touch characteristic of the piano or clavichord. It cannot be said that his hopes were realized, but *peau de buffle* plectra do produce a delightfully tranquil pianissimo. The characteristics of the plectra were assisted in Taskin's dispositions by the assignment of the *peau de buffle* to the rearmost rank of jacks. Thus, Taskin's four-register rebuilds were most often disposed:

$$
\begin{cases}
\quad \rightarrow 8' \text{ quill} \\
\text{- - - - - - - - - - -} \\
\quad \leftarrow 4' \text{ quill} \\
\quad \leftarrow 8' \text{ quill} \\
\quad \leftarrow 8' \text{ } \textit{peau de buffle.}
\end{cases}
$$

It will be noticed that the four-foot jack is placed between the two quilled eights in order to permit the maximum contrast between them.

Peau de buffle [98] is a sort of woolly leather, like thick chamois, which is made from the skins of the Old World buffalo. In the eighteenth century buffalo were kept in the Near East, the Papal States, and the Kingdom of Naples, from whence there was a considerable commerce in their hides, which were in special demand for items of military equipment. A great deal of nonsense has been written about *peau de buffle* by those who fail to distinguish between it and the very much harder cowhide used by modern harpsichord makers as a standard plectrum material. Whatever the historical precedent for the employment of cowhide, it must be emphasized that the *peau de buffle* episode is irrelevant to it.

More fundamental than the *peau de buffle* plectra were Taskin's ingenious knee levers with which he operated the registers. Since his upper manuals have only one stop, there is never need to move its register. Taskin provided one knee lever for each of the other stops in the instrument so that the player could easily vary the registration while playing. The mechanism is shown in Plate XIV. The knee levers were in the form of pommels of square section (figure 6) which were mounted vertically in the bottom of the instrument under the front edge of the key-

---

[98] *Dictionnaire portatif de commerce* (Liége, 1770), "Bufle," I, 382.

board. The player could raise them one at a time with his knees, and they were provided with hitches (the notch in the pommel — plate XIV, figure 6 — engaged in the member of the stand — not shown — through which it passed in order to hitch) to retain them in the raised position. Various arrangements are found, but the levers are most commonly in the following order.

Machine stop	Four foot	Lower quill	Manual coupler	Peau de buffle	Raises peau de buffle jacks

(The knee lever is raised to retire the jack from the string.) The "machine stop" was a simple device to facilitate the employment of the *peau de buffle* as a sudden contrast. It took off the four-foot and both of the quilled eight-foot stops in one motion, leaving the *peau de buffle* as solo. This was accomplished by means of a piece of wood hinged to the bottom of the harpsichord. When the machine stop pommel was raised, this piece rose with it and operated the cranks of the four- and eight-foot trap work by means of blocks glued to its upper surface, which communicated with the trap work through holes in the bottom. It is difficult to understand why Taskin arranged the machine stop to take off the upper-manual eight-foot. The only reason I can think of would be to get the effect of undamped strings sounding sympathetically.

The last knee lever is somewhat mysterious in purpose. A short dogleg is sawed into the rear edge of each *peau de buffle* jack. A batten (Plate XIII, figures 2 through 5) is hinged to the top of the lower-manual rack which engages the doglegs. When the knee lever is operated, the batten rises, lifting all the *peau de buffle* jacks. Possibly Taskin hoped to use the soft leather of the plectra as the pads of a buff stop. His rebuilds usually have no buff stop of the ordinary type. If so, it seems to me that his was a faint hope. The difficulties in regulation would be almost insurmountable, and the pads would be so far from the ends of the strings that one would be more likely to raise the pitch of the note sounded than to obtain the pizzicato buff effect. Possibly Taskin was attempting to obtain a special timbre by undamping one choir of strings. Dampers are such ephemeral objects that the arrangements found in extant harpsichords are not very meaningful. In order for this mechanism to undamp one choir of eight-foot strings, the back eight-foot quilled jacks would have to have no dampers and the choir would normally be damped by the dampers in the *peau de buffle* jacks. This would not have worked well since the *peau de buffle* dampers would not damp firmly when the stop was off.

A more damaging objection to this theory lies in the fact that the back eight-foot jacks were always provided with slots for dampers.

Gerber[99] gives the original credit for the invention, or at least the suggestion, of *peau de buffle* plectra to Balbastre, and we have seen that Balbastre's harpsichord was already fitted with a *peau de buffle* stop in 1770 when Burney was in Paris. According to Gerber, Taskin's role was that of developer rather than inventor. In our own time the Pleyel firm in Paris has inscribed their large harpsichords with a legend giving credit to Wanda Landowska for the suggestion of a sixteen-foot stop. Since the sixteen-foot had been a well-known feature of the largest (German) harpsichords two hundred years before, it is apparent that no great effort of the imagination was involved. I suspect that the situation between Taskin and Balbastre was similar. If a maker can have the public endorsement of a well-known musician, he is often willing to offer the fragile reputation for originality in exchange.

According to a widely quoted[100] letter by the Abbé Trouflaut, originally published in the *Journal de musique* (no. 5) in 1773, Taskin began fitting his *peau de buffle* plectra and knee levers in 1768. Trouflaut says that Taskin chose one register among the usual *three* to be equipped with *peau de buffle*. This sounds as if Taskin applied the invention first of all to his own instruments, and afterwards adapted it to the four-register Ruckers. The 1769 Taskin harpsichord we have described is fitted with a *peau de buffle* register (the back eight-foot), but the tongues appear modern, and it is impossible to say whether or not the disposition is original.[101] The harpsichord has two hand stops and no knee levers. In any case, I feel that the use of *peau de buffle* in a three-register instrument is not advisable since the tone quality of the *peau de buffle* is so unlike the quill that the total ensemble is damaged. Even more serious, the *peau de buffle* is likely to be so much quieter than the upper manual quill that one cannot obtain a proper dynamic balance between the manuals. The *peau de buffle* is an excellent device when it involves the luxury of a fourth register, but it must not be allowed to eliminate the *sine qua non* of the primary 2x8', 1x4', in quill.

We have said nothing about spinets during the eighteenth century be-

---

[99] Ernst Ludwig Gerber, *Historische-Biographisches Lexicon der Tonkünstler* (Leipzig, 1790–1792), II, "Instrumenten-Register" (Clavecin à Peau de Buffle).

[100] Reprinted in La Borde, *Essai sur la musique ancienne et moderne*, I, 347; and *Encyclopédie méthodique*, "Arts et métiers méchaniques" (1785), IV, 9a. See Appendix A.

[101] Another Taskin harpsichord of the same year has a *peau de buffle* stop, but its jacks have also been reworked several times.

cause they do not seem to have played a very important role in France. Plate XV reproduces a contemporary illustration of the spinet. They are found most frequently in the bentside form shown, but sometimes occur in an oblong form with round corners and recessed keyboard. The article on the spinet in the *Encyclopédie méthodique* of 1785 (See Appendix A for the text) treats the instrument first in a historical manner as if it no longer existed. As the discussion proceeds the meaning of the word is silently changed to signify any jack action instrument, and the article ends by discussing harpsichords. In 1761 De Garsault[102] constructed a list of musical instruments in which the existing types were divided into two groups: the "Instruments de grande étendue, propres à exécuter toutes tout sorte de musique de transpositions, autrement Instruments des grands concerts, etc." ("instruments of large range suitable for performing all sorts of transpositions, otherwise instruments of important concerts, etc."), and the insignificant ones, the "Instruments d'amusement." The harpsichord falls into the first category and the spinet into the second. Hullmandel[103] also reveals the contemporary lack of interest in the spinet: "Il ne reste plus de virginales; les épinettes disparoissent, on les démolit pour employer leurs vieilles tables à la construction d'instrumens plus modernes" ("There remain no more virginals; spinets are disappearing, they are being demolished so that their old soundboards can be used in the construction of more modern instruments").

The claviorganum makes its usual appearance in the course of the history of jack action instruments in France. It was termed the "clavecin organisé" and was treated most thoroughly by Dom Bedos.[104] The organ maker was expected to begin with an ordinary three-register, two-manual harpsichord, which was placed on top of the organ case. (See Plates XVI and XVII.) A third manual was provided below the harpsichord keyboards for the organ, and a coupler from the harpsichord lower manual to the organ keyboard was specified. The organ could consist of several combinations of stops, but Dom Bedos gave the following as the most practical: "Un Bourdon de 4 pieds bouché; un Prestant de deux pieds bouché; un Dessus de 8 pieds ouvert; un Hautbois, dont la Basse sera un Basson" ("a four-foot stopped Bourdon; a two-foot stopped [!] Prestant; an unstopped eight-foot in the treble; an Oboe of which the bass will be a Bassoon"). It should be noted that in many small organs

---

[102] De Garsault, *Notionaire ou Mémorial raisonné de ce qu'il y a d'utile et d'interessant dans les connoissances acquises depuis la création du monde jusqu'à présent* (Paris, 1761), "Table."

[103] "Musique," *Encyclopédie méthodique*, p. 286a.

[104] *L'Art du facteur d'orgues*, p. 641.

the stops were divided at c'; this eight-foot would extend upward from c'. The bellows and reservoir were contained in the bench, and there was no pedal board. Dom Bedos specifically mentions the possibility of playing the harpsichord and organ together (as, indeed, the harpsichord to organ coupler would imply) and suggests that the stops can be moved by knee levers.

We find in the claviorganum evidence of that peculiarly French interest in tone color which is expressed in the superb reeds of St. Gervais and Petit Andely and which produced the characteristic rapport between the French composer and his harpsichord. The same discrimination of ear led the French makers of the seventeenth century to enlarge the scope of the Ruckers tonal mechanism by clever disposition. The resulting instrument, the *clavecin à grand ravalement* of the eighteenth century, became the most important single type of harpsichord, both for the literature it inspired in France and the influence it exerted on the makers of central and northern Europe. The English were to derive their own style from the Ruckers design, but the Germans seem to have worked more closely to French models.

CHAPTER FOUR · ENGLAND

The kind and number of harpsichords made in England during the sixteenth century must remain rather conjectural. Our only firm knowledge derives from the names and addresses of a few sixteenth century makers supplied by the archivists and from the cursory descriptions of instruments included in the inventories of the possessions of various noble and royal persons. To what extent these makers produced harpsichords and virginals is unknown. Some seem to have been organ makers who may also have made stringed instruments; others are termed "virginal" makers in various legal documents, but their practice of the craft may not have gone beyond repairs and procurement. Still others are known to have made occasional repairs to "virginals," but their main trade is unknown. (It should be noted that in England until the late seventeenth century the word "virginal" was usually generic for all forms of jack-action instruments.) Not a single instance can be provided in which a sixteenth century English virginal maker is clearly said to have made a specific instrument. The dearth of extant instruments from a period in English musical history notable for composition for the keyboard is a little surprising. One must assume that the majority of instruments in use in England at the time were imported, first from Italy and later from Flanders.

Only one sixteenth century instrument made in England has survived, and it would not be accurate to call its maker English. This claviorganum, now in the Victoria and Albert Museum, London, is inscribed "Lodowicus Theewes me fesit 1579." Lodowicus Theewes, the son of a member of the St. Luke Guild in Antwerp, was admitted to that body himself before emigrating to England (probably as a result of the increasing turmoil in the Low Countries). His claviorganum is Flemish in every detail except in the choice of oak for the case work.

One must endeavor, therefore, to specify the sources of instruments for the sixteenth century musicians of England. Our studies so far make it obvious that Flanders and Northern Italy were the great centers of harpsichord production, and it seems that the makers of both regions exerted a strong influence in England. Four of the sixteen known "makers" of the sixteenth century came from Flanders or from the area of Flemish influence, and the English virginals which still survive from the seventeenth century show that this Flemish influence was not without effect. They also make ridiculous the often repeated dictum that Tabel brought the Flemish style of harpsichord making to England in the early eighteenth century.

But the Flemish style was by no means predominant in sixteenth century England. There are many signs that Italian instruments were known and played. If the seventeenth century English virginals reveal a Flemish heritage, the earliest extant English harpsichords show an equally strong awareness of the Italian principles of design which was not completely purged from the English tradition until the reign of William and Mary. We have already seen that the Englishman Thomas Hariot immediately connected cedar wood with virginals when he saw the towering trees of Carolina — surely an indication of his knowledge of Italian instruments. It has also been noted that "Queen Elizabeth's virginal," which is usually assumed to have been in England since the sixteenth century, was of Italian construction. An interesting if somewhat more ambiguous class of testimony comes from contemporary inventories which often mention "virginals" which were fitted into outer boxes. Sometimes we learn that Englishmen were employed to make outer cases for existing instruments or to line such cases with colorful fabrics. When the instrument is specified to have been of cypress, one would tend to assume an Italian origin. Yet it must be remembered that early French inventories often mention inner-outer instruments, and one cannot be completely sure to what extent this early practice of inserting instruments into outer cases represents various local versions of an older tradition mutually inherited, or the actual importation into France and England of Italian instruments. In France, the existence of such *épinettes* in the workshops of makers seems to imply that they were the local product.

Our best authority on the nature of the harpsichords in use in England during the sixteenth century is the inventory drawn up by the musician Philip Van Wilder in 1553 of the musical instruments at Westminster owned by Henry VIII. Some of the items from that inventory read as follows.

[fol. 201]
[1] Item   an Instrument with a single Virginall and single regall withe a stoppe of timbre pipes of woode vernisshed grene and redde.

[2] Item   an Instrumente with a double Virginall and a double regall with iij stoppes of pipes of woode painted with grene rabesce [arabesque] worke with a foote of wainscott [oak] and the Bellowes lyinge in the same.

[3] Item   an Instrument that goethe with a whele withoute playinge uppon of woodde vernisshed yellowe and painted bleue with six rounde plates of Silver painted with antics garnisshed with an edge of Copper and guilte.

[4] Item   twoo paire of double virginalles thone covered with blacke Leather and the lidde lined with grene bridget [Bruges] Satten and thother covered with redde leather.

[5] Item   a paire of double virginalles covered with blacke Leather partelie silvered the lidde lined with grene bridget satten.

[6] Item   a paire of double virginalles of Cipres in a case of wainscot.

[7] Item   a paire of single virginalles covered with redde leather and the lidde lined with grene bridget satten.

[8] Item   two paire of single virginalles th'one of them havinge Keies of Ivorie and thother of Boxe with twoo cases to them of redde leather ptelie gilte and lined with blacke vellat.

[9] Item   a paire of single virginalles covered with grene bridget Satten with iij Tilles in them[?].

[fol. 202]

[10] Item   two paire of single virginalles covered withe blacke Leather.

[11] Item   one paire of single virginalles covered with redde Leather.

[12] Item   a paire of single virginalles with pipes Vndernith and in a case of timbre covered with blacke Leather.

[13] Item   a paire of single virginalles covered with redde Leather partelie guilte.

[fol. 204]

[14] Fyrste   one newe paire of double virginalles covered with blacke Leather with smale roses printed and gilte upon it the lidde lined with grene Satten and garnisshed upon with redde silke ribonne lozenge wise.

[15] Item   another newe paire of double virginalles vernisshed yellowe and painted allouer with redde rabesce worke the lidde being lined with purple stirconet and havinge the King's armes painted and guilte in the middle of hit.

[16] Item   a litle paire of virginalles single covered with redde Leather in a Case of woode covered with blacke Leather.

[17] Item   twoo faire paire of newe longe virginalles made harpe fasshion of Cipres with keies of Ivorie havinge the kinges armes crowned and supported by his graces beastes within a gartier gilte, standing over the saide keies with two caises to them covered with blacke Leather thinner partes of the liddes to the saide caises beinge of wallnutte with sondrie antickes of white woode wrought in the same.[1]

[1] MS, British Museum, Harl. 1419a, folios 201, 202, and 204.

Henry seems to have possessed twenty-two "virginals" including three claviorgana, one automatic virginal that "goethe with a whele withoute playinge uppon," six "double" virginals, ten "single" virginals, and two bentside harpsichords. Galpin[2] maintains that "single" virginals descended to C and "double" virginals to CC. It seems more likely to me that single virginals had one stop, double virginals two.

Both harpsichords (Item 17) seem to have been Italian to judge by the use of cypress and the outer cases; and the eight-foot virginals (Item 6), of cypress in an outer box of imported oak, was certainly of that tradition. The four-foot claviorganum (Item 12) seems to have been contained in an outer case, which may imply Italian origin. But that supposition is weakened by Item 16, an ottavino covered with red leather in an outer case of wood covered with black leather. No Italian instrument known to me is covered with leather, although that form of adornment was sometimes applied to outer cases. This instrument may have been of an inner-outer type differing from the Italian, the only examples of that method of construction now extant. However, Italian ottavini cannot be as rigidly fitted into the bounds of their particular school as the larger instruments. Many were of a heavier construction than the harpsichords and materials other than cypress were used. Thus, the red leather covering this ottavino does not rule out the possibility that it was made in Italy.

While the list of Henry's instruments does not demonstrate as much dependence upon foreign suppliers as do Praetorius' *Theatrum instrumentorum* or the Dresden inventory (reproduced below, Chapter V), it does show a strong continental bias. Besides the three certain Italian instruments and the two possible ones it seems quite likely that Henry's three claviorgana were Flemish. For, if my supposition is correct that a claviorganum Lewes brought to Greenwich in 1530[3] was based on a Flemish double virginal or 2x8' harpsichord, that fact, combined with the observation that the only extant sixteenth century claviorganum in contemporary English hands was made by the Fleming Theewes, leads

[2] Francis W. Galpin, *A Textbook of European Musical Instruments* (London, 1937), pp. 109, 182.
[3] "Item the vj daye paied to William lewes for ij payer of Virginalls in one coffer wt iiij stoppes brought to Grenewiche iij li." (Sir N. Harris Nicolas, *Privy Purse Expenses of King Henry VIII*, London, 1827, p. 37.) See also H. St. George Gray, "A Virginal by Charles Rewallin," *Connaisseur*, 46:77, for quotations from various sixteenth century documents including the foregoing which mention double virginals. Gray also quotes an interesting remark of Sir Jerome Horsey who bore official gifts to Russia in 1581: "The Empress was especially struck by the loud and musical sounds of some organs and virginalls."

one to believe that claviorgana were rather a Flemish specialty. At any rate, there is no evidence that the English made them, and there is good evidence that the Flemish did. Furthermore, we may guess that the automatic virginal came from Germany where the Biderman family were soon to become famous for such devices. Thus it is possible to conjecture that at least nine of Henry's twenty-two "virginals" were imported.

Until the end of the century the Lord Chamberlain's accounts continue to mention instruments which were apparently fitted with outer cases:

(1558, April 10)
Warrant to deliver to John Grene "coffer-maker," "as much grene velvett as will suffice for the covering of one pair of virgynalls and as much grene satten as shall serve to lyne the same, with passamayne lace of silver for the garnishing and edginge of the same. And that ye paie unto the said John Grene as well for two cases of tymber covered with lether and lyned, th' one being for the aforesaid virgynalls."

Payment also to be made for "a newe key for the aforesaid virgynalls, also for mendynge the iron worke and gildinge of eight squyers to the same. Item for one locke, a pair of hendges, two handles, two hooks, with nailes for the case of the same virgynalls."

(1560, May 28)
Warrant to deliver to William Treasorer, "maker of our instruments five yards of crimson velvett, to cover one payre of regalls, and one yarde of purple satten to line the same. Item for the iron worke of a case for a paire of virginalls aforesaid, covered withe crimson velvett."

(Account ending Michaelmas, 1582)
Warrent for the delivery of crimson velvet for covering, lining and ornamenting divers of the Queen's "regalls and virginalls," and for the payment for covering with velvet four pairs of regals and virginals and for ornamenting the same with gold and silver lacquer; for covering and ornamenting divers virginals with green velvet, and levant leather, and for iron work for the same; for a wooden box lined with velvet for a pair of virginals, etc., etc.

(Account ending Michaelmas, 1593)
Warrant for the delivery of certain black velvet, black satin, ble [glaucus] velvet, scarlet cloth and gold and silver lacquer, for covering, ornamenting and repairing the Queen's virginals.

(1595–6)
Warrant to pay for "14 yards of carnation velvet and eight yards of wrought velvet black and ash colour, employed and spent in covering of our virginals, and for twelve yards of grene velvet to cover a greate instrument, all being garnished with lace of gold and silver and silke riben and sowing silke to them." [4]

[4] Quoted from De Lafontaine, *The King's Musick*. De Lafontaine made extracts

After this date there is no further mention of materials or techniques which seem peculiarly suited to instruments in outer boxes. A few conclusions can be drawn about the instruments pertaining to the virginalist composers of the sixteenth century. We have seen that both Flemish and Italian instruments were common and that harpsichords as well as virginals were in use. We would expect the Italian harpsichords to follow the usual 2x8', single-manual pattern. Little is known about pre-Ruckers Flemish harpsichords, but if we assume that Hans Ruckers continued an older tradition, the standard Flemish type available to English buyers would have been a 1x8', 1x4', single. In the doubtful event that the transposing double harpsichord existed before Ruckers it must be remembered that it was musically equivalent to a single-manual harpsichord. Italian virginals and pentagonal spinets would, of course, have been common as well as all of the various types of Flemish virginals. There is no reason to believe that a two-manual harpsichord was available to sixteenth century English composers. On the other hand, there is no reason to limit modern performances to spinets or virginals. Larger instruments were unquestionably numerous, and it is chiefly the ambiguity of the early use of the word "virginal" that leads one to think of a small rectangular instrument as the medium of Byrd, Bull, and Gibbons.

The Theeuwes claviorganum is the earliest extant 2x8', 1x4' harpsichord, and it is perhaps significant that the next oldest harpsichord made in England (1622) also had three choirs. It seems that English keyboard players not only possessed larger instruments than the virginal but that they sometimes had available the most complex instruments of their time. In this regard it is interesting to note the phenomenal English interest in claviorgana. Among the few sixteenth century instruments of which I have been able to find any trace in England, no less than six were of this type (assuming that none of those in Harl. 1419a was identical to that sold by Lewes in 1530). Besides mentioning those belonging to Henry VIII and the 1579 Theeuwes, Rimbault[5] quotes a description of a large claviorganum with a reed stop from an inventory of 1584: "Item, an instrument of organs, regalls and virginals, covered with crimson velvet and garnished with goulde lace."

It would be interesting to find more about the specific way in which these instruments were used. We know that the Theeuwes claviorganum was placed in the chapel at Ightham Mote, Kent, where presumably it

from the records. Only the sections enclosed in quotations were taken verbatim from the manuscripts.

[5] Edward F. Rimbault, *History of the Pianoforte* (London, 1860), quoting an inventory of Kenilworth Castle (the Earl of Leicester).

was used during services. What role the organ stops played in secular music and to what extent organ and harpsichord were sounded together is difficult to conjecture. There is no mechanical reason why they should not have been so used, and scattered eighteenth century references imply that the combined ensemble was sometimes employed.

If our knowledge of the sixteenth century is conjectural, we reach firmer ground as our studies lead us into the seventeenth century, for a fair number of spinets, virginals, and harpsichords by native English makers of that era are still extant. It must be assumed, however, that many instruments continued to be imported from the continent. Samuel Pepys' well-known remark "I observed that hardly one lighter or boat in three that had the goods of a house in, but there was a paire of virginals in it"[6] implied a very large number of instruments in use in England during the seventeenth century. The twenty-five or thirty spinets, eighteen virginals, and three or four harpsichords of English seventeenth century origin which are extant are hardly numerous enough to meet the case even if allowance is made for the destruction caused by the Fire and the wars of the Commonwealth. We have already seen that Sir Francis Windebank, private secretary to Charles I, purchased a Ruckers harpsichord in 1638. Many of Sir Francis' countrymen must have joined him in importing their instruments from Antwerp, for there are frequent traces of Ruckers harpsichords in England during the eighteenth century. We can assume that many of these had been bought directly from their makers. Italian influence continued to be felt. Indeed, about 1668 we find two Italian makers, Girolamo Zenti and Andrea Testa, connected with the Chapel Royal. But the English seem to have turned away gradually from the Italian style to the imitation of Flemish instruments.

The Haward family was possibly the most important English harpsichord making dynasty of the seventeenth century. Our genealogical information is most incomplete, but one can discern the uncertain lineaments of three Johns, two Thomases, and one Charles in the records of the Joiners' Company.[7] Mace's famous "Pedal" was invented by "Mr. John Hayward of London,"[8] possibly the maker of the 1622 harpsichord at Knole which is described below. Pepys reports buying a spinet from "one Hayward" in 1668 after flirting with the idea of a "harpsichon."[9]

[6] *Diary*, Sept. 2, 1666.
[7] See Boalch's article on Haward and his list of London apprentices in *Makers of the Harpsichord and Clavichord*, pp. 46 and 149. The remarks on the lute stop contained in that article do not take account of the existence of lute stops in seventeenth century harpsichords.
[8] Thomas Mace, *Musick's Monument* (London, 1676), p. 235.
[9] *Diary*, April 4, 1668; July 10, 13, 15, 1668.

The bulk of the surviving instruments are by Charles (dated between 1683 and 1687) to whom we can ascribe one harpsichord, at least eleven spinets, and possibly one virginal.

The earliest extant English seventeenth century harpsichord was made by John Haward of London in 1622. The handsome quartered oak case with its well-proportioned panels outlined by elegant moldings rests upon a carved and arcaded stand. There is no lid, but it seems unlikely that there was ever an outer case since the stand fits the outline well, and care was evidently lavished on the external decoration. This harpsichord is now a hollow shell, lacking soundboard, keyboard, and frame members. The wrest plank and lower guide are still in place but the nuts are gone. The short distance from the front of the instrument to the nameboard implies a single manual which seems to have had fifty-three notes. There were three ranks of jacks. Among the possible ranges the most likely would be C–e''', or GG/BB–d''' with one split sharp in the bass.[10]

This instrument is particularly interesting in that its design shows a mixture of English, Flemish, and Italian styles. Haward seems to have worked at the moment when English harpsichord makers were just beginning to digest the Flemish and Italian influence which had been dominant and to evolve a style of their own. The general concept of the harpsichord is certainly very Italianate. The elongated form (87 inches long, 27⅞ inches wide, 9½ inches deep, with ⅜-inch case sides), light scantlings, and oblique registers are obviously Italian in flavor. Even more typical are certain features of the construction such as the sides which overlap the bottom, the full-length planks which make up the bottom, the diagonal frame members which slope from the top of the bentside to the bottom, and the style of the molding sections. From Flanders came the leather-covered lower guide, a transposing device (see below), and the wrest plank veneered to resemble the soundboard. Among the characteristics which we might dare to call English are the oak case members, the division of the sides of the case into panels, and the dovetailed corners.

The deduction of the original disposition of this harpsichord presents formidable difficulties. There can be no doubt that there were three choirs of strings; the three rows of wrest pins and three lines of mortises

[10] Frequently an extra string and mortise in the soundboard were provided for the lowest key of English virginals (cf. virginal by Thomas White 1651, Castle Museum, York). In case a tone not included in the short octave was needed the string could be tuned to the required pitch and the GG/BB jack placed in the extra mortise (see Plate XVIII). The layout of the harpsichord does not permit this interchange of jacks, but the same end could have been accomplished by splitting the lowest sharp.

in the lower guide are straightforward enough. There is space on the wrest plank for two nuts. One ran along the edge of the gap, and the other was placed between the rows of wrest pins. The difficulty springs from the apparent fact that one choir of strings was longer than the other two. We are forced to this conclusion by the two rows of wrest pins which run obliquely across the wrest plank near the gap (in the space normally occupied by the four-foot wrest pins) and the single row placed parallel to the keyboard and close to that edge of the wrest plank. One might postulate two nuts between the gap and the nearest row of wrest pins, the higher being pierced by holes to permit the strings of the lower to pass through. But two nuts simply could not be fitted into the available distance between the wrest pins and the gap. Furthermore, if the nuts were so arranged all of the wrest pins would have been grouped together at the keyboard edge of the wrest plank; there would have been no point in dividing them into two groups.

Given this stringing, there are two solutions within the usual frame of stops: 2x4′, 1x8′, or 2x8′, 1x16′. Neither seems very likely. No tradition shows any trace of 2x4′, 1x8′, and the idea is not attractive. And the instrument has altogether the wrong shape to have included a sixteen-foot stop at any normal scale even if we could reconcile a sixteen-foot with what we have learned of the historical development of the harpsichord.

A much more likely solution is that suggested by the close ties between Flemish and English makers at this period. The two shorter choirs may have sounded C pitch and the longer, F pitch or G pitch. The relatively great length of the case would make this tuning quite possible even in the bass. Given the apparent position of the nuts and a normal bridge position, the lengths of the two choirs would bear the relationship of 3:4 in the treble, which would be about right for a pitch difference of a fourth. On the Flemish transposing doubles the c″ on the upper manual actually sounded c″, but on the lower manual f′ sounded c″. Therefore the pitch was raised a fifth on the lower manual. Haward seems to have planned his unison choirs so that the c″ key sounded c″, but the single choir would have sounded at f′ or g′ for the same note on the keyboard. Thus the pitch was lowered a fourth or a fifth. With the Flemish transposing keyboards the player could lower the pitch a fourth by transposing an octave down on the lower keyboard, or raise it a fifth by playing notes as written on the lower manual. By providing a transposing choir rather than a transposing keyboard activating the standard choirs, the English were able to use a variable tuning. Assuming that the longer choir could be tuned a fourth or a fifth below the unisons, and employing an octave transposition at the keyboard, one could lower the pitch a fourth or a fifth and raise it a fifth or a fourth. The relatively large range of the keyboard made this transposition feasible. If the longer choir could be raised as high as a major third below the unisons, transpositions of thirds and sixths would be available as well.

A more characteristic product of the mid-seventeenth century English makers was the sort of rectangular virginal illustrated in Plate XVIII. The dark oak case with its wrought-iron hardware opens to a surprising burst of color. The side of the case is divided into panels, the frames of which enclose bands of gilt embossed paper; these often surround a darker, ornately painted center. The interior of the coffered lid frequently was decorated with a pastoral scene or a view of the Mall in St. James Park. The inside of the front flap, which is hinged and hangs down under the keys when the instrument is open, generally shows a similar painting.

One surviving harpsichord, unsigned and undated, fits into this tradition almost too neatly, following the Flemish-inspired English virginals in decor but reflecting Italian influence in scale and lightness of construction.[11] The wrest plank carries an inscription, probably inserted by a repairer, which has been deciphered to read "Jesses Cassus." The outside of the case is divided into panels, each of which is enlivened by the depiction of a seascape. A similar work covers the interior of the lid. The nameboard is treated in the manner of the virginals, and the boxwood key tops, scored with four lines, are identical to those of the virginals. The arcaded key fronts, however, are not typical, for the key fronts of the virginals were usually of embossed leather or paper, gilded to harmonize with the front of the case. It is possible that these arcades are not original.

There is one manual with the range AA–f'''. Its owner reports that the top four keys are spaced differently than the rest and that the key bed shows signs of having been moved. However, the scale is already so short that it is difficult to believe that four notes could have been added to the treble and the whole keyboard moved to the left to accommodate them. It seems more likely that these keys were lost or damaged and replaced by a restorer. There are two choirs tuned to unison eight-foot pitch, but the instrument originally had three registers, two in the gap and one cut-through lute stop. The slides project through the cheekpiece for manipulation. The gap for the lute stop, which is cut obliquely through the wrest plank near the nut, has been covered with wood, but the lower

---

[11] Illustrated in Boalch, *Makers of the Harpsichord and Clavichord*, plates XXI and XXII. I have not been able to examine this harpsichord and am indebted to Robert Johnson of Los Angeles, its owner, for a careful description.

guide still exists. The evidence thus afforded of the English employment of the lute stop long before van Blankenburg's announcement of its invention is supported by another English harpsichord, dated 1683, which shows traces of having been fitted with such a stop. There are one or two undated Italian instruments which may have been made in the seventeenth century which also were fitted with lute stops, and an undated Joannes Couchet harpsichord in the Metropolitan Museum of Art in New York now has one. Thus it seems that the lute stop cannot be ascribed to a single inventor or even to a single school of makers. The idea seems to have been in the air in the seventeenth century, but it was applied most frequently during the eighteenth.

The case of the "Jesses Cassus" harpsichord has an oak bentside and tail, but the rest is of lime with a pine bottom. (This composite construction is also found in a virginal by Stephen Keene in 1668.) The instrument is 64¾ inches long, 33½ inches wide, and 10⅞ inches deep. The bentside is extremely incurved, and the bridge is placed very close to the edge of the soundboard. The scantlings appear to be very light. The scale is as follows.

String	String length (inches)	Distance to plucking point (inches)
f'''	3½	1⅛
c'''	4	1¼
c''	8	1⅝
c'	16½	2¼
c	31⅜	3⅛
C	50⅞	4⅜
AA	52¾	4⅞

The plucking point referred to here is for the first jack in the gap. The plucking point for the lute stop is not available. The second jack in the gap is ⅞ inch behind the first.

This scale is extremely short, even considering the Italian influence we know to have been exerted in England during the period. However, it is not short enough to make it likely that the harpsichord was ever tuned to four-foot pitch unless we apply the remark of Praetorius [12] that the English pitch of the sixteenth century (at least for wind instruments) was a minor third lower than his. It is barely possible that the "Jesses Cassus" harpsichord was tuned to four-foot pitch a minor third flat, but the lightness of construction is against it. Such a pitch would imply a scale of about 13⁵⁄₁₆ inches, which would require a fairly strong case. Nor can it be presumed that the keyboard has been moved to the right in the

[12] See page 63.

instrument to permit the addition of extra notes in the bass (a process which would assign a shorter string to each of the "c's"). Extra notes have been added in the treble, if anywhere, an operation which would lengthen the scale if it involved shifting the keyboard to the left. It is unlikely that the keyboard was moved in this direction because that would imply that the bass range was once even longer.

Thus, unless the width of the case has been changed (a possibility we cannot assess with our present information) it seems that the keyboard has not been moved and that the scale is original. The eight-inch scale at eight-foot pitch is the more believable if we recall that contemporary French harpsichords tended to have short scales (although not this short) compared to their successors and that another extant English harpsichord of the seventeenth century has a shortish scale. There is always the possibility that the harpsichord was designed to sound at a nonunison higher pitch. The scale would permit a tuning of a fourth or fifth higher. This supposition is strengthened by the traces of a transposed pitch we have noted in the Haward harpsichord of 1622. However, Praetorius does not mention a dual pitch in England, and one cannot find traces of other keyboard instruments definitely tuned a fifth high as one can in Flanders. Thus the question is difficult to resolve.

An interesting feature of this harpsichord which may represent its maker's familiarity with virginals is the fact that the nut does not stand on the wrest plank but on a small section of soundboard of its own. The nut and bridge, however, are not of the form ordinarily found in the English virginals but resemble the usual Italian shape. This section was also used by Theeuwes in 1579.

In a harpsichord inscribed "Carolus Haward 1683" (see Plate XIX, figures 1–3 and 8) we find a connecting link between the uncertain groping of the eclectic early English tradition and the stable and independent school of the eighteenth century. The round tail of Haward's instrument may be characteristic of English harpsichords made in the period of transition between the seventeenth century style and that established around 1740 by Kirckman and Shudi. Only three extant English harpsichords have round tails: a Thomas Hitchcock double which was probably made between 1690 and 1720, a small single by Joseph Mahoon in 1742, and this one. The resemblance between the latter and the Hitchcock double in outline and internal construction may be seen in Plate XIX.

The Charles Haward harpsichord is almost exactly the same length (88 inches) as a Ruckers transposing double but it is somewhat wider

(33⅜ inches) due to the greater range (FF–d‴ with no FF♯). The depth of the case is 9¾ inches and the thickness of the cheekpiece and bentside is ⁷⁄₁₆ inch with a somewhat thicker spine (⁹⁄₁₆ inch). The scaling follows.

String	String length (inches)	Distance to plucking point (inches)
d‴	3¾	1⅜
c‴	4½	1½
c″	10⅛	1⅞
c′	19⅜	2¹³⁄₁₆
c	37¾	3¹⁵⁄₁₆
C	66⁹⁄₁₆	5⁵⁄₁₆
FF	73	6⅛

The plucking point given is that of the front jack in the gap. The second jack is ⅝ inch behind the first.

The original wrest plank has been replaced, thus eliminating all trace of the lute stop gap. But evidence of the original lute stop is provided by the mortises made to retain the second jack rail (Plate XIX, figure 8), traces on the key levers of pads at the point where the lute stop jacks would rest, and a mortise in the cheekpiece through which the lute register would have passed. The registers are now controlled by hand stops, but originally they projected through the cheekpiece in the Ruckers manner.

Plate XIX will give a general idea of the shape and construction. Like the "Jesses Cassus," this instrument employed a combination of materials, the cheekpiece and bentside being of rather thin walnut and the spine of heavier pine. Plate XIX, figure 1, shows the belly rail, which is interesting in resembling the type used some years later by Thomas Hitchcock (Plate XIX, figure 11), in which the upper member is horizontal and the lower is vertical. Plate XXI, figure 1, showing the standard eighteenth century English belly rail, will make the distinction clear.

Besides the round tail and the belly rail, other elements bear out the relationship of style between the Haward and the Hitchcock. Both have a vertical batten applied to the outside of the cheekpiece at the front to retain the lock board, and an analogous arrangement of the external moldings. Both have short scales compared to later English practice, although Haward's is shorter than Hitchcock's. On the other hand the Italian-sectioned bridges of the Haward look back toward the "Jesses Cassus" whereas Hitchcock made bridges like those of the later eighteenth century.

One of the most interesting developments in the seventeenth century was the appearance of a harpsichord with stops changed by pedals. Mace gives a good description:

But when we would be most Ayrey, Jocond, Lively, and Spruce; Then we had choice and singular consorts, either for 2, 3, or 4 Parts but not to the organ (as many (now a days) Improperly, and Unadvisedely perform such like consorts with) but to the Harpsicon; yet more Properly, and much better to the Pedal, (an Instrument of a Late Invention, contriv'd (as I have been informed) by one Mr. John Hayward of London, a most Excellent kind of Instrument for a Consort, and far beyond all Harpsicons or organs, that I yet ever heard of, (I mean either for consort or Single Use;) But the Organ far beyond It, for Those other performances before mentioned.

Concerning This Instrument, (call'd the Pedal (because it is contriv'd to give Varieties with the foot) I shall bestow a few Lines in making mention of, in regard It is not very commonly used, or known; because Few make of Them Well, and Fewer will go to the Price of Them: Twenty Pounds being the Ordinary Price of One; but the Great Patron of Musick in his Time, Sir Robert Bolles, (who in the University, I had the Happiness to Initiate, in This High Art) had Two of Them, the one I remember at 30 l. and the other at 50 l. very Admirable Instruments.

The Instrument is in Shape and Bulk just like a Harpsicon; only It differs in the Order of it, Thus, viz. There is made right underneath the Keys, near the Ground, a kind of Cubbord, or Box, which opens with a little Pair of Doors in which Box the Performer sets both his Feet, resting them upon his Heels, (his Toes a little turning up) touching nothing, till such time as he has a pleasure to employ them; which is after this manner, viz. There being right under his Toes 4 little Pummels of Wood, under each Foot 2, any one of Those 4 he may Tread upon at his Pleasure; which by the Weight of his Foot drives a Spring, and so Causeth the whole Instrument to Sound, either Soft or Loud, according as he shall chuse to Tread any of them down; (for without the Foot, so us'd Nothing Speaks.)

The out-side of the Right Foot drives One, and the In-side of the same Foot drives another; so that by treading his Foot a little awry, either outward or inward, he causeth a Various Stop to be heard, at his Pleasure; and if he clap down his Foot Flat, then he takes Them both, at the same time, (which is a 3d Variety, and Louder.)

Then has he ready, under his Left Foot, 2 other Various Stops, and by the like Order and Motion of the Foot, he can immediately give you 3 other Varieties, either Softer or Louder, as with the Right Foot before mentioned he did.

So that thus you may perceive he has several Various Stops at Pleasure; and all the Quick and Nimble, by the Ready Turn of the Foot.

And by this Pritty Device, is This Instrument made Wonderfully Rare, and Excellent: So that doubtless It Excels all Harpsicons, or Organs in the World, for Admirable Sweetness and Humour, either for a Private, or a Consort use.

I caused one of Them to be made in my House, that has 9 several other Varieties, (24 in all) by reason of a Stop (to be Slip'd in with the Hand) which my Workman calls the Theorboe-Stop; and indeed It is not much unlike It: But what it wants of the Lute, It has in Its own Singular Pritti-ness.[13]

Mace's indomitable arithmetic makes it possible to deduce the exact disposition of the "Pedal." With the hand-operated "Theorboe-Stop" and four pedals his instrument gave twenty-four registrations. The only disposition which could provide such results must have disposed four registers and a buff stop (theorboe) on a single manual. Our previous examination of contemporary harpsichords makes it plain that the precise disposition would have been 2x8', 1x8' (lute), 1x4', and buff (that is, the Charles Haward harpsichord plus four-foot and buff). My deduction proceeds as follows.

Let ABCD represent the four pedals. There are sixteen possible combinations: All off, A, B, C, D, AB, AC, AD, BC, BD, CD, ABC, ABD, ACD, BCD, ABCD. Each pedal enters into eight combinations. Therefore, whichever choir the buff affected, it could add only eight more varieties (nine, counting its off position, which has already been assumed in specifying the first sixteen registrations). The total, as Mace said, is twenty-four. Hence each pedal represents a "stop."

"Stops" can only represent registers, coupler, or buffs. Mace's reference to the "Theorboe-Stop" eliminates the buff as a possibility for one of the pedals. A two-manual instrument with three registers and coupler operated by pedal (besides being mechanically unlikely) will not give enough possibilities. For arithmetic purposes it does not matter how the stops are disposed on a hypothetical double, but I assume a normal disposition: 1x8' on the upper and 1x8', 1x4', on the lower. The following seven registrations would be available: 1x8' (upper); 1x8' (lower); 1x4' (lower); 1x8', 1x4' (lower); 2x8' (coupled); 1x8', 1x4' (coupled); 2x8', 1x4' (coupled). Since there would not be enough combinations yielded if a pedal were used for the coupler, each pedal must have operated a register. In view of my previous examination of seventeenth century harpsichords the almost certain disposition was 2x8', 1x8' (lute), 1x4', and hand-operated buff. The only two-manual disposition which would yield enough combinations (since one needs ABCD) would be 2x8', 1x4' on the lower, and a dogleg lute on the upper. This would be pointless. Furthermore, it seems likely that Mace would have mentioned a second manual.

[13] *Musick's Monument*, p. 235.

Thus I conclude that Mace's disposition must have been 2x8′, 1x8′ (lute), 1x4′, and buff on a single manual.

Mace's Pedal is particularly interesting in that a similar instrument was apparently in use at the Chapel Royal during the period of Purcell's connection there (from sometime in the sixties until his death in 1695). Between 1664 and 1683 there are several references to the "pedalls" in the accounts of the Lord Chamberlain,[14] and there can be no doubt that Purcell who, among other things, was "keeper, maker, mender, repayrer and tuner of the regalls, organs, virginals, flutes and recorders"[15] knew them well. He is the only major composer for the harpsichord who can be demonstrated to have played an instrument the stops of which were changed by pedals.

The accounts of the Lord Chamberlain show one item which throws some light on Purcell's instrument. In an entry for September 1675 we find: "a greate harpsichord with three ranks of strings for his Majesty's musick in the hall and in the privy lodgings."[16] The three ranks of strings must refer to 2x8′, 1x4′. Since the harpsichord was considered large it might also have had a lute like the Pedal.

It should be stressed that the Pedal apparently met no generally recognized musical need. After 1683 we hear no more about it until the pianistic taste of the later eighteenth century led various makers to pursue similar experiments.

The obscure moment of transition from the seventeenth century type of harpsichord to that of the eighteenth century is somewhat illuminated by the jottings of James Talbot, Regius Professor of Hebrew at Cambridge.[17] Between 1685 and 1701 Talbot gathered information on the various instruments in use at his time, possibly as the preliminary to writing a book. His notes were preserved by Dean Aldrich of Christ Church, Oxford. (See Appendix A for text and Plate XXXIX for Talbot's sketch of the layout of the instrument, to which the letters in his text refer.) Talbot does not seem to have known much about the harpsichord, but he took the trouble to measure an instrument which appar-

[14] See De Lafontaine, *The King's Musick*, p. 173 (Nov. 3, 1664), p. 200 (Jan. 29, 1667/8), p. 231 (April 27, 1671), p. 253 (April 25, 1673) (all repairs by Hingston); p. 299 (Feb. 7, 1675/6; "To Mr. Charles Haward for mending the harpsichords and pedalls in the Great Hall in the Privy Lodgings and for the private musick for 2 whole years"); p. 300 (Sept. 1675), p. 334 (Aug. 10, 1678), p. 361 (Dec. 25, 1683).

[15] *Ibid.*, pp. 255, 361.

[16] *Ibid.*, p. 300.

[17] Christ Church Music MS 1187. For an account of this manuscript see Anthony Baines, "James Talbot's Manuscript," *The Galpin Society Journal*, I (1948): 9. See also Fétis, *Biographie universelle*, "Aldrich, Henry."

ently belonged to an unidentified lady named Jenny. Unfortunately, he does not record the maker's name. The hasty penmanship and many corrections pose formidable problems to the editor, and the fragmentary quality of the expression does not make for easy interpretation. It should also be noted that the text cannot be taken as a description specifically of the English harpsichord, for Talbot was attempting to treat the harpsichords of all nations in one group. He cites Mersenne and Kircher, and one can occasionally identify material extracted from the former. Certain characteristically French and Italian materials such as cypress or leather-covered registers and *cormier* (wood of the service tree) are listed. His measurements, however, all seem to pertain to one English harpsichord.

The effort to pick out the solid facts of Jenny's instrument from the generalities Talbot listed in the same tables is almost fruitless, and perhaps it is wiser to attempt only a general definition of the English harpsichord as Talbot seems to have known it. Even this conception must be winnowed from information derived from Mersenne and Kircher and the results of Talbot's obvious acquaintance with the Italian tradition. Talbot seems to have known a 2x8' or 2x8', 1x4', single-manual [18] harpsichord, the general dimensions of which were slightly larger than the Ruckers single, model II. However, the English short scale produced a much deeper curve in the bentside than was characteristic of the Ruckers. The lute stop was a possibility. The registers were controlled by hand stops, perhaps inside the nameboard on the wrest plank. The case seems to have been covered with veneer at least on the interior. The keyboard, with its black naturals and ivory topped sharps, had a range of GG–c''' or C–c'''; the instrument was just wide enough to have had the larger range, but four octaves would have fitted more comfortably.

Although we have been unable to define a single archetype of the English seventeenth century harpsichord, certain characteristics appear to have been fundamental. Two eight-foot choirs, a single manual, and a tendency to brighten the ensemble by means of a lute stop rather than a four-foot were certainly basic. Although the Flemish tradition had been based on the 1x8', 1x4', conception, and the Anglo-Flemish claviorganum of Theeuwes had introduced an elaboration of that idea, the English seem to have accepted the Italian point of departure from two eight-foot choirs. Their first excursions carried them to the eight-foot lute stop, and it was only the elaborate Pedal which shows signs of having

[18] The length given for the C string was 60 inches. The total length of the harpsichord (74 inches) must be equal to this plus part of the wrest plank width, the nameboard thickness, the key length, and the distance from the bridge to the tail. There could not have been two manuals.

had a four-foot before 1675. It is significant that in the midst of the Pedal episode Charles Haward was still making 2x8' harpsichords supplied with a lute. Another indication of the English indifference toward the four-foot can be found in the nearly complete absence of ottavini among the products of their makers.

Both the Pedal and the lute stop imply a strong interest on the part of their designers in the expressive possibilities inherent in marked changes of tone color. It is thus somewhat surprising that the "Cassus" harpsichord does not seem to have had the buff stop which could have yielded another timbre very cheaply. (The replacement of the wrest plank in the Charles Haward has destroyed any evidence there might have been of an original buff stop. There is no buff stop in the instrument at present.) It is possible that the characteristic short scale was too easily damped by a buff which, therefore, was not very agreeable. We have seen that the buff was always rare on the short-scaled Italian harpsichords. Mace implies that the normal Pedal had none, although his instrument did.

In 1622 we found no provision for the easy changing of stops. By the time of "Cassus" (ca. 1650) the registers protruded through the cheekpiece in the Ruckers fashion, and even after the development of the Pedal we find Haward using the primitive Ruckers system. Hand stops were used on the Theeuwes but seem not to have been used again until late in the century when Talbot mentions them.

The remaining seventeenth century developments can be briefly summarized. We have observed the tendency of the English harpsichord makers to gradually turn away from the Italianate style characteristic of the early seventeenth century toward the Flemish inspiration found in the eighteenth. We have seen, for instance, that the light scantlings and elegant form of the harpsichord John Haward made in 1622 were transformed into the heavier instrument of his successor, Charles, in 1683. But we are not to find the English suddenly changing their style to an abject imitation of the Flemish as did the French makers toward the end of the seventeenth century. Even the English virginals, more obviously derived from the Ruckers models than any other English type, retained certain native features. The scales, for example, continue to reflect the English preference for short treble strings. This was apparently an Italian heritage, as were the boxwood key tops and multiple roses. The painted and gilded adornment and the oaken cases themselves remained typically English.

The sudden appearance of the oblong English virginals in the seventeenth century is a little puzzling. Like a marching platoon of soldiers they burst into view in 1641. Seventeen dated examples are found in the thirty-eight years between that date and 1679. There are no stragglers, no prototypes, and few variants. The ranges began long by Flemish standards (C–e′′′) and ended longer (GG/BB–f′′′),[19] but this is about the only evidence of evolution to be detected.

The English took over the basic layout of the Flemish *Spinetten* which placed the recessed keyboard to the left of center. The bridge sections and the leather covered mortises for the jacks with independent lower guide are both typical of the Antwerp style. But the boxwood key tops and the wooden pins engaging the rack at the rear of the key levers remind one of the Italian keyboards. On the other hand the proportions of the keyboard and the style of its workmanship are more like those of Antwerp than of Italy.

Several points of resemblance exist between the virginals and the contemporary English harpsichords. Both generally had oak cases or cases largely of oak but with deal spines. And both had shorter treble strings than the Ruckers would have advised. Most of the virginals had scales between 11 and 12 inches although some are as short as 10½ inches, and one (strangely enough, the earliest) is 13 inches. There seems to have been a good deal of random variation in the distance to the plucking point, from 1⅛ inches for an 11¹¹⁄₁₆-inch scale to 3½ inches for an 11¹³⁄₁₆-inch scale, but never with very good results. The best English virginal I have heard had a 13-inch scale; this is by Gabriel Townsend, 1641, now in the Conservatoire in Brussels.

Plate XVIII shows the layout and construction of a typical virginal. Handsome as these instruments were, their tone is not very good. The general quality is thin and unresonant and often rather nasal as a result of the close plucking point. The basses tend to be sour and the trebles feeble.

Sometime shortly after 1650 the northern instrument makers began to imitate the Italian style of bentside spinet, of which the earliest example seems to have been that of Zentis, made in 1631. The earliest English spinet known to me is dated 1660 and was made by Thomas Hitchcock the elder. This is about the time that Zentis was in England,[20] and it may very well have been made under his influence. Charles Haward, Stephen Keene, and John Player were possibly the most prolific of the seventeenth century spinet makers, and their lead was followed in the

[19] Frequently an extra string and mortise in the soundboard were provided for the lowest key. In case a tone not included in the short octave was needed the string could be tuned to the required pitch and the GG/BB jack placed in the extra mortise.

[20] See De Lafontaine, *The King's Musick*, p. 465.

eighteenth century by all of the minor makers. (It is noticeable that Kirckman and Shudi concentrated on harpsichords, apparently leaving the crumbs to their competition.)

The characteristic seventeenth century spinet was rather small (about four and one-half feet long) of walnut with either a curved or mitered tail. Sometimes the nameboard was decorated with marquetry. The keyboards were generally black with inlaid or white-topped sharps, and a common range was GG/BB–d'''. The tone was not good. The bass strings had too little soundboard, and the scale was likely to be short in the treble.

The chief interest of these spinets lies in certain seventeenth century expedients of instrument making which were preserved in them long after other means had been adopted by the harpsichord makers. Among the spinets we find the old-fashioned black naturals and inlaid sharps, rack keyboards, simple tongue sections, short scales, and composite construction fairly late in the eighteenth century. Plate XXIII gives the layout of a typical eighteenth century spinet. Its seventeenth century predecessor would have been similar but somewhat smaller.

We have seen that the seventeenth century harpsichord had a single manual. About the turn of the century the second manual seems to have been adopted by English makers. The first clearly dated evidence we have are two letters from Thomas Day to Edward Hanford dealing with the choice, purchase, and dispatch of a harpsichord destined for Woolas Hall, Pershore, where it remained until 1949.[21] The first letter, dated June 10, 1712, describes an instrument by John Player.

I have been this morning to see another harpsichord: it is of Player's making, with split or quarter notes [Player normally split the bottom two sharps of his spinets in order to fill out the short octave.] like Mrs. Stratford's . . . the upper sets of keys is an Eccho, very soft and in my opinion a little snaffling; but the other sett has two Unisons like Mrs. Stratford's belonging to it, but a more noble sound. The man asks 30 guineas; I believe that the Excellent Harpsichord of 45 guineas will come at 40 if not for 40 lb. It is handsomely vernish'd, with mixt gold and black, and must have a leather cover which will come to 24 sh: the first I mention'd is plain without and has a leather cover to it, tho' not very handsome . . . the Harpsichord I saw to-day has the full compass that Mrs. Stratford's has above; a long Octave to F below. The other Harpsichord is just of the same compass as hers but of a sound and make that is beyond exception . . . I do not find any difference between it and those that cost 80 and 100 guineas.

---

[21] The letters were quoted in the catalogue of Sotheby and Company, London, for a sale held Dec. 16, 1949, in which the letters and the harpsichord to which they pertained were sold. Reprinted, *Apollo* (London), March 1950, p. 92.

But this instrument was rejected in favor of one made by "Josephus Tisserand" of London in 1700. On August 23, 1712, Day wrote:

I sent you word when I went to Mrs. Hanford that I had bought you a Harpsichord . . . I saw it safely put in the wagon . . . You will be pleased to send a cart for it to Pershore, and that, before the wagon can be there, for fear there should not be due care taken in unloading it; for it is heavy and requires strong hands as well as care. When you have got it into the room you design for it, and taken off the cover and Cross Bars that are within the case, you will lay it down as softly as can be, with the open side of the case downwards, and then take up the case from the Harpsichord. Among the shavings you will find the stick and key tied to it . . . I fear one of the nails has razed the leather cover . . . The pins are tied with Packthread, but I hope to have an occasion to send you some sattin lacing for that purpose . . . The lid of the Harpsichord opens in two places; the first will do best for your usual Practice because the more you open it the sooner it will be out of tune. I hope you design to keep it in the grey room, that being as I take it the dryest . . . There are three Setts of Strings, which may be played on either all together, or every one by itself. One Set is an Octave to the other two . . . all together are only a thoroughbass to a Consort: for Lessons, any two sets of the three are more proper . . . If any Jack does not speak it is commonly by reason of the pen hanging on the string; and the way is not to beat the key or shave the Jack, but take your pen-knife and scrape the underside of the pen towards the point as lightly as ever you can; then smooth it with three or four strokes of your pen-knife haft. And if any Jack should not slip down, never shave it, but thrust it up and down, and at the most scrape it gently.

Both the name "Josephus Tisserand" and the style of his harpsichord lead me to believe that the instrument chosen for Mr. Hanford was made by a Frenchman resident in London [22] and therefore is not very pertinent to the history of English harpsichord making. Much more significant for our present purpose is the rejected harpsichord. John Player was born about 1635 and flourished until about 1708. He has left one extant virginal, dated 1664, and several undated spinets which were probably made later. This harpsichord cannot be dated exactly but the comparison of its price to that of the equivalent but handsomer Tisserand leads one to believe that it could not have been very much older than the Tisserand.

Day does not mention any difference in disposition between the two harpsichords, from which I infer that the Player, like the Tisserand, had only three registers, 2x8', 1x4'. There was no manual coupler, but the upper-manual jack was doglegged. Thus Player's harpsichord represents

[22] No reference to Tisserand has been found in the archives of either Paris or London.

an interesting stage in the development of the standard English disposition. Later we are to find the following invariable arrangement which is similar to that of the Player with the addition of a lute:

←Lute (8′)
←8′ Dogleg (also on the lower manual)
- - - - - - - - -
→8′
←4′.

Probably the earliest double harpsichord with the standard English disposition is the famous Thomas Hitchcock instrument [23] in the Victoria and Albert Museum. The date of this instrument has been the subject of some controversy. Boalch argues that Philip James (in *Early Keyboard Instruments*) is in error in assigning a date around 1690 to this harpsichord; he believes that the style is that of some twenty years later. In the absence of similar and dated specimens, I feel that this a question which cannot be resolved simply by an examination of the harpsichord.

Boalch assumes that there were two Thomas Hitchcocks. The first was the maker of two spinets dated 1660 and 1664; he was dead before February 1700, according to the records of the Joiner's Company. The younger Thomas was apprenticed in 1700 for a period of eight years. In that very year we find a spinet by a Thomas Hitchcock which Boalch ascribes to the novice apprentice. At a date Boalch variously reports as 1703 and 1705 Thomas inscribed a spinet jack with his name, the date, and a number which he records as both 54 and 45. This spinet came from the workshop of Edward Blunt who was not young Thomas' master. Whatever permutations of these numbers we choose (James gives no. 54 and 1703), it seems too many instruments to have been made by an apprentice, and even less likely to have been the work of a corpse. Thomas the Younger did not become free (of the Haberdashers' Company) until 1715. It seems to me that either Thomas the Elder lived on after 1700 or that there was another Thomas between the two suggested by Boalch.

In any case, the harpsichord in question (which, incidentally, is not identified "James," as James and Boalch have it, but is inscribed "Tom's D. Harpsichord" on the lowest key of both manuals) could have been made by any of these Thomas Hitchcocks, who cover a span at least from 1660 to 1733. It probably belongs to the period between 1690 and 1720.

[23] Illustrated in Philip James, *Early Keyboard Instruments* (London, 1930). See also Plate XIX, figures 4–7 and 9–13.

Like the 1683 Haward this Hitchcock has a round tail, and the walnut exterior set off by moldings is quite reminiscent of that instrument. The ivory keyboard, however, indicates a later date. Although the disposition is identical to much later English instruments, various features reveal its relationship to the harpsichords of the seventeenth century. The solid walnut case is something unknown in the time of Kirckman and Shudi, and the scale is noticeably shorter than their standard. The range is GG–g‴, a compass often found on Hitchcock spinets. There are three choirs, 2x8′, 1x4′. The disposition is:

←Lute (8′)
←8′ Dogleg (also on lower manual)
- - - - - - - - - - -
→8′
←4′.

There are four handstops, one for each register. The case is 91½ inches long, 33⅛ inches wide, and 9⁵⁄₁₆ inches deep. The cheekpiece and spine are ⅞ inch thick but the bentside is only ½ inch thick, probably to make it easier to bend. The scaling is as follows.

String	Eight-foot string length	Distance to plucking point: lute	Distance to plucking point: front eight-foot
g‴	4⅜ inches	⁷⁄₁₆ inch	2⅛ inches
c‴	6¼	¾	2⅞
c″	12⁷⁄₁₆	1¼	4⅛
c′	26	2	5¾
c	43¼	2⅛	6⅜
C	66⅜	2⅞	8
GG	68¼	3⅛	8⅝

A curious feature is the soundboard which is not laid in with its grain parallel to the spine but at an angle of about 35 degrees. This may be reminiscent of the bentside spinets which often had the soundboard grain oriented at various angles. There are other points of relationship to the spinets of the time: the solid case, not paneled on the exterior but veneered on the inside; the molding in the inner edge of the case above the soundboard and the molding that runs around the lower edge of the case to mount vertically at the junction of bentside and spine; and the "skunktail" sharps (Plate XIX, figure 7). The Hitchcocks continued to produce work in the style of this harpsichord for many years. Boalch illustrates [24]

[24] *Makers of the Harpsichord and Clavichord*, plate XXIX. Spinet numbered 1335. Sulgrave Manor, Northamptonshire.

a spinet by Thomas the Younger, having a very similar case, which was made about 1730.

If the constructional features of Hitchcock's harpsichord reveal a sensitivity to influence which may bespeak a certain uncertainty on the part of its maker, the disposition (except for the lack of a buff stop) was solidly established in the form that all English double harpsichords would follow for the remainder of the eighteenth century. The English makers do not seem to have felt the need for further experiment nor were they influenced by the French instruments which had been rendered so much more flexible by the addition of the manual coupler. We have already seen that the primary elements of the English disposition — the dogleg and the lute stop — were not peculiar to English instruments. About the time Player, Hitchcock, and their contemporaries were developing this disposition, van Blankenburg seems to have been experimenting with his lute stop at The Hague (1708). We now know that he did not invent it as he claimed, for we have found the lute stop in England during the seventeenth century, spasmodically in Italy, and (although the evidence is not clear) in Flanders at the end of the period of the Couchets. We know that van Blankenburg used a dogleg, that the French seventeenth century makers certainly did, and that a double harpsichord by Petrus Ionnes Couchet (1669) in the Gemeente Museum, The Hague, now has one, although subsequent restoration makes it difficult to determine whether Couchet's was original or not. However, the combination of the lute and the dogleg occurs so much more often in England than anywhere else that one naturally thinks of them as English.

An intermediate position between the English disposition and the four-jack disposition with manual coupler that the French eighteenth century makers gave the Ruckers doubles was taken in 1702[25] by the maker of a harpsichord in the Conservatoire, Brussels, marked "H.V.L.," obviously of Flemish origin:

$$\leftarrow 8' \text{ (in the main gap)}$$
$$\rightarrow 8' \text{ Dogleg (also available on lower manual)}$$

- - - - - - - - - -

$$\leftarrow 4'$$
$$\leftarrow 8'.$$

An instrument by Ionnes Daniel Dulcken (1745), now in the Smithsonian Institution, approached the English even more closely by transforming the front eight-foot into a true cut-through lute:

[25] Not 1762, as Mahillon says.

←Lute (8′)
→ 8′ Dogleg (also available on
                lower manual)

- - - - - - - - - -

←4′
←8′.

At first glance the Dulcken disposition seems almost identical to the English, but the experienced player would soon note significant differences. Both are about equally successful in producing rapid alterations between piano and forte or between two violently contrasting tone colors. However, unlike the Dulcken the English disposition offers the possibility of dialoguing one eight-foot (the lute) against another (on the lower manual), an effect often required in contrapuntal textures. Sometimes Dulcken arranged his upper manual so that it could be drawn forward bodily, disengaging it from the dogleg. In this version his disposition is more flexible than the English. Both dispositions, however, would be better if the dogleg were replaced by a true manual coupler.

The period between the time of the Hitchcock harpsichord and the establishment of the workshops of Burkat Shudi (ca. 1729) and Jacob Kirckman[26] (1738) is dominated by the shadowy figure of a certain Hermann Tabel. According to James Shudi Broadwood[27] this worthy learned his trade under the last of the Couchets. Tabel seems to have settled in London about 1700 where both Kirckman and Shudi are known to have worked for him, and Kirckman became Tabel's successor by marrying his widow. Burney referred to him as "the celebrated Tabel,"[28] but Burney obviously was not very familiar with either his life or his work, for he fixed the commencement of Kirckman's employment as 1740, after Tabel's death (1738). Apparently Tabel was a rather insubstantial figure even during his lifetime, for in 1733 he had to insert an advertisement in the St. James's Evening Post denying rumors of his death.[29] If, as many modern authorities hold, Tabel served as the connecting link between the Flemish and the English traditions, it must be observed that he had had a good deal of assistance going back into the mid-sixteenth century. The only element of the Flemish style which

[26] Many authorities spell the name "Kirkman." Kirckman, however, always signed his instruments as we give it.
[27] Some Notes Made by J. S. Broadwood, 1838, with Observations and Elucidations by H. F. Broadwood (London, 1862).
[28] Abraham Rees, ed., The Cyclopaedia (London, 1819), s.v. Jacob Kirckman.
[29] No. 2774, Feb. 22–24, 1733; quoted by Boalch, Makers of the Harpsichord and Clavichord, p. 121.

Tabel might have introduced into England is the dogleg and lute stop disposition which seems to have been in the air in Flanders at the time of his apprenticeship. However, one of the elements of that disposition — the lute — was more indigenous to England than to Flanders, and the dogleg is too obvious (and too widely known) to have required an intermediary. Although it cannot be proved, it seems likely that the traditional role ascribed to Tabel and his posthumous fame were the fabrication of both Kirckman and Shudi in their dotage, a reminiscence of the good old days and a shrewd effort to claim descent from the Ruckers in order to share their eternal glory. The only extant harpsichord signed by Tabel is of dubious origin and similar to many later English harpsichords.

An interesting instrument[30] of the period before the near monopoly by Kirckman and Shudi began was made in 1738 by Joseph Mahoon, who was also the maker of several extant spinets and the round-tailed single-manual harpsichord of 1742 mentioned above. The somewhat lowered case and a strip of vertical molding at the front of the cheekpiece, a vestige of the batten placed there by earlier makers to retain the lockboard, indicate the antiquated style of this 1738 instrument. The case, of plain walnut, is inlaid with a checkered stringing to divide it into the panels which were to be the mark of nearly all English harpsichords after this date. The range, standard until about 1775, is FF–f‴, FF♯ missing. There are two keyboards. Four registers of jacks, one of which is a lute stop, pluck the 2x8′, 1x4′ choirs. The disposition is interesting:

←Lute (8′)
→ 8′ Dogleg (also on lower
              manual)
· - - - - - - - - -
←8′
←4′.

It resembles the Flemish eighteenth century harpsichords in providing a true unison on the upper manual. Since the lute and lower manual eight-foot pluck the identical choir, their dampers would produce interference if both stops were on at the same time. Directions written in a contemporary hand indicate that this effect is to be used in lieu of a buff stop. This expedient is not very satisfactory because the dampers are too far from the ends of the strings to work well as buff pads. There is a tendency for the strings to be too well damped or for a node to form at the damper causing the string to sound at a higher pitch than its fundamental.

[30] Privately owned in England. One of the keys is signed "Broom Smith, 1738."

Harpsichord making in England from the middle of the eighteenth century was dominated by two firms, founded respectively by Burkat Shudi and Jacob Kirckman. A few minor makers continued to practice their trade, and rather late in the century a firm of dealers, Longman and Broderip, sold a fairly large number of instruments which seem to have been made for them by various makers. As we have remarked, most of the less successful makers, such as John Hitchcock and Baker Harris, seem to have devoted themselves mainly to spinets, while the Kirckman and Shudi houses produced almost nothing but harpsichords.

The biographical details of the lives of Kirckman and Shudi [31] are too well documented in standard works of reference to require other than cursory treatment here. Both were born on the continent, Shudi in Switzerland and Kirckman in Germany. Shudi, leaving Tabel about 1728, was the first to set up shop independently. His earliest extant harpsichord is dated in the following year, but it has been so thoroughly restored that it is impossible to authenticate either its date or present form. Kirckman became independent in 1738, but his earliest known harpsichord is dated 1744.[32]

Shudi dated and numbered his harpsichords, a practice which enables us not only to estimate the total of his production but also to calculate his yearly output. The highest number so far discovered on any Shudi harpsichord is 1155. About fifty of his instruments are known to have survived into modern times. Boalch has calculated his yearly output as follows: thirteen instruments per year in the decade 1740–1749, fifteen per year from 1750 to 1769, twenty-three per year from 1770 to 1779, and twenty-five per year from 1780 to 1789. The last instrument is dated 1793.

All of Kirckman's extant harpsichords were made between the years 1750 and 1800, but there is reason to believe that the firm produced a harpsichord as late as 1809.[33] About one hundred ten are known to exist. Thus one is justified in guessing that Kirckman's total production was twice that of Shudi, or about 2000.

Both Kirckman and Shudi appear to have produced three models: a single, 2x8'; a single, 2x8', 1x4'; and a double, 2x8', 1x4', lute. These were usually, but not always, equipped with a buff stop. A little over half

[31] See the appropriate articles in *Grove's Dictionary* and Boalch, *Makers of the Harpsichord and Clavichord*, and William Dale, *Tschudi the Harpsichord Maker* (London, 1913).

[32] Privately owned in New York according to information kindly supplied by Hugh Gough.

[33] Carl Engel quotes Joseph Kirkman (dead 1877) to that effect. See Boalch, *Makers of the Harpsichord and Clavichord*, p. 61.

of the extant instruments have two manuals. James[34] quotes Shudi's usual prices as 35 guineas for the 2x8' single, 40 guineas for the single with four-foot, 50 guineas for a single with swell, and 80 guineas for a double with swell. Kirckman made a few very handsome instruments adorned on the interior with any of several styles of marquetry, which were placed on rather clumsy cabriole stands. Shudi concentrated more on providing musical resources than on fancy woodwork, and his most elaborate instruments were given the extended range, CC–f'''.

Many of the eighteenth century English harpsichords, both double and single, were fitted with register-operating pedals known as "machine stops." This was such a simple addition and so desirable in the late eighteenth century that the original date of the invention is hopelessly obscured by late accretions to existing instruments. On the double the machine stop took the following form. There was one pedal (on the left side of the stand) and a hand stop on the left cheekpiece. When this stop was drawn toward the player the pedal was disengaged and the registers were controlled by the hand stops arranged on the nameboard. When the hand stop was pushed toward the nameboard, all of the registers except the back eight-foot were engaged by a mechanism sliding along the outside of the spine, and the hand stops no longer could be used to control them. When the pedal was in the up position, the registration was 1x8' (dogleg) on the upper manual and 2x8', 1x4' (including dogleg) on the lower. The back eight-foot is here presumed to have been left on. When the pedal was depressed, the dogleg eight-foot and the four-foot were taken off and the lute put on. The registration was then 1x8' (lute) on the upper manual and 1x8' (back eight-foot) on the lower. The machine stop thus provided a sudden transition from forte to piano.

Various versions of the machine stop existed for singles, most often taking off one eight-foot, or one eight-foot and the four-foot, when the pedal was depressed. Sometimes the buff stop was applied to the remaining eight-foot. A second pedal was occasionally provided for the buff stop.

In 1769 Shudi patented a device called the Venetian swell (see Appendix D). This consisted of a cover fitted inside the case over the soundboard and formed of longitudinal louvers rotating on their long axes. When a pedal on the right was depressed, these louvers opened, theoretically providing a crescendo. In practice the Venetian swell was not very successful since the tone was dull when the swell was closed and brightened immediately when the louvers were cracked open. Even

[34] *Early Keyboard Instruments*, p. 42.

with the swell completely open the tone was not as bright and loud as it would have been had the louvers not been there. The whole swell mechanism was hinged so that it could be raised with the lid and retained there by means of the prop.

One is tempted to assume that Kirckman desperately countered this device by providing the "nag's head swell" in which a specially hinged segment of the lid was raised by a pedal. Unfortunately the evidence is not clear. Kirckman intermittently fitted both types of swell, and some of his nag's heads are later than other of his Venetian swells. Furthermore, the nag's head was used on a 1754 Kirckman, that is, fifteen years before Shudi patented his swell. It should be noted that, as with the machine stop, it is simple to add a Venetian swell to an existing instrument. Shudi appears to have used his swell for two or three years before patenting it, but one cannot be certain.

Virtually all of the English eighteenth century harpsichords were veneered. A molding ran around the edge of the case at the bottom (Plate XXI, figure 11). The sides were divided into panels, two or three on the bentside and one each on cheekpiece and tail. The spines often were not veneered. These panels were outlined by an inlaid line of plain boxwood or a more elaborate stringing which appeared in several versions. The stringing in its turn was surrounded by a cross-banding of veneer similar or contrasted to that of the bentside panel. Generally speaking, the earlier instruments were veneered in walnut and the later ones in mahogany. Toward the end of the century satinwood is occasionally found. The more elaborate harpsichords often had veneered lids and sometimes even veneered stands. A molding was always placed on the underside of the lid (Plate XXI, figure 10) to overlap the edge of the case when closed. Interiors are found in dark and light versions. The dark were often in a burl such as walnut and the light in sycamore, maple, or mahogany.

The stands were always of the trestle type, that is, four legs connected by stretchers. The legs could be dismounted from the long stretchers for transport. Various sorts of legs are found: square untapered with a molding cut into the outer arris, turned baluster, a combination of turned baluster and cabriole, and square tapered. The square tapered was the last type to appear. Most stands were mounted on casters.

Large brass strap hinges of a standard pattern were used on most English harpsichords until about 1780. These were sometimes chased. The hinges were complemented by handsome hooks retaining the lid, brass stop knobs, and an escutcheon.

Keyboards were always covered in ivory with ebony sharps. The key fronts (Plate XXI, figure 9) were formed by a molding of sycamore.

The soundboards were not painted. Kirckman and sometimes Longman and Broderip used roses; Shudi, never. There were three types of Kirckman rose, always of gilded metal. The earliest was formed by the initials "J.K." in an intertwined knot pattern. The most common shows King David playing a harp with the initials "I.K." The latest type was stamped rather than cast, and various musical instruments formed the elements of the design.

In the later harpsichords the upper edge of the nameboard was lowered about ¾ inch below the edge of the case so that a music desk could be slipped in as we find in the modern grand piano. The earlier ones show no provision for an integral music desk.

Although these almost mass-produced harpsichords did not have as musical a disposition as their French contemporaries, it is possible that they represent the culmination of the harpsichord maker's art. For sheer magnificence of tone, reedy trebles and sonorous basses, no other harpsichords ever matched them. Their actions were workmanlike, and as furniture they shared the inspired decorum of most Georgian design. As playing instruments they are the most practical of all antiques to restore. The only reproach which might be leveled at them is that they are too good. The tone is so characteristic and luxurious that it almost interferes with the music. English harpsichords are at their best in noble and powerful passages, least successful where clarity and restraint are required.

I have chosen a Kirckman double of the era 1770 as the model for Plates XX, XXI, and XXII, which illustrate how these results were obtained. It is slightly atypical in that the bridge is a little farther from the edge of the case than in most examples, but the harpsichord is even better than most English instruments.

The plates are almost self-explanatory. The casework of these instruments was of oak, the corners dovetailed, and the bottom of deal. Wrest planks were of oak veneered in walnut or mahogany. The frame members were of spruce or pine. The sloping props to the belly rail (Plate XXI, figure 1) should be noted, as well as the absence of blocks supporting the wrest plank, which was retained by stub tenons and many small dowels. This was a poor feature, and the wrest planks of English harpsichords often are found wrenched out of position.

English soundboards average ⅛ inch thick, and many were tapered from bass to treble. The example illustrated is ¹⁰⁄₆₄ inch thick along the spine and at the bentside near the tail (the bass), and it tapers to ⁵⁄₆₄ inch in the treble. Most do not show such a marked taper. They vary from %₆₄ inch to ⅞₄ inch.

Key levers were of pine or lime, and a three-rail key bed with front rail pins (Plate XXII, figure 4) was always used on the lower manual. The upper-manual key bed (Plate XXII, figure 1) was formed by a panel of ½-inch oak to which the three rails were applied. This key bed could be removed by sliding it forward like a drawer.

Jacks and registers were of pear, the registers (Plate XXII, figure 10) either cut out of a solid piece or built up as explained in Chapter VI. Lower guides were cut out of the solid and were not leather-covered. The characteristic form of the jack and its tongue (Plate XXII, figures 5–9) should be noted, particularly the staple at the top. This served both as a back stop to the tongue and as a reinforcement to the jack. English jacks were not tapered.

The lurid final chapters of the history of the French harpsichord are not quite equaled in England insofar as the effort to imitate bird calls and orchestral voices is concerned, but England produced its share of mechanical marvels for all that (see Appendix D for some English patents referring to the harpsichord). Some were sensibly concerned with improvements to the reliability of the instrument. Some are reminiscent of experiments tried on the Continent: the gut-string harpsichord, and the *Geigenwerk*, which reappears in the guise of a "celestina." [35] An English specialty seems to have been the combination piano-harpsichord, patented by Joseph Merlin in 1774. Two examples are known to me. The earlier, now in the Smithsonian Institution, Washington, is inscribed:

Combined
Harpsichord & Grand Piano
Upper Bank Piano
Lower Harpsichord
Robertus Stodart Londini Fecit 1777
Inventor & Patentee Robertus Stodart.

Stodart's role as patentee must refer not to the combination of piano and harpsichord but to the details of the piano action which he had patented that same year. This instrument is fundamentally a piano with a typically short scale (11 inches) and three eight-foot choirs arranged close together in the usual manner of pianos. There are two jacks which pluck the outside strings of each group of three, giving a 2x8′ unison.

[35] See Russell, *The Harpsichord and Clavichord*, p. 177.

The second, in the Deutches Museum, Munich, was a more elaborate effort by Merlin himself. The inscription reads: "Josephus Merlin Privelegiarius Novi Forte Piano No. 80 Londini 1780." Although there is only a single manual, there are four choirs, 1x16', 2x8', 1x4', arranged on three bridges. The sixteen-foot bridge is high enough to permit its strings to clear the eight-foot bridge, but the nuts are contrived so that there are only two levels of strings at the gap: 2x8', 1x16', above, and 1x4' beneath. Three registers of jacks pluck 1x16', 1x8', and 1x4', and the piano hammers strike from above, 2x8', 1x16'. Two pedals control respectively the piano action and the sixteen-foot. There is "Celestial Harpe" which undamps a choir of eight-foot strings, permitting them to vibrate sympathetically. A "Welsh Harp" buffs the sixteen-foot. In addition to all of this, Merlin provided a device to record the improvisations of the fevered performer. A continuous belt of paper is slowly advanced by clockwork while sixty-one little pencils, activated by bell-cranks and trackers, mark the duration of each note played. The resulting record looks a little like a player-piano roll and must be deciphered.

Although Merlin was a formidable inventor in his own right,[36] the proprietor of "Merlin's Cave" of mechanical phenomena, presenting a grateful world with the wheel chair and the roller skate, he was not solely responsible for the music writing device. Fétis documents the claims of several other inventors to that honor.[37] Unfortunately no records of eighteenth century improvisations have ever come to light.

The transition from harpsichord to piano was more orderly in England than on the Continent in that the two pre-eminent firms of harpsichord makers continued to dominate the field after the harpsichord had been finally replaced by the piano. Shudi's name was dropped from the nameboards of the instruments made in his old shop during the nineties, but the firm still exists under the name John Broadwood and Sons. The successors of Jacob Kirckman also continued to make pianos until relatively recent times. Until about 1825 pianos made by Broadwood and Kirckman were almost identical in outward appearance to the harpsichords of fifty years earlier.

[36] See Percy A. Scholes, *The Great Dr. Burney* (London, 1948), II, 202.
[37] See articles on J. F. Unger, J. Hohlfeld, J. Creed, J. Freeke, Engramelle, and, in the supplement, Careyre and Baudouin.

CHAPTER FIVE · GERMANY

No German instruments except a few ottavini have survived which were made before 1700. This is not surprising in view of the disturbances of the Thirty Years War which would have eliminated harpsichord making almost completely in Germany from the time of Praetorius until well after the middle of the seventeenth century. However, even in Praetorius' time most of the instruments in use seem to have been imported, and by the time that harpsichord making was possible again, French influence in Germany was dominant in every field. The typical eighteenth century German harpsichord was strongly influenced by the French type and thus was ultimately derived from the instruments of the Ruckers.

To say that the German makers may not have developed their instrumental type *ab ovo* is not to say that Germans did not know the harpsichord in early times. The word "clavicymbolum," for example, appears in the rules of the Minnesingers in 1404, and there are descriptions and illustrations of jack-action instruments in Sebastian Virdung's *Musica getutscht* (Basel, 1511). A series of makers' names can be provided from the end of the fifteenth century, but this early phase does not appear to have been particularly important or original. Very little trace can be found of a native tradition like that we have seen preceding the introduction of the Ruckers type of harpsichord into England and France.

Since extant harpsichords from the earliest period are lacking, we are forced to turn to documentary sources to glean what knowledge we can of the instruments then in use in Germany. There is not much useful information to be obtained from Virdung and his imitators, Agricola, and Luscinius, beyond the bare fact that they were acquainted with jack instruments.[1] Virdung provides extremely crude illustrations of what he calls a *Virginal*, *Clavicimbalum*, and *Claviciterium*. The distinction between the first two is not clear since both appear to have been small

---

[1] Martin Agricola, *Musica instrumentalis deudsch* (Wittenberg, 1528). Ottomar Luscinius, *Musurgia seu praxis musicae* (Strasbourg, 1536).

rectangular instruments. Because the engraver of Virdung's woodblocks failed to reverse the drawings of the *Clavicimbalum* and the *Claviciterium*, those instruments appear in mirror image, and this must be taken into account in reckoning their ranges. There is also the chance that the engraver reversed the keyboards in his blocks but failed to reverse the string band. Against this grim possibility we are helpless. In any case, Virdung's *Virginal* appears to have had a range of A–b″ (38 keys), top b♭ missing. The *Clavicimbalum* shows the apparent range B–d‴ (40 keys), but it seems likely that the true range was G/B–d‴. The *Claviciterium*, or upright harpsichord, which looks very much like the small portative organs of the period, had a range of F–g″ (38 keys), low F♯ missing. Virdung remarks that the *Claviciterium* had gut strings[2] and was newly invented. This, as we have seen, seems to have been the chronic condition of clavicytheria from 1511 until 1800. Since none of these instruments is longer than about two feet (judging from the keyboards), they must have sounded at four-foot pitch.

In Praetorius' great work,[3] published in 1619, nearly all of the keyboard instruments illustrated are clearly of foreign origin. He shows a Flemish virginal; an Italian pentagonal spinet; an ottavino probably Italian in origin but possibly descended from the *Virginal* or *Clavicimbalum* of Virdung and his copyists; and a clavicytherium, the origin of which is difficult to specify. (See Plates XXV and XXVI for reproductions of these illustrations.) The keyboard brackets of the clavicytherium seem to be Italian in style, but the case outline with the round tail is not typical of seventeenth century Italian instruments. However, this outline is found in France and England later in the century, and it is not impossible that the idea of a round tail goes back to the early seventeenth century in France. Mersenne and Kircher both show a clavicytherium with Italianate keyboard brackets (their plates are too abstract to define the tail form),

---

[2] Virdung gives no description of the *Clavichordium* nor of the *Virginal* except to imply that they were stringed instruments with keys and to illustrate them. On the following page, which shows illustrations of a hurdy-gurdy (*Lyra*), a *Clavicymbalum*, and a *Claviciterium*, he makes the following remarks without specifying to which instrument he is referring: "This is like the *Virginal* except that it has different strings of the gut of sheep, and nails which make it harp. It also has quills like the *Virginal*. It is newly invented and I have seen only one" ("Das ist eben als das virginale/ allein es hat ander saiten von den dörmen [der] schaue und negel die es harpfen machen hat auch federkile als das virginale. ist neulich erfunden und ich hab ir nür eins gesehen"). The fact that the instrument was "newly invented" makes it likely that Virdung intended to refer to the *Claviciterium*.

[3] Michael Praetorius, *Syntagma musicum* (1615–1620). The second volume, *De organographia*, which contains most of the information pertinent to our study, appeared at Wolfenbüttel in 1619.

and Mersenne definitely connects the upright instrument with Italy. Praetorius illustrates three clavichords: two appear to have been of native manufacture, but one is described as of the Italian type. He shows a fine Italian harpsichord which is labeled *"Clavicymbel*, a fourth lower than choir pitch" (see Plate XXIV).

If we accept Mendel's [4] conclusion that Praetorius' two pitches were one tone apart, choir pitch lying a semitone above the modern standard and chamber pitch a full tone above that, the harpsichord Praetorius illustrated (see Plate XXIV) must have been tuned about a major third below modern pitch. However, the whole question is complicated by Praetorius' peculiar use of the terminology of pitch in his discussion. From his account of the history of pitch one gathers that pitch had risen gradually to a level which he regarded as too high. This standard was generally known as choir pitch and seems to have been about a minor third above modern pitch. Praetorius, however, "favors the distinction made in Prague and other Catholic chapels, between choir pitch and chamber pitch." [5] In other words, the pitch usually known as choir pitch has been renamed chamber pitch, and a new standard, one tone lower, has been provided for use in churches. If the "choir pitch" (*Chor-Ton*) in Praetorius' legend refers to the standard nomenclature rather than his, the harpsichord illustrated is only one tone below modern standard pitch, and possibly only a semitone, for Praetorius also remarks that some persons "have presumed to raise our present pitch another semitone higher." [6] It seems likely that Praetorius was using the standard nomenclature, for a short-scaled Italian harpsichord could not sound well tuned a major third below a' (at 440).

In his text Praetorius does not specify the ordinary range or the disposition of the harpsichord, so we are forced to glean what we can from his illustration. It is not quite clear where the keyboard leaves off at top and bottom, and the end blocks begin, but the range is probably C/E–d''', which is usual for an Italian harpsichord of the period. The apparent disposition, 2x8', 1x4', is surprising. One would not expect to find a four-foot choir and certainly not more than two stops. Again, the illustration is somewhat ambiguous and there may have been only one eight-foot choir. Although two bridges, an eight-foot and a four-foot, are clearly shown on the soundboard, the nuts and wrest pins are more difficult to make out. The eight-foot strings are plainly grouped in pairs, indicating

[4] "Pitch in the 16th and Early 17th Centuries."
[5] *Syntagma musicum*, II, 14.
[6] *Ibid.*

two choirs, but the artist could have been led astray in his drawing by the memory of 2x8′ Italian harpsichords. This question cannot be finally resolved, but there is no reason why the instrument could not have had three choirs. No Italian harpsichord of this early date with three choirs survives, but the Ruckers began to fit a third register to their large singles a few years later.

Although Praetorius' remarks on the various jack-action instruments are brief, he is discursive enough to make several comments which deserve our attention. Chapter XXXVII[7] opens the complex question of terminology. It appears that Praetorius' contemporaries were in the habit of indiscriminately applying the term *Instrument* to all keyboard instruments. Praetorius uses *Symphony*, *Spinetta*, and *Virginal* to refer to eight-foot spinets and virginals, and *Spinetta* or *Octav-Instrumentlin* for ottavini; the harpsichord was known to him under various forms of the word *Clavicymbel* as well as *Flügel* or *Schweinskopff*.

In Chapter XXXVIII Praetorius mentions ottavini tuned both a fifth and an octave high. He remarks that the ottavini were generally placed on top of larger instruments, or in them (an interesting parallel to the Flemish double virginals). This practice was to leave its mark on the disposition of the first expressive two-manual harpsichords, and in Germany one will find occasionally the harpsichord with the four-foot on the upper manual, even in the eighteenth century.

Chapter XXXIX deals with the harpsichord itself, and Praetorius, like Mersenne, seems to have known at least one very large instrument:

> The harpsichord or *Gravecymbalum* is a longish *Instrument* which to some is a *Flügel* [wing] because it is almost in that shape: by others (but badly) it would be called a *Schweinskopff* [pig's head] because it ends in a point like the head of a wild boar; and it is of a strong, bright, rather lovely tone and resonance, more than the others, because of the doubled, tripled, even quadrupled strings; just as one I saw which had two *Aequal* [eight-foot unisons], a quint [fifth or possibly twelfth], and a little octave [four-foot] of strings; and quite sweetly and splendidly they rang amongst one another.

The harpsichord that Praetorius knew best was probably considerably simpler than this one with its four choirs. As we have seen,[8] the quint seems to have been in the air in the early seventeenth century, but if it had been very common or very successful it would surely have left more trace in later times.

Praetorius provides in Chapter XL a discussion of the variable intonation keyboard. He suggests that d♯ and g♯ be split and then goes on to

[7] All chapter references are to *De organographia*, pt. 2.
[8] See page 95.

describe a more elaborate keyboard he had seen at Carl Luyton's, organist to the Emperor in Prague. This keyboard had been made in Vienna about 1590, and "not only did it have all chromatic tones, such as b♭, c♯, d♯, f♯, and g♯ in double form throughout, but it was also provided with a special chromatic tone necessary for the enharmonic genus, between the e's and f's such that the instrument had seventy-seven keys in all in its four octaves."

The clavicytherium and claviorganum are mentioned very briefly without adding anything to our information. Then in Chapter XLIII Praetorius raises another of those ghosts which drift thinly over the surface of our subject, too unsubstantial to be defined, yet too persistent to be denied. We have already noted two instruments of more or less Flemish origin which are fitted with a stop of mysterious purpose, and an elaborate Italian version of the same device. Now Praetorius adds another example to our list. "The *Arpichordum*," he writes, "is a *Symphony* or *Virginall* on which a harplike sound [*Harffenirender Resonanz*] is produced by means of a special stop which governs brass hooks [*Messingshäcklin*] under the strings." These instruments all have a set of metal pins which are brought into light contact with the strings by a variety of methods, producing a buzzing noise. One would not normally connect such a buzz with the tone of a harp, but both Praetorius and Virdung seem to have done so. Indeed Praetorius seems to have found this sound to be peculiarly typical of the harp. In Chapter XXXIV he writes: "for the strings of the harp also rattle and crackle [*knirren und schnarren*] if they come into contact with the pegs with which they are fastened into the frame of the instrument, at the bottom. This rattling is usually referred to as harplike sound [*Harffenierender Resonanz*]." And Virdung, in an obscure remark about the clavicytherium, identifies the tone of a harp with the sound of a metal pin touching a vibrating string: "und negel die es harpfen machen" ("and nails which make it harp").

In his *Musica mechanica organoedi* Adlung quotes Praetorius' description of the *Arpichordum* as if he had not seen it himself, but some years earlier he had given a rather full description of one version of the device in the *Anleitung zu der musicalischen Gelahrtheit*.[9] Fifteen years later Sprengel[10] mentions a similar stop: "Sometimes the harpsichord maker puts a second batten behind the buff stop [*Lautenzuge*] on the soundboard side which has the same arrangement as the foregoing except that it is not covered with cloth. If one damps the strings at the same time with the buff stop and with this bare batten, the strings jar, and therefore

[9] Note r to paragraph 246.
[10] P. N. Sprengel, *Handwerk und Künste in Tabelen* (Berlin, 1773), XI, 265.

this last stop is called the *Schnarrwerk* [a term which generally refers to the reed stops of an organ]."

Table 14 summarizes the various types of jack-action instruments described by Praetorius. It seems likely that only the first four types were at all common. The glimpse, brief but startlingly clear, that Praetorius has given us of the instruments in use in Germany at the beginning of the seventeenth century is probably pertinent until near the end of the

Table 14. Jack-action instruments described by Praetorius

Instrument	Type	Range	Disposition	Remarks
Virginal	Flemish style	C/E–c'''	1x8'	*Arpichordum* stop can be fitted
Spinet	Italian pentagonal style	C/E–f'''	1x8'	*Arpichordum* stop can be fitted
Ottavino	Five sided square ends. No nationality can be ascribed	C/E–b''	1x4'	Can be tuned a fifth higher than 8' tone. Often set inside of or on top of a larger virginal
Harpsichord	Italian style	C/E–d'''	2x8', 1x4'	Decorated exterior makes outer box unlikely. Could have had two, three, or four choirs. See next entry below
Large Harpsichord	(Not illustrated)		2x8', 1 x quint, 1x4'	
Clavicytherium	Italian (?) style. Round tail, non-inner-outer	C/E–c'''	1x8'	May have had gut strings since it is said to sound like a harp or cithern
Claviorganum	Virginal or harpsichord mounted on a box containing the organ pipes			

century when the characteristic native instruments began to appear in significant numbers. One indication that this was the case is to be found in an inventory dated 1681 of the musical instruments in the "Churfürstliche Sächssische Jüngste Gerichte- und Instrumentkammer" in Dresden.[11] Five of the items of interest to us are:

1) "1 harpsichord [*Clavicimbul*] with two registers, of cypress with an ivory keyboard to GG, in a black box. It is without flaw except that the soundboard is somewhat cracked."

[11] F. A. Drechsel, "Alte Dresdener Instrumenteninventare," *Zeitschrift für Musikwissenschaft*, 10 (1927–1928): 495–499.

2) "1 virginal [*Instrument*], single strung and rectangular, of which the front board and lock are missing."

3) "1 virginal [*Instrument*], single strung and rectangular, of cypress, somewhat damaged, and half of the lid of the outer box over the keys is broken away."

4) "1 virginal [*Instrument*], single strung and rectangular, with a buff stop [*Lauten Zug*], lacks the lock."

5) "1 harpsichord [*Clavizimbul*] with four registers, one ivory keyboard to GG, without lock."

Most of these instruments are certainly not very ambitious compared to the contemporary French or Flemish productions, and the list has much the eclectic air of Praetorius' *Theatrum instrumentorum*. The first harpsichord and the virginal (3) were certainly Italian since they were made of cypress and inserted into outer cases. Item 2 is of uncertain origin, but item 4, equipped with a buff stop, could not have been Italian. It will be noted that the fifth instrument has the same type of keyboard and an identical compass in the bass as the first. Four registers on a single-manual harpsichord were rare at any time or place. It is possible that the instrument was strung 2x8′, 1x4′, and that the fourth "register" was only a buff stop. In that case the harpsichord would either have been a Flemish single or of native origin.

The Germans were never as fond of the harpsichord as the French, and their country was not to be a world center of harpsichord making like Flanders or Italy. German harpsichords were always few compared to those of other nations. More characteristic products of German makers were the clavichords and organs which encroached on the domain of the harpsichord from opposite sides by absorbing the energies of the makers or by competing at a price far below the cost of a good harpsichord. Makers seem to have been more an item of export than their wares. Burney observes that "the Germans work much better out of their own country, than they do in it, if we may judge by the *harpsichords* of Kirkman and Shudi; the *pianofortes* of Backers; and the organs of *Snetzler*; which far surpass, in goodness, all the keyed instruments that I met with, in my tour through Germany." [12]

As usual we must discount Burney's chauvinism, but we are able to document his observation by pointing out that harpsichord making and the woodworking trades in general were in German hands in Paris during the eighteenth century. In his *L'Art du menuisier ébéniste* Roubo remarks, "Cet établi . . . se nomme *établi à L'Allemande*, (soit qu'il ait été inventé en Allemagne, ou, ce qui est plus vraisemblable, par des

---

[12] *The Present State of Music in Germany*, II, 145.

Ébénistes Allemands, qui sont en très-grand nombre à Paris)" ("That bench . . . is called German, either because it was invented in Germany, or, what is more reasonable, by German cabinetmakers who are very numerous in Paris").[13] Among the Parisian harpsichord makers, Jean Goermans, Benoist Stehlin, Jean Henry Moers, Joseph Treyer ("l'Empereur"), Jacques Malade, and the two Hemsch brothers are all known to have been born in German-speaking countries. There were many others with German names of whose origins we are still ignorant.

There is considerable evidence that the German harpsichord makers carried on their trade in a desultory manner, frequently combining the craft with the career of an organist, organ builder, or even joiner. Johann Karl Jacobsson provides an extremely interesting discussion of the organization of the trade in Berlin toward the end of the eighteenth century. In an article on the harpsichord maker [*Flügelmacher*] he writes:

Not all are trained instrument makers, but some are clever joiners [*Tischler*] who either worked as journeymen with instrument makers and thus came to it, or who acquired a knowledge of the making of keyboard instruments through their own meditations. They abandon the daily exercise of joinery and make only the aforementioned instruments. Thus it is explained that those musical instruments which are entirely strung with metal strings are not always made by special craftsmen, but often by joiners. The case of a harpsichord or clavichord is put together of planks, and thus is pre-eminently the production of a joiner. If such a one understands the layout or stringing of a harpsichord or clavichord he can easily be transformed from a mere joiner into a harpsichord and clavichord maker. And then he is to be considered as an artist who is free of guild regulations, and if he trains an apprentice he seeks stipulations favorable to himself. Yet this does not happen often, for these craftsmen usually take journeymen joiners for the rough work and do the fine work themselves. On the whole the organ maker is the true harpsichord and clavichord maker, and many organ makers take up this work when they do not find opportunity to build or repair organs. In Berlin meanwhile, as we have said, joiners, musicians, and other people enter this occupation, and it is to be presumed that the same state of affairs exists in other cities.[14]

Shortly after the opening of the eighteenth century German harpsichords rather suddenly began to be endowed with the ability to survive into the twentieth. Even the oldest extant instruments can be divided readily into two schools. The first, and possibly the better, was that of the Hamburg makers, dominated by the Hass and Fleischer families. Harp-

[13] Page 803.
[14] *Technologisches Wörterbuch oder alphabetische Erklärung aller nützlichen mechanischen Künste, Manufacturen, Fabriken und Handwerken* (Berlin, 1781–1794), I, 766.

sichords made in Hamburg almost invariably had round tails, lavish decorations, and elaborate dispositions. The makers of the second school were more scattered geographically, and their product was less ambitious. The most eminent members of this group belonged to the Silbermann and Gräbner dynasties, both of which produced instruments in Saxony, although the Silbermann family had an active offshoot in Strasbourg. Kinsky[15] suggests that one of the Gräbners had been trained by Gottfried Silbermann, but I have not been able to find evidence to support this theory.

It is interesting and puzzling that the Silbermanns are praised so much more than the Hass family by the biographical authorities of the period. This fact probably indicates once more the plain tendency of the Germans to confuse the harpsichord and the organ in their aesthetic. Silbermann's fame as an organ builder obscured Hass's great accomplishment as a harpsichord maker. Johann Heinrich Zedler,[16] for example, gives lavish praise to Silbermann in various articles but provides no entry for Hass. One of Zedler's most interesting remarks is this: "Some harpsichords of his [Gottfried Silbermann's] make have been taken to England and were welcomed with especial applause." This is a reversal of the usual trend in which English harpsichords were received with admiration on the Continent. Zedler does not give much information on Silbermann's harpsichords beyond the following: "This famous artist has not only built expensive and large organs, but also the most beautiful *Clavessins* which have two keyboards and provide many changes [of tone]."

The plates (XXVII–XXIX) illustrative of the construction of German harpsichords are taken from an instrument of the Hamburg tradition. In the fundamental layout of string band and plucking points many of these do not vary much from the practice of the contemporary Blanchets and Taskins except where a more elaborate disposition entails changes. Table 15 compares the scaling and plucking points of a single-manual 2x8′, 1x4′, harpsichord made by J. A. Hass in 1764 and a double made by Nicolas and François Etienne Blanchet in 1730. Although the German harpsichord has a slightly longer scale than the French, its strings are relatively more shortened in the bass so that the bass strings of the French harpsichord are actually longer. Except for the extreme treble where the French harpsichord is plucked farther from the nut, the plucking distances represent almost the same percentages of the string lengths and

---

[15] *Musikhistorisches Museum von Wilhelm Heyer, Katalog*, II, 657.
[16] *Grosses Vollständiges Universal Lexicon aller Wissenschaften und Künste* (Halle and Leipzig, 1732–1750). See also Appendix A.

thus are equivalent. The eight-foot bridge of the German harpsichord is slightly farther from the edge of the soundboard than that of the French instrument. This should make the French soundboard less compliant than the German and resonant to a higher frequency at the bridge. Surprisingly the German instrument has the more brilliant tone. Possibly its soundboard is of stiffer wood than Blanchet chose. Another significant factor might be the several small ribs, probably the work of a restorer, which pass under the eight-foot bridge of the Blanchet. These may be loading the soundboard sufficiently to dull the tone.

Table 15. Length of strings and percentage of string length represented by distance to plucking point, German and French harpsichords [a]

	German				French			
	Eight-foot		Four-foot		Eight-foot		Four-foot	
String	Length (inches)	Percent-age to plucking point	Length (inches)	Percent-age to plucking point	Length (inches)	Percent-age to plucking point	Length (inches)	Percent-age to plucking point
f'''	5¼	33%	2⅝	38%	4⁵⁄₁₆	36%	2⅝	53%
c'''	6⅞	29%	3½	36%	6¾	32%	3⅜	44%
c''	13⅝	22%	6⅝	27%	13³⁄₁₆	22%	6¹⁵⁄₁₆	29%
c'	26⁵⁄₁₆	15%	13⅝	18%	27¼	15%	13¾	18%
c	45⅜	11%	25¾	12%	46¾	11%	24	14%
C	65	9%	40½	9%	65	9%	36¼	10%
FF	71⅝	9%	47⅞	9%	72⅛	9%	43½	10%

[a] See text for instruments compared.

Of the six harpsichords of the Hass family which have survived in their original condition, only one has what could be regarded as a normal disposition. The others show aberrations such as a third manual, a third eight-foot choir, a two-foot choir, or a sixteen-foot stop in the same instrument as a lute stop. All are beautifully decorated, and often with rare materials.

The Saxon makers, on the other hand, often made instruments of an almost crude simplicity and usually left them unsigned. We find their harpsichords in stained pine or plain hardwood cases, the spine and cheekpiece reinforced at the front like a breadboard by a vertical piece. The inner edge moldings are often omitted and the keyboards are usually covered with plain ebony or pear stained black. This group of makers also showed less initiative in the more adventurous dispositions. None of their instruments known to me shows original sixteen-foot stops. Two harpsichords survive which might appear to contradict this statement, but I am convinced that the sixteen-foot of neither is original. Political barriers have made it impossible to examine personally either the double harpsichord by Johann Heinrich Gräbner (1774) now in Leipzig or the "Silbermann" double (undated) at the Bachhaus in Eisenach. However, the curator at Leipzig, Paul Rubardt, has assured me by letter that the sixteen-foot choir of the former was not original. There are only two nuts and two bridges. Hence the only change required to add a sixteen-foot would be the substitution of heavier strings. It is more reasonable to assume that this alteration was made than to attempt to justify the present miserable 1x16', 1x8', 1x4', disposition on two manuals. Adlung (see below) mentions the substitution of a sixteen-foot choir for an eight-foot choir but only on 2x8' harpsichords (obviously of a single manual) or on a quadruple-choired instrument.

The Eisenach "Silbermann" (which carries the initials "GS" on a modern music desk as its only identification) is in the same category: a 2x8', 1x4', double harpsichord in which one choir has been changed to sixteen-foot pitch. Friedrich Ernst, who is in charge of the restorations at the Schloss Charlottenburg in Berlin, is of the opinion that the sixteen-foot of this harpsichord is not original. Like the Gräbner at Leipzig, this instrument has only two nuts and two bridges. Both of these harpsichords originally had one of the following dispositions:

$$
\left\{ \begin{array}{l} \rightarrow 8' \\ \text{- - - - - - - -} \\ \leftarrow 4' \\ \leftarrow 8' \end{array} \right. \quad \text{or} \quad \left\{ \begin{array}{l} \rightarrow 8' \\ \text{- - - - - - - -} \\ \leftarrow 8' \\ \leftarrow 4'. \end{array} \right.
$$

Ernst would favor the second.

There can be no doubt, however, that Silbermann, at least, built such instruments. Boalch [17] quotes an item from the *Strassburger Gelehrte Nachrichten* for 1783 which mentions "an unusually large harpsichord with sixteen-foot tone" made by Silbermann, and Jacobsson [18] found the same instrument remarkable enough to be worthy of mention among the inventions newly applied to the harpsichord. This might suggest that sixteen-foot stops were not commonly used by Silbermann.

The harpsichords of Silbermann and Gräbner were not only simpler but were also of lighter construction and shorter scale than their Hamburg counterparts. In Table 16 various constructional details of a sample of instruments of both schools are compared. Table 17 records the disposition of a group of German harpsichords to the extent that the information is available.

[17] *Makers of the Harpsichord and Clavichord*, p. 113.
[18] *Technologisches Wörterbuch*, V, 573 (1793). See Appendix A.

Table 16. Comparison of constructional features of selected German harpsichords

	Date	Maker	School	Number of manuals	Range	Length and width (inches)	Tail form	Bentside material	Material, rest of case	Average thickness of case (inches)
(1)	1710	J. A. Hass	Hamburg	II	FF–f‴	99x39	round	pine	pine	5⁄8
(2)	1720	Carl Conradt Fleischer	Hamburg	I	GG–c‴	92¾x35⅜	round	pine	pine	9⁄16
(3)	1723	H. A. Hasch	Hamburg	II	FF–c‴	93½x37½	round	pine	pine	11⁄16
(4)	1734	H. A. Hass	Hamburg	II	GG–d‴	105x36½	round	oak	oak	11⁄16
(5)	1737	Christian Zell	Hamburg	I	C–d‴	80¾x32⅜	round	pine	pine	¾
(6)	1764	J. A. Hass	Hamburg	I	FF–f‴	90⅝x38⅜	round	oak	pine	9⁄16
(7)	1782?	Carl August Gräbner (?)	Saxony	II	FF–f‴	97½x38⅛	mitered	pine	pine	[a]
(8)	1785	Gottlieb Rosenau	Hamburg	II	FF–f‴	108x41⅜	round	pine	pine	¾
(9)	[a]	[a]	Saxony	II	FF–f‴	84x36⅝	mitered	walnut	walnut	⅜
(10)	[a]	Gottfried Silbermann (?)	Saxony	II	FF–f‴	97x37½	mitered	walnut	walnut	⅜
(11)	[a]	H. A. Hass (?)	Hamburg	II	FF–f‴	94⅝x38	round	pine	pine	9⁄16
(12)	[a]	Gottfried Silbermann (?)	Saxony	II	FF–f‴	103x38⅜	mitered	oak	oak	½

Table 16 (*cont'd*)

	Eight-foot scale (inches)	Decoration of case	Decoration of keyboard well	Key top material		Remarks
				Naturals	Sharps	
(1)	13	paint	paint	tortoise shell	ivory topped	Boalch no. 1
(2)	13¾	paint	paint	ivory	ebony	Boalch no. 2
(3)	13¾	paint	paint	tortoise shell	ivory topped	Boalch no. 3
(4)	13½	paint	tortoise shell and ivory	ivory	ivory and tortoise shell	Boalch no. 5
(5)	12⅞	paint	veneer	boxwood	black stain	Museo de Musica, Barcelona
(6)	13⅝	modern veneer	old veneer	ivory	black stain	Boalch no. 18
(7)	12¾	stained natural finish	stained natural finish	ebony	bone topped	Boalch no. 4. Inscription not visible
(8)	12¾	paint	veneer	ebony	bone topped	Carl Claudius Collection, Copenhagen. Made in Stockholm
(9)	11¹⁵⁄₁₆	natural finish	natural finish	black stain	bone topped	Hug and Co., Basel in 1956
(10)	9½	natural finish	natural finish	ebony	bone topped	Museo de Musica, Barcelona Silbermann-like rose
(11)	12⅜	paint	paint (late veneer)	ebony	bone topped	"Bach harpsichord," Schloss Charlottenburg, Berlin
(12)	12½	natural finish	natural finish	ebony	bone topped	Boalch no. 4

ᵃ Information unavailable.

Table 17. Comparison of dispositions of selected German harpsichords

Date	Maker	School	Man-uals	Range	Choirs	Regis-ters	Disposition
1710	J. A. Hass	Hamburg	II	FF–f'''	1x16', 2x8', 1x4', 1x2'	5	→ 2' → 8' dogleg - - - - - - - ← 4' ← 8' → 16' → 2' Buff stop on upper 8' and 16'
1720	Carl Conradt Fleischer	Hamburg	I	GG–c'''	2x8', 1x4'	3	→ 8' ← 8' ← 4' Buff stop
1722	Johann Heinrich Gräbner	Saxony	II	FF–f'''	2x8', 1x4'	3	1x4' uppr 2x8' lower Buff stop?
1723	Hieronymus Albrecht Hasch	Hamburg	II	FF–c'''	3x8', 1x4'	4	{ ← 8' - - - - - - - → 4' dogleg → 8' ← 8' Buff stop on the back 8'
1734	Hieronymus Albre. Hass	Hamburg	II	GG–d''''	1x16', 2x8' 1x4'	5	← 8' lute ← 8' (p. de b.) dogleg - - - - - - - ← 4' → 8' → 16' Buff on lower 8' and 16'
1737	Christian Zell	Hamburg	I	C–d'''	2x8', 1x4'	3	→ 8' ← 8' ← 4' Buff stop
1764	J. A. Hass	Hamburg	I	FF–f'''	2x8', 1x4'	3	← 8' ← 4' → 8' Buff stop
1774	Johann Heinrich Gräbner	Saxony	II	FF–f'''	2x8', 1x4'	3	1x4' upper 2x8' lower Buff stop

Coupler	Means of expression	Plectra	Remarks
Upper manual slides in to engage dogleg upper 8'. No manual coupler	Hand stops on the wrest plank. Tabs on buff stop battens	quill (leather back 8')	Upper manual 2' has a range of FF–b, 30 notes. Lower manual 2' has a range of FF–c", 44 notes. Boalch no. 1
None	Hand stops on the wrest plank. Tab on buff stop battens	quill	Boalch no. 2
Coupler, type unknown	ª	ª	Keyboard slides sideways to afford a transposition of a semitone. Lowest position gives range of EE–e'''.[b]
Upper manual slides in to couple and to engage dogleg on 4' jack	Hand stops on the wrest plank. Tabs on buff stop batten	quill	The 8' nut has two levels. The back 8' is mounted on the lower level at the nut but crosses top of 8' bridge with the other choirs. Boalch no. 3
Lower manual slides forward to couple	Hand stops on the wrest plank. Tabs on buff stop battens	quill	The *peau de buffle* has been installed in modern times, replacing original quill. Boalch no. 5
None	Hand stops on the wrest plank. Tabs on buff stop batten	quill	Museo de Musica, Barcelona
None	Hand stops on the wrest plank. Tabs on buff stop batten	quill	Boalch no. 18
Coupler, type unknown	Hand stops on nameboard	quill	Now has 1x4', 1x8', 1x16'. Boalch no. 2

(continued)

Table 17 (cont'd)

Date	Maker	School	Man-uals	Range	Choirs	Regis-ters	Disposition
1782?	Carl August Gräbner (?)	Saxony	II	FF–f'''	2x8', 1x4'	3	← 8' dogleg - - - - - - - - ← 4' → 8' Buff stop on back 8'
1785	Gottlieb Rosenau	Hamburg (worked in Stockholm)	II	FF–f'''	2x8', 1x4'	3 (4)	→ 8' - - - - - - - - ← 4' ← 8' Buff stop on upper 8'
ª	Gottfried Silbermann (?)	Saxony	II	FF–f'''	2x8', 1x4'	3	1x8' upper 1x8', 1x4', lower Buff stop
ª	Gottfried Silbermann (?)	Saxony	II	FF–f'''	2x8', 1x4'	3	ª No buff stop
ª	H. A. Hass(?)	Hamburg	II	FF–f'''	3x8', 1x4'	4	← 8' - - - - - - - - → 4' dogleg → 8' ← 8' Buff stop
ª	Gottfried Silbermann (?)	Saxony	II	FF–f'''	2x8', 1x4'	3	1x8' upper 1x8' 1x4' lower Buff stop
ª	ª	Saxony	II	FF–f'''	2x8', 1x4'	3	1x8' upper 1x8' 1x4' lower No buff stop

ª Information unavailable.
ᵇ See Kinsky, *Acta musicologica*, 12 (1940): fasc. I–IV.

Coupler	Means of expression	Plectra	Remarks
Lower manual slides in to engage dogleg on upper 8′	Hand stops on nameboard	quill	Inscription not visible. Boalch no. 4
Upper manual slides in to couple	The buff batten is moved by molded blocks glued to its ends	quill	A lute stop is now blocked up. There were probably originally four registers
	Hand stops on nameboard	quill	Now has 1x4′, 1x8′, 1x16′. Boalch no. 3
Lower manual slides in to couple	Hand stops on the wrest plank		Boalch no. 4
Upper manual slides in to couple (See remarks)	Hand stops on the wrest plank	quill	"Bach Harpsichord." See Appendix G for complete account. Coupler probably originally engaged a 4′ dogleg. Now has a 16′ and is disposed:
	Hand stops on nameboard		Museo de Musica, Barcelona
No coupler. No dogleg	Hand stops on the wrest plank	quill	Hug and Co., Basel, in 1956

In the "Bach Harpsichord" remark the disposition is shown:

$$\left\{ \begin{array}{l} \rightarrow 8' \\ \rightarrow 4' \\ \text{- - - - - - -} \\ \leftarrow 16' \\ \leftarrow 8' \end{array} \right.$$

The harpsichords listed in Tables 16 and 17 represent a typical sample of the productions of German eighteenth century makers. Study of these instruments reveals few tendencies to engage the analytical powers of the historian. All one can say is that the later instruments tend to be simpler and more often to come from Saxony, a fact easily explained by the increasing competition of the pianoforte which discouraged harpsichord makers from undertaking elaborate and expensive enterprises. Even this observation should be qualified; according to Fétis Christian Salomon Wagner made a three-manual harpsichord in 1786 which he called the "clavecin royal." One can also see that the Hamburg makers seem to have eventually given way to the Saxons, although a Swedish imitator of the Hamburg school, Gottlieb Rosenau, was active as late as 1785.

Trendless, the account of German eighteenth century harpsichord making must become static, relying more on description than narrative. The schizoid character of German harpsichord making makes even description desultory. Generalizations are difficult to draw. Fortunately the literature in German is rich enough and specific enough to permit an account of the German harpsichord to be given almost entirely by means of quotations from contemporary documents. Appendix A contains a selection of annotated passages which together with the existing instruments has formed the basis for my remarks.

The tonal design of German harpsichords seems to have been inspired by two distinct bodies of ideas, those of French harpsichord makers and those of the German organ builders. Especially in Hamburg the close association and frequent identity of the German harpsichord makers with organ builders often led them to think of the harpsichord in terms of the organ, and to some extent they attempted to apply the organ maker's concept of tonal design to the harpsichord. In the organ a specific tone color is often achieved synthetically by means of several pipes sounding simultaneously, each of which contributes a group of the partials which are to be combined to produce the desired timbre. We have already pointed out that the organ and the harpsichord differ in that each of the constituents of the organ chorus can be given a very simple tone, whereas each string of the harpsichord produces an extremely complex tone. Thus, the attempt to develop a chorus of stops in the harpsichord stumbles over the fact that one is mixing several already complete harmonic series and the ensemble tone very quickly becomes muddy. It was for this reason that the quint of Mersenne and Praetorius was never very widely adopted. Practically speaking, the harpsichord can employ stops only at intervals of one or more octaves from the fundamental.

The four-foot is successful if discreetly voiced and lends a brittle edge to the tone. As we have seen, it was admitted everywhere as a possible resource of harpsichord disposition. The German makers went further and tried both the two-foot and the sixteen-foot. The two-foot sounded well enough but the effect it produced was not sufficiently distinct from that of the four-foot to be worth the additional complexity it entailed. A large harpsichord by J. A. Hass, 1710,[19] in the Yale University Collection of Musical Instruments, is fitted with a two-foot choir, which is provided with two registers so that two-foot tone can be obtained from either manual. On the upper manual the two-foot is plucked by the first rank of jacks which extends from the bass to b. On the lower manual it is sounded by the last row of jacks which extends another octave to c''. (A two-foot choir cannot be carried to the top of a large harpsichord since the gap is too wide to be spanned by two-foot strings in the treble.) The two-foot tone is rather lost in the total ensemble, and, although of a certain value in light registrations, the discontinuity implicit in its division between the manuals severely limits its usefulness. The two-foot stop has not often been employed by other makers.

The sixteen-foot tone, on the other hand, has had a modern vogue out of all proportion either to its value or to its historical significance. Modern players and harpsichord makers have forgotten that with two exceptions [20] original sixteen-foot choirs occur only on eighteenth century German harpsichords, and even within that tradition they were somewhat unusual. The great name of Bach has been used to justify the widely felt necessity of a sixteen-foot on the modern concert platform, but the supposed ownership by Bach of a sixteen-foot harpsichord cannot be proved. Recent research by the staff of the Institut für Musikforschung in Berlin [21] has deprived the so-called Bach harpsichord in that institution's collection of all pretension to having belonged to Bach, and in any case its sixteen-foot stop is not original.

It is not my intention to rail against those musicians who violate all

[19] The date or signature may be in error since all the other instruments signed by this maker are dated between 1747 and 1768. Documents in the archives at Hamburg show Johann Adolf Hass to have been the son of Hieronymus Albert (usually signed as Albr.) Hass who was born in 1689. It is impossible that the son should have made a harpsichord twenty-one years after his father's birth and it is unlikely that the father could have contrived so complex a production as this one so early in life. See Boalch, *Makers of the Harpsichord and Clavichord*, p. 43.

[20] One is a harpsichord, too late to be of much historical significance, by Joachim Swann in Paris, 1786. Although he worked in Paris, Swann was so Germanic that he even inflected his name to *Swanen* on the nameboard of this harpsichord. However, he signed the jack of another harpsichord he restored, "fait par Joachim Swann." The second exception is a combination piano forte and harpsichord by Joseph Merlin, London, 1780. See p. 164.

[21] Friedrich Ernst, *Der Flügel Johann Sebastian Bachs* (Frankfurt, 1955).

precedent by the incessant employment of the sixteen-foot stop, I might suggest, however, that the specification of a sixteen-foot stop by the majority of modern harpsichord players as an indispensable component of any concert harpsichord is dictated by desperate necessity. Frustrated by the monotonous tone and feeble bass of their harpsichords, these players hope that the sixteen-foot will provide the depth and sonority their eight-foot choirs lack. Seeking a nobility and definition of line, they find only an inflated and muttering obscurity.

This is not to say that the sixteen-foot has no legitimate place in harpsichord registration, but the lower pitch and the slacker strings produce a more complex tone which can easily thicken the total ensemble. The sixteen-foot must be used with extreme discretion in contrapuntal textures, for in the place of the required transparency and sharp delineation of line, one is likely to obtain a clumsy and opaque sound. The sixteen-foot is best at lending weight and power to chordal or homophonic passages. It follows that the so-called Bach disposition (which is found on no genuine old harpsichord) [22] in which the upper manual is given 1x8′, 1x4′, and the lower, 1x8′, 1x16′, is generally inferior to that disposition usually found on eighteenth century harpsichords which placed 1x8′ on the upper manual and 1x16′, 1x8′, 1x4′ on the lower manual. The chief argument which can be advanced for the "Bach-disposition" is that it offers the possibility of dialoguing 1x8′, 1x4′ against 1x8′, 1x16′, which in my opinion is a miserable expedient. The guttural, muffled utterance of the sixteen-foot and eight-foot combination is in sad contrast to the steely fragility of the eight-foot and four-foot. Nor is the Bach disposition as suitable for alternating tutti and solo passages (where the sixteen-foot should come into its own), because one must use the coupler in order to obtain a sixteen-foot, eight-foot, and four-foot tutti. With the more usual disposition one need merely alternate manuals. It is true that the ideal harpsichord should offer certain fairly evenly matched registrations on two manuals, but the Bach disposition carries this principle to an extreme. The two manuals have cruelly severed the body of the tone through the trunk. To the lower manual pertain the nether regions, and to the second manual the unsupported upper work. The harpsichord with sixteen-foot should be considered as a 2x8′, 1x4′, instrument to which has been added a sixteen-foot for special effects, just as Taskin added the *peau de buffle* eight-foot to the 2x8′, 1x4′, conception. The basic structure of the disposition has not been altered, and to do so is to sacrifice the coat for the lace.

[22] See Appendix G for a discussion of the historical basis of the Bach disposition.

Although, as we have seen, the sixteen-foot was usually placed on the lower manual together with an eight-foot and a four-foot, leaving the second eight-foot for the upper manual, sometimes there was no second eight-foot stop. Adlung [23] mentions a harpsichord made in Breitenbach which had two manuals. There was an eight-foot on the upper manual while the four-foot and a sixteen-foot stop were on the lower manual.

The 1x16', 1x8', 1x4', harpsichord seems most unmusical to me; [24] a clear example of the common German tendency to confuse the aesthetic of the organ with that of the harpsichord. A harpsichord is limited indeed which condemns the player to sixteen-foot and four-foot tone on the lower manual and on which it is impossible to obtain the 2x8' unison which should be the sound around which all the more exotic registrations are grouped. The Hamburg makers usually reserved the sixteen-foot for those instruments which already had a full complement of stops. For example, the 1710 J. A. Hass has 2x8', 1x4', and a two-foot on the upper manual from FF–b and on the lower manual from FF–c'' in addition to the sixteen-foot stop. The 1734 Hieronymus Albrecht Hass with sixteen-foot has a lute stop in addition to the usual two eights and a single four.

With all this emphasis on the sixteen-foot stop, sight must not be lost of the extremely important fact that most German harpsichords show the same disposition as the French: 2x8', 1x4', on two manuals with coupler. Even Adlung says that "Harpsichords are rarely single- or quadruple-choired, most often double- or triple-choired."

Apparently four-choired instruments with 2x4' were not unknown although none has survived. Single-manual harpsichords normally were given 2x8', 1x4', although Adlung mentions the possibility of a lute stop, even on one manual, an arrangement we have hitherto found only in England. Halle [25] found the 2x8' disposition the most common although he mentions the possibility of a four-foot.

FF–f''' is the usual range of German harpsichords, but one finds more limited ranges from time to time on even the largest harpsichords. Halle specifies either forty-eight or sixty-one keys (that is, four or five octaves) but extending from GG–g'''. Unless his count is in error in the case of the four-octave instrument he must expect low C♯ to be omitted.

The registers in German harpsichords were controlled by hand stops.

---

[23] *Musica mechanica organoedi*, II, 110.

[24] As a matter of fact, Hiller remarked that "one might wish something else of him [Adlung] than his taste in performance." (*Lebensbeschreibungen berühmter Musikgelehrter und Tonkünstler*, Leipzig, 1784.)

[25] Johann Samuel Halle, *Werkstäte der heutigen Künste*, (Brandenburg and Leipzig, 1764), III, 360.

There is not much trace of the late French or English tendency to change stops with pedals or knee levers. In every country except England the standard means of varying registration until after the era of Bach, Handel, Couperin, and Scarlatti was through hand stops and push couplers. The coupler was unknown in England. The English machine stop came into use after the period under discussion. The very rare exceptions were of local influence and ephemeral duration, a fact which argues powerfully against those modern players who rely on pedals to produce effects unsuitable to the music they pretend to revive.

In Hamburg the hand stops seem to have been even more inaccessible than in England and France, for they were generally placed inside the nameboard on the wrest plank, where the music desk would have interfered with their rapid manipulation. It seems likely that the player established a basic registration for each manual before beginning to play, and limited himself during performance to an alternation of manuals and at brief pauses the shifting of the coupler. The Gräbner-Silbermann type of harpsichord seems to have been somewhat more handy in this regard than the Hamburg instruments since the hand stops were likely to be located on the nameboard. It seems perverse that the most elaborately disposed German harpsichords were equipped with the most inconvenient stop levers.

In the hard light of these mechanical facts one wonders what C. P. E. Bach meant when he wrote: "If the Lessons are played on a harpsichord with two manuals, only one manual should be used to play detailed changes of forte and piano. It is only when entire passages are differentiated by contrasting shades that a transfer may be made. This problem does not exist at the clavichord, for on it all varieties of loud and soft can be expressed with an almost unrivaled clarity and purity." [26]

Did Bach mean that the detailed dynamics must be lost altogether by the harpsichordist, or were they to be captured by the subtler snares of phrasing and agogic accent? Surely, after warning the performer to avoid the fussiness of frequent alternation of manuals he would not counsel an attempt to register dynamics by means of the stops.

During the period when the musical aesthetic for which the harpsichord was supremely fitted was breaking down, the Germans displayed a good deal more common sense than the French. Whereas endless efforts were expended in Paris to endow the harpsichord with the capacity

[26] *Versuch über die wahre Art das Clavier zu spielen* (Berlin, 1753), translated by William J. Mitchell, *Essay on the True Art of Playing Keyboard Instruments* (New York, 1949), p. 164.

for nuance, the German perception of that necessity was reflected in the popularity of the clavichord and later of the piano. Although the German musical journalists and lexicographers reported the French experiments with interest, the German makers were not driven to emulate them on a large scale. Indeed, more effort was expended to elaborate the piano and to give it, perhaps in violation of its essential nature, the power of varying its tone color. The French loved the tone of the harpsichord and attempted to preserve it even after the evolution of their musical taste led them to make demands which it could not fulfill. The Germans, on the other hand, do not seem to have been particularly sorry to see the last of the harpsichord. Their nostalgia was for the organ which, like the harpsichord, was dynamically rigid; hence their attempts to transfer the ability of the organ to vary its timbre to the piano which already possessed the now essential dynamic flexibility.

Even though the German makers avoided the pedals and mechanisms used in England and France they did sometimes make harpsichords with three manuals, probably in an effort to provide quick changes of registration without resort to their inconvenient hand stops. A three-manual harpsichord by Hieronymus Hass, 1740,[27] has stops arranged as follows:

Top manual: Lute 8′
        8′ dogleg (common to top and middle manual)
Middle manual: 8′ dogleg
        4′
        8′
Lower manual: 16′
        2′.

The middle manual can be coupled to the lower thus making all stops except the lute available from the lowest manual.

Most German two-manual harpsichords were fitted with couplers identical to those found in French harpsichords. Occasionally one finds an instrument in which the upper-manual key bed is fixed to the sides of the case while the lower manual slides under it to couple. Another variation was the fitting of long doglegs to the upper-manual jacks. These projections were too short to reach to the lower-manual key levers until that manual had been pushed to the rear, when blocks on the upper surfaces of its key levers mated with the doglegs so that the upper-manual jacks were coupled to the lower manual.

The buff stop is found in most German harpsichords, but the mechan-

<hr>

[27] Illustrated in Raymond Russell, *The Harpsichord and Clavichord*, plates 87 and 88.

ism is sometimes somewhat different than that we have so far encountered. Instead of a batten that moves to the side to bring pads into contact with the strings, a vertically acting batten is used which slides up on inclined planes to carry the pads to the strings (see Sprengel, Appendix A).

Pedal boards appear to have been known to German harpsichord makers. Adlung describes both the pull-down and the type which involved an independent pedal instrument. He mentions with approbation a pedal harpsichord with the disposition 2x8′, 1x16′, which was under expression (see Appendix A). Halle confirms Adlung in the view that pedal boards should obtain sixteen-foot tone (see Appendix A).

German harpsichords give the impression of clean and accurate workmanship, possibly not as deft as the French, but certainly more painstaking. There is more iron work on the interior and the frame parts are extremely well finished. Cases are often made of a variety of woods with a hardwood bentside and softwood spine. The aspect of German case construction that is perhaps of most interest is the precise provision made for the sixteen-foot choir. This seems to have taken three forms. The first, and the least satisfactory, was simply to design a 2x8′, 1x4′, harpsichord and to replace one of the eight-foot choirs with a set of heavier strings, possibly overspun, which were tuned to sixteen-foot pitch. This has two disadvantages. In the first place, one is left with a rather poor disposition. In my opinion, 2x8′ should be the point of departure for all harpsichord registration, and it is not contained in such a disposition. The second objection is that the sixteen-foot scale, being identical to the eight-foot scale, is too short, and the stop is certain not to sound well. This objection can be extended to the modern expedient of making an eight-foot bridge with two levels which carry a sixteen-foot string on top and two eight-foot strings below. I have never seen an old harpsichord that had originally been constructed in this manner.

The second method of providing for a sixteen-foot choir called for a larger case than usual and a third bridge on the soundboard as well as a third nut. The sixteen-foot bridge and nut were higher than the corresponding eight-foot structures and supported the sixteen-foot strings at a level which was higher than the eight-foot strings. Thus the strings would be spaced at three heights: the four-foot lowest, then the two eight-foots, and finally the sixteen-foot. The eight-foot choirs were hitched to a member placed exactly where the bentside would have been if the harpsichord had been disposed 2x8′, 1x4′. This inner bentside had its lower edge mounted to the bottom cross braces and it was high enough for the soundboard to be glued to its upper edge. On the upper surface of the soundboard, just over the edge of the inner bentside, was glued a molded hitchpin rail into which hitchpins were driven. This system is much more satisfactory than the first because the sixteen-foot choir can have a decent scale. The bass sixteen-foot strings, of course, are not twice as long as the corresponding eight-foot strings, but they approach that ideal length for all the notes above tenor c. (In point of fact, the amplitude of vibration for strings twice as long as the bass eight-foot would be too large to cope with, and they would be certain to buzz against each other and against the jacks.) This type of sixteen-foot stop has a tone quality which is closely related to that of the eight-foot and not only blends better in the total ensemble but is of more use as a solo stop.

The third system is simply a variation of the second in which the soundboard is not continuous. It is illustrated in Plate XXVIII, figs. 1, 2, and 3, and Plate XXIX, fig. 13. Instead of crossing over the inner bentside the soundboard is cut off at that point. A narrow, crescent-shaped soundboard is inserted between the outer bentside and the inner bentside, resting on the top of the latter. The level of this sixteen-foot soundboard is enough above that of the eight-foot soundboard to permit the sixteen-foot bridge to be of the same section as the eight-foot bridge and yet to maintain the sixteen-foot strings at a suitable distance above the eight-foot strings. It is possible that the smaller sixteen-foot bridge produces a better tone.

Bridges and nuts of German harpsichords are of an enlarged Italian form and frequently are not tapered. They are sometimes stained black and are not always hooked in the bass.

The natural key heads have an average length of 1⅝ inches. The sharps tend to be considerably longer than those of other traditions (up to 3⅝ inches). It is interesting to recall Bach's opinion on this subject as it was reported by Agricola: [28]

Anyone who is in the habit of placing his fingers properly will know that he need never stretch a finger out straight in playing. Why then does he need such long manuals? As far as the width of the keys is concerned, it is known that particularly in Brandenburg the keys are made narrower than elsewhere, but no man yet has got his fingers stuck between the semitones. Are there giants, then, in Thuringia? A certain organist who wore very wide shoes

[28] Adlung, *Musica mechanica organoedi*, II, 23–24. (Quoted and translated by Hans T. David and Arthur Mendel, *The Bach Reader*, New York, 1945, p. 258.) David and Mendel point out that Agricola (whose note we are quoting) is attacking Albrecht, the editor of Adlung's MS, who had condemned the smaller dimensions. Albrecht came from Thuringia.

had the pedals of his organ, on which he could not play much anyway, spread so far apart that anyone else, wishing to play anything more on these pedals than the bass tone already represented by the little finger of the left hand, could easily have ruptured himself. The French very rightly make even the keys of their harpsichords shorter than in Germany; but no one has yet complained about it. The semitones must anyway be a little narrower at the top than at the bottom. That is how the late Kapellmeister Bach required them to be, and he, for the above-mentioned reasons, also liked short keys on the organ.

The German makers usually used a three-rail key bed and a rack with overrail to limit the key dip (see Plate XXIX, figs. 1 and 3). The balance point was forward of the middle. The key levers were most often of pine. The natural key heads were covered with ebony or hardwood stained black in Saxony and with a variety of materials in Hamburg.

The registers (not of the box type, although that construction is sometimes mentioned by German authorities) were cut out of solid slips of hardwood, and the jacks were similar to those of Blanchet and Taskin.

One common feature of the Saxon school was a nameboard below the level of the edge of the case. Sometimes it was nearly flush with the upper surface of the wrest plank. Often a removable nameboard was slipped in front of the fixed member. This piece was wide enough to reach nearly to the surface of the keys and had to be removed to enable withdrawal of the keyboard.

The great dissimilarity of tone among the German harpsichords by comparison to those of the French or Flemish traditions is plausibly explained by the unsettled condition of several of the most fundamental design characteristics within the German school. One finds a range of scale type from Italian to Flemish, case scantlings varying from very light to very heavy, the alternate employment of light and heavy woods for basic construction, and a great deal of variety in disposition. Thus it becomes difficult to define anything which might be taken as a peculiarly German tone quality. The Hass instruments sometimes have a very hard and clean tone, quite powerful, but a little fatiguing in its brilliance. Those Hass instruments with sixteen-foot tend to sound a little duller and perhaps to suffer from a lack of definition. This observation may appear to contradict our first remarks about the Hass tone color. Yet although the tone of an orchestral triangle is certainly clean and hard, if one were to make a sort of xylophone out of a series of triangles the tone would surely be unsuitable for the clear statement of contrapuntal lines. The tone of many Hass instruments sounds very fine and impressive, but somehow the music slips by, just out of grasp.

Some other German harpsichords have a sound not unlike their French contemporaries. Sometimes the reduction of case scantlings seems to have exactly balanced the shortened scale. A harpsichord said to be by Carl August Gräbner, 1782 (now owned by Ulrich Rück of Nuremberg), with a 12¾″ scale has a hard, bright tone with a powerful but "boomless" bass like the Hass 2x8′, 1x4′, single-manual instrument whose scaling is given in Table 15. Unfortunately, the very short-scaled German instruments which I have seen have not been playable, and no report on the tone can be given.

We finally arrive, as Adlung would say, at the last kind of instrument, and it need not detain us long. The typical eighteenth century German spinet is quite like the contemporary French spinet. The case outline is that which had been derived in the seventeenth century from Zenti by French, English, and German makers. The bentside, unlike those of the English spinets which were S-shaped, was composed of a simple parabolic curve. The usual range was five octaves, FF–f‴, 1x8′. The cases were often veneered in walnut to appear solid and rested on a three-legged cabriole stand. A feature which often distinguished the German spinet from its English or French counterpart was the frame-and-panel lid.

It is noticeable that the Saxon makers, particularly Silbermann, more often identified their spinets than their harpsichords. Several spinets contain the Silbermann rose, a design of intertwined S's within a triangle.

The tone of these spinets, like that of most spinets, is poor. A hard and weak treble passes insensibly into a dead middle register. The tenor is passable and the bass is flat and harsh like an old upright piano. Some, however, are better than others.

The seventeenth century ancestors of these spinets are not more interesting. Most of them were ottavini similar to the instrument illustrated by Praetorius. One, by Israel Gellinger, in 1677, has a bentside and two manuals with one choir of strings, 1x4′, and a case of cypress with Italian decor. We must suppose that it was made as a toy.

The commanding position of German composers in the history of Baroque music forces us to take German harpsichords seriously. If it were not for this fact we should dismiss them as well made but not well thought out. Those of the Saxon school seem to be inferior imitations of the Flemish as altered by the French, and their peculiar characteristics, such as the decor and scaling, are not admirable. The Hass instruments, superb technical achievements, strike us as the grotesque result of the barbarous imposition of tonal concepts appropriate to the organ on the unresisting but equally unresponding harpsichord.

CHAPTER SIX · THE WORKSHOP

To provide an account of the workshops, tools, and procedures of harpsichord makers presents even greater difficulties than those encountered in describing their productions, for those establishments and their traditions have disappeared almost without trace. Written sources which discuss the instruments are meager enough, but the contempt of the typical man of letters for manual labor made it most unlikely that he would find it worth while or within his capacity to describe how harpsichords were made. Clues, of course, can be found in the instruments themselves, but these are seldom sufficient to serve as a basis for a comprehensive account. Thus we are forced to derive what further information we can from sources which are exceedingly scattered and difficult to interpret.

Toward the end of the period, particularly in France and Germany, more writing on the arts and trades was done, but even contemporaries found it difficult to ascertain the traditional processes of the various crafts. Diderot writes of the trials of the early technical writer in the *Encyclopédie* under the article "Encyclopédie" which describes his approach to the problem. Since a great deal of my information is drawn from the *Encyclopédie* it seems worth while to quote him at length.

Then he [the encyclopedist] will sketch out for each workman a rough memorandum whose outlines are to be filled in. He will require each one to discuss the materials he uses, the places from which he procures these, the prices that he pays for them, the tools he uses, the products he makes, and the whole series of operations he performs.

He will compare the memoranda furnished by craftsmen with his own original sketch; he will confer with them; he will make them supply orally any details they may have omitted and explain whatever they may have left obscure.

However bad these memoranda may be, when written in good faith they will always be found to contain an infinite number of things which the most intelligent of men would never have perceived unaided, would never even have suspected, and hence could never have asked about. Indeed, he will wish to know still more, but these matters will be part of the trade secrets which workmen never reveal to anyone. I myself have found by experience that people who continually busy themselves with something are equally disposed to believe either that everyone knows those things which they are at no pains to hide, or that no one else knows anything about the things they are trying to keep secret. The result is that they are always ready to mistake any person who questions them either for a transcendent genius or for an idiot . . . Above all, once he [the encyclopedist] has made the rounds of the workshops over a certain period of time, money in hand, and once he has been made to pay dearly for the most ridiculous fabrications, he will know what sort of people these artisans are — especially here in Paris, where fear of the tax collector keeps them in a perpetual state of mistrust, and where they regard every man who questions them at all closely either as a spy for the farmers-general or as a rival craftsman who wants to set up shop . . . Craftsmen . . . live isolated, obscure, unknown lives; everything they do is done to serve their own interests; they almost never do anything just for the sake of glory. There have been inventions that have stayed for whole centuries in the closely guarded custody of single families . . . There are trades where the craftsmen are so secretive that the shortest way of gaining the necessary information would be to bind oneself out to some master as an apprentice or to have this done by some trustworthy person.[1]

In addition to the articles in encyclopedias there are the commercial dictionaries and technical treatises, which contain a great deal of material that can be applied indirectly. In Germany some of the treatises on organ building have a chapter on harpsichord making. Elsewhere one sometimes finds a work written to puff a particular invention which includes general information on harpsichord building methods. The anonymous *Verhandeling over de Muziek* is a good example of this genre. Inventories of the contents of harpsichord makers' workshops are certainly the most authoritative if enigmatic of evidence.

I have not attempted to divide this discussion of the workshop into national sections since the commercial environment and technical milieu of all Europe were sufficiently uniform to permit a single description. Differences there were, of course. The contrast between the product of the Italians and that of any of the northern schools of makers naturally involved certain differences of technique, and the environment of London in 1700 where the guilds were about dead certainly was not that of the continent where they were to flourish for another seventy-five years. Even so, the traditions of apprenticeship and workshop organization were so conservative in a minor trade like harpsichord making that the work was carried on in much the same way with or without guild regulation.

Under the usual guild practices a boy was bound legally to a master for a period of six or seven years during which he lived with the family

---

[1] Translated by Jacques Barzun and Ralph H. Bowen, *Rameau's Nephew and Other Works* (New York, 1956). © Copyright 1956 by Jacques Barzun and Ralph H. Bowen. Reprinted by permission of Doubleday and Co., Inc.

of his master and worked without compensation. The terms of these apprenticeships were the subject of notarial acts which generally contained stipulations concerning the living standard of the apprentice and his training in the craft. Having completed his apprenticeship, the boy became a journeyman and could hire himself out at will to any master. In several European countries it was traditional for the young journeyman to travel from city to city, working with various masters in order to perfect himself in his trade. In most trades the majority of journeymen never became masters and, indeed, in many places it was almost impossible to do so unless one were the son of a master. Ordinarily this does not seem to have been the case among harpsichord makers, for a great many master makers were not born to the trade.

The guild imposed strict regulation of commerce, regulation which resulted in a minute division of technical processes. It had to be particularly specified, for example, in the statute setting up the Parisian instrument makers' guild that the *luthiers* (stringed instrument makers) be permitted to use the techniques characteristically employed to decorate their works. The abundant litigation resulting from the disputes over those operations which lay between two trades or which were common to both emphasizes the extraordinary degree of control the guilds exerted upon the lives of artisans and the progress of the industrial arts. A typical dispute occurred in 1741 between F. E. Blanchet, in his capacity as an official of the Paris guild of instrument makers, and the guild of *tabletiers* (ivory workers). One of the criteria for establishing the jurisdiction of a guild was the material used in the trade in question. On this basis the ivory workers held that the turning of ivory flutes belonged to them. Blanchet argued that flutes pertained to instrument making.[2] The identity of the eventual victor in this particular litigation does not concern us. The fact to be placed firmly in mind is that a milieu so legalistic and categorized must be extremely discouraging to the inventive worker. An invention which involved the application of a new material or technique to harpsichord making was quite likely to involve a lawsuit with another guild. The niggling detail of the enforcement of the guild statutes is made clear in the following passage from Roubo:

The law which forbids workmen to have heavy tools [*outils d'affutage*] at home is very good because it prevents those who do not have the necessary qualifications from working on their own account. But at the same time it is

---

[2] A most interesting quasi-legal study of the guilds of musicians and instrument makers in Paris is that by Paul Loubet de Sceaury, *Musiciens et facteurs d'instruments de musique, statuts corporatifs* (Paris, 1949).

annoying that that law, good in itself, serves as a pretext for the injustice and violence of certain individuals who, because a workman has a bench at home which serves only to make the tools which are necessary to him for his work (and is too small for anything else) which he can make only on Sundays and holidays at the expense of his rest; that these men, I say, do not blush to use that law to take the only means of livelihood from a weak and defenseless workman, then they refuse to give him work because he has no tools.[3]

The position occupied by harpsichord makers in bourgeois society was perhaps best specified by an *Arrêt au conseil* of July 5, 1582, in which the guilds of Paris were listed and divided into five groups: *meilleurs mestiers* (the best trades); *mestiers d'entre les meilleurs et mediocres* (the trades between the best and the mediocre); *les mestiers mediocres* (the mediocre trades); *mestiers d'entre les mediocres et petits* (the trades between the mediocre and the petty); and *les petits mestiers* (the petty trades).[4] The instrument makers were practicing one of the mediocre-trades, a chastening consideration which is somewhat relieved by the knowledge that the players of instruments were listed close at hand.

We have seen in Chapter 3 that the usual Paris harpsichord workshop was operated by a staff of three men who ordinarily must have consisted of the master, an apprentice, and either a journeyman or the master's son. Apprentices, of course, represented a very cheap supply of labor, but the guild statute prohibited a master from training more than one at a time.

Roubo describes the physical arrangement of the usual joiner's workshop, and it seems likely that the harpsichord maker's establishment was similar although somewhat smaller.[5]

Of all the mechanical arts, joinery [*menuiserie*] is the one in which there are the greatest number of tools, the perfect knowledge of which is indispensable both for the manner of making them and for that of using them; but before entering into the details I believe that I should speak of the shop or *atelier* where joiners work. This is not to say that every joiner must have premises of a standard type but it is merely intended to indicate the dimensions and equipment which are required.

There are two types of joiners' shops, those which are located in rented houses and those which are especially built with frame construction in the form of lean-to sheds.

The first are suitable for cabinetmakers [*ébénistes*; Roubo uses this term to apply particularly to those cabinetmakers who produced veneered furniture], all types of furniture makers, and for carriage builders; it is not that

[3] *L'Art du menuisier*, I, 52.
[4] R. de Lespinasse, *Les Métiers et corporations de la ville de Paris du quatorzième au dix-huitième siècle* (Paris, 1886–1897).
[5] *L'Art du menuisier*, I, 49f.

the ones of which I have just spoken do not sometimes have very large shops, but what I have said applies in general. For *menuisiers de bâtiments* [those who execute the fine carpentry — such as the paneling — in building construction] ordinary shops are hardly suitable in view of the space which they require; thus the majority of them (at least the most prosperous), and those who undertake large projects, have a shop [*boutique*] in their own dwellings where they do their small work and a timber-yard in town where they place their stores of timber and in which they have a shed constructed capable of containing a number of benches equivalent to their requirements. There are others who have no shops but who choose premises large enough to lodge them commodiously and to contain their stores of wood and a workshop of reasonable size. This last method is the best because it permits one to keep an eye on everything, which is impossible if one is lodging elsewhere.

When space is limited and one requires a large number of workmen, one makes the shed double, that is, one places benches on both the ground floor and on a second floor. The shop of M. Menageot in Porte Saint Martin is constructed in this manner and is possibly the best built in Paris as much for solidity as for all the facilities which are provided for the workmen.

The shop of a *menuisier de bâtiments* ought to be twelve and one-half feet in height at least, because the timber is ordinarily twelve feet in length and it is essential to be able to dress it and to turn it end over end without being cramped.

Its depth should be from fifteen to eighteen feet in order that there be three feet between the end of the bench and the sill[6] of the shop, nine feet being the length of the bench, and about six feet at the end so that each workman can have a place for his wood and his work.

As for the width, it must be limited by the available space and by the number of benches one wishes to install, which are ordinarily eighteen to twenty inches in width, and that much again is required between each bench; which works out that each worker needs three feet four inches, which dimension determines that of the workshop by simple multiplication.

The window sills of the shop should be of a height equal to that of the benches so that in the case of jobs of extraordinary length one can let the wood pass over the top while working on it, and thus be supported.

There should be several entrances, the number depending upon the width, which will be closed by doors which should open clear to the top in order to facilitate the entry of wood, and which will be glazed with linen so that when they are closed one can enjoy daylight in the interior of the shop.

The space above the sills must also be closed by frames covered with linen which are raised during the day and held to the ceiling by catches which retain them there.

At the top of the front of the shop there should be a pentroof projecting about 18 inches or 2 feet which will serve to keep water out and to prevent damage to the work and tools.

---

[6] The building was apparently built a little like a screened porch with the wall rising to a height of about 2½ feet. Above that it was enclosed by hinged frames garnished with a translucent cloth.

Near the shop there ought to be an enclosure twelve to fifteen feet square in which there is a fireplace with a mantel six or seven feet off the floor and as wide as possible, that is to say, as wide as is convenient, and facing the hearth there is built a little wall or *banquette* of masonry, 15 or 16 inches in height by seven or eight inches thick and four or five feet distant from the bare wall or back side of the fireplace. The top of the *banquette* should be faced by a piece of wood three or four inches thick, which thickness is included in the height of the *banquette*.

This place is called the *étuve* or *sorbonne*, in workmen's language, and serves to melt and to heat glue, to warm and to glue wood, and to dry glue joints during the winter and in damp weather. It is useful also to have a bench in the *sorbonne* in order to be able to pound and to glue joints on it; lacking a bench one uses the top of the *banquette* which is intended for that purpose as well as for retaining the fire and preventing it from spreading.

The *sorbonne* should be quite tight, and yet well lit, so that one can work there as I have described above: it serves also as a place for the workmen to take their meals; that is why one must take the greatest possible care to make it comfortable, especially during the bad season. It must be built very close to the shop and even be contiguous if that is possible so that wood taken there to be heated and glued is not subject to being wetted, a thing which happens if it is otherwise situated. See the vignette of plate XI [Plate XXXI]: it represents the interior of a joiner's shop with several workmen busy at various tasks.

The workshops of harpsichord makers generally belonged to the type Roubo thought suitable for *ébénistes* and were installed in ordinary houses. It is not possible to provide a very vivid or authoritative description of the premises of any harpsichord maker since no eighteenth century visitors seem to have thought them worthy of special comment. However, if one reads between the lines of the inventories, of which we have printed extracts in Appendix C, a sort of spiritless image can be resurrected.

The establishment of the Blanchet family in the Rue de la Verrerie was a little larger than the average but was probably typical otherwise. There were six floors (five by the Continental system), possibly with a *boutique* on the ground level, living quarters on the second and third floors, a salon on the fourth which was used as a showroom, a smaller *atelier* on the fifth, and various other storerooms on the fourth, fifth, and sixth floors. The *boutique* must have been of fairly good size since it contained four workbenches, but the *atelier* was fitted with only two. The salon was either exceedingly large or very crowded, for we find three large harpsichords and five pianos displayed there at one time. The various Mesdames Blanchet must have found cleaning difficult since even the corridors and stairways were cluttered with instruments and wood.

By contrast, Treyer's establishment was much smaller. In 1779 he inhabited seven rooms of which three were very small. His *boutique* did double duty as kitchen and was on the second floor. The tools and instruments were in one room facing the courtyard. By 1788, however, he had moved into larger quarters and now disposed of eight rooms and a cellar. His 1779 shop was of the standard three-man type, but by 1788 he had increased his workbenches to four.

The tools employed in these workshops were divided into two classes, those provided by the master and those owned by the individual workman. Roubo's pathetic remonstrance[7] demonstrates the degree to which this was a real and legal distinction. (The plate and figure numbers in parentheses refer to Roubo's plates.)

By shop tools [*outils de boutiques*] are understood all those which master joiners are obliged to furnish to their workmen, both those which are used by everyone and those which are provided for each man.

Formerly every sort of tool was furnished but since the practice of piecework has been introduced each man provides all the necessary tools except the large ones called *d'affutage*, such as benches, jointing planes, jack planes, etc., which they cannot be known to possess without their being subject to confiscation, and not only the tools *d'affutage* but all the others which are found at their homes.

The shop tools are of two sorts, as I have said above, viz., those common to all the workmen and those which are for each of them.

The first class includes the ripsaws (XII, 1), and crosscut saws (XII, 3, 4), the handsaws, the squares of all sizes, large marking gauges or beam compasses (XV, 1), large compasses, bar-clamps of all sizes (XVIII, 16, 17), one or more levels, *étraignoirs* [a clamp used in gluing up panels or soundboards] (XVIII, 18, 19), *réglets* [a device for sighting a plank to check whether it is in wind (twisted)] (XIV, 1, 2), tenon-sawing jigs (XVII, 13) of all kinds, small holdfasts [a piece of iron shaped like the figure 7. The stem passes through a hole in the bench in which it jams. The horizontal bar holds the work securely against the bench top.] (XI, 1), *les pieds de biche* [a notched board used to hold the end of a plank being planed] (XIV, 17), the stone for sharpening tools, glue and a copper pot in which to heat it.

The shop tools pertaining to each workman are first, a bench and holdfast, a jointing plane [a large wooden plane used in jointing planks edge to edge] (XIII, 1) and a jack plane [identical to the jointing plane but smaller], two shoulder planes [a narrow plane in which the iron passes completely through from side to side — to be distinguished from the rabbet plane which has a fence or guide to direct it in cutting rabbets] (XIII, 11–17), a smooth plane (XIV, 12, 14, and 15), a hammer, a firmer[8] and a chisel.

---

[7] *L'Art du menuisier*, I, 49f.

[8] It is difficult to reconstruct Roubo's definition of the various types of chisels. He mentions *fermoir, ciseau,* and *bec d'âne*. In modern workshops one distinguishes paring chisels which are quite thin, firmer chisels which are heavier and either beveled or

Roubo proceeds to a long list of tools which each worker was to provide for himself. Since many of these were designed for the particular use of the joiner, we shall not reproduce it here, but provide in its place a list of the tools mentioned by Dom Bedos as essential for the organ maker: a bench with several holdfasts; *pied de biche* (see above); clamps; vise; large and small ripsaws; crosscut saws, both tenon and keyhole (able to saw curves); jointing and jack planes in three sizes; smooth plane; rabbet plane; fillister planes (several sorts); shoulder planes in several widths; compass; beam compass; squares; bevels (a sort of square with an adjustable blade to provide angles other than 90°); marking gauge; firmer chisels in several widths; flat chisel; gouges; mortising chisels; rasps; mallet; brace and bits.[9]

The blades for all these tools, according to Roubo, came from Germany which provided the best steel. Most of the planes of the seventeenth and eighteenth centuries were of wood with the blade retained by a wedge, but there are occasional references and illustrations of metal planes, always in small sizes.

A list of the special tools required by the harpsichord maker is provided in the *Encyclopédie*. Plate XXXII reproduces the illustration of those tools; a translation of the rather obscure captions to that plate accompanies it. Unfortunately for us, the choice of tools made by the editors of the *Encyclopédie* seems a little capricious. Many of the tools illustrated are in no way peculiar to the art of harpsichord making, and we are left uncertain as to the nature of the tools that were used for many processes. I have found no illustrations that depict the various jigs and fixtures harpsichord makers must have used. Treyer's "three tables of forms," his "various pieces of wood with a frame garnished with iron and sheet metal," or Blanchet's "machine to bend the bentsides of harpsichords" would be most interesting to see.[10]

All woodworking operations, including harpsichord making, can be divided into two phases. In the first the material is reduced to planks of appropriate thickness, length, and width. In the second the joints are formed and the finished product is assembled. Most of the great contributions made by modern machinery (at least for the small shop) have been applied to the first phase. The circular saw, jointer, and thickness planer

---

square-edged, and mortising chisels which are the heaviest. All of these types come in various widths. The *bec d'âne* was certainly the mortising chisel and was heavier toward the tip than at the butt. The other two are ambiguous. Both words are cognate to English terms.

[9] Bedos de Celles, *L'Art du facteur d'orgues,* I, 15.

[10] See below, Appendix C, pp. 309, 291, 293.

have greatly lightened the labor required to produce a dimensioned plank. Yet the usual conception of the eighteenth century cabinetmaker in his saw pit reducing tree trunks to planks and planing great shaggy timbers to thickness is exaggerated.

Timber was available in an astonishing variety of dimensions from the merchants of any of the large European cities. Roubo, Sprengel, Savary, and the anonymous *Description abrégée*,[11] among others, specified the commercial dimensions of the various species, and Roubo illustrated timber stacked in a merchant's yard which looks just like its modern counterpart (see Plate XXXIII). Several writers mention that the planks were sawed from the logs by water- or wind-powered sawmills situated in the forests of origin. Illustrations of such mills can be found in the *Encyclopédie*,[12] in Sprengel,[13] and in De Caus,[14] whose plate 25 is reproduced here as Plate XXXIV.

Sawmills driven by water were known in Europe at least as early as the thirteenth century.[15] Apparently one of the first wind-driven sawmills was that built by Cornelius Cornelisz in Holland in 1592. This mill was illustrated in the *Groot Volkomen Moolenboek*;[16] the plate shows two reciprocating saw frames side by side, one fitted with three saws, and the other with four. From that period on Holland seems to have been a center of sawmilling (particularly around Zaandam) and wood dealing in general.

Sawmills seem to have become fairly common on the Continent but they were almost unknown in England. A sawmill was erected near London in 1663 but was soon abandoned as a result of the hostility of sawyers. No further attempt was made until 1767 when a wind driven mill was set up near Limehouse. This was destroyed in a riot but was rebuilt and continued to operate.

Although sawmilling was widely practiced, it seems that most of the smaller-dimensioned timber was resawed by hand sawyers in town, usually by those who made a special trade of it. Roubo makes one direct reference to instrument makers in this connection: "It is not the cabinetmakers who resaw their own wood, but workmen who specialize in this

[11] *Description abrégée des principaux arts et métiers, des instruments qui leurs sont propres etc.* (Paris, n. d.).

[12] "Charpenterie," plates 34 and 35.

[13] *Handwerk und Künste in Tabelen*, plate II.

[14] Salomon de Caus, *Les Raisons des forces mouvantes* (Paris, 1615 and 1624).

[15] A drawing in Villard de Honnecourt's notebook (1235) shows a reciprocating saw driven by a water wheel. Power from the wheel raises the saw which is returned by the spring force of a flexible pole.

[16] By L. Van Natrus, J. Polly, and C. van Vurren (Amsterdam, 1734), vol. I, plate V.

trade and who resaw not only for the cabinetmakers but also for the *luthiers* and in general all those who employ thin wood. These workmen or sawyers are paid by the pound, that is to say, by the weight of wood which is brought to them, which with the loss of wood in sawdust renders the wood nearly two-thirds more expensive, an important consideration." [17]

The woods employed by harpsichord makers varied from country to country, but most of the north European makers required some sort of deal for the cases and frames, a good quality wood for the soundboard, and pear and holly or boxwood for the action parts. In addition, the English makers required oak for the cases as well as various veneers, chiefly mahogany and walnut, but also tulip, satinwood, rosewood, curly maple, and the burls of several species. The Italian makers, of course, used a great deal of cypress. [18]

Savary [19] states that sapin (pine) was regularly sold by Paris merchants in the following dimensions.

Length (feet)	Thickness (inches)	Width (inches)
6	¾	10–18
8	¾	12
9	$1\frac{1}{12}$–$1\frac{1}{8}$	12
10	$1\frac{1}{12}$–$1\frac{1}{8}$	12
12	$1\frac{1}{12}$–$1\frac{1}{8}$	12

The first and second sizes were most suitable for harpsichord cases, but some of the heavier frame members and blocks must have been taken from the longer planks.

A letter printed in the *London Chronicle* for August 21, 1765, gives us an insight into the state of the English timber trade of the time. *Abietacius Negociator* complains that American deal was badly manufactured. He contrasts it to the Norwegian and Swedish deal which was stored in two-inch planks, cut to equal length. He argues that deal should be one-quarter inch thick "as the Hollanders do the German or Dutch oak." Although Norway exported the best deals, the writer favored encouraging the American product. We see that even at that date England was dependent on imports for much of her timber and that her merchants were familiar with the products of many other countries. It seems likely

[17] *L'Art du menuisier* "L'Art du menuisier-ébéniste," p. 799.
[18] See Russell, *The Harpsichord and Clavichord*, p. 125, for documents relating to Cristofori's procurement of cypress.
[19] *Dictionnaire universel de commerce*, IV, 639.

that much of the veneer used in English harpsichords came from Amsterdam. Savary says: "A very extensive commerce in all sorts of wood is carried on at Amsterdam, but particularly in those species which are suitable for dyeing, marquetry and inlay work. The prices vary and diverse discounts are made for large orders and prompt payment." [20]

The soundboard is the one part of the case of a harpsichord in which the specific material used is vitally important. The problem of identifying the most favored wood, however, is a formidable exercise in linguistics and divination. The terms used by various authorities are as follows.

Italian
   Griselini: "Abete." [21]

Dutch
   Verhandeling over de Muziek: "Vuurenhout, dat uit Zwitzerlant koomt."

French
   Mersenne: "Cyprez, cedre, & principalement de sapin."
   Encyclopédie: "Sapin de Hollande."

Spanish
   Nassare: "Pino avete."

German
   Halle: "Tanne."
   Adlung: "Fichttannenholz, Tannenholz."
   Jacobsson: "Tannenholz."

English
   Talbot MS: "Belly best of Firr, sometimes Cedar or Cypress."

We are dealing with four possible genera:

1) The spruces (genus *Picea*). Sometimes called spruce-fir. The needles are arranged singly, making a sort of spiral around the branch. The most important European species for our purpose is the Norway spruce (*Picea excelsa*). This is a large tree with drooping boughs found on most of the European mountain ranges from the Pyrenees north.

2) The pines (genus *Pinus*). Incorrectly known as fir in England. The long needles are arranged in bundles, the number in each varying according to the species. The most important is the Scotch fir or Scotch pine

[20] *Ibid.*, I, 566.
[21] Francesco Griselini's *Dizionario delle arti e de' mestieri* is a word-for-word translation from the *Encyclopédie*; however, it is useful to see how the word *sapin* is translated.

(*Pinus sylvestris*) which has a mushroomlike top in maturity and is indigenous to northern Europe.

3) The firs (genus *Abies*). Sessile needles, often flat. The most important is the silver fir (*Abies pectinata*) which has a straight trunk and conical profile. It is found in the northernmost countries of Europe.

4) The cypress (genus *Cupressus*). This presents no problem. The tree is that pointed evergreen which grows everywhere on the shores of the Mediterranean (*Cupressus sempervirens*). Only the Italians used its wood for soundboards.

So far as dictionary definitions go, the following are the equivalents:

Picea: Spruce, spruce-fir, *Fichte* (German), *épicea* (French).

Pinus: Pine, fir (in Great Britain), *pin* (French), *Kiefer* (German).

Abies: Fir, *abete* (Italian), *sapin* (French), *Tanne* (German), *vuuren-hout* (Dutch).

These specific meanings, however, are obscured by the fact that the words *Tanne*, *Fichte*, *sapin*, pine, and fir are all applied loosely to various genera.

Halle gives the following description of the tree he considered proper for soundboards:

The *Tanne* of the white type in which the knots or needle bundles pull out; torn out, these produce a fluid resin. On each scale of the cone two seed pods are attached of which the top surface is winged. The pointed, longish needles are placed on one side only of the stem where in the *Fichte* they are arranged in rings around it. The wood is soft, fine grained and white with little resin. It is brought to us from Saxony. All sorts of cabinetwork is made of *Tanne* planks. It serves especially for chests and the best quality is made into the soundboards of harpsichords, clavichords, harps, violins, and zithers.[22]

We seem condemned to labor in ambiguity and uncertainty, for even this description does not completely settle the question. Halle specifically rules out the spruces with the word *Fichte* coupled with a correct description of spruce needles. But he is not so successful in distinguishing between the two remaining groups, the pines and the firs. Pine needles grow in clusters, but only firs have their needles on one side of the twig. Fir cones fit Halle's description better than pine cones. Two out of the three elements point to fir, and the word *Tanne*, while not always specific, is more correctly applied to fir than pine. Therefore it seems that Halle really meant that soundboards were to be made of fir. This supposition is strengthened by the fact that Jacobsson specifies *Tannenholz* for the soundboard and *Kienenholz*, or pine, for the case. Thus Halle

[22] *Werkstäte der heutigen Künste*, chap. 22, "Der Tischer" (*sic*).

rules out spruce as a soundboard material, and Jacobsson pine, leaving only fir.

It is very difficult to identify the wood of existing soundboards under the dirt and wax of centuries. Scientific techniques provide the only reliable means of identification. These, however, require that a sample be provided a laboratory, and this is not easy in the case of harpsichord soundboards. I have managed to obtain a small piece of a Ruckers soundboard and part of the belly of an Italian lute of the sixteenth century. The United States Forest Products Laboratory very kindly identified both of these specimens as spruce, probably Norway spruce (*Picea excelsa*). This finding says little in relation to Halle's specifying fir. Possibly both fir and spruce were used.

Soundboard wood came from various sources. Jacobsson mentioned the Black Forest and Bohemia; Halle suggested Saxony; the Swiss editions of the *Encyclopédie* say Lorraine and Switzerland, but the Paris edition called it *sapin de Hollande*. Since the *Verhandeling over de Muziek* states that fir was brought to Holland from Switzerland, the two editions of the *Encyclopédie* were really in agreement. As we have seen, a great deal of thin wood was supplied by Amsterdam dealers, and it was probably in that form that the French makers bought it. A frequent item in the French inventories is *sapin* in *feuilles*, or leaves, for soundboard making, and considerable quantities were often on hand.

As for the criteria to be applied to soundboard wood, most authorities agreed that it should be fine-grained, free from blemishes, nonresinous, and very dry. Diderot's informants told him that it must be without knots or checks, that it must season a long time after having been sawed into leaves and that one should choose only the oldest and the best possible woods for soundboards. Gall specifies that it be somewhat hard and "ringing." Jacobsson warns against the heartwood and resinous varieties and advises the harpsichord maker to use the driest wood he can find. Adlung was even more disturbed by the possibility of oily or resinous substances remaining in the wood. Having said that fine (*subtile*) and dry stock should be sought he advises the maker as follows: "The wood of the soundboard must not be oily. Accordingly, an instrument maker is accustomed to boil out such planks as he is going to use for soundboards. This can be done in a suitable brewer's vat." [23] This practice may often have produced the noticeably chalky texture of some of the German soundboards. Adlung does not mention the fact that a long period of drying would be necessary after such a leaching process.

[23] *Musica mechanica organoedi*, II, 112.

In addition to timber, harpsichord makers had to find wire and pins, wrought-iron stop mechanisms, hardware, buff leather, and crow quills. Pennant remarked that "the quills of ravens sell for twelve shillings the hundred, being of great use in tuning the lower notes of a harpsichord." [24] *Peau de buffle* seems to have been a common article in commerce as a result of its general employment for items of military equipment. Its chief use in harpsichords was not for the Taskin type of plectra but for buff stops, to which end it was almost universally applied.

As might be expected, harpsichord makers do not seem to have made their own hinges and other decorative hardware. Certain initials cast into the back of English hinges might be useful to specialists in identifying the foundries. One of the curious facts about English harpsichord strap hinges is that all the hinges were nearly identical regardless of the maker of the harpsichord, and yet the pattern never seems to have appeared on other types of contemporary furniture.

On the Continent guild regulations would probably have been enough to prevent harpsichord makers from forging their own iron stop mechanisms and wrest pins. In any case, there is no evidence of any forging equipment in the harpsichord shops of which we have inventories. In the bundle of notarial acts which contains the Taskin inventory of 1777 certain accounts of that maker are to be found. Among the items is a debt of 194 *livres* owed by Taskin "au machiniste." It seems likely that this machinist had been supplying him with his metal parts.

Harpsichord makers require thin wire for the strings of their instruments, steel for the treble and brass for the bass. Both of these had been standard items in commerce since the invention of the draw plate in the tenth century. The eighteenth century compiler of the *Dictionnaire portatif de commerce* remarked that

there are several sizes [of brass wire] used in different products. The thinnest is called clavichord wire [*manicordion*] and is used to make the strings of various musical instruments such as the clavichord (whence it takes its name), harpsichords, spinets, and others . . . Considerable shipments of it are made from Laigle and Rugle in Normandy and from the other provinces of France wherever this type of factory is established. From Germany and particularly from the neighborhood of Aix-la-Chapelle comes a great deal of brass wire of all types from the thinnest to the thickest. These wires are sent in coils or packets, circular in shape, of various weights and diameters. Their circular form gives them the name of hoop-brass. A great deal also comes from Sweden. [25]

[24] Thomas Pennant, *British Zoology* (London, 1766), I, 280.
[25] Vol. III, p. 18.

Iron or steel wire seems to have been drawn in many parts of Europe, but the best was supposed to come from Liège. A particular specialty of thin iron wire was made at Cologne. The iron wire used in old harpsichords has a lower carbon content and is much closer to pure iron than the sort we now call music wire. Thus it was much softer and more pliable (see Appendix B).

The question of the precise diameters of the wire used for harpsichord strings is an intriguing one. French, Dutch, German, and English sources provide us with tables of the appropriate gauge numbers of wire to be used for each string, and certain French, English, and Italian harpsichords are inscribed with the pertinent gauge numbers, usually on the nut. The problem is to translate these obsolete gauges into terms of absolute diameter. Perhaps Hugh Gough has been the most successful in this regard since he was fortunate enough to find several English harpsichords which seemed not to have been restrung since the eighteenth century and upon which the gauge numbers were stamped. By measuring the strings with a micrometer he was able to construct a table which Boalch has printed on page 106 of his dictionary of harpsichord and clavichord makers. This system suffers from the damaging possibility that the strings, while old, may not be original and may not conform to the indicated numbers. Even if it is correct it is not of assistance in dealing with French harpsichords. The English gauge numbers and those from Hamburg resemble each other in that the diameter increases with the gauge numbers while the French and most German stringing lists move in the opposite direction, the largest gauge numbers referring to the finest wire.

After consulting many technical dictionaries and treatises on the mechanical arts, I have come to the conclusion that there was not a very rigid correspondence between gauge number and diameter during the epoch of the harpsichord except on a local and temporary basis. The process of wire manufacture, which involved the drawing of wire through a series of die plates of constantly decreasing diameter, was not easily subjected to the imposition of an immutable standard. The die plates were of steel and the holes were formed by punches. After a certain amount of wire had been drawn through a die, the hole became slightly enlarged and the resulting wire was thicker. The very fact that the many discussions of wire manufacture which I have been able to find almost never provide tables of diameters, although the same works contain tables of almost everything else, would seem to indicate that these gauges were not standardized.

Gough found twelve sizes of wire, from no. 3 to no. 14, varying in diameter from .009 inch to .0315 inch. The harpsichord to which his table primarily pertains was one of those large Shudis which descended to CC, which accounts for the rather large diameter of the bass strings. Normally, one would not expect a five-octave harpsichord to require wire heavier than .025 inch, corresponding to English gauge no. 12. Gough's table of equivalents follows.

English gauge number	Diameter in inches
3	.009
4	.010
5	.0115
6	.0135
7	.0145
8	.016
9	.018
10	.020
11	.022
12	.0245
13	.027
14	.0315

Table 18 brings together some of the principal stringing lists. Allowing for the differences between harpsichords and individual prejudices regarding the size of strings to be used, this table seems to demonstrate that all of continental Europe during the seventeenth and eighteenth centuries was operating within more or less the same gauge system while the English system was obviously different. Continental harpsichords in general were probably strung more lightly than the rather heavy English instruments. With this assumption in mind it is possible to construct the following highly speculative table for the continental gauges.

Gauge number	Diameter (inches)	Gauge number	Diameter (inches)
11	.007	4	.0145
10	.008	3	.016
9	.009	2	.018
8	.010	1	.020
7	.011	0	.022
6	.012 [26]	00	.024
5	.0135	000	.026

[26] Géoffrion de Cryseul, *Moyens de diviser les touches les plus correctements possible*, Paris, Lille, Valenciennes, Douay, 1780, 25: "Soit une corde de cuivre d'une grosseur telle qu'il en faille 92 diametres pour un pouce, les clavecinistes la marquent du No. 6." ("If a copper string is of such a size that there are ninety-two diameters in one inch, the harpsichordists mark it No. 6.") This agrees fairly well with our table: 1⁄92 pouce equals .0116 inch.

Table 18. String gauge numbers [a]

	Kirckman	Corrette	Encyclopédie	Dumont	Bendeler	Adlung	Gall	Hasch	Italian	Douwes
f'''	#4 b	#9	#11	#9		#10	#8		#10	
e'''	4	9	11	9		10	8		10	
d#'''	4	9	11	9		10	8		10	
d'''	4	9	11	9		10	8		10	
c#'''	4	9	11	9		10	8		10	
c'''	4	9	11	9		10	8	#9	10	#10
b''	4	9	11	8		9	8	9	10	10
a#''	4	9	11	8		9	8	9	10	10
a''	4	9	11	8		9	8	9	10	10
g#''	4	9	11	8		9	8	9	10	10
g''	4	9	10	8	#9	9	8	9	9	10
f#''	4	9	10	8		9	8	9	9	10
f''	4	9	10	8		9	8	9	9	10
e''	4	9	10	8		9	7	9	9	9
d#''	4	9	10	8		9	7	9	9	9
d''	4	9	9	8		9	7	9	9	9
c#''	4	9	9	7		9	7	9	9	9
c''	4	8	9	7	9	9	7	8	8	9
b'	5	8	9	7			7	8	8	9
a#'	5	8	9	7			7	8	8	9
a'	5	8	8	7			7	8	8	8
g#'	5	8	8	7			7	8	8	8
g'	5	8	8	7			6	8	8	8
f#'	5	8	8	7			6	8	8	8
f'	5	8	8	7	6		6	8	7	8
e'	5	8	7	6			6	8	7	8
d#'	5	8	7	6			6	8	7	8
d'	5	8	7	6			6	7	7	7
c#'	5	8	7	6			6	7	7	7
c'	6	7	7	6			5	7		7
b	6	7	6 or 5	6			5	7		7
a#	6	7	6 or 5	6			5	7		7
a	6	7	6 or 5	6			5	7		7
g#	6	7	6 or 5	5			5	7		7
g	6	6 or 7	6 or 5	5			5	6		7
f#	6	6	5 brass	5			5	6		6
f	7	6	5 "	5			4	6		6
e	7	6	5 "	5			4	6		6
d#	7	5	5 "	4			4	6		6
d	7	5	4 "	4			4	5		6
c#	7	5	4 "	4			4	5		5 brass
c	8	6 brass	4 "	4			3	5		5
B	8	6 "	4 "	4			3	5		5
A#	8	5 "	3 "	4			3	5		4
A	8 brass	4 "	3 "	4			3	4		4
G#	8 "	3 "	3 "	3			3	4		
G	8 "	3 "	3 "	3			2	4		3
F#	8 "	3 "	2 "	3			2	3		

Table 18 (cont'd)

	Kirckman	Corrette	Encyclopédie	Dumont	Bendeler	Adlung	Gall	Hasch	Italian	Douwes
F	9 brass	3 brass	2 brass	2						
E	9 "	3 "	2 "	2			2	3		3
D♯	9 "	2 "	1 "	2 brass			2	2		2
D	10 "	2 "	1 "	2 "			1	2		2
C♯	10 "	2 "	1 "	2 "			1	1		
C	10 "	2 "	0 "	1 "			1	1		1
BB	10 "	1 "	0 "	1 "			1	1		
AA♯	11 "	1 "	0 "	1 "			0	0		
AA	11 "	0 "	00 "	0 "			0	00		
GG♯	12 "	0 "	00 "	0 "			0	00		
GG	12 "	0 "	000 "	00 "			0	00		
FF♯	13 "	00 "	000 "	00 "			0	000		
FF	13 "	00 "	000 "	00 "			0	000		

ᵃ Based on: (1) the nut markings on a Kirckman harpsichord of 1760; stringing lists in (2) Corrette, Le Maître de clavecin, and (3) the Encyclopédie; (4) nut markings on a Nicolas Dumont harpsichord of 1699; (5) remarks by Bendeler, Orgel-Bau-Kunst; (6) remarks by Adlung, Musica mechanica organoedi; (7) a stringing list in Gall, Clavier-Stimmbuch; nut markings on an (8) H. A. Hasch harpsichord of 1723, and on a (9) Baptista Cargnonus Salodiensis harpsichord of 1689; (10) stringing list in Douwes, Grondig Ondersoek. Douwes supposes a short octave. A♯ is the first accidental.

ᵇ Where not otherwise noted the material is assumed to be steel.

One of the small items which was employed in rather large quantities by harpsichord makers was the common, or dressmaker's, pin. For some time I was puzzled by the prodigality which permitted harpsichord makers to cut off the pin heads, using only the shanks for the tongue pivots. In modern days the waste of labor implied by the discarded heads would be negligible, but in the eighteenth century such might not have been the case. One would have expected bits of wire to have been used for the axles. Then, quite by chance, I stumbled upon an eighteenth century description of the manufacture of pins, which was actually a highly refined mass production operation. In this regard it is interesting that Adam Smith used pin manufacture as an example of the efficiency to be gained by the division of labor. The process seemed interesting enough to be worthy of quotation, and the reader will find it in Appendix B in a somewhat fuller early nineteenth century version.

Having obtained his materials the harpsichord maker could set to work. The first step of the modern maker would be to make drawings from which he could prepare the templates used to mark out the instruments. It is remarkable that the old makers do not seem to have worked very much from drawings. In all of our inventories there are only three hints of drawings or templates, and none is very specific. In 1737 Blanchet had some pieces of sheet iron "for harpsichord soundboards" which might have been templates of some sort. The Goermans inventory of 1789 (item 14) shows a package of old patterns "proper for the trade." Item 23 of the Malade inventory of 1781 lists "a plan of a harpsichord" (see Appendix C).

I have seen one Italian harpsichord in which the maker had drawn the plan view of the instrument in full scale on the inside of the bottom.[27] He obviously began by jointing enough planks to form the bottom, made his drawing on this panel and subsequently fitted each part to the drawing like a boy building a model airplane from a kit. This could only have been an Italian technique as the following will make clear.

One of the fundamental differences between the northern and the southern methods of construction lay in the placement of the bottom. The Italians began by making a bottom which they cut to shape. The knees and wrest plank blocks were mounted flush with its edges. Then the sides were nailed and glued to the outside of the bottom, covering its edge. The northerners began by assembling the sides of the case, inserted the frame,[28] and then nailed and glued the bottom to the lower edge of the sides. Under the paint or veneer the edge of the bottom is exposed. This means that the bottom of a northern harpsichord is easy to remove, but it is almost impossible to do so with an Italian. Since the northern makers did not build their instruments on the bottom in the southern style, there would have been no point in their attempting to use it as a pattern in the manner of the Italian maker mentioned above. A corollary to the two methods of construction is the full-length bottom found in Italian harpsichords in which the bottom planks run the full length of the instrument and the northern style in which the planks run lengthwise from the belly rail to the tail but crosswise under the keyboards.

The English harpsichords appear at first sight to have been built in the Italian manner, but a closer examination will show that this is only an illusion caused by the molding which covers the edge of the bottom. At the spine, where there is no molding, the edge of the bottom can be seen.

Like a beaver building his dam, then, the maker constructed his case,

[27] A 1646 Andreas Ruckers (the elder) harpsichord shows much the same technique being practiced by the maker who enlarged it. A drawing was made on the new bottom showing the old soundboard, the pieces to be added, the wrestplank and belly rail, etc. Each part is carefully labeled in Flemish (or Dutch).

[28] Diderot states that the frame was inserted after the bottom was attached to the sides. In any case, the French assembled the sides independently, and the Italians assembled them on the bottom.

guided by experience for the length and by the known size of a keyboard of the projected range for the width. He planed each of his sawed planks smooth with the jack plane and reduced them to the correct width. Diderot prescribes dovetails for all the corners and tongue and groove assembly for the planks making up the bottom. There is a harpsichord by Pascal Taskin (1769), privately owned in Paris, which has dovetailed joints as Diderot recommended, but most French makers, like Ruckers, made corner joints as shown in Plate VI for cheek to bentside and bentside to tail, and mitered the tail to spine. The English, the eighteenth century Flemish, and the Germans usually dovetailed the corners. The Italians mitered all corners.

The French inventories often show bentsides stocked in the workshops. It is curious that in his tremendous treatise on cabinetmaking Roubo never mentioned bending techniques. It should be noted that all of the tortuous curves of carriages, furniture, and building woodwork were sawed out. There are a few hints of the process of imparting the curve to a bentside. In 1726 Blanchet had a "lead trough for soaking bentsides, with the bending form." This device was to be found in his workshop from 1722 to 1766, but its like was not often mentioned elsewhere. Malade, however, had a "machine for bending wood" in 1774. Jacobsson describes the process thus: "The bentside is made out of maple [29] which is softened in water, then clamped to a form with the shape of the curve and there allowed to dry, whereupon the plank holds the curve." [30] The *Verhandeling over de Muziek* says, "it has been in water for several days and then is fastened to a form and dried in a baker's oven." [31]

Blanchet's apparatus must have consisted of the soaking-trough and a form. The curious thing is that there is no mention of heat. Nowadays wood is exposed to hot water or, better, to steam for some hours and then clamped to the form. I have never experimented with simple soaking, but one would have to dry the bentside for a very long time after such a prolonged immersion.

I am inclined to believe that the Italian makers did not ordinarily prebend their bentsides before assembling their harpsichords. To begin with, the Italian bentside was so thin that it could be bent to shape dry, and the Italian bottom, with the knees standing vertically along its edge, is a

---

[29] We have seen that a composite construction, the bentsides of hard wood and the rest of the case of soft wood, is specifically German although sometimes found in England.

[30] *Technologisches Wörterbuch*, I, 766.

[31] Page 193: "eenige dagen in het water gelegt, op eene mal gespannen, en gedroogt op eenen Bakkers oven."

convenient support to which it is easy to fasten even a springy board. I have made copies of Italian harpsichords without pre-bending, and so I can definitely state that it is possible. I once had occasion to remove the bentside of an Italian harpsichord almost three hundred years old, and within a day it had become almost straight. This suggests that it had not been soaked and bent on a form.

Modern makers often clamp several laminates to a form. When the glue between the layers has set, the structure retains the curve of the form. This technique is preferable to steam bending because the curve is more stable in conditions of varying humidity and it is easier to predict the final shape. Diderot may have known something of this technique, for he says: "The concave side FBDG is made of three or four pieces, more or less, in order more easily to give it the curve it must have."[32] Since bentsides never were butted except in *ravalement* it seems that Diderot was indicating a laminated construction, but it is unfortunate that he was not more specific. I have never seen an antique laminated bentside earlier than about 1820.

With the molding plane (see Plate XXXII, figure 31), a molding was cut in the upper edge of each side (before bending), the wrest plank was planed and veneered, and the case was assembled. The bottom was doweled to the sides and the frame and liners installed. Once the case was prepared the harpsichord maker planed the edges of the planks he intended for his soundboard and glued them together. Diderot specifies fish glue for this purpose, but it seems rather unsuitable since it is excessively sensitive to moisture. The *Verhandeling over de Muziek* describes a process of clamping: the soundboard planks are placed side by side on a bench top; they are forced together with wedges and weights are placed on top to keep them from springing upward; the joints are covered with strips of paper at the moment of gluing so that in shrinking it will aid the wedges. This is a technique still used in veneering. However, the use of Roubo's clamps seems a more professional method and more likely to have been generally used.[33]

The soundboard was next planed smooth on both sides and reduced to thickness. Many authorities give ⅛ inch as the normal thickness, but several mention that this could not be taken as an immutable standard, and Jacobsson specifically says that the soundboard was planed by eye. The extreme recommendations for soundboard thickness are ¹⁄₁₆ inch by

[32] "Clavecin," 483b.
[33] Some modern makers hold that any pressure is bad in jointing soundboards since it produces locked-in stresses. They "rub-joint" and use no clamps. In my opinion the locked-in stresses are more than offset by the more certain joint obtained with clamps.

Adlung and a little less than ¼ inch by the *Verhandeling over de Muziek*. The *Verhandeling over de Muziek* describes a rather marked taper from bass to treble, leaving the wood a little heavy around the rose and thinning the soundboard between the eight-foot bridge and the bentside. Adlung and Diderot held that a rose must be cut into the soundboard if no other opening was provided, but Jacobsson, Gall, and Talbot did not find it necessary.

There is a great deal of confusion among authorities as to the nature of the ribbing to be applied to the underside of the soundboard. This obviously reflects the fact that the ribbing could not be seen from the outside and that makers universally regarded it as an important secret on which great stress had been laid as far back as Mersenne's time. "Il faut seulement remarquer que l'vn des principaux secrets de l'Epinette consiste à barrer la table, dont la bonté depend de l'excellente barrure, qui a esté pratiquée en perfection par Anthoine Potin, & Emery ou Mederic, que l'on recognoist auoir esté les meilleurs Facteurs de France" ("It is necessary only to remark that one of the principal secrets of the spinet consists in the ribbing of the soundboard, the quality of which depends on excellent ribbing, which has been practiced to perfection by Anthoine Potin, & Emery or Mederic who are recognized as having been the best makers of France").[34]

Diderot provides a plate which bears no resemblance to any arrangement under any soundboard that I have seen (see Plate XXXV, figure 3). The description which conforms best to the observed facts appeared first in the Swiss quarto editions of the *Encyclopédie*.

The greatest part of these good qualities depend on the quality of the soundboard, on the accuracy of the scale of the bridge and on the arrangement of an interior counterbridge [four-foot hitchpin rail] which is glued to the soundboard between the two bridges and which is called *boudin* in the terms of the trade. This *boudin*, as well as the transverse ribs placed on the bass side of the harpsichord between the terminal side or the straight plank which is on the bass side at the rear of the harpsichord [spine] and the *diapason* or bridge of the four-foot, contribute a great deal to the good quality of the sound when these pieces are arranged according to the true principles of the art.[35]

It will be noted that the cutoff bar is not mentioned. The writer does not seem to have been aware that if the four-foot hitchpin rail serves as "counterbridge" to the eight-foot, the cutoff bar serves the same function to the four-foot. It was always present except in those Italian harpsi-

[34] *Harmonie universelle*, III, 159.
[35] "Clavecin."

chords which were ribbed diagonally from side to side. The transverse ribs extend to the cutoff bar, not to the four-foot bridge.

Kirckman always glued strips of cloth along the underside of the soundboard joints and over the ends of the ribs as reinforcements. It is revealing that he left off the cloth immediately under the bridges, apparently in order not to damp the tone. This precaution, probably an excessive one, suggests that Kirckman would have felt ribs under the bridges to be detrimental to the tone and may indicate that many of the ribs we now find under the soundboards of old harpsichords, French and Flemish as well as English, were placed there as repairs when age had caused the board to crack or deform.

Many of our authorities describe the bending and placing of the bridges and the installation of the soundboard as the next steps. However, it seems likely that most makers made the keyboard and registers next, since the marking out was performed essentially from the keyboard and it would have been exceedingly difficult to glue the bridges to a soundboard already in the harpsichord. For the sake of unity we shall assume that the keyboards and registers have been made and continue with the marking out of the soundboard. Jacobsson gives the following directions for this process:

The harpsichord has two bridges and their spacing is determined by the length of the strings. The front bridge [nut] lies just behind the wrest pins on the wrest plank, the back bridge, however, is on the soundboard running the length of the curve and has the same curved form. The nut runs obliquely across the harpsichord. The mortises in the registers establish the position of the strings very exactly. Thus, one draws lines from the nut on the wrest plank through each mortise in both registers on to the soundboard. One determines the place of the bridge by the length of the strings. These different points give the form and position of the bridge.[36]

Previously[37] Jacobsson had said that the length of each "c" in the instrument was to be marked on a measuring stick. It seems likely that this measuring stick was used to establish the curve of the bridge. Gall proceeds by the same system. The *Verhandeling over de Muziek* gives a Ruckers scale but is not particularly clear about how to obtain it. Having provided only general dimensions for the case, the writer specifies the scale while suggesting that the bridge be as far from the bentside as possible. The wrest pins were to be marked out from the registers by means of mock strings crossing the mortises.[38]

[36] *Technologisches Wörterbuch*, IV, 269.
[37] *Ibid.*, I, 198.
[38] Paragraph 86.

The measuring stick method of marking out can be further documented. Douwes gives directions[39] for the construction of the rack of a clavichord. The spacing of its grooves determines the splaying of the keys and hence the scale. The point is that instead of drawing the clavichord, including the rack, Douwes performs prodigies with a compass, graduating a marking-out stick which is then used as a guide in sawing the grooves in the rack. Dom Bedos[40] teaches the organ builder to mark out his keyboard directly on the panel, using a *règle du clavier* (keyboard ruler). It seems a waste of effort to have to redraw these constructions for each instrument, but there seems to be little doubt that this was in fact done. Modern makers rely greatly on drawings and templates to speed up the process of construction. The high level of production which the old shops were able to attain without these aids is remarkable. However, the old method depended upon the maker's experience to provide automatically a viable shape of case in which to insert string band and action. Thus the conservatism we have found in most schools of harpsichord making had a basis in necessity. If the maker departed far from the instruments he knew, he was likely to get into trouble. The modern maker makes his mistakes on paper and he knows when he commences a harpsichord that it will work. He is much freer to experiment.

The soundboard having been marked out, the bridge was bent, formed, and glued on. In the northern traditions sawed rather than bent bridges are often found. Those bridges with a molding section were always bent but the simpler form of the English, Flemish, and French bridges could more easily be made by sawing a wide plank to the appropriate curve and finishing with plane and spokeshave. Most of the north European harpsichords show a line of nail heads on the underside of the soundboard on the line of the bridges. It is difficult to see exactly how these could have been driven at the moment of gluing on the bridge. They may have been added afterwards as reinforcements. Or perhaps the soundboard was drilled on the centerline of the bridge with a row of holes spaced about six inches apart, nails were inserted from below, and the soundboard was backed by a hard surface (possibly Blanchet's sheet iron, mentioned above). The bridge was carefully drilled from the underside to match, but the holes were left a little undersize and shallow. The glue was spread and the bridge driven down onto the nails with a mallet. The nails then served as positioning pins and clamps.

Nuts were positioned on the wrest plank by a different method. Con-

[39] *Grondig Ondersoek*, p. 98.
[40] *L'Art du facteur d'orgues*, p. 244.

struction lines are often found scribed into wrest planks, and it seems likely that the layout was drawn on the surface of the wrest plank by ordinary drafting means. Kirckman seems to have driven two rows of pins into the wrest plank between which the nut was positioned and glued.

Many northern soundboards seem to have been left unfinished except for the tempera paintings. The third letter of the Duarte-Huyghens correspondence mentions that the soundboard as well as the inside of the lid and the nameboard of Huyghen's new Couchet was to be left white in order that they might be decorated later to his taste. The phrase used is "boden onder de snaren," and one wonders if the instrument was to be unstrung in order to be painted. This remark indicates that the makers usually did not decorate the soundboards themselves. In Antwerp it would have been legally possible for them to do so since they were members of the guild of painters. In Paris the greater sophistication of the painting and the more binding guild regulations make it less likely.

Lorenz Mizler [41] provided a recipe for harpsichord soundboard varnish which he claimed was identical to that used for violins by Jacob Stainer. If so, the violin world should rush to Mizler's door, for Stainer's varnish is of that type mourned as a lost secret. Adlung [42] picked up Mizler's remarks and warned that a varnish for harpsichord soundboards must not be oily, for all fat and oil is the ruination of harpsichord soundboards. The concoction in question is a spirit varnish based on gum copal.

The *Verhandeling over de Muziek* [43] advocates varnishing the soundboard on both sides and states that varnish improves the sound, but the *Encyclopédie* does not mention varnished soundboards at all. I have not seen a harpsichord with a soundboard varnished on the underside. The English harpsichord soundboards most often show signs of having been varnished. The Italian seem to have been usually oiled or waxed, a technique appropriate to cypress but hopeless for spruce, pine, or fir.

Next the lid was jointed, cut to shape, and hinged. In England a molding was nailed and glued to the underside to hide the joint between the case and the lid, but this was not often found in France, Germany, or Flanders. The harpsichord was now ready to be decorated in whatever style was in fashion at the moment. The most elaborate were sent out to be painted by well-known artists, but others received more modest treatment. Ernest Closson has printed the following letter written by Taskin describing the then current Blanchet models.

[41] *Neu eröffnete musikalische Bibliothek* (Leipzig, 1739–1749), II, 266.
[42] *Anleitung zu der musikalischen Gelahrtheit*, p. 564, note c.
[43] Paragraph 88.

Paris, October 6, 1765

Monsieur,

Please accept my duty and I have the honor to reply to your question. The price of a good new harpsichord runs about six, seven, or eight hundred livres — made by Mr. Blanchet, harpsichord maker to the King, who is the *bourgeois* for whom I work; they are *à grands ravallement* [sic], a term of our trade which means two manuals of which each keyboard is composed of 61 keys, which is five octaves. The outside is painted black, white, gray, blue, green, or red with a band of gold running round the outside, and under the lid in the orders of architecture. Occasionally one can find them second hand at 400 to 500 livres and that by the chance of a kept woman being abandoned, and such a present having remained with her by way of gratitude. They can be had from other makers at the price of 400 to 500 livres new, and old or second hand some hundred livres cheaper, but these are productions to provide expense. Many have passed through my hands to have quantities of faults corrected.[44]

The English maker of the eighteenth century would be certain to veneer his case at this point. More rarely the French and Germans might, and the technique was not entirely unknown to the Italians. We have mentioned the early type of Italian harpsichord in which the cypress case was veneered inside and outside with ebony. The most convenient time to do this would be before the planks were assembled. Some Italian spinets were decorated with parquetry designs (a repetitive pattern produced by covering the surface with squares, lozenges, or other simple geometric forms in veneer).[45] In the late eighteenth century the Italians sometimes decorated their non-inner-outer style of cases in the same manner.

The English harpsichord maker either bought his veneer ready sawed from his timber merchant or sawed it out of the log himself. Plate XXXVI, taken from Roubo, illustrates this process. An English source describes the veneering procedure as follows:

The wood used in veneering is first sawed out into slices or leaves about a line in thickness, i.e. the twelfth part of an inch. In order to saw them, the blocks or planks are placed upright, in a kind of sawing-press. See SAWING-MILL.

These slices are afterwards cut into narrow slips, and fashioned divers ways, according to the design proposed; then the joints having been exactly and nicely adjusted, and the pieces brought down to their proper thickness, with several planes for the purpose, they are glued down on a ground or block, with good strong English glue.

The pieces being thus jointed and glued, the work, if small, is put in a

<hr>

[44] "Pascal Taskin."

[45] There is a full treatment of the techniques of parquetry and marquetry in Roubo, *L'Art du menuisier*, "L'Art du menuisier-ébéniste."

press; if large, 'tis laid on a bench covered with a board, and pressed down with poles or pieces of wood, one end of which reaches to the cieling [sic] of the room, and the other bears on the board.

When the glue is thoroughly dry, it is taken out of the press and finished; first with little planes, then with divers scrapers, some of which resemble rasps, which take off the dents, &c. left by the planes.

After it has been sufficiently scraped, they polish it with the skin of a sea-dog, wax and a brush, or polisher of shave-grass; which is the last operation.[46]

This process is suitable for the veneering of flat panels. In the case of curved parts such as harpsichord bentsides the maker had to use a technique which involved spreading the glue, placing the panel of veneer in position, and rubbing it from the center outward with a tool called a veneering hammer. This forced out the excess glue leaving the veneer firmly adhered to the carcass. If necessary, the maker could use a heated iron to remelt the glue. He may have used a shaped caul or sandbag to hold the veneer in place until the glue was quite hard. Plate XXXVII, again taken from Roubo, shows the veneering hammer and heating iron in use.

The characteristic English panel of mahogany or walnut surrounded by a cross-grained band of a similar or contrasting wood was often assembled on the carcass and not according to the method described above in which the individual pieces of veneer were cut to shape on the bench. This assertion can be demonstrated by the existence of certain knife cuts on carcasses of English harpsichord cases which line up with the veneer joints above them. The panel was left oversized and was glued roughly in position, extending beyond its true margins on all sides. When the glue had set fairly well, the panel was trimmed to shape with a knife and a straightedge or cutting gauge (that is, a marking gauge containing a knife blade in the place of the scribe). The inlay line could be glued on next, held in position by pins, or the cross-grained band could be built up piece by piece. One segment of veneer would be glued on, then the next would be placed with its edge overlapping that of the first. A knife cut would pass through both (marking the carcass). The waste wood removed, both pieces were rubbed down well with the veneering hammer, and paper was glued over the joint. When the cross-grained banding was complete, and if the inlay was not in place, a cutting gauge or knife would make the necessary trimming cut parallel to the edges of the panel.

---

[46] *A New Universal History of Arts and Sciences* (London, 1759), II, 531. As so frequently happens, the cross reference to "sawing-mill" leads to nothing; there is no article on this subject.

The waste veneer could be warmed and removed and the inlay strip inserted. Sometimes even the cross-grained tulipwood inlay strips were built up *in situ* in this manner.

Roubo does not seem to have made much use of varnish or other heavy finishes for the surface of veneered work. The French cabinetmakers, however, generally used very hard, smooth-grained woods which could be finished well enough with wax. The more open-grained walnut and mahogany favored by the English required something to fill the grain, and most of the English harpsichords seem to have been varnished. The subject of eighteenth century varnish is one in which feeling runs high, and we must advance with trepidation. Each violin maker and his disciples have a pet theory which is ordinarily revealed just enough to provide mystery but not enough to serve as the basis for discussion.

Varnish, according to Dr. Ure, "is a solution of resinous matter, which is spread over the surface of any body, in order to give it a shining, transparent, and hard coat, capable of resisting, in a greater or less degree, the influences of air and moisture." [47] Generally speaking, there are two types, oil varnishes and spirit varnishes. In the first type resins are dissolved in a hot siccative oil such as linseed oil, usually thinned with turpentine. In the second the resins are dissolved in alcohol.

Since oil varnishes are much more difficult to make, most varnish faddists concentrate on them. However, I am inclined to believe that the spirit varnishes were commonly employed for harpsichords. The only varnish mentioned by Roubo falls into that class. *A New Universal History of Arts and Sciences* [48] does not mention oil varnish but provides several spirit varnishes. Watin, [49] the standard eighteenth century authority on this subject, gives a spirit varnish as the most suitable for violins and other musical instruments. He contrasts the qualities of the various varnishes: "It is the object that one wishes to varnish which must determine which of the three varnishes one should use. If it must be exposed to the outside air and to the injuries of the weather, one should apply oil varnish; if, on the contrary, it will be enclosed, cared for and conserved in the interior of apartments, then one uses spirit varnish, which is every bit as brilliant, has no odor, dries more quickly and is durable, so long as it does not suffer continual exposure to the air." [50]

[47] Andrew Ure, M.D., *A Dictionary of Arts, Manufactures and Mines* (3rd ed., New York, 1842), p. 1270.
[48] "Varnish."
[49] Jean Félix Watin, *L'Art de faire et d'employer le vernis ou L'Art du vernisseur* (Paris, 1772), p. 79.
[50] *Ibid.*, p. 72.

Later editions of Watin's work specify more clearly the difference between oil and spirit varnishes. "For the perfection of the art of the varnisher one would desire either that spirit varnish acquire more solidity or that oil varnish become more brilliant. The former are not very durable; sandarac is too soft, rosin is merely brilliant, alcohol thin. The second are less beautiful; the change that occurs in copal and amber through the violent action of the fire damages their transparency and the oil that one introduces, however clean and white it may be, always dulls them." [51] From this description it seems hardly likely that oil varnish would be chosen for fine furniture. Indeed, the uses that Watin prescribes for oil varnish are connected with the exposed parts of carriages.

The spirit varnish which Watin gives for violins and other musical instruments is made in the following way.

> 4 oz. Sandarac
> 2 oz. Shellac in grains
> 2 oz. Gum mastic in tears
> 1 oz. Gum elemi

Place the above in one *pinte* [93 centiliters, nearly one quart] of alcohol. Melt over a low heat and when the solution has boiled several times add 2 oz. of Venice turpentine.

"Venice turpentine" is a semiliquid crude rosin. Probably the cake rosin would do as well. This formula is very similar to that given by Roubo for the finishing of veneered work and to the so-called "white varnish" of *A New Universal History of Arts and Sciences*.

Of all the parts of the harpsichord the keyboard imposes the most stringent demand on the maker's manual technique. This was even more true in the eighteenth century when the keys were sawed out by hand. The mark of a Taskin or a Kirckman harpsichord is an accurate and handsome keyboard.

The fundamental method of keyboard making has not changed since early times. A panel is jointed to the dimensions of the entire keyboard and the outlines of each key are drawn on its surface. The natural key tops are glued on and any lines to be scored in their surface are scribed. The key bed having been prepared, the panel is positioned on it and clamped there. The holes for the balance pins are drilled through the keyboard panel into the balance rail, and the grooves for the rack are marked. If, like the English harpsichords, the keys are guided by front rail pins, holes for these are drilled before the key tops are applied. This technique of drilling both key and key bed in one operation insures that

[51] Page 326 (1823 ed.).

the keys take the correct position when they are mounted on their pins. Even if the hole has not been drilled in the center of the key, the same error has been made in the key bed and the key remains correctly positioned. The next operation is to saw down the lines between the keys, dividing the panel into the separate keys. This is the moment of truth for the keyboard maker. If his hand is not steady the keys become uneven in width or the spaces between must be widened excessively in order to straighten wavy saw cuts. The edges of the keys are planed to remove the marks of the saw, the sides of the natural key heads are shaped, and the sharps are glued on. If the key fronts are to be formed of a piece of molding, this is glued onto the panel, but if they are arcaded or otherwise discontinuous, they must be added individually after the keys have been separated.

The problem in marking out a keyboard is reminiscent of tempering an octave in tuning, in which process one must spread a discrepancy over several divisions. There are twelve keys in the octave C to B, seven naturals and five sharps. Since there are no sharps between B and C and between E and F, those keys are divided by straight lines perpendicular to the front edge of the keyboard. The octave is thus divided into two unequal sections. The lower section contains five keys, C to E, and the upper section, seven, F to B. The lower section contains three naturals; the upper, four. Plate XXXVIII, figure 1, taken from Dom Bedos, makes this pattern clear.

In order to look well and be comfortable to play on, all the natural key heads must be of exactly equal width. Thus we can define the widths of the two unequal sections of the octave by the number of naturals they contain. The section C to E is three naturals wide, and the section F to B is four naturals wide. In the C to E section there are five keys. For the moment let us assume that the key tails (that is, the portion of the naturals which lies between the sharps) and the sharps are of equal width. Thus, in laying out the key tails and sharps we are dividing the C to E section, which is three naturals wide, into five equal parts. Similarly, the F to B section, which is four naturals wide, must be divided into seven equal parts. Thus each sharp or key tail in the C to E section must be three fifths of a natural in width, but each sharp or key tail in the F to B section would be four sevenths of a natural in width. However, the sharps are usually all of equal width. This increases the discrepancy in size of the tails of the two sections. Under the jacks all of the key levers are of even width. Thus the lines connecting the back of the keyboard to the front cannot be quite parallel.

Dom Bedos gives the following procedure for laying out a keyboard:

Before beginning the keyboards, one must make what is called the *règle du clavier* in the following manner. One will have a rule of fine-grained wood such as walnut or pear, 2¹¹⁄₁₆ inches wide by ¼ inch thick by 27¾ inches long, well planed. The line HP [see Plate XXXVIII] is drawn 1⁷⁄₁₆ inches from one edge with a marking gauge having a fine point. [See Plate XXXVIII, figure 1, which represents that rule half size.] A distance of 26⅗₁₆ inches is taken on that line and the points H and P are marked, one at each end. The distance between H and P is divided into 30 equal parts, which will be the 30 natural key heads representing the four octaves and one note of the keyboard. In order to make that division easily the distance HP is first divided into two equal parts. Next each half is divided into three parts, and finally, one divides each third of each half into five equal parts and one will have made the division into 30 equal spaces.

On the points L, R, M, O, U, Y, Z, X, J, Q, [the dividing lines between the B's and C's and the E's and F's] draw perpendiculars clear across the width of the rule. At all the other points draw perpendiculars which stop at the line HP.

In order to obtain the sharps, divide the width of one key head ah into eight equal parts, five of which are taken to establish the distance ab. With the compass set at the distance ab, mark ce. Divide the distance eb into three equal parts and mark the points d and i. Perform the same operations to the distances MO, UY, ZX. By this means one will have the C♯'s and the E♭'s.

To obtain the other sharps, divide the width VM of a key head again into five equal parts, of which one takes three to establish the distance mo. With the compass set to the distance mo, mark off cg. Divide the distance og into five equal parts and mark the four points, n, p, r, l. Perform the same operations to the distances OU, YZ, XJ. One then will have all the F♯'s, G♯'s, and the B♭'s. As far as the last C♯ is concerned, place it in the middle between the last C and the last D and make it of the width of the other C♯'s. Finally, having accurately and squarely cut off the superfluous ends of the rule on the first and last perpendiculars, follow all the marks with pen and ink. Write the name of each key and each sharp as is shown in the figure and the *règle de clavier* will be finished.[52]

Dom Bedos then marked out his panel by means of the *règle du clavier* and proceeded as we have outlined above. The mortises for the balance pins were cut with a chisel of the width of the pin and did not pass through the key (see Plate XXII, figure 3).

The sides of all the key levers at the front were usually stained black in keyboards equipped with ebony key tops, and the sides of the sharps only were stained in other styles. The *Verhandeling over de Muziek*[53]

---

[52] *L'Art de facteur d'orgues*, II, 246. Adjustment has been made to translate all dimensions from the *pied du roi* into modern inches, to the nearest ⅟₁₆ inch.

[53] Paragraph 74.

remarks that this stain was provided by two or three applications of a strong extract of wine vinegar and iron filings followed by an extract of gallnuts in wine vinegar. The black portions of the levers were then polished with black wax until nothing came off on the cloth. It seems likely that the ebony itself was often treated in this way to ensure its color. Sharps were often made of pear, stained black.

The registers were normally marked out from the *règle du clavier* or the keyboard itself in order to ensure that each jack stood in the center of its key lever. The strings were positioned from the registers. Thus the *règle du clavier* became the original standard from which the entire instrument was laid out. Mersenne worked directly from the keyboard, placing the register blanks across the keyboard and marking on it the midpoint of each key lever. He describes the construction of a spinet with a range of fifty keys.

Il faut aussi marquer la piece aux mortaises sur les bouts des marches, & tracer les mortaises dessus & dessouz; & puis il la faut sier en deux, afin d'en coller vne moitié sur la table, & l'autre sur vne petite table de sapin, que l'on colle apres bien droit vis à vis de la premiere sur les deux barres du fonds: & pour de suiet on fait cette piece, qui est de hestre bien doux, d'onze lignes de large, que l'on rabotte iusques à ce qu'elle soit tres mince & deliée.

Il faut percer cette table de sapin, & eslargir vn peu les mortaises par le dedans: & puis on colle vn morceau de peau de mouton dessus, que l'on coupe nettement de la grandeur desdites mortaises auec vn petit fermoir: & parce qu'il n'y en a que 25, l'on y met de petits entre-deux de grosses chordes d'Epinette, que l'on fait entrer à trauers par des trous faits auec vn poinçon d'aiguille, & puis on les riue par dessouz la table.

(It is also necessary to mark the mortised piece [register] from the ends of the keys and to mark out the mortises above and below; and then they are sawed in two [split lengthwise] in order to glue one half onto the soundboard and the other half onto a small board [54] [*table*] of *sapin* which one afterwards glues accurately *vis à vis* the first part across the two frame members on the bottom: and thus one makes this part which is composed of tender beech, one inch wide, and it is planed until it is very thin and delicate.

(It is necessary to pierce the soundboard and to enlarge the mortises a little inside, and then one glues a piece of sheepskin above and cuts it cleanly to the size of the said mortises [that is, one mortises the sheepskin] with a small firmer chisel: and because there are only twenty-five of them one installs little dividers of thick spinet wires which one causes to pass through holes made with a needle drill and then rivets them under the soundboard.) [55]

The dividers he mentions must have been shaped like a paper staple and

[54] See my remarks on double soundboards in Flemish virginals, p. 48.
[55] *Harmonie universelle*, p. 157.

divided one long mortise into two shorter parts so that two jacks could work side by side.

Diderot deals with the French style of harpsichord register. (The figure references in the following quotation refer to the plate reproduced here as Plate XXXII.)

The register is sometimes covered on top with sheepskin, and this is always the case with spinets in which the soundboard serves as register, that is to say that it is pierced like a register. In order to cut the holes in the leather, one uses the punch [*emporte-piece*] described in the article PUNCH on which one strikes as on a die stamp . . .

PUNCH, a sort of die stamp which harpsichord makers use to make the square holes in registers and guides covered with sheepskin. In one operation the *pelletier* [leather punch?] punches a rectangular hole which has the shape of the mortises in the registers and guides through which the jacks pass: the two others marked [25] and [29] in the plate serve to perform the same operation in two strokes. That which is numbered [25] cut the two long sides of the holes; and number [29], the ends of the same holes. The latter type is used preferably even though it is necessary to strike twice because they are easier to make and easier to sharpen. One cuts these pieces of leather on a well-planed piece of wood or on a sheet of lead. See figures 24, 25, and 29.[56]

Pelletier is defined as fur merchant, but the term must have been used in the trade to mean a leather punch. This four-sided punch is illustrated in Plate XXXII, figure 24.

It seems likely that the French type of register was constructed by mortising a batten first, then gluing the sheepskin to its upper surface and punching the leather from the inside, using the mortises as guides to position the tool. If the leather were punched before being glued in place, the moisture in the glue would alter the length of the strip of leather to the point that the finished register would not fit the keyboard.

Makers seem to have taken two basic approaches to register making, whether in solid wood or leather-covered wood. According to the first method, the register was cut out with one side missing. Thus the mortises could be cut with a fine saw and quickly finished with a chisel. At this stage the register would look like a coarse comb. Then a strip of wood would be glued over the open ends to form the missing side. The joint was often concealed from the top by scoring a line the length of it with the marking gauge. This type of construction is found in all traditions.

[56] "Registre de clavessin" and "Emporte-piece." It should be noted that Diderot's figure numbers have been corrected. Many of his plate references are incorrect. The sort of confusion between plate and text which we find in this article may suggest that he was not directly responsible for the unlikely framing and ribbing shown in his plates.

The second method, equally widespread, was simply to cut out the mortises with a chisel. The English harpsichords are especially notable for their cleanly cut solid registers.

The Italian box slide is particularly difficult to cut out of the solid since the mortises are about two inches deep. The fact that Italian wrest planks were often tapered in width from end to end produced a gap which was not perpendicular to the strings. The mortises of the registers, however, must be oriented so that their long sides are parallel to the strings. Thus a built-up Italian box slide would be likely to show one end of the mortise which was not square. For this reason Italian box slides were usually cut out of the solid. Sometimes, however, they were built up of blocks of the section shown in Plate XXIII, figure 4, which were arranged between the longitudinal sides like biscuits in a box. In order to assure the correct placement of the mortises the maker must have made a set of blocks which were all slightly too thick and planed each as he proceeded. A somewhat similar construction is found on English bentside spinets in which the register is built of blocks assembled in a space provided in the rear edge of the wrest plank.

It is curious that with all the descriptions of jacks provided in the literature, directions for their construction are so rare. The *Verhandeling over de Muziek* [57] describes what must have been the commonest procedure for obtaining the jack blanks. A block of suitable wood of the length of the jacks was planed until its thickness at one end was equal to the length of the mortises in the register, and at the other, to the length of the mortises in the guides. In other words, this block was made equal in thickness to the tapering width of a jack. The thickness of one jack was next marked on the face of the block with a marking gauge, and the blank for one jack was sawed off the edge of the block. The author warns that an allowance must be made so that the jack not be too thin. The edge of the block was planed again, re-marked, and a second blank sawed off. When enough blanks had been obtained, a planing jig was made by cutting a groove into a heavy plank into which a jack would just fit. This groove had a depth equal to the thickness of a finished jack. The face of the jack could be planed by means of this jig until the exact dimension was reached. A similar groove was provided for planing the edge of the jack to the finished dimension, although the width should have been correct in the first place. The jack blanks were individually fitted to the mortises in the registers and numbered accordingly. The *Verhandeling over de Muziek* does not explain how to form the open

[57] Paragraph 90.

mortise, or fork, at the top of the jack. However, many old jacks show scribed lines on the face, and it is obvious that each was marked out with the special marking gauge illustrated by Diderot (see Plate XXXII, figure 14), the fork sawed with a small saw, beveled at the bottom with a chisel, and finished with a file or chisel. Jacobsson [58] mentions an alternative procedure which would be more efficient. With a saw or grooving plane, he cut a groove of the proper dimensions in the end of the block before the individual jacks were taken out. Thus, each jack blank had an open mortise in the top as it was sawed out of the block. The bevel at the bottom of this open mortise would have been provided individually with a chisel.

Two small holes had to be drilled, one for the axle of the tongue and the other for the bristle. It is likely that the bow drill, Plate XXXII, figure 10, was used to drill for the axle, and the hand drill, figure 21, was used for the bristle hole. Nowadays the bristle hole is drilled by means of a revolving piece of music wire supported in a jig. The axle was formed of a dressmaker's pin. Only one side of the fork was drilled and the point of the pin was imbedded in the other. This makes it difficult to remove the tongues of old jacks for repairs.

Tongue blanks were probably sliced off the end of a cross-grained batten of suitable section. The mortises for the quills were punched with the device illustrated in Plate XXXII, figure 13. Many old tongues show a crescent-shaped mortise which fits the form of a quill.[59]

The last process in building a harpsichord is quilling and voicing. Since the maintenance of the quills was a continuing chore of all harpsichordists, many tuning manuals and methods contain instructions in quilling. Possibly the clearest explanations are those of Bendeler, Petri, Halle, and Gall.[60] Further information on the art of preparing plectra can be obtained from the article "L'Art d'écrire" in the *Encyclopédie*, which deals with quill pens, and the article "Chamois" in the same work, which describes the preparation of the buff leather used in *peau de buffle* stops. Gall advises:

[58] *Technologisches Wörterbuch*, IV, 369.

[59] There is fairly sizable literature describing peculiar tongues and plectra of various sorts, designed either for increased stability or special effects. Among the most interesting representatives of these works are the *Verhandeling over de Muziek*, already cited; the *Lettera dell'autore del nuovo cembalo angelico inventato in Roma nell'anno MDCCLXXV* (Rome, n.d.); and F. Hopkinson, "An Improved Method of Quilling a Harpsichord," *Transactions of the American Philosophical Society*, 2 (1788): 185. See Raymond Russell, *The Harpsichord and Clavichord*.

[60] Bendeler, *Orgel-Bau-Kunst*, p. 51; Johann Samuel Petri, *Anleitung zur praktischen Musik* (Leipzig, 1782), p. 367; Halle, *Werkstäte der heutigen Künste*, III, 361; Gall, *Clavier-Stimmbuch*, p. 114.

For quilling harpsichords one should really take only ravens' quills on account of their superior hardness and elasticity. However, these are not very common so most of the time one must settle for the less robust and hard crows' feathers.

Raven and crow feathers are white at one end in the unfeathered part. This white part of the quill is less hard than the remaining black part and is preferably cut away . . .

Now, when one has prepared the feather in this manner, it must be cut as if a toothpick were to be made. One does not cut through it crosswise at all, but obliquely, toward the front side of the quill as if one were cutting a pen. The cut up to the point need be only one half inch long.

This toothpick will next be stuck through the mortise in the tongue and pushed in deep until it sticks. Then the feathered part of the quill behind the tongue is cut off and the projecting part is pushed in as far as possible with the penknife in order that the pointed quill be completely tight. Then any part which still projects from the rear of the tongue is cut off very close to the tongue. We have explained above that the projection of the quill need not be more than one half inch. By the way, the toothpick must be inserted from behind into the mortise, that is, from the side of the tongue where the bristle is found, and in such a way that the surface of the quill left after cutting away the feathered part and replacing the jack is parallel to the bottom.

All fibers must be carefully removed from this inserted quill in order that it not remain hanging on the string.

If the inserted quill is still too long and thus remains hanging on the string one cuts its point as far back as is necessary.

If the quill is still too strong (which is indicated if the tone it draws from the string overwhelms the other tones), one shaves the hollow side while one has the arched side lying on the nail of the thumb of the left hand, taking from it whatever is necessary . . . The width of the point of the quill must be about one half the thickness of a knife-back . . .

When the quill has been corrected according to the above, the point is bent upward slightly — one must not break it, however — so that when the jack is again put into place it curves up a little from the plane of the strings. This bending back of the point makes the quill return better.

One and the same raven or crow quill is sufficient to quill three to four jacks.

The information provided by Gall can be amplified somewhat from other sources. Adlung[61] discusses various plectrum materials. Goose quill is too soft, whalebone soon breaks, and ostrich feathers are no better, besides producing a heavy action. Raven quills seem to be best. They are to be treated with olive oil so that they become tough. He warns against the poor touch produced by uneven quilling or a key dip which is too deep. Petri mentions turkey for the bass notes and sug-

[61] *Musica mechanica organoedi*, II, 106.

gests that the heavy end of the quill be used for the low notes and the weaker small end for the treble. Halle advocates raven feathers for the treble and *indianischer Hünern* for the bass, but Bendeler preferred turkey quills throughout.

The musical employment of the instruments thus cleverly conceived and laboriously made is clearly beyond the scope of this book. I do get the impression however, that the modern style of performance bequeathed to us by the first revivers of the harpsichord has little to do with the tonal and structural concepts I have painfully unraveled in these pages. I should like to hear of the publication of a fourth work to supplement those of Boalch, Russell, and myself, which would put the facts we have provided to their final application in the definition and encouragement of a pure and tasteful style of performance. In recent years the playing of a group of musicians among whom Ralph Kirkpatrick and Gustav Leonhardt are notable has indicated the path to be followed, but as yet there has been no rigorous treatment of the subject in print.

APPENDICES · BIBLIOGRAPHY
GLOSSARY · INDEX

APPENDIX A · CONTEMPORARY
DESCRIPTIONS OF INSTRUMENTS

FLANDERS

GERBIER–WINDEBANK LETTERS. QUOTED FROM SAINSBURY, *Original Unpublished Papers Illustrative of the Life of Sir Peter Paul Rubens* (1859), p. 208.

[To Sir F. Windebank]

Brussels Jan 20/30 1637–8

Right Honorable:

The Virginall I do pitch upon is an excellent piece, made by Johannes Rickarts att Antwerp. Its a dobbel staert stick as called, hath foure registers, the place to play on att the inde. The Virginal was made for the latte Infante,[1] hath a faire picture on the inne side of the Covering, representing the Infantas parke, and on the opening, att the part were played, a picture of Rubens representing Cupid and Psiche, the partie asks £30 starling. Those Virginals wch have noe pictures cost £15: — yr honr will have time enuf to consider on the sum cause I can keepe the Virginal long enuf att my house.

I take my leave and rest

Yor honrs, &c.,
B. Gerbier

[To B. Gerbier]

Westminster, Feb 2 1637–8

Sir:

In a letter apart you are pleased to give me a testimony of yor care of my private little businesse concerning the Virginall, for wch I retourne yu my most affectionate thankes.

If the Instrument, for sounde & goodnesse, be right, I do not much respect the accessories of ornament or paintings, & therefore if yu can meet wth a very good one plaine & wthout these curiousities, I shold rather make choice of such a one. But I will advise wth yr good frende & myne Mr. Norgat,[2] whose skill in these businesses is excellent, & then I will take the liberty to

---

[1] It is always interesting to find evidence of Flemish harpsichords destined for Spain since there seems to have been such a dearth of instruments made in that country.

[2] Edward Norgate, repairer of organs and virginals to Charles I. See Boalch, *Makers of the Harpsichord and Clavichord*, and De Lafontaine, *The King's Musick*.

acquaint yu wth my further desires. Presenting my true love to you & making it my siute to yu to use me as freely, as by yor many civilities you have obliged me to be (Sr)

Yr most faithful true servant
Fran. Windebank

[To B. Gerbier]

Westminster, July 20, 1638

. . . The Virginal, wch you sent me, is com safe, and I wish it were as useful as I know you intended it. But the workman, that made it, was much mistaken in it, and it wantes 6 or 7 Keyes, so that it is utterly unserviceable. If either he could alter it, or wolde change it for another that may have more Keyes, it were well: but as it is, our musick is marr'd. Neverthelesse, I am exceedinglye beholding to you for it and do acknowledge as many thankes to be due to yu, as if it had bene the most exquisit peece in the worlde. In that quality I beseeche you (Sr) comaunde

Yor most faithfull and obliged
true frende to serve you.
Fran. Windebank

[To Sir F. Windebank]

Brussels July 28/Aug 7 1638

Right Honorable:

. . . I have yr honors letter to me of 20/30 July, to which I have no more to say but that I must take patience, the Virginall proves not according expectation; Iff yr honor causeth the same sent to me agayne well conditioned and a just measure of the keyes desired annother Virginall to be; I will cause this to be sould as itt can, and annother made forthwth by Mr. Rickaerts, the same and the best master here, who saith this Virginall cannot be altered, and noe elce made here on saille.

Humbly take my leave and rest yor honrs, &c.,
B. Gerbier

LETTER FROM DE LA BARRE TO CONSTANTIJN HUYGHENS. FROM JONCKBLOET AND LAND, eds., *Musique et musiciens au XVIIe siècle* (1882).

[1648]

. . . As far as the price of harpsichords in Paris is concerned about which you wrote me, I thought I had sent you the facts but possibly, despite myself, I have expressed myself badly. Because the truth is that this master, who is still young, originally discovered the invention of making harpsichords with two manuals, not in the style of Flanders which play only the same strings, but different in that these make different strings sound from each keyboard; and to speak correctly, they are two harpsichords joined together, and as a result, the work is double. In the beginning the first ones that he made were sold for two hundred *écus* [equivalent to three *livres*], although in my opinion they were not very good. At present after making mine and several others, they seem much better to me and he sells them for less than a third. I can certainly tell you and it is true that mine cost me only two hundred fifty *livres* without the painting, but it is also true that he made me a special price because I have put him in the way of earning a profit several times. About those that he sells for only sixty *écus*, they have only one keyboard as I informed you. I have suggested to him one of another contrivance, prettier, for which he asks me up to six or seven hundred *livres*. This one can be completed this year. Thank you very humbly for the good will which you have evidenced to me toward my children; this will oblige them, with me, to seek again for occasions to demonstrate to you that I truly am, Monsieur,

Your very humble servant,
De la Barre

"OF HARPSICHORDS." FROM DOUWES, *Grondig Ondersoek van de Toonen der Musijk* (1699).

[104]

Harpsichords are musical instruments which are very pleasant in sound and are therefore used mostly for pleasure and diversion. They are best for playing readily all kinds of airs and pieces of music. There are various kinds. In some the jacks stand about half way between the bridges[3] and these are the most common; they are called *Muselars*. In some the jacks stand close to the bridge, on the left hand and these are called spinets [*Spinetten*]. The small ones are called sharps [*Scherpen*] because they are high and sharp in sound. There are also other kinds still in which the keyboards are at the one end and the other end runs to a point. These are called *Steertstukken*. They are of varying sizes, some *Steertstukken* are eight feet long, some harpsichords [*Klavecimbels*] are six feet long, some five feet, some four feet and some smaller still. The pleasantness of the tone depends on the soundboard being of the correct thinness and on the ribs under the soundboard lying in the right place. Readiness of speech depends on the strings lying the correct distance away from the jacks, and on the jacks and the tongues being well made. In order to have a good tone, the two bridges must be directed in such a way that the upper octaves vary in length by half, but the lower octaves must no longer be half because the long strings which are much thicker than the short cannot stand nearly so high in pitch. And the lowest octave of all, which has copper strings, can in no case stand so high. Also the harpsichord would be too long if all the octaves should be longer by half.

Therefore I shall say something more about the length of the strings:

A six-foot harpsichord, then, requires that the longest strings,

that is, the top C, should be in length	[c‴]	7	
the second C from the top	[c″]	14	
the third C	[c′]	28	inches
the fourth C	[c]	45	
the fifth C	[C]	59	

[3] Douwes is dealing here with virginals.

This length must be taken between the bridges, for what is beyond the bridge does not affect the ptich.

A five-foot harpsichord requires that
the topmost C should be in length	6½
the second C	13
the third C	25 } inches
the fourth C	39
the fifth C	50

A four-foot harpsichord:
the first or topmost C	5
the second C	10
the third C	18 } inches
the fourth C	31
the fifth C	41

A three-foot harpsichord: [4]
the first or topmost C	3½
the second C	7
the third C	13 } inches
the fourth C	22
the fifth C	31

Thus all these octaves have been fixed at such lengths so that the other strings or notes included between them can also have their proper length, although this is not a matter of very small amounts since one string can well be pulled up a bit tighter than another, which may easily be adjusted in tuning.

But I should add that such harpsichords as are called six foot are not fully six feet in length but about one third of a foot shorter.

Likewise those of five, four and three foot also do not have quite the full length but are usually somewhat shorter which is why I put down these string lengths too.

The notes or keys of harpsichords agree with most organs, namely from C to C [C to c'''], four octaves. But some large *Steert-stukken* [sic] go down further to G or F [GG or FF], like some large organs, and include four octaves and a fifth.

[119]
Order and Manner of Stringing Harpsichords and Clavichords. For this purpose three kinds of strings are made: red, yellow, and white. The red are made of red copper which is the weakest or softest of all and are used for the lowest or deepest basses. The yellow are made of yellow copper [brass], and these are somewhat harder than the red and are used on harpsichords for the next basses. The white are made of iron, are the hardest of all, and also are fine and clean in tone. They are all wound on little wooden reels each with its number from no. 1 through no. 12. The first of them is the thickest and so right through so that the twelfth is the finest.

[4] Probably at four-foot pitch.

Harpsichords, which on account of their pleasant tone are used most for pleasure and entertainment, are strung not only with red and yellow, but mostly with white strings because the white are fine and clear in tone. But clavichords which are used mostly for instruction in the art are fitted with red and yellow strings only, for they do not rust like the white and therefore can last much longer. The thickest are inserted down in the bass as the strings are longest and so on right through so that the finest come up in the treble as shall be set forth here.

To string a six-foot harpsichord: [5]

Note	No. of Wire	
C	1	Copper
D–E	2	
F–G	3	
A–A♯ [6]	4	Brass
B–c♯	5	
d–g	6	
g♯–d′	7	
d♯′–a′	8	Iron
a♯′–e″	9	
f″–c‴	10	

To string a five-foot harpsichord:

Note	No. of Wire	
C	1	
D	2	Copper
E	3	
F–G	4	
A–A♯	5	Brass
B–c♯	6	
d–g	7	
g♯–d′	8	
d♯′–a′	9	Iron
a♯′–e″	10	
f″–c‴	11	

To string a four-foot harpsichord:

Note	No. of Wire	
C	2	
D	3	Copper
E	4	

[5] Douwes' stringing list has been brought into conformity with modern conventions of notation.

[6] Douwes supposes a short octave. This is the first accidental.

Note	No. of Wire	
F–G	5	
A–A♯	6	Brass
B–c♯	7	
d–g	8	
g♯–d♯′	9	
e′–b′	10	Iron
c″–g″	11	
g♯″–c‴	12	

To string a three-foot harpsichord:

Note	No. of Wire	
C	3	
D	4	Copper
E	5	
F–G	6	
A–A♯	7	Brass
B–c♯	8	
d–a	9	
a♯–f♯′	10	Iron
g′–d♯″	11	
e″–c″	12	

To string a little harpsichord of two feet four inches:

Note	No. of Wire	
C	4	
D	5	Copper
E	6	
F–A	7	Brass
A♯–c♯	8	
d–g	9	
g♯–d♯′	10	Iron
e′–c♯″	11	
d″–c‴	12	

[124]
It should be mentioned here that just as the instruments of some are somewhat coarser strung and of others somewhat finer, if however the strings are short and coarse and are pulled up tight they will give a dull or dim tone, and if they are long and fine they will give a thin and rattling tone. Therefore the middle way is best. Likewise it makes little difference whether the strings are red or yellow, but the red can stand somewhat lower in pitch than the yellow. If you wish coarser strings than no. 1 you can buy for that purpose glowed [annealed?] potter's wire as thick as you wish it and scour

the dirt off it. This is very convenient for stringing some notes down in the pedal register too and is very good in tone.

"OF THE HARPSICHORD." FROM VAN BLANKENBURG, *Elementa musica* (1739).

[142]

1. This instrument is not a cymbal with keyboard (as the name seems more to convey), but a horizontal harp whose strings are stirred by means of *Tangenten* [jacks], that is to say touchers, which are called *springers*[7] in France. The instrument which is tapering and narrow at the end is called by us a *staartstuk*, but in France *Clavessin*.

2. It is of this only that we shall treat here. Of the virginals we will say in passing that those whose keyboard stands towards the left are regular and playable. These are called *Spinetten*, but those which have the keyboard on the right hand side are good in the right hand but grunt in the bass like young pigs. It is impossible to prevent this because the jack in falling divides the string into two parts which are of such length that they can sound against each other.

3. At the beginning of the previous [seventeenth] century the best harpsichord had only forty-five keys of which the lowest octave consisted of the eight notes of Guido, C D E F G A B H c, which were threaded through each other for shortening thus: C F D G E A B; this is now called a short keyboard [short octave], but formerly it had the name of a harpsichord with the new extension because in the preceding [sixteenth] century they used to make them only down to F and up to A[8] such as I have seen on organs too in my youth.

4. At that time they were so inexperienced in transposing that in order to transpose a piece a fourth lower they made expressly a special second keyboard in the harpsichord. This seems incredible, but the proof (which is very remarkable) will confirm this [statement]: viz., that the famous Ruckers from the beginning of the previous century [seventeenth] until more than thirty years later only made instruments in which, first, there were for the two keyboards only two [sets of] strings, but nevertheless four registers (for there is no indication even then of a unison), so that one keyboard had to be silent when the other was sounding; secondly, the lower keyboard stood a fourth lower than organ pitch and had at the top five keys too many so that the upper keyboard could have had the same overflow in the bass, but instead of making the beautiful bass of the lower keyboard sound to this end they not only left it without keys but they made in their place a wooden block and next to it a short octave — and this with great difficulty because the keys, on account of the recently mentioned rearranged notes had to reach over each other. This proves how little importance was attached at that time to the filling in of notes in the bass.

[7] This word is used in Germany but never in France. *Sautereaux* has the same meaning, however.

[8] Most sixteenth century harpsichords had a range of C/E–c'''. I do not recall having seen a keyboard end at F.

5. About fifty years afterwards [ca. 1650] these two faults began to be corrected, which was done with very little difficulty since they only had to displace five keys in order to change f into c and to add an octave at the bottom end of the upper keyboard. By this means both keyboards on the harpsichord were fifty keys long, that is to say, four octaves and a b flat below the lowest c above this number. We can see the proof of this by removing a piece of wood by the keyboard in front, for we can see the new wood on the top keyboard and the rearrangement of the numbers where Ruckers had numbered the keys on the lower one.

6. Later on they took the step of adding a third string. N. B. — here it must be remarked that one can fall into an error instead of enjoying an advantage. For you must know that Ruckers laid the bridges on the sound- board as far apart as ever the strings could bear if they were to attain the right pitch. Now suppose that Ruckers' topmost c is six and one-half inches long, then the new c placed next to it and to its left will be seven inches long on account of the curve of the bridge, which is the measurement of the adjacent string a semitone lower than c. I have found various harpsichords harmed by this increase in length, on the one hand through strings break- ing because the instrument cannot well stand so high [a scaling], and on the other through the heavy weight of the strings which press too hard on the soundboard, which is harmful to the tone, as one can prove with mutes or by laying a piece of lead on the bridge. Further it can sometimes happen that the bridge sinks in so deep that the strings touch the octave [strings]. My advice is that you should not increase the Ruckers measure- ment to seven inches but that you should add the new string on the other side of the above-mentioned c near to the unison string which goes with it. This can be done without pressing the soundboard down in the slightest degree. Then you should add a jack in each register, shift the whole key- board a half tone higher, add a key to the string left open in the bass which will then be A. By this means the harpsichord will be improved in tone and can stay in tune and is enriched by the above-mentioned A which is very useful as a fifty-first key in the place where otherwise the fiftieth is as good as useless. This being done, you arrange that by means of a little lengthening the third jack is moved both by the lower and by the upper keyboard, and then the latter is no longer dumb, for you play on the top keyboard *piano* with one string and on the lower *forte* with three strings. But the fourth register, which stands in front, is not only useless but even inconvenient.

7. All harpsichords with two keyboards have nowadays three strings so that the instrument seems to be perfect. At this point it might be asked what moved us to describe it so minutely. There are three reasons for it, of which the smallest is important enough to oblige us to do it: The first is that the harpsichords (which were sold in their maker's lifetime for twenty Flem- ish pounds, the small harpsichords for twelve and the virginals for six) today have reached so high a price that certain *entrepreneurs* have set out to cheat the public by fitting to a small harpsichord (which had only one keyboard, two registers, and forty-five keys) two keyboards with the full number [of keys], and four registers of which the fourth, as was pointed

out above, is useless. This instrument is then called a harpsichord by Ruckers with two keyboards. But the contrary is true, for it is then a forced instrument which perhaps sounds sweet but is certainly soft in tone. They [full-sized harpsichords] can be recognized by their breadth which must be of fifty complete keys and a block at either end between the cheek-pieces. The second reason touches the large harpsichords which some have undertaken to enlarge still further. This I have always seen turn out very badly, for if, in order to place a greater number of strings on the bridge, each space is diminished slightly by means of compasses, the harpsichord will lose the power it received from Ruckers because of the weight of the added strings. The tone of the bass [strings] depends particularly on the space which they have on the bridge. For this reason harpsichord makers should be careful to give them too much space rather than too little. Those who will open the eyes of their intellect can see at once that there is no proportion in giving large strings no more room than small ones.

8. Now we come to the third reason which is a description of the great advantage one can enjoy from the good use of the above-mentioned superfluous [row of] jack[s]. A person might be surprised when we say that we can bring about by this particular means such wonderful and delightful results as will give the ignorant as well as the informed the very greatest pleasure.

9. All that is necessary to this end is to give to the fourth [row of] jack[s], which up to now has been an outcast, a more important office than the other three. This may be done by placing it with its register one and one-half or two inches away from the bridge in the bass and as close to it as possible in the treble. If anyone wishes to know what the effect of this will be, let him take a writing quill and touch a string close to the bridge and then at a distance from it, and he will hear the difference between a spinet tone and a round tone. This is a thing which has been known for a long time. But that by making such a spinet within a two manual Ruckers harpsichord one could produce more than a dozen excellent variations of play (as is done by many registers in an organ), this has been unknown until our time.

10. I applied this discovery in 1708 to a two-manual harpsichord of Joannes Ruckers of the year 1625 and named the four registers *Spinetta*[,] *Unisonus, Cymbalum, Octava,* or to speak in organ fashion, *Trompet, Bourdon, Prestant, Octaaf*; and in order to be able to surprise the listener more quickly through unexpected changes we brought the stops to the front so as to be able to move them while playing with a motion of the hand, by which means we were able to use the keyboards alternately or simultaneously.

11. This instrument made such a sensation at that time that many noblemen, ministers, and even princes did me the honor of coming to hear me play on it, and not being able to understand how it was possible for a harpsichord to produce such a variety of effects, asked me if there was not another instrument concealed in it. Whereupon I removed the rail which covers the jacks and showed them that it all consisted entirely of the four registers, and that one could at will add a lute and a harp of new invention which

does not press the strings, not to mention an improvement in tone which we could introduce into the best harpsichords without affecting the soundboard.

12. In order to enjoy the fruit of a super harpsichord such as this there is need of a master to bring out the fine effects of all the changes and combinations of various tones. But a learner who can only play as he has been instructed can have some pieces made for this purpose. Moreover, this harpsichord is not only convenient but even better for general use too. "But," someone may say, "where is the instrument and where are the pieces?" The first we can show him at any time, and the second we can make up while playing. Thus all difficulty is removed, for the learner is helped at once and in the meantime, if he is well taught, can learn to produce similar effects out of his own head which he can then afterwards do also on a much finer instrument and even on an organ on which all imaginable changes can be found . . .

[174]

11. Further, we will also exhort the learner in order to attain a good discrimination of sound to keep his harpsichord always exactly tuned, and also to learn to tune it himself, which is the best means of training his ear. One should be warned that this instrument is a sort of thermometer which goes up and down with the cold and warmth, so that a person who has a good ear will be able to tell from it whether one room is warmer than the other. Moreover, copper strings drop much more through warmth than iron ones, so that when the weather changes copper and iron strings go out of tune with each other. One would wish that they would rise and fall uniformly. It would help a great deal to this end if they were all of copper, but since they do not sound as clear as iron ones in the treble, harpsichords are seldom made in this way. There is a difference in the string lengths: a top c of iron is seven inches long, but of copper five and one-half; an octave lower down, the measurement of the iron string is fourteen inches, of the copper one, eleven. But the third string is not twice fourteen but about twenty-five or twenty-six inches long, for here the length of the iron strings must decrease in order to be able to place copper and iron [strings] next to each other at the beginning of the bottom octave. The little oblong virginals which are called five-footers are suited to copper stringing, the measurements for which may be investigated. Furthermore, according to the greater or lesser distance between the bridges one can select finer or thicker strings.

SCALES OF VARIOUS HARPSICHORDS. EXTRACTED FROM SPECIFICATIONS GIVEN IN REYNVAAN, *Muzykaal kunst-woordenboek* (1795), p. 114.

"Eight-Foot" Harpsichord

c'''	7"
c''	14"
c'	28"
c	45"
C	62"

"Six-Foot" Harpsichord

c'''	6½''
c''	13''
c'	25''
c	43''
C	60''

"Five-Foot" Harpsichord

8'			4'	
c'''	6''	c'''		3½''
c''	12''	c''		6½''
c'	24''	c'		12''
c	40''	c		23''
C	58''	C		33''

"Four-Foot" Harpsichord [9]

c'''	5''
c''	10''
c'	18''
c	31''
C	41''

"Three-Foot" Harpsichord [10]

c'''	3½''
c''	7''
c'	13''
c	22''
C	31''

FRANCE

"THE HARPSICHORD." From *Encyclopédie méthodique*, volumes entitled *Arts et metiers* (1785).

The harpsichord is a melodic and harmonic instrument in which the strings are made to speak by playing the keys of a keyboard similar to that of the organ. The harpsichord consists of a triangular case which is about six and one-half feet in its longest dimension (see plates X, XI, and XII of *Lutherie*, vol. III of the engravings.) [11]

[9] Possibly strung with brass.

[10] Probably at four-foot pitch.

[11] See Plates XV, XXXV, XL. This article is taken from the *Encyclopédie méthodique* which is a compendium of the various editions of the original *Encyclopédie* from which our plates are reproduced. The plates of the *Encyclopédie méthodique* relative to our subject are identical to those of the *Encyclopédie* except for a reduced format. *Encyclopédie méthodique* plate X corresponds to our Plate XL, plate XI to our Plate XXXV, and plate XII to our Plate XV. Any failure of the letters on these plates to correspond to those of the text is an original error of the editors of the *Encyclopédie* and is not due to our use of first edition plates with a later text.

Figure 1 ACDB of plate X shows a harpsichord.

The sides IF, FD, GC, EL, which form the rim are called sides. The sides are ordinarily of lime wood; they are assembled with dovetail joints.

The bentside FBCG is made of about three or four pieces in order to give it more easily the curvature it must have.[12]

After the sides are prepared, they are joined to the bottom of the case, which is ordinarily of pine one-half inch in thickness, of which the pieces are glued and jointed with tongue and groove joints; the sides are fixed to the bottom on which they must be supported and glued, with points (a sort of little nail) which pass through the bottom and finally enter the sides; then several bars of pine or of lime wood are glued across the bottom. These bars, which are arranged like those of the stand, plate XI, figure 2, must be nailed onto the bottom and serve to prevent warping across the width; the sides of the case perform the same office for the long dimension.

These same bars are fastened against the inside of the sides with points and glue.

One can carry out the same methods that were practiced for gluing organ pipes in reheating to make the glue hold more strongly.

The case being prepared, the wrest plank, which is a piece of oak, AB, plate XI, figure 2, of about three inches in thickness, is fastened to it. The ends are made into tenons and enter tenoned into the lateral sides KBMA, plate X, figure 1, and are held with glue and points in mortises which must not go clear through the sides. The whole is clamped by means of a bar clamp (a woodworking tool) until the glue is dry and the wrest plank well fixed.

After having veneered to the top of the wrest plank a thin piece of the same pine as that of the soundboard so that it appears to be made of the same piece of wood as the soundboard, two nuts are glued, and farther up toward the rear part three rows of holes are drilled to receive the wrest pins, by means of which the strings are stretched.

Next, the bar EF [belly rail] of lime wood or of old pine one-half inch in thickness, is fitted and is placed parallel to the wrest plank from which it is about two inches distant.

This bar, which is glued and mortised into the lateral sides like the wrest plank, is three to four inches wide in some harpsichords; it reaches down to the bottom of the case where it is glued so that the entrance into the case is totally closed from the side of the keyboards. Then one should know enough to plan to make a rose in the soundboard in order to give an outlet to the air contained in the instrument.

Finally, strips of wood [liners] r, s, t, u, figure 2, plate XI, about 8 lines[13] wide by one-half inch thick, are glued around the case to the inside of the sides. These strips must be strongly fastened by points and glue so that they cannot in any way detach themselves.

After these strips are fastened in place about two inches from the upper

[12] Laminated construction! I have never seen this on an old harpsichord.

[13] One line equals ¹⁄₁₂ inch; hence, 8 lines equal ⅔ inch. The dimensions given in lines in this article are consistently rather small. Possibly we should assume that the author estimated a line to be about equal to ⅛ inch.

edge of the sides to which they must be parallel, curved members or forked bars T, V, X, Y, Z, are glued which push on one end against the strips r, s, t, u, of the bentside and the piece GC only, and at the other end against the crosspiece GH that is called belly rail.[14]

These bars represent good practice and resist the pull of strings which tend to draw the bentside toward the wrest plank, as one can judge by the string ii [?] of figure 2.

Nevertheless, some makers neglect to use them. Then they are obliged to give more thickness to the sides to make them able to resist the action of the strings. This renders the instrument more mute. Still one often sees soundboards of unframed instruments warp and become uneven.

Next, a board [nameboard] CD is made which is glued to the front of the wrest plank. This board, ornamented by moldings all around the edge, is joined to the sides with dovetail joints, and it meets the tops of the keyboard as one can see in ST of the first figure, plate X.

The soundboard is made and must be of Holland pine without knots or checks, resawed to a thickness of about two lines. Each plank is well dressed on its surface and edge and should not be more than six inches wide because a soundboard made of wide pieces is more subject to warping and twisting.

One must take care to joint the pieces which make up the soundboard only a long time after they have been sawed out and to choose the best and oldest wood that one can find because, more than on anything else, the worth of the instrument depends on that of the soundboard.

When it is desired to assemble the pieces, they are dressed again on the edges and glued two-by-two with the best fish glue that can be found. When the first pairs are dry, they are dressed again on their outside edges to be jointed together until there are enough to fill the space in the case.

It should be noted that the grain of the wood should run in the same direction as the strings of the instrument, that is to say, lengthwise, not crosswise.

When the soundboard is entirely glued, it is placed upside down on a smooth and well-planed bench. It is planed on this side and scraped with a scraper (a cabinetmaking tool). Then the soundboard is turned over and the same operation is performed again. It is reduced to a line or more in thickness.

When the soundboard is finished, it is ribbed underneath with little strips of pine standing on edge, a, b, c, d, e, f, figure 3, plate XI. These strips are only one and one-half or two lines wide on the base and about one-half inch high. They are flattened at the ends.[15]

These strips meet others still thinner, 1, 2, 3, 4, etc., of the same figure. None of these strips, whether large or small, must be placed along the length of the grain, nor exactly across it. The fewer of them that one uses the better. It suffices when there are enough of them to keep the soundboard from warping and to serve to bond the pieces together which make it up.

[14] I am sure that the frame shown in plate XI (our Plate XXXV) never existed. I suspect that the author is confusing a description given him by an Italian maker with what he had seen of the exteriors of French harpsichords.

[15] I have never seen the style of ribbing shown in this plate, and I doubt that the author of this article had seen it either.

The two bridges ac, db, figure 1, plate X, are placed on the top of the soundboard in the following way: the bridge ac, which is the lower, is about four or four and one-half inches distant from the wrest plank edge. The other, db, which is higher and which is called the big S as the other is called the little S, must be glued about four to five inches away from the bentside BDC whose curvature it must follow.

The bridges must have a very sharp arris on the side toward the vibrating part of the strings. On that arris there are brass or iron nails against which the strings press. Next, a hole R is cut for the rose.

The rose is a very delicate construction of cardboard made in the shape of a watch cock or star, from the bottom of which is erected a little pyramid of the same material.[16] This whole affair is painted and gilded and is pierced clear through. It serves only as an ornament, like the crown of flowers painted in distemper around it.

Between the two bridges ac, bd, there is a row of pins ed, driven obliquely into the soundboard. These pins serve to hook the eyes of the four-foot strings in the same way as the points driven into the molding which runs along the length of the bentside BDC serve to hold those of the two unisons.

All the strings, after having crossed two bridges, one on the soundboard and the other on the wrest plank, are twisted around the wrest pins, by means of which they are given sufficient tension to make them reach the tone that they must produce.

Next, the soundboard is glued down to the liners r, s, t, u, plate XI, figure 2, and to the bar EF. Great care must be taken that it be well applied and glued.

Onto the soundboard and around the sides are glued light limewood moldings. These moldings serve both for ornament and to fix the soundboard to the liners.

Next, the keyboards are made and are placed in the front part of the harpsichord, as can be seen in plate X, figure 1. The key levers must pass under the wrest plank and line up with the underside of the opening xy, figure 2, through which the jacks reach down to the key levers, which make them rise when one pushes down the front part b, d, [key head] and pluck the string corresponding to each by means of a crow quill with which their tongues are armed.

One of the two keyboards is movable. In figure 1 it is the lower keyboard which can be pulled out by means of the knobs X, figure 1, plate X, fixed in the end blocks or sides. Its movement is stopped when it reaches the bar MK which borders the front part of the harpsichord.

The keys of the lower keyboard raise the keys of the second keyboard by means of coupler dogs which line up, when the keyboard is drawn, with pads which are under the levers of the keys of the second keyboard.

They cease to move when the keyboard is pushed because the coupler dog goes beyond the pad or the end of the key of the second keyboard, to the keys of which the first rank of jacks correspond, after having passed through the lower guide and register.

16 This sounds like an Italian style rose.

The registers are strips of wood covered with leather, pierced by means of a punch, [see Plate XXXII, figures 24, 25, and 29] with as many holes as there are jacks and keys on the keyboard.

The registers are placed parallel to the wrest plank between it and the belly rail EF. They have about a line and a half or two lines of free motion along their length.

The lower guide is placed three or four inches below the register and serves to guide the jacks to the keys.

The jacks are numbered from E toward F, according to the succession of numbers 1, 2, 3, 4, 5, etc., in order to identify them and place them in the same position.

Above the top of the jacks is placed, at a convenient distance, a bar AB, figure 1, plate X, which is called a jack rail or simply bar. It is padded with several layers of wool selvages against which the jacks strike without making any noise. This bar can be removed and replaced easily by means of two pins, which are at the end A, and a hook, which is at B.

Of the three registers there is one which is fixed. It is the first from the side of the keyboard. Through it pass the jacks of the second manual. The two others can be moved by two iron levers which attach to their ends.

These levers, which are called *mouvemens* because they make the registers move, have handles S, T, which pass through mortises made for that purpose in the plank at the front of the wrest plank [nameboard]. They are fixed in the middle by a screw which goes into the wrest plank and around which they can turn freely. The end which goes under the jack rail AB has a pin which goes into a hole at the end of the register which this lever must move, so that when the handle S is pushed toward the T side, the register fastened to the end A of the lever SA is moved in the opposite direction from B toward A.

The purpose of the registers is to advance or withdraw the jacks from the strings at will so that the quills of their tongues touch or do not touch the strings.

The harpsichord being thus finished, a lid is made which is a plank of oak or walnut of the same shape as the bottom. This lid is in two pieces, the larger of which covers the strings and which has the same shape as the soundboard ABDC of the instrument, figure 1, plate X. It is hinged to the side AC. The other piece which is rectangular, LABI, and which covers the keyboards and wrest plank, is hinged to the first along the line AB so that it can fold back onto the big piece. The two pieces are raised together and can be held up in that position by a rod of wood which rests on one end obliquely against the side B and at the other perpendicularly against the underside of the lid.

Next the stand PPPP, etc., figure 1 and 4, is made, composed of several legs, B [*sic*], P, P, jointed and glued into a frame c l k g.

This frame, which stands on edge, is covered by another, C K L G, which lies flat and around which moldings are made. It is crossed by several bars H, F, E, B, which serve to render the whole structure more solid.

In the part which is under the keyboards and wrest plank a place is arranged for a drawer N O N, figure 1, and T, figure 4, in which can be kept music books, strings, and other things pertaining to the harpsichord, even the music desk when it is made in such a way that it can be folded.

Next a board is made which closes the front of the keyboard M L I K, figure 1. In the middle of that plank is the lock which closes the whole instrument.

It is necessary to have a music desk, plate X, figure 5, of which the sides l a, i b, are placed on the sides L A, I B, figure 1, of the harpsichord. They are held together by a transverse piece of suitable length so that the battens f, a, g, h [sic; should read fa, gh], catch on the outside of the sides LA, IB. In the middle of the crosspiece is a pivot which fits into a hole in the base of the music desk, e [sic; should read o], which thus can be turned to all sides. On the music desk is placed the book which contains the piece of music it is wished to play. Also on the front part f, g, there are two plates c, d, on which candlesticks and folding arms are mounted in which lighted candles are placed which provide illumination for the harpsichord when one wishes to play at night.

The harpsichord is strung with strings partly yellow, partly white; that is to say, of copper and of steel. Those of copper serve for the bass and the others for the treble.

The yellow and white strings come in several gauge numbers or sizes: the smallest gauge number marks the thickest strings. The first gauge number in the yellow is for the c-sol-ut [great C] of the bass, two octaves below [the C] of the C-clef, which must sound the eight-foot unison.

When the harpsichord is enlarged like the one shown in the plate, one puts on, descending to the bass, yellow strings still larger than the first gauge number. These are marked by o, oo, ooo.

The string ooo is the largest used up until now. It serves for f-ut-fa [FF] of the sixteen-foot. Sometimes also red copper strings are used for *ravalement* [extended bass of the harpsichord] marked by the same ooo, oo, o, 1, 2. These strings are readier of speech and more harmonious than the yellow strings.

Table of string gauge numbers and of the number of each that one must put on, beginning in the bass and ascending according to the series of jacks A 1, 2, 3, 4, 5, 6, 7, etc. B. The first column contains the gauge numbers of the strings that must be put on of each number.

Gauge number of the strings	Number of strings according to the series of jacks	
ooo	2	The bracketed strings can be of red copper if the yellow do not speak well.
oo	2	
o	3	
1	3	
2	3	
3	4	
4	4	
5	4	

White strings which begin at f-ut-fa of the f-clef [f].[17]

6 and sometimes 5	5
7	5
8	5
9	5
10	5
11	9 If the treble goes up to
12	e-si-mi [e′′′].

Gauge no. 12 serves for the four-foot in place of no. 11. Likewise no. 11 serves in place of no. 10 and so forth.

Characteristics of a Good Harpsichord. We will say, according to the *Dictionnaire des arts et métiers*, that the skill of a good harpsichord maker consists in giving his instrument a masculine and at the same time silvery sound, sweet [pithy] and equal in every note.

These good qualities depend in large measure on the choice of the sound-board, on the accuracy of the bridge and the rack, and on the positioning of the interior counter-bridge [four-foot hitchpin rail] which is glued to the soundboard between the two bridges, and which is called *boudin* in technical language.

This *boudin* and the crossbars [ribs] placed along the bass part of the harpsichord between the back or straight side [spine] (which is toward the bass along the rear of the harpsichord) and the four-foot bridge contribute greatly to the good quality of the tone when they are treated in accordance with the principles and niceties of the art.

The lightness of the keyboard and the equality of its resistance in regard to each key is also one of the points that a maker of harpsichords must necessarily observe in giving the exact counterweight relative to the force of the finger which operates the keyboard and in avoiding too much key dip, which makes it awkward to play, nor too little, which makes it hard and even reduces the volume of sound.

The best harpsichords for beautiful tone that we have had up to now are those of the three Ruckers (Hans, Jean, and André), as well as those of Jean Couchet, all established at Antwerp in the last century, who made an immense quantity of harpsichords, a large number of original examples of which are in Paris, recognized as such by true connoisseurs.

Makers are found in our time who have copied and counterfeited Ruckers harpsichords so that one can be fooled by the outside, but the tone quality has always revealed the deception.

Nevertheless, these harpsichords of the three Ruckers and of Couchet, as they came from the hands of these masters, are becoming absolutely useless today because, even though these clever artists understood the tonal part superbly, they succeeded very badly in the matter of the keyboard.

[17] This crossover point seems very high. Modern practice is about one octave lower since the brass strings will not produce so high a pitch.

Besides, these Flemish harpsichords are so small that the pieces or sonatas that are composed nowadays cannot be executed on them. That is why they are enlarged ([mis] *à grand ravalement*).

Enlarged Harpsichords. Harpsichords are called thus that have sixty-one keys in place of the fifty that they had in other times.

Most of the Ruckers and other old harpsichords were made with only two strings per note, but in the enlarged harpsichords, instead of one hundred strings, there are one hundred eighty-three, due to the addition of a *grand unisson* [eight-foot], by means of which the tone becomes still more masculine and majestic.

It is in the art of enlarging the Flemish harpsichords of the Ruckers and of Couchet that Blanchet, a French maker, has perfectly succeeded. Yet he has been surpassed by M. Paschal Taskin, his pupil. Anyway, here is the procedure for enlarging harpsichords.

To accomplish this it is necessary to cut them on the treble and bass side, then to widen and even elongate the whole case of the harpsichord, and finally to add old resonant pine, the most even-grained one can find, to the soundboard to give it its new width and length.

The wrest plank is replaced in this sort of harpsichord which, all considered, keeps of its original state only the soundboard and around two and one-half feet of the old right side.

The accessory parts like the keyboard, jacks, registers, are made now with much more accuracy than the Flemish masters made them in the last century.

A harpsichord of the Ruckers or of Couchet, artistically cut and enlarged with jacks, registers and keyboards by a clever modern maker such as Blanchet, Paschal, has become an infinitely precious instrument.

Keybed of the Harpsichord and of Spinets. This is the part of these instruments upon which the keys are mounted [see Plate XV]. It is made up of three bars of wood [front rail, balance rail, back rail] and two traverses joined to each other. The second bar [balance rail], which is between the two others, is covered with as many pins arranged in two rows as there are keys.

The pins in front serve for the natural keys and the others for the chromatics or sharps. These pins fit into holes which are in each key.

On the first bar, which forms the base of the key bed, is glued another bar called the *diapason* [rack], divided by as many perpendicular saw cuts as there are keys. These saw cuts receive the pins in the ends of the key levers and guide them in their movements.

On the part of this first bar [back rail] which is not covered by the rack, several strips of wool selvage are attached so that the keys do not make any noise in falling back, a thing that would not fail to happen if this bar of wood were not covered.

For the same reason little pieces of cloth are threaded onto the pins of the second bar on which the keys balance, where the keys would touch.

As for the third bar, it is a strip of very thin wood whose purpose is to retain the two sides of the key bed. The keys must not touch this last bar.

The key beds of harpsichords which have two keyboards are almost like those of spinets. It is only the second which differs in that in place of the rack to guide the keys there is a bar furnished with iron pins between which the keys move.

Keyboards of the Harpsichord. The double keyboards of harpsichords shown in figure 8, plate XII of *Lutherie* [see Plate XV], are, as in the keyboards of organs, two rows of keys which line up perpendicularly with one another.

The keys of the second manual are held in position by a guide which is a strip of wood EF, figure 8, furnished with pins between which the keys move, as contrasted to those of the first [lower manual] which are guided by the bar or *diapason* cut across by saw kerfs.

The bed of the first keyboard can be pulled out or pushed in so that when the keyboard is drawn out, the coupler dogs GH, same figure 8, plate XII, are positioned under the key levers of the second manual, where it happens that when the first keyboard is played the movement is communicated to the second as if someone were playing above. This plays those strings which correspond to the jacks of the second keyboard. But when the lower keyboard is pushed in, the coupler dogs pass beyond the ends of the key levers of the second manual which remain motionless when the keys of the first are touched.

The wood of the inside of the keyboards is of the closest grained limewood. The key tops which are glued artistically to the key levers, are of ebony for the natural keys, and of a little strip of beef bone for those of the sharps. In other times these strips were made of ivory, but since these were likely to yellow after a certain time, it is preferred to use the beef bone which always stays white.

Harpsichord Registers. The registers of the harpsichord are strips of wood pierced with as many holes as there are keys in the keyboard. These holes are longer than they are wide to fit the size of the jacks. They are cleared underneath.

The register is sometimes covered above with sheep skin. This is always done in spinets in which the soundboard serves as register, that is to say, it is pierced like a register. To pierce the holes in the leather, punches are used on which one strikes as on an awl to cut them out.

There are as many registers as there are strings for a single key. Thus there are harpsichords with two, three, or four registers which are all placed side by side between the wrest plank and the soundboard of the instrument.

Handstops. The handstop levers of harpsichords are little levers of iron or copper fastened at the center by means of a pin. At one end is a point or hook which catches in the register, on the other end is a little handle by means of which one makes the register move by pushing in the opposite direction to that in which one wishes to move the register.

The wrest plank of the harpsichord is the piece of wood in which are fitted the pins which serve to stretch the strings of the instrument. It is a strong piece of beech or other wood of about the same type fastened into the sides of the harpsichord by dovetail tenons.[18]

[18] Dovetail tenons would be almost impossible to assemble.

On the wrest plank two nuts are glued. The first carries the strings of the four-foot which are fastened to pins which have to pass between the strings of the eight-foot which are the two long unison strings of the harpsichord.

The two choirs of strings which pass over the large nut are attached to the wrest pins of the other two rows.

Each of these ranks has as many wrest pins as there are keys in the keyboard.

The wrest pins are arranged in two lines near one another in this manner: Those of the lower row are those of the front row of the harpsichord and correspond to the natural keys, and those of the upper row or back of the harpsichord correspond to the sharps or chromatics in this way:

	♯ ♭	♯ ♯ ♭	ut re mi fa sol la si ut			
Upper row	o o	o o o	o o o o o	o o o o o	o o o o o	o o o o o
Lower row	o o o o o o o	o o o o o o o	o o o o o o o	o o o o o o o		

Fourth Octave Third Octave Second Octave First Octave

Jacks. In a harpsichord there are as many jacks as strings.

The jack, so called from *saltando* because it jumps when it performs its function, is a little rule of pear wood or other wood easy to cut, a half-inch wide, only a line [actually about ⅛ inch] thick and as long as is suitable, plate X of *Lutherie* [see Plate XL], figure A, and following to bottom of plate.

At its top end this little slip of wood has a cutout AC, a line and one-half wide and about one inch long. This cutout, the lower end of which is cut on the bevel, receives a little piece of white wood which is called the tongue. This piece is beveled on the lower end to fit the bevel on the cutout AC.

When the tongue is placed in this cutout it is fixed in place by means of a pivot D which is a little common pin that runs across the jack and the tongue which must move freely around it.

There is a little hole o, figure k, in the upper part of the tongue through which a pointed crow quill passes. It is thinned as much as necessary so that it is not too stiff, which would give a disagreeable tone to the strings. There is a slot or groove in the rear of these same tongues along the length.

This groove receives a spring e, figure E, which is a hog or boar bristle which always returns the tongue between the two sides of the jack cutout until the bevel of the one rests on the bevel of the other.

The jacks pass through two planks or rules of very thin wood, each pierced with as many holes as there are jacks. These holes are square and line up perpendicularly, those of the registers over those of the lower guide.

The jacks, after having traversed the register and the lower guide, descend perpendicularly to the key levers, each of which is a little seesaw.

From this construction it follows that if one presses a key of the keyboard with the finger, the end of the lever will rise (because they are pivoted) and it will raise the jack which it carries.

The jack in rising will touch the string opposite it by means of the quill in its tongue. It will move the string from its state of rest until its resistance exceeds the stiffness of the quill. Then the string will overcome that stiffness and will bend the quill permitting the string to escape. The string thus freed will make several oscillations producing the tone.

Next, if one releases the key, it will fall back by its own weight. The jack, not being held up, will fall back until the quill touches the string from above. Then, if the weight of the jack exceeds the resistance that the spring or boar bristle already mentioned is capable of producing (as it must always do), the jack will continue to descend, because the spring, in giving, will let the tongue move away from the string so that the quill can pass.

Lower Jack Guide. The lower jack guide is a rule of thin wood covered with leather. This rule is pierced with as many holes as the registers underneath, which they line up perpendicularly. The lower guide is about three inches under the registers on the inside of the harpsichord and above the key levers, so that when the jacks have gone through the registers and the lower guide, they fall directly onto the key levers.

Vertical harpsichord, in Italian cembalo verticale, *in Latin* clavicytherium, *a type of harpsichord that some improperly call* pantalon. The vertical harpsichord is nothing but a harpsichord with a somewhat more narrow case than an ordinary harpsichord, and which is vertical rather than horizontal. Consequently, it requires much less space. Since the jacks are not vertical and cannot fall back by themselves, they are pushed back by a spring wire.

Harpsichords with peau de buffle [buffalo hide] [19] *Invented by M. Paschal.* M. Trouflaut, canon and celebrated organist of the church at Nevers, addressed the following letter in 1773 to the authors of the *Journal de musique.* It will make known the merit of the *peau de buffle* harpsichords invented by M. Paschal Taskin, maker of harpsichords to the court and keeper of the musical instruments of the Royal chamber.

The harpsichord holds one of the first ranks among instruments. The means that it furnishes to unite all the parts of a consort, to form harmonic groups, and to offer to the composer in little space all the possible forms of harmony and melody render it always dear to true musicians.

In spite of the undeniable resources that it offers to talent it is noticeable nevertheless that the unvarying quality of its tone constitutes a real fault.

This instrument was originally very simple, and had at first a single keyboard like our spinets. For several centuries it kept almost the same simplicity.

Then someone thought of doubling the jacks on each key to vary the sound a little.

It was at this time that the first germ of taste was developed in favor of our instrument. Next, the makers thought of putting on two keyboards of which the upper made a single rank of jacks play and the lower made two play.

By this means the loud and soft were obtained, but this loud and soft were always the same and there was no gradation from one to the other.

Eventually a thousand other means of enlarging, decorating and improving harpsichords were invented, but no one attained the goal which should

[19] Trouflaut usually spelled *buffle* with one f, but not always. We follow Larousse.

have been proposed: to gradate the tone as nature and taste suggest to a delicate ear and a feeling heart.

The makers were not the last to notice imperfection, but they preferred the repose of custom to the activity of genius and did not seek to perfect this beautiful instrument nor to place it in a position to execute *forte, piano, amoroso, gustoso, staccato,* etc., and all the other gradations which figure with such charm in modern music.

It was reserved for M. Paschal Taskin to carry his views further and to triumph over the obstacles which had stopped his predecessors. Given to frequent meditations, this artist, as clever as he was modest, determined to try all sorts of materials in order to draw agreeable sounds from them.

In 1768 after repeated experiments he obtained the success that he hoped for.

From among the three ranks of jacks in a harpsichord he chose one in which he substituted pieces of buffalo hide for the crow quills. He put it in the tongues in almost the same way as the quills.

From the effect of this leather on the string of the instrument there resulted delicious and velvety sounds. One increased the sound at will by pressing more or less hard on the keyboard. By this means one obtained rich, pithy and suave tones, voluptuous to the most epicurean ear. Does one desire passionate, or tender, or dying sounds? The *buffle* obeys the pressure of the finger; it does not pluck any more but it caresses the string. The touch, only the touch, of the harpsichordist suffices to bring about these charming variations, and without changing either the keyboard or the registers.

M. Paschal did not limit himself to this valuable discovery. He wished to put the quilled registers to use in order to increase the variety of his instrument.

For that end he devised bars of iron which pass through the wrest plank of the harpsichord vertically from top to bottom. The upper end moves the quilled registers, the lower end stops a little above the knees of the harpsichordist.

By this ingenious and simple mechanism it is possible with the smallest movement of the knee to make this or that stop of quills speak separately or together, or the *buffle* stop alone, or all of the stops of the harpsichord together, so that if one wishes to imitate the effect of a large chorus, of an echo, or of all the shadings of which modern music is susceptible, one succeeds beyond one's hopes without removing a hand from the keyboard.

What a prodigious variety in an instrument apparently so unresponsive. The magic of the sounds that it makes heard today quickly captivates the attention of the auditors, interests his heart, enchants him and ravishes him.

Since 1768 M. Paschal has known how to add to his own discovery. It is in combining the effects of the keyboard and the *buffles* that he has discovered that one can both maintain the same equality of touch and still increase or diminish the tone at will. Consequently, he knew how to place under the foot of the harpsichordist a pull which makes the *peau de buffle* stop and the quill stop move imperceptibly.

This pull receives more or less pressure from the foot and increases or diminishes the tone more or less. Then one easily manages to make felt all the possible variations in execution, and one produces at will successive weak or strong, tender or brilliant sounds, which produces the most flattering surprise.

From the low tenor to the bottom of the bass these harpsichords in *peau de buffle* perfectly imitate the sound of the brass of the *prestant* of the organ, and from the low tenor to the top of the treble that of the transverse flute.

As to their durability, what can be said most precisely is that the first harpsichord in *buffle*, made in 1768, for M. Hebert, Treasurer General of the *Marine*, has retained for five years at least as much and probably more of that equality of strength and elasticity characteristic of *peau de buffle*, a very interesting advantage for amateurs who are disgusted with the harpsichord because of the prompt degeneration of the quills.

I dare to add with confidence that the harpsichord with *peau de buffle* is very much superior to the *piano-forte*. Whatever is clever about these last, they do not fail to have essential faults. While in the establishment of the vendor they are able to please and seduce, but if one casts an attentive glance into the interior, their complication will alarm one in an instant.

Though the trebles are charming, the hard, loud and false basses seem to give consumption to our French ears, an irremediable fault up to the present. If one makes use in this sort of harpsichord of a flute [20] stop, such as one sees some of in Paris, to ameliorate the bass and to reinforce the treble, the consequence is a double mechanism, double expense, double servitude to maintain the tuning of one to the other.

Furthermore, and this is what is most essential, one cannot adapt the mechanism of the *piano-fortes* of London to our French harpsichords. The form and arrangement of the latter have never been able to accept it, whatever the intelligence there may be among the makers. These harpsichords [pianos] finally, however little they may be out of order, whether as a result of transport or of the inclemency of the air, in the provinces are soon condemned to an eternal oblivion where no one is able to maintain them as required. One passes over their extreme dearness in silence.

In the harpsichord with *buffles* of M. Paschal, on the contrary, the bass corresponds precisely with the treble. All the notes on the keyboard are equally sonorous and sweet and always capable of every gradation the artist could desire. Its mechanism can be adapted at very little expense to all old French, Flemish and Italian harpsichords. Once the mechanism is installed, one can still use part of the quilled registers and contrast the sounds, and thus always have something new and agreeable. Through this discovery [this] will become the epoch of the resurrection of the Ruckers, of Geronimi, of Marius, etc. Furthermore, when the harpsichords of M. Paschal go to the provinces, they have nothing to fear from the awkwardness of those charged with their maintenance.

One examines the jack a little bit, its mortise, the *buffle*; then he might want to compare the notes which do not work with those that do; nothing

[20] Probably refers to a combination piano-organ.

is easier and more amusing than to provide a remedy as prompt as it is efficient. A pen knife, chisels, a piece of *buffle*, are all the equipment needed.

The modest price that M. Paschal charges for his mechanism proves that he is more ambitious of being useful than to enrich himself. It must still be remarked that the *buffles* placed in the jacks of the spinet are as pleasant as in the harpsichord except that it is impossible to produce as much variety with a single register.

For his discovery M. Paschal deserves the unanimous approbation of connoisseurs. The best artistes in Paris such as M. Couperin [21] and M. Balbâtre [22] have not stinted their praise of the value of the invention. And the persons of the highest rank at court and in the capital hasten to follow their example, so that M. Paschal has no regret except that of being endlessly occupied in applying his mechanism to old harpsichords and of not having a moment to make his own, which he regards quite properly as being the most fitting to assure his reputation.

Spinet. The spinet is a sort of small harpsichord. It comes in the form of a parallelogram. Others, called *à l'italienne* [see Plate XV] have almost the shape of a harpsichord. Some sound at four-foot pitch, others a fourth or fifth above the harpsichord. Otherwise, it is of the same construction and mechanism.

Spinets have only one string for each key and only one rank of jacks.

The name of the inventor of the spinet or ordinary harpsichord is unknown. Neither the time nor the place where this instrument was conceived is known. Two hundred years ago the spinet was only five feet long and twenty inches wide. It had about thirty keys commencing with the *fa*, the fourth of the prestant, and ending at the C, an octave above the g-clef [f–c′′′].

The mechanism of the keys was almost the same as that of today except that in place of the quill the jack was provided with a piece of leather in almost the same manner as that practiced by M. de Laine,[23] teacher of the

---

[21] Probably Armand-Louis, nephew of François le Grand.

[22] Claude Balbastre, organist and student of Rameau. It will be remembered that Burney called on Balbastre in Paris and saw his elaborately painted Ruckers harpsichord: "one of the unisons is of buff, but very sweet and agreeable; the touch very light, owing to the quilling, which in France is always weak." (*The Present State of Music in France and Italy*, p. 38.)

[23] Boalch refers to a notice in the *Avant-coureur* of 1771 in which De Laine claims to have invented leather plectra for jacks. An earlier account is to be found in the *Mercure de France* for August 1769 from which it seems that De Laine was an active candidate for the honor of having discovered *peau de buffle* plectra and applying a mechanism to the registers of the harpsichord: "Recently a new method of quilling harpsichords has been discovered which combines the advantages of lasting for four or five years without any repair and a still rarer improvement, that of doubling the harmony of the instrument and of rendering its sound more seductive and more agreeable to the ear. The inventor of this method has found the yet more remarkable secret of swelling and diminishing the tone on this instrument which up to then had only had one uniform level. Thus he has been able to apply a mechanism to the harpsichord which makes the sound swell by imperceptible degrees from *pianissimo* to *fortissimo*. This mechanism produces its effect by means of the feet, to which one must adapt the touch of the hand so that the touch should be lighter or heavier according to whether the foot presses the pedal or releases

hurdy-gurdy, and M. Paschal, harpsichord maker, both living in Paris. The jacks of the old harpsichords were not felted at all,[24] so that the sounds were confused. The strings were of gut and consequently the tone sweet and soft. Dampness and dryness threw the instrument out of tune every day. Some of these old harpsichords are still to be found in Paris and in the large cities of the Low Countries and Germany.

Ordinary spinets[25] were six feet long and two and one-half feet wide. They have two keyboards. The upper has one jack on each key. The lower keyboard has two jacks on each key; one plucks a string at eight-foot pitch, the other plucks a string at four-foot pitch.

One can add without much expense a fourth jack close to the nut. This jack draws from the string the sound of a harp. Also, without expense it is possible to put on a little rule sliding in a groove. This rule will be furnished with *peau de buffle* to partly stifle the vibration of the string and make it produce a lute tone.

The best makers of ordinary spinets have been the Ruckers, at Antwerp, who lived at the end of the last century [*sic*; end of sixteenth century is meant], and Jean Denis of Paris. But since the death of the Ruckers, several improvements have been made to their spinets. More range has been given to the keyboards, which had only three and one-half octaves. They began at fa, an octave below the f-clef, and ended at the C, a twelfth above the g-clef [f to c′′′]. An octave has been added to the bass and a fourth to the upper notes while keeping the same spacing and shape. Also, contrivances have been added to imitate the lute and the harp — some have combined it with a little organ which multiplies the pleasure one hundred fold.

About one hundred years ago strings of iron and copper were put into the spinet in place of those of gut, the jacks were armed with quill and felted to stop the vibration of the strings. This fortunate discovery has since been used in all spinets.

"CLAVECIN." From *Encyclopédie méthodique*, volumes entitled *Musique* (1791 and 1818). The article was written by N. Hullmandel.

Harpsichord. The epoch of the invention of the harpsichord is uncertain. Some think that it must be placed in the fifteenth century, others believe it much earlier.

Thirty years ago there existed in Rome a straight-sided harpsichord with

---

it. He adds to that mechanism one of a lute which, coming on or off at the will of the player, gives the instrument the character of the harp or of the plucked instruments. The originator of this discovery has proved the value of his method by several trials. The best masters as well as a number of persons of taste, amateurs and people of the greatest distinction have also applauded this invention. He can apply his mechanism to all harpsichords without involving the basic part of the instrument even for a moment. For these harpsichords one can go to M. de l'Aine, rue Fromenteau on the third floor of the same house as M. Merlin, Procureur du Châtelet."

[24] That is, there were no dampers.

[25] *Epinettes ordinaires*. The term is used in its general sense. The instrument being discussed is the harpsichord, properly the *clavecin*.

twenty-five keys without sharps or flats, which was said to have been brought from the Greece of Julius Caesar's time.

In the same city there is still to be found another harpsichord of which the case, soundboard, and bridges are in white marble. It is estimated to be six hundred fifty years old. The truth of such traditions is too difficult to demonstrate to be worth lingering over.

Boccacio, who was writing in the fourteenth century, mentioned the *cembalo* for accompanying the voice. Whether it was the *harpsichord* which was actually known under that name is doubtful for it is not known whether the *cembalo* was then the *harpsichord* or a sort of instrument having a relationship with the *cymbalum* of the ancients.

No one writing on music before the sixteenth century names the clavichord, the virginal, the spinet, or the harpsichord, but writers of the sixteenth century speak of them as instruments already in use, which leads us to believe them much older. One hardly speaks of a musical instrument before long experience has made its use common and developed its resources.

The most probable of all the traditions is that the Italians invented the clavichord five or six hundred years ago, and then were imitated by the Flemish and the Germans. It is possible to conjecture that in that instrument was the origin of the harpsichord. Its shape is square, it has only one string for each tone, and the only mechanism is a tongue of copper attached to the end of each key beneath the string that it strikes. The advantage of this tongue is to swell and diminish the sound when one presses more or less with the finger on the key; and the inconvenience is that it sharps or flats it [the tone] at the same time. The simplicity of its construction has allowed its length to be reduced at times to under two feet. Some of these instruments have even been designed so that they can be folded. The clavichord is retained in use in Germany because of its convenience, of the little upkeep that it requires, and because in that country where more than in any other research has been made on the art of playing the harpsichord, it has been noticed that practice on the clavichord is very good for improving the touch. The slightest difference of strength in the fingers is noticeable and the least irregularity can make a bad effect.

The disadvantage that these tongues of copper in clavichords have in raising the sound when one augments it, and of not permitting the strings to vibrate freely has led to the invention of plucking the strings with little pieces of quill mounted in sprung tongues set in the top part of thin and flat pieces of wood called jacks. There is one of them beside each string, standing vertically on the keyboard which makes them move. A little piece of cloth is applied to the edge of each jack and has the effect of stopping the vibration of the strings when the key is released.

This new invention was adapted to two instruments which differed only in shape: the virginal, which is square like the small piano-fortes, and the spinet, which resembles a harp lying flat. Only these two instruments and the clavichord appear to have been in use until toward the end of the sixteenth century,[26] the period when the harpsichord prevailed. There are no

[26] As we have seen, the Italians had been making harpsichords one hundred years before the date Hullmandel gives.

more virginals remaining; spinets are disappearing, they are being demolished so that their old soundboards can be used in the construction of more modern instruments.

The harpsichord is constructed on the model of the spinet, and is only, so to speak, the enlargement of it. A larger capacity, two strings at the unison for each note, greater length of strings — these are the things that for a long period were the only distinctions. Hans Ruckers gave this instrument a stronger sound, more brilliant and more animated, in adding to the two strings of the unisons a third choir of thinner and shorter strings than the others and tuned an octave higher.[27] This was called the little octave [four-foot]. Hans Ruckers strung his harpsichords half in copper for the bass and half in iron for the treble. In imitation of the organ he made a second keyboard whose object was to produce nuances,[28] and he caused three choirs to be heard on one keyboard and one on the other. He extended the range of the keyboard to four octaves from C to C by adding four low notes to the forty-five of which it was composed before him.

What especially distinguished this clever maker is the quality, fullness, and equality of tone which he gave to his harpsichords through their happy proportions, through an extreme care in the choice of the wood of which he made the soundboards of his instruments, through the care with which he arranged the grain of the wood of his soundboards so that nothing hindered the vibration, and through the gradation which he observed in their thickness, proportioned to the different frequencies from bass to treble.

The first harpsichords of Hans Ruckers are from the end of the sixteenth century. This maker had been a cabinetmaker at Antwerp. He left his first trade to devote himself entirely to the making of harpsichords. This circumstance proves that these instruments were then well known. Hans and his two sons, Jean and André, who were almost as clever as he, sent an enormous number of them into France, Spain,[29] England, and Germany.

The Italians did not profit by the new progress of the harpsichord and continued to make theirs with two unisons and one keyboard. Since these instruments were almost entirely destined for composers and were used especially to accompany the voice, a sweet sound was all that was sought. The best Italian makers have been Le Prêtre, Zanetti, Le Crotone, Farini,[30] all dating from the early seventeenth century. The last of these makers strung some of his harpsichords with gut strings. Some of them still exist in several cities of Italy, which attests to the advantage of these strings for quality of tone to those of iron or copper.

In France about the same time Richard and other makers acquired a reputation. One hundred years later Blanchet surpassed them in the agreeable tone of his harpsichords, and principally in the extreme lightness of his keyboards, which contributed a great deal to the progress of the instrument in

[27] Hans Ruckers normally made his instruments with one eight-foot and a four-foot. Thus he did not add the four-foot to the two unisons.

[28] Hans Ruckers certainly never made an expressive double harpsichord.

[29] This may partially explain the dearth of Spanish harpsichords.

[30] Apparently Boalch was not familiar with this passage since he does not cite Hullmandel in the notices of any of these makers. Le Prêtre does not appear in his list.

France. Blanchet remade the keyboards of a great number of Ruckers harpsichords to which he added four bass notes and as many in the treble.

The range of the keyboard has since been carried to five octaves. Because of several attempts made over a period of time it can be guessed that the limits of that range will soon be extended.

Such is about the present state of the harpsichord in spite of everything happy or absurd that has been attempted or carried out to refine it or to vary its real sound which has always appeared sharp to delicate ears. Harpsichords have been made which have more than twenty changes to imitate the sound of the harp, the lute, the mandolin, the bassoon, the flageolet, the oboe, the violin, and other instruments. The sounds which have been discovered in the course of experiments, to which no analogue to known instruments could be attributed, have had new names such as *celeste* stop, etc. Among this number of stops there are some that should be worthy of preservation if their fragility did not hinder their general use.

To produce these various effects the ranks of jacks have been multiplied, and in place of quills some have been fitted with whatever material is most suitable to carry out the end in view. The executant can cause these different stops to be heard either together or separately without interrupting himself by means of springs which he moves by means of knee levers and by pedals.[31] Sometimes in order to make the combinations still easier a third keyboard has been added. Finally there is the idea of placing an organ case under the harpsichord and making the pipes connect to the keyboard under the latter. The organ and the harpsichord can be heard together or separately. In combining the variety of stops adapted to the harpsichord to the diverse organ stops for which the space is adequate the number becomes prodigious.

Nuances are missing on the harpsichord. No one has found another method after that of two keyboards of augmenting or diminishing the sound except by advancing or withdrawing the various ranks of jacks successively by means of springs [mechanisms] in order to put them out of reach of the strings or to move them forward. The English, however, have added another method to that one by means of a cover placed above the strings which is divided into well-fitted slats which a pedal separates and brings together gradually in order to let the sound out or to enclose it.

So many complications denote the imperfection of the harpsichord. It calls for too much skill on the part of the workmen and patience on the part of the players. The mechanism is too constraining, and repairs are too often necessary, for instruments that require them frequently are not very rare. Is it then by false and childish imitations that we are to be drawn to it? An instrument where unity and purity of sound and all desirable degrees of loud and soft speak to the heart without wounding the ear meets the requirements of music much better.

Among that mass of inventions one should note the *peaux de buffle* substituted for the quills, which produce a sweet round sound quite different from that given by quill. These leathers, thick at the part where they are fastened

---

[31] I am not aware of any surviving French harpsichords in which the stops are moved by pedals. De Laine seems to have employed pedals in 1769. See note 23 above.

to the jacks and thinned at the other end, can by their flexibility force and soften the sound. In a large number of harpsichords a fourth rank of jacks fitted with these *peaux de buffles* has been added to the three ranks of quills. They give these harpsichords a beauty of sound which would have destroyed the use of quill except that habit too often stops the progress of the arts.[32]

One must not omit the invention of a double bottom under the harpsichord or piano-forte, by means of which strings are fitted which are struck by hammers operated by pedals like those of the organ. Silbermann at Strasbourg and Peronard at Paris have carried out this idea very well. The conception was that of Schobert, the well-known harpsichordist. It enriches the harpsichord with two octaves of low notes and an infinity of harmonic resources.

The harpsichord shares the fault of other keyboard instruments and of those in which the intonation is fixed. An attempt has been made to eliminate this failure to give the difference between the sharps and flats by adding keys. This kind of improvement will be difficult to introduce because of the problems which it presents to executants and to tuners.

The space that harpsichords occupy has caused them to be made in the past with the case standing upright, forming an angle with the keyboard. In these instruments the keyboard and the jack are held together. The weakness of their sound has always caused the horizontal harpsichords to be preferred.[33]

In order to prolong the tone of the harpsichord an attempt has been made to substitute a type of bow for the jacks. The quality of sound which has resulted has not brought great success to this invention.

A more ingenious piece of research, of which the advantage would be unimaginable and which has already excited the emulation of several artists, is that of a machine attached to the harpsichord which could write down the ideas of the player just as he played them. So far this machine has given only such results as to make further efforts desirable and to make us hope for greater success.

It is not astonishing that one should take such pains to perfect an instrument which has been generally disseminated throughout Europe for the past two hundred years and which has become one of the primary ornaments in the education of women. The success of the harpsichord at first must have been very slow. Organists disdained it for a long time. Its short and weak sound made everything that gave a good effect on the organ seem insignificant or ridiculous. The pure, majestic, and prolonged sounds of the organ were better suited to the grave and simple style of the old music. It was possible to feel the advantages of the harpsichord only when the taste for instrumental music spread and gave more fire and lightness to singing and harmony. Then the organists took it up and some demonstrated an astonishing technique. One finds proof of that in a book containing virginal pieces which was used by Queen Elizabeth. One can hardly compare the difficulties devised in the eighteenth century with those of several pieces in that collection.

To the extent that instrumental music has been perfected, harpsichord style

---

[32] An attitude which shows that the great days of the Baroque were indeed over.
[33] There is no reason why the tone of the *clavicytherium* should be weaker than that of the ordinary harpsichord.

has put the changes to the proof. Sixty years ago it still seemed too much like that of the organ. Since then a more just distinction has been made between the two instruments. Harpsichord music has been given the type of harmony and performance, the grace and lightness which is suitable to it. Alberti, Scarlatti, Rameau, Mütel, Wagenseil, then Schobert have wrought this revolution almost simultaneously. The different styles of these composers have served for more than twenty-five years as models for those who have composed for the harpsichord after them. Perhaps Emanuel Bach, for his learned, agreeable and piquant music, has merited the first place among original artists, but since he composed for the piano-forte, in use in Germany before being known elsewhere, he must not be confused with them [harpsichord composers]. He is one of various composers who in giving their music the graduated nuances, oppositions, and a melody suitable to the sound and resources of the piano-forte, have prepared or decided the downfall of the harpsichord.

The undoubted resources of the harpsichord in harmony, and the ease with which it represents on the keyboard the effect of the diverse instruments which make up the orchestra, have assigned it the first rank among the instruments of music. It has become the instrument of composers because it renders them better account of their intentions than any other instrument. It has become that of singing masters because its fixed sounds guide the irresolutions of the voice, always likely to sharp or flat when it is not sustained, and because it accustoms the person who sings to feel all the parts which must accompany him. This use and these advantages of the harpsichord have put it in the position of directing the orchestra in the theater and in concerts. Not twenty years ago it still was habitually used for the *basso continuo* of sonatas or solos executed on other instruments and even in symphonies, although it weakened the effect.

Such a range of uses for the harpsichord shows the extent of the knowledge required by those destined to that instrument. Besides having a clean, brilliant, and rapid technique, embellished by taste and ornaments, and an imagination accustomed to express itself with facility, they must also be good harmonists and good readers to seize at sight the intent and spirit of each composer; and they must know how to give confidence to a singer and ensemble to an orchestra by great accuracy in rhythm and care in indicating the most sensitive and expressive chords.

ENGLAND

"HARPSECHORD." FROM THE TALBOT MANUSCRIPT. Reproduced by kind permission of the Governing Body of Christ Church, Oxford. See Plate XXXIX for Talbot's diagram.

A. the Keys: KK the Foreboard [nameboard] B. C. D. the Restpiece [wrestplank] on wch the Restpins EE of wch 1 2 or 3 rows according to the No. of Strings:[34] D. the Restpiece Bridge wch if single carry's 2 rows of

[34] We see that the four-foot choir was apparently well established by Talbot's time.

Unisons answerable to 2 Stops: [" if double," [35] crossed out] If 3 you have 3 Stops you have 2 or 3 Bridges of [which] the 1st or highest carry's 2 Unisons: the 2nd or lower one row. Unison sounds the octave.[36] if 3 bridges each has a single row.[37] GGG the Stops wch may be 2 or 3: 3rd the Lute Jack.[38] H the Long bridge on wch the Bridge pins I the Octave bridge: L the Movement or Register.[39] Over the Jacks proper the Ruler [jack rail] under wch a List of Flanel or Cloth [a damping strip or pad to deaden the noise of the jacks]. M the Cheekpiece. N the Bending side. O the Little or Mitre-end. P the backside: Q. the Sound-board or belly. — with the Knot [the rose] (disus'd) Under the Keys at Front the Key-pin piece on wch the Key pins at the inward end of the Keys a List to prevent Noise of Jacks: at the ivry end of the Keys runs a Mannichord [40] in wch each Key has its proper Guide to run in. At the end of the Lid near the Keys the Flap fitted by a Hinge.

[MS Page 2]

Harpsichd Germ Geigenwerck [41]   Germ Spinetten
   Harpsichord Spinet Spinett. Germ. Bierdticht [42]
     1 Mannichord Germ Clavichord
      Virginal

Harpsichord Mers. Lat. 61: Gall. 110 [43] Kirch. 16 p. 754. Sc. 4. Fig. 1

Stops of Wallnut Pear: Beach (if solid): if covered wth Leather, beach or Lime. best Leather Calves [44]

Spinet. Mers. Lat. 59. 65. Kirch. ibid. Fig. 2.

Mannichord. Mers. Gall. 114: Lat. p. 63.

Jacks best of Pear wood (with the Beach not so good) Quills ["for Basses Raven" is crossed out] Crow ["quill" crossed out] for Trebles Crow (or Rook (blackest) Raven best for large Inst with long 8ve for 8 lowest Keys.

[35] Talbot seems to have used "single" to mean 2x8', "double" to mean 2x8', 1x4'. Is this a possible explanation for the same terms in inventories of the sixteenth century?

[36] Makes no sense: apparently an error.

[37] I have never seen this arrangement of nuts.

[38] The lute seems to have been the third stop added at least part of the time.

[39] That is, the hand-stop lever. It appears to have been mounted inside the nameboard on the wrest plank. Talbot's sketch is so rough that any conclusions are difficult.

[40] The "mannichord" must be the rack behind the key levers, properly called "diapason" in Latinate terminology. The manichord was identical with the clavichord.

[41] Properly a keyboard instrument with a mechanism which bows the strings.

[42] Possibly *viereckig* (four-cornered) was intended.

[43] References to Mersenne's Latin and French editions, and to Kircher.

[44] Talbot knew both the leather-covered and solid registers. The French made leather-covered registers but both the Flemish and the Italians used solid wood, although their design was quite different.

The Case usually Deal Wainscot [oak] Walnut, Lime, Cypress, Cedar, Cormier.[45] Case usually finier'd within by Cedar Cypress Walnut. The Keys usually of Firr or Lime wood but covered at the end with Ebony: [46] Sharp with Ivory at top. Foreboard of Deal same wth inside of Case as is the Cheekpiece.

Rest-piece usually Pearwood Oak beach without Knots. Pins Iron wire. Rest p. bridge & long bridge Pear Beech, (bending better) sometimes Walnut.

Restpiece of Oak or beach finier'd as Inside of Case:

Barrs usually of Firr never less than 4 never more than 7 [?]. If not let into —— then a piece of Cloth is glued to belly over Barr.[47]

Ruler of Deal finier'd as the inside.

Belly best of Firr, sometimes Cedar or Cypress. best Firr fine grain rare in England

Key-pin piece solid Oak. Frame of Oak or Deal. Sometimes Beach.

Mannichord Lime and Oak . . .

Strings Yellow hard [brass] 12 Numbers 12th biggest wch are to vary Sizes. Copper & Brass. Brass has 12 Nos Copper 6 from No 6 to 12. Iron 6 Nos from Nr 1 to 6. Copper Basses mellower; than Brass Last Wire argentern [silver].

[MS page 3]

Jenny's [48]	F. I. O.[49]				Breadth of Stops	F. I. 8.		
Length of Body Back	6.	2.	0.		Breadth of Stops	0.	0.	5.
Fore-end [width]	2	6.			[registers]			
Cheek piece	1.	6.	4.		Length of Strings for			
Bending side	4.	9.	4.		bridge			
Mitre end	0	9.	4.		Rules for stringing			
Depth round [50]	0	8	5.		bridge [51]			
Depth from Belly to Edge [52]		2	4.		First C	0	4.	7.
Depth of Belly [thickness of soundboard]	0	0	1.		2nd C or cc	0	10.	2.

[45] The service tree. The wood is very hard.
[46] It is noteworthy that the keys were black.
[47] The ribs often had a reinforcing strip of cloth glued over their ends.
[48] Probably the owner of the harpsichord.
[49] That is, feet, inches, and eighths of inches.
[50] If this represents the deviation of the bentside from a straight line it was very curved indeed. If the case was 8⅝ inches high, it was very shallow. The 1683 Haward was 9¾ inches high.
[51] This scale may be transcribed: c‴, 4⅞"; c″, 10¼"; c′, 20"; c, 37⅞"; C, 60".
[52] That is, the distance from the upper edge of the case to the soundboard — about normal.

F. I. O.

Barr thick Bottom [53]	⎤	......o o	3
Largest sound ribs to- ward thickness of half crown	⎬		
Breadth inside to to- ward the broadest pt. of Belly depth of edge at end [55]	⎬	o. I. o	
Toward narrow less		...........o o	6.
Breadth of Key [56]		...............o o.	7+
Sharp distant			
E.F.G.B.C.[57]		..................o. o.	4.
A. G.		..........................o o	4+
of D		...........................o. o.	5.
Breadth of Sharp		...............o. o.	4.
Length of Sharp		...............o. 2.	5
of Head of Key or great end		........o. I	2½
Rest p. bridge from Fore- board [58] on Treble side	⎫⎬	o. 5.	I
on Bass side		...................o 7	7.

F. I. 8.

3rd or c) ....I.	8.	o.
4th or C) ....3.	I	7.
5th or CC) ....5.	o.	o.

For GG N.[11] brass or Copper.[54] CC N. 9 or 8. AA. N. 10 or 9 ["DD" crossed out] N. 8. b♯ EE 7. EE 7 or 6. F. G. 6 or 5. A.B. 5. C. 5. 4. X D 4 to c. 3 to cc. thence to aaa 2. to bbb & ccc. ddd N. 1.

[53] Since this item is bracketed with a remark concerning the ribbing under the sound-board it is possible that Talbot meant that the wedge sectioned ribs were ⅜ inch thick on the bottom where they were glued to the soundboard and tapering to the thickness of a half crown on top. Another possibility is that ⅜ inch represents the thickness of the lower-level frame members. Sound bars the thickness of a half crown throughout their section would be far too light, however.

[54] The stringing list may be transcribed:

$$
\begin{array}{llll}
d''' & - a\sharp'' & - \sharp 1 \\
a'' & - c\sharp'' & - \sharp 2 \\
c'' & - c\sharp' & - \sharp 3 \\
c' & - c\sharp & - \sharp 4 \\
c & & - \sharp 4 \text{ or } \sharp 5 \\
B & -A & - \sharp 5 \\
G & -F & - \sharp 5 \text{ or } \sharp 6 \\
E & & - \sharp 6 \text{ or } \sharp 7 \\
D\sharp & & - \sharp 7 \\
D & & - \sharp 8 \\
C & & - \sharp 8 \text{ or } \sharp 9 \\
AA & & - \sharp 9 \text{ or } \sharp 10 \\
GG & & - \sharp 11 \text{ (Brass or Copper).}
\end{array}
$$

The point of changeover from steel to brass is not specified. In the treble these strings are considerably lighter (ca. .007 inch) than those used by Kirckman (.010 inch), but the bass diameters are like (.0022 inch). The gauge numbers follow the system we have found in the eighteenth century in England. See page 207.

[55] This item and the following may refer to the dimensions of the eight-foot hitchpin rail.

[56] That is, the key head of the naturals.

[57] That is, the width of the various key tails. See page 221.

[58] There is an error here. The nut is always closer to the nameboard in the bass than in the treble. These dimensions may refer to the width of the wrest plank. That of the

F. I. O.

Breadth of Bridge ....o. o 3.
  (generally) ....o o 4.
From Rest piece to Stops
  [that is, width of wrest plank]
  Treble ....o. 7. o.
  on Bass side ....o. 7 2.

[There is one more leaf with a sketch of a jack and several illegible words
which deal with the order of the jacks in the gap and to which choir each
jack pertains.]

GERMANY

PASSAGES FROM PRAETORIUS, *Syntagma musicum*, vol. II, *De organographia*
(1619).

[62] Chapter XXXVIII. Spinet (plate XIV)

Spinet (Italian, *Spinetto*) is a small four-cornered *Instrument*[59] which is
tuned about an octave or a fifth sharp of ordinary pitch, and which is usually
placed on top of or in the large *Instrument*. In Italy the large four-cornered
ones, as well as the small ones, are called spinets without distinction.

In England all such instruments, large or small, are called *Virginall*.

In France, *Espinette*.

In the Netherlands, *Clavicymbel*, and also *Virginali*.

In Germany, *the general* term *Instrument* is applied specifically to designate this particular kind of instrument.

Chapter XXXIX. Harpsichord (plate VI)

The harpsichord or *Gravecymbalum* is a longish *Instrument* which to some
is a wing because it is almost in that shape: by others (but badly) it would be
called a pig's head because it ends in a point like the head of a wild boar, and
it is of a strong, bright, almost lovely tone and resonance, more than the
others, because of the doubled, tripled, even quadrupled strings; just as one
I saw which had two eight-foot unisons, a quint, and a little octave of strings;
and quite sweetly and splendidly they rang amongst one another.

[66] Chapter XLI. Clavicytherium

Has a pointed shape like a harpsichord except that the case and soundboard with the strings are made upright as may be seen in plate XV [see
Plate XXVI]. It produces a sound almost the same as that of the cittern or
harp.

Chapter XLII. Claviorganum

Is a harpsichord or other jack-action instrument in which several ranks of

---

1683 Haward is 5⅝ inches in the treble and 7⅞ inches in the bass. Hence, the gap is
oblique.

  [59] In Chapter XXXVII Praetorius explains that the word *Instrument* is used in two
senses. The first is that of modern English; to cover all the instruments of music. The
second refers especially to the jack-action keyboard instruments.

pipes like those of a positive are built in along with the strings. From the outside however, it looks no different than a harpsichord or jack-action instrument except that in some the bellows are placed behind, and in others inside the case.

Chapter XLIII. *Arpichordum*

Is a jack-action instrument or virginal on which a harplike sound is produced by means of a special stop which governs brass hooks under the strings.

[72] Chapter XLV. Regal (plate IV)

By the word regal we not only understand the reeds with brass resonators found for the most part in the front of the *Brustwerk* of the organ, but this term is also used in royal chapels to designate an instrument in the shape of a small but rather long chest containing one or more ranks of reeds with two bellows attached in back. This instrument can be set on a table and it is very suitable in ensembles and much better than a harpsichord or jack-action instrument, for the harpsichords are too soft in full ensembles and their strings cannot sustain their tone longer than half a measure.

Selected Passages Relating to Disposition and Means of Expression

FROM ADLUNG, *Anleitung zu der musikalischen Gelahrtheit* (1758).

[554]

[Harpsichords] are rarely single- or quadruple-choired, most often double- or triple-choired. The double-choired are at eight-foot pitch, but now and then one of the eight-foots is replaced by an overspun string at sixteen-foot pitch. The four-choired are either strung with two eight-foot strings and two four-foot strings, or one of the latter is left and one replaces the other with a sixteen-foot overspun or plain string [60] . . . It is fine when a harpsichord has two keyboards even if it has only three choirs. It can be arranged so that the upper keyboard works the front row of jacks and the lower controls the remaining rows. If it is desired to sound all the stops together the keyboards can be coupled. Furthermore, more rows of jacks can be fitted so that the lower keyboard can sound all of the choirs without coupling and the upper manual can play one, two, or three stops.[61] With these and the following types of instruments one can add a fifth to the bass and carry the compass up to e''' or f'''. In this case it does not cost so much as with an organ . . .

[note 1 to page 555].

Although this many jacks are bothersome to make there is still another use for them. If a row of jacks plucks nearer to the nut they produce a sharper tone than if they pluck farther from the nut. Sometimes, therefore, several

[60] It is not possible that this be taken literally. The four-foot scale is far too short for a sixteen-foot choir. Adlung probably meant to say that the fourth choir could be a sixteen-foot instead of a second four-foot.

[61] Adlung's methodical enthusiasm seems to be running away with him. One can clearly see the organist's mind at work. Later Adlung describes an upper manual to lower manual coupler. This would make possible these heavy registrations on the upper manual.

rows are made for a single string even though there is only one keyboard . . .
If such a row of jacks is placed very near the nut, and thus is distant from
the other jacks, it sounds almost like a *Spitzharfe* and where I saw it, this
stop was called a *Spinet*.[62]

FROM HALLE, *Werkstäte der heutigen Künste* (1764)

[III, 359]
The two registers are of pearwood and lie between the soundboard and the
wrest plank. They are at eight-foot pitch and are sometimes reinforced by a
third *Kornetregister*.[63] Many harpsichords have double keyboards with two
registers[64] of eight- and four-foot tone plus a buff stop [*Lautenzug*] or
Kornetzug.

[III, 360]
In the keyboard there are 48 or 61 keys from g to g [GG–g‴] five octaves,
the natural keys of black ebony and the sharps covered with ivory. So much
for the single harpsichord.
The double gets two registers plus the *Oktavkornetchen* [?] so that the
largest harpsichord has two or even three keyboards over one another from
twelve-foot [FF]. The greater number of strings requires more bridges on
the soundboard. Otherwise their construction is on the whole the same [as
singles].

FROM ADLUNG, *Musica mechanica organoedi* (1768)

[II, 103]
The keyboard is like that of an organ and consists of four octaves, sometimes five. And I should suggest that this instrument should never be made

---

[62] In English this stop is called lute stop, a fact which has caused endless misunder-
standings between English speaking and German speaking musicologists. The following are equivalents: buff stop or harp stop — *Lautenzug*; Lute stop — *Spinet, Nasal* or
Oboezug. The lute stop is most common on English harpsichords, but I have seen it in
Flanders, and Hass sometimes used it.

[63] Here Halle seems to use *Kornetregister* to mean four-foot, and *Kornetzug* to refer
to some sort of string-shortening stop, but his meaning is not at all clear. See page 328
for a reference to the *Kornett* by J. F. Agricola, and page 270 for Sprengel's remarks.
A very crude illustration (tab. VIII, fig. 47) shows the plan view of a round-tailed harpsichord. According to the legend the four-foot bridge is called *Kornetsteg*. Two parallel
lines drawn across the wrest plank at 30° (from the front at the bass to the rear at the
treble) are lebeled *schräge Kornetregister* (diagonal *Kornetregister*). It is difficult to
guess their purpose. Since they would shorten the treble strings more than the bass,
they could not have actually applied anything to the strings which changed the vibrating length, for the intonation would be damaged hopelessly. Gall distinguishes between
a sort of *Arpichordum* which causes the strings to jar and the "string-shortening *Kornettzug*." If it were not for his remarks we should suggest that Halle's *Kornetzug* fell
into the category of the *Arpichordum* or *Schnarrwerk*. One wonders if Halle understood
the matter himself.

[64] Halle may mean two pitches, eight-foot and four-foot, rather than two stops, although he does not say so: "mit zwei Registieren von 8 und 4 Fus Thon."

otherwise than with five octaves because many keyboard pieces require it and cannot be played with four octaves.

[II, 105]

Some harpsichords are single-choired, others have two strings for each key; still others have three.

[II, 110]

I know of a harpsichord from Breitenbach [65] with two keyboards and three choirs. It consisted of the octave four-foot, eight-foot, and an overspun choir at sixteen-foot pitch. However, it extends to FF in the bass and thus to twenty-four-foot pitch.[66] The four-foot and sixteen-foot are on the lower manual. The former [the four-foot] is at a lower level, has its own bridge, and does not extend as far forward as the other wrest pins nor as far back as the bent bridge, but its curved bridge is a fair distance more to the front and lower so as to give the possibility for the eight-foot and the sixteen-foot to pass over it without touching. Behind the lower bridge, pins are driven into the soundboard to which the four-foot strings are hitched and thence extend forward to their own nut at which a special row of wrest pins is driven (it is important to provide an oak hitchpin rail under the soundboard), between the other strings, on which these strings are wound [hitched]. These will be controlled by the rear-most jacks through the lower manual and produce a good sound. The upper manual controls the eight-foot string by means of the front jacks; and in order to have a forte on the lower manual the two keyboards can be coupled together, not in the manner we have described before, in which by sliding the upper manual the lower is pressed down (in which case one must play on the upper), but if one slides the upper and plays on the lower, the upper also goes because the lower keys lift the upper by means of little slips of wood glued above and below as in the case of the organ coupler. And one can make three manuals in the same way. The keyboards are so arranged that the upper raises the front row of jacks, the others extend somewhat further inward and raise the rest.[67]

FROM JACOBSSON, *Technologisches Wörterbuch* (1793), V, 573.

The court mechanic, Milchmeyer, at Mainz, has devised a new-action *Flügel* which is not much larger than the ordinary and yet contains more

[65] Boalch reports only two Breitenbach makers who might have made Adlung's harpsichord: Johann Heinrich Harrass (died 1714), of whom Kinsky mentions a two-manual harpsichord in the library of the Hofkapelle at Sondershausen; and H. W. Langguth, who is known only through a signed clavichord, dated 1760, which was shown in the International Inventions Exhibition of 1885.

[66] A pipe 8 feet long sounds C. FF requires a pipe twelve feet long. Thus 16-foot pitch at FF would be sounded by a pipe 24 feet in length.

[67] This somewhat clumsily expressed passage seems to indicate an upper to lower and lower to upper coupler. If the upper manual was in one position, the coupling was down; and when it was pushed to the other extreme of its motion, the coupling was up. I have never seen such a coupler.

than 250 variations. It has three keyboards; the lowest can be pulled out and then two persons can play.[68]

[STOP MECHANISM]

FROM SPRENGEL, *Handwerk und Künste in Tabelen* (1773), p. 263.

A harpsichord usually has some handstops [*Registerzüge*] of which later on one must say the needful. It has already been pointed out (page 259) that the two registers fi and dh rest loosely on the wrest plank supports [*Leisten*] he and dg, and that they can be moved somewhat across the width of the harpsichord. Hence the two most important handstops. On the wrest plank [*Wirbelbalken*] ei is a piece of wood, fastened by means of a pin x, and called a stop lever [*Zug*] fg.[69] The pin x stands vertically in this stop lever and thus one can grasp the forward end of the stop lever and push it on the wrest plank in the direction from y to t and back again from y toward s. The rear end of this stop lever is fastened to the register fi. Thus if one moves the stop lever at y from y toward s, the register fi will also be moved and in the direction f toward i. If, however, one pushes the stop lever at y from y toward t, the register, on the contrary, will move from i toward f. All told, one can move the register only $\frac{1}{16}$ *Zoll*,[70] for under the stop lever fg is fixed a pin at f which fits into a mortise in the wrest plank ei and this mortise is only $\frac{1}{16}$ *Zoll* long.[71] If the register fi is moved in the direction of f to i, then one moves at the same time all the jacks which are inserted in the register (page 259) about $\frac{1}{16}$ *Zoll*. In playing, these jacks ordinarily touch the strings to the right of each key,[72] but now, on the contrary, they are withdrawn to such a distance from the said strings, having been moved from f toward i with the register, that their quills do not touch the strings. In this case, only the quills of those jacks in the rearmost register hd strike their strings when they are moved. If, however, one moves the register fi by means of the stop lever fy back again from i toward f, then each quill again stands beneath its string and the jacks of both registers touch the strings in playing. With the first stop

---

[68] This passage is quoted in German by Boalch, *Makers of the Harpsichord and Clavichord*, p. 80. Boalch seems to have found it in *Cramers Magazin* for 1783, from whence Jacobsson must have lifted it. Some of the 250 effects were imitations of the flute, bassoon, clarinet, and harp. See Russell, *The Harpsichord and Clavichord*, p. 102, for a description of a Hieronymus Hass three-manual harpsichord of 1740 which resembles this *Flügel* in some regards.

[69] Sprengel is describing a handstop mounted on the wrest plank rather than on the nameboard. This seemingly inconvenient location was quite common in German harpsichords.

[70] Substantially equal to $\frac{1}{16}$ inch.

[71] Another and better version of this end-stop mechanism is often found in Ruckers harpsichords. A block spanning the gap is placed over all the registers at the treble end. Pins are driven through this block, passing through short slots cut in each register. Thus the motion of the registers is determined by the length of the slots.

[72] Thus Sprengel confirms that the front register ordinarily sounded the shorter unison of the pair. His harpsichord would be disposed:

$$\rightarrow 8'$$
$$\leftarrow 8'.$$

lever moved in the direction f to i, each jack remains standing on its key however, for one moves it very little, namely ¹⁄₁₆ Zoll. A similar stop lever dz moves the rearmost register hd, just as with the front one. Thus at pleasure one can play with the jacks of both registers fi and dh or also with the jacks of either one of the registers.

[MANUAL COUPLER]

FROM SPRENGEL, *Handwerk und Künste in Tabelen* (1773), p. 266. (See Plate XXX.)

When a harpsichord has two keyboards one over the other, it is called a double harpsichord [*doppelten Flügels*]. These vary from the foregoing single ones in the following respects. First, in place of two, there are three registers and the two rearmost (fig. III, fi and hd) pertain to the lower manual just as in a single harpsichord; the front one, however, belongs to the upper manual. Secondly, one can play on either keyboard separately or on both coupled together in such a way that when the lower manual is played its moving keys set the corresponding keys of the upper manual in motion. This is accomplished through the following very simple intermediary: The upper keyboard is in a special frame or slider which can be moved horizontally forward and backward. The lower keyboard, on the other hand, is immovable like that of a single harpsichord. ki of fig. IV shows a key of the lower manual, and lm a narrow bit of wood which stands vertically and rigidly on the rearmost end of the key. When the upper manual is pushed back, the rearmost end of the key of the upper manual stands over the vertical piece of wood ml of the corresponding key of the lower manual. Thus, if the lower key is depressed at the front end k, the rear end l rises and with it the piece of wood lm. The latter thus lifts the rear end of the corresponding key of the upper manual and the keys of both manuals will be set in motion together, for all the keys of the lower manual have the aforementioned arrangement. However, if the upper manual is drawn forward, then the rear of its key disengages the piece of wood ml of the lower keyboard and each manual can be played independently. Generally speaking, the double harpsichord has the same arrangements as the single, and it can have stop levers as well.

FROM *Clavier-Stimmbuch*, EDITED BY GALL (ca. 1795).

The keyboard of a harpsichord generally takes the entire width. One can not only play each keyboard independently on double harpsichords but one can also couple them so that the upper keys move when one is playing on the lower. On the rear end of each key lever of the immovable lower keyboard, fixed and vertical, stands a narrow piece of wood which raises the rear of the corresponding key lever of the upper manual just above, whenever it [the lower key] is played, providing that the sliding lower [probably an error for "upper"] manual on its special key bed has been pushed back.

[SPECIAL EFFECTS]

FROM ADLUNG, *Anleitung zu der musikalischen Gelahrtheit* (1758), p. 557, n. r.

[*Harfenzuge*] [73] — This is also found on the nut and is either a movable batten into which bent pins have been driven or similar bits of wood are provided as may be seen on the *Davidsharfe*. When they are close to the string a harplike jarring [*Harfen mässiges Schnarren*] will be perceived which detracts nothing from the clarity of the tone. The stop affects only one string and the remaining stop is taken off in order to hear it. Praetorius (page 67) calls an *Instrument* with this stop an *Arpichordum*.

FROM SPRENGEL, *Handwerk und Künste in Tabelen* (1773), p. 265.

The maker places six wedges (specially illustrated, Fig. V, a) on the wrest plank ei so that all the wedges are in a line parallel to the registers (fig. III, fi). On all of the wedges lies a batten BC which is exactly the same length as the nut [*Vordersteg*] on the wrest plank. This batten is notched on the underside to fit the wedges exactly. Thus if one pushes this batten in the direction from B to C on the wedges, it is raised, and since it lies only a short distance below all of the strings of the harpsichord it can be raised until it touches the strings. The maker glues red cloth to its upper surface, and if, as in the aforementioned case, the cloth touches the strings, they are damped and this damping is called a "buff stop" [*Lautenzug*].[74] However, the batten leaves the strings again when it is pushed in the direction C to B and the strings of the harpsichord again sound in their usual undamped manner. Sometimes the harpsichord maker installs a second batten on wedges behind the buff stop toward the soundboard of the harpsichord, which batten has the same mechanism except that it is not covered with cloth. If the strings are damped at the same time with the aforementioned buff and with the latter unfelted batten, the strings jar [*schnarren*], and hence this last stop is known as the *Schnarrwerk*. By changing and blending in different combinations these four stops the owner of the harpsichord can change the tone of the strings in many ways. Formerly a cornet stop [*Cornettzug*] was added to the foregoing which shortened the strings; but it has gone out of fashion.

[PEDAL BOARDS]

FROM ADLUNG, *Anleitung zu der musikalischen Gelahrtheit* (1758), p. 556.

One can also add a pedal to such instruments, or what is better make a special pedal instrument [*Pedalkörper*] and set the harpsichord on top. It should be made well so that the tension of the strings does not bend the sides of the case and so that the instrument holds its tuning.[m]

[73] See page 74 for a further account of this device.
[74] Most German harpsichords seem to have had the normal buff stop mechanism in which the buff pads (one for each string of the choir to be damped) stand above the surface of a batten mounted on the rear of the nut. When the batten is moved sideways each pad damps its string.

(m) A very fine harpsichord and an equally good pedal board [*Clavicym-belpedal*] designed to be placed underneath was shown to me by Herr Bürgermeister Vogler [75] in Weimar who let me hear it as well. The harpsichord was strung 2x8', 1x4' and had a range of six octaves CC–c''''.[76] The upper keyboard was disposed 1x8', the lower had the remaining stops; and if the upper manual were pushed in and one played from the lower, the keys were coupled and the action was still light. The stop handles were on the wrest plank [*Decke*, literally soundboard] and were painted vermillion. The jacks were very delicate and light, the quills sloped upwards so that they could not stick.[77] I found the soundboard so thick that one would think it could not sound, and yet I have met no other instrument with a better tone. The inner arrangements of the case were reinforced by a good deal of iron, and iron screws were particularly noticeable in the pedal board case [*Pedalkörper*], chiefly toward the tail where the strings impose the least stress. This *Pedal* was strung 2x8', not overspun, and 1x16', overspun. There was a door in the lid which could be opened to increase the tone. Both cases were nicely veneered.

FROM HALLE, *Werkstäte der heutigen Künste* (1764), III, 363.

Sometimes pedals [*Pedale*] are fitted to harpsichords [*Flügeln*] and clavichords [*Klaviren*] in which the strings are mounted beneath those of the manuals. The *Pedal* obtains sixteen-foot tone and space is accordingly allowed for number 0000000 strings.

FROM ADLUNG, *Musica mechanica organoedi* (1768).

[II, 158]

We arrive finally at the last instrument, the pedal, which will not delay us long because most of its details correspond to those of the clavichord or harpsichord.[78] The pedal keys are made like those of an organ, of the same number, thickness, width and length, provided with springs, pins and so forth. (See chapter 2, paragraphs 27, 28, 29, most of which applies here.) It is a good thing if the parts are screwed together so that they can be taken apart and transported. Then one makes the frame which is not unlike a sawhorse [*Tischbocke*], except that in front the rack-grooves [*Scheiden*] will be cut (par. 27), as was done with the organ. In this case it is different because they must be cut higher,[79] since one cannot determine the point to which they [the keys] will fall in play as can be done with the organ; all the more so if

[75] Johann Caspar Vogler (1695–1765). A favorite student of J. S. Bach. Court organist at Weimar, he was named Bürgermeister in 1735 by the duke who retained his services in that way.

[76] Possibly Adlung is referring to the pitches sounded by the strings rather than to the actual keyboard range. A harpsichord with a keyboard from CC–c''' would be able to sound c'''' when the four-foot stop was drawn.

[77] A quill which slopes upward slightly aids the return of the jack at the moment when the tongue must be cammed backwards by the contact of the underside of the quill with the string.

[78] Adlung is primarily dealing with clavichords in this section.

[79] One would think that Adlung meant lower.

one regulates the device with string.[80] Hence it is not necessary to line them with cloth. The frame should be high enough so that with the box on top and the clavichord on that, it is of equal height to the organ keyboard to which one is accustomed.

[II, 159]

It is well to take the pedal up to d', for one plays things at home more often than on the organ that go up to d'. It is also well to place a lid on the case, for when the soundboard is at least partly uncovered it sounds louder. On this account the lid over the soundboard should be removable.

[II, 161]

The case can not only be made like that of a clavichord, but also in the form of a harpsichord, plucking the strings with quills. This is called a *Clavicymbelpedal*. If the harpsichord sounds well such a pedal is usually fine. It requires no special description for it is like a *Clavicymbel* to make; with only two octaves the jacks are set farther apart since two octaves require the space ordinarily taken by four octaves.

There is a simplified version where one makes no special case or box but arranges that the keys of *Clavichords*, *Clavessins*, *Instruments*, *Lautenwerks*, etc., be pulled down by trackers or cords. These are common and for them one need only drive staples or screws into the key levers of the two lowest octaves, as is done frequently with organs . . . However, the roller board and trackers appear more important than they did because the two octaves are not as extended as they were,[81] hence the cords will arrive at entirely too steep an angle; otherwise it is a good enough compromise.[82] If one wishes to take such an instrument apart, one hangs the cords loosely on the upper or lower part . . . Herr Bach,[83] in Jena, formerly made *Lautenwerken* with pedals which resembled a common theorbo in sound.

Selected Passages Relating to Constructional Factors Affecting Tone

[CASE DIMENSIONS, DETAILS, AND MATERIALS]

FROM HALLE, *Werkstäte der heutigen Künste* (1764).

[III, 358]

One ordinarily gives single harpsichords a length [*Länge*] of eight feet, and the large ones a length of sixteen feet.[84] They are about 3 feet 2 inches

---

[80] Adlung is describing a clavichord in which the special pedal instrument is mounted off the floor and is connected to the pommels of the pedal board by cords.

[81] Adlung had been speaking of a special pedal instrument in which the string band was widened to the spacing of the pedal pommels. In the case of pull-downs he was forced to connect the widely spaced pedals to the narrowly spaced keyboard.

[82] Agricola gives us this note: "However, it is sometimes very unpleasant if one is playing things with obbligato pedal and arrives at a tone on the manual which has already been played from the pedal. This can happen to these unifications [*Compendia*] and on the organ, too. They can be excused by nothing but a pressing need for economy."

[83] See Appendix F.

[84] Halle seems to have confused length and pitch.

in width; however one need not follow these measurements exactly. The bottom will be one inch thick.[85] It is made of pine [*Kien*] or fir [*Tannen-holz*], the drier the better. The spine [*Hinterwand*] will be of ½ inch pine, the bentside of maple,[86] elm or fir. The native maple which one can procure in this region is coarse fibred and bluish instead of white and fine grained as maple should be. Fir, preferably from Bohemia, Upper Lausatia and Silesia, must be dry, fine grained and beautifully white. Elm [*Rüster*] is a very flexible wood, and for that reason the bridges on the soundboards of harpsichords are generally of elm or maple, which conforms almost to the color of walnut [87] but differs in that walnut remains unbendable without softening in water. Fir [*Tannenholz*] is used for the soundboard and it is glued up of planks ⅛ inch thick, and often thinner if they produce a muffled sound on being tapped with a finger while they are in the gluing clamps. The case is generally of maple [88] and the soundboard of fir with the understanding that because the sun burns the fibres of the south side [*Mit-tagsseite*] of a fir harder and stiffer, the preference is given to the north side [*Mitternachtseite*] which sustains the vibrations of the strings better, and whose fibres are more easily set in motion.

[III, 360]

The soundboard will be ⅛ inch thick all over and is made of fir planks glued together and accurately planed.

FROM ADLUNG, *Musica Mechanica Organoedi* (1768).

[II, 103]

We take note first of the case [*Corpus*] of the *Claveçin* or *Clavicymbel*. It is sometimes of soft wood, but those of hardwood are more stable. They are as wide in front as the keyboard so that they ordinarily have space for four or five octaves (which latter is better); to the rear, however, they are quite pointed, almost like a right-angled triangle [45° ?]. The painting, ve-neer, etc., conforms to the maker's whim. Their height is about ½ *Elle*,[89] sometimes more, sometimes less. If the former, they sound more heavy and pompous; the latter, however, produces a more lovely sound. The sides must be of soft or hardwood, and the bottom is made of fir [*Tannenholz*] in order to aid the tone. For in connection with the tone and the movement of the air, both the soundboard and the bottom vibrate to some extent, the sound-board more than the bottom.

[II, 104]

The soundboard over the whole *Clavessin* is made of fine fir [*Tannen-holz*]. For this wood is lighter than most others and it is moved by the air

[85] The bottoms of existing instruments are usually ½ inch.
[86] Although softwoods were often used for bentsides, most hardwoods like maple can be bent more easily after steaming or soaking.
[87] Halle must be thinking of the sapwood of walnut which is very light in color.
[88] Although, as we have seen above, the bottom and spine can be of deal or fir.
[89] An *Elle* is equal to about 25¾ inches according to some authorities and 26.258 inches according to others.

most easily and best aids the tone as a result. However, it must be quite dry. Otherwise it will shrink and split in dry weather, and thus the tone will be deadened by the open crack. The *Boden* [literally bottom] (as the sound-board is sometimes called) is rabbeted into the sides, but the front edge rests on top [of the belly rail], and from the right hand side of the front back to the tail a bridge is set, not far from the side of the case, and the strings are afterwards laid upon it. Still farther toward the bentside metal pins are also driven just as into the bridge in order to mount the strings. In front, near the keyboard, one wrest pin of heavy wire or of forged iron is driven for each string. These must be strong so that they do not bend and thus stand the steadier. Under these a baulk of oak is mounted into which they are driven through the soundboard [90] in order to stand firmly. Brass pins do not stand so well. In front of these wrest pins the strings rest on another bridge [nut].

[II, 112]

Then they [the planks for the soundboard] are glued accurately together. They must not be thicker than about 1/16 of a *Zoll* [91] so that the soundboard may be moved more easily and can be brought into vibration. If one lays something on the bridge, the tone is muted because the vibration cannot take place freely. If one puts something on the soundboard, a key for example, it buzzes; whereupon one sees that the soundboard is put into continuous motion by the pluck. One notes that new harpsichords (as is true of most musical instruments) do not sound as bright [*scharf*] and pleasant [*angenehm*] as they do when they have been played a while. The basic reason is that the wood continually becomes drier and lighter. Therefore some do well to take old boxes for the purpose which have laid for long periods in dry places and so have been quite dried out.[92] Also it is customary to make the soundboard somewhat thicker in the bass for the sake of sonority [*Gravität*].[93] Under the soundboard a countersupport [*Wiederhalt*] is placed.

[90] The wrest plank of German harpsichords was usually veneered to resemble the soundboard.

[91] This seems wrong. As far as I can tell, the *Fuss* at this period equaled 12.357 modern inches; 1/16 *Zoll* is thus substantially equivalent to 1/16 inch. Some Ruckers instruments have soundboards this thin in places, but not over their entire area. Other German authorities give 1/8 inch, which checks with the extant soundboards I have been able to measure. Adlung may have meant that only the treble should be 1/16 inch. See his remarks on taper below.

[92] This sounds like an oblique reference to Maffei, who mentioned in the course of his famous account of Cristofori's newly invented piano forte that "Pesaro made use of old chests that he found in the granaries of Venice and Padua, which were for the most part of cypress wood from Candia and Cyprus." (Trans. Rimbault.)

[93] In point of fact a thin soundboard is resonant to a lower frequency than a thick one, since the thick board is stiffer. Modern piano makers sometimes taper their soundboards in the reverse direction. However, analogy was too strong for the old makers. Thick strings and large bridge sections pertained to the bass and thus, they reasoned, the soundboard should also be thick in that region. Whenever I have been able to detect a consistent taper in a soundboard, it has been, as Adlung says, thick in the bass and thin in the treble.

[II, 113]

For there must be an opening because if the air is enclosed the case [*Corpus*] does not vibrate freely and therefore does not sustain long, and because of this the tone is quite dull [*stumpf*] and lacking all beauty.[94]

FROM SPRENGEL, *Handwerk und Künste in Tabelen* (1773), p. 257.

The length (fig. III, ab) of a harpsichord depends solely on the discretion of the future owner. Of course, the longness of the harpsichord provides the advantage that long and thinner bass strings can be fitted. But the maker understands what to do to manage a short harpsichord as in the case of a clavichord (page 252), that is, to put on shorter but thicker strings. The width bc is determined by the number of octaves the harpsichord possesses, and usually nowadays it has five octaves. Finally, a double harpsichord (one with two keyboards, one above the other) has a deeper case abc than a single harpsichord because the latter has only one keyboard. In general, concerning the dimensions of harpsichord cases, one can say only that they are ordinarily 6½ feet [*Fuss*] long, 3 feet wide and that the depth is optional.

The case of the harpsichord is assembled with almost the same techniques as the clavichord (page 241) except that the bentside ad is made of maple [*Ahornholz*] which is soaked in water, attached to a form with clamps, allowed to dry, and thus bends. In the rear part of this case is the soundboard ad resting on the liners [*Leisten*], almost like that of the clavichord except that the wrest plank is not placed at the rear of the case as it was in the clavichord, but in front of the soundboard and behind the harpsichord keyboard ie. The changed layout of the harpsichord with its keyboard running across the case rather than along the length allots another place to the wrest plank. This last should be 1½ inches [*Zoll*] thick, 8 inches wide, and as long as the harpsichord is wide. On account of its size and strength the maker can make it of oak [*Eichenholz*] while, on the other hand, the smaller wrest plank of the clavichord must always be made of maple (page 247). The planed wrest plank is fastened to the liners or blocks fe and ig which are glued into the case of the harpsichord. On these same blocks, between the wrest plank ie and the soundboard da rest the two registers in which the jacks of the harpsichord are inserted. However, these registers dh and fi are not attached to the aforesaid blocks, but they can be moved slightly across the breadth of the harpsichord. The reason for this will be given below. Each register is as thick as the wrest plank de [95] and a little wider than a jack, which will be presently described more minutely. For solidity the maker must make them of strong pear wood [*Birnbaumholz*]. On each register he cuts as many mortises with the chisel as the harpsichord has keys, and a jack stands in each mortise. The mortise for the jack must

[94] This passage should be set beside the following by Jacobsson (*Technologisches Wörterbuch*, III, 406): "Some cut a hole through the glued up soundboard with a knife. Others, however, find it unnecessary to do so."

[95] Box slides! This may suggest that Italian instruments were common in Germany as late as 1773.

be just of a size so that the jack can be pushed up and down easily in the mortise.

The registers fi and hd lead us to the description of the keyboard of a harpsichord. The keys of a harpsichord turn out to be made and placed on a pin rail and bed as were the keys of the clavichord (page 249). The whole difference lies in the fact that a harpsichord key has no metal tangent but has, on the other hand, two wooden jacks. Both jacks rest independently on the rear end of the key. And since two strings pertain to each key, in playing each string is touched by a single jack. The jack which plucks the string to the right (when one stands facing the keyboard bc) is generally placed in the foremost register fi; but the jack for the left side is in the rearmost register hd. Figure IV will make all of this clear.

FROM JACOBSSON, *Technologisches Wörterbuch* (1781–1794), III, 406.

Soundhole (Music) — the hole in the soundboard which usually is provided only as ornament. It seems that this hole is not for the sound since clavichords and other instruments are made today which do not have it and yet they have a beautiful tone.

Soundboard — it can only be made of fir [*Tannenholz*], because this wood is remarkably elastic, has resonant [*klingende*] fibres, and above all, is not resinous. The small planks of this wood which come from Bohemia and the Black Forest are 6 inches wide, 6 to 7 feet long, and ¼ inch thick, and are those preferably employed. The inner core [heartwood] of the fir has fibers which are too coarse and stiff for this purpose so that only the planks which were split near the heart can be used.[96] On this account they are always narrow. Hence the soundboard is put together out of several narrow planks which are well planed and glued together. The thickness of the soundboard is not established after any positive rule, but is given by the estimate of the experienced eye which the maker has acquired. This much is certain, that each soundboard should be ⅛ inch thick. However, such a thin board could easily warp or crack and split, even though the driest wood had been used. Therefore, it is deemed right to clamp and glue a few ribs underneath, across the width of the soundboard[97] . . . The soundboard of a harpsichord is put together in the same way as that of a clavichord [*Klavier*], and after it has its bridge it is glued into the case of the harpsichord.

[OLD WOOD[98]]

FROM *Schlesische Provinzialblätter*, II (1785), 439. QUOTED AND TRANSLATED BY BOALCH, *Makers of the Harpsichord and Clavichord*, p. 112.

[96] That is, the planks do not pass through the center of the tree but extend from a point near it toward the bark. Consequently, their width can only be less than half of the diameter of the tree.

[97] This section refers to square piano and clavichord soundboards which are ribbed according to a different system than those of the harpsichord.

[98] In exploding, the punctured balloons of musical myth often destroy their de-

"as he [Gottfried Silbermann] travelled from village to village mending the pews in the churches for the peasants, he took away their old pews, which were then over 100 years old, instead of payment."

[Laminated soundboards [99]]

FROM CARL LEMME, QUOTED IN MS., "MUSIKALISCHE ERFINDUNGEN" (1781), collected by Westphal, Bibliothèque Royale, Brussels (Ms. II 4120), p. 6.

In the year 1771 we received an order from a friend who was staying just then in Amsterdam, to send two claviers with the express condition that their soundboards must be injured neither by his proposed tour to Batavia, nor by the heat, nor anything else. We were convinced that the risk was too great for us to depend merely on using good dry wood and sending the claviers off, for in this case we must be absolutely certain.

We set aside on this account a room in which we hung a Fahrenheit thermometer, and specially heated it to the temperature found below the equator; and all experiments were fruitless even when we used the driest baked wood. Even if it did not split in the heat, it did when it was returned to the cold, or at least it warped. Finally we had the idea of making a double soundboard which I called "gepreszten" in my catalogue.[100] Admittedly the fear arose that the tone might lose its perfection. Only unwearying diligence, numerous and often fruitless experiments, and many changes to the specially made clamps satisfied us. The commissioned claviers arrived at the specified place without the least damage, and many more have followed thither with the same good fortune.

[Layout]

FROM HALLE, *Werkstäte der heutigen Künste*, III, 363.

According to the Dresden measurements, the Contra F [FF] string is 7 *Fuss* long [86½ inches] and c''' is only 6 *Zoll* [6³⁄₁₆ inches].[101] Nut and bent bridge on the soundboard must therefore decrease proportionately for

stroyers. Nevertheless, I venture to suggest that there is not much in the myth of old wood, at least insofar as harpsichord making is concerned. I am convinced that good design is far more important. It does seem that a new harpsichord changes rapidly after first being put into use, but this process seems to slow quite soon. In any case, further change is not observable because of the lack of suitable controls. No man has an ear keen enough nor a memory long enough to note the extremely subtle changes that may occur over a period of many years.

[99] This invention, made by Friedrich Carl Lemme (1747–1808), organist and instrument maker in Brunswick, and his father, was also reported by Gerber, Jacobsson, Forkel, and Gall. The text quoted here was published in 1781 in the *Hammerwischer Magazin*, which I have not been able to see.

[100] *Anweisung und Regeln zu einer zweckmässigen Behandlung englischer und deutscher Pianofortes und Klaviere* (Brunswick, 1802). This citation is taken from Boalch. An earlier edition must have existed since Lemme refers to it in 1781.

[101] Giving a 12⅜-inch scale, which falls within the range of variation of the Saxon school (see Table 16).

each string; thus the bridge with its guide pins is bent in the treble and is almost straight in the bass.

FROM SPRENGEL, *Handwerk und Künste in Tabelen* (1773), p. 262.

The measure of the strings [scale] and particularly the stringing of a harpsichord varies very little from what has been said on these subjects above (page 251). The treble strings of a harpsichord will be only a little longer than those of the clavichord since the length of the harpsichord permits the bass strings to be longer as well. Therefore unspun [102] bass strings are chosen for the harpsichord. If the harpsichord is at eight-foot pitch (page 254) the "C" of the highest octave of the treble is 5¼ inches long.[103] A harpsichord has two bridges. The front bridge [the nut] (fig. III, st) lies a little behind the wrest pins on the wrest plank ei. The rear bridge uv, however, is on the soundboard. The distance of these bridges from one another establishes the true length of each string. The mortises of the two registers hd and fi indicate the position of each string. Thus the instrument maker determines the position of the front bridge st on the wrest plank, draws parallel lines with a ruler through each mortise of both registers on to the soundboard ad. Thus he can measure the length of each string from the forward bridge, marking it off on the corresponding line. The length of the strings indicates the position of the rear bridge uv as has been shown on page 255.[104] Both bridges st and uv will be made and attached like those of the clavichord.

FROM JACOBSSON, *Technologisches Wörterbuch*, I, 199.

When a clavichord [*Klavier*] or harpsichord [*Flügel*] is to be strung, the length of the treble strings, and consequently the position of the bridge on the soundboard, must be established beforehand; for which purpose the maker has a rule or measuring stick on which the length of each treble string is marked. The length of all the remaining notes in an octave is regulated by the length of the "C". For example, the string for this note in the fifth or highest octave is 5 *Zoll* [5⅛ inches] for a *Klavier* and 5¼ *Zoll* [5¹³⁄₃₂ inches] [105] for a *Flügel* with eight-foot tone, but that "C" must be twice as long if it has sixteen-foot pitch.[106] The string for this "C" [c″] in the fourth octave must be twice as long, and twice as long again in the third octave [c′].

---

[102] That is, not covered with a coil of lighter wire like the bass strings of a piano.

[103] Giving a 10¹³⁄₁₆-inch scale and identifying Sprengel's informants as belonging to the Saxon school. These Saxon scales are remarkably short for a northern tradition, too short really: although as we have seen, the Saxon makers did use a lighter construction to compensate.

[104] On page 255 Sprengel describes a similar method of marking out a clavichord.

[105] Jacobsson's exact agreement with Sprengel on harpsichord scaling is not accidental. Many of the passages in his compendium are drawn verbatim from Sprengel.

[106] A detail often overlooked by modern designers.

[STRINGS]

FROM BENDELER, *Orgel-Bau-Kunst* (written ca. 1690), p. 48.

If a spinet, harpsichord, etc., does not sound well it is usually to be attributed either to the soundboard, the case [*Corpus*] measurements or to the scale [*Mensur*] which latter might not be correct. It is not enough to say that in this last matter [the scale] the strings are too short. If this or that note can not be held by this or that string I say that it is an instrument which is not *Chormässig* [of the proper size for standard pitch]. But it would be an error to assume that an instrument on which the strings do not hold tune is not *Chormässig*. For even though the case is of beautiful, smooth, and strong wood, the soundboard equally delicately and well made, and the bridge done carefully, the instrument does not sound of itself but only amplifies and strengthens the sound produced by the strings, lovely or unlovely. Accordingly, it is either bright and big, or little and flat, in which it must be understood that the case [*Corpus*] indeed amounts to something in the loveliness or unloveliness but yet it is not the first and basic thing. Unloveliness is produced first and foremost when the length of the string is not proportionate to the note it must give or when it moves too much, which chiefly occurs if the plucking point is too far from the nut even though the quill is not too strong. If for this reason a poor sounding *Instrument, Spinet*, or *Clavicimbel* is to be improved I proceed as follows: I put on c′, *Chormässig*, pluck it quite close to the nut, then a little farther back, and if I do not obtain the most pleasant sound possible I put on a thicker or thinner string and pluck it in the same way; when I have obtained a really good tone I note carefully how far the plucking point is from the pin on the nut and I make the nut so that the plucking point of C I can make twice as long, or even a little longer, and that of c′″ only half as long. When this is settled I string c′ again with thinner and thicker strings until I again obtain a good tone. I take the length of this c′ (from nut to bridge) to be 190 exactly, the string no. 9. Now I will seek the string for f, a fifth below. First of all I say: The proportion 2 affords 190. The exact length which affords the proportion 3 makes 285.[107] I say further: 2 affords no. 9, what does 3 afford? Through the rule of inverse proportion it comes out to no. 6. Now, however, I must see whether the instrument really has a length of 285 on f. I find that it is only 220 and thus from the 285, 65 is gone. Accordingly I say, 285 lost 65, what does 6 lose?

[Bendeler continues his dative-case mathematics, confusing himself between gauge numbers and diameters, diameters and cross-sectional areas, until finally he testily turns on a man who asks him the basic question.]

And suppose you don't find any good tone? Thereupon I answer that it would be difficult to find so badly measured an instrument, be it long or short, on which one would fail to find a lovely tone by changing strings

---

[107] 2:3 = 190:285. Based on the 2:3 relation of vibration numbers in a descending fifth.

and plucking points, and by raising or lowering the pitch an octave.[108] If anyone does not believe this, let him seek the truth himself.

FROM HALLE, *Werkstäte der heutigen Künste*, III, 362.

FF gives a 16-foot organ tone and will be strung with no. 000;[109] normally a harpsichord is strung with brass wire[110] from no. 0 to no. 9 or 10, c''' with no. 10. The rounder a wire is the purer will be the tone, and often a string is not round throughout. If one examines it with a magnifying glass he will see a drawing chip or streak and if he draws it through a narrow die the tone will be improved.

The white strings are of iron and rust easily.

FROM ADLUNG, *Musica mechanica organoedi* (1768), II, 105.

The strings are of hardened wire, either white [steel] or yellow [brass]. The former sound more lovely and stand in tune better, but the latter do not rust and hence last longer. Personally, I prefer to put on yellow strings. On the upper notes they must be light [*Zart*] and their thickness progresses by degrees to the end. However, how high the numbers shall be cannot be established exactly. Some *Clavessins* take heavier strings than others. On some, one can string c''' with no. 8,[111] but others take no. 9 or even no. 10. Smaller sizes are no good because the tone will be weak. If one seeks the reason, it is because all harpsichords are not the same size, or that in one the length of the string from nut to bridge is greater than in another and, therefore, one must mount thinner strings. For a long thick string cannot be pulled up as high as if it were shorter. I advise that if for reasons of sound the *Clavessin* be made somewhat longer that the bridge be placed in such a manner that the length of strings not become too great. The proportion to follow in this respect would be too complicated to discuss . . . If one wishes to overspin from the bass up to c, the bass will be heavier.[112] One can easily try this for himself. I shall not detain myself over it. It is to be noted that many organ makers or harpsichord makers [*Künstler*] give the strings a thinner proportion than could reasonably stand. For example: I string a harpsichord and no. 9 holds well from the top to c'', but no. 8 does not; from b'' to c'' no. 8, but not no. 7, and so forth. So I should do well if I put on no. 10 from the top to c''', and put on no. 9 in place of no. 8, and no. 8 in place of no. 7, etc.,

[108] This may have been true in 1690 but it certainly is not true now!

[109] Obviously neither Hamburg nor Swedish gauge.

[110] This may be the explanation for some of the very short scales we have noted.

[111] These gauge numbers agree with those of Halle, but not so closely with those of Bendeler who would put no. 9 on c'. It is possible that Bendeler was thinking of an Italian harpsichord which is more lightly strung than the heavier types and might just take the wire size on c' that another would have at the top. The gauges of Halle and Adlung agree neither with the Hamburg nor the Swedish nor with the gauges marked on English harpsichords.

[112] And duller. Agricola adds: "However the quills soon rub off the overspinning. Therefore many hold that it is better not to use overspun strings on the harpsichord."

because in damp weather it will not set out so lightly to climb in pitch until the strings break, causing new work and trouble. However, when a harpsichord is strung so that the pitch can be safely raised a semitone, one can be secure. However, one should write down the gauge numbers originally used, from top to bottom, in order that when one [a string] breaks one can mount the correct gauge again. For it is an error, one string being thin, that the next should be thick.[113]

[113] The method Adlung uses to judge string sizes is based on a fundamental fallacy. He strings every note one gauge size too thin on the assumption that a thin string requires less tension to be brought to pitch and therefore will stand a higher pitch than a thick one. Theoretically, this is not so for the following reason: While the thin string requires less tension to come to pitch, it is also weaker, and these two factors are exactly proportional. Length and material being held constant, the pitch that a given tension will produce is dependent on the weight of the vibrating string, and this is a function of the cross-sectional area. The tension that the string can bear is also proportional to the cross-sectional area. Therefore, as the tension required for a given note is reduced by thinning the string, the string is being weakened at exactly the same rate. If strings of equal length were all made of exactly equivalent material, they would all break at the same pitch, regardless of diameter.

Adlung was really trading on a side effect. The process of drawing steel into fine wires seems to produce a structure composed of a hard sheath around a softer core. This sheath is always roughly equal in thickness, and thus occupies a larger percentage of the diameter of a thin string than of a thick one. Therefore, a thin string will actually stand a slightly higher pitch than a thick one. Nevertheless, Bendeler's method is much better. One strings by ear, not by physics.

APPENDIX B · CONTEMPORARY
DESCRIPTIONS OF TECHNICAL PROCESSES

THE MANNER OF WIRE-WORK AT TINTERN IN MONMOUTHSHIRE. From Ray, *A Collection of English Words Not Generally Used* (1674), p. 132.

They take little square bars made like bars of steel, which they call *Osborn-Iron*, wrought on purpose for this manufacture; and strain *i. e.* draw them at a Furnace with a hammer moved by water (like those at the Iron Forges but lesser) into square rods of about the bigness of one's little finger, or less, and bow them round. When that is done they put them into a furnace and neal them with a pretty strong fire for about 12 hours: after they are nealed they lay them in water for a month or two (the longer the better) then the *Rippers* take them and draw them into wire through two or three holes. Then they neal them again for six hours or more, and water them the second time about a week, then they are carried to the Rippers who draw them to a two-bond wire as big as a great packthread.

Then again they are nealed the third time and watered about a week as before, and delivered to the small wire drawers, whome there they call Overhouse-men, I suppose only because they work in an upper room.

In the mill, where the *Rippers* work, the wheel [the water wheel of the mill] moves several Engins [sic] like little barrels, which they also call *Barrels* hoopt with Iron. The Barrel hath two hooks on the upper side, upon each whereof hang two links standing across, and fastened to the two ends of the tongs, which catch hold of the wire and draw it through the hole. The Axis on which the barrel moves runs not through the center, but is placed towards one side, *Viz.* that on which the hooks are. Underneath is fastened to the barrel a spoke of wood, which they call a Swingle, which is drawn back a good way by the calms [cams] or cogs in the Axis of the wheel, and draws back the barrel, which falls to again by its own weight. The tongs, hanging on the hooks of the barrel, are by the workmen fastened on the wire, and by the force of the wheel the hooks being drawn back draw the wire through the holes.

They annoint the wire with train-oil, to make it run the easier. The plate, wherein the holes are, is on the outside Iron, on the inside steel.

The holes are bigger on the Iron side, because the wire finds more resistance from the steel and is streightened [sic] by degrees.[1]

[1] Ure (*A Dictionary of Arts*, p. 1312) provides further details of draw plates which

There is another mill where the small wire is drawn which with one wheel moves three Axes that run the length of the house on three floors one above another.

The description whereof would be tedious and difficult to understand without a Scheme, and therefore I shall omit it.

ON THE MANUFACTURE OF PINS. FROM URE, *A Dictionary of Arts* (1842), p. 961.

PIN MANUFACTURE (*Fabrique d'épingles*, Fr.; *Nadelfabrik*, Germ.) A pin is a small bit of wire, commonly brass, with a point at one end, and a spherical head at the other. In making this little article, there are no less than fourteen distinct operations.

1. *Straightening the wire*. The wire, as obtained from the drawing-frame, is wound about a bobbin or barrel, about 6 inches diameter, which gives it a curvature that must be removed. The straightening engine is formed by fixing 6 or 7 nails upright in a waving line on a board, so that the void space measured in a straight line between first three nails may have exactly the thickness of the wire to be trimmed; and that the other nails may make the wire take a certain curve line, which must vary with its thickness. The workman pulls the wire with pincers through among these nails, to the length of about 30 feet, at a running draught; and after he cuts that off, he returns for as much more; he can thus finish 600 fathoms in the hour. He next cuts these long pieces into lengths of 3 or 4 pins. A day's work of one man amounts to 18 or 20 thousand dozen of pin-lengths.

2. *Pointing* is executed on two iron or steel grindstones, by two workmen, one of whom roughens down, and the other finishes. Thirty or forty of the pin wires are applied to the grindstone at once, arranged in one plane, between the two forefingers and thumbs of both hands, which dexterously give them a rotatory movement.

3. *Cutting these wires into pin-lengths*. This is done by an adjusted chisel. The intermediate portions are handed over to the *pointer*.

4. *Twisting of the wire for the pin-heads*. These are made of a much finer wire, coiled into a compact spiral, round a wire of the size of the pins, by means of a small lathe constructed for the purpose.

5. *Cutting the heads*. Two turns are dexterously cut off for each head, by a regulated chisel. A skillful workman may turn off 12,000 in the hour.

6. *Annealing the heads*. They are put into an iron ladle, made red-hot over an open fire, and then thrown into cold water.

7. *Stamping or shaping the heads*. This is done by the blow of a small ram, raised by means of a pedal lever and a cord. The pin-heads are also fixed on by the same operative, who makes about 1500 pins in the hour, or from 12,000 to 15,000 per diem; exclusive of one thirteenth, which is always deducted for

are probably valid at least for the second half of the eighteenth century: "The French draw plates are so much esteemed that one of the best of them used to be sold in this country, during the late war, for its weight in silver. The holes are formed with a steel punch; being made large on that side where the wire enters, and diminishing with a regular taper to the other side."

waste in this department, as well as in the rest of the manufacture. Cast heads, of an alloy of tin and antimony, were introduced by patent, but never came into general use.

8. *Yellowing or cleaning the pins* is effected by boiling them for half an hour in sour beer, wine lees, or solution of tartar; after which they are washed.

9. *Whitening or tinning.* A stratum of about 6 pounds of pins is laid in a copper pan, then a stratum of about 7 or 8 pounds of grain tin; and so alternately till the vessel be filled; a pipe being left inserted at one side, to permit the introduction of water slowly at the bottom without deranging the contents. When the pipe is withdrawn, its space is filled up with grain tin. The vessel being now set on the fire, and the water becoming hot, its surface is sprinkled with 4 ounces of cream of tartar; after which it is allowed to boil for an hour. The pins and tin grains are, lastly, separated by a kind of cullender.

10. *Washing the pins* in pure water.

11. *Drying and polishing them,* in a leather sack filled with coarse bran, which is agitated to and fro by two men.

12. *Winnowing,* by fanners.

13. *Pricking the papers* for receiving the pins.

14. *Papering,* or fixing them in the paper. This is done by children, who acquire the habit of putting up 36,000 per day [!].

The pin manufacture is one of the greatest prodigies of the division of labor; it furnishes 12,000 articles for the sum of three shillings, which have required the united diligence of fourteen skillful operatives.

ON THE MANUFACTURE OF PINS. FROM THE *Dictionnaire portatif de commerce* (1770), II, 495.

Of all mechanical productions the pin is the slightest, the commonest, the least valuable, and nevertheless one of those which demands the greatest combined effort: whence it follows that this art, like nature, limits its prodigies to small ends, and that the industry is as limited in its views as admirable in its resources. A pin requires eighteen operations before entering into commercial channels.

ON THE MANUFACTURE OF WIRE. FROM THE *Dictionnaire portatif de commerce* (1770), III, 19.

Fil de fer [iron wire] is also called *fil d'archal.* The famous M. Ménage, that clever etymologist, derives this word from *filum* and *aurichalcum;* [2] but the most sensible among those who deal in it believe simply that a Richard Archal, having invented the method of drawing the iron through the apertures of a die plate, left his name to this merchandise, which is quite commonly called *fil de Richard.*

The first iron which runs from the ore when it is smelted, being the most ductile and strongest, is saved for the making of *fil d'archal.*

[2] M. Ménage is followed by Larousse in this etymological conjecture.

There is iron wire of various thicknesses, diminishing regularly from around 6 *lignes*[3] to the very finest, or from a half *pouce*[4] to ⅒ *pouce* in diameter.[5] These fine wires are called *du manicordion* [clavichord], the same name that is given to the brass wire with which (along with the iron) one makes some of the strings of harpsichords, psalteries, clavichords, and other similar musical instruments.

A good deal of iron wire is made in France, in Switzerland, and in Germany, where it can be obtained from Hamburg and the regions around Cologne and Liège. The best is that from Liège. The Swiss is quite good; the least esteemed is French because it is sharp [*aigre*, probably "brittle"] and not homogenous. There is a mill established near S. Grand-Villard à Marvillard, in Alsace.

The thin iron wire comes particularly from Cologne; there are from 8 to 10 sizes which are shipped in barrels of about 2000 pounds.

Although the French get a good deal of it directly from Hamburg, the English and the Dutch cause a very large quantity to enter by Bordeaux which comes to them by the return of their fleets from the Baltic Sea.

Sweden furnishes a great deal of *fil d'archal* to other countries.

The Hamburg iron wire is distinguished by numbers according to the diameter; the finest is called *fil à carde*,[6] and several sizes are included under this name. At the point where the largest *fil à carde* ends, no. 00 begins, and no. 0, no. ½, no. 2, no. 3, no. 4, no. 5, and no. 6 follow. The last number is nearly as large as one of the strongest goose quills.

The kinds which are used most are no. 00, no. 0, and no. ½. The consumption of the others diminishes as their size increases.

German *fil de fer* is packed in packets each weighing 4 lbs. 12 oz., at 100 pounds per mark. The packets of Swiss wire weigh ten pounds per packet.

[3] In Paris a *ligne* (one-twelfth of a *pouce*) equaled about .095 inch, but in Brussels it was nearer .123 inch. The work from which this passage is taken was published in Liège. The fact that 6 *lignes* is taken as equal to ½ *pouce* makes the Paris measure more likely. The Brussels *pouce* contained only ten *lignes*.

[4] The *pouce* equaled 1.666 inches in Paris, .987 inch in Brussels.

[5] A harpsichord uses strings of about ¹⁄₁₀₀ *pouce* in diameter. "Pouce" here is probably a misprint for "ligne."

[6] A *carde* (card) is a sort of wire brush used to comb out the fibres of wool and cotton before spinning.

APPENDIX C · INVENTORIES OF THE WORKSHOPS OF FRENCH HARPSICHORD MAKERS AND OF INSTRUMENTS IN THE HANDS OF FRENCH MUSICIANS

INVENTORIES OF WORKSHOPS

Note: Most of these inventories were prepared by notaries with the help of harpsichord-maker experts on the various occasions when it was necessary to specify the exact amount of an estate. Normally these occasions would arise at the time of a marriage, the death of a member of the family, or the maker's own death. It will be seen that the care with which they were prepared varies a good deal. Hence comparisons of one to another must be made with caution. Monetary values are given in *livres*, the French equivalent of the English pound. There were twenty *sols* or *sous* to the *livre*, and twenty-four *livres* to the *louis*. The following texts are excerpts and contain only the merchandise and tools, not the household goods or other properties.

THE WORKSHOP OF JEAN DENIS. ARCHIVES NATIONALES, MINUTIER CENTRAL, LIV, 356, JAN. 12, 1672.

A spinet stand and a harpsichord stand	3 l.
A harpsichord at eight-foot pitch, made of cedar	90 l.
A spinet four feet long, the soundboard painted	44 l.
A spinet two feet four inches long, the soundboard painted	36 l.
A small harpsichord with one choir, five feet long	66 l.
A harpsichord with one keyboard, four-foot pitch, the soundboard painted	50 l.
A spinet three and one-half feet long, the soundboard painted	40 l.
An ear-shaped [?] spinet, the sound board painted, with its marbled case, four and one-half feet long	60 l.
A two-foot eight-inch spinet with two cases, the soundboard painted [*a lachure* ?], a landscape on the lid	44 l.
A short little bentside [?] spinet	110 l.
A four-and-one-half-foot spinet, the soundboard painted, three octaves	10 l.
A three-foot two-inch clavichord	25 l.
A two-foot ten-inch clavichord	25 l.

A little German spinet veneered in ebony that plays by itself, with its drum on which are three different pieces   18 l.

A spinet in the form of a harpsichord with two half keyboards one like the other and playing at the octave, one of the other   40 l.

A four-and-one-half-foot spinet with its soundboard and its keyboard   18 l.

A little two-foot eight-inch spinet nearly finished, the keyboard with its pins and the jacks made   25 l.

A harpsichord commenced, with one keyboard and two choirs, with its key frame, rack [*diapaison*[1]], and wrest plank   20 l.

A small single-manual harpsichord with its keyboard, mortised register [*diapaison*], and wrest plank   8 l.

A finished harpsichord with two keyboards   120 l.

A bentside [?] spinet five feet long with two keyboards, finished   36 l.

A single-manual harpsichord case   9 l.

Twenty-eight boards etc. . . .

THE WORKSHOP OF PIERRE BAILLON. ARCHIVES NATIONALES, MINUTIER CENTRAL, CXXI, 135, JAN. 23, 1682. PRINTED BY NORBERT DUFOURCQ, "PIERRE BAILLON," P. 196.

First, an unfinished harpsichord of cedar wood[2] with the *termes* [sides?] with their mortises, soundboard, keyboards covered [i.e., with key tops covered] and its stand, taken together at   50 lt

Item   a walnut harpsichord stand, without columns, taken at   100 s

Item   a large oblong virginal painted in imitation of marble and finished, taken at   20 lt

Item   an unfinished spinet *à l'italienne* with its keyboard, lid and soundboard, taken with the piece for closing said keyboard   9 lt

Item   two spinet cases in walnut with their soundboards and prepared unfinished parts [?] taken at   10 lt

Item   a harpsichord case with its two finished keyboards with its lid, registers and bridges, taken at   30 lt

Item   A harpsichord case with its two covered keyboards and its registers and bridges unfinished, taken at   15 lt

Item   An unfinished four-foot spinet, taken at   20 lt

Item   two unfinished spinets at the fourth [i.e., a fourth sharp], taken together   15 lt

Item   an unfinished clavichord, taken at   40 s

Item   five clavichord cases, taken at   50 s

Item   another clavichord case with its keyboard in the white, taken at   30 s

Item   six keyboards of linden wood, taken together   3 lt

[1] This word is variously used to refer to the keyboard rack, the string band, the register, or any part which is accurately spaced out.

[2] This is the only example of which I am aware of a non-Italian making an instrument of cedar.

Item a little spinet with its keyboard, taken at — 20 s

Item four unfinished harpsichord key frames, two for spinets, twenty-four bundles of roughed out jacks, a number of *picquot* [shims?] for gluing soundboards, three harpsichord wrest planks, a large spinet and an archviol body, and a spinet and an archviol, all taken together — 11 lt

Item a case of *sapin* [fir?] and its lid, three spinet cases, two harpsichord lids, and two dozen of clamps, taken together — 100 s

Item five benches and two large rip-saws, several planks of *sapin* for soundboards, eight jointing planes, three shoulder planes, four *varlopes a ongle* [large planes with nails or claws — perhaps fences?], four smooth planes, a fillister plane and several molding tools, taken together — 20 lt

Item four oil stones, two rules of copper, several spring saws [i.e., fine saws made from clock springs], four bit braces, several roughed out sharps and several drawers of worthless marquetry, taken together — 18 lt

Item some pieces of marble and a plate of engraved copper for borders,[3] taken together — 3 lt

Item a positif and a spinet on top, [a claviorganum] taken at — 120 lt

Item four organ bellows, a vox humana stop and a wardrobe of oak and several organ pipes of lead and wood, taken together — 40 lt

Item a harpsichord lid painted with a landscape, a case and a round table top, a wooden screw clamp, tools used to make clamps, a bundle of moldings and two spinet lids, taken together — 4 lt

Item two large iron vises, a lathe equipped with tools, taken together — 8 lt

Item four organ books[4] and two for the harpsichord, bound in *bazanes* [sheepskin], taken together — 30 lt

Item ten organ books and twenty-six harpsichord in white [i.e. unbound?], taken together — 180 lt

Item one hundred thirty-three tin plates of the Livre d'orgue of Mr. Le Begue weighing together two hundred and three pounds taken at ten sols the pound, making at that price the sum of — 101 lt 10 s

Item Ninety plates also of tin of the livre de claversin of the said Mr. Le Begue weighing together one hundred ten pounds taken at ten sols the pound, making at that price the sum of — 55 lt

Item eighty plates also of tin of the new Livre d'orgue of the said Mr. Lebegue which are not yet completely engraved, weighing together one hundred fifteen pounds at the rate of ten sols the pound making at the said price the sum of — 57 lt 10 s

---

[3] French instruments were sometimes decorated along the edge above the soundboard with printed papers.

[4] Baillon engraved Lebègue's first and second *Livre d'orgue* and the *Premier livre de clavecin.*

THE WORKSHOP OF PHILIPPE DENIS. ARCHIVES NATIONALES, MINUTIER CEN-
TRAL, LXXII, 178, JULY 21, 1705. PHILIPPE WAS THE THIRD SON OF JEAN I.

Item Two benches, one of service wood [Pyrus (Sorbus) domes-
tica: the sorb-apple tree] and the other of beech, two iron
holdfasts, three jack planes, two smooth planes, a dozen of
small tools such as chisels and files, four saws two of which
are hand saws [probably tenon or dovetail saws], a harpsichord case and its lid without soundboard or keyboard,
thirty planks of various sizes both poplar and linden, a
dozen of small tools almost worn out, and an old table top
of beech, the whole taken together   62 l.

THE WORKSHOP OF LOUIS DENIS. ARCHIVES NATIONALES, MINUTIER CENTRAL,
IX, 566, AUG. 18, 1706. LOUIS WAS THE SECOND SON OF JEAN I.

1 small harpsichord with 1 manual, painted in the style of a cameo
[*en camaillen*, possibly for *camaïeu*].   60 l.
Chisels and other tools suitable for harpsichords   3 l.
3 packets of brass strings   11 s.
3 harpsichords with 2 manuals, 1 of which has the ex-
tended range   175 l. times 3
1 spinet *à l'Italienne* [5] without lid   40 l.
1 other spinet half made and one other without keyboard which is
about one-quarter made   30 l.
In the city, another harpsichord with 2 manuals   175 l.
and 2 oblong spinets   30 l.

THE WORKSHOP OF NICOLAS BLANCHET. ARCHIVES NATIONALES, MINUTIER
CENTRAL, CXV, 403, JULY 17, 1722. FOR THE FRENCH TEXTS OF THE FOL-
LOWING DOCUMENTS RELATIVE TO THE BLANCHET FAMILY SEE PIERRE
J. HARDOUIN, "HARPSICHORD MAKING IN PARIS, PART I," THE 1793 INVEN-
TORY OF THE WORKSHOP OF PASCAL TASKIN MAY BE FOUND IN THE GAL-
PIN SOCIETY JOURNAL, NO. 13 (1959).

Item a small harpsichord, three spinets, and another small harpsichord in pieces, all Flemish   500 l.
Item two new harpsichord cases without soundboards, with bottoms and lids, two keyboards, registers and jacks for one
harpsichord   160 l.
Item two covered keyboard blanks with four key beds   100 l.
Item a case for a spinet at eight-foot pitch with the rest of the
materials, six wrest planks one for spinet, three harpsichord
. . . and three bars [?] with front pieces   44 l.
Item six harpsichord soundboards in the rough   60 l.

---

[5] That is, with a bentside.

Item   two benches equipped and one unequipped, six holdfasts, three large hammers, three small hammers and four nippers, all of iron   80 l.

Item   fourteen planes large and small, and seventeen tools for molding and grooving   16 l.

Item   two tenon saws, a rip saw, and eighteen other saws of which three are not mounted, one plier and two bit braces   24 l.

Item   two glue pots, two vises, one large and one small, several tools such as firmer chisels, mortising chisels, gouges, bits, bellows, files, round-nosed and flat pincers, compasses, set squares, bevels, presses and clamps, go bars [6] and a resawing vise   74 l. 10 s.

Item   seventy-two planks of pine and deal for making harpsichords   40 l.

Item   an old Flemish harpsichord   300 l.

Item   one hundred seventy-seven planks of lime wood, six timbers of pear and sorb apple wood to make jacks   108 l.

Item   six hundred leaves of pine for making harpsichord sound-boards   210 l.

Item   nine hundred sheets of bone to make sharps and enough sawed-out jacks for three harpsichords   24 l.

Item   sixteen keyboards, the requirement for eight harpsichords   16 l.

Item   fifty-four pounds of ebony in thin sheets   81 l.

Item   six old harpsichord lids, three others from Flemish virginals   10 l.

Item   three old harpsichord stands, with a machine for bending harpsichord bentsides   8 l.

Item   fifty pounds of strings in boxes, and one hundred fifty spools   115 l.

Item   seven pounds of nails for keyboards and to hitch strings and for bridges, about five thousand small nails, and keyboard cloth and locks, and five pounds of iron wire   16 l. 5 s.

THE WORKSHOP OF FRANCOIS ESTIENNE BLANCHET. ARCHIVES NATIONALES, MINUTIER CENTRAL, CXV, 445, JAN. 15, 1726.

Item   thirty-five large keyboard blanks for harpsichords and thirty-six small   145 l.

Item   two spinet blanks, ten harpsichord wrest planks, and another for spinet   20 l.

Item   eight *membrures* [7] of lime wood   8 l.

Item   seventy-two *toisos* [probably for *dosses*, a squared log] of lime wood, four spines [?], and forty-three *toises* of heavy pine   73 l.

Item   two large Flemish harpsichords with extended compass   2400 l.

Item   three small harpsichords all by Jean and André Riqueurs [Ruckers]   1050 l.

[6] Flexible bars jammed between the ceiling and work on a bench to serve as clamps.
[7] Planks 3″ by 6″ by 9′, 12′, or 15′ in length (Roubo, *L'Art du menuisier*).

Item	ten Flemish virginals all Ricquerses	800 l.
Item	two harpsichord cases with their lids and their soundboards cut out only	160 l.
Item	a spinet case and two harpsichord lids	60 l.
Item	wrest pins enough for fifteen harpsichords	75 l.
Item	a large harpsichord by Riquerse without extended compass	900 l.
Item	five hundred sheets of pine to make soundboards	900 l.
Item	three benches with their tools	80 l.
Item	jacks roughed out for twenty harpsichords, sheepskin for slides, and English glue	129 l.
Item	ebony cut out for about eighteen harpsichords, and a Turkey oil stone	99 l.
Item	seven spines with their jack rails for harpsichords, seven bentsides, wood cut out for fourteen harpsichord key frames [?], and planed up frames for the interior of harpsichords with *emboitures* [possibly refers to frames for frame and panel lids] for the lids, and an old Flemish virginal soundboard	80 l.
Item	harpsichord strings in all gauge numbers and tongues for the jacks, with key fronts [?] for twenty harpsichords	60 l.
Item	a device to glue ribs to soundboards, and a lead trough for soaking bentsides, with the bending form	45 l
Item	several things such as bridges, moldings, jack rails, *porlines*,[8] ribs for soundboards and moldings	30 l.
Item	Iron handstops for harpsichords, iron work for harpsichords, and moving parts covered with leather [probably registers]	26 l.
Item	jointing plane and smooth plane irons, and brand new firmer chisels, and iron wire	5 l.
Item	hand clamps, resawing vises, rip saws, vises, several saws large and small, molding tools, grooving planes of various sorts, old firmer chisels, files, triangles, squares, and two bit braces with several bits, and rasps for wood	110 l.
Item	three bottoms and two soundboards for harpsichords, ten planks of poplar nine feet long	75 l.
Item	new sharps for six or seven harpsichords and four blocks for printing Flemish paper	25 l.

THE WORKSHOP OF FRANCOIS ESTIENNE BLANCHET. ARCHIVES NATIONALES, MINUTIER CENTRAL, IX, 646, MAY 9, 1737.

First	three harpsichords by André Ruckers	1700 l.
Item	three other harpsichords by Jean Ruckers, and four Flemish virginal soundboards	1600 l.
Item	two other harpsichords made by the said Sieur Blanchet, another used, and a spinet	890 l.
Item	a repair to a harpsichord commenced	160 l.

[8] May be related to the English *purlin* (origin obscure): a long timber binding the rafters of a roof together. Hence, liner.

Item several irons and pieces of sheet iron [*feuilles de taule*, possibly for *tôle*, a thin sheet of iron or steel [9]] for the soundboards of harpsichords, five pounds of harpsichord strings, and crow quills, and bristle, some pieces of leather and cloth for registers and keyboards, a thousand iron wrestpins, about two thousand jacks and as many tongues, ebony cut out for eight keyboards, ten keyboards worth of sharps and wood to veneer them [that is, keytops], with eight pounds of Flemish glue, eighty pounds of ebony in the log, a piece of boxwood, eighty pounds of old lead, fourteen pounds of old copper, several things as much for harpsichords as for their outfitting, with key frames and panels, and blocks for the printing of papers, pieces of oak [!] for the ribs of the soundboard, three harpsichord bottoms, several pieces and rules of oak and pieces of lime wood, and two machines for ebony and registers,[10] one hundred ninety-six planks of poplar and lime, seven hundred thin sheets of pine 466 l. 6 s.

Item three equipped benches, thirty-three saws of various types, ten smooth planes, three vises, two oil stones, a grindstone, seventy-four clamps, three bit braces, fifteen pounds of nails and iron wire, several pincers and compasses of iron and copper, three pounds of nails and copper wire, several small hammers and other tools of various types 292 l.

THE WORKSHOP OF FRANCOIS ETIENNE BLANCHET. ARCHIVES NATIONALES, MINUTIER CENTRAL, CI, 511, DEC. 18, 1761.[11]

Item a small harpsichord, a harpsichord case, a spinet, all in bad condition 46 l.

Item twenty small boxes in which are small nails, tacks, a steel pincer, a *porte vice*,[12] two nippers, twenty files, ten small hammers and six chisels 48 l.

Item one thousand little tongues for the jacks, five hundred jacks, the garniture of two registers [that is, the leather to cover two registers(?)], one hundred fifty pieces of rough soundboard wood, a bench with its holdfasts 78 l.

---

[9] See pages 215 and 210.

[10] Both Dom Bedos and Roubo show devices contrived to produce battens of very accurate thickness. The roughly planed piece is drawn under a knife which is fixed a determined distance above the bed of the machine. The ebony referred to must have been for keytops.

[11] It must not be assumed from this inventory that the Blanchet firm had fallen upon evil times. François I had just died and during his illness François II had taken the work in hand to his own house.

[12] Perhaps for *vis*, a screw; hence a tool having some connection with screws, possibly a screwdriver.

Item   another bench of walnut with its holdfasts, thirty tools for making moldings, three pounds of harpsichord strings, eighteen panels large and small, a machine for bending harpsichords, nine *planches* [13] for harpsichords   61 l.

Item   eighteen planks of various woods, ten little clamps for gluing, a bench of beech with its holdfasts, twenty-two *voliges* of various sizes, ten saws, six hundred sharps garnished and ungarnished [that is, with and without bone tops], six clamps   72 l.

THE WORKSHOP OF FRANCOIS ETIENNE BLANCHET. ARCHIVES NATIONALES, MINUTIER CENTRAL, CI, 545, JUNE 18, 1766.

First   a harpsichord with hammers, with its stand, both painted black   400 l.

Item   another harpsichord without keyboard and without legs, made by Mr. Jacquet   12 l.

Item   another old harpsichord with its soundboard   36 l.

Item   another harpsichord painted black   450 l.

Item   another harpsichord without soundboard   21 l.

Item   boards of soundboard wood   60 l.

Item   twenty boards of lime wood   20 l.

Item   thirty boards of poplar   15 l.

Item   six boards of pear wood   5 l.

Fifteen thin boards of poplar   6 l.

Sixteen other *volliges* and three *planches* [14]   9 l.

Six bent boards   6 l.

Item   A quantity of short ends of boards   6 l.

Item   a small bench   9 l.

Item   ten small tools, files, nippers, wood rasps, saws, firmer chisels, chisels, compasses, small vises, and pincers   18 l.

Item   a large bench   18 l.

Item   another small bench   6 l.

Item   three other benches and their appurtenances such as jointing planes, jack planes, and smooth planes   37 l.

Item   twelve bench holdfasts   12 l.

Item   twelve medium and small saws   9 l.

Item   three other rip saws   10 l.

Item   twenty-four molding and grooving tools   9 l.

Item   a machine to bend the bentsides of harpsichords   9 l.

Item   twenty-four clamps and bar clamps   12 l.

[13] According to Roubo a *planche* or *volige* was six, nine, twelve, or eighteen feet long by one, one and one-quarter, one and one-half, one and three-quarters, or two inches thick.

[14] The notary seems to have distinguished between *volliges* and *planches* although Roubo held them to be the same. The difference can only be one of dimensions. Since soundboard wood seems to come in *planches* one might assume that a *vollige* was a bit thicker.

Item a large iron vise   6 l.
Item two glue pots   1 l.
Item two grindstones   3 l.
Item a quantity of small tools used in the shop, such as firmer
      chisels, mortising chisels, hammers, and pincers   12 l.

THE WORKSHOP OF PASCAL TASKIN. ARCHIVES NATIONALES, MINUTIER CEN-
TRAL, CL, 621, APRIL 29, 1777.

First a green ornamented harpsichord with four registers [reg-
      iltes; possibly for registres: registers] and handstops
      [mouvements¹⁵]   750 l.
Item a harpsichord decorated with depictions of children   650 l.
Item a light green harpsichord with gold bands, four registers
      [regiltes] and handstops [mouvements]   600 l.
Item five piano forte[s] at fourteen louis each   1680 l.
Item two unfinished harpsichords with their stands   400 l.
Item a sort of foreign forte piano   48 l.
Item a harpsichord painted gray with gold bands   650 l.
Item two little Ruckers harpsichords for the purpose of having
      their soundboards removed   120 l.
Item a spinet with extended compass painted puce   84 l.
Item two little work benches in the workshop   12 l.
Item one hundred twenty different tools such as saws, firmer chis-
      els, nippers, hand vises, pincers, all tools used in keyboard
      instrument making   15 l.
Item three hundred twenty-seven planks of soundboard wood   215 l. 5 s.
Item four work benches and their associated tools   60 l.
Item sixty different planes, curved, mounted, and otherwise   24 l.
Item twelve holdfasts   12 l.
Item three iron bar clamps   6 l.
Item eighteen small and medium sized iron clamps   9 l.
Item twelve wooden clamps with screws   6 l.
Item twelve saws mounted in wood   15 l.
Item a grindstone for sharpening tools   3 l.
Item an oilstone for tools   2 l.
Item one hundred small tools such as firmer chisels, saws, rasps,
      files, drills, hand vises, flat pincers, gouge   30 l.
Item one hundred ends of wood as much lime as poplar and pine
      and oak, for harpsichords   24 l.
Item twelve bridges and four-foot hitchpin rails [boudins¹⁶] for
      harpsichords   12 l.

¹⁵ In the Encyclopédie the word mouvement is used for the handstops. When a more
elaborate mechanism involving knee levers or pedals is intended, the word is usually
resort, or spring (remember how characters in Gothic novels were forever touching concealed springs to open secret doors). It is possible, however, that these harpsichords had
knee levers.
¹⁶ In the Encyclopédie this word is defined as the contre-chevalet or four-foot hitchpin

Item	three old pairs of keyboards	6 l.
Item	twelve planks of thin poplar	6 l.
Item	twelve planks of thin pine	6 l.
Item	twenty-four bottoms for piano cases	12 l.
Item	a quantity of wood for harpsichord cases	15 l.
Item	twelve wooden clamps	9 l.
Item	a packet of little wooden laths	4 l.
Item	a small quantity of spinet soundboard wood	9 l.
Item	twenty-four thin planks of lime wood and poplar	15 l.
Item	a small quantity of wood for the frames of various productions	15 l.
Item	several planks of lime and poplar	9 l.
Item	several frames and planks	6 l.
Item	a small harpsichord with limited compass	220 l.
Item	another harpsichord with one keyboard	120 l.
Item	another harpsichord with limited compass	220 l.
Item	one thousand to twelve hundred unfinished harpsichord jacks	36 l.
Item	fifty-two sharps for harpsichord keyboards, three hundred harpsichord wrestpins	10 l. 18 s.
Item	several spinet music desks	3 l.
Item	two pairs of trestles on which to place harpsichords	40 s.
Item	about three pounds of strings for harpsichords	12 l.
Item	four pounds of iron pins for keyboards	4 l.
Item	two violins from Lorraine, considered very old	6 l.

"ACCOUNT OF WHAT PASCAL TASKIN OWES TO VARIOUS PRIVATE PARTIES."
FOLDED INTO INVENTORY OF THE WORKSHOP OF PASCAL TASKIN, ARCHIVES
NATIONALES, MINUTIER CENTRAL, CI, 621, APRIL 24, 1777.[17]

[Among the entries:]

To the machinist	194 l.
To the cabinetmaker for various jobs	778 l. 10 s.
Another bill from the same cabinetmaker	93 l. 14 s.
To Mr. Beck [18] in London	660 l.
To Mr. Caron,[19] violin maker	416 l.

THE WORKSHOP OF PASCAL TASKIN. ARCHIVES NATIONALES, MINUTIER CENTRAL, XIV, FEB. 22, 1793.

In the shop on the fifth floor facing the street:
4 benches, 24 l.; six jointing planes, 10 l.; twelve jack or small planes, 3 l.; 46

---

rail. Larousse defines it as a half cylindrical molding. Since both the four-foot hitchpin rail and the frames of French harpsichords were rounded, it could have referred to either.

[17] This account is evidence that Taskin did not do all his metal or wood work himself.

[18] Probably Frederick Beck (fl. 1774–1794), 4 Broad Street, Golden Square, London. A maker of spinets and pianos.

[19] Caron (fl. 1779–1793) seems to have been Taskin's colleague, *luthier* by appointment to Marie Antoinette, at Versailles.

items such as small grooving planes, molding planes and others, 6 l.; an iron jointing plane, a bar of iron and two planes also of iron, 15 l.; 17 *pièces montés d'un vert en marqueterie* [?] 8 l.; 30 items such as chisels, firmer chisels, gouges, and mortising chisels, 3 l.; 30 items such as files and iron rasps, several planks garnished with drills and bits of different sizes not meriting more ample description, 3 l.; 18 items such as nippers, vises, and pincers to cut iron and copper, 9 l.; 58 iron clamps of different sizes, 58 l.; 12 iron holdfasts, 12 l.; 2 small iron vises, 4 l.; six iron bar clamps of different sizes, 4 l.; 3 glue pots with their —— of yellow and red copper, 9 l.; 4 bit braces, 16 items, small planes and shoulder planes, 4 l.; 1 iron drill [?] and iron screw die, 1 small anvil, 4 l.; 1 grindstone on its base with its handle, two wooden holdfasts, 5 iron hammers, 3 triangles, 5 l.; 28 wooden hand-screw clamps, 6 l.; 21 items, wooden clamps of different kinds, 2 l.; 2 bundles of iron wire, 6 l.; various little coils of copper wire and a package of *Baillette* [?] also in yellow copper, 5 l.; 1 tap with its *mures* [?] and different little ——, 7 coils in copper, 3 small ——, 6 l.

1 drawer in which are 5 punches, different little locks and hinges, 15 key panels in lime wood of which 3 are covered with ebony, 15 l.; 45 handstops [?], 3 l.; 1 small crucible, 1 assortment of old pieces of iron, 3 l.;

It is recognized by both parties as regards the enlarged harpsichord carrying the name of Ruckers that it is sent to Pascal Taskin by Citizen Dourlan of Lille to be repaired, that it has a keyboard by Lerman with a stand and a music desk, 72 l.; 1 piano by Boulebart [20] in mahogany with 4 screw legs, 144 l.; 1 bellows . . .

In another room:

2 benches with their appurtenances complete and each with its holdfast, 15 l.; 66 items of tools (etc.).

20 boxes of harpsichord strings . . . 350 spools of harpsichord strings . . . 8 curved pieces, 7 planks . . . *voliges* of wild pear wood . . .

1 discarded harpsichord case without subsidiary parts with one old spinet, 3 l.; 3 piano cases without lids, 18 l.; 3 pianos by Gille de Broule in mahogany with lids and stands, 144 l.

800 harpsichord jacks, strips of several kinds of wood, 12 l.; several harpsichord actions [?], glue pot with its water jacket in red copper, 1 piano lid, 1 oilstone, 4 l.

In a room on the second floor:

1 piano, 144 l.; *id.* 144 l.; *id.* 200 l.; 2 pianos, 300 l.; 1 harpsichord by Dumont,[21] 48 l.; 2 unfinished harpsichords, 200 l.; 1 small table organ, 24 l.

In a drawing room:

1 piano, 200 l.; 1 piano without name, 240 l.; 2 pianos, 190 l.; 1 piano made by Paschal Taskin, 1 harpsichord, 300 l.; 1 similar piano of the same maker, 200 l.; one harpsichord with three registers and one keyboard, 120 l.; 1 harp-

---

[20] Probably Buntebart, partner (1769–1778) of Zumpe, maker of square pianos in London. Even Gille de Broule may be the same man.

[21] Nicolas Dumont, a Parisian harpsichord maker. In addition to the information provided by Boalch I can note that the Stehlin inventory of 1774 shows a yellow harpsichord by Dumont, dated 1695, and that in 1789 Goermans had a black harpsichord of his make. Taskin restored several harpsichords by Dumont.

sichord by Richard,[22] 120 l.; 1 harpsichord by Hans Rukers worked on by Paschal Taskin with 4 registers and mechanical stops, 600 l.

In another room:

2 old harpsichords, 72 l.; 2 other harpsichords of which one is by François Blanchet, the other by Raron [?], 144 l.; 1 harpsichord with 4 registers by Jean Laquerre Ruckers [?], *fabriqué*[23] by Paschal Taskin, 600 l.; 1 little harpsichord with three, with three unisons and 3 registers by Paschal Taskin, 144 l.; a new one with its soundboard and keyboard unfinished, 9 l.; 1 harpsichord, a false Ruckers, 60 l.; 1 case of a false Ruckers harpsichord, 3 l.; 1 harpsichord without name with three registers, 2 keyboards, its lid and stand, 24 l.

In a room:

1 harpsichord carrying the name of Ruckers, *fabriqué* by Mr. Taskin, not finished, with its base and lid, with 4 registers, 100 l.; 1 other similar harpsichord, repainted, with its mechanism, 150 l.; 1 case of a similar harpsichord, 36 l.; 1 other similar harpsichord case, 24 l.; 1 Rukers harpsichord with its keyboards, 100 l.; 4 new unfinished harpsichords made by Paschal Taskin of which three have their keyboards, stands and lids, 200 l.; 1 black harpsichord with its . . . stand, with 2 keyboards, with the name of Germain,[24] 60 l.; 1 bad harpsichord suitable for burning, 3 l.; 1 spinet by Blanchet, 24 l.; 6 hammers, 2 bundles . . .

In another room:

1 bench with its small holdfast, 2 small lots of iron, 6 l.; 50 small tools useful for the trade, 3 l.; 12 items such as nippers and pincers, 5 l.; 5 squares, one of which is of copper, 2 small hold-fasts, 1 wooden level, 5 small wooden hand clamps, 2 —— 2 iron hammers, 1 bit brace, 2 small —— mounted in wood, 3 stones, 7 l.; 11 copper runners for the bottoms of cabriol legs, 4 candle holders, 3 castors of wood with copper ends, 1 small lot of old hinges, 1 of old iron pins, 24 leaden rosettes, 7 l.

2 cabinets with 5 small drawers full of bad pins . . . 1 barrel organ, 1 cithern, 1 transverse flute, 3 l.

1 harpsichord carrying the name of Jean de Rukers repaired by Paschal Taskin, on its stand, music desk, enlarged compass, 200 l.

1 black harpsichord with gold bands on its stand, music desk and lid, enlarged range, 150 l.

1 harpsichord by Jean Rukers in gold and its gilded stand, somewhat enlarged range,[25] 150 l.; 1 other English harpsichord veneered in mahogany, with the declaration that it has been valued only according to the work done on it up to this date, 60 l.

several small boxes containing small nails of copper and iron and old screws, 9 l.; 1 box containing 5 harpsichord mechanisms in iron, not complete, 5 l.; various strips of *peau de buffle*, sheep skin and cloth, 2 l.; 8 boxes containing

---

[22] Probably Michel Richard of Paris.

[23] Literally, made. Probably means enlarged and rebuilt.

[24] Either Jean or Jacques Goermans.

[25] A *ravallement*. A range between four and five octaves. A *grand ravallement* has been translated as "with enlarged range" or simply, "enlarged." It is taken to mean a five-octave range, FF–f‴.

—— for keyboard garnished with their bone, 8 l.; 2 boxes full of strips of ebony for harpsichords, 3 l.; 2 small smooth stones, 1 bellows and 4 mallets of iron with 3 plane irons, 3 l.; 2 candlesticks in white iron, iron molding planes, 1 brush for the business, 1 l.

1 Forte-piano in the style of a harpsichord [en faveur de clavecin, probably for façon de clavecin], not finished, 48 l.

In a room on the fifth floor, facing the court:
3 forte pianos in the style of harpsichords of which one is painted with their covers and bases, all three not finished, with keyboards, 84 l.; 1 piano case, 12 l.; 1 unfinished forte piano, 73 l.; 1 English oak forte piano with its legs, 240 l.; 1 harpsichord with its keyboards unfinished with 4 registers and other parts, not pointed, 72 l.; various bridges or boudins [either four-foot hitchpin rails or soundboard ribs], 2 l.

In an attic above:
4 quarters of rosewood, each 2 feet 4 inches long, 8 l.

In a small room:
40 sheets of ebony, 15 l.; 1 cybalum by François Blanchet with its legs, 9 pairs of keyboards fit for burning . . . 1 bench, 3 l.; 1 walnut spinet with enlarged range, on its 4 round legs, 18 l.; another spinet with short range and without legs, 3 l.; 1 small forte piano in the shape of a harpsichord made by Pascal Taskin, 800 l.; 1 small spinet by Paschal Taskin, 40 l.; 1 forte piano, 200 l.; 1 English forte piano, 400 l.; 2 gilded forte pianos by Sehart, 500 l.; 2 other forte pianos of which 1 is by Boutebard and the other by Longue-mann,[26] 450 l.; 1 combination piano-organ reworked by Paschal Taskin, 500 l.

THE WORKSHOP OF PIERRE DE MACHY. ARCHIVES NATIONALES, MINUTIER CEN-TRAL, LXII, 340, APRIL 26, 1726.

First	a walnut harpsichord with two manuals	100 l.
Item	another harpsichord with a case painted black	100 l.
Item	another harpsichord and its stand, the case is painted black	80 l.
Item	another harpsichord with a walnut case	100 l.
Item	another harpsichord with a walnut case	80 l.
Item	another harpsichord with a walnut case	80 l.
Item	another harpsichord with a case painted black	80 l.
Item	another harpsichord with a case painted black	70 l.
Item	another harpsichord with one manual with a pine case	45 l.
Item	a pedal stand [?] with a pine case	45 l.
Item	four harpsichords with pine cases	400 l.
Item	five spinets with walnut case	125 l.
Item	another spinet whose case is also walnut	20 l.
Item	another long, square virginal	20 l.
Item	another long, square virginal whose case is of pine painted black	15 l.
Item	another small spinet with its stand, the case is painted	12 l.
Item	another long, square virginal taken with its stand	20 l.

[26] Probably Longman and Broderip of London.

Item a theorbo in its case 3 l.
Item two wooden benches and several tools 30 l.

THE WORKSHOP OF JEAN FERCHUR. ARCHIVES NATIONALES, MINUTIER CENTRAL,
Y 15323, JAN. 30, 1729 (scellé).

A harpsichord in its white pine box with two keyboards and enlarged range,
equipped with all its strings, ready to play, on a gilded wood stand . . .
Two pine harpsichord cases without strings, with their soundboards, without
keyboards; another harpsichord also of pine, painted black, with soundboard and keyboard . . .
A harpsichord which belongs to Mons —— rue de la Verrerie; several tools
serving the profession of harpsichord maker . . .
A bench with its holdfasts, planes, large planes, etc. . . . the said profession,
several planks of pine . . . to make harpsichords
[A further inventory includes:]
A harpsichord made by Belot the father, the said harpsichord enclosed in a
box painted black with gold bands and mounted on its stand, also painted
black . . . similar gilded decoration having painted on the inside of the
said harpsichord a representation of Parnassus
Another harpsichord, the said gilded inside and on top, made by Pierre
Denis.

THE WORKSHOP OF JACQUES BOURDET. ARCHIVES NATIONALES, MINUTIER CEN-
TRAL, XCI, 758, MARCH 2, 1737. BOURDET WAS RECEIVED INTO THE GUILD
IN 1679, WAS AN OFFICIAL IN 1689, AND DIED IN 1737. HE WAS THE
FATHER OF JACQUES GUILLAUME BOURDET, THE MAKER CITED BY BOALCH.

A harpsichord numbered one, made by Philippe Denis 60 l.
A harpsichord numbered two, by the same maker 70 l.
A harpsichord numbered three, made by Jacques Meurice 60 l.
A harpsichord numbered four, made in part by Philippe Denis 60 l.
A harpsichord numbered five, made by Vaudrez [Vaudry] [27] 60 l.
A harpsichord numbered seven, made by Menuier 60 l.
A harpsichord numbered eight, made by Vaudry 50 l.
A harpsichord numbered ten, made by Louis Denis 60 l.
A harpsichord numbered eleven made by [space left] 50 l.
A harpsichord numbered twelve, made by Louis Denis 80 l.
A harpsichord numbered thirteen with one keyboard, made by
Pierre Richard 24 l.
A harpsichord numbered fourteen, made by Vaudry 60 l.
A harpsichord numbered fifteen, enlarged, by Jean Ruckers 440 l.[28]
A small harpsichord numbered sixteen 24 l.

[27] Antoine Vaudry, Rue du Platre, Paris. On April 20, 1733, he took Nicolas Lefevre
as apprentice (XXIII).
[28] It is interesting to note the high value placed on the Ruckers harpsichord as compared to the French instruments.

A small flageolet stop for a barrel organ
Eleven spinets made by different makers taken at seven *livres* apiece   77 l.
Two clavichords and six music desks   24 l.
—— Declared that Mr. Bourdet has in his possession an enlarged Flemish harpsichord by Belot [29] on its gilded stand which has been visited by Mssrs. Blanchet and Nadry [?] and is rented by Jehan Sincea, which harpsichord has been purchased by the said Sincea.

THE WORKSHOP OF JEAN MARIE GALLAND. ARCHIVES NATIONALES, MINUTIER CENTRAL, LXXXIII, 461, MAY 14, 1755. SEE PIERRE J. HARDOUIN, "HARPSICHORD MAKING IN PARIS, PART I," FOR THE FRENCH TEXTS AND BIOGRAPHICAL DETAILS OF GALLAND.

Item	a harpsichord by the elder Ruckers with a small compass [*a petit ravalement*]	400 l.
Item	two harpsichords with full range	700 l.
Item	a counterfeit Ruckers harpsichord with a small compass	200 l.
Item	two small harpsichords with two unisons [2x8′]	200 l.
Item	a counterfeit Dumont harpsichord	120 l.
Item	two folding harpsichords in two pieces of which one has split sharps and the other a small compass	50 l.
Item	another folding harpsichord in three pieces and with split sharps	50 l.
Item	three small folding harpsichords at the octave [four-foot pitch]	216 l.
Item	a harpsichord by Louis Denis of small compass	150 l.
Item	a spinet *a l'Italienne* of medium range [*a ravalement ordinaire*]	72 l.
Item	another spinet *a l'Italienne*	36 l.
Item	three spinets at the octave	72 l.
Item	two folding dulcimers	24 l.
Item	two other square dulcimers	24 l.
Item	a *carillon* made of thin metal bars	24 l.
Item	a *carillon* of small bells with keyboard	24 l.
Item	four barrel organs	80 l.
Item	an outfit consisting of a bench, planes, saws, chisels, hammers, and other tools used by the said Sieur Galland	36 l.

THE WORKSHOP OF JEAN MARIE GALLAND. ARCHIVES NATIONALES, MINUTIER CENTRAL, LXXXIII, 468, MAY 30, 1760.

Item	a table organ in walnut with one keyboard and one reed stop	240 l.
Item	a walnut harpsichord with two unisons, on two trestles	48 l.
Item	another harpsichord with two keyboards and three choirs, with its cover, [*surtous*] of wood painted blue, made by Denis, on its wooden stand, with its music desk	150 l.

[29] That is to say, the *ravalement* was performed by Bellot.

Item	another harpsichord painted black with cutouts [probably ornamented by the technique of *découpage*], on its stand, also painted black, with three choirs, ivory sharps	200 l.
Item	another harpsichord painted red with gold bands, two manuals and three choirs, on its stand	300 l.
Item	another harpsichord painted black with gold bands, two manuals, three choirs	48 l.
Item	a spinet *a l'Italienne* on its stand, of four octaves, painted black in the Chinese style	36 l.
Item	a walnut folding harpsichord in two pieces, and with three choirs	60 l.
Item	a square walnut spinet with medium range [*a ravalement*]	42 l.
Item	a small octave spinet, painted black, bronze bands, with its stand	48 l.
Item	another small spinet without stand, painted black and red, at four-foot pitch	24 l.
Item	a folding four-foot harpsichord in walnut, two choirs at unison	42 l.
Item	a square walnut spinet with one choir by Philippe Denis	18 l.
Item	another octave spinet covered with paper	12 l.
Item	a folding dulcimer	14 l.
Item	two other square dulcimers [to be played with] drumsticks	24 l.
Item	a *carillon* made of thin metal bars, of two octaves, covered with paper	18 l.
Item	a *carillon* with seventeen small bells, painted yellow, and its stand, also of wood, painted yellow	18 l.
Item	a bench, five planes, and several tools such as chisels and drills, taken together with several saws and files	15 l.

THE WORKSHOP OF HENRI HEMSCH. ARCHIVES NATIONALES, MINUTIER CENTRAL, CIX, 728, SEPT. 28, 1769. FOR THE FRENCH TEXT SEE HARDOUIN, "HARPSICHORD MAKING IN PARIS, PART III."

Item	a harpsichord made by the said deceased	300 l.
Item	four other harpsichords with enlarged range also made by the said deceased	1200 l.
Item	a harpsichord made by Goujon which has for name Hans Ruckers	350 l.
Item	a harpsichord by Joanes Ruckers	450 l.
Item	a harpsichord by Ruckers	500 l.
Item	a harpsichord by Roze	120 l.
Item	a dilapidated small harpsichord	18 l.
Item	a spinet painted black	24 l.
Item	a walnut spinet with medium range	10 l.
Item	two other spinets also with medium range	108 l.
Item	a spinet at the octave	30 l.
Item	a walnut spinet with medium range	50 l.

Item	a *cimballon* [?] with two keyboards, not finished	20 l.
Item	another small *simballon* [?] in walnut, also not finished	19 l.
Item	five small instruments such as spinets and clavichords, all of them dilapidated	19 l.
Item	fourteen harpsichord cases, mounted [probably means with strings], without being finished or their subsidiary parts prepared	120 l.
Item	two old stands, old lids and ends of wood not worth description	12 l.
Item	three benches with their tools	10 l.
Item	fifty-three wooden screw clamps both large and small	20 l.
Item	around one hundred tools such as hand saws, turning saws [?] firmer chisels, chisels, files, rasps for wood, taps and other tools	30 l.
Item	fifty-six planks six feet long of poplar	22 l.
Item	thirteen curved planks of the same wood	6 l.
Item	forty-eight planks of poplar six feet long	20 l.
Item	two planks of oak six feet long	40 l.
Item	six planks of willow	5 l.
Item	twenty-eight bundles of twenty-four or twenty-five to the bundle of pine for the soundboards of harpsichords	224 l.
Item	three planks of walnut	5 l.
Item	three *membrures* of beech	2 l.
Item	about two pounds of harpsichord strings on spools, about seven hundred harpsichord wrest pins and about half a dozen of harpsichord keys [possibly tuning keys], and three organ pipes	19 l.

THE WORKSHOP OF JEAN JACQUES MALADE. ARCHIVES NATIONALES, MINUTIER CENTRAL, XX, 677, FEB. 9, 1774. FOR THE FRENCH TEXTS AND BIOGRAPHICAL DETAILS OF MALADE SEE HARDOUIN, "HARPSICHORD MAKING IN PARIS, PART II."

In the attic:

First	seventy-four planks of poplar wood six feet long, taken at eight sols the plank	29 l. 12 s.
Item	twenty-one planks of lime, nine feet long	26 l. 5 s.
Item	twelve planks of oak, six feet long	6 l. 12 s.

In the work-room:

Item	three hundred twenty-five planks of soundboard wood	156 l.
Item	two woodworking benches six feet long, each with its outfit composed of a holdfast, two jointing planes, a miter plane, and a smooth plane	30 l.
Item	six molding planes of different types, two shoulder planes, two grooving planes, a curved plane and another toothing [plane]	5 l.
Item	sixty tools such as files, rasps, firmers and chisels, gouges, and mortising chisels	15 l.

Item   eight nippers and pincers of which two with latches, a spring compass, three other plain ones, two small hand vises, an iron plane, a vise weighing ten pounds on a stand, two bit braces of which one has an iron butt, five bench hammers, a drill equipped with a dozen of bits, with four large saws and two small   18 l.

Item   two screw-boxes and their taps, and thirty-two wooden screw clamps used in gluing   12 l.

Item   a drill bit mounted on its chassis and a collection of various small tools not worth describing   4 l.

Item   an oil stone, two dozen packets of jacks   6 l.

Item   two pounds of strings as much iron as copper for harpsichords, at four *livres* the pound   8 l.

Item   three coils of iron wire of different sizes weighing thirty-six pounds   15 l.

Item   a device for bending wood   3 l.

Item   seven large panels, eleven small, three harpsichord wrest planks, and various other pieces of glued-up wood   24 l.

Item   four large gluing clamps and twelve small   4 l.

Item   fifty pounds by weight of ebony   20 l.

Item   thirty pounds by weight of boxwood   9 l.

Item   a harpsichord made by the said Mr. Malade   500 l.

Item   four harpsichords ready to receive strings and keyboards   300 l.

Item   an old harpsichord stand of carved and gilded wood   6 l.

THE WORKSHOP OF JEAN JACQUES MALADE. ARCHIVES NATIONALES, MINUTIER CENTRAL, Y 11973, MAY 18, 1781 (*scellé*).

. . . a musical instrument called a forte piano with its keys and strings, carrying the name of the deceased and the year 1780.
. . . a harpsichord with its keys and strings belonging to Mr. Lemaire.

THE WORKSHOP OF JEAN JACQUES MALADE. ARCHIVES NATIONALES, LIV, 992, MAY 26, 1781.

In the workshop on the fourth floor, in a small room to the right on entering:

First   three logs of ebony sawed into sheets about two and one-half feet long, and another four feet long also sawed into sheets, the whole weighing ninety-eight pounds   40 l.

2. Item   a harpsichord in the white without its stand, not finished, with the name Stelle [30]   120 l.

3. Item   a piano on its four legs, in cherry, perfect and complete   200 l.

4. Item   one hundred sixty-seven planks of pine on a support   80 l.

5. Item   one hundred eighty planks of various lengths and widths, with a quantity of short ends of planks   44 l.

6. Item   nine key panels of lime wood   12 l.

[30] Probably Benoist Stehlin. See texts that follow.

7. Item a quantity of jacks — 18 l.

8. Item two spinet cases and a key panel, with a quantity of short ends of planks — 12 l.

9. Item a table with a frame serving as a template, two templates of different wood [31] — 6 l.

10. Item two bundles of bridges, a bundle of guides [*guides*, possibly lower guides or registers] two bundles of moldings, a bundle of *boudins* and a sack of horsetail [32] — 12 l.

11. Item a small box containing a bundle of boxwood, a quantity of unfinished sharps, some short ends of ebony, and some leather for registers — 18 l.

12. Item twenty-five clamps or iron screws, of which nine are large and sixteen small — 15 l.

13. Item twenty-four small boxes containing iron wrest pins, nails, hinges, and hitchpins for harpsichords — 9 l.

14. Item a box full of small grooving planes, two small boxes of punches, a drawing case — 18 l.

15. Item twenty-four stop mechanisms of copper large and small, and three of iron — 6 l.

16. Item a bench with a holdfast of iron and all its equipment, five items — 18 l.

17. Item forty-eight items, files and other small tools serving the profession, two tools for wire drawing, seven hand saws, a clock spring [33] — 15 l.

18. Item a bit brace with its bits and two screw drivers, two dies and their taps, a hand vise, two copper compasses, nippers, pincers, a bow drill in wood, four small packets of brass wire and eight rosettes in lead — 10 l.

19. Item four hammers of which three are without handles, and four small tool handles — 6 l.

20. Item a packet of off-cuts of buff leather, a music desk, and a quantity of small pieces of wood good for a piano — 3 l.

21. Item two writing tables of which one is with a drawer, an iron chandelier with candle holders of copper, two arms of white iron with flowers and two lights — 6 l.

22. Item a dilapidated spinet in walnut — 6 l.

23. Item two saws of which one a rip saw, and the other a press saw [see Plate XXXVIII], with a plan of a harpsichord — 6 l.

In the said shop, at the end:

24. Item a harpsichord on its carved stand, music desk, keyboard, jacks, and four registers, all in the white, not finished — 300 l.

[31] Very ambiguous. I have translated *calibre* as template. A "frame serving as a template" could be some sort of building form or jig.

[32] A plant growing in marshy places. Its dried stems are abrasive and were used for smoothing and polishing wood.

[33] Roubo suggests that small saws be made of clock springs.

25.	Item	another harpsichord with its soundboard and its registers, the lid not finished	
26.	Item	a harpsichord case with its bottom	96 l.
27.	Item	six other harpsichord cases in the white	36 l.
28.	Item	a harpsichord painted green, old, without stand and without being enlarged	144 l.
29.	Item	an old harpsichord in black painted wood	24 l.
30.	Item	a piano case to be mounted [with strings ?], between the two windows	9 l.
31.	Item	one hundred forty-three planks of pine hung in the air	60 l.
32.	Item	one hundred fifty-six bars of various woods in the corner by the fireplace	72 l.
33.	Item	forty pieces of wood for harpsichords, and keyboards, part hung up and part on the floor beside the fireplace	6 l.
34.	Item	four music desks and three cross pieces [?], two harpsichord lids and two small ones, not finished	3 l.
35.	Item	four bent pieces of walnut plank, and a plank of oak in the corner to the right	12 l.
36.	Item	ten wrest planks of oak and several ends of planks of various sizes hung on the wall between the partition and the fireplace	6 l.
37.	Item	forty-seven wooden screw clamps of various sizes	9 l.
38.	Item	twenty-four molding tools with a grooving plane, two taps for wood with their screwboxes	18 l.
39.	Item	three small vises, forty-six items such as firmer chisels, files, and others	18 l.
40.	Item	ten planes or shoulder planes	6 l.
41.	Item	twelve saws of various sizes	6 l.
42.	Item	two bit braces, twelve bits, five small terrieres [?], six files, hand vises and nippers	12 l.
43.	Item	three bar clamps, six holdfasts in iron of various sizes, a vise, a small anvil on its block, an iron plane, three packages of iron wire of various sizes	9 l.
44.	Item	two benches with their vises and two drawers	12 l.
45.	Item	twelve jointing planes and small planes, two mallets, four iron hammers with their handles	12 l.
46.	Item	a quantity of wood in pieces, prepared for pianos, in a harpsichord case	12 l.
47.	Item	thirty ends of planks and planks two and one-half feet long, and other ends of planks of various woods and various lengths, not worthy of description, with six clamps of white wood	60 l.

In the attic:

48.	Item	forty-three planks of poplar in thin planks	12 l.
49.	Item	fourteen planks of lime, five feet long	12 l.
50.	Item	eleven planks of oak of various lengths and thicknesses	6 l.
51.	Item	eleven planks of various lengths and thicknesses	8 l.
			12 l.

52. Item   seven planks and four short ends of pine   10 l.
53. Item   ten planks of lime of various lengths   15 l.
54. Item   eleven planks of pear of various lengths and widths   8 l.
55. Item   four planks and three pieces of mahogany   48 l.
56. Item   a quantity of ends and planks of various woods of which
        the greater part is only fit for burning   6 l.

Plus 2 harpsichords and a forte piano which are rented.
At the house of Dame Dupre, rue Ste. Barbe:
      Item   a harpsichord with two manuals by Jean Ruckers with
          extended compass on its stand of deal   450 l.
At the house of Sieur Beck, harpsichord teacher, Rue du Cimetiere, St. Andre des-Arts:
      Item   a forte piano without maker's name, on its oak stand   120 l.
At the house of Commissioner Simoneau, Rue Aubry-le-Boucher:
      Item   a harpsichord by Hemsch, with one keyboard and ex-
          tended compass   200 l.

THE WORKSHOP OF BENOIST STEHLIN. ARCHIVES NATIONALES, MINUTIER CENTRAL, Y 11263, JULY 11, 1774 (scellé).

Item   a Flemish harpsichord with enlarged range in its box[34] and on its legs, of wood painted gray and gilded
Item   another unfinished harpsichord with enlarged range in its box and on its legs, of wood painted gray and gilded
Item   an unfinished harpsichord with enlarged range in its box of white wood, without legs

THE WORKSHOP OF BENOIST STEHLIN. ARCHIVES NATIONALES, MINUTIER CENTRAL, XLIX, 813, JULY 15, 1774. FOR THE FRENCH TEXT SEE HARDOUIN, "HARPSICHORD MAKING IN PARIS, PART II."

[In the salon:]
First   a harpsichord made by Jean Ruckers in one thousand seven hundred and thirty [sic] and extended in compass by the said deceased, resting on its stand of water green outlined in gold, with its top painted to represent a portico and other historical subjects   800 l.
Item   another harpsichord made by Mr. Stehlin, painted gray and also outlined in gold   390 l.
Item   a harpsichord on its stand made by the said Mr. Stehlin, of which the case is not painted   300 l.
Item   a woodworker's bench of oak equipped with its iron holdfast, a large and a small jointing plane, two hammers, a hatchet, four saws of different sizes, forty-five tools, chisels, files, bits, gouges, firmer chisels, all in iron with wooden handles, a

[34] Probably does not mean much of anything; a legal phrase to indicate that a harpsichord consists of a harpsichord case.

small hand vise, two bad pincers, a bit brace, three marking
gauges, a rabbet plane, the whole being tools used by
luthiers . . . with an iron plane   30 l.

[The remainder of the items were in another house.]

Item a harpsichord with its white wooden case and its stand in
painted oak, made by the deceased and equipped with all
its parts   200 l.

Item two other unpainted harpsichord cases with their soundboards painted in water color and all the dependent parts
ready to be assembled   300 l.

Item twelve unpainted harpsichord cases without stands, of
which eleven are equipped with their panels [?] and keyboards, and the twelfth without panels, all supplied with
their parts ready to be strung   1200 l.

Item a harpsichord painted yellow made by Nicolas Dumont in
Paris in 1695, with all its parts and strings   80 l.

Item another harpsichord in very bad condition with neither jacks
nor strings, made in Paris by Louis Denis   10 l.

Item four bad spinets all dilapidated   24 l.

Item thirty-five ends or planks of lime and other kinds of wood
used in instrument making, twenty-five wooden clamps of
various sizes, a brass rabbet plane with wooden handle, two
gimlets with wooden handles, seven trestles and stools of
wood, a wooden cabinet   40 l.

Item a woodworker's bench in oak equipped with an iron holdfast,
two jointing planes, an iron hammer, three harpsichord stands   8 l.

THE WORKSHOP OF JOSEPH TREYER, SOMETIMES CALLED L'EMPEREUR. AR-
CHIVES NATIONALES, MINUTIER CENTRAL, CXVI, 513, JAN. 19, 1779. FOR
THE FRENCH TEXTS AND BIOGRAPHICAL DETAILS OF TREYER, SEE HARDOUIN,
"HARPSICHORD MAKING IN PARIS, PART II."

First ten spinet cases   600 l.

Item nine unfinished harpsichord cases   800 l.

Item a harpsichord painted green with gold bands and cabriole
legs, made by l'Empereur   300 l.

Item a small case in walnut with its keyboard, on a columned
stand   100 l.

Item a square virginal and a small harpsichord, both Flemish, very
bad state   75 l.

Item four pairs of trestles on which to place unfinished instruments   8 l.

Item *two cupboards, three benches and their tools and vises,*
[The words in italics have been crossed out] three benches
of which one with vises   100 l.

Item two jointing planes and two jack planes, three smooth planes
and six small planes, two shoulder planes, *a resuvais* [?] with
screw, six molding tools of various sizes, an iron vise, an iron

anvil mounted on its block, twenty-four bits of various sizes, a dozen of files of various sizes, twelve firmer chisels, twelve gouges, six saws, two for marquetry, a small drill, two pincers, two nippers, three hammers, four mallets, two tuning hammers   72 l.

Item   about eight hundred sheets of pine from various countries suitable for making the soundboards of harpsichords   300 l.

Item   about one hundred fifty planks of walnut, two hundred of poplar, twelve of pear   300 l.

Item   a harpsichord made by Jerome,[35] painted black, on its cabriole stand, with two manuals   [150 l. erased]   75 l.

Item   another harpsichord painted to resemble marble, mounted on its cabriole stand, with two keyboards and extended range, taken as old   73 l.

Item   two hurdy-gurdies and a violin, each in its case   63 l.

THE WORKSHOP OF JOSEPH TREYER. ARCHIVES NATIONALES, MINUTIER CENTRAL, XLIII, 551, SEPT. 3, 1788.

Item   a spinet case with its keyboard and stand   24 l.

Item   an old harpsichord with two manuals, with its stand, not finished . . .   150 l.

Item   four small hammer harpsichord cases, each equipped with its keyboard, not finished, only two of which are equipped with their lids   204 l.

Item   five other spinet cases, provided with their keyboards and their stands   120 l.

Item   two harpsichord cases without keyboards or stands or soundboards   18 l.

Item   a spinet in buff leather [that is, with *peau de buffle* plectra] with its stand   60 l.

Item   another old spinet [with one?] register, of wood   18 l.

Item   a small black harpsichord   6 l.

Item   another grey harpsichord with gold bands, with its stand, made by Gougeon [Goujon]   120 l.

Item   another harpsichord in walnut, foreign   6 l.

Item   another old harpsichord painted black   6 l.

Item   two harpsichord cases, completely new   12 l.

Item   an old harpsichord provided with only one bridge   10 l.

Item   eight harpsichord bentsides   4 l.

Item   six panels of which three large and three small   6 l.

Item   a small square spinet, with a small dulcimer   3 l.

Item   thirty-four clamps, as many with screws as without   6 l.

Item   fourteen music desks, as many large as small, without bases   3 l.

Item   a vise and an anvil on its block, taken with a hammer   12 l.

[35] A maker otherwise known only by an advertisement in *Les Affiches et annonces* in 1767.

Item	about twenty bad tools, files, chisels, saws, and others, taken with a sharpening stone	1 l.
Item	an old bench and a poor clamp	3 l.
Item	two large packages of crow quills	3 l.
Item	a bench equipped with two vises	6 l.
Item	six saws, mounted	3 l.
Item	about sixty items of tools such as bits, squares, hammers, and others	3 l.
Item	a box containing a drill, sixteen bits, and other tools	1 l. 10 s.
Item	an iron plane garnished with copper	3 l.
Item	twenty large screw clamps, and twelve small	7 l. 4 s.
Item	three clamp irons with screws	1 l. 10 s.
Item	nineteen shoulder planes, smooth planes, jointing planes, and grooving planes	8 l.
Item	a quantity of old iron scraps and pieces of wood together with the five old drawers containing them	3 l.
Item	thirteen bridges with the forms [*modeles*, probably forms for bending the bridges]	2 l.
Item	three tables of forms [36]	3 l.
Item	a pile of pine made up of two hundred thirty sheets for harpsichord soundboards, six feet long and six inches wide	115 l.
Item	another pile of one hundred eighty sheets of pine about ten inches wide	100 l.
Item	twenty planks of lime, fourteen inches wide, one inch thick and seven feet long	20 l.
Item	another quantity of similar wood of various sizes and widths	18 l.
Item	sixteen planks of walnut wood, eleven feet long by different widths and thicknesses	20 l.
Item	ten pieces of walnut, six feet long, ten inches wide, and about five inches thick	48 l.
Item	seven square pieces, three inches by various widths	3 l.
Item	twenty-eight pieces of walnut of various lengths and widths and one inch thick	30 l.
Item	two other planks nine feet long and one foot wide	2 l.
Item	thirty planks of deal of various lengths and widths	36 l.
Item	a quantity of lime for keyboards	6 l.
Item	various pieces of wood with a frame garnished with iron and sheet metal [evidently a jig]	8 l.
Item	two *tables* [?] of walnut, six and one-half feet long by eighteen inches wide, five inches thick	12 l.
Item	three hundred pieces of bone for sharps, with the basket that holds them	4 l.
Item	twelve wooden screw clamps	4 l.
Item	three taps with their die and two bow [drills?]	3 l.

[36] Bending forms for bridges, moldings, and other small parts often consist of a curved piece of wood nailed to a flat surface. The part to be bent is steamed or soaked and clamped to the form to dry. This is probably the device here so cryptically described.

Item   a bench equipped with its vises and various pieces of wood   24 l.
Item   a bow drill with its bow   3 l.
Item   four harpsichord soundboards with another small old
       soundboard   4 l. 10 s.
Item   two dozen small thimbles of copper suitable to receive
       the battens [probably prop sticks for the lids] of harpsi-
       chords   2 l. 8 s.
Item   two harpsichord hammers [tuning hammers], three pincers,
       and various small tools such as knives   3 l.
Item   a harpsichord by André Ruquer with its stand and action
       [*mechaniques*; perhaps a knee-lever mechanism] and key-
       board, not finished   200 l.
Item   eight pieces of plank suitable to make soundboards of harpsi-
       chords, of various widths and thicknesses   3 l.
Item   a harpsichord with the name, L'Empereur, with its action
       [*mechaniques*] mounted on a stand   300 l.
Item   a quantity of ebony of various lengths and widths, and a box
       of ebony   15 l.
Item   various short pieces of boxwood   1 l. 4 s.
Item   various pieces of iron suitable for mechanisms   6 l.
Item   eight harpsichord locks in copper and their keys   6 l.
Item   sixty small square hinges in copper   6 l.
Item   a box full of various hinges of copper and of various pieces of
       iron   6 l.
Item   a box full of iron wrest pins turned together [that is, a set, all
       of a size (?)] and five small wooden planes   4 l.
Item   thirty tools of various kinds such as bits, files, chisels,
       and others   1 l. 10 s.
Item   two coils of brass wire and iron wire   12 l.
[This document also notes that Treyer owed a painter-varnisher 201 l. and
that the latter would return a harpsichord case then being painted only after
payment. Thus we see that Treyer and presumably other harpsichord makers
did not do their own painting.]

THE WORKSHOP OF JACQUES GOERMANS. ARCHIVES NATIONALES, MINUTIER
CENTRAL, XLVI, 538, MAY 6, 1789. FOR FRENCH TEXT AND BIOGRAPHICAL
DETAILS OF JEAN AND JACQUES GOERMANS, SEE HARDOUIN, "HARPSICHORD
MAKING IN PARIS, PART I."

First No. 1st two old forte pianos   144 l.
Item No. 2 a forte piano by M. Goermans   144 l.
   3   a forte piano by Frederick Bark [37]   200 l.
   4   a small unison harpsichord [that is, with two eight-foot stops
       only] with one manual by the said Goermans   120 l.
   5   an old harpsichord by Dumont painted black   150 l.

[37] Probably Frederick Beck of London.

6	a piano in the shape of a harpsichord in mahogany by M. Goermans	
		150 l.
7	an old English piano in the shape of a harpsichord	150 l.
8	a square forte piano by M. Goermans	200 l.
9	a forte piano of the same shape, not finished	72 l.
10	five forte pianos by M. Goermans	720 l.
11	three forte pianos by M. Goermans with their keyboards and lids, without their soundboards, the said forte pianos not completed	
		150 l.
12	a forte piano in walnut all dilapidated	84 l.
13	three hundred iron wrest pins for stringing forte pianos	6 l.
14	a package of old patterns [*modeles*] suitable to the trade, and a drawer of tools consisting of little planes, molding planes, old saws	
		6 l.
15	a brass lathe for turning between centers, taken with some iron pins	
		4 l.
16	eleven sets of wrest pins for forte pianos	22 l.
17	three iron smooth planes	9 l.
18	a box containing various tools useful to the trade	9 l.
19	six drawers containing various tools such as hand saws, bit braces, drills, bits, files, compasses, pincers, punches, stop mechanisms iron work for pianos, copper candle holders colored gold, and various other small tools serving the trade of keyboard instrument maker	
		72 l.
20	a brown violin lacking strings and bridge	3 l.
21	a horizontal harpsichord with its stand without keyboard	100 l.
22	a forte piano in the shape of a harpsichord with painted soundboard made by M. Goermans	
		36 l.
23	a small model of a forte piano with its little stand	12 l.
24	four harpsichord cases of various sizes	24 l.
25	six benches of which four with their vises	48 l.
26	a clamp for clamping wood	6 l.
27	twelve sets of keyboard ivories	72 l.
28	two square forte pianos	30 l.
29	three forte piano cases	72 l.
30	an odd [*de fantaisie* (?)] harpsichord	72 l.
31	three old harpsichords to be taken to pieces	36 l.
32	an old harpsichord made by M. Goermans	72 l.
33	an old spinet	24 l.
34	four planks of mahogany eight feet in length and four thin planks of the same wood six feet long and of various widths	
		40 l.
35	one hundred thin planks of white wood six feet long and of various widths	
		40 l.
36	two hundred forty little pieces of pine for veneering the wrest planks of harpsichords and forte pianos with [to match?] their soundboards	
		36 l.
37	two hundred leaves of soundboard wood for harpsichords	100 l.

38 four lots of pine five feet long   24 l.
39 sixty four pieces varying in length of thin sheets of pine for
    making forte pianos   12 l.
40 four planks of walnut   9 l.
41 twenty-four planks of lime wood of mixed lengths, widths, and
    thicknesses   18 l.
42 two bent pieces with various pieces of thin planks and ends of
    planks   9 l.
43 twelve pieces of planks and thin planks of various lengths   9 l.
44 three old vises, two with supports, two little anvils   15 l.
45 twenty-one planes, some jointing planes and some jack planes   24 l.
46 three grooving planes, three rabbet planes, six marking gauges,
    three mallets, two squares   6 l.
47 seven holdfasts, two glue pots, three irons to heat wood   9 l.
48 three taps with their dies, and three bits, four bit braces, and
    two drills mounted in wood and a bow [probably a bow drill]   12 l.
49 fourteen saws mounted in wood, as many large as small   12 l.
50 a hand saw with two other saws mounted in iron, and one mar-
    quetry saw, a plate of copper with divisions [possibly a ruler or
    protractor, or a marking-out jig]   9 l.
51 two drawers full of unfinished jacks   6 l.
52 two pieces of ebony and one of boxwood   40 s.
53 fifty hand clamps   24 l.
54 a trowel and its trough [possibly for gesso work], with some rem-
    nants of iron wire   9 l.

THE WORKSHOP OF LOUIS HENOCQ. ARCHIVES NATIONALES, MINUTIER CEN-
TRAL, XLII, 652, JAN. 12, 1791. FOR THE FRENCH TEXT AND BIOGRAPHICAL
DETAILS OF LOUIS HENOCQ, SEE HARDOUIN, "HARPSICHORD MAKING IN
PARIS, PART II."

Item a harpsichord made by the said Mr. Henocq   200 l.
Item a harpsichord made by Andre Ruckers with a carved stand
      and music desk   300 l.
Item an old harpsichord in bad condition, painted black   36 l.
Item a square octave virginal   24 l.
Item another square virginal and its stand   30 l.
Item an old forte piano and its stand   96 l.
Item a bench with its vise   6 l.
Item three jointing planes   3 l.
Item seven planes with curved soles, two rabbet planes and two
      ordinary smooth planes, an iron smooth plane, seven molding
      planes, four iron holdfasts, a bar clamp, a heating iron, four
      hammers, a copper glue pot, four squares, four marking
      gauges, an English square, a drill and its accessories, a rip
      saw and four other saws, and two marquetry saws   47 l.

Item two bit braces with their bits, a bow drill, and a quantity of
white iron and bits   6 l.
Item three punches and two little dies in a drawer, a dozen files and
rasps, round and flat and rat tail   6 l.
Item a dozen firmer gouges and mortising chisels, nippers, round
and flat pincers, three little saws held on wooden plaques   6 l.
Item a dozen screw clamps, nine sheets of boxwood, and four little
ends of mahogany   12 l.
Item some pieces of oak and beech, linden and walnut, and a thin
plank of pear, some pine and sheets of templates [*fouillé de
modelles*]   12 l.
Item some ends of iron wire to make small wrest pins, three or four
pieces of leather, and six packages of old wrest pins and iron
nails   3 l.

INSTRUMENTS IN THE HANDS OF FRENCH MUSICIANS

This compilation is based on documents in the Archives Nationales, Minutier Central.

Date	Instruments	Owner
1617	Three small spinets of which two are covered in cloth of gold braided with two gold bands, and the other covered with satin. A *panodion* [?] [38] the color of red Morocco. A double spinet [*espinette*] [39] painted green inside and out. A harpsichord with two stops, painted green. Another double harpsichord.[40] A clavichord covered with black leather. A spinet with a small keyboard.	J. Lesecq (organist)
1623	A large spinet covered with leather and ornamented with iron *alentour*. [?] A small spinet of white wood.	Bienvenu (organist)

[38] Perhaps for *pantalon*: a term sometimes used for the cimbalom.
[39] *Espinette* at this period was used rather indiscriminately and might refer to a harpsichord-shaped instrument. *Clavecin* is translated here as "harpsichord" and *epinette* as "spinet," unless it is qualified by *carré* in which case it is translated as "virginal." The instrument referred to as a double spinet might have been a double virginal (mother and child) or a two-stop harpsichord.
[40] Probably with two stops and one manual.

Date	Instruments	Owner
	A large spinet of white wood with a keyboard of ebony and ivory.	
1626	Two small spinets and one harpsichord	J. and M. Lesecq
	Ten lots of wood for spinets and clavichords.[41]	
	Five spinet trestles.	
	A spinet covered with red leather.	
1636	A medium harpsichord covered with red leather and a clavichord and a small spinet.	S. Biermant (organist)
1639	A large harpsichord.	Henry Housse (organist)
1648	A spinet.	R. Dubuisson (organist)
	A bad spinet.	
1653	A large harpsichord.	R. Dubuisson
	A small square virginal with a stand, covered.	
	A mediocre spinet, covered.[42]	
1655	One of the last of his make [Couchet] with two keyboards like that of M. de Chamboniere which is very excellent, and such as I believe no one has made after this poor Couchet, whom [which?] I regret extremely.	Constantijn Huyghens (Letter to DuMont, organist in Paris).
1662	Two harpsichords of which one has two keyboards and is painted on the soundboard and protected with a cover, the other with one keyboard.	Nicolas Gigault (organist)
	Three spinets.	
	A clavichord.	
	Another double clavichord [that is, with two choirs].	
1664	A small spinet two feet long.	Charles Racquet (organist)
	A large spinet covered with red leather and lined inside with green damask.	
	A large spinet three and one-half feet long covered, and ornamented inside with a silver border.	

[41] Lesecq must have been a maker as well as organist at St. Eustache.
[42] Probably identical to the spinets in the previous item.

Date	Instruments	Owner
1671	A harpsichord with its parts, on its stand of walnut pillars turned and a *tirouer* [possibly for *tiroir*, a drawer].	François (I) Couperin [43]
1677	A large walnut harpsichord with two keyboards. A small spinet of *largetterie* [?] wood. A single manual harpsichord with a case of pine. A spinet with two manuals the two ends of which are covered with red morocco.[44]	J. Racquet (organist)
1678	A spinet by Jerosme which comes out of its box. A large harpsichord with two keyboards by Ph. Denis. A harpsichord on its stand. Pieces of wood for spinets.[45]	—— de Hardel (lutenist)
1679	A harpsichord with two keyboards, [and at Arcueil] a spinet covered with red leather.	Michel de la Guerre (organist)
1684	A clavichord. A harpsichord with one keyboard of marbled wood. A harpsichord.	Henri Dumont (organist)
1684	A pedal board harpsichord. (The harpsichord with two keyboards that goes with it is already sold.)	Jean Lebègue (organist)
1685	A large harpsichord. A small harpsichord. A small harpsichord with one keyboard. Four spinets of which two are of walnut and two marbled. Three clavichords.	Antoine Fouquet (organist)
1688	A single-manual harpsichord on its black painted wooden stand with twisted legs.	Guillaume Gabriel Nivers (organist)

[43] See Pierre J. Hardouin, "Quelques documents relatifs aux Couperins," *Revue de musicologie*, 37 (Dec. 1955): 111.

[44] The word *épinette* is probably used in its general sense. A two-manual harpsichord is intended. Possibly the sides of the keyboard well were covered with red leather.

[45] De Hardel must have been a maker as well as lutenist.

Date	*Instruments*	*Owner*
1689	A spinet by Louis Denis.	Antoine Mahieu (dancing master)

1691 A harpsichord with one manual and three choirs.
A harpsichord with two choirs.
A harpsichord with one keyboard and three choirs with a keyboard for transposing.[46]
A small Flemish harpsichord by Ruckers with one keyboard and two choirs.

Jean Henry D'Anglebert

1699 A harpsichord with two keyboards in its case.

André Raison (organist)

1701 A harpsichord with two keyboards at the unison [eight-foot pitch].
A pedal harpsichord at the octave [four-foot pitch], all at chamber pitch.
A spinet *à l'Italienne* at the tone [eight-foot pitch] in walnut.
A harpsichord with one manual at unison with the tone in pine.
A square virginal at the octave of the tone with bass strings of silver, the inside painted with a landscape.
Another small spinet also at the octave of the tone and *à l'Italienne*.
An unfretted clavichord with one hundred strings, at the unison, mounted with brass strings.

Nicolas Gigault [47]

1702 A small spinet.
A harpsichord with three keyboards.
A harpsichord with one keyboard *enchassé* [?] above.

Claude Jacquet (organist)

1704 A harpsichord mounted on its stand with iron screws.

Marin de la Guerre (organist)

1707 A spinet with one keyboard.

Simon Lemaire (organist)

1711 A small Flemish harpsichord with two keyboards.

Gabriel Garnier (organist)

---

[46] Transposing double harpsichords never had three choirs of strings. This instrument may have had a manual which slid sideways a few semitones.
[47] Compare to the 1662 inventory.

Date	Instruments	Owner
1714	A harpsichord . . . with ebony lines.	Guillaume Gabriel Nivers (organist)
1714	An old spinet.	E. Houssu (organist)
1715	Five harpsichords of which one Flemish one is by André Ruckers painted black like ebony with gold lines. A small harpsichord by Jean Ruckers. Two harpsichords by Dufour of which one has an enlarged range in the bass only, and the other is extended in treble and bass. Another harpsichord by the said Dufour with one manual. A small spinet by Hierosme. A small old spinet.	Louis Garnier (organist)
1720	An old fashioned walnut harpsichord.	Louis Thomelin (organist)
1721/2	Two harpsichords of which one is by Ruckers and the other by Blanchet. A harpsichord with flowered marquetry. Three spinets.	Gabriel Garnier (organist)
1727	A Flemish harpsichord.	J. B. Buterne (organist)
1728	A large harpsichord with two manuals on its stand painted black like ebony, walnut music desk. Another ordinary harpsichord with two keyboards also on its stand of walnut. Four small spinets of which one is on its stand of wood *a la capucine* [?]. Two small harpsichords with one keyboard, each 100 l.	Nicolas Couperin (organist)
1732	A small spinet. A harpsichord. Two spinets.	Antoine Fouquet (organist)
1738	A spinet with its keyboard, strings, and jacks.	Louis Thomelin (organist)
1740	A harpsichord with its keys of ebony and ivory. A small spinet . . . A clavichord . . .	Guillaume Marchand (organist)

Date	*Instruments*	*Owner*
1744	A harpsichord with enlarged compass by Rastoin, the father.	René Drouart de Bousset (organist)
1753	A harpsichord with full range. A psaltery	Charles Alexandre Jollage (organist)
1757	A Flemish harpsichord by André Ruckers	M. Forqueray (organist)
1760	A harpsichord with enlarged range which lacks the jacks and keyboards. An ordinary harpsichord, out of order. A psaltery.	P. Fi——[?] (organist)
1761	A harpsichord with two manuals in its case, painted green with gold bands.	Charles Alexandre Jollage (organist)
1761	A harpsichord in good condition by André Ruquestre with a cover of printed callico. A clavichord in good condition.	Jean Landini (organist)
1761	A small harpsichord with one keyboard by Bellot. A harpsichord by P. Belot in blue outlined and gilded.	N. G. Forqueray (organist)
1763	A wooden Flemish harpsichord by A. Ruckers. A wooden Flemish harpsichord by Havet A spinet.	Christ. Chiquelier (Keeper of Instruments to the King. Taskin's predecessor.)
1765	Two harpsichords of which one has pedals [48] without name of maker, and the other by Ruquer of Antwerp. A spinet.	Joach. Gigault (organist)
1772	A harpsichord.	Pierre Claude Fouquet (organist)
1789	A painted harpsichord, decorated with a landscape on the inside and with a mechanism to graduate the sound. Another harpsichord with a religious painting of which the outside is not finished.	Armand Louis Couperin (organist)

[48] It is impossible to say whether this means pedals to change the stops or a pedal board.

Date	Instruments	Owner
	An English forte piano.	
	A large large spinet with [?] keyboard by Mr. Blanchet.	
	A small octave spinet.	
	A clavichord.	
	A small organ.	

APPENDIX D · INVENTIONS APPLIED TO THE HARPSICHORD

ENGLISH PATENTS [1]

October 22, 1730 — no. 521.

Harris, John: "A new invented Harpsichord, upon which (having only two Sets of Strings) may be performed either one or two Unisons, or two Unisons and one Octave together, or the Forts and Pianos, or Loud and Soft, and the contrary may be executed as quick as Thought, and also Double Basses, by touching only single Keys, whereby hard Divisions on the Bass Part may be well played in a double manner without the Thumb and Finger together, which could not well be executed otherwise; [and Shakes may be here performed, which cannot be done by the Thumb and little Finger together.] [2] that besides the above mentioned Advantages a great deal of time and Trouble will be saved in Quilling and Tuning the said Harpsichord, and it will keep much longer in Tune than any Harpsichords that have Octave Stops, and consequently will not be so expensive to keep the same in good order as those Instruments which are made in the Common Way, neither can any double-key'd Harpsichord be so serviceable and useful as the Peticoner's new-invented Harpsichord, although the Expence is vastly greater."

December 17, 1730 — no. 525.

Barton, Wm.: "Pens of Silver, Brass, Steel, and other Sorts of Metall, which will improve the Tone of the said Instruments, and last many Yeares without Amendement; Crow and Raven Quills, of which they are now made, requiring frequent Charge and Trouble."

December 30, 1741 — no. 581.

Plenius, Roger: "Lyrachords which are harpsichords strung with catgut." [3]

[1] Extracted from *Abridgements of Specifications Relating to Music and Musical Instruments, A.D. 1694–1861*, Office of the Commissioners of Patents for Inventions (London, 1864).

[2] The interpolated passage is taken from an advertisement of Harris, quoted by Rimbault. Harris' harpsichord may have had an octave coupler, or possibly, a string-shortening cornet stop which raised the pitch an octave by touching each string in the middle.

[3] This was apparently a *Geigenwerk*. For a contemporary description and illustration

Also a set of "bended levers," weights, sliders, etc. to keep harpsichords in tune. Also: "set of plectrums, wherewith to strike the strings of the said instruments instead of quills, which plectrums, being made of ivory, tortoiseshell, or other materials . . . with regulating screws behind the said tongues." Also metal jack-slides, key levers in the form of square tubes. Also: "octave strings are kept in tune full as long as the unison strings by means of iron or other metall pegs or screws which are fixt in the body of the harpsichord, and appear through the belly thereof, and to which the said octave strings at one end are fastened to the tops of the said pegs or screws."

July 10, 1745 — no. 613.
Plenius, Roger: "Stop which imitates the Welch harp." This was a vertically operating buff stop. Also key buttons, keys bushed with leather underneath, closed-top jacks, etc.

December 18, 1769 — no. 947.[4]
Shudi, Burkat: "A piece of mechanism or machinery by which the harpsichord is very much improved . . . a cover extending the breadth of the harpsichord, and from the front board of the harpsichord to the ruler, of an indefinite number of valves which with their frame extend the breadth of the harpsichord, and the length hereof from the ruler to the small end, which valves are opened and shut by a number of small levers equal to the number of valves inserted or fixed in an axis spindle or bar turned by a pedal."

December 28, 1770 — no. 977.
Haxby, Thomas: "A new single harpsichord containing all the stops of a double one, which by the use of one pedal only, produces every increase, diminution, and variation of tone that a double one is capable of performing . . . A single harpsichord of two unisons, octave, lute and harp, which by the use of one pedal only (which pedal has a connection with several sliding tumblers, springs, &c.) produces ten variations of stops, also an increase and diminution of tone (either gradually or instantaneously) from the softest stop to the full harpsichord, or from the full harpsichord to the softest stop."

August 29, 1772 — no. 1020.
Walker, Adam: "Celestina" or *Geigenwerk*. The patent refers to the whole instrument but Walker sometimes attached it to existing harpsichords.[5]

September 12, 1774 — no. 1081.
Merlin, Joseph: "A new kind of compound harpsichord, in which, besides

of the lyrachord see Eric Halfpenny, "The Lyrachord," *The Galpin Society Journal*, 3 (March 1950): 46.
[4] This is the well-known Venetian swell.
[5] See "Letters between Hopkinson, Jefferson, and Burney," Raymond Russell, *The Harpsichord and Clavichord*, p. 177. (Jefferson ordered a harpsichord from Kirckman with Walker's stop.)

the jacks with quills, a set of hammers of the nature of those used in the kind of harpsichords called Piano Forte, are introduced in such manner that either may be played separately or both together at the pleasure of the performer, and for adding the aforesaid hammers to an harpsichord of the common kind already made, so as to render it such compound harpsichord." [6]

December 28, 1774 — no. 1092.

Gillespy, Samuel: "New-Constructed Principle of Putting on the Quills to Strike the Strings of a Harpsichord with a Peddle and Swell, which raises the Top, brings on the Tone, and Swells a new Celestial Stop, at the same time Preserving the Instrument compleat." The Celestial stop seems to have been a sort of *Tangentenflügel* in which the striking surface was composed of leather, cloth or wood.

[6] There is a harpsichord of Merlin's make in the Deutsches Museum in Munich to which this device has been fitted.

ABSTRACTS OF FRENCH INVENTIONS

Date	Purpose and nature of invention	Inventor	Remarks	Source
1678	"Languettes Impériales," plectra of a new and more stable design calculated to avoid the mechanical difficulties of ordinary crow quill plectra and bristle springs. The plectra were spiral in form and possibly were made of metal.	Jean Baptiste de la Rousselière	De la Rousselière's treatise on the subject contained one hundred forty-nine pages, but the author avoided grappling with his subject with almost uncanny skill. He never properly described the *Languette Impériale*. Presented to the Académie Royale des Sciences in 1679.	*Mercure de France*, 1678, p. 109. J. B. de la Rousselière, *Traité des languettes impériales* (Paris, 1679).
1698	A monochord to be used in tuning the harpsichord. It consisted of one string, one key and one jack. A calibrated movable bridge gave each note of the temperament octave.	Estienne Louilé (music master)	Presented to the Académie in 1699. Louilé also invented a metronome in 1696.	Estienne Louilé, *Nouveau système de musique*, Paris, 1698. Also Gallon, *Machines et inventions approuvées par L'Académie*, 1666–1754 (Paris, 1735, 1777), I, 189.
Before 1699	A four-string monochord to be used in tuning the harpsichord.	Louis Carré (geometrician)	Presented to the Académie "before 1699."	Gallon, *Machines et inventions*, I, 102.
1700	Folding harpsichord for traveling.	Jean Marius (maker)	Many examples survive. Presented to the Académie in 1700.	Gallon, *Machines et inventions*, I, 193.
1708	Keyboard instrument with mechanically bowed strings.	Cuisinié	Presented to the Académie in 1708.	Gallon, *Machines et inventions*.
1712	*Vis-à-vis* harpsichord with two keyboards at each end to be used for duets.	Philippe Denis (maker)	Ruckers had made something like this instrument one hundred years earlier but he did not provide two equal instruments in one box.	*Mercure de France*, 1712 (April), p. 216.
1716	Four types of piano action.	Jean Marius (maker)	Presented to the Académie in 1716.	Gallon, *Machines et inventions*, III, 83.

Date	Purpose and nature of invention	Inventor	Remarks	Source
1725	"Clavecin pour les yeux." Colored jacks are intended to provide a visual translation of aural music.	Le Père Castel	A philosophical disputation continued for years, especially in the *Mercure*. Castel's invention is discussed in the *Encyclopédie*, "Clavecin oculaire."	*Mercure de France*, 1725 (Nov.), p. 2552; 1726 (Mar.), p. 445; 1726 (Apr.), p. 650; 1726 (May), p. 929; 1751 (Dec.), p. 7; 1755 (Apr.), p. 160; 1755 (July), p. 144.
1727	Metal plectra to provide greater stability of regulation.	Thevenart (maker)	Presented to the Académie in 1727.	*Mercure de France*, 1727 (Nov.), p. 2495. Gallon, *Machines et inventions*, V, 11.
1732	Alteration to harpsichord bridge so that both eight-foot strings could be of equal length.	Bellot (maker)	Presented to the Académie in 1732. His surviving instruments do not show this device.	*Histoire de l'Académie*, (Paris, 1732), p. 118.
1742	Keyboard instrument with mechanically bowed strings.	Le Voir	Presented to the Académie in 1742.	Gallon, *Machines et inventions*, VII, 183.
1759	Crescendo and variation of tone through knee levers.	Welman	Presented to the Académie in 1759. Precedes Taskin.	*Histoire*, 1759, p. 241.
1765	Claviorganum. Two manuals, one for the organ and one for the harpsichord. Fitted with a crescendo knee lever which advanced a buff stop.	Jean Antoine Berger	Presented to the Académie in 1765.	*Almanach Dauphin* (Paris, 1777), p. 45. *Annonces, Affiches de Paris*, 1770 (Sept.), p. 151; 1765 (Oct. 23).
Between 1766 and 1780	Nonenharmonic keyboard.	Pascal Taskin (maker)	Made to the order of M. Chiquelier, *Garde des instruments de la musique du Roi*.	De la Borde, *Essai sur la musique* (1780), I, 344.

324

Date	Purpose and nature of invention	Inventor	Remarks	Source
1768	"Clavecin acoustique." Imitated several instruments and even the voice.	De Virbés (organist)	Presented to the Académie in 1768.	Mercure de France, 1768 (Jan.), p. 207; 1773 (Apr.), II, 194; 1776 (June), p. 208; Almanach Dauphin, 1777, p. 46; E. I. Gerber, Lexicon (1790–1792), II, table, and II, 39.
1769	Leather plectra (probably peau de buffle) combined with pedals to advance the registers by degrees to provide a crescendo. Also a pedal controlled buff stop. It was claimed that these plectra lasted four or five years.	De l'Aine (music master)	The Encyclopédie states that the crescendo does not work well because the plectra hang on the strings when the register is in the advanced position.	Mercure de France, 1769 (Aug.), p. 205. Almanach Dauphin, 1771, "Delaine."
ca. 1770	Music noting device to record improvisations.	Marie Dominique Joseph Engramelle	Assisted Dom Bedos in his discussion of mechanical instruments.	De la Borde, Essai, II, 622. Fétis, "Engramelle."
1773	Device to provide crescendo.	De la Pleigniere (Ecuyer du Roi, Caën)	Details not given although the inventor states they are not secret.	Mercure de France, 1773 (April), II, 197.
1776	Upright harpsichord with a light action. (2 x 8', à grand ravalement, 8-feet high with stand.)	Gosset (luthier at Rheims)	"Convenient for apartments."	Mercure de France, 1776 (Sept.), p. 187.
1782	Nonenharmonic keyboard.	L'Abbé Roussier	Presented to the Académie in 1782.	Roussier, Mémoire sur le nouveau clavecin chromatique de M. de Laborde (Paris, 1782).
1787	Harpsichord or piano with a series of replaceable keyboards for growing children.			Mercure de France, 1787 (Apr.), p. 191.
ca. 1790	Screw regulated wrest pins. Two ends of one piece of wire provided unisons as in the modern piano.	Pascal Taskin (maker)	A piano with this device by Taskin in 1790 is to be found in the Palais de Versailles.	Encyclopédie méthodique, Musique, I, 288.

APPENDIX E · THE PEDAL

The inconclusive information bearing on the identity of the maker of the "Pedal" is as follows:

1) John (I) Haward: Maker of the 1622 harpsichord at Knole. There was a maker of this name resident in the Parish of St. Helen Bishopsgate in 1649. In 1658 an apprentice, Corney Barres, was bound to "John Haward the Elder," implying that John I was still alive.

2) John (II) Haward: A maker of this name admitted to the Joiners' Company in 1647–48. He is probably not identical with John I because several apprentices were bound to a John Haward between 1622 and this date. Therefore John I must have been a member already.

3) John (III) Haward: Admitted to the Joiners' Company by patrimony in 1652. It seems more likely that he was the son of John I than John II.

Boalch suggests that John I died in 1667 (although he does not state his exact reasons for so believing). The earliest reference to the Pedal is 1664. Therefore it is quite possible that John I invented it. On the other hand, John II and John III were also flourishing by that date and either might have been responsible.

Mace implies (as Boalch points out) that several makers produced Pedals: "because Few make of Them Well." Mace, himself, may not have dealt directly with the inventor when he obtained his own example, for his phrase is vague: "an Instrument of a Late Invention, contriv'd (as I have been informed), by one Mr. John Haward of London." It seems reasonable to assume that several of the members of the Haward family made pedals occasionally.

APPENDIX F · THE GUT-STRINGED HARPSICHORD

Frequent references to the gut-stringed harpsichord are to be found from the earliest times until the end of the eighteenth century, but there are no extant instruments which are identifiable as having been fitted with gut strings. The vague outlines of this phenomenon are made still more dubious by the fact that any of the short-scaled Italian harpsichords might originally have had gut strings. I have conducted certain simple experiments which demonstrated that gut can easily be brought up to modern pitch at a ten-inch scale.[1] Since gut strings are much thicker than those of steel or brass, the layout of a complex instrument is difficult to accomplish in the limited space available. Therefore the makers would have had a strong motive to keep gut-stringed instruments simple. This motive would have been reinforced by the instability in tuning of gut-stringed instruments which would have made a multichoired gut-stringed harpsichord almost impossible to keep in tune. Thus it seems reasonable to guess that the 1x8′ Italian harpsichords might have been specifically planned for gut strings. It must be remembered, however, that several German sources refer to more elaborate dispositions.

The following selection of the most important references to the gut-stringed harpsichord are arranged by order of the period to which the texts refer rather than by the exact date of origin.

1511. VIRDUNG, *Musica getutscht* (Basel).

[Speaking of the *clauiciteriũ* or the *clauicimbalũ*:] This is like the *virginale* except that it has different strings of the gut of sheep, and nails which make it harp. It also has quills like the *virginale*. It is newly invented and I have seen only one.

ca. 1778. V.A.L. IN THE *Encyclopédie*, "Epinette" (Geneva).

Two hundred years ago . . . the strings were of gut and consequently the tone was sweet and soft; dampness or dryness put the instrument out of tune every day. One still finds a few of these old harpsichords in Paris and in the large cities of the Low Countries and Germany.

[1] I am bound to report that gut strings on an Italian harpsichord sound very badly. For purposes of comparison it is interesting to note that the violin has a 10½″ scale on the A string and nearly 16″ on the E string which was formerly of gut!

1791. HULLMANDEL IN THE *Encyclopédie méthodique, Musique* (Paris), I, 286b.

[Farini] mounted some of his harpsichords with gut strings. There are still some of them in several Italian cities which attest to the advantage of these strings over those of iron or copper for the quality of tone.

1636. MERSENNE, *Harmonie universelle* (Paris), bk. III, p. 104.

Strings of gut, silk, gold, or silver can also be put on the spinet, but experiment reveals that those of gut are not as suitable as those of brass because they change their pitch too easily in wet or dry weather and are not as uniform or equal in every part as those of metal; and those of silk are still more uneven than those of gut.

1732. WALTHER, *Musicalisches Lexicon*, "Fleischer," (Leipzig).

Fleischer, Johann Christoph: a very famous and experienced maker . . . [who made a] theorbo harpsichord with sixteen-foot tone, and a lute harpsichord with eight-foot tone. The former had three registers of which two were strung with gut and the third with metal. The latter had two gut-stringed unison choirs. The remarkable fact was that the gut strings held their tuning at least as well as the metal.

1768. AGRICOLA IN A FOOTNOTE TO ADLUNG, *Musica mechanica organoedi* (Berlin), II, 139.

The writer of these footnotes remembers about the year 1740 having seen and heard a lute-harpsichord in Leipzig which had been suggested by Mr. Johann Sebastian Bach, and made by Mr. Zacharias Hildebrand.[2] It was of smaller size than the usual harpsichord but otherwise was like any other. It had two choirs of gut strings and a so-called little octave four-foot of brass strings. It is true that in its regular setting (that is, when only one stop was drawn) it resembled the theorbo more than the lute. But when the stop which on harpsichords is called the buff stop, which was just like that of harpsichords, was drawn with the cornet stop,[3] it was almost possible to deceive even professional lute players. Mr. Friderici[4] also made similar instruments, but with a few changes.

[2] Of Münsterberg, organ builder, pupil of Gottfried Silbermann (Boalch).

[3] It is not clear whether the cornet stop was simply the four-foot, or whether it consisted of some sort of movable batten on the soundboard or wrest plank which could carry a set of pins into contact with the strings forming a node at the midpoint, thus causing the pitch of the string to rise one octave. On page 266 above there are two quotations from Halle which seem to bear out the assumption that the cornet stop and the four-foot were identical. On the other hand, we find Sprengel referring to the cornet stop as "string-shortening"; Gall follows him in stating that, "The string-shortening *Kornettzug* is obsolete" (see page 270). In the next breath Gall adds, "The four-foot turns up on harpsichords too"; thus it seems that he distinguished between the four-foot and the cornet stop.

[4] The surname of at least five related instrument makers.

1750. THE "SPECIFICATIO" OF J. S. BACH'S ESTATE. QUOTED FROM MENDEL, *The Bach Reader,* p. 193.

"1 Lauten Werck . . ." [lute-harpsichord]

1768. ADLUNG, *Musica mechanica organoedi* (Berlin) II, 135.

Up to now I have seen no other example than that made in Jena by J. N. Bach,[5] which, however, is certainly very successful. It is almost in the shape of a harpsichord and the strings run toward the tail. Since lute strings vary in thickness not in length, it is done that way here; at least the variation in length is not so pronounced as in the case of the harpsichord. As a result the tail of the instrument is not as narrow and pointed. The rest of the case is similar as is the soundboard, keyboard, jacks (which pluck with ravens' quills), the wrest pins etc. The difference lies chiefly in the strings and bridges. These must be gut lute strings, otherwise the instrument would not have a lute tone, and their length must bear a true proportion to their length on the lute. Strictly speaking, one should have a specific string for each key as regards thickness, but where could one find so many [sizes] as there are keys from C to c'''. Thus one must take the string length from a lute by means of a compass, this is, from the bridge to the point where the finger stops the string, and these lengths are to be laid out on the lute-harpsichord. Then the front row of wrest pins are set out as in the harpsichord, but one should not fit a bridge like that of the harpsichord, for each string has its own bridge which rests on the soundboard and is not more than an inch tall, and preferably not that large. If one begins with bass C as does the lute, the length of the lute string from nut to bridge is measured and the same length is laid out on the string of the lute-harpsichord from the front bridge [nut] toward the rear, and the small bridge is placed wherever the length ends. C♯ should be a little shorter but the same thickness string can be used. The rear bridge is placed slightly farther forward, as much as the distance involved in a semitone on the lute. There is a particular string for D on the lute, hence we provide its full length here. The D♯, however, loses as much in length as the string shortens when I stop D♯ on the lute. And so it goes with the following: where a lute string has more than one stop length, then one retains one string size for several courses on the lute harpsichord and makes it ever shorter as much as it loses in length on the lute through stopping the string. So it goes to c'''. The rest one can supply for himself.

However, the strings on a lute do not rest on wire [pins] but only on the wooden bridges above and below. It must be this way on both bridges if the tone is not to be spoiled. No pins are inserted, as on the harpsichord, but the strings simply run over the wooden bridges and are affixed to the hitchpins. One must avoid any arris in order that they do not cut. Although there can be no sharp corners as the strings lie free on the bridges, yet one can make

[5] Johann Nikolaus Bach (1669–1753). He does not appear to have been a full-time professional maker although Adlung reports that he paid him sixty Reichsthaler for a three-manual lute-harpsichord. Agricola considered this "eine erschreckliche Summe." Adlung mentions (II, 138) that Johann Georg Gleichmann also made lute-harpsichords.

slight grooves in which they lie. In order to prevent the force of the quills raising the strings, screw the bridge on from underneath through thin four-cornered blocks, two by two. If the soundboard is planed quite thin like that of the lute and the length of the strings is justly proportioned to their thickness, and they lie on wood, and the pluck takes place by means of the jacks exactly as when it is done by the finger, then it must necessarily sound like a lute, and indeed, of the best grade and with much more charm, for the resonance will be stronger since the soundboard is larger and because so many strings lie there quite free, producing a simultaneous sound when other strings harmonious to them are plucked. Thus Mr. J. N. Bach has deceived the best lutenists when he has played and not permitted his lute-harpsichord to be seen, for one would swear that it was an ordinary lute [6] . . . Mr. Bach makes two or three keyboards, one *forte*, as when the lute plays in its usual way (indeed, if it plays its loudest the tone is still rather weak), the next *piano*, the third *piu piano*, and in this way one gets over the difficulty somewhat.[7] The only question is this: How are the strings arranged? Answer: It works out very badly if one uses doubled strings or even tripled as on the harpsichord.[8] Rather one lets all the keyboards pluck the one string with their jacks. The jacks are near one another, three by three, as on the harpsichord, each in its mortise. The quills are of equal stiffness, and even so, one register of jacks plucks more strongly than another. How does that happen? Answer: The front row plucks very close to the nut, hence the tone is loud. The next rank, on the middle keyboard, plucks farther from the nut, and this produces a weaker tone. The back row is most distant from the nut and thus plucks most softly.

[6] Adlung gives tips for imitating the style of the lutenists.
[7] That is, that of imitating the dynamic variation of the lute.
[8] Below (II, 138) Adlung seems to contradict this statement: "The lute has two strings per course in the bass and one in the treble. The lute-harpsichord must be made in the same way."

APPENDIX G · THE BACH DISPOSITION

An unsigned, undated harpsichord once believed to have belonged to Bach is the only extant old harpsichord known to me which might bolster the case for the so-called Bach disposition. This is No. 316 of the *Staatliche Sammlung für Musikinstrumente* in the charge of the *Institut für Musikforschung* at the Schloss Charlottenburg in Berlin. It cannot be absolutely proved that its present disposition is not original but presumptive evidence weighs heavily against it. The harpsichord has been restored many times as physical traces and inscriptions on the interior indicate. The case is of pine with a round tail, and the general form and dimensions strongly suggest the Hamburg school. At present there are four choirs and four registers arranged in the Bach disposition. There are only two bridges on the soundboard in the normal positions for the four-foot and eight-foot choirs. Three nuts at three levels are placed on the wrest plank. The lowest carries the four-foot, the second the two eight-foot choirs, and the highest, the sixteen-foot. These distinct levels are maintained in the choirs of strings at the gap so that the jacks pluck at three different heights in the customary arrangement for four-choired instruments. In the treble the eight-foot choirs pass through holes drilled into the eight-foot bridge considerably below its top, but as soon as the bridge has curved a bit away from the gap both eight-foot and sixteen-foot strings are pinned to the top of the bridge. The distance of the bridge from the gap permits this arrangement without destroying the assignment of the choirs to three levels at the plucking points.

This arrangement carries no internal evidence of the disposition at the time the harpsichord left its maker's hands. The wrest plank has obviously been reworked and the present distribution of the eight-foot bridge pins in the treble could easily have been made at a late date. Fortunately a relatively unaltered harpsichord made by H. A. Hasch (Hass) in 1723, now in the Musikhistorisk Museum, Copenhagen, is very close to No. 316 in basic dimensions and may represent the original form of the latter.

	Hasch 1723	*No. 316*
Length	93½″	94⅝″
Width	37½″	38″
Cheekpiece	29½″	29⁹⁄₁₆″
Range	FF–c‴	FF–f‴

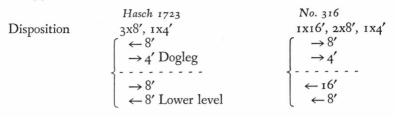

Disposition

	Hasch 1723	No. 316
	3x8′, 1x4′	1x16′, 2x8′, 1x4′

Hasch 1723:
- ← 8′
- → 4′ Dogleg
- - - - - - - -
- → 8′
- ← 8′ Lower level

No. 316:
- → 8′
- → 4′
- - - - - -
- ← 16′
- ← 8′

	Hasch 1723		No. 316	
	8′ scale	8′ plucking point	8′ scale	8′ plucking point
c‴	7¹⁄₁₆″	2⅛″	6½″	1⅞″
c″	13¾″	3¹⁄₁₆″	12⅜″	2½″
c′	25½″	3⅞″	26⅛″	3¼″
c	44⅝″	4¾″	42⅞″	4″
C	62⅝″	5¹¹⁄₁₆″	60½″	4¹⁵⁄₁₆″

Hasch placed the three eight-foot choirs on one nut with two levels, 1x8′ on the lower level, and 2x8′ pinned to the top of the nut. The upper manual slid in to couple. In the half-way position it engaged the dogleg of the four-foot jack. The resulting registrations were:

With coupler completely disengaged:
    Upper: 1x8′
    Lower: 2x8′, 1x4′
With coupler in the intermediate position:
    Upper: 1x8′, 1x4′
    Lower: 2x8′, 1x4′
With coupler completely engaged:
    Upper: 1x8′, 1x4′
    Lower: 3x8′, 1x4′

It will be noted that the Hasch harpsichord had *two* strings at the top level, *one* string at the intermediate level, and one string at the lowest level. At the gap No. 316 now has *one* string at the highest level, *two* strings in the intermediate position, and one on the bottom. The back eight-foot register of No. 316 which now plucks at the intermediate level has an old mortise in each tongue about one-quarter inch above the present quill, indicating that it once plucked at the higher level. This suggests that No. 316 once had its choirs arranged in the same manner as the Hasch. An overspun sixteen-foot string vibrates with too much amplitude to be safely placed at the same level as an eight-foot choir. One needs all possible space to avoid its buzzing on the backs of the adjacent jacks. Therefore we may assume that the arrangement of the choirs in No. 316 was altered to permit the safe substitution of a sixteen-foot choir for the third eight-foot choir.

As I have noted, the present orientation of nuts on the wrest plank of No. 316 does not look old. It will be observed that its scale *and* plucking points are consistently shorter than those of the Hasch. This fact also supports the hypothesis of an alteration from 3x8′, 1x4′, to 1x16′, 2x8′, 1x4′. Where Hasch was able to place 3x8′ choirs on one two-level nut, the rebuilder of No. 316 had to provide a third nut, farther from the gap in order to get as long a sixteen-foot scale as possible. To find sufficient space on the wrest plank he was forced to move the eight-foot nut forward, thus shortening the eight-foot scale and plucking points to a degree most unlike the Hamburg school.

The present upper manual of No. 316 is too long to have operated a dog-leg jack, but its antiquity is rather dubious. The jacks themselves show enough evidence of alteration and rearrangement to make credible the assumed elimination of the dogleg projection which once reached to the lower manual.

Thus in No. 316 we are faced with an instrument which easily could have been altered to its present highly unusual disposition from the observed disposition of a very similar and absolutely authentic harpsichord. Further evidence suggests that this was, in fact, done. The provision for the present sixteen-foot choir does not resemble that ordinarily made by Hass or other makers. We usually find a special sixteen-foot bridge sufficiently distant from the nut to give a decent scale. The case of the harpsichord is enlarged enough to permit adequate space for soundboard around this sixteen-foot bridge. The following comparison of No. 316 to a 1710 J. A. Hass (now in the Yale University Collection of Musical Instruments) and a 1734 H. A. Hass (now in the Conservatoire Royal de Musique, Brussels) indicates how the sixteen-foot choir has been crammed into an undersized case in No. 316.

	1710	1734	No. 316
c‴	13⅞″	14¹⁵⁄₁₆″	10″
Length	109″	105″	94⅝″

No. 316 fits into the Hass tradition so neatly if one assumes an original 3x8′, 1x4′, disposition, and so badly if one accepts the present disposition that I am forced to relegate its sixteen-foot choir to the limbo of late accretions.

APPENDIX H · THE CLAVIORGANUM

The idea of combining an organ with a harpsichord seems to have been hit upon very early and to have been applied intermittently throughout the history of the harpsichord. Extant claviorgana are extremely rare, but the following may be cited as fine examples:

1) Alexander Bortolotti (1585), Conservatoire Royal de Musique, Brussels.

    1 manual
      GG/BB–c'''
        Harpsichord: 1x8', 1x4'
        Organ: 4' flute (wood), quint (wood), 2' prestant

2) Lodowicus Theewes (1579), Victoria and Albert Museum, London.

    1 manual
      C–c'''
        Harpsichord: 2x8', 1x4'
        Organ: 5 stops

3) Jacob Kirckman and John Snetzler (1750), Privately owned, United Kingdom.[1]

    2 manuals
      FF–f'''
      (no FF♯)
        Harpsichord: 2x8', 1x4', lute
        Organ: 5 stops

Several authorities mention the claviorganum. Among these are Bottrigari (1594), Praetorius (1619), Charles Butler (1636), Kircher (1650), Nassare (1723), Adlung (1758 and 1768), Burney (1771), Dom Bedos (1778), and the *Encyclopédie méthodique* (1791).[2] Like the *Geigenwerk* and the clavicytherium, the claviorganum was never common and was regarded everywhere as something of a phenomenon. Adlung remarked that they were more

---

[1] See Boalch, *Makers of the Harpsichord and Clavichord*, p. 67.

[2] Bottrigari, *Il Desiderio*, p. 10; Praetorius, *Syntagma musicum*, pt. II, chap. XLII (see Appendix A); Butler, *The Principles of Musick*, p. 93; Kircher, *Musurgia universalis*, I, 67; Nassare, *Escuela musica*, I, 465; Adlung, *Anleitung zu der musikalischen Gelahrtheit*, p. 563, and *Musica mechanica organoedi*, II, 98; Burney, *The Present State of Music in France and Italy*, p. 103; Dom Bedos, *L'Art du facteur d'orgues*, II, 641; and *Encyclopédie méthodique, Musique*, I, 286b.

numerous in his younger days than at the time of writing (1758). We quote several of the most informative discussions of the claviorganum.

FROM BUTLER, *The Principles of Musick in Singing and Setting* (1636), p. 93.[3]

And these latter curious times have conjoined two or more in one: making the *Organ* and the *Virginal* to go both together with the same keys: yea & with the same keys to sound divers pipes of the *organ* (grave & acute) by reason of the new-invented divers stops.[4]

FROM DUFOURCQ, *Remarques sur le clavier*, p. 225. A contract for the installation of organ stops in a harpsichord. Archives Nationales, Minutier Central, XXIV, 347, fol. 355.

[Paris, November 8, 1637]
Being present the nobleman, Pierre Chabanseau [*sic*], Sieur de la Barre, organist to the King and Queen, party of the first part, and Valeran de Heman, maker of organs, living in Paris, Rue Sainct Martin, Parish of St. Laurent, party of the second part. The parties stating that they were about to enter into litigation concerning the execution of a contract agreed on between them ten or eleven years ago before notaries for the construction of five stops under a harpsichord, undertaken by the said de Heman for the said Sr. de la Barre for the consideration of 200 *livres* . . . the said parties have compromised the said difference as follows: to wit that because of failing to satisfy the said Sr. de la Barre on the stipulations of the said contract, the said de Heman has promised and promises in place of the said five stops to provide three stops to the said Sr. de la Barre during next Pentecost, to wit, a stopped flute four feet long, sounding eight-foot, which stop will be of cypress wood, plus another stopped two-foot stop, sounding at four-foot, of the same wood, and the other stop a *musette* reed of copper at eight-foot pitch, the said stops will be divided [*couppez*] wherever the said Sr. de la Barre pleases. Plus two bellows of which the sides will be of beech and the top and the bottom of oak or of lime, garnished with good leather inside and out, and the said de Heman will provide everything required for the perfection of the said project which will render it well and properly made and finished in the express opinion of experts and men acquainted with these matters, the said Sr. de la Barre will furnish a harpsichord to make the said organ play which the said de Heman agrees to return in the same condition that it was delivered to him . . .

[Signed] Pierre Chabenceau
de Heman
Contesse Chapellain

[3] Butler apparently had views on the reformation of English spelling and couched his treatise in a curious orthography which I have thought best to suppress. He was also the author of a grammar and a manual for bee-keepers.
[4] The claviorganum was well known in England at an early period. See p. 136.

FROM NASSARE, *Escuela musica* (1723–1724), p. 465.[5]

Those called Claviorgana [*claviorganos*] are instruments which produce their sounds in two different ways, one by means of metal strings, and the other by means of pipes [*flautas*] like the organ. Ordinarily these are of pyramidal shape, having the keys at the base or widest end. It has a wind chest [*secreto*] like that in Organs, although no larger than is necessary for two or three rows of pipes, which are in the single cavity [*cóncavo*]. It is commonly a flute [*flautado*] of an intonation of seven fourths [*siete quartas* ?], with octave; and some are wont to carry another rank at the quint [*quincena*].

The material of the majority of said pipes is wood of square section, and they are accommodated lengthwise in the cavity. The wind chest is as long as the whole of the keyboard and a little more, and is accommodated below the latter; but it is no wider than the keys at the part where they are played. The reservoir [*arca del viento*], which is a little less than the whole wind chest, has the bellows outside the body of the instrument, but they are not always permanent on it, since they are taken off when it is not required that the pipes should sound. They are skilfully accommodated, so that they are fitted in position whenever needed, and are taken off with the same facility. They are movable, because as the instrument occupies so much space, it may occupy less without them, when it is not necessary that they should be in position. The wind chest has its pallets [*ventillas*] which are opened with stickers [*pisantes*]: it also has its sliders [*registrillos*], for in those which have more than one flute, the wind chest carries as many sliders as there are ranks of pipes additional to it in the said instrument. All this is with respect to the pipe work [*cañutería*]; with respect to the strings I will say now that these run over the empty space [*cóncavo*] and are of steel. The lowest string of the bass is of a length of about ten *quartas* [83.7 inches] and they run in diminution up to the highest in the treble, which in order that it may have the proportionate sound, is of a length of somewhat less than a *tercia* [10.35 inches] and somewhat more than a *quarta* [8.37 inches].[6]

Instruments of this kind are ordinarily a tone lower than the natural tone; and without doubt the Ancients had two reasons for setting them so, the one that it was necessary that the instrument would be of a length of eleven to twelve *quartas* [124¾ inches to 133 inches], which it ordinarily is, so that the pipe work might be accommodated within the space; and the length being such, the string cannot attain the natural tone, wherefore it is necessary that it be lower. The second reason is that in times when instruments of this kind were performed on more than now, they were fre-

---

[5] It is unfortunate that the single extended description of the harpsichord and claviorganum in Spanish that I have been able to find should have been written by such a pedant as Nassare. He seems to have been caught in his cant to the point of being utterly unable to describe what lay before his eyes. The present translation was very kindly procured for me by Raymond Russell, but I am responsible for the interpretation of the technical terms.

[6] An impossibly long scale if the range goes much above c″. Nassare is probably thinking of c″, in which case the scale is a short, Italian type.

quently used for accompanying natural voices; and for more restful singing it was convenient that they should have a tone lower than the natural. And although it is conjectured that these are the reasons why these instruments have a lower tone, there is no doubt that they can be at the usual pitch; since, although it be a *quarta* less in length, the accommodation of the pipe work in it can involve little or no difficulty; because, if the latter is to be in the natural tone, its length has necessarily to be less.

. . . Among stringed instruments this is one of those possessing the greatest number and the most delectable of notes, and I do not know why the use of it has been lost; since one finds only the occasional one, although I conjecture that the lack of artificers is the reason why it is not more performed upon in these times.

. . . The material has to be, as in all the other instruments, very solid massive wood, except for the soundboards [*tapas*], and these, as in all the instruments as I have already stated, are to be of fir [*Pino avete*], which is to be of the finest or minutest grain.

. . . The sounding of the strings alone is achieved by not giving air to the pipes; but when the stop is pushed in, so that the jacks are supported by the keys,[7] and air is given to the pipe work, everything sounds together.

The jacks [*martinetes*] are to be of strong and heavy wood; strong, so that as they are delicate parts they may have durability; and they are to be very smooth, so that they rise and fall swiftly without any check. It is necessary that they be of heavy wood, so that they fall quickly. The part in which they are is commonly called the register [*diapason*], because in it are distributed the sounds of the strings, the jacks being disposed so that each strikes its respective string. This part is also to be of strong wood of square section; the thickness of it depends upon how much the *cóncavo* of the instrument rises above the keyboard, and the artificer must use his discretion, so that there remains sufficient space between the said register and the keyboard for a hand to be inserted to adjust whatever may be necessary; but the part must always be of a thickness little less than two *dedos* [ca. 1½ inches], which together with another two or three *dedos* which there may be of distance from it to the keys, suffices.[8]

. . . Everything that I have said is very essential for the instrument of the Claviorganum; and although I have not stated the proportions in which the pipes must be, because I leave it for when I write of those of the Organ, I only advise that the strings run an octave below the flute [that is, four-foot organ, eight-foot harpsichord].

. . . Of all these kinds of harpsichords [*clavicordios*], with which I have dealt, there is no doubt that the most pleasing are those which are least prac-

---

[7] Nassare describes a rather unlikely mechanism in which each jack is supported by a narrow block on the rear of the key. When the stop is "off" the jacks do not rest on the blocks and do not move with the keys. Small projections on the jacks prevent them from falling through the registers. I suspect that Nassare did not understand how a stop is canceled on a harpsichord by retiring the plectra from the strings and invented something plausible to do the job.

[8] It will be noted that the registers are of the box type, implying an Italianate tradition.

ticed, such as the Claviorgana, and those which carry three choirs of strings. They are more costly to make, and without doubt this will be the reason for their not being in greater use, and on account of there being few artificers in Spain and this has caused me to give these rules, with which, and what can be seen in others, they may be successfully constructed.

FROM ADLUNG, *Musica mechanica organoedi* (1768), II, 98.

Furthermore I have seen a *Positiv* made in almost the same manner in which the pipes stood at a high pitch, and above them there was an *Instrument* which worked from the same keyboard. Now the *Positiv* had its own register so that it could be obtained solo, or it could be taken off and the stringed instrument played alone since that part could be stilled and made to play again by means of a stop knob as is to be seen in harpsichords (see below, par. 528).

FROM DOM BEDOS, *L'Art du facteur d'orgues* (1768), II, 641.

We will suppose that this harpsichord is large and *à ravalement* from "F" to "F" bass and treble.[9] That is to say that the keyboards will be of five octaves. We will further suppose that one wishes to install a four-foot stopped diapason, a two-foot stopped prestant; a *dessus* at eight-foot, unstopped, an oboe of which the bass will be a bassoon. After one has seen how these stops can be gotten in one will perceive that the rest of the job is similar to the organization of the piano forte [that is, combining a piano with an organ].[10]

[9] Dom Bedos should have said *à grand ravalement* for an FF to f‴ keyboard.
[10] Dom Bedos gives a thorough explanation of the process of making the organ part of the claviorganum. He provides two plates, reproduced here as Plates XVI and XVII.

APPENDIX I · THE TRAITÉ DES INSTRUMENTS DE MUSIQUE OF PIERRE TRICHET

Trichet's manuscript, composed about 1640, serves to illuminate and steady the pedantic fancies of Mersenne. Trichet, a lawyer of Bordeaux, seemed to his twentieth-century editor[1] to have been a bit more realistic than the learned humanist. Thus we might fairly hope to unravel some of the mysteries of the *Harmonie universelle* by consulting Trichet's sober pages. To some extent this hope is realized in his discussion of the spinet and the manner in which one spinet was placed on the top of another. Unfortunately, the profoundest riddle in Mersenne, that of the eudisharmoste, is not solved, for Trichet follows the holy father so closely that one is forced to conclude that he was not writing from his own experience but that of Mersenne, which leaves us more or less where we were.

"OF THE SPINET"

The spinet [*espinette*] is a very commonly used instrument at this time, both in France and elsewhere. I believe that it was formerly unknown since one does not find the word in the works of the Greek and Latin authors which remain to us from antiquity. One of the principal parts of the spinet is the keyboard composed of forty-nine keys similar on the outside to those of the organ and equal in number as I have said in the first book . . .

The keyboard of the spinet is different from that of the organ only in that the keys are lengthened quite far in order to support and move the jacks which enter through little openings made in the mortise [sic].[2] Each jack being of suitable length is furnished at the top with a little tongue cleverly set within and easily moved by a little spring made of hog's bristle which must pass through a little hole that is made in the jack, finally to return accurately to the tongue which must be pierced together with the jack by an iron wire that serves as an axle. At the top of the tongue a point of crow quill is inserted and passes through to pluck the string. Beside the tongue on the top of the jack a little saw cut is made in which to insert and attach a little piece of scarlet cloth which stops the continuing sound of the string after the jack

---

[1] François Lesure (Neuilly-sur-Seine: Société de Musique d'Autrefois, 1957). The selections from *Traité des instruments de musique* are translated here with the kind permission of the publishers.

[2] Further on Trichet speaks of the soundboard as the *"table supérieure."* The *mortaise* may thus be the lower guide.

is lowered. Furthermore a flat bar of wood covered with cloth on the underside is placed above the jacks against which they strike, not being able to leap higher or to make any noise because of the cloth. It is also necessary to cover with cloth the ends of the keys which support the jacks in order to prevent noise. It is enough to glue the cloth at the two ends without placing glue in the middle so that this part touches the jacks more softly. The upper table of the spinet should be of very thin pine [*sapin*] rather than of any other kind of wood, and it must be pierced obliquely in as many places as there are jacks to make them pass through to meet the strings, the material of which is ordinarily steel or brass. It is necessary to lay out and arrange the angle on the two bridges glued to the soundboard [*table de dessus*], one drawn out in a straight line and the other broken into two. The strings are fixed at one end by immovable nails or pins [*pointes*], and at the other end wrapped around movable iron wrest pins which are turned by means of a key combined with a little iron hammer that has a small hook in the middle of its head to twist the ends and form the eyes of the strings that one wishes to attach. One can use either yellow or white strings,[3] but white strings are used in the treble because they are stronger and can be tuned higher. It is necessary to have several different sizes, at least from four to six, to equip a spinet suitably. The smallest and most delicate, which are of the first size, are used for the treble, and the others which follow continually increase in size by degrees until the last and lowest string. Before stretching the strings across the bridges the soundboard should be made smooth and polished by rubbing it with shavegrass in the same way as one polishes the keys of a keyboard made of boxwood, ivory, or ebony.

After the invention of simple spinets some subtle spirits of our century, not content that each key have a single string, have sought means to fit others and to multiply them in a marvelous way. They have succeeded so well that it is now possible for anyone to have double, triple, and quadruple spinets — that is to say with two, three, and four stops; some[4] have even managed to make spinets of such ingenuity that by playing on the keyboard of one, the other plays likewise. This is done in this way: it is necessary that one of the spinets be large and the other smaller and that they be tuned — if one wishes — an octave apart. But I note that one can play them separately. Nevertheless one can join them by removing the jack rail of the large one and placing the smaller spinet on the other. But it is necessary to make them so that the jacks of the large one exactly meet the ends of the keys of the small one, to which end one must make openings underneath at the place where the keys end. To play them it is necessary to use the lower keyboard and through its design one will see that the upper keyboard will obey the lower without being touched as far as one can see.

But there is another way to make two spinets play together, or even a spinet and an organ, using the keyboard of a spinet placed on the other or on an organ made expressly. This can be done easily if one keyboard corresponds exactly to the other and is directly above. As many coupler dogs [*vergettes*]

[3] That is, brass or steel.
[4] I have read *quelques-uns* for *qu'aucuns*.

as there are keys are arranged between the two keyboards so that each key has its coupler dog which can reach from the upper key to that which corresponds to it underneath. And finally, so that these coupler dogs cannot fly out [extravaguer], it is necessary to have one or two thin panels and to make in them as many holes as there are coupler dogs through which they can slip easily if one has made the holes accurately and in the right place. By this means, in striking the keys of the upper keyboard, one will push down those of the lower keyboard, which is the opposite of the preceding operation. When the spinet and the organ are joined together one gives them the name *espinette organizée,* and Michel Praetorius calls it *claviorganum* . . .

I leave all these new inventions to say another word about the simple spinet, more frequently used. I say then that it is a very suitable instrument for those who are sedentary and who rarely leave the house, but chiefly for girls. That is why it is called in latin *virginale.* It is also called *harpsichordum* in my opinion because it resembles a reversed harp. But *spinetta* is the commonest and most used name. It is possible to say of the spinet that it does not have the convenience of the lute in being easily transported here and there, but that in any case it has the advantage over [the lute] of being able to remain in tune longer and of holding tune without being touched for a whole month, where it is necessary to tune the lute every minute . . .

"OF THE HARPSICHORD [*clavecin*]"

Since the harpsichord is a modern instrument it should not be found strange if the name that has been given it is also new. Jules de l'Escale and the translator of Jean Heyden [5] call it in latin *clavicymbalum,* and others *clavicitherium.* If it conforms to the spinet in the appurtenances of its keyboard, which has a number of keys equal to that of the clavichord [*manichordion*] and the organ, it differs in its shape and in the arrangement of its strings. The construction and form of the harpsichord is almost triangular while that of the spinet resembles a parallelogram of which the length exceeds the width. In the harpsichord the strings run longwise from the end of the front piece to the far end, as much from the other end as from the cut-off end [*retranchement*]; and in the spinet they run crosswise. Moreover in the arrangement of the parts of these two instruments there is this dissimilarity, that the keyboard of the harpsichord is at one end while the place for the keyboard of the spinet is always in the middle as is that of the clavichord. The tone and sound that result are almost the same, but the sound of the harpsichord is more powerful and brilliant [*esclattant*]; also spinets are not usually made like harpsichords with two or three keyboards and seven or eight stops,[6] each of which can be produced separately, or can be played alternately by changing them, mixing them, and joining all of them together in the same way as is done on the organ. This is achieved by means of springs and registers easy to draw that cause the jack to pluck

[5] Hans Haiden, author of *Commentatio de musicali instrumenti,* Nuremberg, 1605; and *Musicale instrumentum reformatum,* Nuremberg, 1610; inventor of a *Geigenwerk.*

[6] The passage which follows is obviously adapted from Mersenne.

whichever rank of strings one wishes. If one is content to have a single keyboard with registers [7] but nevertheless one desires to vary the stops a little, one manages it so that the keyboard can be pulled out a little and pushed in when necessary, and by this means the ends of the keys will meet the rank of jacks that one wishes to put into action. Some find this easier than to have three keyboards and several registers sometimes badly adjusted.

[7] That is, movable registers.

BIBLIOGRAPHY

Abridgements of Specifications Relating to Music and Musical Instruments, A.D. 1694–1861, Office of the Commissioners of Patents for Inventions, London, 1864.

Adlung, Jakob, *Anleitung zu der musikalischen Gelahrtheit*, Erfurt, 1758.

——— *Musica mechanica organoedi*, Berlin, 1768. Facsimile by Bärenreiter, Kassel, 1931.

Affiches, annonces, et avis divers, Les. A bi-weekly periodical publication, Paris, from May 1751. Extracts are printed in De Bricqueville, q.v.

Agricola, Martin, *Musica instrumentalis deudsch*, Wittenberg, 1528.

Arnault de Zwolle, manuscript, MS fonds Latin 7295, Bibliothèque Nationale Paris. Edited by G. le Cerf and E. R. Labande, *Instruments de musique du XVᵉ siècle*, Paris, 1932.

Artusi, Giovanni Maria, *L'Artusi, ovvero delle imperfezzioni della moderna musica*, Venice, 1600.

Bach, Carl Philipp Emmanuel, *Versuch über die wahre Art das Clavier zu spielen*, Berlin, 1753. Translated by William J. Mitchell, *Essay on the True Art of Playing Keyboard Instruments*, New York, 1949.

Baines, Anthony, "James Talbot's Manuscript," *The Galpin Society Journal*, vol. 1 (1948).

Barbour, J. Murray, *Tuning and Temperament*, East Lansing, Mich., 1953.

Bedos de Celles, Dom François, *L'Art du facteur d'orgues*, Paris, 1766–1778.

Bemetzrieder, Anton, *Leçons de clavecin, et principes d'harmonie*, Paris, 1771.

Bendeler, Johann Philipp, *Orgel-Bau-Kunst*, Frankfurt, 1739 (written ca. 1690; originally published under the title *Organopoeia*, Frankfurt and Leipzig, n.d.).

Benelli, Alemanno. *See* Bottrigari, Ercole.

Berner, Alfred, "Zum Klavierbau im 17 und 18 Jahrhunderts" in (Kongress-Bericht) *Gesellschaft für Musikforschung*, Lüneburg, Germ., 1950.

Blankenburg, Quirinus van, *Elementa musica*, The Hague, 1739.

Boalch, Donald, *Makers of the Harpsichord and Clavichord*, London, 1955.

Bonanni, Filippo, *Gabinetto armonico*, Rome, 1722.

Bontempi, Giovanni Andrea, *Historia musica*, Perugia, 1695.

Bottrigari, Ercole (pseudonym for Alemanno Benelli), *Il Desiderio ovvero de'concerti di varii stromenti musicali*, Bologna, 1590. A facsimile of the second edition, Venice, 1594, was edited by Kathi Meyer, Berlin, 1924.

Bricqueville, Eugène de, *Les Ventes d'instruments de musique au XVIII siècle*, Paris, 1908.

Broadwood, H. F., ed., *Some Notes Made by J. S. Broadwood, 1838, with Observations and Elucidations by H. F. Broadwood*, London, 1862.

Bruni, Antonio Bartholomeo, inventory of instruments abandoned by *émigrés*, ed. by J. Gallay, q.v.

Burbure, the Chevalier Léon de, *Recherches sur les facteurs de clavecins et les luthiers d'Anvers*, Brussels, 1863.

Burney, Charles, *A General History of Music*, London, 1776–1788.

—— *The Present State of Music in France and Italy*, London, 1771.

—— *The Present State of Music in Germany, the Netherlands, and United Provinces*, London, 1773.

Butler, Charles, *The Principles of Musick in Singing and Setting*, London, 1636.

Carbassus, M. l'Abbé, *Lettre de M. l'Abbé Carbasus à M. de —— sur la mode des instrumens de musique*, Paris, 1739. Variously ascribed to the Abbé Goujet and François Campion; addressed to Voltaire. Reprinted in the *Encyclopédie méthodique*, "Arts et métiers méchaniques," IV, 9.

Caus, Salomon de, *Les Raisons des forces mouvantes avec diverses machines tant utilles que plaisantes aux quelles sont adioints plusieurs desseins de grotes & fontaines*, Paris, 1615 and 1624.

Chapman, R. E. See Mersenne.

Closson, Ernest, "L'Ornementation en papier imprimé des clavecins anversois," *Revue belge d'archeologie et d'histoire de l'art*, 2 (1932): 105.

—— "Pascal Taskin," *Sammelbände der Internationalen Musikgesellschaft*, 1910–1911, p. 234.

Corneille, Thomas, *Dictionnaire des arts, et des sciences par M.D.C. de l'Académie Française*, Paris, 1694.

Corrette, Michel, *Le Maître de clavecin*, Paris, 1753.

Couperin, François, *Apothéose, composé à la memoire immortelle de l'incomparable M. de Lully*, Paris, 1725, "Avis."

Cryseul, Géoffrion de, *Moyens de diviser les touches les plus correctements possible*, Paris, Lille, Valenciennes, Douai, 1780.

Dale, William, *Tschudi the Harpsichord Maker*, London, 1913.

David, Hans T., and Arthur Mendel, *The Bach Reader*, New York, 1945.

Day, Thomas, letters to Edward Hanford, quoted in *Apollo*, London, March 1950, p. 92.

Denis, Jean, *Traité de l'accord de l'espinette*, Paris, 1650.

Description abrégée des principaux arts et métiers, des instruments qui leurs sont propres etc., Paris, n.d.

Dictionnaire portatif de commerce, Liège, 1770.

Diderot, Denis, and Jean le Rond d'Alembert, eds., *Encyclopédie ou Dictionnaire raisonné des sciences, des arts, et des métiers*, Paris, 1751–1758, 28 vols. in folio, of which eleven consist of plates. Various editions in smaller format from 1777, especially in Switzerland. The additional information in these editions combined with a good deal of new material was incorporated into the *Encyclopédie méthodique, ou par ordre de matières par une societé de gens de lettres*, Paris, from 1782. As the title implied, all the articles under one general subject were collected together. Thus there were many alphabets in place of the single one of the earlier publication. Pertinent articles are found in the volumes entitled, *Arts et métiers méchaniques*, and particularly in vol. IV, *Instrumens de musique et lutherie (art du faiseur d')*, 1785; and in *Musique*, 2 vols., 1791 and 1818.

Diderot, Denis, *Rameau's Nephew and Other Works*, translated by Jacques Barzun and Ralph H. Bowen, New York, 1956.

Doni, Giovanni Battista, *Commentarii de Lyra Barberina*, Florence, 1763 (written ca. 1635).

——— *Compendio del trattatto dei generi e modi della musica*, Rome, 1635.

Doursther, Horace, *Dictionnaire universel des poids et mesures anciens et modernes*, Brussels, 1840.

Douwes, Klaas, *Grondig Ondersoek van de Toonen der Musijk*, Amsterdam, 1699.

Drechsel, F. A., "Alte Dresdener Instrumenteninventare," *Zeitschrift für Musikwissenschaft*, 10 (1927–1928): 495.

Dufourcq, Norbert, "Pierre Baillon, facteur de clavecins, d'orgues, graveur de musique et organiste français," *Music, Libraries and Instruments*, London, 1961, p. 196.

——— "Remarques sur le clavier (clavecin et orgue) dans la première moitié du XVIIᵉ siècle," *La Musique instrumentale de la renaissance*, Paris, 1955, p. 275.

Encyclopédie. See Diderot.

Encyclopédie méthodique. See Diderot.

Ernst, Friedrich, *Der Flügel Johann Sebastian Bachs*, Frankfurt, 1955.

Fétis, F. J., *Biographie universelle des musiciens*, Brussels, 1835–1844.

Gall, ed., *Clavier-Stimmbuch, oder deutliche Anweisung wie jeder Musikfreund sein Clavier-Flügel, Forte-piano und Flügel-Fortepiano selbst stimmen, repariren, und bestmöglichst gut erhalten könne*, Vienna, n.d.

Gallay, J., ed., *Un Inventaire sous la Terreur, état des instruments de musique relevé chez les émigrés et condamnés*, Paris, 1890.

Galpin, Francis W., *A Textbook of European Musical Instruments*, London, 1937.

Garsault, de, *Notionaire ou Mémorial raisonné de ce qu'il y a d'utile et d'intéressant dans les connoissances acquises depuis la création du monde jusqu'à présent*, Paris, 1761.

Gerber, Ernst Ludwig, *Historische-Biographisches Lexicon der Tonkunstler*, Leipzig, 1790–1792.

Gray, H. St. George, "A Virginal by Charles Rewallin," *Connaisseur*, 46:77.

Griselini, Francesco, *Dizionario delle arti e de' mestieri*, Venice, 1769, "Fabbricatore di clavi-cembali." A word-for-word translation from the *Encyclopédie*.

Halfpenny, Eric, "The Lyrachord," *The Galpin Society Journal*, 3 (1950): 46.

Halle, Johann Samuel, *Werkstäte der heutigen Künste*, Brandenburg and Leipzig, 1764.

Hardouin, Pierre J., "Harpsichord Making in Paris, Part I, Eighteenth Century," translated with a technical introduction and explanatory footnotes by Frank Hubbard, *The Galpin Society Journal*, no. 10 (1957); "Part II," *ibid*, no. 12 (1959); "Part III," *ibid*, no. 13 (1960).

———"Quelques documents relatifs aux Couperins," *Revue de musicologie*, 37 (Dec. 1955): 111.

Hariot, Thomas, *A Briefe and True Report of the New Found Land of Virginia*, London, 1588.

Hawkins, Sir John, *A General History of Music*, London, 1776.

Hiller, J. A., *Lebensbeschreibungen berühmter Musikgelehrter und Tonkünstler*, Leipzig, 1784.

Hirt, Franz Josef, *Meisterwerke des Klavierbaus*, Olten, Switz., 1955.

Hodsdon, Alec, and Cecil Clutton, "Defining the Virginal," *The Musical Times*, May 1947.

Hopkinson, Francis, "An Improved Method of Quilling a Harpsichord," *Transactions of the American Philosophical Society*, 2 (1788): 185.

Hubbard, Frank, "The *Encyclopédie* and the French Harpsichord," *The Galpin Society Journal*, 9 (1956): 37.

———"Two Early English Harpsichords," *The Galpin Society Journal*, 3 (1950): 12.

Huguenot Society, London, *The Publications of The Huguenot Society*, vol. 10.

Jacobsson, Johann Karl, *Technologisches Wörterbuch oder alphabetische Erklärung aller nützlichen mechanischen Künste, Manufacturen, Fabriken und Handwerken*, Berlin, 1781–1794.

James, Philip, *Early Keyboard Instruments*, London, 1930.

Jeans, Susi, "The Pedal Clavichord and Other Practice Instruments of Organists," *Proceedings of the Royal Musical Association*, 77 (1950–1951): 1.

Jonckbloet, W. J. A., and J. P. N. Land, eds., *Musique et musiciens au XVIIᵉ siècle, correspondence et oeuvre musicales de Constantin Huygens*, Leyden, 1882.

Kinsky, Georg, "Kurze Oktaven auf besaiteten Tasteninstrumenten: Ein Beitrag zur Geschichte des Klaviers," *Zeitschrift für Musikwissenschaft*, 2 (1920): 65.

———*Musikhistorisches Museum von Wilhelm Heyer in Cöln, Katalog*, Cologne, 1910.

Kircher, Athanasius, *Musurgia universalis*, Rome, 1650.

———*Neue Hall- und Thon-Kunst*, Nordlingen, Germ., 1684.

———*Phonurgia nova*, Kempton, Germ., 1673.

Kirkpatrick, Ralph, *Domenico Scarlatti*, Princeton, 1953.

La Borde, Jean Benjamin de, *Essai sur la musique ancienne et moderne*, Paris, 1780.

Lafontaine, Henry Cart de, *The King's Musick*, London, 1909.

La Lande, Joseph Jérôme de, *Voyage d'un français en Italie*, Paris, 1769; 2nd ed., 1786.

Lespinasse, R. de, *Les Métiers et corporations de la ville de Paris du quatorzième au dix-huitième siècle*, Paris, 1886–1897.

Lesure, François, "La Facture instrumentale à Paris au seizième siècle," *The Galpin Society Journal*, 7 (1954): 11.

Lettera dell'autore del nuovo cembalo angelico inventato in Roma nell'anno MDCCLXXV, Rome, n.d.

Luscinius, Ottomar, *Musurgia seu praxis musicae*, Strasbourg, 1536.

Mace, Thomas, *Musick's Monoment*, London, 1676.

Maffei, Scipione, "Nueva invenzione d'un gravecembalo etc.," *Giornale de letterati d'Italia* (Venice), vol. 5 (1711).

Marcuse, Sibyl, "Transposing Keyboards on Extant Flemish Harpsichords," *The Musical Quarterly*, 38.3 (July 1952): 414.

Mendel, Arthur, "Pitch in the 16th and Early 17th Centuries," *The Musical Quarterly*, vol. 34 (1948); pt. 1, Jan., p. 28; pt. 2, April, p. 199; pt. 3, July, p. 336; pt. 4, Oct., p. 575.

Mercure de France. A weekly periodical publication, Paris, 1672 to 1825.

Mersenne, F. Marin, *Harmonie universelle, contenant la théorie et la pratique de la musique*, Paris, 1636; divided into nineteen books which form several treatises. My references are drawn from "Le Traité des instrumens," which is composed of seven books. This has been translated by R. E. Chapman, *Harmonie universelle, The Books on Instruments*, Nijhoff, The Hague, 1957. All translations in this volume, however, are my own.

Mizler, Lorenz, *Neu eröffnete musikalische Bibliothek*, Leipzig, 1739–1749.

Natrus, L. van, J. Polly, and C. van Vurren, *Groot Volkomen Moolenboek*, Amsterdam, 1734.

New Universal History of Arts and Sciences, A, London, 1759.

Nicolas, Sir N. Harris, *Privy Purse Expenses of King Henry VIII*, London, 1827.

Pennant, Thomas, *British Zoology*, London, 1766.

Pepys, Samuel, *Diary and Correspondence of Samuel Pepys*, Esq., F.R.S., ed. Rev. Mynors Bright, M.A., New York, 1884.

Petri, Johann Samuel, *Anleitung zur praktischen Musik*, Leipzig, 1782.

Pierre, Constant, ed., *Le Conservatoire national de musique et de déclamation, documents*, Paris, 1900.

——— *Les Facteurs d'instruments de musique, les luthiers et la facture instrumentale, précis historique*, Paris, 1893.

Pols, A. M., *De Ruckers en de Klavierbouw in Vlaanderen*, Antwerp, 1942.

Praetorius, Michael, *Syntagma musicum*, 1615–1620. The second volume, *De organographia*, which contains most of the information pertinent to this study, appeared in Wolfenbüttel, Germany, in 1619. The plates (*Theatrum instrumentorum*) were published in the following year. Facsimile of *De Organographia* and the *Theatrum instrumentorum* was published by Bärenreiter, 1958, Wilibald Gurlitt, ed.

Ray, John, *A Collection of English Words Not Generally Used . . . with catalogues of English birds and fishes: and an account of the preparing and refining such metals and minerals as are gotten in England*, London, 1674.

Rees, Abraham, ed., *The Cyclopaedia*, London, 1819.

Reynvaan, Joos Verschuere, *Muzykaal Kunst-Woordenboek*, Amsterdam, 1795.

Rimbault, Edward F., *History of the Pianoforte*, London, 1860.

Rombouts, Ph., and Th. van Lerius, *Les Liggeren et autres archives historiques de la gilde anversoise de Saint Luc*, vol. I, Antwerp, 1872; vol. II, The Hague, n.d.

Roubo, André Jacob, *L'Art du menuisier*, Paris, 1769–1774. In three parts: "L'Art du menuisier, première partie" (1769); "L'Art du menuisier, seconde partie" (1770); "L'Art du menuisier-carrossier, première section de la troisième partie" (1771); "L'Art du menuisier en meubles, seconde section de la troisième partie" (1772); "L'Art du menuisier-ébéniste, troisième section de la troisième partie" (1774).

Russell, Raymond, *The Harpsichord and Clavichord*, London, 1959.

Sachs, Curt, *The History of Musical Instruments*, New York, 1940.

——— *Sammlung alter Musikinstrumente bei der Staatlichen Hochschule für Musik zu Berlin, beschreibender Katalog*, Berlin, 1922.

Sainsbury, W. Noël, ed., *Original Unpublished Papers Illustrative of the Life of Sir Peter Paul Rubens*, London, 1859.

Sartori, Claudio, *Bibliografia della musica strumentale Italiana*, Florence, 1952.

Savary des Bruslons, Jacques, *Dictionnaire universel de commerce*, Paris, 1759–66 (1st ed., 1741). The best edition was that augmented by Cl. Philibert, Copenhagen, 1759–1766, 5 vols. in folio.

Sceaury, Paul Loubet de, *Musiciens et facteurs d'instruments de musique, statuts corporatifs*, Paris, 1949.

Scheurleer, D. F. Lunsingh, "Over het Ornament en de Authenticiteit van bedrukte Papierstrooken in twee Clavierinstrumenten," *Mededelingen van de Dienst voor Kunsten en Wetenschappen*, Gemeente Museum, The Hague, 6 (1939): 45.

Schlick, Arnolt, *Spiegel der Orgelmacher und Organisten*, Mainz, 1511. Reprinted by Robert Eitner, *Monatshefte für Musik-Geschichte von der Gesellschaft für Musikforschung*, 1 (1869): 101. Edited by Ernst Flade with modernised spelling, Bärenreiter-Verlag, Kassel and Basel, 1951.

Scholes, Percy A., *The Great Dr. Burney*, London, 1948.

Shortridge, John D., "Italian Harpsichord Building in the 16th and 17th Centuries," *U. S. National Museum Bulletin*, Washington, D.C., no. 225 (1960).

Smith, Robert, *Harmonics or the Philosophy of Musical Sounds*, London, 1759.

Sprengel, Peter N., *Handwerk und Künste in Tabelen*, Berlin, 1773.

Straeten, Edmond van der, *La Musique aux Pays-Bas avant le XIXe siècle*, Ghent, Brussels, 1867–1888.

Talbot, James, MS description of musical instruments, Christ Church Library, Oxford, Music MS 1187. See Baines.

Todini, Michele, *Dichiaratione della galleria armonica eretta in Roma da Michele Todini, Piemontese di Saluzzo nella sua habitatione posta all'arco della Ciambella*, Rome 1676.

Trichet, Pierre, manuscript, ca. 1640, Bibliothèque Sainte-Geneviève, Paris. Edited by François Lesure, *Traité des instruments de musique*, Neuilly-sur-Seine: Société de Musique d'Autrefois, 1957.

Trouflaut, l'Abbé, A letter describing Taskin's *peau de buffle* stop, originally printed in the *Journal de musique*, no. 5 (1773), reprinted by De La Borde, I, 347.

Ure, Andrew, M.D., *A Dictionary of Arts, Manufactures and Mines*, 3rd ed., New York, 1842. The first edition appeared in London in 1839.

Verhandeling over de Muziek, The Hague, 1772.

Vicentino, Nicola, *Descrizione dell' arciorgano*, Venice, 1561.

——— *L'Antica musica ridotta alla moderna pratica*, Rome, 1555.

Villard de Honnecourt, MS notebook deposited in the Bibliothèque Nationale, Paris. Written ca. 1235.

Virdung, Sebastian, *Musica getutscht*, Basel, 1511.

Walter, Johann Gottfried, *Musicalisches Lexicon oder musicalische Bibliothec*, Leipzig, 1732.

Watin, Jean Félix, *L'Art de faire et d'employer le vernis, ou L'Art du vernisseur*, Paris, 1772.

Weckerlin, J. B., *Nouveau musiciana*, Paris, 1890.

Westphal, Joh. Jacob Heinr., ed., MS "Musikalische Erfindungen," Bibliothèque Royale, Brussels (MS II 4120).

Wilder, Philip van, MS inventory of musical instruments at Westminster, 1553. British Museum, Harl. 1419a.

Zarlino, Gioseffo, *Instituzioni harmoniche*, Venice, 1558.

Zedler, Johann Heinrich, *Grosses Vollständiges Universal Lexicon aller Wissenschaften und Künste*, Halle and Leipzig, 64 vols., 1732–1750. Four-vol. supplement, 1751–1754.

GLOSSARY

Arcade
> The shaped vertical front of the natural key. The design is formed by a rotating cutter (see Plate XIII, figure 8).

Arpichordum
> A stop which is like a buff stop except that the strings are touched by metal pins which produce a buzzing sound. Described by Praetorius in *De Organographia* (Chapter XLIII). Other authorities mention a similar device.

Back eight-foot
> The rank of 8′ jacks which are farthest from the player. Since they pluck the string at a point distant from its end the tone is dark and flutey. The back 8′ is always on the lower manual.

Back-plucked
> String plucked far from the nut thus producing a round and flutelike tone.

Back rail
> The cross member of a key bed which supports the rear of the key levers. It is padded with cloth or felt.

Balance pin
> The pin which passes through the key at the fulcrum and is driven into the balance rail. The balance rail pin prevents the key from slipping in and out or twisting from side to side.

Balance point
> The point along the length of the key lever at which it is balanced.

Balance rail
> The center rail of a three-rail key bed, or the front rail of a two-rail key bed. It serves as the fulcrum for the keys.

Balance rail pin
> See balance pin.

Bar clamp
> A long wooden or metal clamp consisting of a bar and a sliding member which is often fitted with a screw. It is used for clamping wide objects. Hanging on the wall to the right in the vignette of Plate XXXI are several bar clamps of varying lengths.

Beat
> A throbbing or undulating effect taking place in rapid succession when two notes not quite of the same pitch are sounded together. (O.E.D.) If two tones are one cycle per second apart in pitch there will be one beat per second.

Belly rail
   The frame member which supports the edge of the soundboard nearest the player (see Plate XXXV, figure 2, EF).
Bentside
   The curved side of a harpsichord or spinet case.
Bentside spinet
   That form of spinet which has a bentside (see Plate XXIII).
Bit brace
   The cranked metal or wood holder for an auger-bit. (Plate XLI, figure 21.)
Boom tone
   The bass-drum-like tone of the bass note which is at the resonant frequency of the air enclosed in the case of an instrument.
Box resonance
   The pitch at which the air enclosed in the case of an instrument resonates. It is usually around C for five-octave harpsichords.
Box slide
   A type of register found mainly in Italian instruments and English spinets. It is from one to three inches thick and requires no lower guide (see Plate III, figure 4).
Bridge
   The curved strip of wood glued to the top of the soundboard. The strings rest on it and are maintained in position by bridge pins. The bridge transmits the vibration of the strings to the soundboard.
Bridge pin
   The pins driven into the bridge to position the strings and to define the end of the vibrating segments of the strings.
Bristle
   The spring, originally of hog's bristle, which maintains the tongue in a forward position (see Plate XXII, figures 5 and 9).
Buff batten
   The strip of wood loosely held against the vertical front of the nut carrying the buff pads on its upper surface. It can be moved a short distance sideways to cause the buff pads to partially damp the strings, producing a muffled tone (see Plate XXIX, figure 10).
Buff pad
   The pad, usually of leather, which is glued to the top of the buff batten.
Buff stop
   As many soft leather pads as there are notes, mounted on a movable batten which is placed next to the 8-foot or 16-foot nut. When the batten is moved sideways the pads damp one choir of strings, resulting in a harplike tone (see Plate XXIX, figure 10). Sometimes called harp stop or theorbo stop (16-foot) or, in error, lute stop (a mistranslation of the German *Lautenzug*).
Cap molding
   The molding on the upper edge of an Italian instrument case (see Plate II, figure 8).
Cheekpiece
   The short side of the case of a harpsichord to the right of the keyboard.

Chinoiserie
A style of painted decoration in imitation of oriental lacquer work.

Chisel, firmer
A chisel of medium weight, often with beveled sides.

Choir
All the strings of one stop, equivalent to one string per key.

Clavichord
An oblong stringed instrument with keys. A brass tangent mounted in the rear of each key lever strikes the string(s) when the key is depressed.

Cutoff bar
The largest of the ribs glued to the underside of the soundboard. See Rib.

Cyma
A molding of S-section (see Plate XIX, figure 9).

Damper
The felt pad on the jack which damps the string when the key is released (see Plate XL, figure F).

Deal
Any one of several soft woods.

Disposition
The complement and arrangement of stops on a harpsichord. The following convention has been adopted to express a given disposition. An arrow symbolizes a rank of jacks and the direction it faces. Thus → 8′ indicates a rank of jacks that is plucking an eight-foot string to the right. A single-manual harpsichord with two choirs of eight-foot strings might be diagramed thus:

$$\rightarrow 8'$$
$$\leftarrow 8'.$$

A three-register double might be diagramed:

$$\left\{ \begin{array}{l} \rightarrow 8' \\ \text{-- -- -- -- -- -- --} \\ \leftarrow 4' \\ \leftarrow 8'. \end{array} \right.$$

In this example the rank of jacks above the dotted line is understood to be on the upper manual; those below the line on the lower manual. The brace symbolizes a manual coupler. A harpsichord with two choirs of eight-foot strings is indicated thus: 2x8′. A disposition designated as 2x8′, 1x4′, 1xlute would indicate a three-choir harpsichord with two eight-foot choirs, one four-foot choir, and an extra rank of jacks plucking one of the eight-foot choirs close to the nut.

Dogleg jack
A jack which has a piece removed from the front edge permitting it to be engaged by either manual. A dogleg jack in position is shown in Plate XX, figure 2. Pascal Taskin sometimes made the cutout on the rear edge of the back row of eight-foot jacks so that they could be raised by a batten hinged to the top of the rack.

Double bentside
An S-shaped bentside (see Plate XIX, figures 3 and 13).

Double harpsichord
  A harpsichord with two manuals.

Double virginal
  A virginal with an ottavino inserted in the side next to the keyboard.

Drawstop
  A hand stop which is operated by being pulled out.

Eight-foot choir
  One string per note at eight-foot pitch.

Eight-foot hitchpin rail
  The molding on the soundboard at bentside and tail into which are driven
  the pins that hold the eight-foot strings.

Eight-foot pitch
  The pitch of a choir of strings that are at unison with a piano. The note c″
  sounds 523.3 cycles per second. A stop of open organ pipes at eight-foot
  pitch would require a pipe eight feet long at C.

Eight-foot stop
  A rank of jacks sounding strings at eight-foot pitch. It could have various
  timbres depending on the plucking point and the plectrum material.

End block
  The blocks at either end of the keyboard.

End stop mechanism
  The mechanism which regulates the motion of the registers.

Ensemble
  All of the stops of a harpsichord which are designed to be played together.
  The *peau de buffle*, the lute stop, and the buff stop are usually excluded
  from the ensemble.

Epinette
  Literally spinet. Often used in France as a general word to refer to any
  jack-action instrument including at times the harpsichord.

Epinette à l'italienne
  Literally "Italian-style spinet." Used in France during the seventeenth and
  eighteenth centuries to refer to bentside spinets.

Eschequier
  An early keyboard stringed instrument (see page 2).

Exaquir
  See *Eschequier*.

Expressive double harpsichord
  A two-manual harpsichord in which the extra manual is used to vary the
  dynamic level or timbre rather than for transposition.

False inner-outer
  That style of Italian instrument in which the case and the instrument are
  integral but in which the details of decor are contrived to produce the
  appearance of a separate instrument in an outer case.

Foreshortening
  The reduction in length of the bass strings of an instrument below the
  dimension derived by doubling the length of the string an octave above.

Four-foot choir
  One string per note at four-foot pitch.

Four-foot hitchpin rail

The curved member glued to the underside of the soundboard into which the four-foot hitchpins are driven (see Plate VII, figure 2).

Four-foot pitch

That pitch which is one octave above eight-foot pitch.

Four-foot stop

A rank of jacks sounding strings at four-foot pitch.

Frame

The structural members in the interior of an instrument (under the soundboard) which strengthen the case.

Frame, lower level

A reinforcing member fastened to the bottom of a harpsichord.

Frame, upper level

A reinforcing member crossing the harpsichord from side to side which is not fastened to the bottom.

Front eight-foot

The rank of jacks which is nearest to the player of all the eight-foot jacks. Usually on the upper manual. Since the plucking point is closer it has a more nasal tone than the back eight-foot.

Front-plucked

String plucked close to the nut thus producing a nasal tone.

Front rail

The cross member of a key bed which is at the front, under the key heads. It is lacking in two-rail key beds.

Front rail pin

The guide pin under the key head or sharp, driven into the front rail of the key bed, which controls the lateral movement of the key levers. Characteristic of English keyboards.

Gap

The space between the belly rail and wrest plank into which the registers fit.

Geigenwerk

A keyboard instrument with strings ordinarily of gut which are sounded by rosined wheels producing a tone like that of a bowed instrument (see Praetorius, *Syntagma musicum*, plate III).

Hand stop

A lever operated by the hand which moves a register or the buff stop batten.

Harpsichord

To be distinguished from the spinet and the virginal. The harpsichord has a bentside. The strings are parallel to the key levers.

Hitch (of a pedal or knee lever)

A device to hold the knee lever or pedal locked "on" against the spring tension of the mechanism.

Hitchpin

The pin which retains the end of a string opposite the wrest pin.

Hitchpin rail

The molding or rail into which a hitchpin is driven.

Holdfast
> A piece of iron forged in roughly the shape of a figure 7. Used to clamp work down to a bench (see Plate XLI, figure 24e).

Ictus
> The accent resulting from the transients produced at the instant of plucking a string.

Inner edge
> The inner edge of the case above the soundboard and wrest plank.

Inner-outer
> That style of Italian instrument in which the instrument is distinct and separate from a decorated outer box.

Instrument
> A term used in Germany during the seventeenth century for jack-action instruments in general.

Jack
> The plucking mechanism of a harpsichord, spinet, or virginal (see Plate XXII, figures 5 and 9).

Jack blank
> The carefully dimensioned blocks from which the jacks are made.

Jack rail
> A bar of wood, felted on the underside, which is mounted above the jacks and limits their upward motion.

Just scale
> A scale in which the string length is doubled for each octave of descent.

Key bed
> The frame on which the keys are mounted (see Plate III, figure 1).

Keyboard brackets
> The elaborately profiled ends of spine and cheekpiece at either side of the keyboard of an Italian harpsichord. Also the profiled pieces at either end of the projecting keyboard of an Italian spinet or virginal.

Key dip
> The amount a key is depressed in playing.

Key frame
> See Key bed.

Key front
> The vertical front of a natural key head. See Arcade and Molded key front.

Key head
> The wide part of the front of a natural key.

Key lever
> The whole key from front to back.

Key panel
> The glued-up panel from which the keys are sawed out.

Key top
> The ebony, bone, ivory, or boxwood veneer applied to the top of a natural key.

Knee
> A triangular brace on the interior of an Italian harpsichord (see Plate II, figure 2).

Knee levers
> Vertical-acting pommels mounted in the stand which change the stops. Characteristic of late eighteenth century French harpsichords (see Plate XIV, figures 1 and 6).

Leaf spring
> A spring made of a flat blade of metal as opposed to a spring of coiled wire. Brass leaf springs are often found in Italian jacks in place of bristle.

Leather plectra
> Plectra made of hard cowhide. To be distinguished from *peau de buffle* which is much softer and coarser in texture.

Ligne
> In English, line. Equals ⅟₁₂ inch.

Liner
> The strip of wood glued around the inside of the case of an instrument to which the soundboard is glued.

Livre
> French monetary unit equivalent to the pound sterling.

Lock board
> The board which closes up the front of a harpsichord. It is usually fitted with a lock.

Lower edge molding
> The molding running around the lower edge of the outside of an instrument.

Lower guide
> The lower bearing for the jacks (see Plate XXII, figure 10).

Lute stop
> A rank of jacks which pluck an eight-foot choir very close to the nut producing a nasal tone. The register is placed in a special gap which slants across the wrest plank parallel to the nut (see Plate XX, figure 1). See Buff stop.

Machine stop
> A device operated by a pedal or knee lever which operates several stops at once (see Plate XIV, figure 1).

Manual
> A keyboard.

Manual coupler
> A device which causes the keys of different manuals to move together. In harpsichords the upper manual is always coupled to the lower (that is, the upper manual keys move when those of the lower manual are depressed).

Marking gauge
> A tool consisting of a rod of hardwood having a point or knife blade protruding near one end, and a fence which can be fixed to the rod at any point. Used to score a line in a board parallel to an edge.

Marquetry
> Inlaid decoration made by sawing through several layers of different colored veneers and assembling the elements so as to obtain contrasting designs and backgrounds. The whole is then glued to a solid ground.

Molded key front
The vertical front of the natural key embellished with a molding (see Plate XXI, figure 9).

Mortise
A square or oblong hole.

Multiple-division keyboard
A keyboard with more than twelve keys per octave.

Mutation stop
A stop at a pitch other than unison or octave with the ensemble of the instrument. Designed to be used simultaneously with the other stops.

Nag's head swell
A specially hinged segment of the lid which can be raised by means of a pedal to produce a crescendo.

Name batten
The removable batten above the keys on which the maker of an instrument often inscribes his name.

Nameboard
The fixed part of the case of a harpsichord or bentside spinet which is placed transversely above the keys. To be distinguished from the name batten which is screwed or pegged to it.

Nonenharmonic keyboard
A keyboard with more than twelve divisions per octave. It is intended to permit the performer to distinguish between enharmonic notes.

Non-inner-outer
That style of Italian instrument in which the case and the instrument are one and the same. No camouflage is applied to make it appear to be an inner-outer instrument.

Nut
The bridge in a harpsichord or bentside spinet which is glued to the wrest plank. In a virginal or pentagonal spinet it is the left-hand bridge, nearest the line of the jacks.

Octave span
The dimension of a keyboard from the lower edge of a C to the lower edge of the C an octave above.

Ogee
A molding of S-section. See Cyma.

Ottavino
A virginal or spinet at four-foot pitch.

Outer case
The decorated outer box of an Italian instrument.

Outline
The outline of an instrument seen in plan view.

Overrail
A projecting rail felted on its underside which is mounted to the top of the rack. Serves to limit the key dip (see Plate VI, figure 2).

Overspun string
A string in which a core is covered by coils of wire smoothly wound on.

The purpose of the cover is to add mass without stiffening the string. In antique instruments limited to sixteen-foot choirs.

Ovolo

A molding of the section illustrated in Plate II, figure 10.

Paper, block-printed

The ornamental paper, printed from wooden blocks, which was used to adorn the inside and sometimes the outside of Flemish instruments. It is occasionally found in French instruments.

Peau de buffle

Buffalo hide. A stop of jacks with plectra made of *peau de buffle*.

Pedal

A device operated by the foot to change the stops or to open a swell.

Pedal board

A keyboard played with the feet as in the organ.

Pentagonal spinet

The most common type of Italian spinet (see Plate XXV, figure 2).

Pitch

That quality of a musical tone which is dependant on the comparative rapidity of the vibrations producing it. Also the general level of pitch of a choir of strings or of an entire instrument compared to some sort of standard such as a″ = 440.

Pitch C

The C an octave above middle C. At eight-foot pitch, pitch C (c″) sounds 523.3 c.p.s. (in equal temperament).

Plane, fillister

A narrow wooden plane in which the iron extends all the way across the sole (see Plate XXXI, figure 1: the plane farthest from the viewer under the bench).

Plane, jack

A rather large plane used for rough work (see Plate XXXI, figure 1).

Plane, jointing

A very long plane used to make long joints as in soundboards or lids (see Plate XXXI, figure 1).

Plane, smooth

A small plane used for finishing the surface of planks (see Plate XXXI, figure 1).

Plectrum

The piece of leather or quill projecting from the tongue which plucks the string.

Plein jeu

Full harpsichord. The fullest registration of which an instrument is capable.

Plucking point

The point at which a string is plucked relative to the nut. The smaller the distance to the plucking point the more nasal the tone. Sometimes in the case of a four-foot choir that is sounded by the back jacks the plucking point in the treble is beyond the middle of the string. In such cases, although it is still specified by the measurement from the nut, the percentage of the string length represented by the distance from the plucking point to the bridge must be used to predict the nasality of the tone.

Pull-down pedals

A pedal board which is connected to the lower manual by cords. When a pedal is depressed the corresponding key is pulled down, sounding the note.

Quarter, on the (quartersawed)

The orientation of a plank sawed out of a tree trunk so that the broad face is on the radius of the trunk. Wood sawed this way shrinks far less across the grain than that sawed on the slab, and presents a figure of parallel striations rather than the whorls characteristic of the chordal or slab cut.

Quill

The most common material for plectra. Crow or raven quill was most sought after.

Quilled jack

A jack with a quill plectrum.

Quint

Ordinarily a stop which sounds an octave and a fifth above eight-foot pitch. It is possible that Mersenne's quint was only a fifth above eight-foot pitch.

Rack

A board with equally spaced vertical slots sawed into it which is fixed on edge behind the key levers. Metal pins or wooden blades mounted in the ends of the key levers slide in these slots and guide the keys in their motion (see Plate III, figures 1 and 4).

Rack pin

The pin mounted in the end of the key lever which engages the rack.

Rank (of jacks)

A row of jacks, one for each key, mounted in a register and plucking a choir of strings.

Ravalement

A French term referring to the extension of the original range of a harpsichord. *A petit ravalement*, four octaves' range; *à ravalement*, between four and five octaves' range; *à grand ravalement*, five octaves' range.

Regal

A small reed organ.

Register

The mortised batten in which a rank of jacks is mounted (see Plate VI, figure 3, and Plate XXII, figure 10).

Rib

One of the smaller bars glued to the underside of a soundboard. To be distinguished from a cutoff bar. Plate II, figure 4, shows a soundboard with four ribs. Figure 3 shows a soundboard with a cutoff bar and one rib.

Roller board

A contrivance used in organs to conduct the movement of the keys to the pallets of a much wider wind chest. In principle it is similar to the trap work shown in Plate XIV, figure 1. Vertical motion is converted into the rotary movement of a roller in both cases.

Rose

The ornamental rosette set into a hole cut into the soundboard. Usually of cast metal in North European instruments and of parchment and veneer in Italian instruments. It is almost never cut into the wood of the soundboard as in the lute.

Round tail

The far end of a double bentside.

Scale

The length of the strings of an instrument. Since they double in length for each octave of descent most of the string lengths can be calculated if that of one string is known. The usual convention is to specify the length of c″. (In the case of eight-foot choirs the shorter string is usually measured.)

Scantlings

The thickness of the parts which make up the case and frame of an instrument.

Scrolled cheeks

Decoration of the right and left sides of the keyboard well with fret-sawed appliqués reminiscent of the front of an Italian harpsichord in its outer box.

Short octave

The lowest octave of a keyboard in which several chromatics are omitted. The most common kinds are the C short octave (Plate IV, figure 7) and the G short octave. In the C short octave, symbolized C/E, the lowest note of the keyboard appears to be E but actually sounds C. Apparent F♯ sounds D, and apparent G♯ sounds E. A♯ is the first chromatic. In the G short octave, symbolized GG/BB, the lowest note of the keyboard appears to be BB but actually sounds GG. Apparent C♯ sounds AA, and apparent D♯ sounds BB. F♯ is the first chromatic.

Shorter eight-foot string

The eight-foot string to the right of its jack. Each string of this choir is slightly shorter than that of the left-hand choir because of the angle of the bridge.

Shove coupler

A manual coupler which is operated by sliding the upper manual toward the nameboard.

Sixteen-foot choir

One string per note at sixteen-foot pitch.

Sixteen-foot pitch

That pitch which is one octave below eight-foot pitch.

Sixteen-foot stop

A rank of jacks sounding strings at sixteen-foot pitch.

Slab, on the (Slab sawed)

The orientation of a plank sawed out of the tree trunk so that the broad face is perpendicular to the radius of the tree. It is characterized by a pattern of whorls rather than the parallel striations of wood cut on the quarter.

Spine

The straight long side of a harpsichord or bentside spinet. The side of the case of a virginal which is opposite the keyboard.

Spinet

In modern usage, any jack-action instrument which is not a virginal, a harpsichord, or a clavicytherium. There are a variety of case shapes such as the Italian pentagonal spinet and the bentside spinet. All have in common strings which are more or less perpendicular to the key levers.

Split sharp

A sharp divided into two halves, the rearmost raised. It is used to provide two pitches either to fill out the short octave or to give extra nonenharmonic notes.

Stop

One of the sounds of which an instrument is capable. Examples are a sixteen-foot stop, a buff stop, and a lute stop.

Stop lever

The lever which turns a stop off and on.

Stop mechanism

The mechanism which turns the stops off and on.

String band

The choirs of strings as viewed from above.

Stringing

A narrow band of inlay, either of plain wood or a composite patterned strip.

Stringing list

The list of the strings of a harpsichord giving the diameter and kind of wire used for each.

Tail

The short piece which forms the pointed end of a harpsichord case.

Tail angle

The angle of the tail to the spine. An angle approaching 90° is said to be square, a medium tail angle is about 60°, and a pointed tail angle approaches 45°.

Tail piece

See Tail.

Temperament

The adjustment of the intervals of the scale in keyboard instruments so as to adapt them to the purposes of practical harmony: consisting in slight variations of the pitch of the notes from true or "just" intonation in order to make them available in different keys (O.E.D.). Some or all of the resulting intervals cannot be expressed in rational numbers.

Temperament, equal

The division of the octave into twelve equal intervals or semitones.

Temperament, mean-tone

A system of tuning with flattened fifths and pure major thirds. Certain keys are favored at the expense of others.

Three-choir harpsichord

A harpsichord with three choirs of strings, normally 2x8', 1x4'.

Tongue

The pivoted part of a jack in which the plectrum is mounted (see Plate XXII, figure 6).

Transients

The nonperiodic vibrations which produce the clicking sound heard at the instant of plucking a string.

Transposing double harpsichord

A two-manual harpsichord in which C of the upper manual is over F of the lower manual. Both manuals pluck the same two choirs. The effect is simply to change the name of one and the same pitch. A tone with the frequency of 523.3 can be called c'' or f''.

Transposing keyboard

A keyboard which effects a transposition mechanically. The commonest type slips sideways so that the keys may be made to lie under any one of several jacks and thus sound tones higher or lower than those normally assigned to each note.

Trapwork

A system of levers, cranks, and springs which transmits the motion of the pedals or knee levers to the registers, to the buff stop, or to the manual coupler.

Tuning hammer

The metal key with mortised end used to turn the wrest pins in tuning. A primitive form which explains the name is shown under figure 2 of Plate XXV. See also Plate X.

Unison

A term used in several languages to refer to eight-foot pitch or to a stop at that pitch.

Variable intonation

Used of keyboards with more than twelve divisions per octave contrived to distinguish certain enharmonic notes.

Venetian swell

A tightly fitting cover over the soundboard composed of rotating slats which can be opened by means of a pedal to provide a crescendo. Found only in late eighteenth century English harpsichords.

Virginal

A term used in a general sense in England until the middle of the seventeenth century to cover all jack-action instruments. After that it was limited to oblong single-choired instruments, the strings of which are more or less perpendicular to the key levers, and with both nut and bridge resting on the soundboard.

Wolf tone

In tuning, a harsh interval. In instrument making, a bad note, either false or metallic.

Wrest pin

The metal pin with oblong top which holds one end of the string and is turned in tuning. It is driven into the wrest plank.

Wrest plank

The heavy hardwood timber into which the wrest pins are driven.

Wrest plank blocks

The blocks glued to the side of the case on which the wrest planks of some harpsichords are mounted (see Plate II, figure 2).

INDEX

PLATES

Whenever possible the plates relevant to a single type of instrument have been based on a particular extant example. These instruments are noted in the legends. Sometimes, however, no one instrument seems completely typical or it has not been possible to examine it with the necessary minute precision. In these cases the plates represent a composite of several instruments. The effort has always been to show the most typical details and dimensions.

PLATE I

Plan and elevation of an Italian harpsichord. The strings for each C have been indicated on the plan. Based on an instrument inscribed "F.A. 1677" owned by David Aronson of Sudbury, Massachusetts (78″ long, 28⅝″ wide, 7⅝″ high; 10¹³⁄₁₆″ scale).

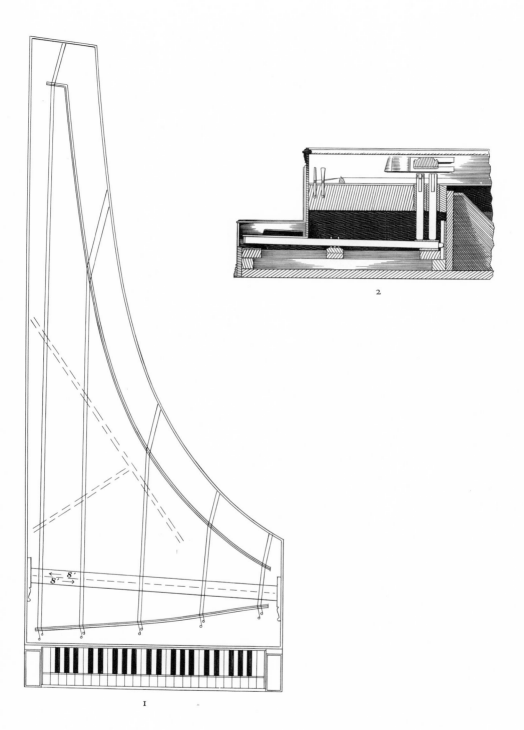

8'
8'

1

2

PLATE II

Interior of an Italian harpsichord.

Figure 1. Detail of jack rail mounting block.

Figure 2. Instrument with soundboard and spine removed, showing the frame.

Figure 3. Underside of soundboard showing style of ribbing used occasionally.

Figure 4. Underside of soundboard showing the more usual style of ribbing.

Figure 5. Detail of the bass end of the bridge.

Figure 6. Section of a soundboard rib.

Figure 7. Molding often used to outline soundboard and wrest plank.

Figure 8. Section through the cap molding at the upper edge of the case. (The exterior of the instrument is to the left.)

Figure 9. Detail of an alternate treatment for the front of the instrument.

Figure 10. Another molding used to outline the soundboard.

Figure 11. End of the jack rail.

Figure 12. Molding at lower edge of case.

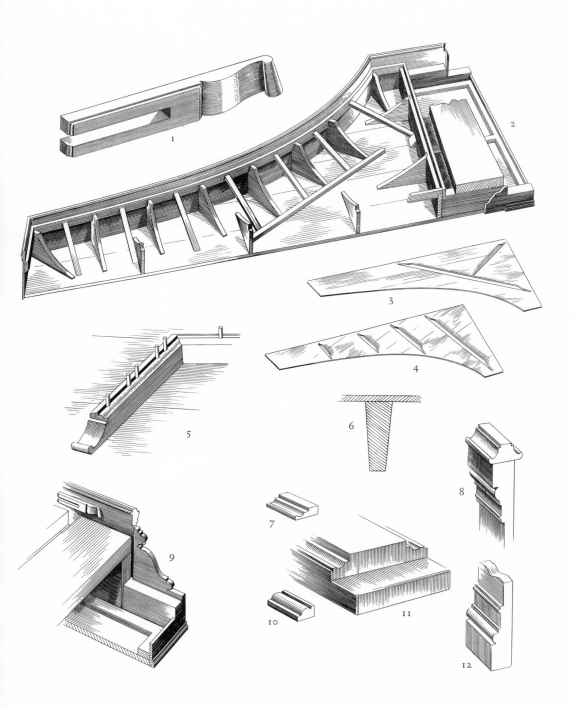

1

2

3

4

5

6

7

8

9

10

11

12

PLATE III

Action of an Italian harpsichord.

Figure 1. Key bed showing the rack and usual three-rail construction.

Figure 2. Key head and sharp. The natural key top is of boxwood. This sharp is ivory topped although many Italian sharps are of ebony or black-stained wood. This arcade is more ornate than most.

Figure 3. Typical Italian jack and register. This style of register is not as common as the box slide shown in figure 4. It requires a separate lower guide and overlaps the wrest plank or soundboard upon which it rests. The jack shows the gauge marks which guided the maker in cutting it out.

Figure 4. Typical Italian jack in a box slide. The rear of the key lever and the rack are shown. This jack has a bristle spring at the rear of the tongue. A flat leaf spring is somewhat more common. The plectrum is of quill although leather is sometimes found in Italian harpsichords.

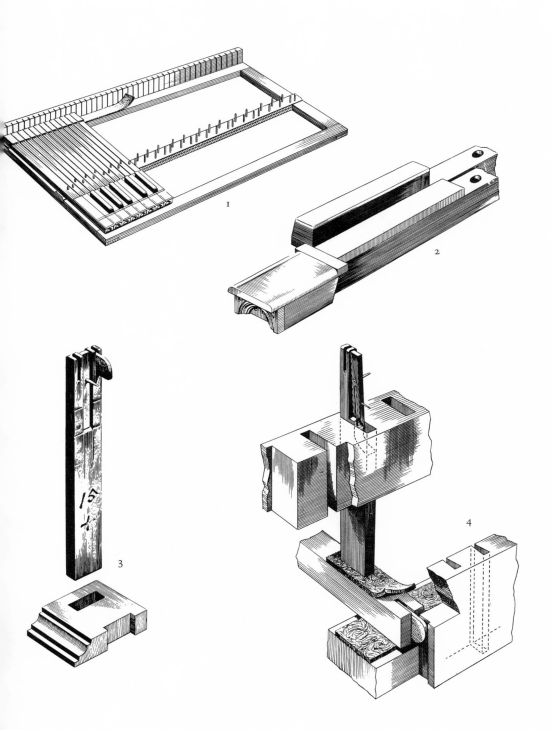

PLATE IV

Italian virginal of the false inner-outer construction.

Figure 1. The virginal with soundboard removed. Note the hitchpin rail to which the soundboard is glued.

Figure 2. Underside of the soundboard showing typical ribbing and the box slide.

Figure 3. Section showing front and back of the virginal. The way in which the cypress veneer ends immediately below the liner may be seen clearly.

Figure 4. One style of jack rail (in section).

Figure 5. The end of another type of jack rail.

Figure 6. Typical jack rail mounting block.

Figure 7. Plan of the virginal. The rose is omitted as was sometimes the case. The strings for each C and the top F have been indicated. The usual arrangement of the C short octave is shown.

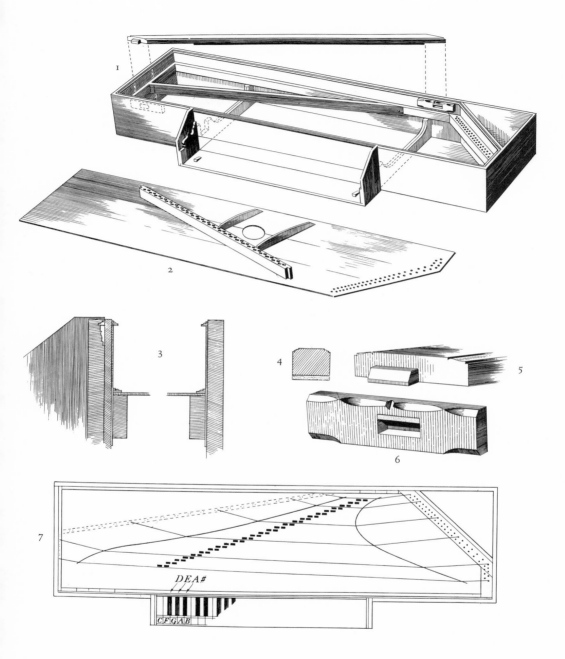

PLATE V

Harpsichord, from Zarlino, *Instituzioni harmoniche*, I, 164. This drawing, although crude, shows the typical deeply incurved Italian bentside and the scrolled cheekpiece and spine. A keyboard with nineteen divisions to the octave is shown. The range is unusual and is possibly not intended to be taken literally; it was perhaps reduced by the draftsman in order to avoid fine detail.

Difficile eſt,niſi docto homini tot tendere chordas.
Alciat. Embl. 2. lib. 1.

PLATE VI

Plan, elevation, and detail of a Flemish harpsichord by Hans Moermans, 1584 (83" long, 33½" wide, 9" high; 14½" scale). The instrument is disposed 1x8', 1x4', with a range GG/BB–f''', similar to Ruckers model III.

Figure 1. Plan. The strings for each C and the top and bottom notes have been indicated on the plan.

Figure 2. Elevation. Note the typical two-rail key bed with metal pin rack and overrail to limit the key dip.

Figure 3. Detail at the cheekpiece showing projecting registers. End motion of the registers is regulated by the two pins which pass through elongated holes cut through the registers.

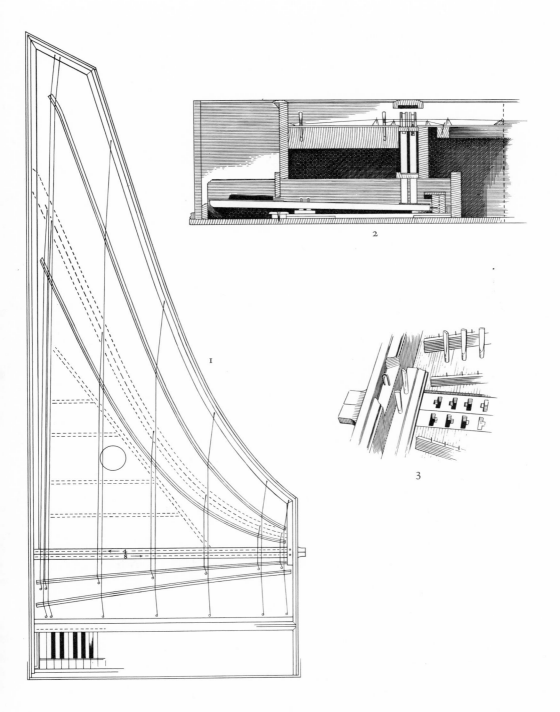

1

2

3

PLATE VII

Interior of a Flemish harpsichord (model IV).

Figure 1. Instrument with soundboard and spine removed, showing the frame. A small hinged opening in the spine gives access to the space between the belly rail and the first frame for storage of tools and supplies. In the treble the four-foot hitchpin rail rests on a small block glued to the rear face of the upper belly rail, and in the bass it is let into the liner.

Figure 2. Underside of the soundboard showing ribbing and four-foot hitchpin rail.

Figure 3. Molding at upper edge of nameboard.

Figure 4. Molding at upper edge of case.

Figure 5. Molding surrounding the soundboard (used as an eight-foot hitchpin rail).

Figure 6. Section of the cutoff bar.

Figure 7. Section of a soundboard rib.

Figure 8. Section of the four-foot hitchpin rail in the bass.

Figure 9. Section of the four-foot hitchpin rail at the halfway point.

Figure 10. Section of the four-foot hitchpin rail at the treble end.

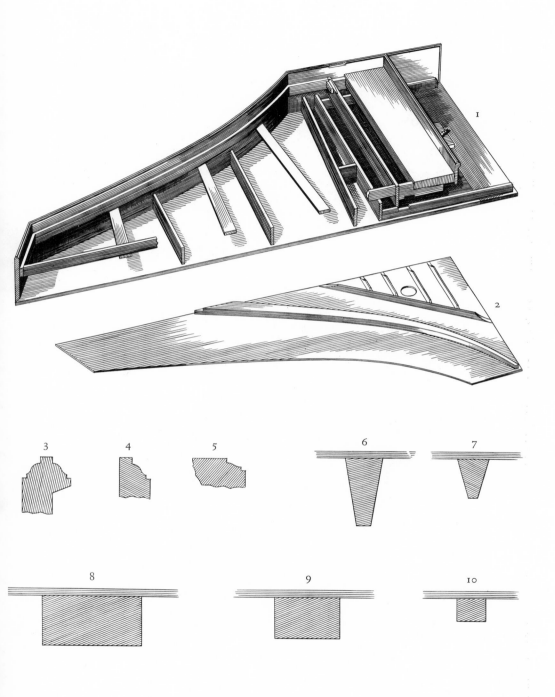

I

2

3   4   5   6   7

8   9   10

PLATE VIII

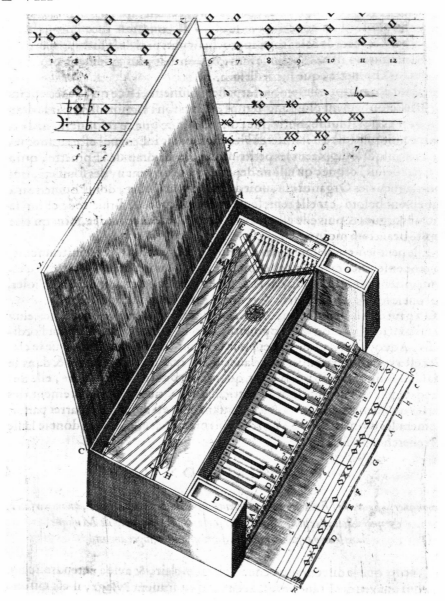

Ottavino, from Mersenne, *Harmonie universelle* (bk. III, p. 108).

The mitered bridge is similar to that of a Richard ottavino (1693) and another by Hans Ruckers (the Younger), both in the Conservatoire at Paris.

The keys are mislabeled. The keyboard range as drawn is B–f″ (G/B–f″). The Richard ottavino has a keyboard compass of GG/BB–c‴. Both of these instruments are at four-foot pitch which gives them an actual range of g/b–f‴ and G/B–c⁗ respectively. The G short octave was typical of French seventeenth century instruments.

The leather strip through which the jacks work is clearly visible as are the trefoiled arcades (also used by Richard).

PLATE IX

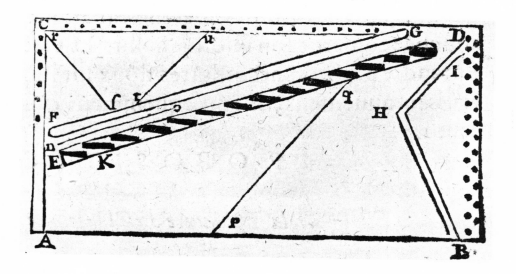

Plan of an ottavino, from Mersenne, *Harmonie universelle* (bk. III, p. 161)
showing bridge (BHD), nut (FG), ribs (rs, tu, pq, no), and the leather
covered register (ED).

PLATE X

Harpsichord, from Mersenne, *Harmonie universelle* (bk. III, p. 111). The instrument is disposed 1x8', 1x4', with a range C–c''' (chromatic), no hand-stops or projecting slides shown. Note the mitered bass end of the eight-foot bridge (an Italianate feature). There is no evidence of an outer case and the shape is more Flemish than Italian.

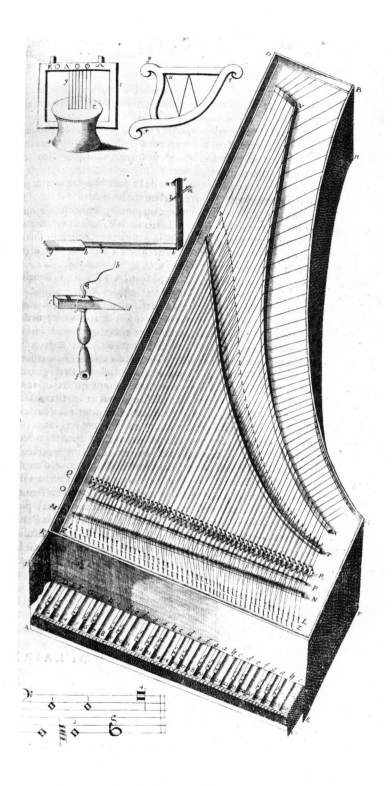

PLATE XI

Plan and elevation of a French harpsichord. Based on a harpsichord signed by Henry Hemsch and dated 1756, at the New England Conservatory of Music in Boston. Strings for all the C's and the top and bottom F's are indicated on the plan. The sides of the lower-manual key bed are dotted in on the elevation so that the edge of the upper-manual key bed may be seen. Note that the upper-manual key bed slides in a recess cut into the lower-manual key bed. As drawn the upper manual is in the forward position and the coupler is "off." If it were pushed back to the dotted line, the ends of the upper-manual key levers would be over the coupler dogs and the manuals would be coupled. The key beds are raised off the bottom of the instrument by battens shown in Plate XII, figure 1.

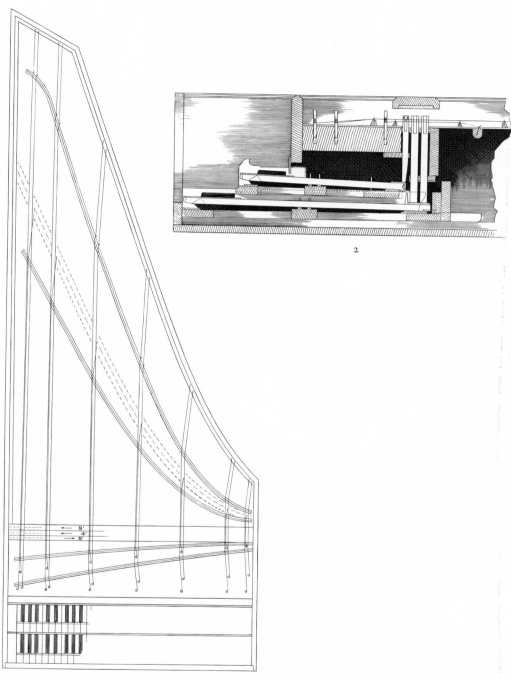

1

2

PLATE XII

Interior of a French harpsichord. Based on a harpsichord made by Pascal Taskin in 1769 (Boalch no. 1).

Figure 1. Instrument with the soundboard and spine removed, showing the frame. Note the rounded frame members and the T-section upper belly rail.

Figure 2. Underside of the soundboard showing the ribs and the four-foot hitchpin rail.

Figure 3. Section of the four-foot hitchpin rail at the bass end.

Figure 4. Section of the four-foot hitchpin rail at the treble end.

Figure 5. Section of the cutoff bar.

Figure 6. Section of a soundboard rib.

Figure 7. Molding section at upper edge of case.

Figure 8. Molding section at upper edge of nameboard.

Figure 9. Section of the molding surrounding the soundboard and used along the bentside and tail as the eight-foot hitchpin rail.

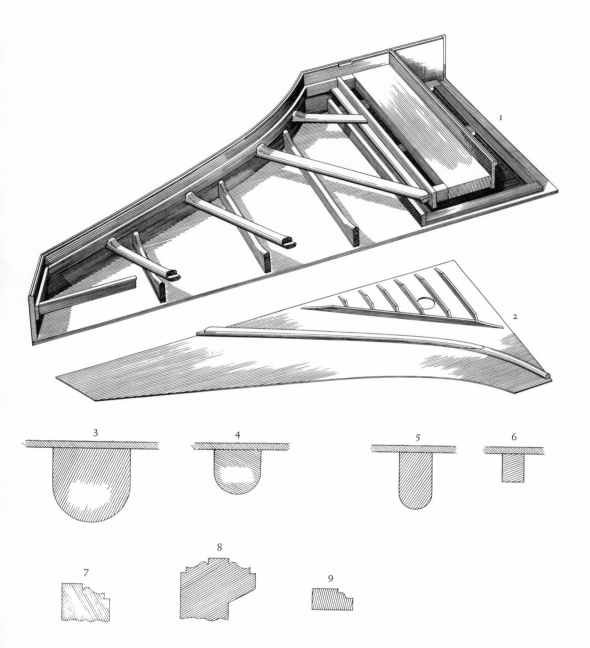

1

2

3 4 5 6

8

7 9

PLATE XIII

Action of a French harpsichord. Based on keyboards by F. E. Blanchet (1758) and action by Taskin (1781) for a Couchet harpsichord (1680), the property of Mr. Edwin Ripin of Forest Hills, New York (Boalch no. 6).

Figure 1. The rear of the key levers (uncoupled position) showing the coupler dog and indicating the motion necessary to couple the manuals.

Figure 2. French keyboards assembled. Note how the upper manual slides in a stopped groove on the inside edge of the sides of the lower-manual key frame. Note also the method of pinning the upper-manual keys at the rear. (The lower-manual key levers are guided by metal pins sliding in a rack.)

Figures 3, 4, and 5. Mechanism used to raise the rear rank of jacks. The knee lever crank transmits motion to the right as indicated by the arrow. The inclined planes shown in figure 4 lift the sliding batten. The hinged strip shown in elevation in figure 5 is raised slightly. The hinges are of parchment. The spring (figure 3) returns the sliding batten when the knee lever is released.

Figure 6. Rear of lower-manual key lever showing the metal rack pin and coupler dog.

Figure 7. Rear of upper-manual key lever showing the mortise for its back rail pin to pass through.

Figure 8. Natural key head. Note the deeply rounded ebony key top scored with three lines, the slight overhang above the arcade (sometimes gilded), and the deep undercutting of the key head to save weight.

Figure 9. A Taskin upper-manual jack. Note the tapered tongue and the deep bristle groove. The jack itself is tapered in both width and thickness from top to bottom, but too little to show in the drawing.

Figure 10. Various views of an upper-manual key lever. Note the undercutting and the bent lever.

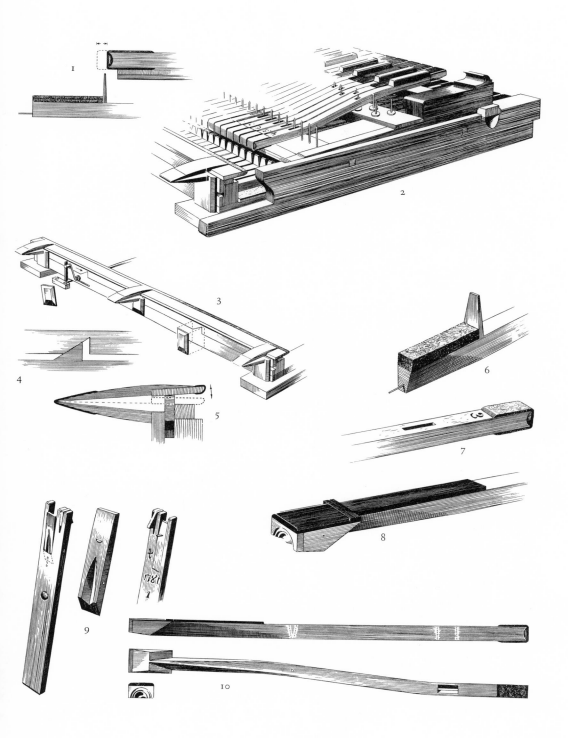

PLATE XIV

Knee lever mechanism of a French harpsichord. Mechanism was installed by Pascal Taskin (1781) in a harpsichord by Couchet (Boalch no. 6).

Figure 1. General view of the mechanism showing the knee levers and the trapwork. The knee levers were actually mounted in the stand (not shown) and were hitched by being raised and pushed to the right. A pin (shown in figure 6) prevented them from falling out entirely. The second and third knee levers are loosely connected so that it is easy to raise and hitch them simultaneously while the other knee is used to put "on" the *peau de buffle*.

Figure 2. Detail of the risers on the spine. The riser for the upper-manual eight-foot register is different from the others since it has to pull rather than push the stop "off."

Figure 3. Detail of the ends of the registers (the rearmost three). See figure 2 for the end of the upper-manual register.

Figure 4. Trapwork for the coupler. The crank is connected to the upper-manual key bed. I suspect that a leaf spring was originally used in place of the coil spring shown. A new bottom has removed any trace of the original spring.

Figure 5. Detail of the risers partially disassembled. The leaf springs catch under the tabs on the ends of the registers (figure 3) and pull the stop "on." The risers push them "off." The upper-manual register is pushed to the right by the spring, and pulled "off" by the riser.

Figure 6. Knee-lever pummel showing retaining pin and notch for the hitch.

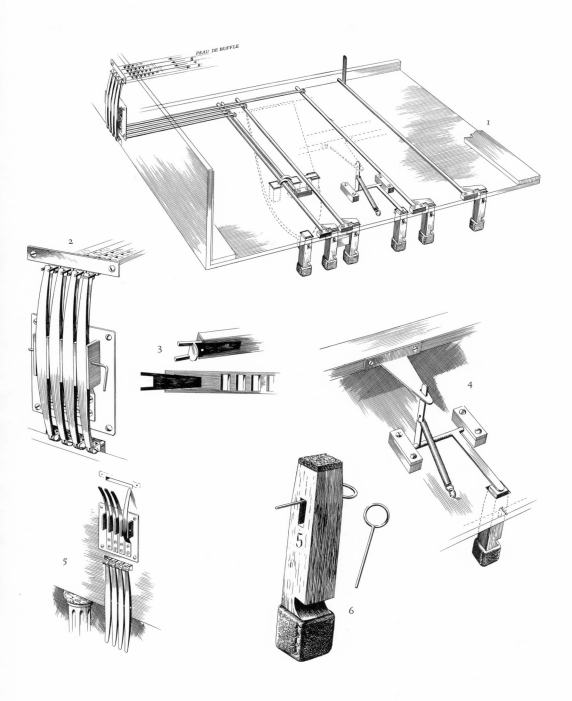

PEAU DE BUFFLE

1

2

3

4

5

6

PLATE XV

Spinet and keyboards, from the *Encyclopédie* ("Lutherie," seconde suite, plate XVI). The legend given with this plate in the *Encyclopédie* reads:

Figure 6. *"Epinette à l'italienne"* (bentside spinet).

Figure 7. Psaltery or *"tympanon"*; a and b, its hammers.

Figure 8. Double keyboards of a harpsichord.

Figure 9. Key bed of a spinet.

The parts so carefully labeled with letters in figures 8 and 9 are unidentified. These are:

Figure 8. D, the rack of the lower manual; HG, a row of coupler dogs; Cd, the upper-manual end block; AB, the lower-manual end block upon which the upper manual slides; F, the upper-manual back rail with its guide pins. No provision is shown to limit the sliding motion of the upper manual.

Figure 9. AB, the rack; CP, the balance rail; EF, the front rail. Note the square balance rail punchings.

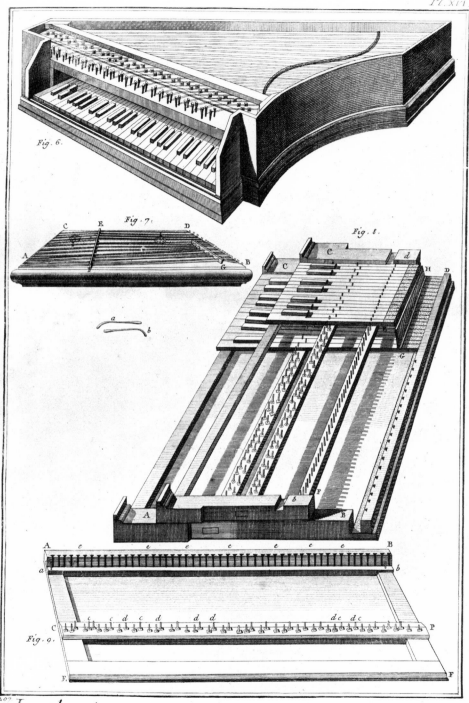

Pl. XVI.

Fig. 6.

Fig. 7.

Fig. 8.

Fig. 9.

Lutherie, *Suite des Instruments à cordes et à touches, avec le Psalterion Instrument à cordes et à baguettes*

PLATE XVI

Plan and front elevation of a claviorganum, from Dom Bedos, *L'Art du facteur d'orgues* (plate CXXXV).

Figure 1. Plan of the claviorganum showing a typical two-manual French harpsichord to which a third manual for the organ has been added. The bellows and reservoir are in the bench. The harpsichord rests on the organ case. According to the engraved scale the harpsichord is about 93 inches long.

Figure 2. Front elevation. No hand stops are shown for the harpsichord. Those for the organ are at either side below the manuals.

Figure 3. Elevation of the bellows and reservoir.

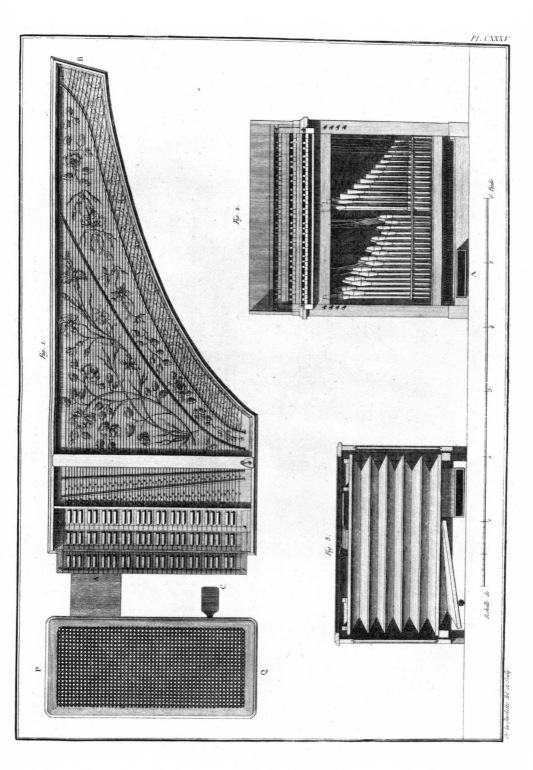

PLATE XVII

Interior and side elevation of a claviorganum, from Dom Bedos, *L'Art du facteur d'orgues* (plate CXXXIV).

Figure 1. Plan view of the interior showing stopped flutes and the wind chest.

Figure 2. Side elevation. Note that the organ keyboard can be coupled to the lower manual of the harpsichord. The upper manual of the harpsichord slides in as usual to be coupled to the lower. Thus the whole instrument can be played together from the lower manual of the harpsichord. Unfortunately no details of the harpsichord's internal construction are shown. The harpsichord disposition is 2x8′, 1x4′, three registers with manual coupler. The compass is FF–f′′′.

Pl. CXXXIV.

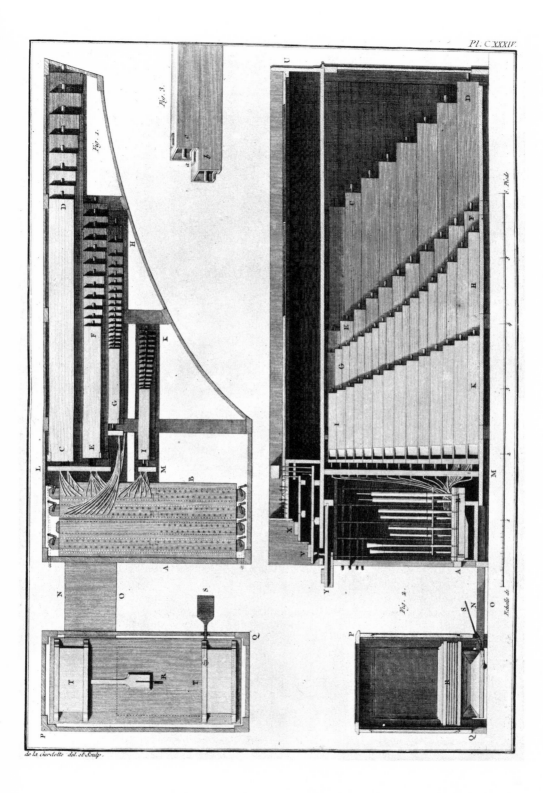

PLATE XVIII

English virginal.

Figure 1. Interior view of the instrument. Note how the rear edge of the lower guide is high enough to be glued to the underside of the soundboard (figure 6) while the soundboard rib (figure 2) meets the projections on the front edge of the lower guide.

Figure 2. Underside of the soundboard showing ribs and mortises for the jacks.

Figure 3. Key bed with rack and overrail to limit the key dip.

Figure 4. Plan. Note the close plucking point. There is one extra mortise and string in the bass. The jack from the last note (C) can be placed in this mortise. It continues to rest on the C key but plucks the extra string which can be tuned to any desired pitch.

Figure 5. Detail of the rack.

Figure 6. Elevation. Note the construction of the lower guide.

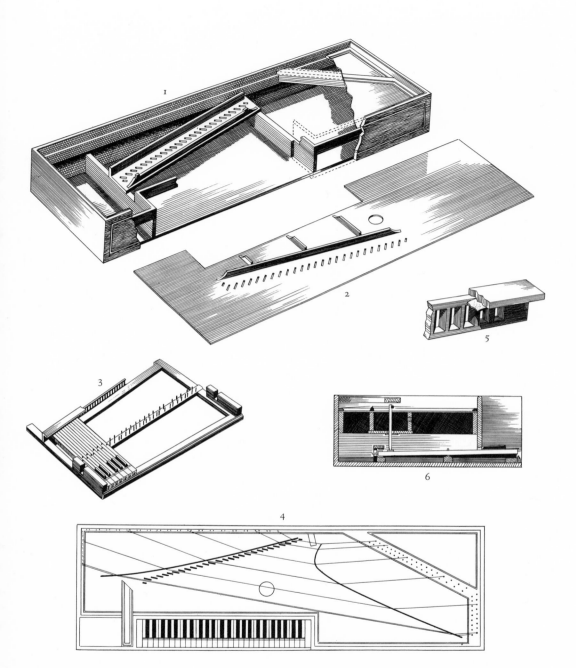

PLATE XIX

Two transitional English harpsichords: Carolus Haward, 1683, property of Sir William Worsley, Hovingham Hall, Yorkshire, and Thomas Hitchcock, undated, Victoria and Albert Museum, London.

Figure 1. Interior of the Haward harpsichord. Note the full-depth frames running diagonally across the instrument, a design much superior to that used in mid-eighteenth century English instruments. The belly rail is also interesting. Compare to figure 11.

Figure 2. Key bed of the Haward harpsichord. Note the two-rail (Flemish) construction and the curious cutouts in the balance rail.

Figure 3. Plan of the Haward harpsichord. The lute stop has been blocked up but originally existed as drawn. The grain of the soundboard is parallel to the spine.

Figure 4. Molding around the inside of the upper edge of the Hitchcock case.

Figure 5. Molding around the outside lower edge of the Hitchcock case.

Figure 6. Eight-foot hitchpin rail of the Hitchcock.

Figure 7. Key tops of the Hitchcock. ("Skunk-tail" sharp and ivory natural with ivory arcade.)

Figure 8. Jack rail hold-down block from the Haward showing provision for the lute stop jack rail.

Figure 9. Lid-edge molding of the Hitchcock.

Figure 10. Molding at the junction of the spine and soundboard in the Hitchcock.

Figure 11. Interior of the Hitchcock. Note the similarities in frame and belly rail to the Haward.

Figure 12. Lower-manual key bed of the Hitchcock. Note the pins between the keys under the nameboard.

Figure 13. Plan of the Hitchcock. The direction of grain in the soundboard is canted about 30° from that of the spine.

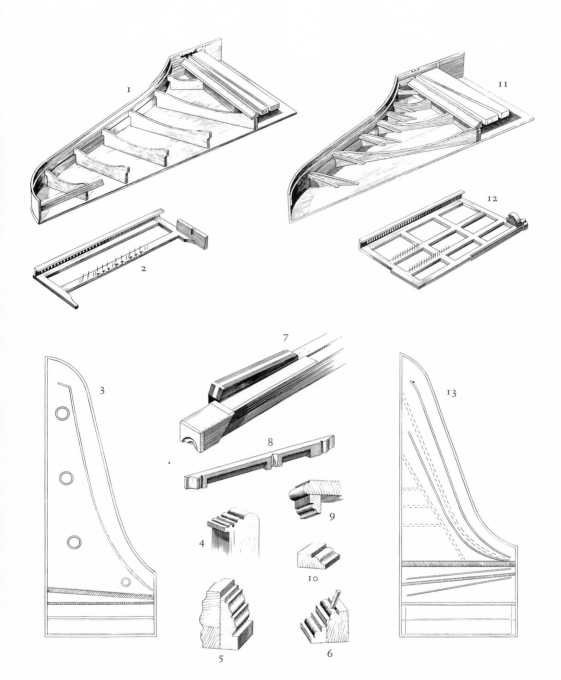

PLATE XX

Plan and elevation of an English harpsichord. Based on an undated J. and A. Kirckman, the property of Charles P. Fisher of Framingham, Massachusetts (91½" long, 36¾" wide, 12" high; 13³⁄₁₆" scale). The nameboard is missing from this instrument, but the I.K. rose is present.

Figure 1. Plan. The strings for top and bottom F and all of the C's are indicated. Note the characteristic curve of the bentside in which all of the curvature is concentrated in the treble end.

Figure 2. Elevation. Note the dogleg jack (front eight-foot) which operates from either manual, and the absence of a coupler. The top of the nameboard has been lowered to accommodate a music desk. In earlier English harpsichords the top of the nameboard was flush with the upper edge of the instrument.

Figure 3. Section of the four-foot hitchpin rail to show the undercutting in the treble. The bottom edge in the drawing is the one which is glued to the soundboard. The undercutting begins below c'.

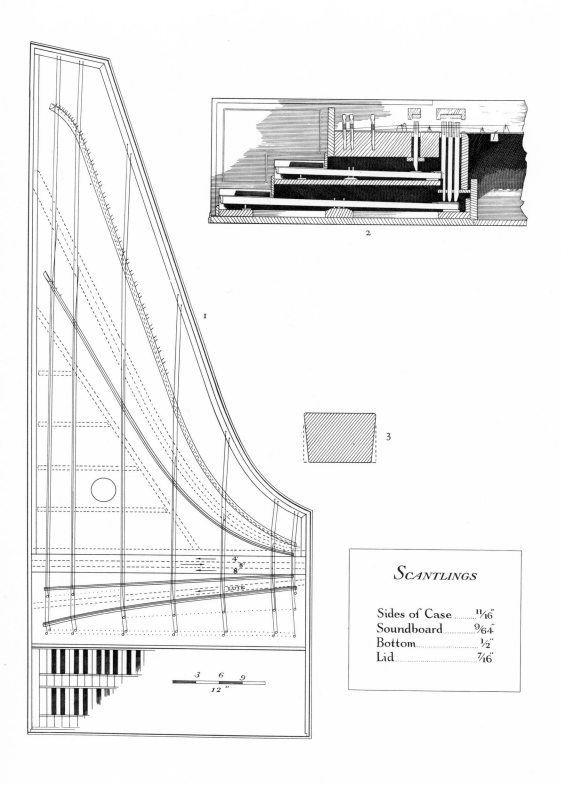

1

2

3

4'
8'
8'

LUTE

3   6   9
12"

SCANTLINGS

Sides of Case...............¹¹⁄₁₆"
Soundboard...........⁹⁄₆₄"
Bottom...............½"
Lid...............⁷⁄₁₆"

PLATE XXI

Interior of an English harpsichord.

Figure 1. Instrument with the soundboard and spine removed showing the frame. Note the sloping braces to the belly rail, a typically English feature. The notch in the liner on the spine is to receive the bass end of the four-foot hitchpin rail. The block nailed and glued to the rear edge of the belly rail in the treble (also shown in figure 2) supports the treble end of the four-foot hitchpin rail.

Figure 2. The underside of the soundboard showing the ribs and the four-foot hitchpin rail. Each joint in the soundboard is reinforced by a glued-on strip of cloth (as is also the case with the ends of the ribs).

Figure 3. Section of the four-foot hitchpin rail in the bass.

Figure 4. Section of the four-foot hitchpin rail in the treble.

Figure 5. Section of the cutoff bar.

Figure 6. Section of a soundboard rib.

Figure 7. Section of the eight-foot nut showing the buff stop.

Figure 8. Section of the eight-foot bridge.

Figure 9. Molding section used on the key fronts.

Figure 10. Molding section on the under edge of the lid.

Figure 11. Molding section at lower edge of case.

Figure 12. Section of the four-foot nut.

Figure 13. Section of the four-foot bridge.

Figure 14. Section of the eight-foot hitchpin rail.

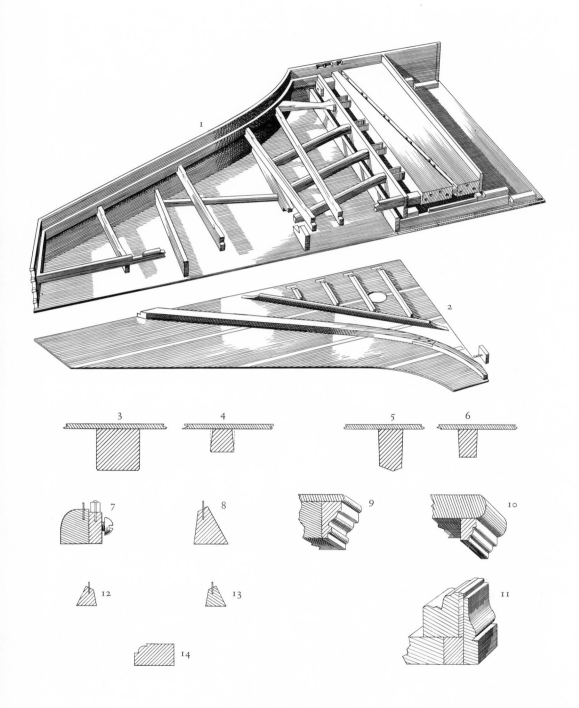

PLATE XXII

Action of an English harpsichord.

Figure 1. Upper-manual key bed with several keys in place. The key bed is made of a panel of oak. Note how the rear pads begin to divide as the lute jacks separate from those in the gap. Note the front rail pins, an exclusively English feature.

Figure 2. Key head with the ivory removed from the tail showing the mortise for the front rail pin.

Figure 3. Section of the key lever at the balance rail pin showing the form of the mortise.

Figure 4. Lower-manual key bed. Note the front rail pins and front rail cloth to limit the key dip.

Figure 5. Jack (from the lute stop). Note the staple at the rear which limits the back motion of the tongue and stiffens the top of the jack.

Figure 6. The tongue (rear view). Note the characteristically English shape and the pad at the top to prevent it clicking against the staple.

Figure 7. The tongue (front view).

Figure 8. Quill plectrum.

Figure 9. Cutaway view of the top of a jack. Note the form of the holes drilled to retain the bristle.

Figure 10. Jack in position in the register and lower guide. Note the clearance given in both register and guide.

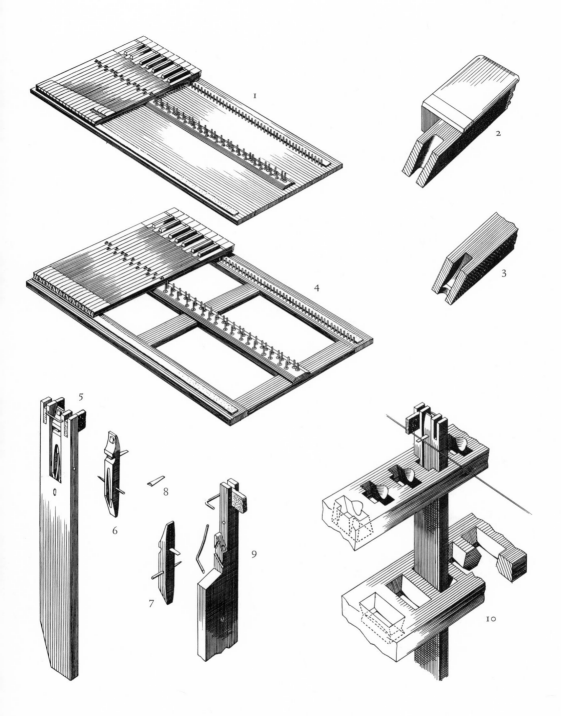

PLATE XXIII

English bentside spinet. Based on an unsigned spinet, the property of Edwin Ripin of Forest Hills, New York.

Figure 1. Instrument with the soundboard and spine removed showing the framing. The wrest plank and nut are dotted in.

Figure 2. The upper side of the soundboard showing the bridge. The ribs are dotted in.

Figure 3. Detail of the rack. The pins between the key levers are made of wire. Note the overrail to limit the key dip.

Figure 4. Detail of the box slide which is built up of blocks.

Figure 5. Construction diagram to clarify the layout of the blocks used in constructing the box slide.

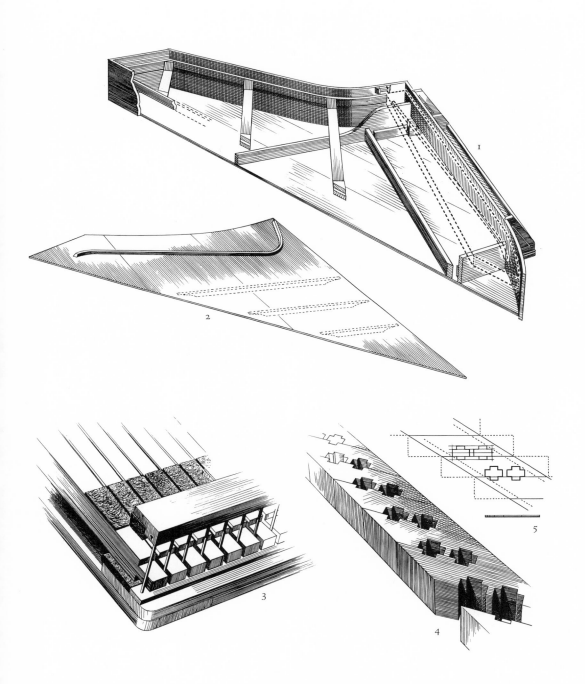

1

2

3

4

5

PLATE XXIV

Harpsichord, from Praetorius, *Theatrum instrumentorum* (plate VI). Praetorius labels the figure "Harpsichord, a fourth lower than choir pitch" (see text for discussion of pitch). This harpsichord is very long, measuring on the scale Praetorius provides about 102 inches. The scale would be about ten inches if one can trust the accuracy of the drawing. This seems too short for such a low pitch. The range is C/E–d''' and the disposition appears to be 2x8', 1x4'. Note the decorations on the outside of the spine, possibly indicating that it had no outer box. In all respects except for the four-foot, this instrument is typically Italian.

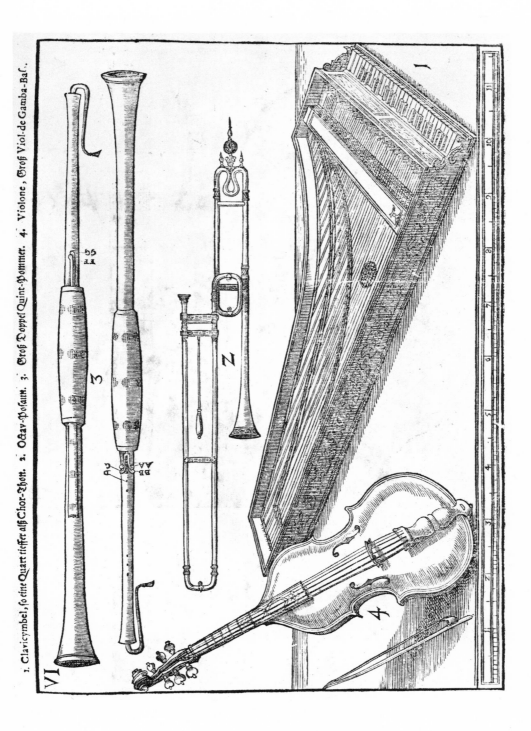

VI

1. Clavicymbel, so eine Quart tieffer alß Chor-Thon. 2. Octav-Posaun. 3. Groß Doppel Quint-Pommer. 4. Violone, Groß Viol-de Gamba-Baß.

PLATE XXV

Spinet and virginals, from Praetorius, *Theatrum instrumentorum* (plate XIV). Note the spools of wire, the tuning hammer with a hook for making eyes in the strings, a pen knife, pieces of quill, and the hand vise (special purpose unknown).

Figure 1. Typically Flemish virginal about 64 inches long by 19 inches wide. (Compare to Ruckers model V at 66–68 inches long by 18½–19½ inches wide.) The range (C/E–d‴) is one note higher in the treble than the Ruckers. Note the split sharps. The scale (c′ located by counting down wrest pins) is about 13½″, within the range of Ruckers variation. Praetorius' legend specifies that this is at choir pitch.

Figure 2. A typical Italian pentagonal spinet. The range is C/E–f‴, a common range for Italian instruments of this type.

Figure 3. Ottavino, nationality difficult to specify. Range C/E–a″ at four-foot pitch.

XIV

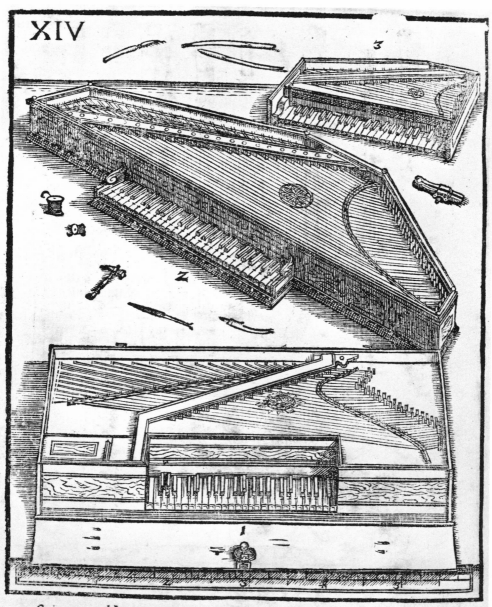

1. 2. Spinetten; Virginal (in gemein Instrument genant) so recht Chor-Thon.
3. OctavInstrumentlin.

PLATE XXVI

Clavicytherium and clavichords, from Praetorius, *Theatrum instrumentorum* (plate XV).

Praetorius labels the figures thus: Fig. 1. Clavicytherium (upright harpsichord). Fig. 2. Clavichord, Italian style. Fig. 3. Ordinary clavichord. Fig. 4. Octave clavichord.

It is impossible to measure the scale of the clavicytherium since the nut is not shown. However, the dimensions (52½" high by 32½" wide) make it quite possible that the strings were of gut as Virdung said (see Appendix F). The range is C/E–c‴.

Note that the woodblock cutter failed to reverse the clavichord in figure 3.

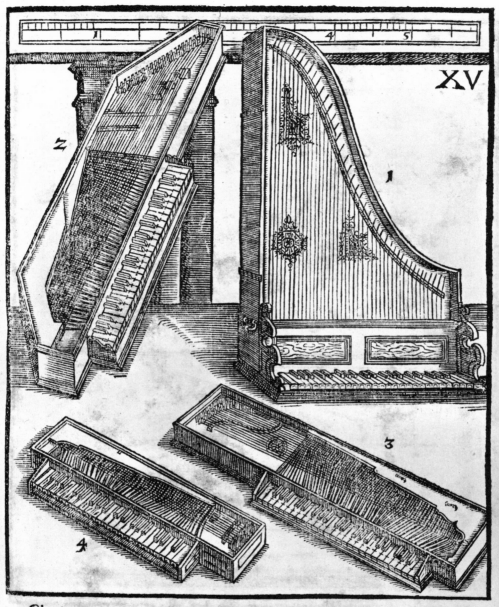

XV

1. Clavicytherium.   3. Clavichordium , Italianiſcher Menſur .
2. Gemein Clavichord.   4. Octav Clavichordium.

PLATE XXVII

Plan of a German harpsichord. Instrument by J. A. Hass, 1710 (Boalch no. 1).

Figure 1. Plan. Note the hand stops on the wrest plank. Disposition: Five choirs (1x16′, 2x8′, 1x4′, 1x2′); two manuals FF–f‴ and no manual coupler. The lower manual slides in to engage a dogleg on the upper manual eight-foot jack, thus coupling that stop to the lower manual. There are two two-foot registers, each plucking the same choir of strings. The two-foot choir itself is incomplete with a range of FF–c″.

Upper manual:	Quill 2′ →	(FF–b, 30 notes)
	Quill 8′ →	(Dogleg engages block on sliding lower manual)
(no coupler) . . .	. . . .	
	Quill 4′ ←	
Lower manual:	Leather 8′ ←	
	Quill 16′ →	
	Quill 2′ →	(FF–c″, 44 notes)

Reading from the nameboard back the order of the nuts on the wrest plank is: (1) 16′; (2) 8′; (3) 4′; (4) 2′. Reading from left to right the order of the hand stops is: (1) upper-manual 2′; (2) 16′; (3) lower-manual 2′; (4) 4′; (5) lower-manual 8′; (6) 8′ dogleg.

Figure 2. Layout of the wrest pins. The top rows of pins are for the 16′ strings. The middle rows are for the up-looking 8′ and the bottom rows are for the down-looking 8′.

Figure 3. Section showing the relative positions of the strings over the registers. The top string is the 16′; the next two strings, directly opposite one another, are the two 8′ strings; the next one down, on the left, is the 4′ string; the lowest, on the right, is the 2′ string. Note that the strings are not directly under one another but are offset slightly.

Figure 4. Plan view of one course of strings showing bridges (solid lines) and hitchpin rails (dotted lines). The jacks rise through the open space in the middle of the course.

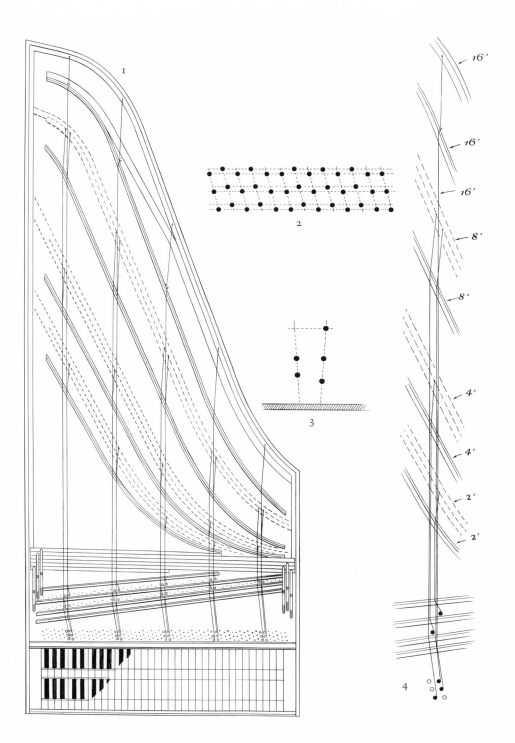

PLATE XXVIII

Interior of a German harpsichord. Instrument by J. A. Hass, 1710 (Boalch no. 1).

Figure 1. Instrument with spine and soundboard removed showing the framing. This drawing was made before restoration (by William Dowd) revealed the presence of one more frame like that from the bentside to the belly rail. It extends from the spine-junction of the frame nearest the tail to the curved tail. Note the eight-foot hitchpin rail which is glued to the frames. It is reinforced by iron angles where it crosses the frames. These angles are on the side away from the viewer and could not be shown. (See Plate XXIX, figures 12 and 13, for details of the frames and of the eight-foot hitchpin rail.)

Figure 2. Underside of the soundboard showing the ribs and the four-foot and the two-foot hitchpin rails. When the instrument was opened up by Mr. Dowd it was found that there was a cutoff bar in the usual position, and only two ribs.

Figure 3. Sixteen-foot soundboard, mounted at a higher level than the eight-foot soundboard. (See Plate XXIX, figure 13.)

Figure 4. Manuals showing end block detail. The upper manual is supported by the light colored block (fixed to the case) which is behind the dark lower-manual end block (see Plate XXIX, figures 1 and 4).

Figure 5. Rear of lower-manual key lever in perspective and section. Note the block which engages a dogleg on the upper-manual jack when the lower manual is pushed in.

Figure 6. Plan view of a lower-manual key. Note the enormous length and the tortoise shell key top.

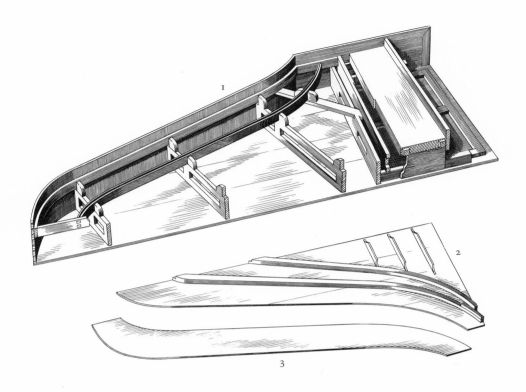

I

2

3

4

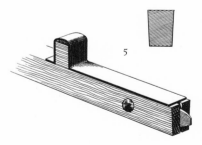

5

6

PLATE XXIX

Action of a German harpsichord. Instrument by J. A. Hass, 1710 (Boalch no. 1).

Figure 1. Upper-manual key bed. Note the guide pins between the key levers. Also observe that it is wider than the lower-manual key bed. Thus it rests on the blocks glued to the spine and cheekpiece (Plate XXVIII, figure 1) while the lower-manual key bed slips between them. This permits the lower manual to slide in and out while the upper manual remains stationary.

Figure 2. Detail of plan view of the balance rail showing the cord running next to the balance pins, serving as a fulcrum for the keys.

Figure 3. Key heads. The natural key top is of tortoise shell.

Figure 4. Lower-manual key bed. The bass end block has been removed to show detail.

Figures 5 and 6. Details of metal hand stop levers.

Figure 7. Detail of hand stop levers in position.

Figure 8. Leathered lower-manual eight-foot jack, rear view.

Figure 9. Same jack, front view.

Figure 10. Detail of bass end of buff stop battens showing the knob by which they are moved. The nearest buff stop damps the upper-manual eight-foot choir; the further one damps the sixteen-foot choir.

Figure 11. Elevation of the sixteen-foot nut (seen from the bass end) showing section of the nut and the buff stop batten.

Figure 12. Elevation of a frame member showing the eight-foot hitchpin rail and the reinforcements at the ends.

Figure 13. Detail of an intersection of a frame member and the eight-foot hitchpin rail. The sixteen-foot soundboard is to the right and the eight-foot soundboard is to the left.

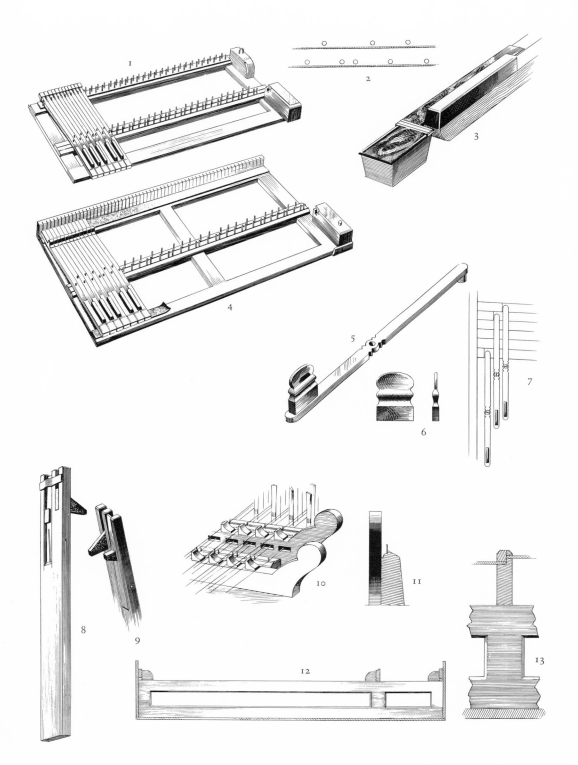

PLATE XXX

"The musical instrument maker," from Sprengel, *Handwerk und Künste in Tabellen* (plate VI). See the excerpts from Sprengel in Appendix A. Note that the harpsichord in figure III has the double bentside characteristic of the Hamburg style. Figure I is a clavichord.

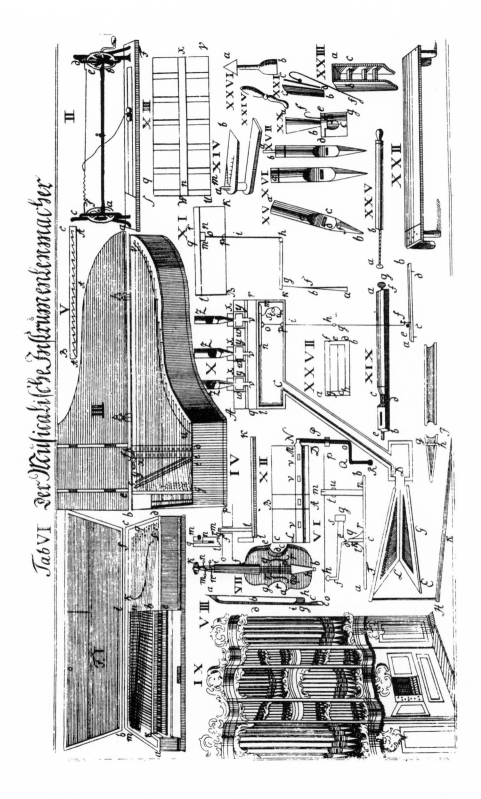

Tab VI   Der Musicalische Instrumentenmacher

PLATE XXXI

"Interior view of the shop of a woodworker," from Roubo, *L'Art du menuisier* (plate II).

Vignette. A French woodworking shop in 1769.

Figure 1. The bench. Roubo calls particular attention to the holdfast (a), and the holes made for it in the top and legs of the bench. On the shelf under the bench are several planes. Reading from the largest toward the viewer they would be (1) jointing plane; (2) jack plane; (3) large smooth plane; (4) smooth plane. Behind the jointing plane is what appears to be a shoulder or rabbet plane.

Figure 2. Bench leg with a holdfast in position.

Figure 3. Detail of a vise.

Figure 4. Section of a vise and holdfast.

Figure 5. Bench dog. (See also c in figure 1.) Used to brace work against in planing.

Figure 6. Metal part of bench dog.

Figure 7. A container screwed under the bench top, able to be swung out, to contain cutting lubricant for sharpening tools.

Figure 8. A mallet.

Figure 9. A hammer.

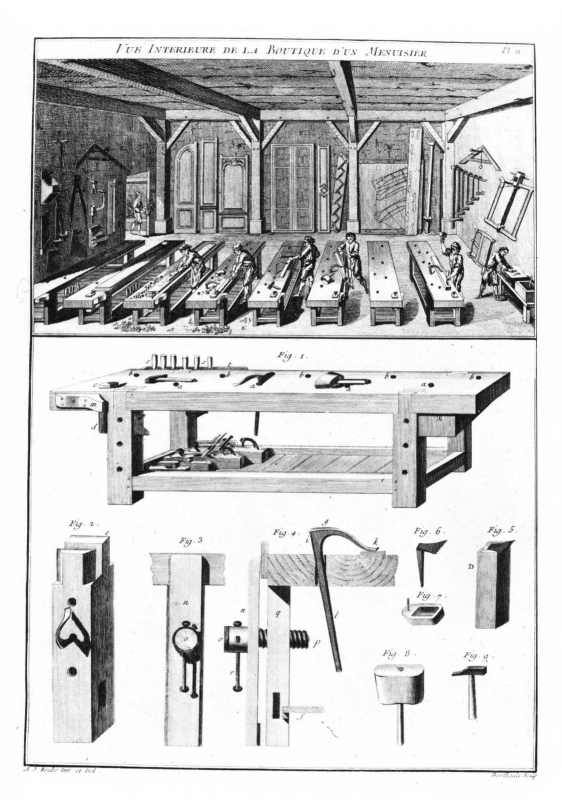

Fig. 1.

Fig. 2.

Fig. 3.

Fig. 4.

Fig. 6.

Fig. 5.

Fig. 7.

Fig. 8.

Fig. 9.

A. J. Roubo Inv. et Del.

Berthault Sculp.

PLATE XXXII

"Harpsichord making tools," from the *Encyclopédie* ("Lutherie," plate XVII, seconde suite).

Figure 10. *Tourniquet.* A bow drill for drilling small holes.

Figure 11. *Presse.* A clamp.

Figure 12. *Lissoire.* Literally, a polisher. Probably mislabeled. It appears to be some sort of marking gauge.

Figure 13. *Languetoir.* A device to punch the mortises for quill in the tongues. Note that the mortise seems to be punched from both sides. The lower punch is obviously too long.

Figure 14. *Trace-sauteraux.* A marking gauge with several accurately positioned scribers. Used to mark out the jacks.

Figure 15. *Fraisoir.* A broach. Probably used to make a round hole square as in the keyboard mortises.

Figure 16. *Double-frontal* (?). A bit for drilling holes.

Figure 17. *Frontal* (?). A bit.

Figure 18. *Longuet* (?). Literally, something elongated. Possibly a form of adze. Purpose unknown.

Figure 19. *Cisailles.* A chisel.

Figure 20. *Fraisoir à vis perdues.* A broach used in setting screws.

Figure 21. *Voie de sautereaux.* A drill or reamer used for jacks. It could ream or drill the tongue-pivot hole or the hole in the jack which receives the pivot.

Figure 22. *Arme ou scie à main.* A hand saw.

Figure 23. *Passe-partout.* A floor-board saw. The convex toothed edge makes it possible to start a cut away from the edge of a plank.

Figures 24, 25, 29. *Emporte-pieces.* Punches. Used to punch the oblong holes in the leather which tops the registers. The punch in figure 24 cuts on all four sides at once. Those in figures 25 and 29 are a pair, each of which cuts two sides.

Figure 26. *Plumoir.* A "quiller." Perhaps a sharp knife used for voicing.

Figure 27. *Accordoir.* A tuning hammer. Note the hook for forming the eyes in the strings.

Figure 28. *Traçoir.* A "tracer." Purpose unknown. Possibly used as a marking-out tool.

Figure 30. *Scie à main.* A dove-tail or tenon saw.

Figure 31. *Rabot à moulures.* A molding plane. Could be used for the molding around the upper edge of the case.

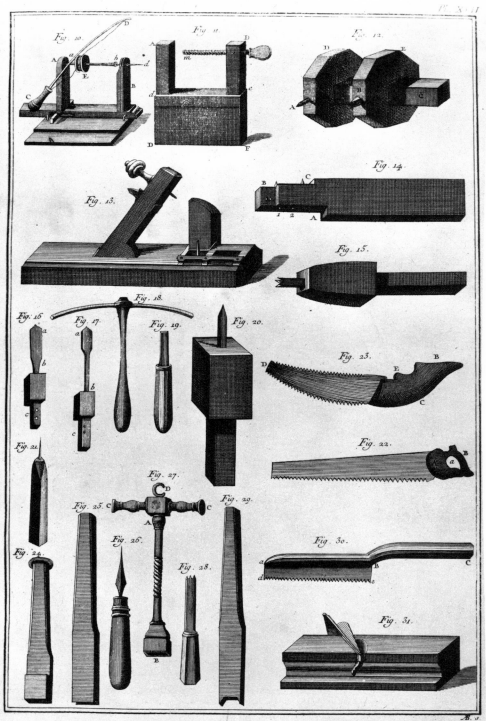

Pl. XVII.

Fig. 10. Fig. 11. Fig. 12. Fig. 13. Fig. 14. Fig. 15. Fig. 16. Fig. 17. Fig. 18. Fig. 19. Fig. 20. Fig. 21. Fig. 22. Fig. 23. Fig. 24. Fig. 25. Fig. 26. Fig. 27. Fig. 28. Fig. 29. Fig. 30. Fig. 31.

Lutherie, Outils propres à la Facture des Clavecins.

PLATE XXXIII

"The way to pile or cut up wood," from Roubo, *L'Art du menuisier* (plate 4). Note that neatly sawed and dimensioned boards were stocked. Figures 5–12 do not concern us directly. Roubo is explaining how to take straight, clear pieces out of warped, checked, or knotty timber. The sawyer's marks shown on several planks are found occasionally in harpsichords.

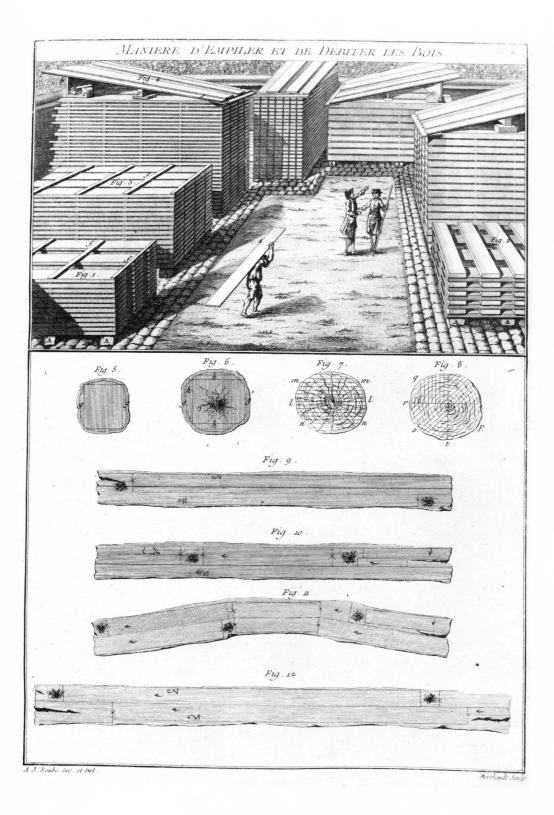

MANIERE D'EMPILER ET DE DÉBITER LES BOIS.

Fig. 4.

Fig. 3.

Fig. 1.

Fig. 2.

Fig. 5.

Fig. 6.

Fig. 7.

Fig. 8.

Fig. 9.

Fig. 10.

Fig. 11.

Fig. 12.

A.J. Roubo Inv. et Del.

Berthault Sculp.

PLATE XXXIV

Seventeenth century water-powered sawmill, from De Caus, *Les Raisons des forces mouvantes* (plate 25).

The following description is from the 1615 edition but the plate was taken from the edition of 1624.

"This machine is very common in the mountains of the country of the Swiss. With it they saw large numbers of fir planks. The said machine is very necessary in a large city or in a forest where wood is sawed, whether into planks or into other forms. This one here is not at all like those of the said Swiss because they feed the wood into the saws by means of toothed wheels with a ratchet; but because of the repairs which are often required to the said toothed wheels, I always endeavor to avoid using them as much as I can. Thus I have used two weights of about two or three hundred pounds each, of which one is marked A. The other must be imagined at the end of the rope B (because if it had been drawn it would have interfered with the view of the mechanism of the pivot C, by means of which the saws move up and down perpendicularly). [The plate was altered between 1615 and 1624 to avoid this problem.] The ropes to which the said weights are attached will be fastened to the rear of two sliding wooden pieces which move along two other fixed wooden pieces by means of some little pulleys which can be placed inside the saw frame. Thus the counterweights always pull on the sliding wooden pieces. The timber that one wishes to saw will be held between the sliding pieces as they advance. The up-and-down motion of the saws will saw the timber with great efficiency. One can use two, three, or four saws, or even more in the frame, as far apart as one wishes the planks to be thick. When the piece of wood comes to the end, a man or two with a lever turn a winch which has a strong rope attached that will draw the said piece back and raise the weights again. Then the said piece of wood is moved sideways a little in order to make the saws bear on it again."

De Caus is probably thinking of sawing several planks from the side of a large timber. Having resawed it once it must be pushed to the side so that another plank or set of planks can be slabbed off. De Caus' gravity feed is not as clever as he thinks for the wood would bear on the saws on the up-stroke as well as on the down-stroke, overheating them and blunting the points of the teeth. A ratchet feed is the only way to avoid this.

PLATE XXXV

Interior of a harpsichord, from the *Encyclopédie* ("Lutherie," plate XV, seconde suite).

Figure 2. "Interior of the harpsichord. Framing of the case." This is not a typical harpsichord frame. Traces on the interior of a 1646 Andreas Ruckers harpsichord, the property of William Post Ross of Berea, Kentucky (not listed in Boalch), indicate that such a frame was installed in it by an eighteenth century restorer. Probably he had seen this plate. Otherwise I have never seen a harpsichord with this frame.

Figure 3. "The soundboard seen from below." This ribbing is not at all typical of any harpsichord making tradition.

Figure 4. "Harpsichord stand." The author of the article, "Clavecin," indicates that frames glued to the bottom of the harpsichord (not shown in figure 2) were arranged in the same way as those on the stand.

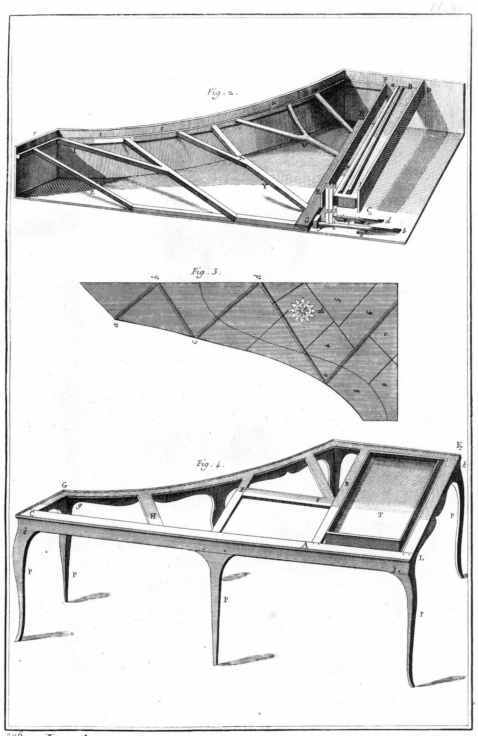

Fig. 2.

Fig. 3.

Fig. 4.

Lutherie, Instruments à cordes et à touches Suite du Clavecin.

PLATE XXXVI

"Method of resawing veneer, with details of the vise saw," from Roubo, *L'Art du menuisier* (plate 278).

Figure 1. Plan view of the vise saw, so-called because it is used to resaw logs held in the vise.

Figure 2. Side view of the vise saw. Note the screw device which tightens the saw blade.

Figures 3, 4, 5, 8, and 9. Details of the arrangement to tighten and hold the saw blade.

Figure 6. Side view of the saw, "four inches wide or less."

Figure 7. Edge view of the saw, "$\frac{1}{12}$ inch thick on the side with the teeth and gradually thinning toward the back." Note that there is no set to the teeth.

Figure 10. Sawing veneer with the vise saw.

Figure 11. The upright sawing vise.

Figure 12. Hack saw. Used for small pieces of hard wood, tortoise shell, ivory and mother of pearl. The blade must be "very thin with no set, and they are thinned toward the back so that they go easily. This is done by taking lengthwise strokes with a file until it is thinned as much as is judged proper. Then it is honed with grease [on a stone] to smooth out the inequalities made by the file. This operation is called *démaigrir* [thinning] in workmen's terms." Roubo mentions that these blades must be harder than those of ordinary saws. Tempered steel is used. He suggests clock springs (an item which turns up occasionally in the inventories of harpsichord makers' workshops).

Pl. 278.

MANIERE DE REFENDRE LE BOIS DE PLACAGE, AVEC les Developpements de la Scie a Presse.

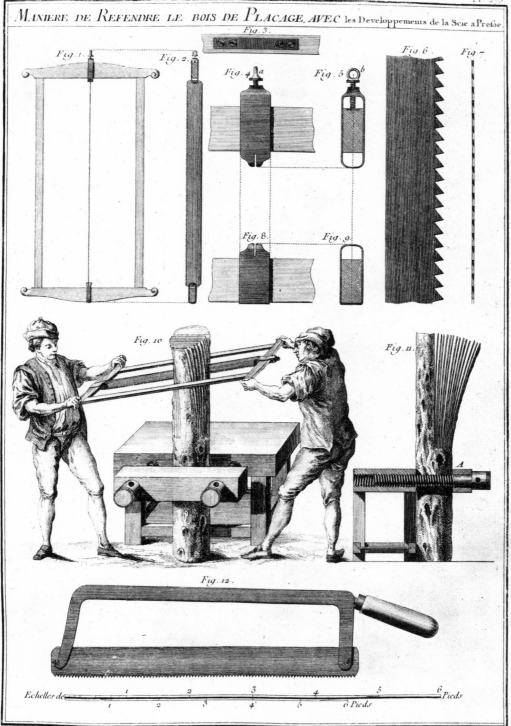

Fig. 1. Fig. 2. Fig. 3. Fig. 4. Fig. 5. Fig. 6. Fig. 7. Fig. 8. Fig. 9. Fig. 10. Fig. 11. Fig. 12.

Echelles de ....1................2................3................4................5................6 Pieds

A. J. Roubo Inv. Del et Sculp.

PLATE XXXVII

"The way to veneer and the tools for veneering," from Roubo, *L'Art du menuisier* (plate 294).

Figure 1. Wooden screw clamp.

Figure 2. Metal clamp.

Figures 3, 4, and 5. Veneering hammers with round and flat faces.

Figure 6. A sponge.

Figure 7. Joint used in assembling the wooden clamp.

Figures 8 and 9. Veneering iron.

Figure 10. Veneering, using the veneering hammer and the veneering iron. The basic procedure in veneering according to Roubo was as follows: (1) Rub the veneer on the glue side with the hammer to make it concave. (2) Damp the outside of the veneer with a sponge to prevent it from curling away from the carcass when the glue wets it. (3) Heat the glue side of the veneer. (4) Spread glue on the veneer and carcass. (5) Put veneer in place quickly. (6) Rub hard with the veneering hammer. Squeeze the glue out. (7) Tap all over with hammer to see if it is well glued. (8) In veneering large pieces the work must be reheated with the veneering iron.

Pl. 294

MANIERE DE PLAQUER, ET LES OUTILS PROPRES AU PLAQUAGE.

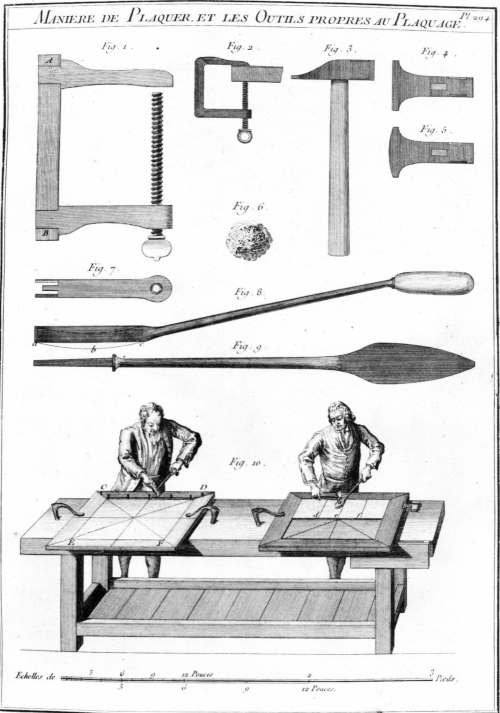

Fig. 1.

Fig. 2.

Fig. 3.

Fig. 4.

Fig. 5.

Fig. 6.

Fig. 7.

Fig. 8.

Fig. 9.

Fig. 10.

Echelles de ... 3 ... 6 ... 9 ... 12 Pouces ... 2 ... 3 Pieds.

A. J. Roubo Inv. Del. et Sculp.

PLATE XXXVIII

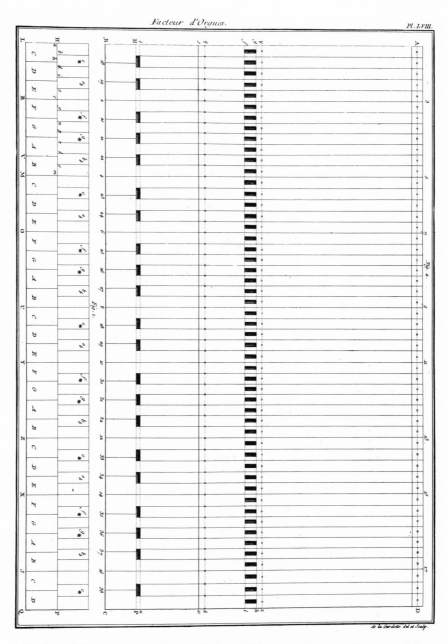

Pl. LVIII.

Keyboard layout, from Dom Bedos, *L'Art du facteur d'orgues* (plate LVIII).

Figure 1. Head scale. The key heads lie between the lines LQ and HP. The key tails and sharps are above the line HP.

Figure 2. Layout of the key panel. This is a keyboard for organ, not harpsichord. However, the dimensions are quite similar.

PLATE XXXIX

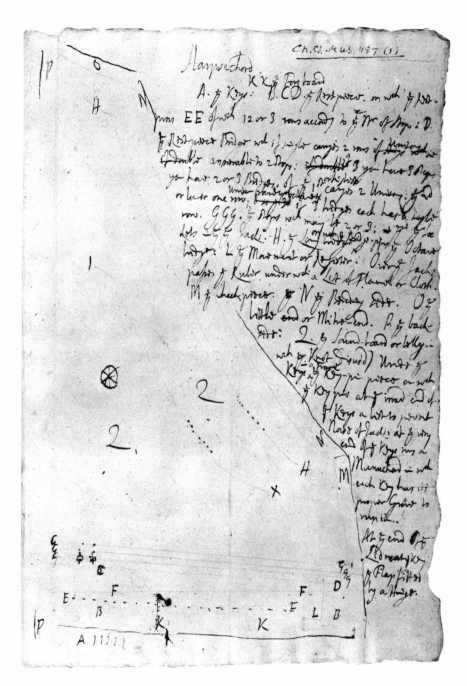

First page of the Talbot manuscript. See Appendix A for text.

PLATE XL

Harpsichord, from the *Encyclopédie* ("Lutherie," plate XIV, seconde suite).

The legend reads: Fig. 1. Harpsichord mounted on its stand without its lid. 5. Music desk of the harpsichord. A. Jack without a tongue. E. Jack with its tongue. F, f, G, H, I. Jacks. K, L. Tongues. M. Pivot.

The harpsichord is a typical French double, probably 2x8', 1x4', with manual coupler and a range of FF-f'''. The music desk was designed to span the case, resting on the spine and cheekpiece. I can see no reason for the curved shape of the damper (figure F) which would be difficult to make.

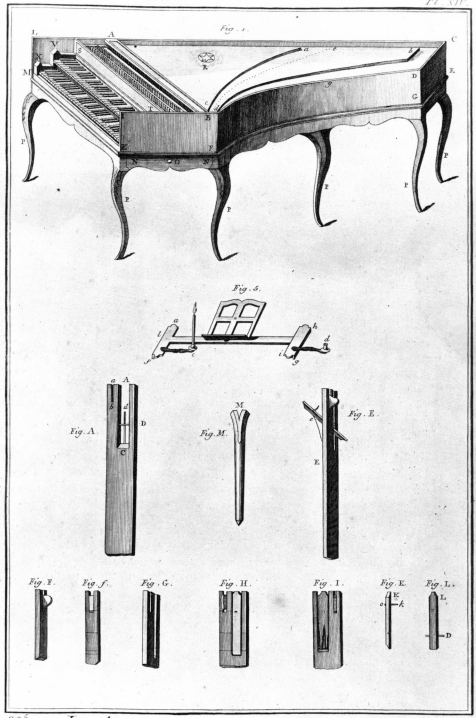

Pl. XIV.

Fig. 1.

Fig. 5.

Fig. A.

Fig. M.

Fig. E.

Fig. F.   Fig. f.   Fig. G.   Fig. H.   Fig. I.   Fig. K.   Fig. L.

Lutherie, Instruments à cordes et à touches, Clavecin.

PLATE XLI

The instrument maker's workshop, from the *Encyclopédie* ("Lutherie," plate XVIII, seconde suite).

The legend reads: The vignette shows an instrument maker's workshop where several journeymen are busy at various products of that trade.

Figure 1. A workman planing the soundboard of an instrument placed on the bench.

2. A workman busy making the head of a harp. It may be seen that he is drilling the wrest pin holes.

5 [*sic*]. A workman finishing a violin.

4. Another who is painting the column and the head of a pedal harp. The head is mounted on a stand for the convenience of the worker (see a). At b is the body of a bass that has just been glued and which is clamped with screw clamps until it is dry.

5. The sounding box of a harp detached from the column and head which the worker (figure 4) is painting. c — the soundboard. d — the iron fitting which connects the column and the sounding box. e — two dowels or iron pins which connect the head to the sounding box.

6. Pedal harp, strung and all finished.

7. f. A hurdy-gurdy in the form of a lute all finished. The rest of the shop contains different wind and stringed instruments.

[At the bottom of the plate]

8. *Marteau* [hammer].

9. *Lime* [file].

10. *Vrille* [gimlet].

11 & 12. *Perçoirs à main de différens calibres ou alésoirs* [drills or reamers of different sizes].

13. *Ciseau* [chisel].

14. *Bec-d'âne* [mortising chisel].

15. *Pinceau à vernir* [paint brush].

16. *Petite scie à main*, a-*porte-scie d'acier*. b-*son manche*. c-*lame de la scie* [small hand-saw, a-the steel saw-frame. b-its handle. c-the saw blade].

17. *Fausse équerre* [bevel].

18. *Equerre* [square].

19. *Petite happe en bois garnie de trois vis* [small wooden clamp with three screws].

20. *Happe simple en bois* [plain wooden clamp].

21. *Vilbrequin de fer*, d-*la meche ou le forêt* [bit-brace, d-the drill, or bit].

22. *Pinces plates* [flat pincers].

23. *Tourne-vis* [screwdriver].

24. *Etabli*. e-*valet*. f-*pot à la colle* [bench. e-holdfast. f-glue pot].

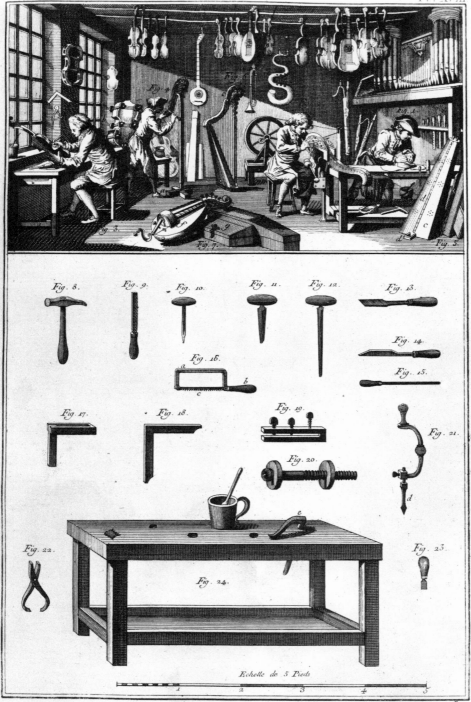

Pl. XVIII

Lutherie, Ouvrages et Outils.